Children's
Literature
Review

Guide to Gale Literary Criticism Series

For criticism on	Consult these Gale series
Authors now living or who died after December 31, 1959	*CONTEMPORARY LITERARY CRITICISM (CLC)*
Authors who died between 1900 and 1959	*TWENTIETH-CENTURY LITERARY CRITICISM (TCLC)*
Authors who died between 1800 and 1899	*NINETEENTH-CENTURY LITERATURE CRITICISM (NCLC)*
Authors who died between 1400 and 1799	*LITERATURE CRITICISM FROM 1400 TO 1800 (LC)* *SHAKESPEAREAN CRITICISM (SC)*
Authors who died before 1400	*CLASSICAL AND MEDIEVAL LITERATURE CRITICISM (CMLC)*
Authors of books for children and young adults	*CHILDREN'S LITERATURE REVIEW (CLR)*
Dramatists	*DRAMA CRITICISM (DC)*
Poets	*POETRY CRITICISM (PC)*
Short story writers	*SHORT STORY CRITICISM (SSC)*
Black writers of the past two hundred years	*BLACK LITERATURE CRITICISM (BLC)*
Hispanic writers of the late nineteenth and twentieth centuries	*HISPANIC LITERATURE CRITICISM (HLC)*
Native North American writers and orators of the eighteenth, nineteenth, and twentieth centuries	*NATIVE NORTH AMERICAN LITERATURE (NNAL)*
Major authors from the Renaissance to the present	*WORLD LITERATURE CRITICISM, 1500 TO THE PRESENT (WLC)*

ISSN 0362-4145

volume 51

Children's Literature Review

Excerpts from Reviews,
Criticism, and Commentary
on Books for Children
and Young People

Deborah J. Morad
Editor

GALE

DETROIT • LONDON

STAFF

Deborah J. Morad, *Editor*

Sara Constantakis, Charity Ann Dorigan, Alan Hedblad, Motoko Fujishiro Huthwaite, Paul Loeber, Carolyn C. March, Malinda Mayer, Thomas McMahon, Adele Sarkissian, Gerald Senick, Diane Telgen, Martha Urbiel, Kathleen L. Witman, *Contributing Editors*

Karen Uchic, *Technical Training Specialist*

Joyce Nakamura, *Managing Editor*

Susan M. Trosky, *Permissions Manager*
Sarah Chesney, Edna Hedblad, Michele Lonoconus, *Permissions Associates*

Victoria B. Cariappa, *Research Manager*
Corrine A. Stocker, *Project Coordinator*
Michele P. LaMeau, *Research Specialist*
Jeffrey D. Daniels, Tamara C. Nott, Norma Sawaya, Tracie A. Richardson, Cheryl D. Warnock, *Research Associates*
Phyllis P. Blackman, *Research Assistant*

Mary Beth Trimper, *Production Director*
Cindy Range, *Production Assistant*

Christine O'Bryan, *Desktop Publisher*
Randy Bassett, *Image Database Supervisor*
Robert Duncan, Michael Logusz, *Imaging Specialists*
Pamela A. Reed, *Imaging Coordinator*

Library of Congress Catalog Card Number 76-643301
ISBN 0-7876-2079-3
ISSN 0362-4145
Printed in the United States of America

10   9   8   7   6   5   4   3   2   1

Contents

Preface   vii
Acknowledgements   xi

Preface

Literature for children and young adults has evolved into both a respected branch of creative writing and a successful industry. Currently, books for young readers are considered among the most popular segments of publishing. Criticism of juvenile literature is instrumental in recording the literary or artistic development of the creators of children's books as well as the trends and controversies that result from changing values or attitudes about young people and their literature. Designed to provide a permanent, accessible record of this ongoing scholarship, *Children's Literature Review (CLR)* presents parents, teachers, and librarians—those responsible for bringing children and books together—with the opportunity to make informed choices when selecting reading materials for the young. In addition, *CLR* provides researchers of children's literature with easy access to a wide variety of critical information from English-language sources in the field. Users will find balanced overviews of the careers of the authors and illustrators of the books that children and young adults are reading; these entries, which contain excerpts from published criticism in books and periodicals, assist users by sparking ideas for papers and assignments and suggesting supplementary and classroom reading. Ann L. Kalkhoff, president and editor of *Children's Book Review Service Inc.,* writes that "*CLR* has filled a gap in the field of children's books, and it is one series that will never lose its validity or importance."

Scope of the Series

Each volume of *CLR* profiles the careers of a selection of authors and illustrators of books for children and young adults from preschool through high school. Author lists in each volume reflect:

- an international scope.

- representation of authors of all eras.

- the variety of genres covered by children's and/or YA literature: picture books, fiction, nonfiction, poetry, folklore, and drama.

Although the focus of the series is on authors new to *CLR*, entries will be updated as the need arises.

Organization of This Book

An entry consists of the following elements: author heading, author portrait, author introduction, excerpts of criticism (each preceded by a bibliographical citation), and illustrations, when available.

- The **Author Heading** consists of the author's name followed by birth and death dates. The portion of the name outside the parentheses denotes the form under which the author is most frequently published. If the majority of the author's works for children were written under a pseudonym, the pseudonym will be listed in the author heading and the real name given on the first line of the author introduction. Also located at the beginning of the introduction are any other pseudonyms used by the author in writing for children and any name variations, including transliterated forms for authors whose languages use nonroman alphabets. Uncertainty as to a birth or death date is indicated by question marks.

- An **Author Portrait** is included when available.

- The **Author Introduction** contains information designed to introduce an author to *CLR* users by presenting an overview of the author's themes and styles, biographical facts that relate to the author's literary career or critical responses to the author's works, and information about major awards and prizes the author has received. The introduction begins by identifying the nationality of the author and by listing the genres in which s/he has written for children and young adults. Introductions also list a group of representative titles for which the author or illustrator being profiled is best known; this section, which begins with the words "major works include," follows the genre line of the introduction. For seminal figures, a listing of major works about the author follows when appropriate, highlighting important biographies about the author or illustrator that are not excerpted in the entry. The centered heading "Introduction" announces the body of the text.

- **Criticism** is located in three sections: **Author's Commentary** (when available), **General Commentary** (when available), and **Title Commentary** (commentary on specific titles).

  - The **Author's Commentary** presents background material written by the author or by an interviewer. This commentary may cover a specific work or several works. Author's commentary on more than one work appears after the author introduction, while commentary on an individual book follows the title entry heading.

  - The **General Commentary** consists of critical excerpts that consider more than one work by the author or illustrator being profiled. General commentary is preceded by the critic's name in boldface type or, in the case of unsigned criticism, by the title of the journal. *CLR* also features entries that emphasize general criticism on the oeuvre of an author or illustrator. When appropriate, a selection of reviews is included to supplement the general commentary.

  - The **Title Commentary** begins with the title entry headings, which precede the criticism on a title and cite publication information on the work being reviewed. Title headings list the title of the work as it appeared in its first English-language edition. The first English-language publication date of each work (unless otherwise noted) is listed in parentheses following the title. Differing U.S. and British titles follow the publication date within the parentheses. When a work is written by an individual other than the one being profiled, as is the case when illustrators are featured, the parenthetical material following the title cites the author of the work before listing its publication date.

  Entries in each title commentary section consist of critical excerpts on the author's individual works, arranged chronologically by publication date. The entries generally contain two to seven reviews per title, depending on the stature of the book and the amount of criticism it has generated. The editors select titles that reflect the entire scope of the author's literary contribution, covering each genre and subject. An effort is made to reprint criticism that represents the full range of each title's reception, from the year of its initial publication to current assessments. Thus, the reader is provided with a record of the author's critical history. Publication information (such as publisher names and book prices) and parenthetical numerical references (such as footnotes or page and line references to specific editions of works) have been deleted at the discretion of the editors to provide smoother reading of the text.

- Centered headings introduce each section, in which criticism is arranged chronologically; beginning with Volume 35, each excerpt is preceded by a boldface source heading for easier access by readers. Within the text, titles by authors being profiled are also highlighted in boldface type.

- Selected excerpts are preceded by **Explanatory Annotations,** which provide information on the critic or work of criticism to enhance the reader's understanding of the excerpt.

- A complete **Bibliographical Citation** designed to facilitate the location of the original book or article precedes each piece of criticism.

- Numerous **Illustrations** are featured in *CLR*. For entries on illustrators, an effort has been made to include illustrations that reflect the characteristics discussed in the criticism. Entries on authors who do not illustrate their own works may also include photographs and other illustrative material pertinent to their careers.

Special Features: Entries on Illustrators

Entries on authors who are also illustrators will occasionally feature commentary on selected works illustrated but not written by the author being profiled. These works are strongly associated with the illustrator and have received critical acclaim for their art. By including critical comment on works of this type, the editors wish to provide a more complete representation of the artist's career. Criticism on these works has been chosen to stress artistic, rather than literary, contributions. Title entry headings for works illustrated by the author being profiled are arranged chronologically within the entry by date of publication and include notes identifying the author of the illustrated work. In order to provide easier access for users, all titles illustrated by the subject of the entry are boldfaced.

CLR also includes entries on prominent illustrators who have contributed to the field of children's literature. These entries are designed to represent the development of the illustrator as an artist rather than as a literary stylist. The illustrator's section is organized like that of an author, with two exceptions: the introduction presents an overview of the illustrator's styles and techniques rather than outlining his or her literary background, and the commentary written by the illustrator on his or her works is called "illustrator's commentary" rather than "author's commentary." All titles of books containing illustrations by the artist being profiled are highlighted in boldface type.

Other Features: Acknowledgments, Indexes

- The **Acknowledgments** section, which immediately follows the preface, lists the sources from which material has been reprinted in the volume. It does not, however, list every book or periodical consulted for the volume.

- The **Cumulative Index to Authors** lists all of the authors who have appeared in *CLR* with cross-references to the biographical, autobiographical, and literary criticism series published by Gale Research. A full listing of the series titles appears before the first page of the indexes of this volume.

- The **Cumulative Index to Nationalities** lists authors alphabetically under their respective nationalities. Author names are followed by the volume number(s) in which they appear.

- The **Cumulative Index to Titles** lists titles covered in *CLR* followed by the volume and page number where criticism begins.

A Note to the Reader

CLR is one of several critical references sources in the Literature Criticism Series published by Gale Research. When writing papers, students who quote directly from any volume in the Literature Criticism Series may use the following general forms to footnote reprinted criticism. The first example pertains to material drawn from periodicals, the second to material reprinted from books.

[1]T. S. Eliot, "John Donne," *The Nation and the Athenaeum,* 33 (9 June 1923), 321-32; excerpted and reprinted in *Literature Criticism from 1400 to 1800,* Vol. 10, ed. James E. Person, Jr. (Detroit: Gale Research, 1989), pp. 28-9.

[1]Henry Brooke, *Leslie Brooke and Johnny Crow* (Frederick Warne, 1982); excerpted and reprinted in *Children's Literature Review,* Vol. 20, ed. Gerard J. Senick (Detroit: Gale Research, 1990), p. 47.

Suggestions Are Welcome

In response to various suggestions, several features have been added to *CLR* since the beginning of the series, including author entries on retellers of traditional literature as well as those who have been the first to record oral tales and other folklore; entries on prominent illustrators featuring commentary on their styles and techniques; entries on authors whose works are considered controversial; occasional entries devoted to criticism on a single work or a series of works; sections in author introductions that list major works by and about the author or illustrator being profiled; explanatory notes that provide information on the critic or work of criticism to enhance the usefulness of the excerpt; more extensive illustrative material, such as holographs of manuscript pages and photographs of people and places pertinent to the careers of the authors and artists; a cumulative nationality index for easy access to authors by nationality; and occasional guest essays written specifically for *CLR* by prominent critics on subjects of their choice.

Readers who wish to suggest authors to appear in future volumes, or who have other suggestions, are cordially invited to contact the editor. By mail: Editor, *Children's Literature Review,* Gale Research, 27500 Drake Road, Farmington Hills, MI 48331-3535; by telephone: (800) 347-GALE; by fax: (248) 699-8065.

Acknowledgments

The editors wish to thank the copyright holders of the excerpted criticism included in this volume and the permissions managers of many book and magazine publishing companies for assisting us in securing reproduction rights. We are also grateful to the staffs of the Detroit Public Library, the Library of Congress, the University of Detroit Mercy Library, Wayne State University Purdy/Kresge Library Complex, and the University of Michigan Libraries for making their resources available to us. Following is a list of the copyright holders who have granted us permission to reproduce material in this volume of **CLR**. Every effort has been made to trace copyright, but if omissions have been made, please let us know.

COPYRIGHTED EXCERPTS IN *CLR,* VOLUME 51, WERE REPRODUCED FROM THE FOLLOWING PERIODICALS:

The ALAN Review, v. 10, Fall, 1982; v. 13, Winter, 1986. Both reproduced by permission.— *Appraisal: Science Books for Young People,* v. 19, Fall, 1986. Copyright © 1986 by the Children's Science Book Review Committee. Reproduced by permission.—*The Booklist,* v. 62, October 15, 1965; v. 66, November 1, 1969; v. 72, November 1, 1975. Copyright © 1965, 1969, 1975 by the American Library Association. All reproduced by permission. —*Booklist,* v. 78, June 1, 1982; v. 78, June 15, 1982; v. 80, November 1, 1983; v. 80, February 1, 1984; v. 81, September 1, 1984; v. 81, October 1, 1984; v. 81, April 1, 1985; v. 82, September 15, 1985; v. 82, March 1, 1986; v. 82, May 15, 1986; v. 83, December 1, 1986; v. 83, March 1, 1987; v. 84, November 1, 1987; v. 84, April 15, 1988; v. 84, May 1, 1988; v. 84, July, 1988; v. 85, September 1, 1988; v. 85, December 1, 1988; v. 85, December 15, 1988; v. 85, May 1, 1989; v. 85, May 15, 1989; v. 86, September 1, 1989; v. 86, September 15, 1989; v. 86, December 15, 1989; v. 86, May 1, 1990; v. 86, August, 1990; v. 87, November 1, 1990; v. 87, July, 1991; v. 87, August, 1991; v. 88, September 15, 1991; v. 88, October 15, 1991; v. 88, March 1, 1992; v. 88, March 15, 1992; v. 88, June 1, 1992; v. 88, July, 1992; v. 89, December 1, 1992; v. 89, January 15, 1993; v. 89, July, 1993; v. 89, August, 1993; v. 90, January 1, 1994; v. 90, May 1, 1994; v. 91, September 1, 1994; v. 91, October 15, 1994; v. 91, January 1, 1995; v. 91, February 1, 1995; v. 91, March 15, 1995; v. 91, April 1, 1995; v. 91, August, 1995; v. 92, October 1, 1995; v. 92, December 1, 1995; v. 92, January 1 & 15, 1996; v. 92, May 1, 1996; v. 92, June 1 & 15, 1996; v. 93, September 1, 1996; v. 93, October 1, 1996; v. 93, October 15, 1996; v. 93, December 1, 1996; v. 93, December 15, 1996; v. 93, February 1, 1997; v. 93, March 1, 1997; v. 93, March 15, 1997; v. 93, June 1 & 15, 1997; v. 93, August, 1997; v. 94, October 1, 1997; v. 94, October 15, 1997. Copyright © 1982, 1983, 1984, 1985, 1986, 1987, 1988, 1989, 1990, 1991, 1992, 1993, 1994, 1995, 1996, 1997 by the American Library Association. All reproduced by permission.—*Books for Keeps,* n. 40, September, 1986; n. 44, May, 1987; n. 46, September, 1987; n. 69, July, 1991; n. 80, May, 1993; n. 88, September, 1994; n. 92, May, 1995; n. 105, July, 1997. © School Bookshop Association 1986, 1987, 1991, 1993, 1994, 1995, 1997. All reproduced by permission.—*Books for Your Children,* v. 20, Autumn-Winter, 1985; v. 21, Autumn-Winter, 1986; v. 25, Autumn, 1990; v. 27, Spring, 1992; v. 30, Spring, 1995; v. 30, Summer, 1995; v. 31, Summer, 1996. © *Books for Your Children* 1985, 1986, 1990, 1992, 1995, 1996. All reproduced by permission.—*Bulletin of the Center for Children's Books,* v. 19, June, 1966; v. 19, July-August, 1966; v. 25, September, 1971; v. 25, July-August, 1972; v. 33, October, 1979; v. 34, May, 1981; v. 35, April, 1982; v. 36, September, 1982; v. 37, July-August, 1984; v. 38, June, 1985; v. 39, April, 1986; v. 39, May, 1986; v. 40, September, 1986; v. 40, February, 1987; v. 40, April, 1987; v. 41, October, 1987; v. 41, March, 1988; v. 42, October, 1988; v. 42, January, 1989; v. 42, March, 1989; v. 42, July-August, 1989; v. 43, September, 1989; v. 43, October, 1989; v. 44, October, 1990; v. 44, March, 1991; v. 44, April, 1991; v. 44, June, 1991; v. 45, October, 1991; v. 45, November, 1991; v. 45, April, 1992. Copyright © 1966, 1971, 1972, 1979, 1981, 1982, 1984, 1985, 1986, 1987, 1988, 1989, 1990, 1991, 1992 by The University of Chicago. All reproduced by permission./ v. 46, January, 1993; v. 46, March, 1993; v. 46, April, 1993; v. 47, October, 1993; v. 47, May, 1994; v. 48, September, 1994; v. 48, November, 1994; v. 48, January, 1995; v. 48, April, 1995; v. 48, May, 1995; v. 48, June, 1995; v. 49, October, 1995; v. 49, December, 1995; v. 49, January, 1996; v. 49, March, 1996; v. 49, May, 1996; v. 49, July-August, 1996; v. 50, September, 1996; v. 50, December, 1996; v. 50, January, 1997; v. 50, February, 1997; v. 50, March, 1997; v. 51, February, 1998. Copyright © 1993, 1994, 1995, 1996, 1997, 1998 by The Board of Trustees of the University of Illinois. All reproduced by permission.—*Catholic Library World,* v. 54, December, 1982; v. 67, March, 1997. Both reproduced by permission.—*Children's Book News,* v. 3, November-December, 1968. Reproduced by permission of Baker Book Services.—*Children's literature in education,* n. 14, May, 1974 for "A Dead Pig and My Father" by Nina Bawden. ©1974, Agathon Press, Inc. Reprinted by permission of Plenum Publishing Corporation and Curtis Brown Ltd (London) on behalf of Nina Bawden./ v. 8, Summer, 1977 for "Recent World War II Fiction: A Survey" by David L. James; v. 22, March, 1991 for "The Writer and the Reader in Carrie's War," by Barbara Freedman; v. 24, December, 1993 for "The Making of Anya or A Tale of Two Villages" by Michael Morpurgo. © 1977, 1991, 1993,

Michael, photograph by James Ravilions.—Napoli, Donna Jo, photograph. Reproduced by permission of Donna Jo Napoli.—Park, Ruth, photograph by Patrick Niland. Reproduced by permission of Ruth Park.—Wisniewski, David, photograph. Davis Studios. Reproduced by permission of David Wisniewski.

Children's
Literature
Review

Nina (Mary Mabey) Bawden

1925-

English author of fiction, nonfiction, and autobiography.

Major works include *Carrie's War* (1973), *The Pepper-mint Pig* (1975), *Kept in the Dark* (1982), *The Outside Child* (1989), *Granny the Pag* (1996).

For more information on Bawden's career prior to 1976, see *CLR,* Volume 2.

INTRODUCTION

One of Britain's most highly esteemed novelists, Bawden is distinguished by her ability to take conventional plots and give them a significance, resonance, and reality uncommon to most children's fiction. Targeting mainly elementary readers, her novels feature young people either facing unusual adventures or new family circumstances; whatever their problems, however, Bawden's protagonists have a rich emotional center which brings them believably to life. The key to the success of her fiction, many critics observe, is that she is able to combine an entertaining, exciting plot with a depth of characterization and theme, making her work accessible to a wide range of readers. Reviewers have also praised her ability to include realistic adult figures in her stories, thus creating a world which reflects real children's concerns about family and society. While her adventure stories may portray young people involved in political intrigue or criminal mystery, they also use family relationships with siblings or parents to reveal character and enrich the story. Other stories focus on children who feel like outsiders, and their experiences often reveal greater truths about life as a whole. Ethel L. Heins once noted that Bawden's "singularity lies in her emotional realism and her respect for young readers," while Peter Hunt summarized: "Her confrontation of the central problem of adults writing for children—the establishment of a satisfactory viewpoint—[has] confirmed her as one of the most subtly innovative of modern writers for children."

Biographical Information

Bawden was born in London, England, and spent her first twelve years in the suburbs of that city. Her father was a marine engineer who was often away at sea while she and her younger brother enjoyed a conventional middle-class lifestyle with their mother. Even at a young age, Bawden was fascinated with literature, using reading and writing to experience places more interesting than her "quite exceptionally boring" neighborhood. Britain's involvement in World War II, however, led to an abrupt change of scenery as she and her brother were among the many children who were sent away from

London to safer parts of the country. She was first relocated to a mining village in South Wales and later to a more pleasant farm in Shropshire. The dislocation gave Bawden an insight into what she calls "the outside child," a character that figures prominently in many of her children's novels.

Bawden did not start her career writing for children, however. After earning degrees from Oxford University where she studied politics, economics, and philosophy, Bawden published her first novel, the adult thriller *Who Calls the Tune* (1953; U.S. edition as *Eyes of Green*). Even before writing directly for a young audience, Bawden was already giving child characters important roles in her fiction, as in the novel *Devil by the Sea* (1957; abridged version for children, 1976). Wanting to explore themes from a different point of view, and being challenged by her own children to write something for them, she published her first children's novel, *The Secret Passage* (1963; published in the U.S. as *House of Secrets*). Since then, the author has produced works for adults and for children in equal measure, earning accolades for both, including a Carnegie Medal commendation for *Carrie's War* and a Booker Prize nomination for the adult novel *Circles of Deceit* (1987). The only difference in writing for two audiences, the author has noted, is in the point of view; otherwise, as Marcus Crouch stated, Bawden "brings to these books the same formidable technical equipment, the same standards and the same dedication that she devotes to her other books which, in the publisher's eyes at least, are intended for adults."

Major Works

Bawden's earliest novels for children contain several familiar elements of mystery and adventure stories: a motherless family sent to live with an apparently uncaring relative (*The Secret Passage; The Runaway Summer,* 1969); a set of friends trying to uncover a secret or a crime (*The Witch's Daughter,* 1966; *A Handful of Thieves,* 1967); or a group of children finding themselves somehow involved in political intrigue (*On the Run,* 1964; published as *Three on the Run,* 1965). Even these early works earned critical praise for the considerable skill in characterization, pace, and setting that Bawden brought to them; a *Junior Bookshelf* critic found them distinguished by their "memorable . . . depth of aim." While these early plots often hinted at serious issues, the 1971 novel *Squib* dealt more directly with social problems in telling of a neglected and mistreated young child who presents a puzzle to the four children who encounter him in a park. Bawden turned to a historical setting for the first time with *Carrie's War,* focusing the action on the coming of age of a girl who has been evacuated to the Welsh countryside during World War II. Another award-winning historical novel followed. Set at the turn of the century, *The Peppermint Pig* proved that Bawden was equally at home with slice-of-life family portraits as with adventure stories.

Suspense and adventure have continued to play a major part in Bawden's novels, however, at the same time that friendships and family relationships are developed in realistic detail. The thriller *Kept in the Dark,* for instance, places three children with their estranged grandparents. As the children try to determine how they fit into this new situation, they discover the existence of an older half-brother whose erratic behavior endangers the entire family. The story of an unknown half-sibling—a situation that actually occurred in Bawden's own family—is explored from the opposite perspective in *The Outside Child,* which follows the efforts of a thirteen-year-old to discover why her existence has been kept a secret from her younger half-siblings. There are no dark secrets in the 1988 novel *Keeping Henry* (also published as *Henry*); instead Bawden creates a powerful portrait of a family, separated by the evacuations of World War II, whose struggles to remain united are somehow mirrored in the moods of their pet squirrel. One of Bawden's most recent works, *Granny the Pag,* showcases her ability to create memorable, believable characters. In this novel about a custody battle, Cat's untraditional, motorcycle-riding grandmother has her ability to care for Cat challenged by Cat's newly successful actor parents. In portraying how the actions of adults jeopardize the Cat's

security and peace of mind, Bawden once again demonstrates her ability to realistically portray the emotional lives of children. As Elaine Moss noted: "Nina Bawden is not merely the technically efficient teller of a good yarn; she is an author whose gift for understanding adults and weaving them into integral role in her children's stories makes her a significant writer for the young."

Awards

Bawden earned a Carnegie commendation in 1973 for *Carrie's War,* which also received the 1993 Phoenix Award from the Children's Literature Association, while *The Peppermint Pig* won the *Guardian* Award for children's fiction in 1975. *Kept in the Dark* received a nomination for the Edgar Allan Poe Award in 1983, and the adult novel *Circles of Deceit* was nominated in 1987 for Britain's prestigious Booker Prize. Bawden received a Commander of the British Empire citation for services to literature in 1995, and was the British nominee for the Hans Christian Andersen Award in 1996.

AUTHOR'S COMMENTARY

Nina Bawden

SOURCE: "Through Literature of Life?" in *Signal,* No. 11, May, 1973, pp. 102-07.

[The following excerpt is from a speech Bawden delivered at a National Book League conference held in Birmingham in November, 1972. Bawden presents her perspective on whether fiction has a place in helping young people to cope with the social problems that surround them.]

A children's book should, like any good novel, hold an honest mirror up to life. And by that I don't mean that children should necessarily be given books about themselves, matching social class to social class, colour to colour, but that the emotional landscape in their stories should be one they recognize. Not just situations, but the emotions those situations arouse. And that's where one runs into trouble, particularly if you're writing for children under twelve, as I do—perhaps because it's an area in which adults themselves feel insecure. Like the teacher who wrote to me about the television serial of *The Runaway Summer* and said she thought it was "highly dangerous viewing" for children. I think she reacted so strongly not because Mary's parents were getting divorced but because the child herself was portrayed as having some rather unpleasant thoughts about her parents as a result.

It's important in children's books to write about relationships between children and adults, I think. I know when I was young this seemed to me to be something I couldn't get from books and wanted to. Everyone learns, after all, through story; it's the way you learn to look at yourself and other people and discover what the world is like. Books for children that leave out the adults, leave out a large area of human relationships—an area which, when I was a child, was the source of some of my worst fears. Not pleasurable fears like the excitement of nicking dolls from Woolworth's, but cold, flattening, draining fears like did my mother love me, why were my parents quarrelling downstairs? Books that don't take account of children's fears will never mean much to them, and books can help by bringing fears out into the open. It's reassuring for a child to know others have felt the same way. A letter saying "I didn't know anyone else felt like that" is one of the rewards of writing for children.

Not that I ever intended to write about "problems" for children, simply to place what I hope are exciting adventure stories in a world that is real to them, and include situations and feelings they know. Adventure stories are important to children, not just the what-happens-next excitement, but because they can see themselves taking part in the action and test themselves: would they be brave in such a situation, or would they run away? Few children have a chance to do this in real life.

The difference between writing for children and for adults can be seen in *Squib,* which is a story about an ill-treated child. To have written about the little boy himself would not only have been too horrifying but also morally confusing: one would have had to consider the ignorant foster mother and her stupid husband. And young children, pre-adolescents, still inhabit too morally structured a universe for this. As Chesterton said, "Children are innocent and love justice, while adults are wicked and naturally prefer mercy."

Nina Bawden

SOURCE: "A Dead Pig and My Father," in *Children's literature in education,* No. 14, May, 1974, pp. 3-13.

One of my earliest memories is standing in Tilbury Docks, near London, looking at a dead pig in the water. It was floating belly upwards, a tight yellowish balloon, veined with blue. It was surrounded by several planks of wood that were being pushed into the side by a passenger liner that was coming into dock. When these planks crowded together and bumped the swollen-bellied pig, it bobbed in the water and squeaked.

I was four years old. I know how old I was because my mother was standing beside me, holding my baby brother. He was wrapped in a shawl and he had a face like a wet, wrinkled prune. He was two months old and he had been born just after my fourth birthday.

We were standing on the dockside, my mother and my baby brother and me, because my father's ship was coming in. He was a marine engineer, coming home from Australia after a long time away and he hadn't seen my baby brother so this was an important occasion. My mother said, 'Look at the big ship, Nina. See if you can see Daddy.'

But I was more interested in the dead pig. I went on watching it as it bobbed and squeaked in the water.

Children don't always feel what adults expect them to feel, nor see what adults expect them to see. They inhabit the same world but they look at it so differently. This is why they are so rewarding to write about, so *useful* to the novelist. Novelists have always used children, as Henry James used his little heroine in *What Maisie Knew,* to comment on the hypocrisies and follies of society. They move, as it were, in the undergrowth; they have their ears to the ground, and their eyes are unclouded. They are detached, attentive and sometimes quite cruel observers of what goes on in the adult world because, although it is their world too, their interests in it are basically quite different. A dead pig, to a four-year-old, can be more interesting than the father she has not seen for years and has almost forgotten. . . .

We [Bawden and her mother] were both there together, caught up in the same, highly charged, emotional situation, but we each saw it quite differently. And the important difference between writing for adults and writing for children is not style or subject matter, though those things come into it, but the point of view you're looking from.

I should say, before I go on, that by writing for children I mean writing for pre-adolescents from about ten to thirteen or so. The child I am writing for, is, I suppose, the child I used to be, and since my childhood came to an end, more or less, when the war broke out and I left home for the first time, I have a fairly clear, fixed picture of that child and her emotions and preoccupations in my mind. I do not write for older children—although any literate teenager could read my adult novels—and I do not think there is any point in writing specifically for them. I believe, indeed, that the growing tendency in children's fiction to give more critical attention to books for adolescents than to those written for a younger audience is a slightly pernicious one.

Of course, a statement like that, once made, must immediately be qualified. There are some novels that are especially suitable for teenagers, some fantasies, some historical stories, and there are occasional books, like that marvellous, stylized comedy, *The Strange Affair of Adelaide Harris,* that appeal enormously to them. But in general, it seems to me that most modern novels aimed deliberately at this older age group are often watered down adult fiction; thin gruel, rather foolishly served to people who not only should be cutting their adult teeth on more solid food, but, given the choice, would prefer to. Dr Johnson may not have been right when he said that babies do not want to read about other babies, but I am quite sure that most adolescents don't want to read about other adolescents, or at least not in a selectively limited way. They may read children's books, consciously slipping back into childhood from time to time for a number of reasons and no harm in that, but once they've crossed the bridge—so to speak—emerged from childhood, what they want to read about is the new world they've just entered. They are concerned with their own position in it, of course, but *not* in the way in which it is being presented in those novels that are written about what are presumed to be exclusively teenage problems. We all know the story about the mother who went to the library to get a suitable novel for her fifteen-year-old and was asked by the librarian, 'What's his problem?'

Literature has a function in education, obviously—we all learn about the world and our place in it through story—but it is not a branch of the social services, supplying advice about drugs or sex, what to do about VD or where to get an abortion, which is the sort of subject that seems to appeal to the writers who have decided to cash in on this particular market, or work out their own emotional hangups by passing them on to the young. As a view of adolescence this seems not only unpleasantly prurient, but as curiously unrealistic as the romantic Victorian view of childhood as a state of innocence from which we have all fallen. And even when good novelists write for adolescents they tend to give a narrower picture than they should, write, over-sensitively, about 'growing up,' as an exercise in nostalgia, or as an escape, perhaps, from the spiritual and emotional confusion of being really grown. Which is not to say one should not write *about* adolescence, only that one should do so in the mainstream of fiction for adults, from an adult point of view, so that the book is there on the shelves along with Tolstoy and Salinger and Graham Greene and Kurt Vonnegut and can be judged beside them.

Now, having cleared that bit of ground, let's turn to the children. When I started to write it never occurred to me to write for them. Why should I? I was grown up. I wrote three books before I even used a child as a fictional character and when I did, in *Devil by the Sea,* it was only, initially, to give an extra turn of the screw to a thriller. But as I wrote that book the child in it, a fat, unattractive nine-year-old who became hopelessly involved with a murderer, began to fascinate me. She was a liar as well as being fat and plain, and when she tried to explain to her parents what was happening to her—which she only half understood, anyway—they either misinterpreted what she told them or assumed she was lying as usual. She was locked in her small, nightmarish world as they were locked in theirs, and there was no communication between them.

That child was part of me, of my own remembered past, far more so than any adult character I had invented up to that time, and, as I developed her, I began to see clearly for the first time, for *myself,* how true it is that the child is father to the man. This is something Wordsworth knew long before Freud. Writing about children

you have to hold in your head what they will become when they are grown. Writing about adults, you must be able to see what they once were. You go back to the beginning so you can see how things became as they are. This is why I write as I do, alternately for adults and for children. I find the one kind of book feeds the other.

But to begin with, although I wrote several novels after *Devil by the Sea* with children in them—*Tortoise by Candlelight, A Little Love, a Little Learning,*—the story was always told from the adult standpoint. That is, the adult looking back and using the child's innocence and fresh sensibilities as a way of commenting on the accepted assumptions of society and so getting a double view of what seems to be going on. We, the writer and reader, think we know what the adults are up to. The child will only partly know. To him, criminal actions, say, or gross sexual misconduct, may only appear as lying or cheating, unkindness, thoughtlessness—cruelty of one kind or another towards other people. I say 'only'. What, in truth could be worse? Hurting people is a greater crime than robbing banks. The very fact that the child has a partial view and is ignorant of some more trivially nasty aspects of adult behaviour, serves to put them in perspective and so make an important moral point.

Writing *for* children is not easier than writing for adults: it is different. The storyline, clearly, has to be stronger. Children may say, if asked, that they have enjoyed a highly praised book without much of a plot, but then children will often give the answer they think is expected. They are naturally courteous in this way like some primitive tribes. The clue to what they really enjoy is what they reread, what they go back to, and this is almost always a book with a strong narrative line.

Not that they are unsubtle. Most of the subjects I write about for adults I write about for children, too: personal relationships, emotions, motives—the extraordinary gulf between what people say and what they really mean. The only real difference—or so it seems to me—between writing for children and writing for adults is a difference of viewpoints. When I wrote my first children's novel I just became eleven years old again.

And that wasn't so difficult. Time travel is not simply a device dreamed up by science fiction writers. We can all travel backwards, whenever we fancy, inside our own heads. You remember the physical sensation of, say, a stocking stuck on the blood of a grazed knee, the smell of dog dirt on the path by the railway line, and the emotional memories follow at once. . . .

Writing for children I remembered, too, the kind of books I had enjoyed as a child. Adventure stories, of course. All children like adventure, and not just for the excitement of what happens next. You don't have to read Anna Freud to know that children enjoy Jack killing the giant. But more important than that basic fantasy is the fact that children are, by and large, singularly helpless. In real life they can't make anything happen. All they can do is stand by and watch. In adventure stories they can see themselves taking part in the action and not only that. They can also test themselves, measure themselves against the characters in the book. Would *they* be brave in such a situation, or would they run away? Would they be honest, or would they lie?

Remembering what I had enjoyed when I was young, I remembered what I had missed in children's books, too. The grown-ups, apart from a wicked stepmother or uncle, were always flat, peripheral figures with no emotions and no function. The books offered to me in my childhood left out the adult world, and even when they didn't, entirely, they never presented adults as children really see them. Parents and teachers were usually shown as kind, loving, distant figures—emotionally hygienic, you might say. Not only were they never beastly to children except in a stereotyped, fairy tale way, but they were never beastly to anyone. They were never the uncertain, awkward, quirky, *dangerous* creatures that I knew adults to be. Since it was the adults who had written these books, it was reasonable to assume that they didn't want to give themselves away; show themselves to us children, to their *enemies,* as they really were. I think, when I started writing for children, I wanted to put this right. To include the grown-ups as solid characters whose roles were as important in a child's life as I knew them to be, and also to EXPOSE them. And of course, recognizable meanness in adults is something children do enjoy reading about. A boy wrote to me about *A Handful of Thieves* and said, 'I liked that book because Fred's Mum is sometimes nasty to his Gran the way my Mum is sometimes nasty to my Gran. I made my Mum read that book.'

Not that children are perfect, either. But what they do have, however they behave, is a strong sense of right and wrong, an awareness, if you like, of good and evil. They are often aware of their own badness in a way adults sometimes forget. When I was young, I often felt very bad and wicked. All children do—I know this now, but I didn't know it then. The children in the books I had read never seemed to have the kind of dark, angry feelings that worried me. They were often naughty in a jolly way, but they were never bad. None of them felt as I did when I was nine years old, no one in the world.

When I was nine, I went to stay with my grandmother for the summer. She lived in Swaffham, in Norfolk. My grandfather had just died and I was to keep her company. She had been born in 1860, married a coach painter, had four children—an ordinary life, but it didn't seem ordinary to me. That summer I stayed with her she told me stories, about her girlhood and young womanhood—about her whole life. . . .

I was fascinated by my grandmother's stories, by the glimpses they gave me of an adult world which was rather different from anything I had been shown before. . . . There is all the difference in the world between hearing something at your grandmother's knee and reading it in print. Writing for children, you should

never pretend things are other than they are, but you can, and should, leave out things that are beyond their comprehension. Answering their questions, their doubts and fears, is one thing. Clobbering them over the head with the facts of life, quite another.

A good book for children, like a good book for adults, should hold an honest mirror up to life; reflect the emotional landscape they move in, tell them what they want to know. And what they want to know, what they want to understand, is their own situation. What they see from their point of view, not what the adult sees, looking back. And their view is necessarily limited. They cannot understand, for example, the desperate anxiety, the helpless love, that parents feel for them. My novel, *The Birds on the Trees,* is about the family of a boy who takes drugs. It is an adult novel because although the central character is a boy of eighteen with a younger brother and sister, the theme of the book is the parents' helplessness, their bitter sense of failure. The boy takes LSD and goes mad. His father and mother try to explain to their eleven-year-old daughter what has happened to him but she cannot understand it. She understands that her brother is ill because he has gone to hospital. People go to hospital because they have appendicitis, or something like that. She explains his illness this way because the real situation is beyond her comprehension. She is aware of her parents' fear and the fact that they are so engrossed with her brother that they no longer seem to care about her. So, since appendicitis is not very dreadful, and people recover from it, the real reason they have ceased to love her must be something they have not told her. They love Toby more than they love her because she is, quite probably, adopted.

Children relate what happens about them to themselves. Blame themselves. If you include an adult situation in a children's book, you must look at it from their side. The child, Mary, in *The Runaway Summer,* sees her parents' divorce as her fault. They are getting divorced because she is so horrible that they no longer love her. You could write an adult novel as Henry James did, round this subject. I chose to write about Mary for children, an adventure story, in which she finds an immigrant boy on the beach and hides him from the uncertain, dangerous world where no adult can be trusted. She doesn't want to know, or be told, how her parents feel; all she wants to know is how the divorce will affect her.

There is no other way she can look at it. The central fact of a child's life is that everything that happens to her depends on the uncertain whims of the adults. As Mary shouts at her Aunt Alice, 'Children don't have any say; they just have to do what they're told. They have to wear what they're told and eat what they're given and live where they're *put.* It's not fair. . . .'

It's not fair. The old childhood cry—and we should listen to it, because it tells us something important. Children inhabit, as few adults do, a morally structured universe. Things are right or they are wrong, or unfair, black or white. You can show them a few shades in between if you are cunning, but not too many or you will confuse them, disturb their sense of moral judgment which they have to develop, slowly, for themselves, or they will never judge soundly later.

In writing for children, if you take your role seriously and believe who you are writing for is important, you must remember this. My children's novel, *Squib,* is about a battered child, a neglected, pale little boy that four other children meet in the local playground. But it is not about Squib himself but about the children who rescue him and the fantasies that they pin on him. The littlest ones think he is being fattened up by a wicked witch for her supper, an older boy thinks he has been kidnapped and held for ransom, a girl pretends he is her young, drowned brother come back. To have written the truth about Squib would not only have been too horrifying—and I do not think one should deliberately horrify children—but also too complicated. It would have meant considering the ignorant people who had ill-treated him and admitting that they might be pitiable, too. And I think that would have been too morally confusing for children who need to feel the ground is firm under their feet. As [G.K] Chesterton said, 'Children are innocent and love justice, while adults are wicked and naturally prefer mercy.'

I used the same theme in my next adult novel. When I had finished *Squib,* I found myself wondering what would have happened to a child like that when he grew up. However carefully he was tended later there would still have been this gap, this terrible space in his life, when normal emotional growth had been suspended. I thought of the war, when I had been evacuated to Wales. Suppose there had been a little girl, treated as Squib had been. . . .

And so I wrote *Anna Apparent,* about a child who is treated by her foster parents like an animal—thrown scaps of bread, forced to sleep, like a dog, in a barn. She is rescued and brought up by a silly but well-intentioned woman, appearing to grow and develop quite normally, but there is always this gap in her life which affects not only her but all those about her.

Writing the same story for adults, you see, but looking at it from a different point of view; trying to understand what happens later, when the same child is grown. The final effect, not just the immediate one. The long view, for which you need an adult perspective, both in writer and reader.

It is possible, occasionally of course, for the two views to come fairly close. When I finished *Anna Apparent,* in the way that one thing leads to another, I found I was still thinking about the war and my own experiences as an evacuee, a child far from home, suffering in some ways but still surviving, adapting, learning about other people.

I started my latest children's book, *Carrie's War,* with a mother going back to the mining valley where she had lived during the war and telling her children what happened to her there. It was the first time, starting a novel, that I had actually wondered whether this was a story for adults or for children. But I didn't wonder long because I soon discovered that although Carrie appears to be telling it to her own children, she is not really telling it from the point of view of a grown woman looking back over her shoulder, but from the point of view of the child she was when it happened, a twelve-year-old girl putting her own interpretation, which is still a child's interpretation, on what goes on around her. She and her young brother are living with a mean, difficult man with a huge chip on his shoulder. The little boy sees him, quite simply, as an ogre. He learns to keep out of his way and has no interest in why he behaves as he does. Nor has Carrie, really. She sees that he tries to be nice, in his way and is, up to a point, sorry for him, but although she is told that he had a harsh, cold, early life, she does not really relate this to his present behaviour.

Quite simply, he does not really concern her. What does concern her are her own feelings about her small brother and about the kind woman, Hepzibah Green, who lives in a house called Druid's Bottom. Hepzibah may or may not be a witch. She feeds the children vast, comforting meals and tells them wonderful stories. One of the stories is about the screaming skull that belongs to the house. If it is ever removed, the walls of the house will crumble. . . .

Carrie half believes this. Towards the end of the book, for what seems to her a very good reason, she throws the skull into the horse pond. That night the house catches fire and she blames herself for it until thirty years later when she comes back to the valley and understands fully what happened.

If I had been a grown-up writing that story, I suppose I might have used the episode of the skull in some other way, as a symbol for some deep, inadmissible feeling of guilt. And perhaps it was, too. But since it wasn't a grown-up telling it, but the twelve-year-old girl that still lurks inside me, it was just the terrible thing Carrie did that she couldn't tell anyone but that she knows will haunt her for ever.

There you have it. My secret is out, as they say. As far as I am concerned, the only real difference between writing for adults or for children is whose eyes I am looking through. My mother's—standing on Tilbury Docks and wishing her wretched child would smile and be nice. Or the little girl's, standing beside her and watching a dead pig in the water, instead of her father's ship coming in.

Nina Bawden

SOURCE: "The Outside Child," in *The Horn Book Magazine,* Vol. LXVII, No. 6, November-December, 1991, pp. 688-94.

[Bawden adapted the following article from a speech she delivered at the Children's Literature New England "Homecoming" conference held at Saint Michael's College in Colchester, Vermont, on August 8, 1990.]

Long ago, in the Second World War, we had a squirrel called Henry. My mother was living with my brothers on a farm in central Wales, and I stayed with them in the holidays. During term I lived in a mining valley in south Wales, which was where my school had been evacuated; we lived with mining families and went to school in the local grammar-school building mornings or afternoons and in Welsh chapels the rest of the time. I made use of that experience in a book called *Carrie's War.* I say "made use of" rather than "wrote about" because *using* is what most writers do, squeezing out every drop of drama they can about what has happened to them and adding a few imaginative frills and fancies along the way. Forty-five years after our squirrel came to live with us, I wrote *Henry,* a novel which is about him, and about my brothers, my mother, and me, and about the part of our wartime life that was spent in a wild part of Wales, on a farm.

Henry was very important to all of us, for a number of different reasons. Writing about him, and my family, I began to understand, for the first time in forty-five years, why he was so important in our lives and what he had really meant to each of us—especially to me.

I lived the first twelve years of my life in a quite exceptionally boring suburb of London. My father was in the merchant navy, and we lived near the London docks, but not near enough to enjoy the huge excitement and bustle of great ships coming and going—that was something we only saw when my father's ship came in and we went to meet him. We lived in a small house with a long skinny garden and nowhere to play except the dusty park that was guarded by a dragon of a park keeper, a man whose natural instinct when he saw a child was to shout at it. My mother—who had been brought up in the country, in a small town in Norfolk, and was still missing her childhood home, and perhaps even her own mother—thought that our suburb was featureless and ugly and that no one but dullards would live there if they had any choice in the matter. Even if she hadn't told me this, I would have known the grass was greener elsewhere; that there was a better life than ours, a life where people lived in beautiful houses and had interesting conversations and exciting adventures. I had read about this life in books. Reading, which is supposed to improve the mind, had simply added to my discontent. Although I loved my mother and my brothers, home, to my mind, was a place to get away from. And since, like all children, I was a prisoner, I escaped into books.

Literature is not an imitation of life as, say, a picture by Van Meegeren is an imitation of a Vermeer. A book is not less real than life. Certainly, when I was young, the stories that I read and the people in them were real to me, as real as my own thoughts and dreams. More real in a way. I felt that I knew more about the characters I read about than I knew about the people around me. This is true of all readers to some extent; even if they keep an ear to the ground and an eye to the keyhole, what they learn about their friends and their family is limited to what they see and hear, while what they can know about an author's characters can be anything the writer chooses to tell them. You cannot really know the innermost thoughts and emotions of someone who exists only in life; there is always some secret chamber they prefer to keep hidden. But characters in books can be filleted, laid out on the slab, explored, exposed. Understood.

If, as a child, I was more aware of the revelations in novels than is perhaps usual, it may have been because our suburban street was so respectable and shut away—people keeping themselves to themselves behind their curtained windows—that it seemed to me they must have something to conceal. After all, in books people lost all their money, died, went to prison—why should our neighbors be immune to these disasters? Or it may simply have been that my family was exceptionally secretive. Whispers surrounded me in my childhood; voices fell when I entered a room. "Never ask your father to show you his birth certificate," my mother once hissed at me. I have no idea why she said this, since I was only about nine years old at the time and that particular question must have been about the last I would have thought of asking him. I was rising fifty before I found out that my grandfather, my father's father, was not a lighterman on the Thames as I had always been told, but an Italian ship's cook called Achille Benati—a much more romantic ancestor altogether. My father's mother had been married to a lighterman, but he had died, leaving her with two sons, and she had rented a house in East London, on East India Dock Road, near the London docks, and turned it into a lodging house. She took in merchant seamen as lodgers—no one below the rank of first mate, my father once told me, in case I should think it was a low-class establishment. But he didn't tell me about the Italian ship's cook.

Achille Benati married my grandmother a month before my father was born and then, some years later, deserted her for a much younger woman, a stewardess on a passenger liner. He was never heard of again. My father, who had been christened Mario Angelo Benati, decided, when he left school to be apprenticed to an engineering workshop in the docks, to take his mother's first husband's surname. I suppose he was ashamed of his real father's defection. I don't know. I never asked him. As far as I know, he never knew that I knew. When I found out, he was very old, and it seemed too delicate a matter to discuss with him if, as I assumed he did, he thought it shameful.

On the other hand, it may have been my mother who chose to keep it dark. Certainly, it was she who decided that my brothers and I should not be told the other important family secret. I had once told her that I remembered falling down the stairs when I was very young, so young that I was still wearing nappies, and I remembered that there had been another child there, at the bottom of the stairs, who was a lot bigger than I. My mother became mysteriously agitated and told me I had "too much imagination," which I knew was a crime as far as most adults were concerned. The truth, as I found out eventually, when I was twenty-six, was that my father had been married before he met my mother and his wife had died when their baby was born. When my mother and father were married some four years later, my mother looked after the little girl, my half sister, but there were some family complications of an obscure but passionate kind, and the day I fell down the stairs she accused the poor child of pushing me out of jealousy. There was a monumental scene, and our father took my sister away to live with some cousins. He took her away in a taxi, she remembers, gave her a huge box of chocolates to comfort her, and then left her with these cousins whom she had never met before. For many years after that—twenty-five years, in fact—she knew about me and my brothers and saw pictures of us when she went on board my father's ship, but we never knew of her existence. And it was sixty years after I had tumbled down the stairs in my nappies that I decided to write a book about what I thought might have been my sister's experience. *The Outside Child* is not a "true" account of what happened in my family all those years ago. How could it be? I was only about nine months old. I never met the women who brought my sister up. They were so implacably opposed to my mother—and by extension to her children—that I never visited my sister while they were alive. Jane Tucker's aunts were based on my mother's older sister and the friend—an honorary aunt to me—with whom she lived. They lived in a seaside town where we sometimes went for summer holidays, and when I wanted to draw a picture of a home that my young heroine would never want to leave—where she was more truly at home than she could ever have been in her father's family—I could think of nothing better than their friendly, happy house that was always open-windowed to their pretty garden. And I must have imagined it all fairly accurately, because when she read the book, my sister said that what I had written seemed true to her, to her memories of how she had thought and felt.

This family habit of keeping skeletons locked up in a number of cupboards was useful background for a novelist. It taught me to keep my ears and eyes open if I wanted to find out what really went on, what secrets people were hiding. No one was likely to tell me, I knew. Adults had such curious ideas about what was suitable for children. You could never trust them to tell you the truth about anything. And when the war came, and I was evacuated, I took my detective instincts along with me and put them to work on the various families I lived with in the mining valleys of south Wales, giving these no doubt blameless people dramatic and sometimes criminal pasts that would have surprised and shocked them had they known.

I didn't miss my London suburb. I missed my mother and my brothers, but I didn't miss my home. Life in other people's houses, even if not always comfortable, was much too interesting to leave room for being homesick.

My novel *Carrie's War* is based on my own wartime story. Carrie, who is twelve in 1939, and her brother Nick, who is younger, are sent away from London as the bombs start to fall, just as I was sent away. They leave the city in a darkened train as I did, not knowing where they are going, with labels around their necks as if they are parcels. I remember that when I asked my teacher why we had to have labels, she answered that if the train was bombed and we were blown to bits, the labels would be useful to identify our bodies. Carrie and Nick arrive, as my brother and I did, in a Welsh mining village and are lined up by their teachers so that the local people can come and pick the children they want to take into their homes as members of their families. Carrie is certain that no one will choose her and her brother. Nick has eaten too many sweets on the train and looks dreadful. Carrie is afraid that no one will want a boy who looks as if he might be ill, and a nuisance. She hisses at her brother, "'Why don't you smile and look *nice*.'"

Now this did not actually happen to my brother and me. He did live briefly in my mining valley before he went to stay with our mother and our younger brother, but he arrived on a different train and we only found out we had been sent to the same town several days later. Even that is not true, now that I think about it; he had been sent to a quite dreadful boarding school for the sons of merchant seamen from which he ran away—how and when he arrived in Wales I simply do not know. But I did know what it felt like to be sure no one would want me, because that was how I felt. And though the story of *Carrie's War* is not mine, or only partly mine, the feelings she has about being separated from her family for the first time, sent to live with strangers, are those I remember. You settled in, so that if your mother or father came, you grew shy; they didn't belong in this new life. And you didn't belong in theirs, either.

To some extent, people are one's home, of course. Mother and father, husband or wife, children. But the place is important, too. Carrie and Nick are at home with their foster mother, Auntie Lou; they are even at home with her disagreeable brother, the ogre-like Councillor Evans. But they find their safe place somewhere else altogether: in the house where Mr. Evans's invalid sister lives with Mister Johnny and Hepzibah Green. Carrie and Nick go there Christmas Eve, along an old railway line and down a dark *cwm* through the yew trees of Druid's Grove. Mister Johnny, who is retarded and has a cleft palate, frightens them without meaning to, and they run, stumbling and terrified, toward the dark house, where a door opens like magic and they fall through it to "light, warmth, and safety."

Hepzibah Green was a woman my grandmother used to tell tales about. She is in *The Peppermint Pig* as well, only there she is called Hetty MacGregor. Since I was always in trouble when I was growing up, Hetty—or Hepzibah—was the sort of woman it comforted me to imagine existed: sensible, kind, always understanding. But the house in *Carrie's War*, which is called Druid's Bottom, belongs in central Wales, in the Marches, not in the mining valleys. My mother and my younger brother were evacuated there, to one huge room in what seemed to us a most beautiful farmhouse, looking over green fields and bare, heathery mountains, in the heart of the country. We all loved it as soon as we saw it. My brothers both lived there all the time with my mother; I only went there in the holidays from school. But I loved it as much as they did, if not more, because I wasn't there all the time. I helped on the farm; I fed chickens, milked cows, rode the farmer's wife's ponies, and tormented the Herefordshire bull. My mother's nostalgia for her country childhood had always convinced me that the country was superior to town; living in the country for the first time, I saw for myself that it was true. The old house, with its flagged ground floor and polished oak upper floors, was beautiful to me; so was the valley; the hills and the fields. For years after we left, it was the only place I ever thought of as home; it was where I always longed to go when I was lonely or frightened, when things went wrong in my life. I put the farmhouse into *Carrie's War* without realizing that I was doing so. When I finally decided to write about Henry, the red squirrel my seven-year-old brother shot out of a tree with his big brother's catapult, all the happiness I had known there came back. It was as if *Henry* had given it a habitation and a name. That farmhouse, in that valley, was the only place I ever really felt homesick for.

I have chosen to discuss *Carrie's War* and *Henry,* which are both set back in the forties, in World War II, because that is the only time I have known a kind of homelessness. It was nothing compared to what happened to less fortunate children in the rest of Europe, of course, but it gave me at least a shadowy idea of what it might be like to be a refugee, with no safe place to go, belonging to no one. Perhaps, indeed, that long-ago experience is why outside children have always interested me: not only Jane Tucker in *The Outside Child,* but Squib, the abused child who is worse off than anyone, for whom home is not even a last resort—"the place where, when you have to go there, they have to take you in"—but a place of terror and physical danger. And there is also Mary in *The Runaway Summer,* who is safe enough with her grandfather but unwanted by her divorced parents.

On the other hand, of course, it is possible that outside children are in fact inherently more interesting. People on their own, up against it, in some kind of crisis, are much more intriguing than people for whom life is straightforward and easy. You want to see how they make out. My own feelings about awkward children, the ones who don't fit, may have been colored by my mother's nostalgic view of home life. She was the youngest of four and much fussed over. She told me the story

of the peppermint pig, the pet pig my grandmother bought from the milkman for a shilling. When I wrote it down, she was furious with me because I had given the family a tramp for a grandfather. There had been one, in point of fact; he was as real as the poor pig who went to the butcher at the end of the year, but he didn't fit with the picture she had made for herself of a respectable, acceptable family. She said, "I don't see why you always have to stir things up, Nina."

I had thought stirring things up was a writer's job, really. But it is not only mothers who don't always care for it.

I believe that the great joy of fiction is that one individual speaks straight to another: writer to reader across all sorts of barriers—race, country, sex, age. If this essay contains random thoughts, it is because I think that is what writers are best at: saying what seems to them most immediate—not important, or fitting in with some tidy theory, but their individual idiosyncratic view, which operates in what Vladimir Nabokov called "that delicate meeting place between imagination and knowledge."

GENERAL COMMENTARY

Elaine Moss

SOURCE: "Nina Bawden: An Author for Today," in *Signal,* No. 4, January, 1971, pp. 28-33.

At a social gathering of children's book people I once said to a fellow reviewer that Nina Bawden was the kind of writer I should like to see brought into the limelight: her adventure stories are accessible to a wide readership, her characters deeply but unfussily observed, her themes contemporary and her backgrounds vivid and various. He looked at me with amazement, granted all I said, took a sip of red wine and then dismissed my championship of Miss Bawden with the remark, "But her books are so poorly produced—no illustrations."

I was dumbfounded. Was he right? Were the books poorly produced? I couldn't remember: those I knew had been so good to read. And unillustrated? Was it possible that I had created in my mind's eye the terrifying picture of the flood in Kenya—"great chunks of red mud, trees, huts being thrown up into the air then gobbled up by the water" (this was the starting point for Ben Mallory's adventures in *The Secret Passage* and *On the Run*)? Had I really never seen an artist's drawing of Polly-Anna, the informing five-year-old twins ("We *saw'd* her, Simon") with their funny round faces and blobby noses (minor but memorable characters who bob up, from time to time, in the pages of *The Runaway Summer*)? Did I conjure up for myself so clear an idea of the cosmography of the sleasy suburb which is the setting for Miss Bawden's most compelling novel, *A Handful of Thieves?* I left my drink untouched and rushed home to find out.

True, true. . . . Nina Bawden's books (apart from *The Witch's Daughter*) are unillustrated. But badly produced? Five lively jackets by Shirley Hughes outweigh one undistinguished effort (for the author's first children's book) by Alan Breese. Paper, print and margins? Reasonable. An occasional example of poor proof-reading, I'll admit, but no child, once drawn into a Bawden story, will care a fig that there isn't a picture to be seen, because her words create such vivid images; and if, here and there, inverted commas fail to close themselves . . . ? My friend the expert will mark it up (quite rightly, for we are nothing if not guardians of standard) against the book, but the young reader will already be at the end of the next paragraph and over the page.

Before I am relegated for ever to the ranks of the Philistines let me say that I do think book production is important: but it is not of over-riding importance. The medium is the medium. It must be kept in its place. If I had to choose between drawing attention to a first-class piece of writing addressed to a wide audience but presented, physically, in a second-rate style, and a classy piece of writing for the intellectual few, smartly produced to catch the adult eye, I would choose to consider the former on the grounds that books are primarily words, and words are for communication.

It takes true talent to write well for the many. This is Nina Bawden's gift. Take the opening page of *The White Horse Gang*:

> "Hey Mum, do you know what?"
> No answer.
> "Hey, Mum."
> No answer.
> "MUM."
> Sam bellowed with the full force of his lungs. His face turned red as a plum.
> "I'm not deaf, dear. There's no need to shout."
>
> Mrs. Peach stopped cutting up steak for the dogs' dinner and looked at Sam in the kindly but somehow *unseeing* way she looked at most human beings most of the time. Though she was fond of Sam, she would really have been more interested in him had he been a dog. Though Sam knew this, he did not resent it—indeed, from his point of view, the situation had its advantages. Other mothers fussed their sons about washing behind their ears and keeping the house tidy. Mrs. Peach fussed over her salukis instead: she was too busy grooming them and getting burrs out of their coats to worry over such an unimportant thing as a bit of dirt on the back of a boy's neck. As a result, Sam confined his washing activities to as small an area as possible: if he washed his face he stopped short at his jaw line so that he often looked like a dark boy wearing a fair, freckled mask. Today he had omitted even this trifling attention. Looking at him in her abstracted way, Mrs. Peach thought he looked exceptionally well and brown.
>
> "What did you want, dear?" she asked.

This sets the mood exactly for a light-weight comic-

kidnap story (not, in fact, one of Miss Bawden's best) in which adult eccentricity plays its part. And *On the Run* begins even more beguilingly with bored Ben bouncing his ball along a wall which connects a row of London gardens:

> Suddenly the ball landed on a crumbly brick and shot forwards and sideways at an awkward angle. Ben lurched to catch it, missed, lost his balance and fell forward—not off the wall, but on to it, so that he ended crouched in an undignified position on hands and toes with his bottom sticking up in the air.
>
> The whole of his stomach seemed to turn over. He was, for a moment, badly frightened. Not because he had so nearly fallen, but because the top of the wall just in front of him was covered with jagged spikes of broken glass. The first spike—a wicked piece that looked like the top of a broken bottle—was only an inch away from his nose. If he had not been agile—or lucky—he would have fallen right on top of it and cut his face to pieces. He eased himself down carefully to sit astride the wall and saw that the broken glass continued all round the small garden that lay just in front of him, on his right side. And his ball had bounced into it.
>
> It had bounced—though of course he didn't realize it at the time—straight into adventure.

Another triumphant entry.

And once inside, the pace never lets up. Miss Bawden, a seasoned writer of adult detective fiction, is past-master at plot construction, at surprise moves, at improbable people coming up with plausible solutions to knotty problems, and at chapter ends which are simply invitations to read straight on. At random, I choose the end of Chapter 10 from *The Witch's Daughter*:

> Tim crawled back to the inner cavern on hands and knees, one hand on the wall of the tunnel. At least he had not come far, he could find his way back. But the brief journey taught him one thing: he could never, in this frightful darkness, find his way back through the maze of tunnels to the beach. There was nothing they could do. They would have to stay here, until help came.
>
> *If* help came . . .

Beginnings and endings are all very well, but what matters most is the meat in the sandwich. Nina Bawden is not merely the technically efficient teller of a good yarn; she is an author whose gift for understanding adults and weaving them into integral roles in her children's stories makes her a significant writer for the young.

Children live in their own world but it is a world circumscribed by adults—at home, at school, on the paper round. Lesser writers of children's adventure stories pit gangs of kids successfully against bands of criminals—but mature authors write about resourceful, nimble-witted, single-minded children who know themselves to be part of a bigger, more complex social system, a system which is governed by laws and has power to protect: a system which, dull and prosaic though it may seem, is, in the stories as in real life, the secure background from which they can confidently operate.

So, in the best Bawden stories, adults are not whisked off at a moment's notice on lecture tours to Australia or (who will be the first in on this one?) hijacked in Jordan so that a family is left to its own resources with dire but thrilling results. The children in Miss Bawden's books are always aware that Mum will wonder where they've got to; they ring up (albeit with cock-eyed excuses) to keep faith with their parents. Their adventures are within the framework of family and neighbourhood and because of these boundaries—which readers experience in their own lives—the stories are more real, the heroes easier to identify with and root for.

Nina Bawden is as concerned with the fears and emotions and small pleasures of Grans and maiden aunts (so often dismissed as comic characters) as she is with the relationships between children. And they are not exceptional Grans and aunts either. They use irritating quotations and phrases *ad nauseam:* "as old as my tongue and a little older than my teeth"; "by the time that happens I'll be ready for my box." They fuss about manners and they tend to keep themselves up tight. But they are lonely, ordinary people with qualities of heart and understanding to which the children respond, each in his own fashion. In *The Secret Passage* and its sequel *On the Run,* the way Aunt Mabel is seen to develop (slowly and painfully, like an ice-berg subjected to the unfamiliar attentions of the thawing sun) from spinster boarding-housekeeper, all spit-and-polish, to wise, sympathetic protective mother-figure (capable of passionate defence of Ben when he's in trouble) as the orphaned Mallory children increasingly become "her family", is truly remarkable; no less remarkable than the way Ben, in the same two books, grows from protected youngest child (whose mother was swept away in that Kenyan flood) into a resourceful, independent, determined, self-sacrificing, adventurous boy whose loyalty and directness get him both into, and ultimately out of, a sticky situation. For he becomes self-appointed protector of an exiled African princeling whose life is threatened by the rebels who overthrew his father's regime in Tiga. (It was Ben's ball, you will remember, which bounced him into this adventure.)

Groups of children have their own identity, but it is an identity which is a composite of the individuals belonging to the group. Because Miss Bawden carefully explores each individual she is able to create groups whose aspirations and conflicts spring not from arbitrary ideas or superficial pressures but from deep-seated characteristics and passions. Her best group, the five children who form the Cemetery Committee (so called because it meets in a junk yard) in *A Handful of Thieves,* is as real to me as are my own children's friends. See with what ease Miss Bawden suggests their characteristics

and throws light on their families. In the following piece they are discussing where they can have their firework party: Aristotle is the guy who has become dismembered in a battle between the Cemetery Committee and the nightwatchman at the junk yard.

> Algy had to be home by seven on Saturdays, so we started back along the path. None of us felt much like talking, and Rosie was particularly gloomy. From time to time she sighed and said, "Poor Aristotle . . ."

> To cheer her up Sid and I began to discuss where we should build the bonfire on Firework Night. Rosie had the biggest garden of all, and the best-tempered mother, but we couldn't light a fire there, because it would frighten all the animals. Sid hadn't got a garden, nor had Clio. Mine was too tidy for bonfires, and as for Algy—well, it would have been easier to ask the Queen if we could light a small fire in the front of Buckingham Palace, than to ask Algy's mother.

> "It's not going to be much fun anyway, now Aristotle's gone," Rosie said drearily. "There's no point in doing *anything,* if we haven't got a guy."

> "Well even if we haven't," I said, "we can light a pretty good fire in my Gran's back yard. I'll ask her if you like, she never grows anything there, she says there isn't enough sun, and it's full of good rubbish we can burn."

Who would believe that this decision to use Gran's yard would be the factor that was to transform the Cemetery Committee into a Handful of Thieves? For it is during the firework party that Fred discovers that Gran's new lodger, Mr. Gribble—"a thin man with a fat man's voice"—has run off with Gran's savings, the forty pounds that she always kept in a teapot on the shelf. The Committee is determined to bring Mr. Gribble—an Alastair Sim character who chats up old ladies and enlists their sympathies in his "good causes"—to justice. After tracking him down, Fred and the "dim, but decent and dogged" Algy—against Sid's sober advice—break into Gribble's new lodgings to try to recover Gran's money, thus becoming, in the eyes of the law, a "handful of thieves." Here Miss Bawden uses the adult background she has carefully built up round the "Thieves" to make the point that no one must take the law into his own hands and that the police, despite their calm, slow, ponderous manner, act like lightning when necessary.

Violence threatens: Mr. Gribble nearly kills Algy who, intoxicated by the chase, acts with foolish bravado. When the adults step in, the "Thieves", far from being resentful, are relieved. Because the reader knows them all so well he shares their understanding that some things are too hot for kids to handle.

But few topics, in Miss Bawden's view, are too difficult for children to understand if the approach is right—that is to say if these topics slide naturally into a realistic and fast-moving story. In her books she introduces, with minimum fuss and sentimentality but with deep feeling (as often expressed in "covering up" as in displays of emotion), the death of the Mallorys' mother *(The Secret Passage),* the remarriage of their father *(On the Run);* a disturbed child of divorcing parents—"Nice people are so *boring*" *(The Runaway Summer);* and a blind child—"Do be *quiet* or I can't see" *(The Witch's Daughter).* World political events provide the mainspring for two of the books—and why not? African rebellion is behind *On the Run,* and the plight of the Kenyan Asians forces itself, in the person of Krishna Patel, an illegal immigrant found on the beach, to be felt by sad and selfish Mary, heroine of *The Runaway Summer.*

Nina Bawden, through her humorous, lively, unpretentious adventure stories, both entertains her young readers and opens their eyes to the world around them. In her best books—*On the Run, A Handful of Thieves* and *The Witch's Daughter*—(a book in which a wild girl on the lonely island of Skua learns the meaning of friendship—and a blind child outwits a jewel robber)—adventure "creeps up from behind" and its course is dictated not by superficial coincidence but by the reactions of each character, child and adult, to every new circumstance as it occurs. Because Miss Bawden delights in bringing together in her stories children from widely different backgrounds (the three children in *On the Run* are middle-class Ben; Liz, a street-urchin "wanted by the Welfare"; and Thomas, an African prince in exile) the readership for her books is bound by neither class nor colour. Nina Bawden is an author for today. To claim more for her would be an extravagance. It is enough.

Peter Hunt with Nina Bawden

SOURCE: "The Handicaps of Being a Child: Peter Hunt Talks to Nina Bawden," in *The Times Educational Supplement,* No. 3959, May 15, 1992, p. 11.

In her new novel for children, *Humbug,* Nina Bawden allows herself a "private joke". Her resilient eight-year-old heroine, Cora, is looking through the library of her elderly mentor, Ma Potter. The books include "books for children, and books for grown-ups, and books (of the best kind, Ma Potter said) that were books for just everyone. Some of these Cora had read, like *The Wind in the Willows* and *Stig of the Dump* and *The Peppermint Pig.*"

The Peppermint Pig won Bawden the *Guardian* award in 1976, and, as a book for "just everyone" stands neatly between the 21 novels "for adults" (*Circles of Deceit* was shortlisted for the Booker in 1987) and 17 "for children" that she has written since 1953. In a sense, the books are all of a piece, they all explore communication; the differences are in what the characters and the readers can understand. "When you write a novel," Bawden says, "you have to know what's gone before—the background, the whole thing—and then you have to distil what happens for children—and maybe they'll be able to see it and maybe they won't."

She began to write for children because, as she explained in Edward Blishen's *The Thorny Paradise* in 1975, "I began to feel indignant on behalf of the child I had been, and so on behalf of all children—those passionately aware human beings imprisoned in a uniquely humiliating disguise." As Albert Sandwich says in *Carrie's War* (1973): "I wish I was grown up . . . It's a fearful *handicap* being a child. You have to stand there and watch, you can never make anything happen. Or stop things you don't like."

In 1992, Bawden says she feels the same. In her books, children are often hemmed in by not-too-admirable adults, but "It's not the author's business to make parents marvellous for children". And if the adults in her books are "quirky or dangerous", then so be it: "Interesting people are not bland."

Bawden's earlier books for children such as *A Handful of Thieves* (1967) and *The Runaway Summer* (1969) were adventure stories with strong characterisations ("I like books in which things happen to real characters"). *Squib* (1971) marked a change in direction: "I think that until I wrote *Squib* I was always bothered by the fact that it seemed that you had to create a kind of artificial story in order to write a novel for children. I think with *Squib* I realised that you didn't have to—that you could just approach it in a different way."

And so, although the central action of *Squib* is about an abused child, "the adventures are really the children's fantasies". The dislocation between how the child characters see the world, and what readers of various abilities might see as actually happening was developed in *Carrie's War*—arguably one of the best three post-war children's books—and *The Peppermint Pig.* By 1988, with *Keeping Henry* ("a kind of footnote to *Carrie's War*") and 1989 with *The Outside Child* the difference between her two kinds of books had narrowed.

There are other connections. *Squib* led directly to her adult novel *Anna Apparent* (1972) about the results of child abuse. In *Tortoise by Candlelight* (1963), *The Birds on the Trees* (1970) and other novels, she was "using children to make a comment about the adult world", whereas, in writing for children she makes some concessions to childhood. "You wouldn't dream of putting an unhappy ending in a child's book, and if you can't always put in a happy ending, you have to put in one that's rational and reasonable." Nor does she like or see the point of "the hideous and horrifying books for children" such as those by Robert Cormier.

But teachers do worry about her rather bleak vision of the adult world. "I'm not," she replies, "a branch of the social services. The only responsibility of an author is to write a good story well . . . You have got to be honest and truthful. You can't go around putting health warnings on books."

Take, for example, the episode in *Humbug* when Cora

runs away and is looked after by a strange tramp overnight. Nina Bawden is rather affronted by the suggestion that in this day and age that is an irresponsible episode. Certainly, children are molested, but, she says, "One of the terrible things you can do to children is to make them feel that everywhere people are dangerous and it's not so". Children can understand things more subtly than that.

She is basically optimistic. *Humbug,* she thinks, is "about a little girl who is faced with somebody who was a monster—a really depraved, evil child—something no grown-up understands, and she has to rely on her own resources". Cora learns to recognise and to some extent deal with evasions and lies and half-truths—humbug, in fact. She does not defeat the evil—it is self-defeating—but she survives, and there is a happy ending. But to make the confrontation work, Cora has to be abandoned by almost everyone, and behind the child-sized drama lies a world where every adult is flawed, unreliable, and weak. Where Bawden sees Cora's white lies to her absent parents on the phone at the end of the book (so they won't worry) as "good humbug", they can be read as yet more deception.

Nina Bawden spends half the year in her house in Islington, which backs on to Regent's Canal, and the other half in Greece, where she finished her adult novel *Family Money* last year. This year, she is working on *The Real Plato Jones,* set in England and Greece, and developing the clever boy character from *The Outside Child.* It promises to continue her explorations of the ambiguities of the adult-child relationship, and how children understand and cope with the pasts of the adults around them. These themes, together with her confrontation of the central problem of adults writing for children—the establishment of a satisfactory viewpoint—have confirmed her as one of the most subtly innovative of modern writers for children.

TITLE COMMENTARY

📖 *THE SECRET PASSAGE* (1963; published as *The House of Secrets,* 1964; reissued, 1992)

Hazel Rochman

SOURCE: A review of *The House of Secrets,* in *Booklist,* Vol. 88, No. 14, March 15, 1992, p. 1356.

First published in England and the U.S. in 1963, this reissue is one of those enjoyable, old-fashioned adventures, where middle-class children find themselves suddenly wrenched from their loving home and placed in the care of an ugly guardian. Their mother has died of pneumonia, their father's had a breakdown, and John, Mary, and Ben have been sent from their idyllic farm in Kenya to live with cross Aunt Mabel in her shabby boardinghouse in England. The great closed-up house next door holds secrets; there's an orphan, a "witch," and treasure; and there's a happy ending where everybody finds family, happiness, and lots of money. The fairy-tale patterns are immensely satisfying, of course, but the realistic story seems dated, perhaps because hunger and homelessness have become too close for cozy play and easy resolution. Seven-year-old Ben's plan to earn money begging doesn't sound as funny and naive as it did 30 years ago. Bawden's best books rely less on wild coincidence and unexpected transformation than this one does: not only does fierce Aunt Mabel turn out to be a loving angel, but so does the gruff rich old "ogre" next door, who helps the poor waif from the orphanage, who's an unappreciated musical prodigy. . . . All those who can suspend disbelief will enjoy the adventure, as they identify with the brave, honest, "upright" children and their delicious, shivery terror.

📖 *ON THE RUN* (1964; U.S. edition published as *Three on the Run,* 1965)

Ruth Hill Viguers

SOURCE: A review of *Three on the Run,* in *The Horn Book Magazine,* Vol. XLI, No. 4, August, 1965, pp. 385-86.

An account of children escaping from adults—wicked or merely obtuse—inevitably has strong appeal. Here the differences represented by the three escapees add to the interest: Ben, an English country boy visiting his widower father in London; Lil, a sly, unschooled city child alone while her mother is in the hospital; and Thomas, son of Chief Okapi, the prime minister of an East African country, and a pawn in a political conspiracy. The story verges on fantasy, but the children are real; the naturalness with which each sees the others as friends, accepting without question their different backgrounds and cultures, is childlike and convincing.

Ruth P. Bull

SOURCE: A review of *Three on the Run,* in *The Booklist,* Vol. 62, No. 4, October 15, 1965, p. 218.

An ingeniously plotted story relating the escapades of three children of distinctly different character and background: Ben, a country lad, who is visiting his widower father in London; Lil, a cockney girl, who is evading the protective care of the welfare lady while her mother is in the hospital; and Thomas, son of an imprisoned African Prime Minister, who is in constant danger from the political intrigue resulting from a revolution in his native country. To protect Thomas, the three decide to run away and seek safety near an English seaside town. The characters are well-drawn, the action well-paced, and the children's adventures realistically and excitingly presented.

Zena Sutherland

SOURCE: A review of *Three on the Run,* in *Bulletin of the Center for Children's Books,* Vol. 19, No. 10, June, 1966, pp. 157-58.

First published in England in 1964 under the title *On the Run,* an adventure story with some weak aspects and some very strong. The small print and the vocabulary level make the book fairly difficult for a reader who would be interested in children as young as the three protagonists seem to be; the characters are well-defined, but several of them hint of stereotype. The relationships are good, and the story has pace and some suspense, but the plot is contrived, and it needn't have been. Ben (one of the three Mallory children of *The House of Secrets*) is now eleven; he meets Thomas, an African boy who is being kept under surveillance in the house next door; Thomas, whose father is a political prisoner, is the pawn in a power struggle and he has a good uncle and a bad uncle. Ben discovers that Thomas is to be kidnapped by his bad uncle, so the two boys decide to run away. The third member of their trio is a small, tough Cockney girl who is hiding out alone so that she won't be taken by "The Welfare" while her mother is in the hospital. And so on. The children are an interesting trio, and they could easily have met under more credible circumstances.

Stuart Hannabuss

SOURCE: "Beyond the Formula: Ways of Extending the Obvious for Children & Young People," in *Junior Bookshelf,* Vol. 46, No. 4, August, 1982, pp. 123-27.

Adventure stories often succeed because the characters in them are action men, ciphers, with little personality complications to clutter up the onrush of plot. Nevertheless the human interest factor is pretty strong, in children as well as in adults, and identikit people like the Hardy Boys eventually pall. It is sad to think that *Crossroads* and *Dear Heart* are all that is left. The problem often found here is that the moment characters become a bit unusual, the action line becomes obscure. This is so in books like *Josh,* fascinating technical innovations for sure, but too much in the way of a good story to succeed on a mass level. The action line does not need to be thrown out of the window, however, as Nina Bawden has proved time after time. *On the Run,* for instance, is a classic tale of escape and pursuit: three children, one the son of a threatened African diplomat, run away, are followed by credible villains, survive some treacherous hours in a cliff-face cave, travel psychologically through a moving and ambitious range of feelings of fear and suspense and exhilaration, until the sinister plot is finally unmasked. The author does not stop there: she gives value for money in terms of excitement, and makes the story very accessible to a wide number of readers, but she also makes sure that the reader knows what the characters really think and feel. They are aware of the difficulties of running away; they know what it is to be frightened and not understood by adults (even by those they trust); they fall out with each other; they experience a testing mixture of fear and excitement when they sleep in the cave and then have to escape from the tide. At the end, the issues in some cases are beyond them, and yet they know that what they have done has brought things out fairly in the end. Nina Bawden knows children well and provides a strong thread of story, around which all sorts of rich, unpredictable elements are woven. These are there for the taking, depending on how individual children respond. Such books are there, too, for the child tired of the obvious: and, more elusively for parents etc., for the child who does not fully know that he is tired of the obvious. Anticipation, after all, is one of the secret ingredients of successful book provision.

THE WHITE HORSE GANG (1966)

Virginia Kirkus' Service

SOURCE: A review of *The White Horse Gang,* in *Virginia Kirkus' Service,* Vol. XXXIV, No. 4, February 15, 1966, p. 181.

There is nothing very startling about this story, set in a small, out-of-the-way English town, nor is there a great deal of point to it, but unobtrusively it offers some very pleasant moments with its precise and often humorous indications of the three young characters who formed the White Horse Gang. The three are nine-year-old Sam, his cousin Rose, and Abe, the poorest, shabbiest, toughest, and hence the most sought after little boy in the town. They plan and execute minor misdemeanors, and dare and scorn each other into accomplishing "dangerous" (mainly by local superstition) feats. Their biggest project was to kidnap an insufferable younger boy named Percy, but after they gave up on the idea, Percy attached himself to them and refused to go home. The three involve themselves in some stock situations, but they seem refreshing and genuine.

Margery Fisher

SOURCE: A review of *The White Horse Gang,* in *Growing Point,* Vol. 4, No. 9, April, 1966, p. 673.

> Other mothers fussed their sons about washing behind their ears and keeping the house tidy. Mrs. Peach fussed over her salukis instead. She was too busy grooming them and getting burrs out of their coats to worry over such an unimportant thing as a bit of dirt on the back of a boy's neck.

With a mother like Mrs. Peach, Sam finds life pleasant—but he is not completely happy. He would like to be more like his hero, Abe Tanner. Abe is only two years older than nine-year-old Sam but he is adult in his attitude to life and, besides, he can belch robustly whenever he wants to. Sam's campaign to win Abe's friendship seems in danger of interruption now that cousin

Rose is coming to stay, but Rose turns out to be a help rather than a hindrance. For one thing, Abe seems intrigued by her insouciance and her obvious admiration of him; and then, it is Rose's idea that the three of them should form a gang, with secret names and secret plans. At first these plans are innocuous—though Miss Pennyfather the school teacher, victim of some of their tricks, might not agree. But the White Horse Gang becomes over-ambitious. Rose has got the idea from Abe that her parents, who are in America on business, probably won't come back for her at all. To comfort her, the boys determine to raise the money for her fare, but the only way they can think of doing this is to kidnap Percy, the persistently clinging, spoilt son of the rich Mountjoys, newly come to the little Shropshire town. The consequences of this exploit, and the danger that comes to the children in Gibbet Wood, make them look at people rather differently.

This may sound like the blue-print for a story for ten-year-old readers, with its remote setting and its sensational adventure, in which children triumph by their own courage and resource. But have we really read this story before? Certainly not with such a clever knitting together of the unlikely and the domestic. Not with such expert handling of the plot, so that new characters are brought in at just the moment when the book needs them—Abe's blind and witch-like grandmother, so much on the spot, balancing absent-minded Mrs. Peach, and the matter-of-fact efficiency of school in deliberate contrast to the dark wood and the imaginative fears it provokes. Certainly not with such good dialogue and character-drawing. On the face of it the adult characters are types—rich, fussy Mrs. Mountjoy, trenchant grandmother, mysterious Farmer John—but each becomes an individual in conversation. As for the children, the relationship between them is beautifully handled. Very naturally Abe draws off a little as he looks into a possible future; very naturally Sam and Rose change from prankish jokes to thoughtfulness and back again. I would expect children of very varying standards of intelligence to enjoy this book, but many of them I think will find it particularly satisfying by contrast with the steady stream of stories published for them in which adventures *are* improbable and *stay* improbable.

Junior Bookshelf

SOURCE: A review of *The White Horse Gang,* in *Junior Bookshelf,* Vol. 30, No. 3, June, 1966, p. 176.

Sam, aged nine, greatly admires an older boy, Abe, and longs for his friendship. The chance comes when Sam's cousin Rose comes to stay with him. Together with Sam and Abe she forms the White Horse Gang. They explore the countryside, plan to kidnap a small boy and then things go wrong. A wolf escapes from a local circus and attacks Abe's home and the novel culminates in an exciting chase.

This is a fairly conventional story and the characters run true to type. But is this type true to life? Would a nine-year-old boy behave in this way? It would rather seem to be the way adult writers of children's books expect, or think, children behave. The book is well written, but the plot is too loose. It should be suitable for 9-11 year-olds, but many of them will find it rather heavy. To become a child again and see life through his eyes is something only very few writers achieve.

Barbara Wersba

SOURCE: A review of *The White Horse Gang,* in *The New York Times Book Review,* June 26, 1966, p. 26.

Nina Bawden writes about childhood as though she had never left it. As though, indeed, she were still exploring its terrain—scraping her knees and forgetting to blow her nose. This, coupled with the fact that she writes well, makes **The White Horse Gang** a more important book than its title indicates. Ostensibly a mystery, it is really the study of three English children in a small town: Abe, Sam and Rose. Discovering that Rose misses her parents, who are abroad, the boys decide to kidnap a little milktoast named Percy and use the ransom to send Rose to America. Well and good, except that Percy—who has been overprotected by his mother—adores being kidnapped and refuses to go home. While there is high comedy in this situation, and genuine suspense in a subplot concerning a haunted forest, the author's main concern is the children. Understanding that they are at once amoral and upright, cold-blooded and sensitive, she presents them with marvelous candor; and if a few threads of plot remain untied at the end, it hardly matters. Her story rings true.

Zena Sutherland

SOURCE: A review of *The White Horse Gang,* in *Bulletin of the Center for Children's Books,* Vol. 19, No. 11, July-August, 1966, p. 174.

First published in England, a story that has a country setting, touches of sophistication and humor, and a nicely unified plot. There are, in the plot and in some of the characterizations, tendencies to broad exaggeration that weaken the story somewhat. Sam is a boy (All Boy type) whose slight crush on a tougher boy is mitigated when an attractive girl cousin visits, and—in a manner described with sympathy, perception, and humor—the boys vie for her attention. The gang of three decides that, in order to send Rose to America so she can join her parents, they must have money. How? By kidnapping the small and detestable Lord Fauntleroyish Percy Mountjoy. Their idea is deplorable, but the reprehensibility seems the less because of the ridiculous reversal of roles. Young Percy, away from his mother, revels in being a kidnappee. There is a contrived last dramatic touch when a wolf escapes from a local circus and endangers the boys, but the book ends with a rather touching scene in which Rose and Sam have a last meeting with the third member of the White Horse Gang, and it is clear that they are still children, while Abe, tougher and more mature, has moved toward adult status.

📖 THE WITCH'S DAUGHTER (1966)

Virginia Kirkus' Service

SOURCE: A review of *The Witch's Daughter,* in *Virginia Kirkus' Service,* Vol. XXXIV, No. 13, July 1, 1966, p. 624.

It's too bad Nina Bawden hasn't written as exceptionally for children as she has about them in her adult novels. Perhaps the transatlantic transition has something to do with it—the vocabulary outstrips the interest level of this age; and there are certain elements in this wistful half world, somewhere just between reality and fantasy, to which American readers are less attuned. The witch's daughter is Perdita, her name means lost, and she's almost eleven, orphaned, considered "foreign" and very much alone on the little Scottish island of Skua. She also has the gift of second sight. Then there are the Hoggart children who prove to be her first friends—Janey who is blind, and her brother Tim. Between them they become involved with a beachcomber, with a burglar who leaves them stranded in a cave, with some jewels, and, for Perdita most disillusioning of all, with just who and what kindly Mr. Smith, her protector, is. Girls will respond more than boys to the story in which the adventure is subsidiary to the gently sentimental appeal.

Publishers Weekly

SOURCE: A review of *The Witch's Daughter,* in *Publishers Weekly,* Vol. 190, No. 12, September 19, 1966, p. 75.

Another way for a reviewer's day to be one of sweet content is to discover that a remarkable writer has gone and topped herself—a difficult feat when the writer is Nina Bawden. But she does it, in her latest story, ***The Witch's Daughter.*** She captures you with her first line, "The Witch's daughter sat on a rock in the bay." You sit enthralled as Miss Bawden conjures up a bleak Scottish island before your very eyes, an island peopled with unique characters—among them a blind girl who is fiercely independent, a villain who is quite a likable fellow. And the spell she weaves will linger on long after you have read her last magic word.

Diane Wagner

SOURCE: A review of *The Witch's Daughter,* in *The New York Times Book Review,* November 11, 1966, p. 44.

Perdita, an illiterate Scottish girl, lives on the island of Skua with her foster mother, housekeeper for a secretive man named Smith. Patiently, she waits for company until the mainland steamer arrives with two children aboard: Tim Haggart and his blind sister, Janey. Tim goes with his father to hunt for orchids in Carlin's Cave, but instead of finding flowers, they discover a ruby-colored stone. Returning to Skuaport, Tim meets Perdita, wearing a diamond around her neck, given her by one of Mr. Smith's visiting friends. Is this the start of a search for pirates' loot, left in the sea-cave by the dragons'-teeth rocks. Or could there be another explanation?

Nina Bawden, author of other equally exciting adventure novels, has written a credible suspense story, with a likeable and resourceful cast. A plausible plot, superior dialogue, and an appropriate setting also work into a dramatization as gripping as the story of Tom and Huck hiding from Injun Joe. ***The Witch's Daughter*** should delight all children who have ever dreamed of searching for buried treasure.

Junior Bookshelf

SOURCE: A review of *The Witch's Daughter,* in *Junior Bookshelf,* Vol. 30, No. 6, December, 1966, p. 376.

This is a fast-moving story of hidden jewels, desperate criminals and amateur detection, rather than the fairy-tale suggested by the title, and set in the Western Isles of Scotland, whose wildness is captured excellently by Shirley Hughes' illustrations. Perdita, a lonely child, has second sight. She has come to trade on it so that the other children fear her, to the relief of the mysterious Mr. Smith for whom her guardian works, for it suits his nefarious purposes that Perdita should not attend school and talk with others. His downfall begins with the arrival on the island of a naturalist and his children. Tim, the elder, is an amateur geologist whose first find is unexpectedly a large ruby in which a dangerous interest is displayed by Mr. Smith. Ten-year-old Janey is blind.

The plot moves fairly predictably, but the book, like the author's earlier ones, is memorable for its depth of aim. The heightened mental senses of Perdita are contrasted with Janey's heightened physical senses, both of which save lives. There is a sympathetic yet realistic picture of the selfishness of the handicapped child and the vanity of the child who is "different." Perdita has to face the waning of her powers as she learns to mix with others, and as in real life, black and white are not sharply defined: Mr. Smith's nemesis is tragedy for Perdita, to whom he was kindness and security. The end is very moving.

📖 A HANDFUL OF THIEVES (1967)

Jean C. Thomson

SOURCE: A review of *A Handful of Thieves,* in *School Library Journal,* Vol. 14, No. 1, September, 1967, pp. 114-15.

Nina Bawden's cheerful mystery is peopled by neighborly types who are at their ease in an uncontorted plot. When Fred's grandmother discovers that gentle Gribble, a trusted lodger, has run off with her teapotful of savings, she tells the children to forget the incident; she fears the family will think her a dotty old lady incapable of caring for herself. The children, however, take the law into their own hands. Though they track down the criminal, they are caught red-handed in the wrong hotel room and arrested. When this twist is straightened out, all embark on a flashy Keystone Cops pursuit of the thief which sustains the spirit of the story at the expense of real suspense. The narrator Fred is the main character, but friends Sid and Algy are also well portrayed, in fact, it is bespectacled Algy who really captures the thief, such heroism earning for him a freer home life and the new respect of his fellows. *Three on the Run* is still the author's best; the later books seem to be coasting along on that book's energy and reputation.

Margery Fisher

SOURCE: A review of *A Handful of Thieves,* in *Growing Point,* Vol. 6, No. 4, October, 1967, p. 984.

The Cemetery Committee (what a likely name for children to give themselves!) meets in an old car on a deserted racing-track. Here they grudgingly accept giggling Cleo as a new member: here they torment the bronchial caretaker: from this innocent headquarters of would-be detectives they are dragged when Gran's savings are stolen and, because she is too proud to call in the police, they must somehow find the thief. Here are utterly believable boys and girls, their personalities substantiated by what we see of their family life. Here is utterly plausible action against back-street petty crime, and a superb use of first-person narrative. From Fred's opening sentence—'This is the story of how we became a gang of thieves'—the story develops its own special logic, artistry and power.

Junior Bookshelf

SOURCE: A review of *A Handful of Thieves,* in *Junior Bookshelf,* Vol. 31, No. 5, October, 1967, p. 318.

Like the earlier Bawdens, this is something more than simply a good mystery, though it can be enjoyed for its sleuthing and suspense alone, and the absence of high crime and phenomenal juvenile detectives plus the presence of a moral somehow seems likely to put off readers because their sympathies for the central characters ensure their personal involvement with the petty crime perpetrated when Gran's savings are stolen by a small-time con man. For once it really *matters* that the thief should be caught, much more than if he had taken a millionairess' diamonds or atomic secrets, because Gran is real, vital and yet vulnerable, for if adults come to hear of her foolishness her independence will be threatened. So her grandson, who narrates the story, and four

other youngsters try to trace the thief and retrieve Gran's forty pounds on their own and do some breaking and entering themselves, thus becoming the "handful of thieves" of the title. A realistic old woman, Gran realises she was wrong to pledge them to secrecy just as she has earlier realised the consequences of the theft, and the reader is left in no doubt about the end not justifying the means. The five children are well differentiated and their problems with the adult world are subtly suggested; they are likable, lively and entirely credible throughout. Only the thief is caricatured—and quite entertainingly—for amongst its other virtues the book portrays lower-class people and scenes without the tone of patronage which mars most books attempting to show how the "other half" lives. This is not about some "other half", but about people. The dialogue and Fred's terms of reference ring true throughout, the background is the shabbier section of an industrial town but there is none of that consciousness of slumming shown by many authors now struggling to depict the proletariat who never shared their own world of nannies and pony clubs. Like a good adult mystery, this succeeds as light entertainment and leaves the reader with several new ideas to think over as well.

Patience M. Daltry

SOURCE: A review of *A Handful of Thieves,* in *The Christian Science Monitor,* November 2, 1967, p. B15.

Nina Bawden's is a recipe certain of success. Excellent characterization, a thorough-going mystery, fast action, enough suspense to keep 9-12's reading, and convincing dialogue. The thieves here are a gang of young Londoners—three boys, two girls—who get on the wrong side of the law when they try to steal back some money stolen from the grandmother of one of the boys. Miss Bawden rightly makes no concessions toward the argument that it is all right to do to others what they did to you, while she keeps an even balance between tough-minded independence and family warmth and security. She can, when necessary, even invoke sentiment without being embarrassing.

The Times Literary Supplement

SOURCE: "Ganging-Up on the Grown-Ups," in *The Times Literary Supplement,* No. 3431, November 30, 1967, p. 1151.

The first page of **A Handful of Thieves** is as compelling an opening as one could hope for. The second paragraph sorts out the characters, places the action and the gang are ready to begin their progress towards becoming thieves and bringing a criminal to justice.

> My friends are Rosie, Sid Bates and Algy. We are the ones who really did it all, though some other people helped a bit, like Sid's Uncle William and

even Rosie's ghastly friend Clio who we have to put up with because Rosie likes her. My name is Peter Henry McAlpine but I'm always called Fred, I'll explain why later. I am thirteen now but when this happened I was eleven and two months. My sister Jinny was fourteen then but she doesn't come into the story much except to complain about my grammar and to suggest a different way of putting things, nor do my Mum and Dad. The most important member of my family in this book is my Gran, and as she began it all I had better start with her.

Fred's gang is the Cemetery Committee whose Den is a broken-down Humber saloon at the bottom of the side of a disused motor racing track. When Fred's Gran is robbed of her savings by the sinister lodger, the Committee is sworn to secrecy lest she be considered unable to look after herself. A Gran is a natural ally where parents exert pressures, so that the Committee decide to track down the thief. They rush into a pursuit which is both dangerous and comic. The adults take over when they should.

This is a most distinctive gang, with each child a different person to his parents and to his peers. The story bounces along, so flexible is the prose, so deliberate the telling. Young readers will enjoy the energy of the characters and adults admire the craftsmanship which conveys the quizzical self-regard of the storyteller, who varies between being totally engrossed in his narrative and humorously portraying his friends. A considerable achievement.

THE RUNAWAY SUMMER (1969)

Ruth Hill Viguers

SOURCE: A review of *The Runaway Summer*, in *The Horn Book Magazine,* Vol. XLV, No. 5, October, 1969, p. 533.

The story of two children's efforts to hide a Kenyan boy who, they believe, has entered England illegally is reminiscent of the author's *Three on the Run.* At the beginning of the book, Mary is one of the most disagreeable children in fiction. The feeling that her parents do not want her has made her cherish her unhappiness so stubbornly that she will not respond to the kindness of her aunt and her grandfather, with whom she has come to live. Her discovery of Krishna Patel and her determination to save him from the authorities lead her to seek help from a neighbor boy, Simon. He is just the friend Mary needs, and she begins to emerge from her unpleasant shell. The plot moves rapidly and the characters are appealing.

The Times Literary Supplement

SOURCE: "Yet More Problems," in *The Times Literary Supplement,* No. 3529, October 16, 1969, p. 1199.

The Runaway Summer is a skilful enough variation of the familiar Bawden formula: a girl and two boys; a mixture of social (and racial) backgrounds; a hunt, a hiding place; a hint of political drama in the machinery. Mary, not unlike her namesake in *The Secret Garden,* is moody and resentful. Her worldly parents, "always quarrelling and banging doors" and now in process of divorce, have left her with grandfather and old-fashioned Aunt Alice in their house by the sea. In her sullen and angry way she makes a friend, a nice, responsible, serious boy called Simon (a policeman's son, by the way), who, among other self-assumed burdens, does his unavailing best to keep in order an untidy and noisy family of younger siblings. Mary asks Simon's help in hiding a Pakistani boy, apparently an illegal immigrant, whom she has found on the beach; they take him to Simon's secret haunt—a tiny island on a weed-grown lake in a neglected estate near by. Though the boy informs them from time to time that his wealthy uncle is waiting for him in London (in "Buckingham Palace Terrace") his casual air is taken not for assurance but for fantasy.

Still, the relationship of the three children is excellently caught—the misunderstandings, the moments of rapport. The adults—all but the suave, amused Pakistani uncle (he *does* turn out to live near Buckingham Palace)—are less convincing. The immigrant motif places the tale in our immediate time. But Aunt Alice (who, by rough calculation, can't be much more than 40) could hardly be more out of touch with the world today. Moreover, no kindness of heart could ever overcome, for a child, her physical unattractiveness so precisely laid down by Miss Bawden at the start. Simon's family, too, wavering at different social levels, seem dashed off at different times of writing: this was less avoidable when novels appeared in serial form, but today suggests either haste or irresolute vision. Of course, if the tale were less effective, these flaws would be less worth mentioning.

Ruth P. Bull

SOURCE: A review of *The Runaway Summer*, in *The Booklist,* Vol. 66, No. 5, November 1, 1969, p. 345.

Somewhat similar in plot to the author's *Three on the Run* but featuring a spirited heroine who masks the misery caused by her unconcerned parents under a hostile and defiant attitude. While staying with her grandfather and an aunt in an English seaside town, Mary enmeshes herself in an embarrassing web of lies and participates in some illegal activities when, with the help of a local boy, she befriends a boy from Kenya who has been smuggled into England and hides him from the police. Eventually all turns out well and through her unorthodox but enlightening experiences, Mary learns to adjust to reality without losing her innate spirit. Characters are very real and the plot intriguing.

Arlene Ruthenberg

SOURCE: A review of *The Runaway Summer,* in *School Library Journal,* Vol. 16, No. 4, December, 1969, pp. 47-8.

This latest of the author's stories for younger girls is an intriguing combination of adventure, suspense, and a penetrating portrait of an angry child whose parents are divorcing each other and her. After stealing some candy (she wanted to do something *really bad*), Mary unexpectedly rescues a refugee boy from India and is plunged into another typical Bawden mystery. At first, she and a friend are afraid to go to adults for help; but complications finally force them to do so, and that aspect of the story is happily resolved. Not so for Mary's personal problems which realistically end in a compromise: the lonely child faces rejection by parents and tries to adjust to living with "rabbity" Aunt Alice and Grampy. Life won't be ideal, but she will cope somehow, less angry now. The pace of the story is rather slow and it may be too drawn out to hold the attention of some readers. However, the English scene is excellently portrayed, the characters capably delineated, and the suspense maintained satisfactorily in this better than average book.

SQUIB (1971)

M. Hobbs

SOURCE: A review of *Squib,* in *Junior Bookshelf,* Vol. 35, No. 4, August, 1971, pp. 233-34.

As always, Nina Bawden's great strength is her portrayal of such a wide range of real people. Squib is a strange withdrawn little boy in the park with whom the two younger Tite children strike up a wordless friendship, and through him the other characters reveal themselves. In the forefront is Kate, a lonely child with a sense of guilt, and of inadequacy at her lack of cleverness, seeking compensation for her drowned brother in the fantasy that Squib is his reincarnation, or even actually Rupert. She makes Robin Tite uneasy by her determination to get to the bottom of such matters as Squib's bruises, and her pathetic anxiety to look after the neglected baby of a selfish young wife. The warm ordinary Tite family are very much individuals: large capable Mrs. Tite, ex-Olympic swimmer; Robin, keen on Greek rather than something useful like Science, with his own fantasy of Squib, kidnapped from rich parents; determined Prue; fearful, obstinate Sammy; and their comfortable married sister Emerald, who provides a not-too-easy happy ending. Even Kate's widowed mother is measured by Squib: withdrawn into her book-illustrating, she cannot face the responsibility of adoption. The "loner" from the motor-cycle gang, kind in his way to the little ones; the old people of the Home, lost, slightly mad, or keeping ends up like the Indian army colonel; and the drunken labourer beating his sluttish wife on the caravan site and stumbling past Kate with hopeless eyes, are also rounded pictures. It is a haunting tale.

Margery Fisher

SOURCE: A review of *Squib,* in *Growing Point,* Vol. 10, No. 4, October, 1971, p. 1807.

Reviewers' shorthand often speaks of children 'identifying' with a character in a story or being reassured by a domestic situation comparable with their own. No doubt sooner or later someone will produce actual proof of this—not that this is likely to make any difference to writers who know where they are going. We may be sure that Nina Bawden didn't write *Squib* to reassure any child that happiness can come from misery; it is enough that she is deeply interested in relationships and in the cross-reference, so puzzling and so educative to the young, between one way of life and another. In one of her customary mixed groups of children, Kate Pollack, whose mother illustrates children's books, finds comradeship with Robin, whose mother cleans for the Pollacks and who is usually clobbered with a small sister and brother. Amusing Sammy and Prue in the park, the older children sometimes see a skinny little boy whose hints of being tied up in a laundry basket hold a fairytale terror for them all. The rescue of Squib is as blundering as one might expect and it brings the children alarmingly close to adult brutality but their concern for the child has contributed something important towards the final decision about his future. How much of all this a young reader will understand, or even want to notice, is something no research would be likely to discover; this kind of book—honest, uninhibited and soberly written—a reviewer is justified in assessing as a novel.

Ethel L. Heins

SOURCE: A review of *Squib,* in *The Horn Book Magazine,* Vol. XLVII, No. 5, October, 1971, p. 482.

The author is especially good at intermingling children of divergent cultures and social groups; and she is sensitive to the plight of the underprivileged. And one feels that her stories, containing varying mixtures of intrigue and suspense, as well as interestingly defined characters, could be made into exciting films for children. Kate is a lonely child living with her busy artist-mother; she does a good deal of baby-sitting, not because she needs the money she earns but because she thrives on the responsibility. She and her friend Robin, son of her mother's cleaning woman, are concerned about a strange little boy called Squib—a pale, silent, staring shadow of a child—who plays in the park with Robin's younger brother and sister. It is easy for Kate to invent a daydream-fantasy in which Squib is actually her own little brother, said to have been drowned with her father in a summer holiday accident four years before. Kate and Robin, with the two younger children, discover that Squib lives with a rough, violent foster-mother who mistreats him in every possible way. Trailing the two of them to their sordid home in an abandoned bus near a quarry pit, the horrified children are determined to effect a daring rescue. As the events of the story are perceived through the understanding of the frightened younger children, of imaginative Kate and practical Robin, and of the sober, dependable parents, tensions rise and are resolved.

Zena Sutherland

SOURCE: A review of *Squib,* in *Bulletin of the Center for Children's Books,* Vol. 25, No. 11, July-August, 1972, p. 165.

Seven years old, small, pale, always alone, the shy boy refused to answer to any name but "Squib" when the other children questioned him. Kate Pollack, who was eleven, was especially concerned about him—he was the same age her brother would have been if he were alive—but each of the other children worries too. Squib doesn't talk much about himself, but he lives in an old people's home, and one of the boys has seen Squib's pale face at a tower window. The children hear a woman threaten him: "Basket for you, that's what you're asking for . . ." The children's attempt to rescue Squib from a situation they don't quite understand but know is wrong, somehow, provides a dramatic and satisfying ending. The relationships among the children, and the family situation of each, are drawn with perception and warmth, and the story is written with just-bearable suspense.

CARRIE'S WAR (1973)

The Time Literary Supplement

SOURCE: "Returning to the Scene," in *The Times Literary Supplement,* No. 3709, April 6, 1973, p. 383.

It is natural enough for children's writers to want to use their own childhood experiences, but it may also be a useful escape from coming to terms with the contemporary young. This certainly isn't the case with Nina Bawden, who has shown over and over again that she can write about the present, and only now, in her eighth children's book, goes back to the time when she was herself a child. Miss Bawden has always been a clever writer, immensely readable and accessible yet often thought-provoking and mind-stretching. But *Carrie's War* is something different, it is altogether more moving, richer and stranger than anything she has achieved before. If it is not partly autobiographical, it certainly feels as if it is.

The story begins in the present. Carrie, widowed with children, returns to the small Welsh town to which she and her brother had been evacuated during the war. "We were so happy here, Nick and I. I thought—I hoped that was all I'd remember." But of course it isn't. Carrie had done "a dreadful thing, the worst thing of my life" all those years ago, and returning to the place she has to tell her children and us what led up to it and the bizarre people the two London children found themselves among. Bizarre they may be, but never caricatures: Samuel Evans, the tyrant grocer ("Dirt and sloppy habits are an insult to the Lord"), Hepzibah Green and her charge, poor Mister Johnny Gotobed, and the dying Mrs Gotobed wearing her old ball dresses in her quiet house, not because she is mad but because Albert Sandwich had suggested that he'd like to see them. "I would hate to be ordinary," Albert said.

Carrie's War makes most other books seem pale and ordinary indeed, but there is bread and butter in it too and its richness is not indigestible or overpowering. The construction is skilful and the subtle promise of a happy ending immensely satisfying.

Margery Fisher

SOURCE: A review of *Carrie's War,* in *Growing Point,* Vol. 12, No. 1, May, 1973, p. 2164.

A flashback can be a stumbling block to impatient young readers, but there is a proper reason why *Carrie's War* starts thirty years after, when a widow returns with her children to the Welsh valley where she and her brother had lived as evacuees. All her life Carrie had believed, irrationally, that she had been the cause of the fire that ruined the house at Druid's Bottom where she and her brother Nick had found happiness and a more relaxed way of life than Councillor Mr. Evans the grocer and his timid sister Lou could provide for them. In this fine novel a whole world is created in which adults and children have their problems and sometimes, in the confused, imperfect way of real life, begin to understand each other a little. Carrie and Nick realise there is a family feud and that Mr. Evans will never speak to his older sister again (though he is quick enough to check her possessions after her death) but they are not old enough to understand how devious and how inconsistent people can be. Nick hates the grocer with his mean, nagging ways; Carrie, though she has moments of sympathy for him, believes almost to the end of her stay that he has acted wickedly towards Hepzibah, who has looked after his ailing sister for so many years. The virtue of the story lies in its completeness, the way children and adults enjoy equal rights in the action, the way the children fret and even suffer because in their inexperience their lives have to be ordered for them. None of this would mean much, though, without the author's notable power to draw character. Carrie and her brother; Mr. Evans with his agonised grumbling about the use of the stair carpet ("Up and down, back and for, in and out, messing and humbugging about"); Albert Sandwich, an evacuee full of worldly wisdom who sees a lot but often deserves Hepzibah's affectionate comment of "Mr. Albert Uppity Know it all"; even frail sister Dilys, comforting her last days by wearing her ball dresses one by one and prinking before Albert's appreciative eye—I can't remember a more fascinating set of people in any of Nina Bawden's books nor any whom children could recognise so readily, so lucid and quick and appropriate are the words, actions and thoughts with which this brilliant writer has endowed them. It is a joy to have books to offer to the young which can match the classic Victorian family stories for humour and feeling.

Mary M. Burns

SOURCE: A review of *Carrie's War,* in *The Horn Book Magazine,* Vol. XLIX, No. 3, June, 1973, pp. 274-75.

Carrie's children were puzzled by their mother's determination to visit an obscure, nearly deserted Welsh mining town, until she revealed that she and their Uncle Nick had once lived there as children—evacuated from London during the early years of World War II. Beginning with a description of their arrival ("[l]abeled like parcels"), Carrie told of their first impressions of the miserly shopkeeper, Mr. Evans, and of his well-meaning but bullied sister. The contrast between their former comfortable status and the drab monotony of the new environment might have been unbearable had they not discovered Druid's Bottom, a once-elegant mansion, where they were mothered by the housekeeper, Hepzibah Green, intrigued with strange little Mr. Johnny Gotobed, and befriended by Albert Sandwich, another evacuee. From Hepzibah, Carrie learned about the legend of the screaming skull and the curse placed on the old house—a story which suddenly became a sinister reality as a series of tragic events undermined her newfound security. Thirty years later, Carrie's children shared in the resolution of the mystery, which had shadowed their mother since childhood. By deft handling of the story-within-a-story, the author has produced a sophisticated blend of diverse elements without sacrificing the credibility of the young heroine. The homely but frustrating details of everyday life during wartime—life relatively unthreatened by immediate danger but affected by political events—add another element to the developing body of literature dealing with childhood experiences during World War II.

Barbara Wersba

SOURCE: A review of *Carrie's War,* in *The New York Times Book Review,* June 3, 1973, p. 8.

Seven years ago I remarked in these pages that "Nina Bawden writes about childhood as though she had never left it. As though, indeed, she were still exploring its terrain—scraping her knees and forgetting to blow her nose." I feel that those words are still true, but the tenor of children's books has changed so radically in the past decade that *Carrie's War* left me oddly disappointed— as though a promise had not been kept.

The promise, I think, is in the nature of Miss Bawden's talent—which is huge—and the disappointment comes from the fact that this talent does not seem to have grown. Children's books, for good or ill, are now so wide-open in their approach to life that anything can happen between their pages—and usually does. Miss Bawden, meanwhile, is still writing a particular kind of

English mystery in which the reader is scared, but not too scared, in which people are evil, but not too evil, and in which happy endings abound. Perhaps it is unkind to criticize her for conventionality, but one knows that she is better than this and longs for something wilder, more daring, more personal.

Her characterizations are indeed well done, and the reader is genuinely moved by Carrie and Nick—a brother and sister who have been evacuated to Wales during the World War II bombing of London. And if the children are real, even more convincing are Mr. Evans and his sister Auntie Lou, who take the youngsters in and offer them a home. Mr. Evans is so mean that he forbids Carrie and Nick to go upstairs more than twice a day (lest they wear out the carpet) and he is so fanatically "Chapel" that an air of leaden religion hangs over the house. But he is a villain with a troubled heart and by far the most interesting person in the book.

As to the mystery, it concerns the children's involvement with Mr. Evans's other sister, Mrs. Gotobed, who is an invalid and lives in a haunted house along with a kindly witch and a simpleton. This latter character, Mister Johnny, might have walked directly out of a Truman Capote short story and fascinated me no end. Alas, there is not enough of him or of anyone else, since all these figures take second place to the plot. How one wishes that Miss Bawden would forget about plot and step through the looking glass of herself—where the real mysteries wait.

A. R. Williams

SOURCE: A review of *Carrie's War,* in *Junior Bookshelf,* Vol. 37, No. 4, August, 1973, pp. 262-63.

Carrie's War is not much about the War itself. The evacuation of Carrie and Nick from London is little more than a device to get them into the different, not just the safer, environment of Wales. From that point their encounters with other people, normal or eccentric, could have occurred at any time and anywhere; the War raises its head mainly through the sporadic contacts with their mother who has evacuated herself to Scotland. The real story is sandwiched between Carrie's initial visit to Wales and her return thirty years later, and an entertaining story it is, full of incidents and characters whose sense of humour, though at times disguised, makes all concerned human. The Welsh background is skillfully used, though in convincing moderation, and Faith Jaques' illustrations have just the right flavour of old-fashionedness which makes them authentic for readers of another generation.

David L. James

SOURCE: "Recent World War II Fiction: A Survey," in *Children's literature in education,* Vol. 8, No. 2, Summer, 1977, pp. 71-9.

Carrie's War is . . . successful in penetrating to the roots of violence. Away from the shelling and the bombing in the cities and with no heroics whatever, Nina Bawden's seventh children's book deals with two very middle-class evacuees, Carrie and Nick, who spend their war in the narrow, suspicious household of Councillor Evans, a volatile and tyrannical Welshman. The major characters are firmly drawn: Nick, a stubborn little boy with a strong sense of injustice, very dependent on his sister; Carrie, his sensitive elder sister; Albert Sandwich, the third evacuee, full of practical wisdom, and billeted at the mysterious Druid's Bottom; Mr Evans, at first an evil tyrant but finally a pathetically lonely figure; Auntie Lou, his oppressed sister who ultimately marries Harper Cass, an American serviceman. Three other characters add an exotic dimension to the story, which dallies with recurring theme in Nina Bawden's novels, the supernatural. Hepzibah Green, the supposed witch and adversary of Mr Evans, is caretaker of Druid's Bottom and of Mister Johnny, the simpleton whose frantic communications either baffle or show strange insight. Finally there is frail Mrs Gotobed, "an old lady with silvery hair piled high and a pale invalid's face" who lives in the past and whose will provides much of the plot's mystery.

The external war is only felt in passing, for this is primarily a story about Carrie Willow's developing awareness of others, her process of understanding other people's mystery and misery. Two scenes stand out from a host of others: the haymaking scene which is joined by Mr Evan's hearty son Frederick, "a broad, beefy soldier with a very big bottom." He taunts Mister Johnny and is in turn attacked with a pitchfork. Also remarkable is Carrie's farewell to Mr Evans, where she begins determined to return his gift of what she thinks is a stolen ring and ends by hearing his unhappy love story:

> The girl in the photograph smiled out, rather older now, her hair in a bun, one hand touching her cheek. Mr Evans said, "See that ring she's got on? That's the one you've got now. I bought it for her, see, with my first wages, and when she gave it back, I gave it to you. So there's a bit of old history you've got with that ring."
>
> Carrie swallowed hard. "When she gave it back?"
>
> "Don't parrot, girl! You heard me!"

Carrie's War is not a book about the war written down to the child's level, but simply one about children in wartime. It is a novel likely to promote understanding and sympathy with the more unpleasant and bizarre qualities of adults, and in a subtle way it has much to say about the need for power and the sources of violence.

Barbara Freedman

SOURCE: "The Writer and the Reader in *Carrie's War,*" in *Children's literature in education,* Vol. 22, No. 1, March, 1991, pp. 35-43.

Nina Bawden's novel *Carrie's War* is an account of a child's struggle to understand the motives and feelings of the adults by whom she is surrounded while an evacuee in Wales during the London blitz of 1939. Bawden's artistry lies in her ability to make a fictitious set of circumstances seem real—so real that the reader believes all that takes place, indeed experiences it, unaware of how her or his own personality and past experiences are seeping into the spaces between the author's words and the two are intertwining.

The purpose of this essay is to separate the two strands and identify their particular fibers. This will be done by analyzing the means by which Bawden speaks to the reader, lures the reader into the world of the characters, and creates reader reactions that add to the text itself. This is the essence of Wolfgang Iser's "phenomenological" theory of literary criticism [published in *Reader-Response Criticism*]. As he describes it, the "artistic" elements of the author and the "aesthetic" elements of the reader confront one another, forming a dynamic literary work which "must lie halfway between the two."

As with any book, before there can be a reader there must be an author, and the relationship that the author sets out to establish with the reader depends partially upon the audience the author is hoping to reach. When studying the manner in which the reader's perceptions influence the reading of the book, it is important, therefore, to identify the author's "implied reader." Thus the first section of this piece will uncover this persona in the manner used by Aidan Chambers in his application of Iser [in *Signal*]. Then a more in-depth study will be made of the implications of Iser's theory in the analysis of *Carrie's War.*

In *The Thorny Paradise,* Bawden discusses her works for children and openly refers to "the child I write for," stating that "I wanted to write, not as a grown-up looking back, but as a former child, remembering the emotional landscape I had once moved in, how I had felt, what concerned me." An examination of such literary elements as style and point of view in *Carrie's War* yield evidence to support Bawden's assertion that the ideal reader is a child, in this case a child roughly twelve years of age who is spoken to through the protagonist, twelve-year-old Carrie, and who may share her level of perception about human nature.

While the tale is told in the third person, the world is shown through Carrie's eyes; her secret thoughts and emotions are revealed. She listens to and observes the people around her, seeking meaning in their words and actions. The reader is privy not only to Carrie's opinions of others, but also to her struggle to form those opinions, as she agonizes to distinguish fact from facade. To illustrate: When Carrie learns that Mr. Evans, the seemingly hateful man in whose house she is living, was loved by his estranged sister, Dilys, until her death, Carrie believes that he will be happy to learn that Dilys's intentions for the disposition of her property were not intended to spite him. Instead, Mr. Evans is furious.

Both Carrie and the youthful reader must work hard to make sense of his unanticipated reaction.

Further evidence that the primary reader is meant to be a child is derived from the observation that few experiential demands are placed on the reader. The explanation for the need to send the children to Wales is kept simple, a mere device to cast Carrie and her brother, Nick, into this strange situation. Their naval officer father is barely mentioned, and their mother, who has gone to Glasgow to aid the war effort and be nearer her husband, is unimportant to the book and nearly absent from the children's thoughts. What is dwelt on is a situation with which any child reader may identify: a sudden abandonment by parents and the equally sudden appearance of a blustering old man who threatens the children's happiness. Thus, a modern-day fairy-tale premise is established. From the moment the children are "labeled like parcels" and banished on a train to Wales, there to wait helplessly in a line until chosen by an adult, any child reader can sense and resent the powerlessness of their situation.

Clearly, the author is taking Carrie's side right from the outset, and according to Chambers, this is another crucial point in the recognition of the implied reader. He asks if the author "forges an alliance with children." In Bawden's own words, she intentionally narrates her stories "through their eyes, from their side." She makes the reader sympathize with Carrie and her confusion. By viewing the world through Carrie, the child reader bonds with her in the early pages of the book. As Carrie watches and listens and comments on the virtues and vices of others, the reader shares her judgments of Nick as "Greedy pig. Garbage can" or Auntie Lou as "nice" but "stupid." Always the perspective is Carrie's, whether she is forming her own opinions or listening to those of others.

Nina Bawden's style also points to an implied child reader. She relies on fairly short sentences with few adjectives. Carrie's feelings rely on childlike insights. Upon her arrival in the Welsh valley, Carrie "had already begun to feel ill with shame at the fear that no one would choose her, the way she always felt when they picked teams at school. Suppose she was left to the last!" Portraying childhood feelings and referring to ordinary occurrences that children may recall from their own pasts lend believability to the ensuing events.

"Affinities between oneself and someone outside oneself" are established, as Iser puts it, or as others might put it, the child reader "identifies" with the child Carrie. This allows the contemporary child to be taken beyond the everyday world. Then, as the child follows Carrie's efforts to understand what lies behind appearances, the child reader can begin to learn not to make harsh judgments of others when hidden circumstances may be determining their behavior. Therein the major theme of the story unfolds. As Aidan Chambers remarks, Nina Bawden manages to unmask "adult characters to a remarkably complex degree without loss of definition for her young readers." He cites *Carrie's War* as "a very fine example of how an author can deploy her craft in the creation of an implied reader."

Bawden effectively employs flashback, as well. At the book's opening Carrie is presented as an adult, returning to the village in Wales and tormented by remorse for a past deed. Carrie then tells the tale of her childhood experience to her own children. This establishes the novel's overall wistful tone and produces a powerful suspense. The reader is drawn in, eager to learn what terrible thing Carrie might be responsible for that could still haunt her thirty years later. As Jane Langton describes it [in *Horn Book*], in reference to children's fantasies, "the writer must set his stakes high, as soon as possible." So for Carrie, and thus for the implied reader, the stakes seem painfully high and one is impelled to read on.

The text then offers conflicting hints at explanations of events, past or future, to which the reader is not yet privy. Expectations are short-circuited and "the opportunity is given to us to bring into play our own faculty for establishing connections—for filling in the gaps left by the text itself." This "indeterminacy," as Iser describes it, is required to set the reader's own thoughts in motion: "The literary text needs the reader's imagination, which gives shape to the interaction of correlatives foreshadowed in structure by the sequence of the sentences."

As an adult cannot experience a child's reactions, however, the adult reader's interactions with the text cannot be those of the author's implied reader. The adult recalls childhood and identifies with the child Carrie but brings to the reading a more sophisticated knowledge of the seeming inconsistencies in human behavior and the subtle effects of environment upon character development. An adult may bring to Carrie's perceptions of Mr. Evans more a sense of sad understanding than the sense of revelation that younger readers might feel.

The adult reader, in addition, is more sensitive to the presence of recurring symbols within a book. The children hear the train whistle as they arrive in the valley, and Nick vomits up both his fears and his lunch. It is heard again, in the background, as Carrie receives her birthday kisses from Albert, a clue to the potential that their relationship holds. Nick, meanwhile, is shielding his ears from the sound, which is a screamed reminder of that initial expulsion from their real home. Finally, a shrill train whistle blends with Carrie's cry as she sees Druid's Bottom aflame from her place on the train as she leaves the valley. To the reader the train whistle is a piercing measure of the children's time in Wales, a cry of fear just as the children have felt fear upon their arrival and upon their departure from this hiatus in their normal lives. It foretells isolation and sorrow.

Another small moment in the book occurs as Carrie and Albert discuss the death of Dilys. Albert disturbs an ants' nest and remarks on the speed with which the ants respond to protect their eggs. He comments that "people wouldn't act so fast, though. Not conditioned to it. They'd stop and think and wonder and while they were doing that someone's great boot would come down—crump—and that 'ud be the end of them."

This casual observation, which a child reader may overlook, causes an adult reader to reflect upon the characters in the book. Mr. Evans and Dilys, a once close brother and sister, have spent bitter years of "thinking," as the boots of life "crumped" down around them. The grown-up Carrie of the book's opening passages has spent thirty years of "thinking" and "wondering" and feeling guilty over an event as yet unrevealed. Humans do react slowly and do ponder and waste years in regret and anguish. The child reader lacks the years and the wisdom to relate to this sorry situation, but the adult reader has the accumulated experience which can allow such symbolic connections to be made.

A third symbol which the adult reader is likely to notice is the double meaning inherent in the title, *Carrie's War*. For as "Carrie thought of bombs falling, of the war going on all this year they'd been safe in the valley; going on over their heads like grown-up conversation when she'd been too small to listen," a more personal war rages within her. Through such unstated associations the reader seeks and finds patterns, or what Iser refers to as the "gestalt" of the text.

Patterns, often illusory, are woven and then unraveled as the reader searches for some stable framework within which all the text's details can be neatly fit. Iser claims that, in truth, "the inherent non-achievement of balance is a prerequisite for the very dynamism of the operation." As the text refuses to cooperate with our expectations of characters and situations, negating them time and time again, the reader must search for new patterns from clues given, desperately hoping to close all gaps and tie up all loose ends, and bringing parts of himself or herself into the book in the process. Scattered throughout the text, foreshadowing and irony play key roles, adding to the reader's tension as events are anticipated and negated. At times premonitions dramatize the irony in the characters' reactions to circumstances.

Paradoxically, Nick wishes to remain at the Evanses' house despite the hostility he feels toward Mr. Evans, for he has grown "used to it." Then, as Carrie and Nick first experience Druid's Bottom, it is mentioned that it "was, perhaps, the most important journey they ever made together." The reader fears for the children as they hesitantly enter the yew grove and a "gobbling" noise terrified them. Yet the prediction of the trip's significance becomes a positive force as they reach the house, "a warm, safe, lighted place. . . . Coming into it was like coming home on a bitter cold day to a bright, leaping fire. It was like the smell of bacon when you were hungry; loving arms when you were lonely; safety when you were scared." Thus, on the return trip, Mister Johnny's gobble has become a comfort and Nick now wishes never to return to the Evanses for "that lovely,

bright, happy kitchen had made the Evanses' house seem colder and bleaker than ever." Hepzibah and Mister Johnny, the two characters at Druid's Bottom who had seemed mysterious and bizarre, have shown themselves to be the most unconditional in their love for others. And yet Carrie feels that she must hide her pleasure in them, when around Mr. Evans.

Nina Bawden deftly molds these twists and ironic turns and, as "preintentions" are dashed, the reader is constantly challenged to reevaluate what has gone before. "This is why the reader often feels involved in events which, at the time of reading, seem real to him, even though in fact they are very far from his own reality," as Iser states it.

Other instances of foreshadowing and irony occur via the symbolism of the spent, dying Dilys adorning herself each day in one of the opulent but faded gowns of her youth. Her appearance in her favorite dress, which she had been saving for last, foretells her death. Ironically, that happens on the very day that Mister Johnny strikes out against societal ridicule, in the form of the ignorant Frederick. This is a warning to the reader of the difficulty to come in finding a new home for Mister Johnny after Dilys's death.

Iser feels that the author's words, by suggesting meanings beyond the print of the page, allow and at times force the reader to link together the incidents in the book through "the process of anticipation and retrospection that leads to the formation of the virtual dimension, which in turn transforms the text into an experience for the reader." Nina Bawden weaves a rich tapestry of impressions about characters which constantly impel the reader to negate past conclusions in an effort to arrive at a consistent view of each character's personality and motivations. Her portrayal of Mr. Evans, for example, continually forces a reevaluation of his character.

When the children are taken to their temporary Welsh home by Mr. Evans's younger sister, "Auntie Lou," it is clear from her mouse-like scurrying that she fears her brother's temper. Then, as the children shiver in bed, they hear his voice booming below and fashion a mental image of a seething "ogre." This initial childish exaggeration is negated on the following day when they learn that he is "just a tall, thin, cross man with a loud voice" who is always to remain "Mr. Evans"; a more personal appellation would be unthinkable. Nick, however, continues to perceive him as a villain after Mr. Evans catches him illicitly munching on cookies. Because Nick had stolen the cookies, Carrie cannot be so cavalier in condemning Mr. Evans. The reader assesses this incident, remembering Mr. Evans's temper, but also his earlier attempt at friendliness with the children through his one-line joke about "the human race."

His character is under constant scrutiny by the reader, who must determine whether or not Mr. Evans is hoping to exploit Carrie as a source of information about Dilys's household. The reader must also consider Hepzibah's and Auntie Lou's explanations of how Mr. Evans's early loss of his father and his youthful poverty had affected his life and his feelings toward his sister, Dilys, who had led a life of frivolity and wealth as part of the mine-owning family who had caused the Evanses so much misery.

Carrie, and the reader, wrestles with a tangle of impressions, of anticipations and negations, seeking a single, lucid portrait of the man. These gaps, too, are heightened by the author's shrewd use of irony. The more Nick hates Mr. Evans, for example, the less Carrie is able to give up on him. Also, Mr. Evans's apparent cruelty to others becomes gradually more understandable as Carrie realizes that life has been cruel to him.

This ambiguity rises to a crescendo when Albert suggests that Mr. Evans may have stolen Dilys's will in order to evict Hepzibah and Mister Johnny from Druid's Bottom. The question of his character takes on a new urgency. Is he evil or merely foul-tempered? The reader struggles with Carrie, with each new negation hoping that he could not be so coldly calculating, yet fearing the worst. When, at last, he is found innocent of these charges (there had been no will), Mr. Evans appears a broken man, more to be pitied than feared. His inability to communicate tenderness and his stubborn ill-temperedness have cost him Auntie Lou's loyalty and have left him with nothing to remember Dilys by but an ancient, discolored photograph and a ring. The sadness is deepened by his having given that garnet ring, symbol of a past bond of love between himself and Dilys, to Carrie, his wordless gesture of love for her. Mr. Evans cannot be excused for all of his gruffness, yet he can be understood and pitied. That may be as far as the implied child reader can carry a revised attitude toward him, but the adult reader may even empathize with him.

Similar gaps are opened, to be closed by the reader's perceptions, as inconsistencies arise in the actions of other characters. Readjustments of past cues are demanded by new disclosures. The "nice" but "stupid" Auntie Lou, portrayed from the outset as a skittish shadow of a woman, takes bold action in appearing before the puritanical Mr. Evans in a lacy blouse and lipstick. Carrie is shocked by her idiocy, but it is Nick's insight that negates the reader's view of Auntie Lou as he explains to Carrie that Auntie Lou "only did it to take him off you."

Suddenly the reader perceives a new strength in Auntie Lou which somehow must be reconciled with her past timidity. The love and warmth brought into the cavernous household by the presence of the children have given Auntie Lou a secret source of new resolve and hope for a cheerier future. She negates expectations again when she elopes with an American soldier. Yet the different facets of her personality do come together. Too cowardly to face her brother, she leaves a farewell note on the kitchen table, adding poignancy to his feelings of betrayal.

Hepzibah presents a third major gap in the reader's comprehension of the characters and their relationships to one another. Mr. Evans plants the idea in Carrie's mind that Hepzibah is an exploiter, rather than a care-giver, of Dilys. His unkind references to her act upon Albert's more kindly conjectures concerning her witch-like talents. Carrie's uncertainties about the possibility that this big-hearted woman could be a witch, along with her uneasiness over the supposed presence of ancient Druid spirits in the valley, cause Carrie to become unreasonably disturbed by the "cursed" skull, long a fixture of Druid's Bottom.

That skull, presenting another gap as the reader wonders if the supernatural might be at work, illustrates the author's use of the readjustment of the focus. As Iser discusses such a device, small details, seemingly insignificant when presented, must later be reexamined and given new meaning. The tale of the skull is introduced into the story as a minor anecdote concerning the family into which Dilys had married. This perception is shockingly negated when the skull becomes pivotal to Carrie's later years of guilt, for she tosses it into the horse pond in anger at Mr. Evans and for thirty years fears it to be the cause of a fire in which she believes Albert, Hepzibah, and Mister Johnny died. This emotional climax probably signals the point at which the implied child reader and the adult reader most widely diverge. The thought of Carrie's guilt may agonize the child reader, as it does Carrie, but the adult reader, while horrified at the apparent death of three much cared for characters, understands that Carrie's feelings of responsibility for the tragedy are totally unwarranted. The child reader may identify with Carrie's shame, whereas the adult reader wishes to comfort her.

Happily, the reader need not suffer long, for this frightening event rapidly leads to the most joyous negation in the entire book. As the reader is returned to the present day, and the children of the grown-up Carrie venture down to the ruins of Druid's Bottom, it is discovered that Albert, Hepzibah, and Mister Johnny are alive! The child reader realizes that often children are not at fault in situations where they have felt responsible and have burdened themselves with pent-up guilt. This makes for a surprisingly happy, and welcome, ending to a richly satisfying novel.

The effect of all the gaps in what the reader is told about the motivations of the characters in the story, as well as the ways in which the reader must reconcile what is foreshadowed with what is later disclosed, causes the reader to enter into the emotional tangle of the tale. The reader connects newly revealed bits of information to nearly forgotten ones and gains new understanding of what has gone on before and what might be yet to come. Along with Carrie, the reader searches to distinguish the truth from the illusion and in the process arrives at Iser's "virtual dimension" of the text, that union of the artistic and the aesthetic, of author and reader.

The reader leaves the book, not happy that *Carrie's War*

has ended, but happy that Carrie's "war" has. The implied child reader comes away from the experience enriched by a deeper comprehension of the complexities of human character, with less of an inclination to judge self or others too harshly on scanty evidence.

Nina Bawden's subtle skill and the personal experience upon which the reader draws work together to shade in the ambiguities and ironies of the story so that each reading is a harmonious completion of the book. The single reader cannot, however, presume to have found "the" completion of the book, for, as Iser observes, "the reading process is selective, and the potential text is infinitely richer than any of its individual realizations." As Nick frequently does, each reader must arrive at her or his own "best thing."

THE PEPPERMINT PIG (1975)

Philippa Pearce

SOURCE: "Pigs and Parsons," in *The Times Literary Supplement,* No. 3813, April 4, 1975, p. 362.

Nina Bawden's *The Peppermint Pig* was written "in happy memory of my grandmother". The book is fiction, but it has a peculiar warmth and vividness to it. It centres on the fortunes of the narrator's Greengrass grandmother and her children—the younger ones, Theo and Poll, especially—with a consciousness of other Greengrass forebears stretching comfortably back into Norfolk mists of time. It buttonholes the reader with its first words, in a reminiscence of an earlier generation: "Old Granny Greengrass had her finger chopped off in the butcher's when she was buying half a leg of lamb. She had pointed to the place where she wanted her joint to be cut, but then she decided she needed a bigger piece and pointed again. Unfortunately Mr. Grummett, the butcher, was already bringing his chopper down. . . . "

Butchery has to play an important part in the story. The four young Greengrasses, with their mother, move from London to live with their Norfolk aunts, while their father goes off to make money in America. They are genteel—not crampingly so—but poor.

Their mother does dressmaking, and, to help the family resources, takes in a pint-pot-sized pigling—a "peppermint pig", roughly on the analogy of a peppercorn rent. Theo and the pig are both undersized, but in a year flourish and grow. The eponymous animal becomes not only huge, but a family pet. Yet he is still valuable pork, and the elder Greengrasses literally cannot afford to ignore that. The pig is killed. Poll, given a puppy beforehand to console her for the loss she has never allowed herself to foresee, is inconsolable. The book is honest. But life goes on, sweeping the pig into the past and Poll and Theo and the others towards growing up.

The life and death of the peppermint pig is only one thread in the Greengrass history. As a whole, the story has not the wonderful inevitability of *Carrie's War* (an exceptionally good book can dog an author for years, almost snapping at its creator's heels), but its incidents are brightly coloured and crisply told, with a sense not only of pigs fattening but also of human beings growing taller and perhaps wiser.

Poll, for instance, coming home alone by country lanes in the dusk, gets lost. Darkness falls; she finds herself by a spot reputedly haunted by a phantom coach; and then the coach comes.

She hears the drumming of hooves, the rattling of iron-shod carriage-wheels; sees the lights of lamps, and the pallor of the coachman's face under his hat—all bearing down upon her, swamping her in an appalling terror. The coach passes: it was only the nine o'clock mail coach, after all. But Poll has learnt real fear: now "the fear that walked with her was a dark dream in her mind and had no shape at all".

Jean Fritz

SOURCE: A review of *The Peppermint Pig,* in *The New York Times Book Review,* May 18, 1975, p. 8.

A peppermint pig, according to the milkman who took a shilling for it, is a pig that's not worth much, a runt, a token of a pig. Nevertheless Nina Bawden's peppermint pig is worth a great deal to the Greengrass family. It becomes a special pet, has the run of the house and is the cause of considerable emotion in 9-year-old Poll, who finds out in the end what can happen to a pig, special or not, when a family is in debt to a butcher. So the pig is one of the major elements of this plot. And so is Mr. Greengrass, though he makes only brief appearances. We worry that he won't appear at all. He's off in America seeking his family's fortunes while his family, shunted off to relatives in the country, try to make ends meet.

Poll's brother, Theo, small for his age (a runt like the pig, he thinks), is another element. In one moment he can worry that his father may have left his comfortable job in London because he committed a theft; in the next moment he himself can on a sudden impulse steal an egg at the market. Because he's unlucky, he's seen by Noah, his special enemy, and because Poll is afraid, he gives in to a long agony of blackmail.

But it's no use trying to pin down the threads of a Nina Bawden book. It is like listing the ingredients of a cake when it's the taste you're after. And Nina Bawden is a master at capturing the taste of growing up. The loving that can turn so quickly into hating. The ridicule that can give way to compassion. The sudden, sad insight into a brother who for all his cleverness will always be lonely. The surprises that even an enemy can contain. The miracle of morning after a long siege of illness.

The story is webbed with a delicate network of interpersonal complications, and it is this network, with Poll at the center, that gives the book its emotional texture, far more important than the events themselves.

Patricia Stubbs

SOURCE: A review of *The Peppermint Pig,* in *The School Librarian,* Vol. 23, No. 2, June, 1975, p. 142.

The author is honoured among reviewers—rightly so: her material is the daily bread of life, and when compared with the emasculated pulp of so much children's fiction shines forth as the true nourishment it is. Here domestic event and interaction of character are set in Norfolk at the turn of the century; and the novel's dedication (to Mrs Bawden's grandmother) gives the clue to the warm, nostalgic but not sentimental tone. She recreates a lost world of flannel and country fairs (aided by the fine illustrations) with affectionate precision, viewing most of the events with art and fidelity through the consciousness of Polly, her tough and tender heroine. Polly learns that experience is difficult, that piglets grow to pigs who die to allow her to eat. The reader experiences her pang, but honours the author's truthfulness, rejoicing at the plain yet crisp and perceptive style. Yet the rigorous standards Mrs Bawden merits reveal a slightly episodic and predictable cast to the book; and Hester Burton's *The Henchmans at Home,* with a similar Norfolk period setting, perhaps establishes the era more solidly. But *The Peppermint Pig* has a low-key claim which must be heard.

Margery Fisher

SOURCE: A review of *The Peppermint Pig,* in *Growing Point,* Vol. 14, No. 3, September, 1975, pp. 2691-92.

In the lives of the young the passage of time is apt to be marked by matters which to adults might seem almost irrelevant. *The Peppermint Pig* tells the story of Poll and Theo, who went with their mother, older brother and sister to a Norfolk town (Norwich, it would seem) to spend a year with their father's schoolmistress sisters while he went to America. The reasons for his departure were not altogether clear to Poll, who was nine at the time, or to thoughtful Theo, rather more than a year older. There had been something about stolen money, something about an uncle with a fruit farm in California, and phrases were overheard about a taste for roving and adventure. In any case, this was for Poll and Theo the year when father went away, the year when they came to know strict, loving Aunt Sarah and jolly Aunt Harriet and met the tramp in the summer-house who turned out to be their grandfather; it was the year when they discovered the depth, extent and influence of Family. But it was, above all, the year of the peppermint pig Johnny, the runt who became a beloved, house-trained family pet, who went to tea with lonely Lady March and whose final fate taught Poll a bitter lesson about points of view.

Time and relationships are all-important in this story. It opens with irresistible drama, "Old Granny Greengrass had her finger chopped off in the butcher's when she was buying half a leg of lamb". It is one of those anecdotes enshrined and embroidered in families. It is told by an unnamed and invisible narrator who is child to one of the old lady's great-grandchildren—Poll, at a cautious guess. Certainly Poll is the centre of the story; even Theo's sufferings at the hand of nasty Noah Bugg are seen through the eyes of his observant little sister, who realises but never fully understands the tortuous way his mind works. But Poll is no isolated child. She is the centre of a family, members past and present, of a world of people all endowed with individuality through Nina Bawden's vigorous, particularised narrative and dialogue. Substantial in background, unerring in its reflection of the social patterns of the turn of this century, this is a fine example of the work of a novelist who has never reserved a particle of her skill when writing for the young.

DEVIL BY THE SEA (1957; U.S. edition, 1959; abridged edition for children, 1976)

Kirkus Reviews

SOURCE: A review of *Devil by the Sea,* in *Kirkus Reviews,* Vol. XLIV, No. 15, August 1, 1976, p. 847.

Bawden's impressively crafted psychological suspense story was published as an adult book in 1958, and its shifting viewpoints and piercing characterization still set it apart from novels written specifically for YA's—who will sympathize but not automatically identify with the intense, perverse child heroine Hilary, and will catch dispassionate glimpses, also, of her inadequate mother's contradictory impulses and of the dotty old killer's interior blubbering. The setting is a British seaside town at the end of summer, where a little girl is found murdered after Hilary has seen her going off to the marsh with a sinister club-footed old man that Hilary's almost diabolically angelic little brother has proclaimed to be the devil. Hilary's own feelings toward the man vary from terror to pity to fascination . . . toward the end, her panic when he chases her through an amusement park gives way, when he catches up with her on the beach, to a serene trust that is even more chilling. At last, in the police station, absorbed in her own disillusionment with the adult world and oddly indifferent to her recent peril, she says that he is not the devil, only a poor old man. And, if superior story-telling weren't enough, that reminder alone, in these days of satanic exploitation, might justify the YA reissue.

Publishers Weekly

SOURCE: A review of *Devil by the Sea,* in *Publishers Weekly,* Vol. 210, No. 8, August 23, 1976, p. 75.

Originally published for adults in 1957, this tense, highly literate and moving story is about to be offered to younger readers. The author has an almost superhuman knowledge and understanding of a child's feelings. Hilary is nine with a pampered younger brother and a teenaged stepsister who resents caring for the children. Theirs is a rum household altogether with an ineffectual father, a pretentious mother and a dotty elderly aunt. Hilary tries to convince them that she has seen the "Devil" make off with a little girl who has been murdered, but they all, for various reasons, dismiss her report. She's at the mercy of the old man she calls the Devil, actually a pathetic pedophile. The narrative builds inexorably to a haunting climax. Readers will be impressed by the story, no less by the compassion which the author expresses for all the players in the drama, no matter what their failings.

Ann A. Flowers

SOURCE: A review of *Devil by the Sea,* in *The Horn Book Magazine,* Vol. LII, No. 6, December, 1976, p. 629.

Although the story includes the murder of a child and is full of tension and excitement, the book is distinguished by a particularly dispassionate portrayal of character. It is based mainly on the perceptions of nine-year-old Hilary, fat, ugly, and clever, who—with her younger brother Peregrine—witnesses the child Poppet being led away by the old man whom they call the Devil because of his club foot. Although Hilary is immediately aware that something is wrong, neither then nor later can she get anyone to believe her story until it is almost too late. Hilary is a complex, disconcertingly inconsistent child; she is alternately maternal and sadistic to her brother and is frequently misunderstood by her family. Her coldly ambitious but sometimes compassionate mother, her ineffectual but loving father, her soppy and resentful half sister Janet all fail her somehow, bringing her finally to the dawning realization of the limitations of adults and of the beginnings of her own maturity. The strong characters and the subtle relationships among even the minor ones, and the suspenseful interweaving of the strands of the plot make a striking book for readers accustomed to more bland fare.

M. Hobbs

SOURCE: A review of *Devil by the Sea,* in *Junior Bookshelf,* Vol. 41, No. 1, February, 1977, pp. 29-30.

Writing on realism in children's books, . . . Nina Bawden said "It is important in children's books to write about the relationship between children and adults", and "Books can help by bringing fears out". Her present book is a condensed (and powerfully condensed) version of one brought out in 1957, and is concerned with both these points. I would join issue with her on them as exemplified here, though I agree with her in principle. I feel she analyses the relationship between nine-year-old Hilary's

strong sense of guilt and her self-centred mother's rejection of her podgy, irritating but clever daughter (no-one praises her for her intelligence), and shows the motivation of the other adults' behaviour, in a way that will be clear to adult readers but not to younger ones. They will scarcely find one likable adult in the book, and little hope for Hilary's future. Adults will recognise more easily, for instance, the idle mother's chance of redemption in earning her living and taking responsibility for others after her husband's death—he is perhaps the most likable character but, preoccupied with his secret illness, he too rejects Hilary frighteningly unjustly before he dies. Secondly, it may help to bring out children's secret fears of nasty old men, but Hilary's rescue in the nick of time is lucky rather than inevitable, though perceptive readers will have been reassured by a previous reference to something she thought in later life. She realises that Dotty Jim, a pathetically understandable reject of society, has murdered one little girl. Her priggish little brother identifies Jim as the Devil, because of his club-foot "hoof", and in Hilary's terrible guilt-feelings for the peccadilloes which the adults exaggerate into crimes, she is drawn irresistibly to the old man because wicked people belong to the Devil. The deep hopelessness of the situation, the wonderful pictures of the family locked in their unhappy, selfish worlds, the stepsister in an arid non-love-affair, the old aunt obsessed with her beach-combing finds, even casual passers-by who consider the slightest unusual move too great though a life is in danger, are all the more depressing because so powerfully drawn. It is an unforgettable story, and Nina Bawden may rightly argue that such things may happen, but it is as much of an extreme, and I would argue an unnecessarily disturbing one, as the golden world of *Anne of Green Gables.* One may argue that children's fears are "helped" because Hilary is shown to forget her experience immediately after the police questioning, but the reader does not forget.

📖 *REBEL ON A ROCK* (1978)

Kirkus Reviews

SOURCE: A review of *Rebel on a Rock,* in *Kirkus Reviews,* Vol. XLVI, No. 6, March 15, 1978, pp. 304-05.

Readers of *Carrie's War* (1973) will be predisposed to follow the adventures of Carrie's daughter Jo, whose new stepfather Albert Sandwich (remember Albert?) takes the family vacationing in a lovely country currently suffering under dictatorship. Jo is flattered at the start when Albert involves her in his touchy mission of delivering smuggled messages to citizens of Ithaca; later, though, she's outraged when he seems to go along with hotel guest Herr Schmidt's approval of the regime. But Jo eventually learns what Albert had guessed all along—that Herr Schmidt is in reality the exiled leader Platonides, and the father of a boy her age with whom Jo had become friendly. Jo begins her first-person story by announcing that "When I was twelve I stopped a war";

in the end you see that this less-than-heroic feat is accomplished when she inadvertently reveals the would-be revolutionary's identity to the dreaded, torturing regime. But Jo no sooner makes that revelation than she reports that Platonides will only be kept under house arrest for two years, when a new revolt will bring him to democratic power. It's a disappointingly easy resolution, and the visiting exile's behavior is sometimes hard to credit. A smaller story then, for a smaller war; but Bawden's keen and sympathetic sense of happy-family abrasions and pre-adolescent anxieties brings Jo and her problems very close to home.

Marjorie Lewis

SOURCE: A review of *Rebel on a Rock,* in *School Library Journal,* Vol. 24, No. 8, April, 1978, p. 81.

This junior spy-thriller is a walloping good adventure in spite of its improbable and coincidence-ridden plot. Twelve-year-old Jo, the narrator, her mother, older brother, and small adopted brother and sister (who are Black) are taken on what Albert, her charming, mild-mannered stepfather, calls a "vacation." At first, being in an exotic country is fun—but soon Jo has reason to believe that Albert is a spy involved in a plot to overthrow the tyrannical dictator and restore the President to his rightful place. In a remote village dominated by an ancient fortification on a rock, Jo meets a young boy who tells her he is the son of the President-in-exile, and dreams of the rebellion to come. False identities, secret passages, and a chance remark ingenuously blurted by Jo's little sister move the plot along, ending with the tragic quelling of the revolution. Jo's prologue, however, updates it all and readers learn of the eventual restoration of the President and defeat of the dictator. Inter-family relationships are treated with wit and warmth and played against the background of a life-or-death struggle. Skillfully put together and suspense filled, it's Bawden, not at her best, but well worth reading.

Margery Fisher

SOURCE: A review of *Rebel on a Rock,* in *Growing Point,* Vol. 17, No. 2, July, 1978, pp. 3362-63.

It is not easy to present for young readers a child's involvement in dangerous criminal matters: either violence and crime are likely to be minimised or the tone of the book may show an uneasy compromise between adult and young interests. This can be seen from the slightly altered edition of Nina Bawden's adult novel *Devil by the Sea,* published last year, which was directed to her wide junior public but which remained obstinately an adult book. Her new story, *Rebel on a Rock,* no less mature in its style and attitudes, is unmistakably a story for children of eleven or twelve to enjoy. For some of them it will remain a simple adventure but some will attend to the way action is shown to affect character and character to shape action, the tug of influences that makes her delusively simple junior novels so stimulating. Readers will be attracted first, inevitably, by the fact that this is a sequel, in which they can meet the heroine of *Carrie's War* as a woman with two children of her own and two adopted and with Albert Sandwich as her second husband. Albert is making a return visit to the fictitious but recognisable country of Ithaca; there is some mystery about his purpose and his behaviour, as twelve-year-old Jo and her brother Charlie quickly notice. Jo has much of the young Carrie's generous nature but temperamentally she is less sensible and more impetuous; it is only too likely that she should stop a war (as she claims in the opening sentence of her own narrative) when she interferes on behalf of her holiday friend Alexis without realising the political intricacies of the dictator-ridden country. Serious and veracious enough in the way it is described, the unhappy situation in Ithaca is still scaled down (not diminished) to Jo's own capacities. She gives us a child's view in which what actually happens to Alexis and his father is no less and no more challenging and perplexing to her than the relationship with her stepfather which she is trying to work out. Shot with comedy, with an utterly sure and natural sequence of scene and dialogue, the book has a total unity of tone and purpose.

Marcus Crouch

SOURCE: A review of *Rebel on a Rock,* in *Junior Bookshelf,* Vol. 42, No. 5, October, 1978, pp. 262-63.

Surely Miss Bawden is the supreme professional among present-day children's novelists; she brings to these books the same formidable technical equipment, the same standards and the same dedication that she devotes to her other books which, in the publisher's eyes at least, are intended for adults.

Because of this professionalism, she does well even when, as in the present case, her plot is a little less than her best. This is, in one sense, a sequel to *Carrie's War* (which showed her at her very best). Jo, the central character, is Carrie's daughter, and Carrie herself plays a small part in the story. Father is dead and Carrie has married again, to Albert Spy-boots. They are off to Ithaca on holiday, with brother Charlie and the adopted Alice and James, both coloured. Ithaca is vaguely Balkan and suffering under a dictatorship, and Albert is somehow involved with the Underground—hence the spy-boots. Jo has gone for the holiday, but she becomes caught up involuntarily in the plotting through her friendship with Alexis, who is the son of the opposition leader and far too clever for his own good.

Miss Bawden excels in the atmosphere of place. The cautious, repressed capital, and the village of Polis are drawn beautifully, with no fussy detailed description, just the essential touches applied lightly. She is equally at ease with her characters, the principals shown in depth, the lesser actors drawn in brisk light lines. They are all people, not types or caricatures, even Miss Emmeline and Miss Ottoline the Yankee tourists.

A lesser writer would not have resisted the temptation to make Jo the pivot of a successful revolution. Miss Bawden knows that things do not work like that in life or art, only in formula stories. So the revolution flops before it has even got started, and the return of democracy to Ithaca is postponed to a more opportune time. Jo is left with some memories and a deeper understanding of one page in the history books, also with the chance of going back, if she has the courage.

What appears to be a book of adventure, albeit with a contemporary twist, turns out to be also a book about growing up, its pains and ecstasies shown with a quiet tenderness that has in it neither sentimentality nor condescension.

THE ROBBERS (1979)

Zena Sutherland

SOURCE: A review of *The Robbers,* in *Bulletin of the Center for Children's Books,* Vol. 33, No. 2, October, 1979, pp. 21-2.

Solitary and happy, nine-year-old Philip lived with his grandmother in an apartment in a seaside castle; his mother was dead, his father a peripatetic television reporter. When his father married an American, Philip went to London for what he thought was a visit; it proved to be a long stay. Precocious and articulate, Philip made only one friend, Darcy, a street-wise boy whose family (an arthritic father, brother Bing who was a street peddler, Bing's black wife Addie, a beautiful and sensitive woman) made Philip welcome. It is when Bing is sentenced for selling stolen goods that the two boys, desperate, plan their robbery of a rich neighbor's home. The deed is particularly significant because Philip's ethical sense is so strong; it is his sympathy (Bing jailed; Addie pregnant) and loyalty to Darcy that make him break his own code. And it is in the disparate reactions of his cold, bullying father and his understanding grandmother (who goes to see Addie) that Philip finds the answer to the question of his future: he chooses to live with his grandmother. The characterization is superb, perceptive and trenchant; the writing style is polished, the book beautifully structured.

Ethel L. Heins

SOURCE: A review of *The Robbers,* in *The Horn Book Magazine,* Vol. LV, No. 6, December, 1979, pp. 661-62.

Because his mother is dead and his father is a globe-trotting TV news commentator, Philip has been brought up by his grandmother; the widow of a famous general, she occupies one of the Queen's "Grace and Favour" apartments in an ancient castle. Living in cozy intimacy with the wise and gentle old lady, Philip has become an unusual little boy—at once both naïve and sophisticated for a nine-year-old. Then his father remarries, settles in a London house, and insists that Philip—much against his will—come to live with him. Enrolled in a rough-and-tumble city school, Philip is terrorized by a pair of bullies but is befriended by a neighborhood boy, Darcy Jones, and his proud but troubled family. Shouldering the burdens of his elders, Darcy in desperation tries some petty burglary, while Philip, in an outpouring of love and loyalty, joins in the escapade; and both boys run afoul of the police. In a story less rich and complex than most of her fiction for children, the author writes with instinctive sensitivity in simple, artless prose and makes some subtle statements about friendship, justice, hypocrisy, and innocence.

Margery Fisher

SOURCE: A review of *The Robbers,* in *Growing Point,* Vol. 18, No. 5, January, 1980, pp. 3627-28.

The best authors, in fact, are those who don't cram their readers with comment but invite them to bring their own wits and associations to their reading. *The Robbers,* short as it is, is full of hints that people are unpredictable, complicated, devious. In a canal-side district of London a lad of thirteen lives with a crippled father, an older brother who sells 'antiques' on a market stall, and a black sister-in-law: over the water, a television newsman of some repute, settled in an expensive house with a young second wife, summons his nine-year-old son Philip who has lived happily with his spry grandmother in her Grace and Favour castle residence. The class basis for the story is precise and important, both for the plot and for the interaction of the characters. Nina Bawden sees clearly how far friendship is possible between, for instance, Darcy's proud father and Philip's self-centred, casual one, and how far Addie, who accepts racial antagonism with her own sturdy philosophy, can help Philip to adjust to a new kind of life and to the new ideas which Darcy's friendship forces on his attention. Philip is old in his manner but not in experience and he is ill-prepared for the experimental house-breaking which he and Darcy attempt, pathetically innocent and incompetent in their intentions. This is not, as it might sound, a sensational story. It is always character that counts with Nina Bawden. Motive, action, setting—everything is simple, clear-cut and selective, and totally adequate for the task of creating a particular corner of London in which believable people speak, act, suffer and learn from their mistakes.

Marcus Crouch

SOURCE: A review of *The Robbers,* in *Junior Bookshelf,* Vol. 44, No. 3, June, 1980, pp. 138-39.

Nina Bawden is the supreme professional among writers of children's fiction. Technically her novels are flawless. What is a great deal more, in addition to her crafts-manship and the integrity of her research she has heart. Her creations are no lay figures made to go through their motions in furtherance of the plot but real people whose problems matter not only to themselves but to society.

The Robbers is vintage Bawden. Philip is an intriguing character, a little boy who has, in a way, enjoyed a sheltered childhood and not been softened by it. His mother dead and his father too busy to bother much, he has been brought up, in a Grace and Favour apartment of a Kentish castle, by his wise and sensible grandmother. Then father marries again and Philip has to live with him. It is not too bad a change. The new stepmother, who looks like—and is—a Red Indian, is kind and understanding, and Philip's new friend Darcy is both good company and tough enough to frighten the school bullies away. Philip comes to love Darcy's family at least as much as his own. But Darcy's barrow-boy brother is sent to prison for receiving and the family's world begins to break up around them. When Philip stumbles into trouble with the law he is horrified to find that there are really two laws, one for Darcy and one for the son of a respectable TV presenter. In a strong climax Philip learns how to make the best of a bad job and his smug father takes an unexpected beating.

All this is told in a quiet tone, without dramatics but with plenty of drama. All the portraits are crisply drawn—the book might have been better without Charles Keeping's illustrations which are far too explicit and which seem in conflict with the author's concepts—and the school, home and play backgrounds beautifully done. A winner, as a novel and as the television play which must surely follow.

WILLIAM TELL (1981)

Kirkus Reviews

SOURCE: A review of *William Tell,* in *Kirkus Reviews,* Vol. XLIX, No. 23, December 1, 1981, p. 1465.

Bawden retells the legend of William Tell in direct, dignified prose, with concrete words that make a strong impression but none of the contrived details with which another author might attempt to do so. First, she shows us the bountiful Alpine area where "the people could have been happy and prosperous"; the harsh, fat, lazy Austrian bailiffs and soldiers whose tax demands render the people "thin and sullen and frightened"; and the worst bailiff, Gessler, whom we see jealously throwing an old farmer out of his warm stone house. Then come: William Tell's refusal to salute Gessler's hat, his famous forced feat of marksmanship in the marketplace, a storm on the lake which allows him to escape on the way to prison, and his shooting Gessler through the heart—"'So perish all tyrants,' he cried"—which inspires the people of Switzerland to successful revolt. A stirring tale, relatively underexposed here—everyone knows about

the son and the apple, but how many American children know the whole story?—and emphatically illustrated in this Swiss illustrator's [Pascale Allamand] hearty prim-itivist style.

Jane E. Gardner

SOURCE: A review of *William Tell,* in *School Library Journal,* Vol. 28, No. 6, February, 1982, p. 64.

While many children have heard the incident of William Tell shooting an arrow through an apple on his son's head, fewer are aware of other deeds of this Swiss hero. This attractive picture book tells the story of Tell's re-sistance to despotic authority from his refusal to bow before the bailiff's hat (which resulted in the apple in-cident) to his killing of the cruel ruler and his role in the establishment of Switzerland as a nation. Bawden in-cludes the major incidents in Tell's legendary life, por-traying a historical superhero with both great courage and integrity as well as physical strength. The clearly written, simple sentences and large type help make it accessible to young children. Full-page illustrations are done in a folk-primitive style, utilizing flat color and pleasing details such as flower-filled window boxes. The pictures well suit the rural historical setting of the book; an attractive, useful picture book.

KEPT IN THE DARK (1982)

Nancy C. Hammond

SOURCE: A review of *Kept in the Dark,* in *The Horn Book Magazine,* Vol. LVIII, No. 3, June, 1982, pp. 296-97.

"It's only not knowing that's frightening," Noel assures his younger brother and sister when their father's ner-vous breakdown forces their mother to deposit them abruptly at their grandparents' manor house. Heretofore estranged, Noel, Clara, and Bosie grow to know and to adjust to their autocratic grandfather and shy, appeasing grandmother. Then twenty-three-year-old David moves in. The existence of the young man, grandchild of their grandfather's first marriage, had been concealed; now the abused American orphan seeks love with a ven-geance. He longs to be part of a happy family, yet he is incapable of acting in ways that will allow it, and his erratic, violent behavior—presumably psychopathic—is both pathetic and terrifying. But by eschewing such labels and describing the ambiguous scenes from the points of view of the children, the author forces us to confront David as they must; we cannot distance him with psychological terms. Each child's initial response is characteristic. Yet as David—precariously skirting destruction—swigs Grandpa's whiskey, provocatively kiss-es twelve-year-old Clara, aims Grandpa's old army gun at Noel, and releases the hand brake when Grandpa steps in front of the car, he acts as a catalyst upon the other characters; they are strengthened and tempered.

Their deliverance is bittersweet when David flees, erroneously convinced that his grandparents have summoned the police. The title of the rich, trenchant book is apt; protection and deception, tolerance and manipulation, relationships and perception are all examined in a suspenseful psychological thriller.

Patricia Craig

SOURCE: A review of *Kept in the Dark,* in *The Times Literary Supplement,* No. 4138, July 23, 1982, p. 790.

The domestic emergency, usually involving illness in a parent, is a standard device in juvenile fiction for getting the children of the family into an unaccustomed setting where alarms and misadventures can suitably occur. The leading characters are often parked on eccentric relatives whom, due to some long-standing estrangement, they now meet for the first time. A runaway daughter, an unadvantageous marriage, and pigheadedness on the part of one or both her parents, will likely emerge as the causes of the old family quarrel. The daughter, the mother of the present set of children, will have taken up with someone unsuitable, in the rigid parents' view, on account of his profession (artistic) and financial prospects (poor). She will have made her bed, and never regretted lying on it. Nothing but desperation will now bring her to ask a favour—childminding—of the unrelenting old pair.

The grandparents, however, will prove less unrelenting than their behaviour over the years has suggested. It will be up to the children to endear themselves to the standoffish old couple, in the interest of reconciliation and prospective emotional expansiveness. They may do this by means of cuteness (though this particular trait has no credibility for a present-day readership), adaptability, resourcefulness or an unapologetic spirit. Whatever the requisite quality, they will manifest it in the course of coping with some further emergency or bother which afflicts the grandparents in their turn. Things, after some close shaves and unanticipated pickles, will end satisfactorily for everyone.

Nina Bawden, who took a different story-book ploy (the father wrongly accused of theft) and used it to exceptionally good effect in *The Peppermint Pig,* now does the best she can with the unoriginal incidents outlined above. She has several advantages over earlier users of this particular plot—terseness, edginess, scorn for the highly artificial dangers to which children in books were traditionally exposed. The danger that looms over inoffensive Noel, stormy Clara and posing Bosie (who plays the baby and the family chef as it suits him) in *Kept in the Dark* is genuine enough, and the author makes no bones about communicating a thoroughly undiluted sense of apprehension, rising at moments to panic. The family contains another grandson, David, a fat young man, stupid almost to the point of psychopathy, who imposes himself on the household. David's threatening friendliness is not to be resisted. The children, taken in at first, and guilty of some significant indiscretions, are soon pandering to their cousin's insane relish for happy family life—for the old people's sake, of course, as much as their own.

There are some inconsistencies in the book, and some implausibilities too. The grandparents are really less eccentric than unlikely (he gruff but not altogether unbending, she wizened and flighty)—and would they really have kept their daughter in ignorance, all her life, of the existence of her half-brother (David's father)? David is a satisfactorily frightening figure, because of his unpredictability and constant need of placation; but we are kept quite in the dark about how he manages to survive on his own (his visits to his grandparents are relatively infrequent). Nina Bawden is too accomplished an author to write anything resembling "case-history" stories, but in this novel there are one or two gestures in that direction. "Social problem" fiction is all very well, but was it really necessary to lumber poor Bosie with so unpalatable a defect as thieving—safely in the past or not? ("I stopped stealing last year . . . On my birthday", he rather pertly announces). And did the author have to involve him in an escapade that verges on delinquency in order to effect a suitable outcome for her story? These are trifling obstacles in an exhilarating course, but they get in the way of complete enjoyment of the narrative.

E. Colwell

SOURCE: A review of *Kept in the Dark,* in *Junior Bookshelf,* Vol. 46, No. 4, August, 1982, p. 148.

This suspense story for older boys and girls is told with the author's accustomed skill and feeling for atmosphere. Three children are staying with their grandparents for the first time, for their mother is estranged from her parents because of her choice of career and husband. Then David arrives and the whole atmosphere of the house changes. Who is he and why has he such an influence over their stern irascible grandfather? The story of this sinister young man is revealed gradually until he disappears as strangely and unexpectedly as he arrived.

Prejudice, misunderstanding, secrets which are kept for the wrong reasons, make this an interesting read for young people. The oddness of some of the characters—the children's grandmother once an actress, the devious housekeeper who torments her mistress so cruelly; the three children themselves who are so different in character yet bound together by family feeling—add to the fascination of the story. The open ending will intrigue readers and perhaps suggest that no one is wholly bad, not even David.

ST. FRANCIS OF ASSISI (1983)

Kirkus Reviews

SOURCE: A review of *St. Francis of Assisi,* in *Kirkus Reviews,* Vol. LI, No. 17, September 1, 1983, p. J-145.

With the direct prose and primitivist pictures that made an eloquent picture book of *William Tell* (1981), Bawden and [Pascale] Allamand give us another, but very different, legendary medieval figure: the saint who disowned his inheritance for a life of poverty, charity, and peace. "When people offered him bread, he asked them for stones. He wanted to help the priest rebuild his church. He grew thin and pale but he was glad to be poor. . . . Now that he owned nothing, he felt rich in a different way." Bawden tells of miracles, of apologizing to stones as well as preaching to the birds, and of the Pope saying to Francis: "Go and roll with the pigs. That is all you are fit for." ("Nobody washed much in those days, and the Brothers hardly at all," she has explained.) So Francis finds a pig sty ("Brother Pig, may I join you?"), wallows in dung, and returns to the Pope even dirtier. Bawden's account, entirely free of second-hand sentiment or premeditated piety, seems as fresh as if St. Francis had just passed through, followed by tales of his remarkable behavior.

Paul Heins

SOURCE: A review of *St. Francis of Assisi,* in *The Horn Book Magazine,* Vol. LIX, No. 5, October, 1983, p. 589.

In a second collaboration between the author and the artist, another gratifying combination of words and pictures. Both the text and the illustrations are spacious in effect, for the uncrowded words in large type on each left-hand page are faced by a full-page pictorial composition enhanced by the constant use of perspective—as is often found in early Italian paintings. Based on the traditional legends of the life of the well-known ecumenical saint, the story not only recounts the familiar episodes but—for example—tells how Saint Francis preached to the fish as well as to the birds; and in telling about his angelic vision, the author describes the stigmata the saint received without mentioning them by name. The unpretentious, flowing narrative style and the somewhat primitive drawing in the luminous full-color pictures are in keeping with the profound simplicity of Saint Francis of Assisi.

Publishers Weekly

SOURCE: A review of *St. Francis of Assisi,* in *Publishers Weekly,* Vol. 224, No. 17, October 21, 1983, p. 68.

Bawden, author of notable books for adults and children, tells about the life of St. Francis in graceful, uncomplicated prose that beginners can readily grasp. Allamand illustrates the story with paintings in glorious colors and an appropriately childlike simplicity, vivid scenes of rural Italy in the 13th century. The story and pictures follow Francis of Assisi from his youth as a rich, pleasure-loving companion to his peers, through his gradual commitment to living as a beggar for Christ. The founder of the Franciscan order, St. Francis has been honored mostly for his charity and love of all creatures.

Sharron McElmeel

SOURCE: A review of *St. Francis of Assisi,* in *School Library Journal,* Vol. 30, No. 4, December, 1983, p. 52.

St. Francis, the 13th-century founder of the Franciscan Order, is feted in this romanticized story of his life. As with the lives of many saints some events will seem unbelievable; but other events in this story could very well have occurred but seem to have no collaborative source. (No sources or documentation for any events or the material as a whole are cited.) Some examples include an episode describing how Francis rolled in pig dung in order to receive the Pope's blessing and the episode in which Francis abandons his youthful aspiration to become a knight when he meets another knight in threadbare clothing. He subsequentially gives up his rich clothing to this knight, and returns home. (Other sources attribute his failure to become a knight to his ill health.) Omissions include the treatment of Clare, Francis' companion and friend in devotion to Our Lady of Poverty; she is mentioned only once, briefly. San Damiano, a church which figured often in Francis' life, is not mentioned by name at all. "The marks of the nails . . . " assumes that readers of picture-book age will possess prior knowledge of the stigmata to deal with that information meaningfully, as no additional explanation is made. Allamand has included many details in the background and foreground of each full-page illustration, while successfully maintaining the focal figure in each picture. Clear bright colors and stylicized figures characterize the paintings.

📖 *THE FINDING* (1985)

Zena Sutherland

SOURCE: A review of *The Finding,* in *Bulletin of the Center for Children's Books,* Vol. 38, No. 10, June, 1985, p. 180.

In the hands of a lesser writer, the situation and developments used here could easily have become maudlin or melodramatic. Bawden, however, has firm control over her material and discrimination about its treatment, in a fine story about an adopted child who is quiet and gentle and greatly loved. What disrupts Alex's life is the fear that he is upsetting his family because he has inherited a fortune, so he runs away to make things easier for them. This crisis is deftly handled, with a building of suspense as the story moves back and forth from the plight of the runaway to the fearful apprehension of his family. Characterization and dialogue are excellent.

Margery Fisher

SOURCE: A review of *The Finding,* in *Growing Point,* Vol. 24, No. 2, July, 1985, p. 4458.

Adoption brings its own problems and not always at a time when they might most readily be solved, as Nina Bawden [has] shown in **The Finding.** Abandoned as a baby on the stone Sphinx on the Embankment, Alex was adopted by an intelligent and affectionate couple who made sure that he was contented with their family pattern and that the sporadic wrangles with his older sister Laura caused only momentary trouble. He is hardly old enough to face the bewildering change in the direction of his life, just after his eleventh birthday, when through the mischievous interference of his grandmother he finds himself dragged along in her wake to console a lonely old friend and, after her sudden death, learns that he has inherited a considerable fortune from her. The comfortable routine of family life is upset, especially by Gran's unwise fantasies about his true identity; faced with Laura's jealousy and his mother's dismay at besieging reporters and incessant telephone calls, he runs away and is befriended by one of those dirty, eccentric London individualists that Nina Bawden draws so well. Old Poll's houseful of spivs and prowlers could have been dangerous for Alex if it had not been for her effortless control of their predatory plans; but though she releases him from danger it is left for him in the end to accept his adoption and to believe in the genuine affection of his adoptive parents, so that though we last see him once more asleep in the arms of the Sphinx we can be sure that this is only a halfway stage to true happiness. Plain prose, incisive dialogue, sparklingly real people, make up one more of Nina Bawden's accomplished studies of people whose impetuous, disordered, sudden behaviour is disciplined within the conventions of fiction.

E. Colwell

SOURCE: A review of *The Finding,* in *Junior Bookshelf,* Vol. 49, No. 4, August, 1985, p. 183.

As always, Nina Bawden has written a story which poses interesting problems and relationships. Alex is found abandoned between the paws of the Sphinx on the Embankment. He is adopted and is happy as a well loved member of his family until he is eleven. Unexpectedly an old lady leaves him a considerable sum of money. Bewildered and upset by the envy and enmity this causes, Alex feels that everyone is angry with him and runs away to London. An odd group of people whose activities are outside the law most of the time, provide shelter until he is found once again between the paws of the Sphinx.

An engaging story, it has dramatic surprises and interesting characterization. Here is Alex's forthright sister, his busybody of a grandmother, the old lady's scheming nephew and his rescuers, a gallery of rogues. At the centre is Alex himself, sensitive, loving and insecure.

Yet another memorable child joins the many Nina Bawden has created!

Roger D. Sutton

SOURCE: A review of *The Finding,* in *School Library Journal,* Vol. 32, No. 1, September, 1985, p. 130.

Alex was found as a baby, swaddled in the arms of one of the Sphinxes guarding Cleopatra's Needle on the Thames. Eleven years later he inherits a fortune from an elderly woman to whom it has been suggested by Alex's grandmother that he is the son of her long-gone daughter. Unable to handle the pressures of publicity and the impact upon his family, Alex runs away. The story is fleshed from the structure of myth, beginning with Alex's Moses-like "finding," his displacement from home, flight into the city where he is taunted and beaten (plagued by a shower of toads). Alex is rescued by the oracular Poll, a Fagin-like woman who reveals the secret of his identity. Alex's family provides a human, contemporary jostling to the ancient story—his gentle father; his mother, always trying to "be fair" to her children; the meddling grandmother; and, most intriguing, Alex's sister Laura: "Alex was the person she loved best in the world, and she enjoyed making him sad because then she could comfort him." This dithers around a bit as Bawden sets up the running away, and there is a jarring ESP note in the denouement, but the mystery and quest elements should keep readers involved.

PRINCESS ALICE (1985)

Margery Fisher

SOURCE: A review of *Princess Alice,* in *Growing Point,* Vol. 24, No. 2, July, 1985, p. 4472.

Adopted into the middle of a mixed family, Alice does what she can to offset the fecklessness of the Maclusky's own older children and to look after the younger Vietnamese twins and the Maclusky baby; now and then she gets a little tired of her self-imposed duties but when her father, an African prince, comes to visit and suggests she might like a change of scene, it is 'Dad' she wants to stay with, for he has time to talk and to explain her place in the family. A shrewd, sympathetic picture of a modern family, illustrated [by Phillida Gili] in the most beguiling washes of vivid paint which seem casual but which at a second look reveal all kinds of amusing domestic details and invoke a serene mood of family affection.

Tony Bradman

SOURCE: "Family Feelings," in *The Times Literary Supplement,* No. 4296, August 2, 1985, p. 862.

With its imperfect adults and a child facing large, disturbing issues which could dramatically affect the rest of her life, *Princess Alice* is unmistakably Nina Bawden's sort of story. Not that it is as gloomy as such a description might suggest. The subjects touched on may be so, but the text has a very light touch.

The Alice of the title is a black child, one of several children of different races adopted by a genial and chaotic white couple. Alice is a very tidy person, while those around her (the household includes numerous dogs and cats) are very definitely not. Her life is a continual struggle to keep small brothers and sisters clean and toys tidied away, while no one else—particularly her mother—is at all bothered by the mess.

So far so good. But then Alice's African father turns up, and it transpires that he is a prince, which makes Alice a princess. His visit is disturbing for her. What must he think of her adoptive family's fecklessness and mess? Will he drag her off to live in luxurious—but lonely—splendour in Africa, far from the family she now realizes she loves? Alice is confused, and wonders whether she really is a princess or not. And which of her two fathers should she now think of as the "real" one? All, however, is well in the end. The African father returns to his palace, the adoptive father is waiting for Alice at home. He also sorts out Alice's confusion on her regal status, by telling her that "all his daughters are princesses" to him.

It is a well-told story with a happy ending and charming illustrations by Phillida Gili, whose style seems just right for showing the chaotic Maclusky household—but there remain some nagging doubts. Alice's real mother is mentioned all too briefly, and little attempt is made to explain Alice's adoption. Most children will also want to know why such a wealthy and powerful father couldn't have looked after his own daughter. Indeed, the difference between real and adoptive parents is made so wide (not only in colour) that the central issues of adoption and "belonging" lose their impact. I have a feeling that adopted and black children (and those children who are both) may feel a little dissatisfied after they have finished the book.

Roger Sutton

SOURCE: A review of *Princess Alice,* in *Bulletin of the Center for Children's Books,* Vol. 40, No. 1, September, 1986, p. 2.

This odd story takes its cue from the common childhood fantasy of being switched, stolen, or adopted from a rightful royal lineage. Alice Mary is adopted, as are three of the other five Maclusky children. One day her natural father, an African prince, visits Alice Mary ("Princess Alice") in London, and tells her what life would be like if she lived with him. "You would not have to do anything. You could sit on a silk cushion and eat sweetmeats all day." Alice Mary declines. "I don't think Mrs. Maclusky could manage without me." The

Prince sends her back home with a gold and ruby bracelet and proffers an invitation for the whole family to come visit him in Africa. Mr. Maclusky asks Alice, "Do you want me to do some explaining?" Well, yes. The overly peculiar plot is not helped by excessive details and an occasionally arch tone; the illustrations of Alice Mary's home and multi-racial family are cheerfully cluttered, but awkwardly drawn.

Colin Mills

SOURCE: A review of *Princess Alice,* in *Books for Keeps,* No. 44, May, 1987, p. 20.

A gentle and sensitive tale about a little girl living with her adoptive parents and visiting her real father, an African prince. The domestic scenes are well handled; the author has the skill to show the relaxed and easy-going family in the banter and the conversations. The meeting with father is tensely drawn.

The harsh edges are rather too readily smoothed over—but eights to tens will want to explore the issues themselves. The pictures are splendid: readers will feel they've actually been inside the Ritz.

KEEPING HENRY (1988; U.S. edition published as *Henry*)

Betsy Hearne

SOURCE: A review of *Henry,* in *Bulletin of the Center for Children's Books,* Vol. 41, No. 7, March, 1988, p. 130.

Henry is a baby squirrel adopted by a family waiting out the London Blitz on a country farm during World War II. With her characteristic subtlety of craft, Bawden develops scenes and dialogue that bring the reader to realize what Henry means to the narrator, her two brothers, and her mother as they all await her father's return from naval duty. The youngest, Charlie, is particularly touching in his desperate attachments to any strong male figure—a farm hand, an Italian prisoner of war—and in his vague fears about the father he can't quite remember. His question of whether his dad will like the squirrel clearly translates into one of whether his dad will like Charlie. There are many realities here, death in a neighbor's terminal illness, her son's decision to stay with his father on the farm afterwards. This is a story that speaks of family unity in the face of dislocation and separation.

Ilene Cooper

SOURCE: A review of *Henry,* in *Booklist,* Vol. 84, No. 16, April 15, 1988, p. 1429.

A story's obvious complexities are often what give it

richness. In this remembrance of World War II, Nina Bawden has written a story whose apparent simplicity belies its deep power.

The unnamed narrator, a girl seemingly about 12 or so, has been evacuated with her mother and two brothers from London to the Jones family's farm. The narrator attends a boarding school, but summers are for her family and during this special summer a new member is added—a baby red squirrel, who little brother Charlie has shot out of a tree with his slingshot.

Almost immediately, the squirrel, named Henry, becomes the focal point of all their attentions. For the mother, Henry is a new baby to love and nurture as her children grow older; the one who will take her mind off her husband's absence while he's away at war. For Charlie, Henry is something to count on, while the narrator and her other brother, James, find the squirrel a happy diversion in the midst of troubled times.

As farmers, the Jones' have a different view of Henry. To them, wild animals are not meant to be house pets. Still, they understand the necessity of making the best of a bad situation. Mrs. Jones is dying; Abel, her son, longs to go to work at his uncle's horse farm, but his father needs him at home, so his dream is thwarted.

Those who read this story at a surface level will nevertheless find much to like. Bawden's descriptions of Henry and his antics delight even those least susceptible to the animal's charms. And while for some it may seem as though the story simply recounts how the narrator's family found a squirrel, which they raised and loved, and how the narrator one day accidently let him go, readers whose perceptions stretch beyond the printed word will find much more. Henry symbolizes all the family has lost—stability, carefreeness, youth. Like his caretakers, Henry has been ripped from his home; his own adaptability gives the family hope that they too can adapt.

Yet little by little, the family's love becomes a prison for Henry. When the narrator returns from boarding school, she finds that there is now a cage for the animal. She is told it is only to keep visitors away who might harm Henry, but it is also to make sure he does not leave—as the normalcy of their lives has left.

One day when she is alone, the narrator takes Henry outside as she had often done in the past, but this time he jumps away and darts into the trees, not to return. While there is anguish, there is also comfort—albeit temporarily—when their father comes home on leave.

The book's unstated message, that life changes, it ebbs and flows, is both heartening and poignant. For the family, and for the Joneses, what must be borne shall be borne, with the hope of better days being the force that keeps will alive. The loss of Henry closes another door for the family—trying to contain joy rarely works—but Henry's memory warms them as they continue their struggle through difficult days.

Kirkus Reviews

SOURCE: A review of *Henry,* in *Kirkus Reviews,* Vol. LVI, No. 9, May 1, 1988, p. 688.

One of Britain's best novelists for children returns to the setting of *Carrie's War*—Wales during WW II, refuge for many of London's children—with an autobiographical story.

Not realizing that he has caused a disruption in the squirrels' lives that equals his own family's displacement after the bombing of their street, Charlie brings a baby squirrel home to his mother and older brother and sister, who are living with a Welsh farmer's family. Accepting the irremediable ("our mother" finds nurturing small creatures irresistible), the family takes Henry in. Like Farley Mowat's unforgettable owls, he's a rambunctious character with a will of his own; like his adoptive family, he adapts and makes a place for himself, roaming free; but in the end, as they try to protect him by caging him more as he matures, he escapes to freedom.

Bawden's characters always have an intense reality that ensures readers' empathy; their particular experiences illuminate our own—here, the delicate balances involving nurture and captivity, family unity and growth. Henry himself is entrancing; and though her humans are a little stiff, wildlife illustrator [Joyce] Powzyk renders him beautifully in soft pencil. The book's design is unusually attractive, with full-page illustrations bordered in squirrel red-brown. A treasure to be shared aloud.

Deborah Singmaster

SOURCE: A review of *Keeping Henry,* in *The Times Literary Supplement,* No. 4447, June 24, 1988, p. 716.

Unlike Nina Bawden's previous books for children, *Keeping Henry* is directly autobiographical. When the author's London home was bombed in the Second World War, she went to live on a Welsh farm with her mother and two brothers; her father was serving in the Navy. For nine months they were joined by another refugee, the squirrel Henry, catapulted out of his nest by Charlie, the younger of the author's brothers. Only a few weeks old and three inches long, Henry needed no taming. He regarded all humans as trees—to be leapt on, explored and used for food storage. Charlie justified keeping Henry by pronouncing him "Nature Study", and now, years later, Bawden's new book proves Charlie's point. This is nature study at its best—first-hand, affectionate observation of a creature rarely seen at close quarters and never in such *unnatural* circumstances. We learn about Henry's diet, about his curious treatment of apples and lead pencils, about his sleeping habits—favouring a sleeve and then a coat pocket until he is able to construct himself a nest of stolen underwear and odd socks. He is a combination of scamp and sprite, mischievous and magical.

Henry is only the golden kernel of this rich evocation of a child's wartime billet: cramped quarters, pumped water, Tilley lamps, the earth closet in the garden with its three holes and cut up pages from the *Dairy Gazette* or *Farmer's Weekly* hanging from a nail. Their hosts, the Joneses, and the farm hands are vividly remembered, but it is the author's mother, to whom the book is dedicated, who is most closely scrutinized: a woman who had a way with animals, a compulsive educator, a mother who nursed high hopes for her children—too high perhaps.

> Girls should have the same chance as boys to do what they wanted, she always said, meaning the things she would have liked to do, like exploring Tibet to look for the Yeti, or travelling alone into dangerous jungles to make friends with savage, wild animals—the sort of things that made me feel hollow inside just to think about. I didn't want to stay at home and darn socks but I could never, I thought, be as brave as my mother.

It is impossible not to detect in this adolescent narrator the genesis of other prickly young teenagers who feature in many of Bawden's novels for children and adults. Here too, in her time on the Joneses' farm, was the inspiration for the recurring theme of children separated by misfortune from parents, or loving grandparents, and billeted for better or worse in temporary homes, as in *Carrie's War.*

After Bawden's most recent children's novels, which have contained a strong undercurrent of violence, embodied in characters like the sadist Jake in *The Finding* and maladjusted David in *Kept in the Dark,* her latest book is a welcome return to the mood of her earlier work, where unfairness and hardship abound but evil is kept at bay. Not that there is anything sentimental about *Keeping Henry*—Mrs Jones dies (and is most summarily mourned), animals suffer, Henry is not for keeps. It is, after all, a true story, but so artfully remembered and retold that it will charm both children and adults alike.

📖 *THE OUTSIDE CHILD* (1989)

Betsy Hearne

SOURCE: A review of *The Outside Child,* in *Bulletin of the Center for Children's Books,* Vol. 43, No. 1, September, 1989, p. 3.

Suddenly and accidentally, thirteen-year-old Jane Tucker learns that her widowed father—a ship's engineer whom she rarely sees—is remarried and has two younger children. Inevitably, she defies her adoptive aunts to locate her half-sister and brother. What she doesn't expect to find is a dark secret that seems to spark violent hostility from her stepmother. The realistically piecemeal revelation of Jane's suppressed memory, together with a careful delineation of her friendship with a boy whose family is separated, makes a taut story with faultless char-

acterization as well as sustained pace. Bawden's style in this first-person narrative is deceptively simple. Because of that, young readers will find themselves absorbed in complex relationships where the strengths and shortcomings of each individual charge the plot without making it melodramatic. The circumstances of Jane's discovery are unusual, but her situation, and the consequent emotions, are not.

Ilene Cooper

SOURCE: A review of *The Outside Child,* in *Booklist,* Vol. 86, No. 1, September 1, 1989, p. 65.

At 13, Jane Tucker is satisfied with her life. She lives with her Aunt Bill, an artist, and tiny Aunt Sophie, who plays the drums. Her father, away at sea much of the time, sees Jane when he can. But then, inadvertently, Jane learns she does not have a complete picture of her family. Mr. Tucker remarried years ago and has three young children Jane knows nothing about. Obsessed with meeting her siblings, Jane and her friend, Plato Jones, devise elaborate strategies for orchestrating an encounter. But like Pandora with her ill-fated box, Jane lets loose all sorts of unexpected difficulties when she re-opens the relationship. Bawden's novel is a carefully plotted psychological portrait of a girl needing links to a family that exists only in her imagination. There is hardly a misstep, until the book's final pages where Jane's stepmother, Amy, the key to the secrets surrounding Jane's early years, offers her explanations. Although Bawden intends this character to be subtle and shifting, Amy is almost too enigmatic, which dilutes the book's ending. Having said that, the quality of Bawden's writing remains far superior to that of most of today's authors. Reading her books is always an energizing experience—this one is no exception.

Marcia Happ

SOURCE: A review of *The Outside Child,* in *School Library Journal,* Vol. 35, No. 14, October, 1989, pp. 130-31.

Her mother dead and her father "away at sea most of the time," 13-year-old Jane has been adopted and raised by a pair of loving, eccentric aunts, secure in the knowledge that they are all the family she wants and needs—until, on a rare visit to her father's ship, she discovers a picture of two younger children among the familiar family photographs on his desk. Thus she first learns of Annabel and George, her father's children by his second wife. More bewildered than embittered by her discovery, Jane imagines herself an "outside child," her nose pressed against the window looking in at the cozy family to which by rights she should belong. With her best friend, Plato Jones, as a willing accomplice (and clearly against the wishes of all the adults involved), she sets out to find Annabel and George, with no fixed plan and near tragic results. Jane's is a tale of innocence and experience, one that comes full circle in a way that should be—but is not quite—satisfying. She begins content with her unconventional family, certain that, for her, it is the best and only possibility. Once this certainty is shattered, she struggles to complete the family circle as she imagines it, only to find the reality unequal to the dream. In the end, she embraces the family (and friend) she's always loved, her love strengthened by the knowledge and acceptance of other realities. While Plato is a fully realized secondary character, the adult characters are another story. As vividly drawn as they all are, it is never quite credible that any of them would participate in such a deception or fail to set things right when the truth is finally revealed. Where Paula Fox's portrait of a difficult character makes *Village By the Sea* work, *The Outside Child* founders on extraordinary circumstances never quite made real. Still, if less than successful as a whole, this is fully engaging from page to page. Bawden's prose is arresting, creating a rich tableau of crystalline moments and remarkable (if not quite believable) characters. And that's more than enough to propel readers from beginning to bittersweet end.

Cathryn M. Mercier

SOURCE: A review of *The Outside Child*, in *The Five Owls*, Vol. IV, No. 4, March, 1990, p. 62.

Jane Tucker is a confident, trusting, and responsible thirteen-year-old. Her mother died shortly after childbirth and her captivating father spends most of his time at sea, leaving Jane to be raised by the unusual but loving Aunt Bill (short for Wilhemina), an artist, and Aunt Sophie, a musician. Exploring his cabin during a visit to her father's ship, Jane stumbles across a photograph of two children, hauntingly familiar but certainly unknown to her. This one secret quickly multiplies into many, and the hard-won stability in Jane's life is forever disrupted. With the help of her faithful best friend, Plato, Jane seeks to uncover the truths too long kept hidden from her. In lives shrouded by secrecy, the children triumph over adult conspiracy.

British author Nina Bawden creates feisty young characters who value family and commitment above all else. The children care and don't lightly risk breaking adult trust. One questions the reliability of the adults in the novel. Except for Aunt Bill and Aunt Sophie, the adults seldom act from other than selfish motives and leave many questions unanswered. Why has Mr. Tucker kept his second family hidden from Jane? Why has his mother remained silent? What is the source of his present wife's instability? Bawden has realized the tensions between child and adult with acute perspicacity, despite glossing them over in a deceivingly easy resolution.

Compelling honesty and the drive for family connections ground the novel. The intimacy of a winning first-person narrator, fluid prose, and generous insights unify and enrich it. Early adolescents, themselves struggling with issues of inclusion and exclusion, will welcome *The Outside Child* especially for the integrity of its likable young characters.

Marcus Crouch

SOURCE: A review of *The Outside Child*, in *Junior Bookshelf*, Vol. 55, No. 5, October, 1991, p. 221.

This is the story of Jane, told by herself. The first-person narrative is managed with immense skill, so that the reader is never conscious of the incongruity of so fluent and eloquent a story coming from a thirteen-year-old. Jane's mother is dead, her father at sea (he is a ship's engineer), and she lives with Aunt Sophie and Aunt Bill, both rather too old and too eccentric to have the charge of a young girl. The arrangement works well. She has the support of Plato, an ugly, asthmatic boy, younger than herself but with far more than his share of intelligence and enterprise. Apart from horrible Maureen who lives next door and is a 'fat white slug' of a girl, all goes reasonably well. Then a secret slips out. Jane has more family than she knew. Father married again, and has two children, with another on the way, and his second wife Amy, for reasons unknown, will have no contact with Jane. With Plato's help Jane sets out to find her half-brother and sister. At first it is something more than a game, not quite as serious as real life, but always potentially dangerous. Then the inevitable happens; Amy finds out what is happening and there is a violent explosion. But why is Amy so hostile? Jane has her theories, supported, she thinks, by childhood memories, but what is the truth. An apparent reconciliation with Amy clears up nothing. Truth is never simple, and perhaps it is not important after all. But in facing her problem Jane has grown up.

This is the work of a major novelist. Only the youth of the principal characters marks it as one for the children's-book list. The exquisite writing, the subtle and profound exploration of character, the control of major and minor figures, and the presentation in a vivid and original setting, all are the work of a sophisticated and fully equipped artist. There is much fun to balance the drama and the heartache. Perhaps the book will need a very special kind of child reader, preferably one with a background as eccentric as Jane's, for fullest enjoyment, but there is much for any child troubled with the bewildering absence of logic in an adult world. Sensible parents will see that the book is just as much for them.

HUMBUG (1992)

M. Hobbs

SOURCE: A review of *Humbug*, in *Junior Bookshelf*, Vol. 56, No. 3, June, 1992, p. 117.

This is another splendidly perceptive book by Nina Bawden. Her heroine Cora sees the adults—her parents, brother and sister and grandparents, and the terrible neighbours, Aunt Sunday and her evil if beautiful little daughter Angel—with frightening clarity. As the youngest and least useful of the family, she knows she is powerless to avoid spending the time while her grandmother (who should have looked after her in her parents' absence) is in hospital, and she is every bit as unhappy as she foresees. Luckily, she has a fellow victim in Aunt Sunday's house, Angel's grandmother, who has been forcibly persuaded to leave the house and gardens she loves to live with the pair. Though they assume she has accepted the feeble, deaf *persona* they have wished on her, however, she is still, when she dares be and when alone with Cora, an intelligent, wise old woman. She teachers Cora to recognise when people are talking humbug, and to use the word itself as a talisman in times of trouble. (She later, equally usefully, shows her that there is a good kind of humbug, for the sake of the hearer's peace of mind.) The unpleasant pair next door specialise in making both Cora and the grandmother uncertain of themselves: Cora has come to believe she is unwanted by her parents and by the rest of the family. When Angel gets her accused of theft, however, she has gone too far. Cora runs away, the real state of affairs is revealed, even down to the truth about Angel's father, and Cora knows her family loves her in their own way, though she has no illusions about them. Cora's terrifying impotence when she is the only one who can see, beyond the surface, the truth about Aunt Sunday and Angel is most powerfully conveyed, and the narrative, enhanced by Ian Newsham's little black and white vignettes and illustrations, is wonderfully gripping.

Kirkus Reviews

SOURCE: A review of *Humbug,* in *Kirkus Reviews,* Vol. LX, No. 14, July 15, 1992, p. 918.

With miraculous skill, Bawden places yet another set of vibrant characters in a compelling plot seasoned with cold reality, the warmth of enduring relationships, and moral ironies. Cora, eight, and her older brother and sister are to stay with their grandparents for six months while their parents are in Japan. When Granny is hospitalized, Cora is moved next door, where "Aunt Sunday" (no relation) has a daughter her age. Pretty Angelica's manner with adults befits her name, but she's actually a cruel, deceitful child whose adoring mother is in terror of her wiles. Fortunately, Sunday's mother, "Ma Potter," a retired headmistress in failing health who is virtually captive in the household, befriends Cora, sharing her books and her philosophy on dealing with posturing and untruths: "I.G.N.O.R.E." what can't be helped, especially when it's "humbug." Still, when Angelica accuses Cora of stealing a ring and even Grandpa believes her lies, Cora flees in distress and anger. By the time she's brought home, though, Granny is also there and truth once again prevails—except, of course, in the social niceties.

Much of the tension here grows out of the characters' complexity. Shown in dozens of revealing glimpses and

background details: Cora, brighter than her jealous older sister, has weathered cruel teasing before and often fibs but is fundamentally honest and kind; some of the reasons for Angelica's spite go back two generations and some are self-perpetuating, but that doesn't excuse them. A splendid, thought-provoking story.

Ann Darnton

SOURCE: A review of *Humbug,* in *The School Librarian,* Vol. 40, No. 3, August, 1992, pp. 99-100.

When circumstances force Cora to stay with her grandparents' neighbours, Aunt Sunday and her daughter Angelica, she is amazed to find that no one else appears to see that Angelica is not the angel she likes to pretend. To Cora it seems that once out of the years of early childhood, people's perceptions become clouded. Rather than the plain truth, they see what they expect to see or, more worryingly, what they feel most comfortable with. As Angelica makes her life more and more miserable, the 'games' which adults play among themselves in order to hide from unpalatable reality mean that it is impossible for Cora to communicate her distress. Only someone very old, Angelica's grandmother, Ma Potter, is able to share the eight-year-old's clarity of perception and come to her assistance. It is Ma Potter who teaches Cora the expression 'Humbug', a talisman intended to remind her that it is she who is in touch with the truth.

Nina Bawden has once more written tellingly about the problems of a child who feels in some way an outsider. While the story is related in an amusing way, the real distress and frustration that Cora feels is also made very apparent.

Publishers Weekly

SOURCE: A review of *Humbug,* in *Publishers Weekly,* Vol. 239, No. 42, September 21, 1992, p. 94.

A victim of adult convenience, eight-year-old Cora is temporarily boarded with a very unpleasant girl named Angelica and her equally disagreeable mother, "Aunt Sunday." The only saving grace is the bond she forms with another unhappy boarder, Sunday's invalid mother, Ma Potter. But when Angelica frames Cora as a diamond thief, even Ma Potter's brand of no-nonsense grandmothering is scant consolation. Cora's ultimate solution to her problem is to run away, but, through the wisdom of Ma Potter, she (and the reader) receive a tool to put painful and confusing experiences in perspective. Ma Potter, meanwhile, gaining some overdue insight into her own life, offers the priceless and humorous comfort of experience to Cora by saying at a particularly uncomfortable moment, "Cheer up. They can't shoot us." Well-rounded, recognizably vulnerable adult characters play well against Cora's very childlike dilemma. Bawden has once again struck the perfect balance between high-spirited storytelling and thoughtful content.

THE REAL PLATO JONES (1993)

Kirkus Reviews

SOURCE: A review of *The Real Plato Jones,* in *Kirkus Reviews,* Vol. LXI, No. 19, October 1, 1993, p. 1269.

When Plato (Jane's supportive friend in *The Outside Child,* 1989) accompanies his mother Maria to her father Nikos's funeral in rural Greece, Plato's self-image is thrown into chaos. His family history is complex: because Nikos betrayed guerrillas to the Nazis in order to save hostage civilians in his village of Molo, he's still scorned—while Welsh grandfather "CLJ," who escaped the Nazis to hide with the help of Plato's great-aunt Elena, is revered. Along the way to reconciling himself to Nikos's terrible, still debatable choice, Plato squabbles—at the rare times they're together—with his sorely missed sister Aliki (who lives in New York with their dad; Plato and Maria live in Britain); learns more about his past from Elena and CLJ; grows—suddenly and emblematically; and, on a second visit to Greece (with Jane as guest), gets his own chance at heroism when Molo is almost destroyed by fire (cf. *Carrie's War*). Interestingly, heroism is demanded of everyone on this occasion, so no one wins distinction for it (or is allowed to enjoy hubris), though Plato's family is finally accepted as a result; and it remains to the nice, rich Greek who's been courting Maria to help Plato grasp the truth: more than bits of Greek and Welsh, he can be himself, though it's "harder than belonging to a tribe . . . [to be] A Citizen of the World." The conclusion may be a bit tidy; but the path that Bawden's wonderfully individual characters take to it has enough unexpected turns to keep readers enthralled, while the subtext concerning the vexed nature of heroism—and nationality—is provocatively explored.

Ethel L. Heins

SOURCE: A review of *The Real Plato Jones,* in *The Horn Book Magazine,* Vol. LXX, No. 2, March-April, 1994, p. 197.

Readers will recall the delightfully precocious Plato Jones, the half-Welsh, half-Greek boy who appeared as a willing accomplice of his friend Jane Tucker in *The Outside Child.* Now Plato stars in a story of his own, while Jane is a supporting character. On the brink of adolescence, Plato is an oversensitive worrier—a myopic, asthmatic, "weedy little runt." His grandfather is Constantine Llewellyn Jones—called CLJ—a Welsh classical scholar who went to Greece during World War II and gave heroic aid to the Resistance. Betrayed to the Germans by a local villager, CLJ spent a perilous year in hiding before his ultimate rescue. Years afterward, Plato's Welsh father and his Greek mother met and married. But now they are divorced; his father and younger sister have moved to New York, while Plato, solicitous about his mother, has chosen to remain with her in England. Then his mother is summoned to Greece, for her father is

dying; she and Plato arrive in the old man's village, where the neighbors confront them with unexplained sullen antagonism. From his redoubtable great-aunt Elena, Plato is stunned to learn that it was his Greek grandfather who, faced with an agonizing decision about the fate of the villagers, actually betrayed CLJ, while it was Elena alone who dramatically saved his life. Back at home and still confused, Plato longs to unravel the mystery of the past. Only when he visits CLJ in Wales and talks with the wise old man is he able to make sense of his family's history. Plot, character, and the author's sensitivity to the disparate cultures of two groups of people all work together to form the fabric of a complex, exciting story of heroism, honor and dishonor, forgiveness, loyalty, and love. Plato's first-person narration is literate, witty, and often hyperbolic; below the surface, however, there lurk crosscurrents of intense human feelings, for Nina Bawden's singularity lies in her emotional realism and her respect for young readers.

Marcus Crouch

SOURCE: A review of *The Real Plato Jones,* in *Junior Bookshelf,* Vol. 58, No. 2, April, 1994, p. 62.

We have already met Plato, in Nina Bawden's *The Outside Child* (1989) when he appeared as the heroine's confidant and also to some degree as the catalyst of the story. Here he occupies the central position and Jane takes on the minor rôle. In each story the principal character is also the narrator, not the easiest of devices but one which Ms Bawden carries off with great expertise.

Plato Jones has a problem of identity. He has a Welsh father, now living in a different menage in America, and a Greek mother. He lives with her in England, which does not help him to decide who he really is. When he goes with his mother to his grandfather's funeral in Greece identity becomes an urgent issue. His grandfather on the Welsh side is CLJ or Jones-the-Spy who had played a prominent part in the Greek Resistance during the War. What part his Greek grandfather had in those events is not clear to him, but the equivocal reception he encounters in the Greek village makes him more than curious about the past. The local view is that Nikos Petropoulos betrayed his brother-in-law to the Nazis. The truth, as it gradually emerges from the mists of the past, is just as disturbing but not so simple. By the time that Plato has completed his discoveries he decides that, reconciled as he is to his Welsh/Greek blood, his aim is 'to be a World Citizen. In the meantime, both my grandfathers fit very comfortably inside my own skin.'

As always with this writer the plot, exciting as it is (and there is a magnificent description of the forest fire that threatens the Greek village and Plato's family), is not allowed to divert attention from the personal and moral issues that it raises. This is serious stuff lightly garbed in the narrator's humour. Plato, 'a weedy little runt' in his own view, is one of Ms Bawden's best creations, but there are others, Mother who 'gets more Greek by the minute', little sister Aliki who confounds Plato by being taller than he, Tasso the wealthy Greek who seems set to become Plato's stepfather (he could do worse), even Plato's headmaster, whom we glimpse only through him and who, it appears, is 'against education'. Better than the plot, better than the characters, is the style which makes every word pull its full weight and through which every page sparkles with wit and truth. Here is an outstandingly fine writer at the height of her powers.

Maurice Saxby

SOURCE: A review of *The Real Plato Jones,* in *Magpies,* Vol. 9, No. 5, November, 1994, p. 32.

How good it is to be able to review a book of real literary merit that is also a gripping read. To use a cliche: this is a book I couldn't put down. For two reasons: I really wanted to know the source of Plato's anxiety; and I was enjoying Nina Bawden's clear, crisp, unpretentious prose, her deft characterisation and her ability to recreate the atmosphere of a small Greek village. I could see it all happening. There is an "issue" involved. Plato's parents are divorced and he has divided loyalties. But the problem is deeper: "I'm half Greek, so that half of me wants to sit about in cafes laughing and talking. The other half, the Welsh half, is much sterner and gloomier." And there is still more to his perplexity. There is a mystery surrounding his Greek grandfather who was involved with his Welsh one during World War II. Was Nikos really a traitor? The reader, like Plato, is forced to think through some tough ethical questions. The perceptive reader will come to realise the trap of "pinning labels" on people, and will grow a little in human understanding.

This is a tender book, wise and thought-provoking. It is also a beautifully crafted novel that puts the ubiquitous teenage problem novel in proper perspective.

📖 *IN MY OWN TIME: ALMOST AN AUTO-BIOGRAPHY* (1995)

The Times Literary Supplement

SOURCE: A review of *In My Own Time: Almost an Autobiography,* in *The Times Literary Supplement,* No. 4791, January 27, 1995, p. 33.

Since her first book, **Who Calls the Tune,** was published in 1953, Nina Bawden has written nineteen novels for adults and seventeen for children. Given that much of her fiction is based on incidents from her own life or from the lives of her immediate family (she herself says that, taken together, all her novels and books for children form "a kind of coded autobiography"), one is tempted to ask whether there can be much left for her to write about. Bawden's use of her experiences as the raw material for her novels almost amounts to an obses-

sion—she writes of wanting to "make use of all my life, all memory, wasting nothing", an approach which has, however, clearly benefited her as a novelist. Like her novels, her memoir reveals her gift for close observation and her sensitivity in analysing human relationships; though without the discipline which the novel form necessarily imposes, her descriptions have a tendency, at times, to drift into superfluous detail.

Bawden subtitles her book "Almost an Autobiography", for it is not a consecutive, chronological narrative, but a series of vignettes of significant events in her life: her evacuation to the country during the war, her time at Oxford (including brief cameos of Richard Burton and Margaret Thatcher, the latter a "plump, neat, solemn girl with rosy cheeks", who started college the same year as Bawden), and the loss of her son Niki, a diagnosed schizophrenic. Throughout it all, the family remains the focal point of her life, a fact reflected by the book's intimate tone. In describing the period leading up to the death of her son, Bawden writes with a frankness and honesty that one can only admire; nevertheless, her intense absorption in the minutiae of family life ultimately makes this a less compelling account of her life than one might have hoped.

Hazel Rochman

SOURCE: A review of *In My Own Time: Almost an Autobiography,* in *Booklist,* Vol. 92, No. 7, December 1, 1995, p. 616.

Like the autobiographies of Beverly Cleary, this is for YAs and adults who remember loving Bawden's children's stories and are curious about her life and times. In **Carrie's War** (1973), **Henry** (1988), **Humbug** (1992), and many other thrilling, honest novels, Bawden has written about young people searching to find out who they are, often in Britain in wartime. Looking back on her own life, she finds no literal parallels in her fiction ("All writers are liars. . . . They make use of their own tragedies to make a better story. They batten on their relations"), but her quiet, wry, lovely sentences re-create the big and the small things in her life, some of which have shape-shifted into her stories. This is a book especially for those who want to write themselves.

Mary M. Burns

SOURCE: A review of *In My Own Time: Almost an Autobiography,* in *The Horn Book Magazine,* Vol. LXXII, No. 3, May-June, 1996, pp. 354-55.

A kaleidoscope of impressions rather than a literal, chronological rendering, Nina Bawden's memoirs are perhaps more revealing of her art and life than any number of conventional biographies might allow. In the first chapter she asserts that "family stories . . . tell us who we are and help to shape our lives." In the last she comments: "A writer's work may be a coded autobiography, but only a very close friend could decipher it." In between, she presents a series of reminiscences, including recollections of her grandmother's stories, incidents from her early school days, memories of World War II and the evacuation of children from London, details of her education at Oxford (where she met Richard Burton and Margaret Thatcher), plus observations on her marriages, motherhood, development as a writer, and service as a magistrate. Perhaps the most moving sections are those devoted to her oldest son, a schizophrenic, and to her mother's last years. References to her novels, especially those written for children, offer insight into the process by which a writer fashions raw material into a polished work of art. Although these passages are likely to pique the interest of those concerned with Nina Bawden the writer, the book as a whole evokes Nina Bawden the person. And what a fascinating, multifaceted person she is!

GRANNY THE PAG (1995; U.S. edition, 1996)

Jo Goodman

SOURCE: A review of *Granny the Pag,* in *Magpies,* Vol. 11, No. 2, May, 1996, pp. 41-2.

Cat's granny is known as Pag simply because Cat misspelled pig one day, but she certainly is different. Not every child is brought up by a granny who rides a Harley-Davidson, has very strange visitors (she is a retired psychiatrist), owns nine old cats and four old dogs and whose clothes are falling apart, but Cat likes her that way—even though she smokes! However Cat's neglectful parents, and her rather conventional headmaster, are not at all convinced that Pag is the best person to bring her up—although she has been doing so for 12 years—so they set out to separate them. But Cat is resourceful, she has been told that children have legal rights, and she is determined to fight for hers. Nina Bawden has here another convincing story about a girl who refuses to leave those in authority to make important decisions about her. The relationship between grandmother and granddaughter is loving but unsentimental, and the highly individual characters are completely convincing. Another very good book from this accomplished writer.

Elspeth S. Scott

SOURCE: A review of *Granny the Pag,* in *The School Librarian,* Vol. 44, No. 2, May, 1996, p. 71.

A quick plot summary could make this sound like a 'problem novel', but with Nina Bawden nothing is ever that simple. Catriona Brooke has lived for most of her life with her grandmother—the Pag of the title—when her now-famous parents decide they want her back. Her grandmother, an eccentric retired psychiatrist who rides a Harley Davidson, is not an obvious guardian for a 12-year-old girl and Catriona has to fight to put her case. There is a sub-plot involving bullying at school and a single-parent family. But this is no formula social issues story. Nina Bawden's characters have depth and personality and, although the narrator is Cat herself, we see more than simply her point of view. As Cat takes on the school, the social services and the law in her quest for justice and the right to have her opinions taken seriously, we see her develop and mature, and her relationships with her parents and her grandmother are changed forever. This is a subtle, funny, moving book and is highly recommended.

Suzanne Julian

SOURCE: A review of *Granny the Pag,* in *Voice of Youth Advocates,* Vol. 19, No. 2, June, 1996, p. 92.

When Cat is a little girl she is left with her unusual grandmother by her parents who want to pursue their career rather than raise a daughter. Cat is so upset by this that she wants to make her grandmother feel bad, so she writes a note that says "Granny is a pig" but instead of "pig" she writes "pag." As Cat learns to love her grandmother, the word Pag becomes a term of affection between them. Life becomes complicated for eleven-year-old Cat because she is embarrassed by her motorcycle riding, cigarette smoking grandmother, she is picked on by the school bully, and she finds out her parents decide they want her back. Cat feels helpless but is determined to fight, so she hires a lawyer. Her grandmother supports her decision and together they win the custody battle. Even though Cat is allowed to live with her grandmother, she realizes that things can still change as the story ends with Cat's grandmother almost dying while they are swimming during their vacation in Greece.

Each character has her own personality which comes alive in the pages of this book. The tension in the story comes from the bully at Cat's school, the custody battle, and her relationship with her family. Touches of humor lighten the mood of the book and present a balanced and realistic picture of a girl who is embarrassed by her grandmother's clothes and behavior but loves her so much she can't imagine living with anyone else, including her parents. Because the writer is British some of the terms used may be confusing to the reader but the story is still understandable and enjoyable.

Nancy Vasilakis

SOURCE: A review of *Granny the Pag,* in *The Horn Book Magazine,* Vol. LXXII, No. 5, September-October, 1996, pp. 591-92.

Cat has often wished that the Pag were "soft and powdery" like other grandmothers instead of a semi-retired psychiatrist who wears dusty long black skirts pinned together with a huge brooch to hide the ripped places or jeans and motorbike leathers when she's riding about on her Harley. Cat lives with the Pag in a house filled with dogs and cats and visited occasionally by the few frail and peculiar patients her grandmother still sees. Now that Cat is twelve, her actor parents have given up their itinerant life and want her to come live with them. Horrified at the thought of leaving the Pag and moving in with Lisa and Daddy-O, who remind her of a pair of Barbie dolls, Cat visits a lawyer on her own to find out what her rights are. An ancillary plot concerning a school bully who terrifies Cat until she comes to understand *his* particular frailty is only mildly diverting and never convincingly integrated into the major storyline. The best part of the book is the mix of interesting characters that make up Cat's eccentric family, and Bawden's clear-eyed, if not groundbreaking, exploration of how dangerous life can seem to children when their sense of family stability is jeopardized.

Steve Rosson

SOURCE: A review of *Granny the Pag,* in *Books for Keeps,* No. 105, July, 1997, p. 25.

Pags, in case you didn't know, are special people—'the sort of people who make all the really important things happen'—and Catriona's granny Polish refugee, retired psychiatrist, cigarette-smoking, Greek island holidaying, Harley-Davidson riding Dame Halina Lubinorska is definitely a Pag. Catriona has been brought up by her whilst her feckless parents have continued their theatrical careers which now see them starring in a popular TV soap. When Mum decides she wants Cat back to complete the show-biz smart home they have just acquired, Cat decides to take action—well, you would resist living with a woman who called you Precious-kins. Told in the first person, the spunky heroine has a nice line in ironic asides and the book carries a number of important messages about families and relationships.

Additional coverage of Bawden's life and career is contained in the following sources published by Gale Research: *Contemporary Authors New Revision Series,* Vol. 54; *Children's Literature Review,* Vol. 2; *Dictionary of Literary Biography,* Vol. 161; *Major Authors and Illustrators for Children and Young Adults; Something about the Author,* Vol. 72; and *Something about the Author Autobiography Series,* Vol. 16.

Kate Duke

1956-

American author and illustrator of picture books.

Major works include *The Guinea Pig ABC* (1983), *Guinea Pig Board Books* (*Bedtime, Clean-up Day, The Playground, What Bounces?*) (1986), *Aunt Isabel Tells a Good One* (1992), *Archaeologists Dig for Clues* (1997).

INTRODUCTION

The author and artist of concept books, original fantasies, nonfiction, and adaptations of fables and poems, all in the picture book format, Duke is celebrated for creating imaginative, engaging works for preschoolers and elementary graders that are both instructive and filled with fun. Although she has profiled a variety of anthropomorphic animals in her stories—mice, pigs, squirrels, moles, and others—Duke is best known as the creator of beguiling guinea pigs, characters featured in several of her picture and board books. These charming creatures participate in daily activities, often with surprising results, and serve as visual examples of concepts such as addition, the alphabet, and spatial relationships. Rebecca Lazear Ozrent noted, "The heroes of Ms. Duke's stories are no ordinary guinea pigs. They are whimsical creatures with serious ideas who always seem to be suppressing a giggle, particularly in the face of disaster." Duke is also well known as the author of two self-illustrated books featuring the talented tale-spinner Aunt Isabel, an Auntie Mame-like mouse, and her enthusiastic niece and collaborator Penelope. Although her works are recognized for their lighthearted, humorous approach, Duke subtly addresses themes such as "a friend in need is a friend indeed" and the importance of celebrating one's personal triumphs while providing information on subjects such as archaeology and the ingredients of a successful story. Duke generally uses simple, brief texts in her works; as an illustrator, she is noted for creating watercolor-and-pen drawings that reflect her gift for caricature, attention to detail, and ability to convey a complete story—including character, action, and feeling—in a minimum of lines. She also includes cartoon-style illustrations, dialogue balloons, and whimsical borders in several of her works. In addition to her self-illustrated titles, she has provided the pictures for the works of such authors as Joanna Cole, Barbara Baker, Miriam Schlein, and Raffi. Duke illustrates these picture books—retellings, fiction, and nonfiction—in her characteristic watercolor and line, and her art is praised for both complementing and amplifying the texts it accompanies.

Biographical Information

Born in New York City as the eldest of four children,

Duke was inspired to become a writer and artist by her early love of books. "Both my parents were and are great readers," she explained, "and we children were always amply supplied with books. My experience of the world of literature was satisfying from the start, for my parents seemed to enjoy reading to me as much as I enjoyed being read to." Although she was an active child—she rode bikes and roller-skated in the city and played in the country during summers with her grandmother—Duke was an avid reader. She recalled, "I read in the summer and in the winter, in the city and in the country in school and on vacation. I liked books that had adventures in them, and books with talking animals, and books that made me laugh. I still do!" Among her favorite literary characters were Nancy Drew and Doctor Dolittle—"I yearned passionately to be able to talk to the animals as he did," Duke commented; however, her most influential discovery was Harriet the Spy, whose exploits "prompted me at age eleven to start following pedestrians around my neighborhood, taking notes on their every 'suspicious' move. I think I owe Harriet my first conscious awareness of the act of writing as important and meaningful work." At about the same time, Duke discovered that she could draw; she recalled, "In art class one day, the picture of a dog that I was copying from a how-to-draw book came out looking pretty much like a dog. Since my artistic abilities had not previously been particularly notable, I remember being quite surprised by this new development. Pleased, of course, but definitely surprised."

After high school, she attended Duke University in North Carolina for a year and then "floundered around for a while," as she described it. Back in New York, Duke took art classes, which reminded her of her childhood affection for picture books. "I got the idea," she recalled, "that I could write stories to go with my pictures, and turn them into books for children. I hoped that the children who read them would love them as much as I loved the books I had read as a child." In 1983, Duke became a full-time author and illustrator of children's books. In discussing one of her most popular works, *Aunt Isabel Tells a Good One,* which introduces the basics of storytelling through the imaginative tales of a stylish mouse, Duke related, "I've been enormously pleased to find that teachers like to use *Aunt Isabel Tells a Good One* to help their students learn about writing. One reason the book works well in the classroom must be because the way Aunt Isabel and her niece make up the story is honestly the way *I* made up the story: by asking questions. I wrote the first draft of *Aunt Isabel* as if I were talking to another person. This other person kept asking (or sometimes telling) me what we should put in the story next, and I wrote down both the questions and the answers. Later I imagined the two 'voices' as mice, and named them Aunt Isabel and Penelope."

Duke, who currently lives in Connecticut and is married to cartoonist Sidney Harris, is a frequent lecturer at schools and other places where children are gathered. "Since writing and drawing are both solitary pursuits," she explained, "I try to make a point of getting out into the real world. A little human contact is important in keeping one's equilibrium. Indeed, one of the greatest pleasures I have these days is in going out to visit schools and talk to children about what I do. These occasions are a chance to get in touch with my books' intended audience and to recharge my memories of what it was like to be a child. I don't have children of my own, so it's a real treat to be able to interact with them once in a while. I'm always cheered and inspired by their energy and imagination. Plus, they laugh at my jokes!"

Major Works

Duke's first book, *The Guinea Pig ABC,* is perhaps her best known work. An alphabet book that is based on adjectives rather than the usual nouns, this work depicts guinea pigs who cavort within each letter of the brightly colored illustrations. The letters are props for the pigs, who act out words such as bouncy, high, mean, and kind. Karen Strang Hanley commented, "The cunning cavies steal the show in this fresh and stylishly executed, full-color alphabet book—a sheer delight," while a

critic in *Kirkus Reviews* noted, "What gives the book a visual edge. . . is the way the guinea pigs' doings are built into the form of the letter" A reviewer in *Publishers Weekly* said, "In the vanguard of artists making their debut in picture books, Duke simply charms one with her antic imagination"; the critic concluded, "Every one of the examples. . . are all so different from most ABCs—Duke doesn't settle for the obvious word or situation anywhere." Ann A. Flowers predicted that *The Guinea Pig ABC* was "destined perhaps to become a classic." Duke's next book, *Guinea Pigs Far and Near* (1984), introduces children to prepositions and to words of similar or opposite meanings by using her "sprightly company of entertainers," in the words of a critic in *Publishers Weekly*, to illustrate words such as apart, away, behind, and beside.

With *Guinea Pig Board Books,* four small volumes directed to very young children, Duke addresses the concepts of playing, cleaning, experimenting with physics, and going to bed. In her review in the *Horn Book Magazine,* Margaret A. Bush commented, "Duke's cheery guinea pigs transfer well into the smaller, simpler presentation"; in assessing the fourth title, *What Bounces?,* in which an errant guinea pig climbs up on a kitchen stool, creates a mess, and tumbles off before being comforted by its mother, Bush noted that "children are likely to respond with interest and concern." *What Would a Guinea Pig Do?* (1988) demonstrates how the guinea pigs clean the house, bake a cake, and play "let's pretend" in their own inimitable fashion. A critic in *Publishers Weekly* noted, "Duke's pigs make disasters look like terrific fun" and adds that "the entire book is a joyful offering." Starr LaTronica called *What Would a Guinea Pig Do?* a "delightful addition to the series" while Rebecca Lazear Okrent concluded, "As in all the best books, the rules for living are discrete. You have to be looking for them." Duke returned to the concept book genre with *One Guinea Pig Is Not Enough* (1998), an addition primer in which a group of guinea pig siblings is introduced one by one, enjoying activities with each other before returning to their parents. A reviewer in *Publishers Weekly* commented, "Duke adds another feather to her cap with this" and concluded that the book is "an exuberant and clever introduction to math."

In addition to her works featuring guinea pigs, Duke is the creator of several other well-received picture books with animal characters. In *Roseberry's Great Escape* (1990), an updated version of an Aesop's fable that Duke dedicates to Aesop, an adventuresome pig who has traveled widely and made many friends decides that he is going to settle down. Choosing a sheep meadow for his home, he is rescued from becoming dinner for the shepherd by the friends he has made on his travels. He learns that home "is where you feel at home and where you are among friends" and decides to resume his nomadic life. Mary M. Burns claimed that Roseberry "is one of the most engaging pigs to appear in recent years, demonstrating once again that few can match Kate Duke's versatile and economical line in the portrayal of porcine protagonists." Leslie Barban added, "Large, loose-lined watercolor illustrations will captivate young listeners or beginning readers, and Roseberry's hard-earned lesson will enlighten them." With *Aunt Isabel Tells a Good One,* and *Aunt Isabel Makes Trouble* (1996) Duke created two of her most popular works. These books, which feature the storytelling mouse Aunt Isabel and her young niece Penelope, are noted for Duke's clever use of the story-within-a-story format as well as for the stylistic touches in her illustrations. In the first book, Penelope, who is spending the night with her aunt, asks for a bedtime story; Aunt Isabel obliges by telling the tale of two royal mice, talented Lady Nell and brave Prince Augustus, who defeat some evil cockroaches. Isabel is aided in her storytelling by Penelope, who asks pertinent questions that affect the direction of the tale. In the second book, Penelope requests a naptime yarn and receives one from her aunt that again features Lady Nell and Prince Augustus; in this work, Nell is the main character, foiling a robbery by the cockroach gang with her strong pitching arm while making it in time to see Prince Augustus on his birthday. Penelope again adds direction and humor to the tale, this time with interruptions that lead to several good-natured twists. In her *School Library Journal* review of *Aunt Isabel Tells a Good One* Lori A. Janick wrote, "An entertaining way to introduce children to the elements of storytelling while providing an impetus for their own creative endeavors." Beth Tegart, who reviewed *Aunt Isabel Makes Trouble* in another issue of the same periodical, commented, "Little Penelope and her aunt make a great team" and called the work an "ideal book for curriculum connections in language arts."

With *Archaeologists Dig for Clues,* Duke departs from her characteristic portrayals of animals to create a book that blends fact and fiction to introduce young readers to the profession of archaeology. Duke structures her work around the story of a boy and his friends who accompany their archaeologist friend on a dig for artifacts from the Archaic Era in a local cornfield. Disappointed when all they uncover are rocks and pebbles, the volunteers are told by Sophie that the fun of archaeology is in the detective work on the site and in the laboratory uncovering information about ordinary people from bygone years. Duke provides her audience with scientific information about archaeology in a straightforward narrative, defining terms and processes while interweaving the techniques used by archaeologists into the story; she also provides sidebars with additional facts and activities. Hazel Rochman noted, "The affected blond kid who worries about dirtying her sneakers ends up getting totally involved ("Cool!"). So will many readers." Comparing *Archaeologists Dig for Clues* to works by Aliki and Joanna Cole, an author whose works have been illustrated by Duke, a critic in *Kirkus Reviews* noted, "Readers will feel as if they're taking an active part in an archaeological dig in this informative entry"; the reviewer concluded, "With her inviting approach to a complex process, Duke ensures that this eye-opening field trip will inspire dirt diggers and treasure-seekers everywhere."

Awards

The Guinea Pig ABC won the IRA-CBC Children's Choice Award from the International Reading Association and the Children's Book Council and was named the Library of Congress Book of the Year in 1983. In the same year, the book was designated as an honor book for illustration by the *Boston Globe-Horn Book* Award committee and was named to the *Horn Book* Honor List. In 1985, *Seven Froggies Went to School* won the IRA-CBC Children's Choice Award, while the four *Guinea Pig Board Books* were named to the Year's Top Prizes Selection by *Publishers Weekly* in 1986. In the same year, Guinea Pig ABC won the Children's Picture Book of the Year from *Redbook* magazine. *What Would a Guinea Pig Do?* was chosen by the American Booksellers Association for its Pick of the Lists in 1988. *Aunt Isabel Tells a Good One* was named the Children's Book of the Year by the Bank Street Child Study Children's Book Committee and won the IRA-CBC Children's Choice Award in 1989; the title was also featured on television and radio programs for children. Duke also received several additional child- and adult-selected awards for her books and has received prizes for the works she has illustrated for other authors.

TITLE COMMENTARY

📖 *THE GUINEA PIG ABC* (1983)

Kathleen Brachmann

SOURCE: A review of *The Guinea Pig ABC,* in *School Library Journal,* Vol. 30, No. 2, October, 1983, p. 148.

Duke's version of yet another alphabet book is a credible attempt at presenting the ABC's in a slightly different manner. Each letter of the alphabet stands for an adjective: *A* is for *awake, B* is for *bouncy, C* is for *clean,* etc. Acting out these examples is a bevy of droll, engaging guinea pigs whose antics are sure to amuse. It is here that Duke's idea falters, though. One of the criteria for an effective ABC book is that the objects or ideas portrayed must be easily identifiable and meaningful to the intended age group; adjectives are much more difficult to portray than objects. Most of the ideas come across remarkably well, to Duke's credit, but a few will take some explaining. For example, an illustration of an obviously ailing guinea pig in bed, with a second guinea pig offering flowers, is meant to portray *kind,* though *sick* comes to mind first. Other examples of this sort occur too frequently for the book to conform to accepted standards of what an alphabet book should be. While the appealing guinea pigs are irresistible and the letters themselves are large and brightly colored, this ABC book does have some conceptual problems.

Karen Strang Hanley

SOURCE: A review of *The Guinea Pig ABC,* in *Booklist,* Vol. 80, No. 5, November 1, 1983, p. 406.

Lively guinea pigs parade through this clever alphabet of descriptive adjectives. Enormous, serified capital letters appear in black-lined boxes on every page, while the featured word is set against a crisp-white field below. Within the parameters of each letter, vivacious guinea pigs artfully illustrate the concept at hand: perching dubiously on the crossbar of *H* for *High;* playing a sneaky trick *(Mean);* and swinging from a clothesline *Upside-down.* The cunning cavies steal the show in this fresh and stylishly executed, full-color alphabet book—a sheer delight.

Kirkus Reviews

SOURCE: A review of *The Guinea Pig ABC,* in *Kirkus Reviews,* Vol. LI, No. 21, November 1, 1983, p. J-185.

An old-fashioned, large-format alphabet book, with a single large picture per letter, in which a guinea pig (or two) illustrates what the word says—sportively, and more-or-less humorously. For Juicy, a guinea pig is gobbling watermelon; Kind is represented by a sickabed guinea pig (thermometer, bandage, etc.) and a guinea-pig visitor, with flowers. What gives the book a visual edge, though, is the way the guinea pigs' doings are built into the form of the letter: the watermelon is cradled in the loop of the J, the guinea-pig patient is under the K—while, in two of the most imaginative examples, a guinea pig stands High on the H, and steps on the Wobbly W. As alphabet books go, this is totally unremarkable; as a set of pictures (drawn with some character), it's wholly pleasing—a homespun, direct alternative to lots of artifice.

Publishers Weekly

SOURCE: A review of *The Guinea Pig ABC,* in *Publishers Weekly,* Vol. 225, No. 2, January 13, 1984, p. 69.

In the vanguard of artists making their debut in picture books, Duke simply charms one with her antic imagination. Illustrations in blithe colors introduce children to the alphabet, each huge letter a prop for the gaggle of darling guinea pigs who act out appropriate words. On the cross line of A, a little fellow leaps from his bed, his nightcap flying, as a "friend" beats a tattoo on his drum, signifying "Awake." P, a giant cactus, snares another guinea pig's coat for "Prickly"; Y supports a table where a benign adult gives a birthday cake (with one candle) to a baby, identifying "Young," etc. Every one of the examples begs to be described; they are all so different from most ABCs—Duke doesn't settle for the obvious word or situation anywhere.

Ann A. Flowers

SOURCE: A review of *The Guinea Pig ABC,* in *The Horn Book Magazine,* Vol. LX, No. 1 February, 1984, pp. 42-3.

An amusing ABC book features guinea pigs whose actions illustrate an adjective for each letter of the alphabet—except for "Zzzzzz," which stands for Z. The idea is cleverly carried out: *Kind* is pictured by a concerned guinea pig tendering a bouquet to an ailing friend, and *mean* by a sly, sniggering animal pulling a chair from beneath an innocent friend who is about to sit. *Rich* is shown by a fully dressed guinea pig tycoon, sitting in a pleased way on a pile of gold pieces which prove, on examination, to be carrot slices. Even the guinea pigs on the title page carry letters spelling out "OH BOY." An astonishing variety of expressions is achieved with economy of line; one sees guinea pigs distressed, dubious, and delighted. With great ingenuity each bright-colored illustration, one to a page, is built around a featured letter; the overall feeling is one of gaiety and happiness. The author's first book—destined perhaps to become a classic.

GUINEA PIGS FAR AND NEAR (1984)

Publishers Weekly

SOURCE: A review of *Guinea Pigs Far and Near,* in *Publishers Weekly,* Vol. 226, No. 8, August 24, 1984, p. 80.

The sprightly company of entertainers who appeared first in *The Guinea Pig ABC* play a return engagement in Duke's new opus. The text is limited to captions defining words in the brightly colored, action-packed pictures. Each scene represents a complete story involving suspense, comedy and adventure. For starters, a girl guinea pig boards a railroad car and her little brother climbs into the car behind her. The coupling breaks and they are separated, their headlong flight demonstrating the words "apart," "far," "near" and, finally, together again. Other words of similar and opposite meanings are fun to learn as they are acted out by the irresistible troupe: "behind," "beside," "between," "among," "ahead," "across," "aboard," "away," etc.

GUINEA PIG BOARD BOOKS (BEDTIME, CLEAN-UP DAY, THE PLAYGROUND, WHAT BOUNCES?, 1986)

Margaret A. Bush

SOURCE: A review of *Guinea Pig Board Books: Bedtime, Clean-Up Day, The Playground,* and *What Bounces,* in *The Horn Book Magazine,* Vol. LXII, No. 5, September 10, 1986, p. 578.

Both Kate Duke and Helen Oxenbury excel in conveying

feeling and character with an impressive economy of line. Duke's cheery guinea pigs transfer well into the smaller, simpler presentation; three of the titles [*Bedtime, Clean-up Day,* and *The Playground*] convey the flavor of everyday events as experienced by an energetic youngster—a mischievous day of household chores with Mother, the pleasures of the playground, and reluctant bedtime preparations. The fourth book [*What Bounces?*] is a story of downright naughtiness, in which the young guinea pig climbs up on a stool and drops items from the refrigerator to see which of them will bounce, creating a thorough mess, into which the errant child tumbles to be retrieved and soothed by Mother. Though Mother's calm response seems a little unrealistic to the adult reader, children are likely to respond with interest and concern.

📖 WHAT WOULD A GUINEA PIG DO? (1988)

Publishers Weekly

SOURCE: A review of *What Would a Guinea Pig Do?,* in *Publishers Weekly,* Vol. 233, No. 4, January 29, 1988, p. 429.

The Guinea Pig ABC came first, then four guinea-pig board books and *Guinea Pigs Far and Near.* Now these little furballs face three problems: how to clean a house (Stick a hose in and rinse it out? Get someone else to clean it?), how to bake a cake (recipes are abandoned) and how to be somebody else (through the addition of feathers or high heels). Duke's pigs make disasters look like terrific fun, and the only foreseeable problem with this book is to make sure that small guinea-pig fans don't take some of these situations to heart and start baking and cleaning in similar fashion. The artist's palette is a crazy quilt of pastels on a bright white background; small ballrooms identify the cartoon-style dialogue, and the entire book is a joyful offering.

Rebecca Lazear Okrent

SOURCE: A review of *What Would a Guinea Pig Do?,* in *The New York Times Book Review,* June 5, 1988, p. 50.

Annie Dillard once observed that since housework was never discussed in any book she'd read, it must not

From Aunt Isabel Tells a Good One, *written and illustrated by Kate Duke.*

exist. Of course she's wrong. All great works of fiction are about housekeeping, and we read them to find out how the characters cope. Take Tolstoy's "Anna Karenina," for example, or Kate Duke's wonderfully instructive new book, *What Would a Guinea Pig Do?*

Granted, Anna wasn't done in by carpet stains; neither will these guinea pigs demonstrate the best way to dust. But the message from both authors is that you do have to keep after these things. And if children are going to learn the rules of housekeeping from books (as well as from our fine example), they could find no better teacher than Ms. Duke, who served up a memorable alphabet in *Guinea Pig ABC* and handily presented prepositions and spatial relations in *Guinea Pigs Near and Far*.

The heroes of Ms. Duke's stories are no ordinary guinea pigs. They are whimsical creatures with serious ideas who always seem to be suppressing a giggle, particularly in the face of disaster. In this newest installment we learn what they do when confronted by life's more perplexing questions. For instance, "What if a guinea pig wanted to clean up his house? What would he do?" He'd try any number of amusing, inept approaches until he got it right. Then he'd have a party and start all over again. Rule No. 1: Children, learn to celebrate your successes.

Or, "What if some guinea pigs wanted to bake a cake? What would they do?" They would choose the most impossibly complicated recipe, with disastrous results. They do show signs of uncharacteristic disappointment when removing their cake from the oven, but they are resilient critters. What they do next is eat their cake and proclaim it perfection. Rule No. 2: Cheerful cooperation saves the day! And finally, "What if a guinea pig wanted to be like somebody else? What would she do?" She would gamely try on the tiger's stripes and other outrageous traits that the little creature is not naturally heir to. Particularly winning in this episode is the absolute loyalty and tolerance of the chameleonlike guinea pig's friends, who are amused, or even appalled, by her transformations, but are right there when she's ready to be a guinea pig again. And really, what better?

The text is minimal and easy to read. The brightly colored illustrations, with bold ink outlines, are cheerful and captivating. As in all the best books, the rules for living are discrete. You have to be looking for them.

Starr LaTronica

SOURCE: A review of *What Would a Guinea Pig Do?*, in *School Library Journal*, Vol. 35, No. 9, June-July, 1988, p. 90.

The rambunctious rodents of *Guinea Pig ABC* (1983) and *Guinea Pigs Far and Near* (1984) return to answer these questions: "What if a guinea pig wanted to clean up his house? . . . What if some guinea pigs wanted to bake a cake?" and "What if a guinea pig wanted to be

like somebody else?" The irrepressible cast romps through each situation in merry mayhem, emerging undaunted for new adventures. ("What would a guinea pig do after he cleaned his house? . . . Have a party to celebrate—and start all over again!"). Bright watercolor illustrations outlined in black are filled with energy and convey most of the action and humor. Dialogue appears in small asides within the illustrations, creating a challenge for story hour presentation, but enhancing enjoyment for individual readers. A delightful addition to the series.

📖 *TINGALAYO* (written by Raffi, 1989)

Kirkus Reviews

SOURCE: A review of *Tingalayo,* in *Kirkus Reviews,* Vol. LVII, No. 8, April 15, 1989, p. 629.

[Raffi's *Five Little Ducks* and **Tingalayo** are] charming additions to the popular singer's "Song[s] to Read," with music (melody plus chords) as well as the entire texts given on the last pages. . . . [Tingalayo] is a donkey in a catchy calypso song. With vigorous black line and colors that evoke the Caribbean setting, Duke shows the comically mischievous donkey going much too fast or slow, sneaking off to a carnival, and even going on a nighttime boat ride before returning to his master. Fine, imaginative expansions of the songs, these also stand confidently on their own as picture books.

Debby Jeffery

SOURCE: A review of *Tingalayo,* in *School Library Journal,* Vol. 35, No. 12, August, 1989, pp. 137-38.

Duke's cartoon-like illustrations show Tingalayo, a mischievous donkey, running away from his owner to attend the carnival. He dances and sings but remembers home and gets back just in time for dinner. Set in the West Indies, the colorful and humorous pictures expand the simple song and provide a satisfying read/sing. Both [*Five Little Ducks* and **Tingalago**] have the music and chords included. Both titles are well done and give a visual dimension to these popular children's songs, which will be successful for story times and general library use.

📖 *IT'S TOO NOISY!* (written by Joanna Cole, 1989)

Kirkus Reviews

SOURCE: A review of *It's Too Noisy!,* in *Kirkus Reviews,* Vol. LVII, No. 19, October 1, 1989, p. 1483.

[Aliana Brodman's *Such a Noise!* and **It's Too Noisy!** are two] new versions of the Yiddish story immortalized in Zemach's *It Could Always Be Worse* (1976). The primer-language Cole edition admits to its ethnic origins only in the CIP and in some of the details of the illustrations, which are comic and lively but no match for Zemach's earthier humor, fine sense of place, and underlying compassion; in Cole's version, the Rabbi is referred to as "the Wise Man." This will be acceptable and useful only to those not offended by what seems to be a halfhearted attempt to suppress the story's origins. . . . Except for comprehensive collections, stick with Zemach.

Karen James

SOURCE: A review of *It's Too Noisy!*, in *School Library Journal,* Vol. 35, No. 16, December, 1989, pp. 93-4.

In this retelling of a Yiddish folktale, Cole has so simplified the text that the tale loses all its poignancy and subtle humor. A poor farmer lives in a small house with his wife, parents, and lots of children. The house is too noisy so the farmer seeks advice from the wise man who tells him to bring the chickens indoors. Every time the farmer complains about noise, the wise man tells him to bring in more animals. His last piece of advice is to send all the animals outside again—and in comparison, the house seems quiet. Duke's illustrations are in keeping with the text. They present the story as a comic romp. Her sturdy blond peasants, rendered in bright watercolors, cavort maniacally. One especially irritating expression—a u-shaped, open-mouthed grin with the eyes drawn up in slits—recurs frequently on their faces. In fact, everyone seems to be having a fine time except the farmer. This compares unfavorably with Margot Zemach's excellent version, *It Could Always Be Worse* (1977). Her retelling, in both text and pictures, conveys the drudgery of too many people living in a small space and provides a contrast that makes the humor of the Rabbi's solution all the more enjoyable. Children will probably respond to Cole's repetition of the noises in the house and, since they are accustomed to the frenetic action of television, may find humor in the illustrations, but Zemach's version is richer and far more satisfying.

Patricia Maclachlan

SOURCE: "Discovering Ourselves in Other Places, Other Times," in *Los Angeles Times Book Review,* December 17, 1989, p. 7.

We see ourselves in *It's Too Noisy!*, Joanna Cole's retelling of an old Jewish folk tale. A farmer lives in a little house with his noisy family and wishes for peace and quiet. The farmer seeks out a wise man who wields ancient wisdom to help the farmer to appreciate the loving clamor that surrounds him. The text is rhythmic, and Kate Duke's numerous watercolor illustrations evoke a world where much more is happening than words can depict. While the farmer doubts the Wise Man's words, for instance, the Wise Man's cat—just as smart as a cat can be—smiles reassuringly. My favorites are the pigs,

who, unlike most humans, are wise enough to be as happy at the beginning of the tale as they are at the end.

📖 *ROSEBERRY'S GREAT ESCAPE* (1990)

Leslie Barban

SOURCE: A review of *Roseberry's Great Escape,* in *School Library Journal,* Vol. 36, No. 5, May, 1990, p. 83.

In this updated version of a familiar tale from Aesop, a wayfaring pig finds out that "home is where you *feel* at home, and where you are among friends." Roseberry, an adventurous pig, has always done "things ordinary pigs never dreamed of," such as taking flying lessons from birds, or digging underground with the moles and badgers. One day he realizes that wandering has its drawbacks: he sometimes eats food he dislikes, and he is often stuck, unsheltered, in the rain. A green meadow where sheep graze looks like the ideal place for setting up a home, until Roseberry learns that the shepherd wants to make a juicy ham out of him. The friends he has made on his journeys rescue him, and Roseberry celebrates the great wide world and all the animals who make him at home among them. Duke's lovable characters wiggle and prance in amusing, frolicsome pictures, dancing about while they eat or shimmering with delight while they dig up dinosaur bones. Large, loose-lined watercolor illustrations will captivate young listeners or beginning readers, and Roseberry's hard-learned lesson will enlighten them.

Publishers Weekly

SOURCE: A review of *Roseberry's Great Escape,* in *Publishers Weekly,* Vol. 237, No. 19, May 11, 1990, p. 258.

Roseberry is a pig on the go. No dull farmyard life for him—the world is his oyster, and he's eager to partake of all it has to offer. The roving life has its down side, however, and one rainy day Roseberry begins to think about settling down. A meadow populated by the fluffiest sheep this side of Little Bo Peep seems to offer the domestic bliss he seeks—but he changes his mind when the shepherd tries to put pork on the menu. With the help of his friends, Roseberry escapes and resumes his nomadic existence. Duke's book is dedicated to Aesop, and although the moral at the end—"A home is where you feel at home, and where you are among friends"—may seem somewhat familiar, readers will probably be too captivated by the snappy tale and tongue-in-cheek watercolors to notice.

Mary M. Burns

SOURCE: A review of *Roseberry's Great Escape,* in *The Horn Book Magazine,* Vol. LXVI, No. 3, May-June, 1990, p. 322.

Roseberry, a peregrinating porker with a knack for making friends, suddenly grows weary of adventuring and decides that he is ready for "a comfortable, ordinary life." Coming upon a green meadow where contented sheep are peacefully grazing, he throws caution aside for the promise of a bucolic life. He is warmly greeted by the doting shepherd who proclaims his fondness for fat little pigs. But, as Roseberry soon discovers, that particular fondness translates into a gastronomic experience rather than pastoral concern. With a little help from his old friends, the birds and fish, he resumes his proper place in the world, sagely observing, "'Meadows and shepherds may be good for sheep, but they are not necessarily good for a pig.'" In true picture story book fashion, text and illustration are dependent upon each other in the development of situations and characters. There are wonderfully exaggerated touches in every picture—such as the bows that decorate the curly heads of the pampered sheep. As for Roseberry, the central character, he is one of the most engaging pigs to appear in recent years, demonstrating once again that few can match Kate Duke's versatile and economical line in the portrayal of porcine protagonists.

DON'T TELL THE WHOLE WORLD! (written by Joanna Cole, 1990)

Publishers Weekly

SOURCE: A review of *Don't Tell the Whole World!*, in *Publishers Weekly*, Vol. 237, No. 41, October 12, 1990, p. 63.

From the author and illustrator of *It's Too Noisy!* comes this sprightly retelling of a folktale about a woman who "would always tell every secret, no matter how big or how small." Dressed in her long frock and bonnet, the effervescent Emma walks through town letting all kinds of information flow from her lips. Her husband, John, is not pleased when Emma announces that he wears flowered underwear, but he loves her so dearly that he forgives her immediately. Yet John faces a serious dilemma when he finds a box full of money while plowing his field. The money will let them pay rent to their crotchety landlord, Mr. Snood, but John is afraid to let Emma know about his discovery. In an appealing plot turn, Emma saves the day by doing what she does best—babbling profusely. Duke's pastel palette and affable characters lend snappy support to Cole's amusing text. This is fine story-telling, charmingly illustrated.

Hazel Rochman

SOURCE: A review of *Don't Tell the Whole World!*, in *Booklist,* Vol. 87, No. 5, November 1, 1990, p. 525.

Illustrated with ebullient, cartoon-style pictures in ink and wash, this is a comic folktale about a woman who just can't keep a secret. To her husband's embarrassment, she even tells the neighbors that his underwear has flowers on it. But he loves her all the same, and when he finds some buried treasure on the farm, he works out a clever way to handle her talkativeness and to trick the greedy landlord. Cole treats the simple characters with affection, and the read-aloud audience will enjoy the mischief.

Judith Gloyer

SOURCE: A review of *Don't Tell the Whole World!*, in *School Library Journal,* Vol. 36, No. 12, December, 1990, p. 74.

A retelling of an old folktale about a wife who cannot keep a secret and her husband's outlandish ruse to keep others from believing her story of buried treasure. Duke sets the story in a rural 19th-century America. While Cole quickly shows that Emma can't keep a secret, her text and Duke's pictures clearly show John's affection for his wife. The villain of the piece is the landlord, old Mr. Snood. When John finds a money box while plowing the field, he knows it's only a matter of time before Emma tells and Snood comes to claim the treasure, so he thinks of a plan. This version has a folksy rhythm and flavor that should please storytellers. A humorous counterpart to John's talkative wife is his ox, who with a look or a nod of its head seems to offer sage advice. The soft pastel watercolors reflect the gentle humor of the tale.

GOOD NEWS! (written by Barbara Brenner, 1991)

Kirkus Reviews

SOURCE: A review of *Good News!*, in *Kirkus Reviews,* Vol. LIX, No. 12, June 15, 1991, p. 796.

[A] story pivoting on the exaggeration of news as it's passed along. Canada Goose is sitting on four eggs; as word travels around the pond, they become eight "monster" eggs. Both repetitions and minor variations serve the humor as well as the needs of the beginning reader. The illustrations are lively and appropriately comic; they also help define less familiar species like wood duck and muskrat.

LET'S GO DINOSAUR TRACKING! (written by Miriam Schlein, 1991)

Publishers Weekly

SOURCE: A review of *Let's Go Dinosaur Tracking!*, in *Publishers Weekly,* Vol. 238, No. 37, August 16, 1991, p. 58.

Conventional wisdom suggests that this teaming of a

science writer with a picture book illustrator should have worked (witness the success of Cole and Degen's *Magic School Bus* series), but this fact and fiction mix just doesn't jell. One problem may be the broken narrative line: it's difficult to follow a story that seems merely wrapped around a collection of facts. Additionally, in both text and art the boundaries between imagination and scientific observation blur and often disappear totally. The nameless scientist and the three anonymous, dinosaur-crazy kids move abruptly through time and space in search of fossilized tracks without the aid of any device to facilitate or justify the action. Though there's much information here and some very appealing art, these talented collaborators will certainly disappoint their intended audience.

Joanne Schott

SOURCE: A review of *Let's Go Dinosaur Tracking!*, in *Quill and Quire,* Vol. 57, No. 12, December, 1991, p. 28.

Here is a book that meets children at the point of one of their great enthusiasms. It then leads them to discover some of the ways scientists work to solve puzzles, and shows how discoveries sometimes lead to new questions. Schlein uses the topic of dinosaur footprints, revealing what can be learned from their location, number, depth, and from the distance between them. Though she presents the information simply enough for even the youngest dinosaur fan, the principles of investigation that accompany the facts serve to introduce the scientific method. It will be a rare reader who does not catch both the urge to find out and the joy of solving a scientific puzzle. Duke's illustrations are an integral part of the process. Her lively trio of child investigators and an energetic grandfather who follow tracks, asking and answering questions as they go, will carry the reader along with their obvious delight in discovery. Schlein and Duke have produced a book that is fun to read, is educational in the best sense, and shows a real understanding of its audience.

Cathryn A. Camper

SOURCE: A review of *Let's Go Dinosaur Tracking!*, in *School Library Journal,* Vol. 38, No. 1, January, 1992, p. 106.

Footprints seem to be this season's discovery in children's dinosaur books, as noted by the recently published *On the Tracks of Dinosaurs* (1991) by James Farrow. Schlein's contribution makes available some of this same information in a format that's more appealing to younger children. She uses a fictional premise of an elderly paleontologist, who zips around the world with his grandchildren in order to examine discoveries of dinosaur footprints. The factual text and playful illustrations interact well with one another, moving readers through the book without bogging them down in details.

A glossary helps decode multisyllable names, and a beach experiment will help readers puzzle out how scientists determine a dinosaur's size by the prints it leaves behind. An enjoyable book that covers the basics of prehistoric tracking well.

AUNT ISABEL TELLS A GOOD ONE (1992)

Publishers Weekly

SOURCE: A review of *Aunt Isabel Tells a Good One,* in *Publishers Weekly,* Vol. 238, No. 52, November 29, 1991, p. 51.

Aunt Isabel is delighted to have her niece Penelope spend the night, and a made-to-order story is part of the package. Asking for guidance from Penelope along the way, Isabel weaves a story of a handsome prince and the enigmatic Lady Nell who can "fiddle like a cricket, sing like a dove and wiggle her ears." Isabel may ask for help, but she is clearly in charge here, insisting on "a little Danger" and "Villains" to flesh out her tale. No passive heroine awaiting the prince's marriage proposal, Nell tackles adversity in fine fashion. In a stylistic departure for the gifted artist (*The Guinea Pig ABC; Roseberry's Great Escape*), fanciful mice—somewhat reminiscent of Helen Craig's illustrations for the Angelina books—take the spotlight here, and the delicate watercolors brim with fairy-tale characters and atmosphere. Especially appealing are the artwork's winsome borders, adorned with tiny, appropriate decorative touches—sandwiches in the frame's corners when Nell is following a trail of crumbs, for example. Though the running conversation between narrator and Penelope at times detracts from the action, the diverting story-within-a-story is an inviting opportunity for youngsters to double their fun.

Lori A. Janick

SOURCE: A review of *Aunt Isabel Tells a Good One,* in *School Library Journal,* Vol. 38, No. 3, March, 1992, p. 214.

When Aunt Isabel makes up a story for her niece Penelope, the tale she tells of Lady Nell and Prince Augustus is occasionally clichéd but redeemed by a clever ending. As the young mouse helps her aunt weave the plot, Isabel provides a gentle lesson in story-making. The story within a story works mainly because of Duke's exuberant portrayal of her endearing mice. Children will identify with bright-eyed, feisty Penelope and will wish that they had a quirky aunt like Isabel (she's dressed in a 1920s flapper dress and sports a feathered headband). Because of the switches in narrative, the book would be best shared one-on-one or used as a language-arts supplement. An entertaining way to introduce children to the elements of storytelling while providing an impetus for their own creative endeavors.

Journal of Adolescent & Adult Literacy

SOURCE: A review of *Aunt Isabel Tells a Good One,* in *Journal of Adolescent & Adult Literacy,* Vol. 40, No. 8, May, 1997, p. 669.

Reluctant to head off to bed one night, young Penelope begs her Aunt Isabel to tell her a story. Aunt Isabel informs Penelope that a good story requires just the right ingredients and then proceeds to stir up a wonderfully delicious tale of Prince Augustus and Lady Penelope and their daring adventure as they defeat two villainous foes. What makes this picture book a perfect choice for a secondary classroom is the way in which the story unfolds. Using the story-within-a-story format. Duke has Aunt Isabel ask young Penelope about where to set the story and how to put some excitement into the tale. As Aunt Isabel tells her niece, "A little Danger is good for a story." Penelope grumbles about this "problem part" but later admits that the story would be fairly dull without it. Use this charmingly illustrated tale to teach the elements of plot or to provide an immediately accessible example of dual plot lines.

SHOW-AND-TELL FROG (written by Joanne Oppenheim, 1992)

Stephanie Zvirin

SOURCE: A review of *Show-and-Tell Frog,* in *Booklist,* Vol. 88, No. 19, June 1, 1992, p. 1766.

Though part of the same Ready-to-Read series as *How Do You Make a Bubble, . . . Frog* is for children slightly more advanced in reading skill. The vocabulary used is still quite simple, but Oppenheim abandons rhyme and nonsense to tell an actual story, challenging kids to do more than simply read the words in front of them. Duke's illustrations, which add flashes of humor to the straightforward telling, follow Allie's little green frog from the moment it disappears from the box under the bed to its reappearance in Allie's classroom—right where it was meant to be all along.

IF YOU WALK DOWN THIS ROAD (1993)

Virginia Opocensky

SOURCE: A review of *If You Walk Down This Road,* in *School Library Journal,* Vol. 39, No. 6, June, 1993, pp. 72-3.

The friendly forest folk in Shady Green are understandably curious about the newcomers walking down the road, stopping in at every home. Grandmommy Cottontail lives on the hill, the Lizard family in the log, Ma and Pa Squirrel and their young ones frisk in their tree, and, at the far end of the town where no one lives, there's the perfect home for Mouse and child. Each of the neighbors comes bearing home-warming gifts. The text is in brief rhythmic questions and replies: "Who has a house with a view of the sky? Old Brown Owl has a view of the sky." Soft watercolor illustrations burst with humorous detail and activity totally appropriate to the homes and residents. Bug's Buggies Used Mobile Homes sells shells on wheels to homeless (though clothed) snails; Mole's walls are hung with picks and shovels; the squirrel kids have several games underway using nuts for balls. Illustrations demand multiple readings and the gentle, welcoming story will linger with the picture-book crowd.

ONE SATURDAY MORNING (written by Barbara Baker, 1994)

Kirkus Reviews

SOURCE: A review of *One Saturday Morning,* in *Kirkus Reviews,* Vol. LXII, No. 20, October 15, 1994, p. 1404.

A typical day in the life of a family of people, illustrated as bears. And the day is truly typical. Mama makes a cup of tea; Lily joins her for toast; they go for a walk in the park; the baby misbehaves; Papa's lunch gets cold. The book succeeds on the one level on which an early reader must succeed: It is utterly simple. (The word "spaghetti" is the only challenge for even the most basic reader.) But it doesn't reach beyond that. Surprises are kept to a minimum, the biggest plot twist being the discovery of Papa's hat in Daisy's carriage. There's no law saying an early reader has to be a thriller, but Baker makes Arnold Lobel's *Frog and Toad* look like a Tom Clancy potboiler. The pictures are cozy, an example of an illustrator making the best of a humdrum subject. While placidity may be a virtue when writing for the early reader set, *One Saturday Morning* crosses over the line into boredom.

Gale W. Sherman

SOURCE: A review of *One Saturday Morning,* in *School Library Journal,* Vol. 40, No. 11, November, 1994, p. 72.

In *One Saturday Morning,* readers meet a loving family of bears and follow them through their busy day. Baker's delightful story features a typical family dealing with the wants and needs of four youngsters at different ages and stages. Duke's watercolor-and-pen illustrations are filled with humor and will delight children. Viewers can't help but notice the numerous pictures featuring family members reading amid the calm and chaos. Though written for beginning readers, it will be a toss up as to who enjoys the book more—kids or parents. This is a winner; buy several copies.

Chris Sherman

SOURCE: A review of *One Saturday Morning,* in *Booklist,* Vol. 91, No. 9, January 1, 1995, p. 827.

From Archaeologists Dig for Clues, *written and illustrated by Kate Duke.*

From Mama Bear's attempts to have a few quiet minutes to herself to Papa Bear's spaghetti lunch with the kids, the busy Saturday activities of each member of the Bear family are featured in six easy-to-read chapters. Baker's bears are a close-knit family, but the smaller bears have a hard time being heard and must learn to stand up for themselves. Beginning readers will enjoy the humor of familiar family situations and appreciate the happy solutions that inevitably follow each mishap. Duke's bright watercolors, which grace each page, enhance the warmth and bustle of the story.

📖 *AUNT ISABEL MAKES TROUBLE* (1996)

Kirkus Reviews

SOURCE: A review of *Aunt Isabel Makes Trouble*, in *Kirkus Reviews*, Vol. LXIV, No. 18, September 15, 1996, p. 1398.

From the creator of endearing guinea pigs comes the second sweet book about mice heroines and cockroach villains.

Employing the same story-within-a-story format readers will recognize from *Aunt Isabel Tells A Good One* (1992), Aunt Isabel spins a naptime yarn for Penelope; every time Aunt Isabel seems ready to come to a close, Penelope says, "BUT," thereby forcing the tale in a new direction. The fairy-tale takeoff stars Lady Nell, a penniless princess who tries to reach her prince's castle in time for his birthday, stopping only to thwart a band of marauding cockroaches. The technique of constant interruption on the part of Penelope may mimic child listeners, but is not as effective as the device used in the first book, which threaded whats, whens, and whys into an already well-told story. Jaunty watercolor illustrations are replete with detail, from the matchbox mouse furnishings and pierced ears to the hidden thieves. The chatty style is lighthearted and the plot full of good-humored twists and turns, even if the pace occasionally lags. Children will anticipate the satisfying outcome and surely applaud the mouse heroine who chews bubble gum and hurls a mean cherry drop. Mice and princesses are a tried-and-true winning combination, and readers of the first book as well as fans of Angelina Ballerina will not be disappointed.

Beth Tegart

SOURCE: A review of *Aunt Isabel Makes Trouble,* in *School Library Journal,* Vol. 42, No. 10, October, 1996, pp. 91-2.

Aunt Isabel is at it again. This time, the storytelling mouse and her niece Penelope tell a tale in tandem about Lady Nell, pitcher for the East Woods nutball team. Dressed in a fetching pink-and-white uniform, Lady Nell sets out to visit her true love, Prince Augustus, for his birthday. Along the way she encounters Cocky the roach and his gang, who are terrorizing the village. Using her nutball skills, she subdues the evil insects and saves the town. Refusing a cash reward, she balloons up and away to reach Augustus's castle in time for the party. Little Penelope and her aunt make a great team. The story-within-a-story technique is clever and appealing. Duke's charming watercolor illustrations in pastel shades neatly complement the fast-paced, well-written text. An ideal book for curriculum connections in language arts.

Publishers Weekly

SOURCE: A review of *Aunt Isabel Makes Trouble,* in *Publishers Weekly,* Vol. 243, No. 42, October 14, 1996, p. 83.

The second Aunt Isabel title (the first was **Aunt Isabel Tells a Good One**) continues to celebrate the joys of storytelling while providing a splendid showcase for Duke's sunny, winningly detailed watercolors of anthropomorphized animal life. This time, Aunt Isabel, an Auntie Mame-like mouse, spins a yarn concerning a famous nutball player, Lady Nell, and her efforts to visit her boyfriend Prince Augustus on his birthday. Her over-energetic niece Penelope, however, offers near-constant interjections ("But—"), just as Aunt Isabel anticipates: "I'll start and you'll keep but-but-butting in. That way we'll make a lot of trouble for this story, and keep it full of surprises." Lady Nell, pictured here as a grown-up version of the baseball-uniform-wearing Penelope, ends up foiling a sandwich-shop robbery planned by a gang of cockroaches and being feted by a grateful village before finally arriving at Prince Augustus's castle in the nick of time. Duke expertly juggles the two levels of narrative, vividly capturing both the what-will-happen-next excitement of the interior story, as well as the fun of creating and listening to it.

Stephanie Zvirin

SOURCE: A review of *Aunt Isabel Makes Trouble,* in *Booklist,* Vol. 93, No. 4, October 15, 1996, pp. 432, 434.

Aunt Isabel mouse told a fine yarn last time (*Aunt Isabel Tells a Good One* (1992). She's also in great form here, with her spirited, argumentative niece Penelope providing lively vocal commentary that keeps Aunt Isa-

bel on her toes and the story, about feisty Lady Nell, full of surprises. It's a good thing nutball season is over for Lady Nell the mouse because it's her true love's birthday. Unfortunately, she's been so busy she forgot about his party and his present. What is she to do? Aunt Isabel keeps her niece spellbound with Lady Nell's plight (Nell's heroic besting of the villainous cockroach gang is especially exciting), but not so enthralled that Penelope forgets to interrupt regularly, prompting Aunt Isabel to send the story off in a new dramatic or funny direction. The watercolors are lively and sweet (although the insect villains are a shade wicked), with plenty of hiding cockroaches to keep kids actively involved in the goings-on. Clever, funny, and inviting.

ARCHAELOGISTS DIG FOR CLUES (1997)

Hazel Rochman

SOURCE: A review of *Archaeologists Dig for Clues,* in *Booklist,* Vol. 93, No. 7, December 1, 1996, p. 662.

In this lively, informative title in the Let's-Read-and-Find-Out Science series, a boy and his friends go on a dig in a local cornfield with their archaeologist friend Sophie. The children are disappointed when they don't find treasure or a mummy; all they dig up are rocks and pebbles and dust. But Sophie explains that archaeologists love garbage and that the fun is in the detective work, on the site and in the lab, finding out how ordinary people lived long ago. In addition to the main narrative, sidebars provide facts and activities ("What Would Your Garbage Tell about You?"), and the cartoon-style color drawings add informality, excitement, and comic relief. As is the norm now in concept books, it's taken for granted that the cast is ethnically diverse; one scientist in the lab is in a wheelchair. The affected blond kid who worries about dirtying her sneakers ends up getting totally involved ("Cool!"). So will many readers.

Kirkus Reviews

SOURCE: A review of *Archaeologists Dig for Clues,* in *Kirkus Reviews,* Vol. LXIV, No. 24, December 15, 1996, p. 1797.

Readers will feel as if they're taking an active part in an archaeological dig in this informative entry in the Let's-Read-and-Find-Out Science series, reminiscent of Aliki's *Digging for Dinosaurs* and entries in the Magic School Bus series.

Student volunteers accompany Sophie, the archaeologist, to an unnamed dig in a cornfield, where remains of people from the Archaic Era are being uncovered. Scientific information is spelled out in a straightforward text, defining terms—*artifact, midden,* and *feature*—as well as processes, e.g., wet-screening dirt. Dialogue balloons show the students' questions and reactions to their discoveries, while a pet beagle's comments provide comic relief. Inserts complement the text by highlighting comparisons between past and present, how tools were made, and what a basket of modern garbage can reveal. The need for meticulous record-keeping and expert analysis is also included: There is a behind-the-scenes look at a lab plus a complete picture of field work, including the long hours, hot sun, and tedious sifting of dirt. With her inviting approach to a complex process, Duke (***Aunt Isabel Makes Trouble***) ensures that this eye-opening field trip will inspire dirt diggers and treasure-seekers everywhere.

James E. Ayres

SOURCE: A review of *Archaeologists Dig for Clues,* in *Science Books & Films,* Vol. 33, No. 5, June-July, 1997, p. 146.

Through the use of attractive cartoons and a brief text on each of this book's 28 pages, typical archaeological activity at a 6,000-year-old prehistoric Archaic-period site is fairly and accurately depicted. The text and dialogue of the cartoon characters follow the scientific methods employed by archaeologists as they progress from the discovery of a site, to its excavation and the recovery and care of artifacts, then to the recording of information in the laboratory, and finally, to the special studies and analyses required to interpret their findings. Descriptions and explanations of the important and necessary techniques of archaeology, including measuring, bagging, and labeling artifacts, dry and wet artifact screening processes, photography, note-taking, and mapping are skillfully woven into the story. The fact that no mention is made of the last step in every archaeological project—preparing a final report—is an unfortunate, but hardly fatal, omission. Other concepts, such as the "trash midden" and "feature," and activities such as flint knapping and carbon dating of wood, also are briefly explained. The author mentions that archaeologists are not treasure seekers; rather, they look for and find the everyday remains of ordinary people in an attempt to reconstruct past human behavior. Another important message presented is that archaeology should not be done on one's own; instead, professionals must be involved. Duke's book stresses the seriousness of the subject, while emphasizing the fun, excitement, and sense of discovery resulting from a volunteer experience in archaeology. The material could be used to support class projects and for general awareness. It is written with 5- to 9-year-olds in mind.

ONE GUINEA PIG IS NOT ENOUGH (1998)

Publishers Weekly

SOURCE: A review of *One Guinea Pig Is Not Enough,* in *Publishers Weekly,* Vol. 245, No. 5, February 2, 1998, p. 88.

Duke (***Aunt Isabel Tells a Good One***) adds another feather to her cap with this addition primer. The book's title comes from the opening vignette, which finds a single, sad guinea sitting by a checkerboard. But this guinea pig is soon joined by a peer to make "two smiling guinea pigs," and the story is off and running. The gang of guinea pigs grows one by one during a romp through a sunny, playground-like landscape; large, colorful numerals take center stage in each scene, providing the audience with easy-to-follow visual cues. To drive home the notion of numeric language, the appropriate equation (e.g., $1 + 1 = 2$) is printed in the lower-right corner when each stage of addition is completed. Duke connects each successive vignette with zest and imagination: for example, the "five flying guinea pigs" who are gleefully bouncing on a trampoline land smack in the middle of another guinea pig's elaborate sand castle, creating "six sorry guinea pigs." At last, nine guinea pigs, cranky after their long day, are pacified by a 10th, "big" guinea pig; returning home, they are reunited with their parents for a total of 20 guinea pigs—"and twenty," Duke concludes, "is plenty." With mixed media drawings that bubble with energy from beginning to end, this is an exuberant and clever introduction to math.

Additional coverage of Duke's life and career is contained in the following source published by Gale Research: *Something about the Author,* Vol. 90.

Nancy Garden

1938-

American author of fiction and nonfiction.

Major works include *Fours Crossing* (1981), *Annie on My Mind* (1982), *Peace, O River* (1986), *Mystery of the Night Raiders* (1987), *Dove and Sword: A Novel of Joan of Arc* (1995).

INTRODUCTION

Garden's success in creating powerful works in a variety of genres attests to the range and scope of her writing abilities. Her fiction and nonfiction for elementary and middle graders often explore the supernatural realm, as they are peppered with occult characters and unexplained events. In her works for older readers, she tends toward realistic renderings, addressing such sensitive issues as racial tension, homosexuality, and teen drug use and suicide. Best known for her landmark novel *Annie on My Mind*, Garden sympathetically and graphically depicts a love affair between two teenage girls. *Annie on My Mind* received great critical acclaim, and Garden is praised not only for treating a topic previously considered taboo in adolescent literature, but also for her complex and convincing characterizations of Liza and Annie as they fall in love and face ostracism by their community. Mary K. Chelton notes that the novel is "clear, consistent, at times lyrical, but best of all gut-level believable." Selected by both *Booklist* and the American Library Association as a Best Book of 1982, *Annie on My Mind,* however, was later the subject of a federal court case after a Kansas school district voted to remove it from library shelves. The ban was declared unconstitutional and the novel was reinstated in the school library, a victory that Garden undoubtedly contributed to by her testimony at the trial about violation of free speech under the First Amendment. Published nearly ten years later, Garden's *Lark in the Morning* (1991) also offers a fresh angle on homosexuality in young adult fiction. As a young female protagonist comes to terms with her sexual identity, her relationship with another female becomes a source of emotional support for her as she helps two teen runaways escape from their abusive relatives. Garden deals with some of the same themes in two of her earlier nonfiction works, yet presents issues about identity on a larger, national scale. *Berlin: City Split in Two* (1971) examines the post-World War II division of this German city and its effect on inhabitants, and the story in *What Happened in Marston* (1971) was inspired by the race riots of the 1960s.

In her fiction for younger readers, Garden connects events to the mystical and the fantastic. Her "Fours Crossing" sequence—comprised of the titles *Fours Crossing, Wa-*

tersmeet (1983), *The Door Between* (1987) and *The Joining*—features a resourceful teen protagonist who battles the evil will of a local hermit to preserve her hometown of Fours Crossing. In the "Monster Hunters" series, preteens Brian, Mumbles, and Dark solve mysteries while narrowly escaping the wrath of such supernatural villains as witches, werewolves, and vampires. What these and other similar works by Garden have in common is both their appeal to horror fans and faithfulness to the genre; such books as *Prisoner of Vampires* (1984) and *My Brother, the Werewolf* (1995) are at once absurdly humorous and chillingly gory, "sure to be popular," noted Sally Estes, "with those who like to be scared but not terrified." Despite mostly strong reviews, and special recognition for the groundbreaking *Annie on My Mind*, Garden does not take success for granted, ever mindful of the audience for which she writes and her reasons for doing so. "I write for young people because I like them," she commented, "and because I think they are important. Children's books can be mind-stretchers and imagination-ticklers and builders of good taste in a way that adult books cannot, because young people usually come to books with more open minds. It's exciting to be able to contribute to that in a small way."

Biographical Information

Garden was born in Boston, Massachusetts, in 1938. Both of her parents were positive influences during her childhood. Her father, an American Red Cross executive, instilled in her the belief that girls could achieve anything that boys could—even if they had to work twice as hard to receive credit for their accomplishments; her mother, a social worker and psychologist, was not only an excellent role model, but Garden's "best friend and confidante." By the time she was ten, Garden had lived with her parents in two other cities in Massachusetts as well as in Manhattan, Scarsdale, and White Plains, New York. As an only child, she was somewhat isolated, and although she made a few very close friends, they were often lost because of the frequent moves her family had to make. Several illnesses—from colds to measles to scarlet fever—often kept her at home, and she became an avid reader, discovering Anna Sewell's *Black Beauty,* Hugh Lofting's *Dr. Dolittle,* and the works of Rudyard Kipling. She later attended the Lincoln School, a private institution run by Quakers, where her love of theater flourished. After a stint of acting in summer stock productions in New Hampshire, she enrolled in the Columbia School of Dramatic Arts, working on lighting design and directing plays. However, upon realizing how difficult it would be to make a living in the field, Garden gave up her dreams of becoming first an actress and then a director; instead she studied at Columbia Teachers College, majoring in speech and earning her master's degree in 1962. She supplemented her income with office work, and at one of these jobs, she met budding artist and illustrator Barbara Seuling, with whom she later collaborated on a children's book. Her first published book, *Berlin: City Split in Two,* appeared in 1971, followed by other nonfiction titles, including *Vampires* (1973), *Werewolves* (1973), *Witches* (1975), and *Devils and Demons* (1976). Garden next turned to fantasy, and in 1981 she produced *Fours Crossing,* the first in a series of novels set in a small New Hampshire town. *Annie on My Mind* was published the following year, and she had begun to establish herself as a successful writer of books for young people. Since then, Garden has written over twelve books and spends time giving lectures about writing at schools and libraries. Split ting her residence between Massachusetts and Maine each year, she enjoys "woods and sea, fresh air and quiet."

Major Works

In the novel *Fours Crossing,* thirteen-year-old Melissa, whose mother has recently died, comes to stay with her grandmother for the summer and soon befriends a boy named Jed. The plot turns fantastical when some mysterious force prevents spring from arriving in Fours Crossing; Melissa and Jed take it upon themselves to outsmart a sinister hermit—whom they learn is the culprit—only to be captured and imprisoned by him. Garden steeps this work and others in the series in Celtic mythology and pagan lore, creating a mood of magic and suspense; Melissa confronts the hermit, gaining greater insight into the origins of his evil intentions in each subsequent book, until, in *The Joining,* she finally succeeds in putting him to rest and thus saves the town. In *Annie on My Mind,* main characters Liza and Annie meet one afternoon at the Metropolitan Museum of Art in New York. They become best friends and then lovers after a long, romantic courtship. What sets Garden's novel apart from others treating the subject of adolescent homosexuality is the resonance and accessibility of the girls' relationship; readers are drawn into the compelling story of Liza and Annie, come to know them well, and can identify with their feelings of anticipation, rapture, and fear as they fall in love and face losing each other. At the end of the story, which is told from Liza's point of view in simple, direct prose, Garden preserves their relationship, as Liza and Annie, who have incurred the wrath of their community and are now at separate colleges, reaffirm their love. *Peace, O River* is another novel exploring friendship, love, and disillusionment among its teen characters, as they grapple, along with their parents, with issues of prejudice, pacifism, and the disposal of nuclear waste. Kate, who returns to her family's home in River View, Massachusetts, after living away for four years, becomes a self-appointed peacemaker among her feuding classmates—some of whom live in an affluent neighborhood, and others who reside in nearby Hastings, a working-class town across the river. The tension between the young people, and the violence that ensues, reflects a larger battle between the two communities. Regarded by critics as powerful and discomfiting, *Peace, O River* closes on a bittersweet note; town members eventually realize the importance of peace and unity as they band together to prevent the selection of one of the two towns as a nuclear waste site. Unfortunately, their truce comes after the accidental death of a central teen character.

Similar to the "Fours Crossing" sequence that deals with the occult, Garden's "Monster Hunters" series—detailing the adventures of Brian, Mumbles, and Dark—is geared for preteen readers. In *Mystery of the Night Raiders,* Brian learns that the cows on his grandparents' farm in Vermont are dying of unknown causes, a situation certain to bring the family financial ruin. A fan of Sherlock Holmes, he employs the help of friends Mumbles and Dark to solve the mystery, and, in doing so, faces two hard truths—that a supernatural force is responsible for the death of the cattle and Brian himself is slated to be a vampire's next victim. Garden succeeds in building a strong measure of suspense and brings the story to a satisfying conclusion, sowing the seeds for Brian's next sleuthing job. A dramatic departure from her previous books, Garden's *Dove and Sword: A Novel of Joan of Arc* is a historical novel set in fifteenth-century France, recounting the life, mission, triumphs, trial, and execution of Joan of Arc. Informed by extensive research into the political and social history of the times, *Dove and Sword* nevertheless offers a modern perspective. Told from the point of view of Gabrielle, a fictional friend of Joan, the novel treats the twentieth-century reader to commentary on the inferior status of women of this period and the atrocities of war. Joan is presented as a celebrated hero, a worker of miracles, but an enigma as well, in a work that *Publishers Weekly* noted "achieves the highest goals of historical fiction—it vivifies the past, robustly and respectfully, then uses its example to steer the audience toward a more courageous future."

Awards

Annie on My Mind was selected as a *Booklist* Reviewer's Choice and an ALA Best Book in 1982. It was also placed on the ALA Best of the Best list, 1970-83. *Fours Crossing* was on the William Allen White Award Master List, 1983-84.

AUTHOR'S COMMENTARY

Mary K. Chelton

SOURCE: "VOYA Interview with Nancy Garden," in *The VOYA Reader,* The Scarecrow Press, Inc., 1990, pp. 270-74.

Since, in our opinion, the publication of *Annie on My Mind* was a landmark in adolescent literature dealing with same-sex love relationships, we decided to interview the author, Nancy Garden, by mail to find out more about how she came to write such a neat book.

MKC: Tell us about yourself and how you started writing adolescent literature.

NG: I've written for my own pleasure since I was about eight years old, and I've written no matter what other kind of work I've been doing (various jobs, acting, theatrical lighting design, teaching, editing). I suppose one reason I started writing for young people is that I remember my own childhood and adolescence vividly—but the main reason is that I think kids are fascinating, wonderful people and an unusually receptive, sensitive, and honestly critical audience.

MKC: What else have you written besides *Annie?*

NG: *Annie* is my tenth book—my fourth published novel. (I say "published" because I have boxes of unpublished manuscripts that never quite worked.) My first novel was *What Happened in Marston*, which, much to my delight, was shown as an ABC After School Special last November. They retitled it *The Color of Friendship*—an apt choice, because the story is about a black boy and a white boy who are friends in a racially tense town. *The Loners* is about a boy—a loner—who falls in love with a girl who is mentally ill and has been experimenting with drugs; its theme, I suppose, is that one can't

always save the people one loves from disaster. My third novel was a "realistic fantasy" called *Fours Crossing*, about a girl who goes to New Hampshire in March to visit her grandmother and finds that it's still deep winter. Together, she, a boy who becomes her best friend, and a partly magic dog solve the mystery of why spring hasn't come. My nonfiction books are a history of Berlin, Germany, showing how it came to be divided (*Berlin: City Split in Two*); a book about writing and solving codes and ciphers (*The Kid's Code and Cipher Book*), and four books on occult subjects (*Vampires, Werewolves, Witches, Devils and Demons*). I've also written various educational materials, and a few works for hire, the most recent of which is a retelling of some Grimms' tales (*Favorite Tales from Grimm*) to go with Mercer Mayer's illustrations that should be out this fall.

MKC: How did you decide to write *Annie on My Mind?* (Did you have trouble finding a publisher, or in not making it a "punishment" story of some sort?)

NG: In a way, I've been writing *Annie* since I was about 17, which is when I started trying to write about two women falling in love. My first attempts were plays, and embarrassingly autobiographical. In my early twenties, I wrote a terribly melodramatic adult novel (which I at least had the sense not to try to have published); it was less autobiographical but fairly bleeding with *Sturm und Drang* and what I called "soapboxing"—me getting on my soapbox and preaching instead of telling a story; stylistically, it had strong echoes of Radclyffe Hall, whom I admired greatly while I was growing up. *Annie*'s most immediate predecessors were a book called *Summerhut* and, after that, an untitled novel with a school theater setting. These were a bit better, I think, than my earlier attempts, but still not right. I did try to get *Summerhut* published, and found some interest in it—one editor, Jim Giblin, was kind enough to comment on several versions of it and on a very early version or two of *Annie*—but I eventually put *Summerhut* and the other book aside and started all over again with a new story and new characters. The subject is so close to me and there was so much I wanted to say about it that I was still having a great deal of trouble not soapboxing. My tendency to overstate my theme—to tell instead of show—plus the fact that I was writing about some of my own deepest feelings led, I think, to my difficulties in working out a viable unautobiographical plot and in writing characters who were people instead of ideas.

So, as you can see from all that, I did have trouble with *Annie,* but the trouble was more with myself than with the outside world. By the time I had a gay novel ready to show anyone—*Summerhut*—publishers had become much more openminded than they were back in the 50s when I started out.

You also asked if I had trouble not making *Annie* a "punishment" story. From the very first, that's exactly what I did *not* want to do. I wanted to write a book with a happy ending, unlike those I'd read. And again, by the time I was ready to show anything to a publisher, the editors who saw *Summerhut,* at least, were beginning to be ready to accept a gay love story with a happy ending.

MKC: What is the main message you wished to convey in *Annie?* or What is the theme of *Annie?* ("Message" makes my question seem to assume a didactic intent which I don't mean.)

NG: That being gay and being happy are by no means mutually exclusive. That although being gay can be difficult, it is difficult more because of the way gayness is and has been perceived by many straight (and, unfortunately, some gay) people than because of any flaw inherent in homosexuality itself. I wanted to try to give straight kids some insight into what being gay truly means; that having a preference for one's own sex does not mean one is "sick" or criminal; that gay people fall deeply in love just the way straight people do. I also wanted to show both gay and straight kids that being gay doesn't necessarily mean aping the opposite sex, either in manner or in sex roles.

MKC: Had you read other titles of the adolescent literature genre on same-sex relationships? (e.g., *Trying Hard to Hear You, Happy Endings Are All Alike, Hey Dollface,* etc.) If so, had they influenced you in any way?

NG: Yes. They influenced me—as did gay books for adults—especially at first, in that they strengthened my resolve to write an openly gay love story for young adults that ended happily, one that treated homosexuality without hedging. And later, as more young adult books at least touched on homosexuality, they encouraged me by showing that the subject was becoming less taboo. As you probably know, one of the earliest YA books (if not the earliest) to deal with homosexuality or related issues in any depth was John Donovan's *I'll Get There, It Better Be Worth the Trip* (1969). In that book, the protagonist and his best friend care deeply about each other and have a brief homosexual episode which scares them—well, scares the protagonist, anyway. They decide not to continue that part of their relationship, and there's nothing really to indicate that they are likely to grow up gay. But nevertheless the book was a landmark in that it actually treated the subject openly. (It also delivered an important message to straight kids: that one homosexual incident doesn't necessarily mean one is gay.) *I'll Get There* encouraged me enormously, as did the increasingly more explicit books that followed it, and I feel greatly indebted to Donovan and to all other YA authors who published books about the subject before I did.

MKC: Why did you even use teachers in the plot, given the myth of the seductive gay teacher which anti-gay groups love to promulgate?

NG: I'm delighted you asked that! The main reason was to try to help shatter that very myth. I wanted to show that it is ridiculous to suppose that gay teachers go around seducing their students or that they try to influence them to become gay; the truth is that the vast majority of gay

teachers keep their homosexuality to themselves. I certainly did when I was teaching and various of my friends have also. What's important, though, is that even when gay teachers are "in the closet" they are sometimes unwilling—but sorely needed—role models for gay kids. I remember teachers who I thought were gay, and their very presence plus that possibility comforted me and made me feel less alone and more hopeful. I wish more people would realize that gay kids have few—if any—positive role models while they are growing up. Most people around them, from their own parents to the people shown on TV commercials, are straight. I remember when I was in high school my lover and I often speculated about adults we knew who might possibly be gay—how desperately we needed their help, and how impossible it was for us to seek it out—for of course back then it was risky even to mention homosexuality in a general way. I'd like to see the day come when a gay teacher who realizes a gay kid is in trouble could identify himself or herself to the kid and try to help, the way a sympathetic heterosexual teacher can advise a straight teenager who is having problems adjusting to his or her emerging sexuality or with the opposite sex. I can understand the fear the uninformed people have about openly gay teachers, but again I long for the day when those people realize gay teachers don't—and wouldn't—seduce their students any more often than straight teachers do, which certainly isn't often! We let men teach girls, for heaven's sake, and women teach boys; it's really no different. As to straight students suddenly wanting to be gay because a teacher they admire is gay—well, for one thing, one doesn't "decide" to become gay, and for another, being gay is, even nowadays, too difficult to be a seductively attractive lifestyle for most people—perhaps especially for kids, who after all have constant peer, family, and environmental encouragement to grow up straight.

MKC: What are you working on now—post *Annie?*

NG: I'm working on a sequel to *Fours Crossing,* called *Watersmeet*—with the same editor, by the way, Margaret Ferguson, who worked with me on *Annie.* She's a wonderful editor—perfect would not be too strong a word—and it's both an honor and a pleasure to do any book with her. And I've just finished the rough draft for a new realistic YA novel, which I'll be revising this winter or spring and getting ready to send off. That one's not about being gay, but I expect a future book, or books, of mine will be.

MKC: Anything I forgot or didn't have sense enough to ask?

NG: No, not at all, but there's something I'd like to say, and that's that Farrar, Straus, Giroux—especially Margaret, of course, but everyone there whom I've encountered—has been wonderful about *Annie.* I never have felt the slightest wavering of their support, and I think their deciding to publish *Annie* in the present climate of growing censorship is an act of great courage, for which I shall always be tremendously grateful.

Nancy Garden

SOURCE: "Banned: Lesbian and Gay Kids' Books Under Fire," in *Lambda Book Report,* Vol. 4, No. 7, November-December, 1994, pp. 11-13.

My eyes were barely on the road, because I was imagining the cover of my young adult novel, **Annie on My Mind** curling, blackening, melting, as flames consumed it.

Farfetched fantasy? No. My book was burned last fall by religious fundamentalists in Kansas City, Missouri. Since then, it has been banned in a school district there, and is now the subject of a lawsuit brought by several kids and their parents.

There's nothing like a censorship attempt against one's own book to sensitize one to similar attempts against others, and to the issue of censorship in general.

According to Judith Krug, Director of the American Library Association's Office for Intellectual Freedom, there were 40 reported challenges (complaints) to or outright bannings of gay books (adult and children's) in 1991, 64 in 1992, 111 in 1993, and 56 from January, 1994 to July 15, 1994. A little arithmetic will show you that so far this year's figure is comparable to last year's. Krug estimates that the incidents her office hears about represent at most only a quarter of the actual ones; most are never reported. Michael Willhoite's picture book *Daddy's Roommate* was the most challenged book—book, not just gay book, and not just children's book—in 1993 and so far maintains that position in 1994. The third most challenged in 1993 was Lesléa Newman's *Heather Has Two Mommies.*

Kids' books have always been prime targets for censors; protecting "innocent" and "impressionable" minds from "evil ideas" is a popular pastime of people—some sincere but others politically motivated—on the religious right. *Daddy's Roommate,* said challengers in North Carolina, "promotes a dangerous and ungodly lifestyle from which children must be protected." *Promote* is a key word used not only in challenges to individual books but also in those states with proposed legislation or ballot initiatives seeking to deny expenditure of public funds for materials on homosexuality for kids, or seeking to deny kids access to such materials.

But I write gay YAs because of the appalling suicide rate among gay adolescents, not to "promote" homosexuality, and because of the loneliness and confusion most gay kids face as they struggle to discover, understand, and accept themselves. Michael Willhoite, who writes for younger kids, told me, "I wrote *Daddy's Roommate* for kids of gay parents because their lives were not being addressed. . . . Children need to see their lives reflected in their literature."

Lesléa Newman expresses a similar view. "[The subject] resonated with me as a Jew, also. . . . Nothing reflected my reality in picture books when I was a child. . . . If I have an 'agenda,' it's that every child in the country should be proud of who they are and what their family is."

Jacqueline Woodson, whose forthcoming book *From the Notebooks of Melanin Sun* is about an African-American boy whose mother falls in love with a white woman, says, "My goal is . . . to show the one queer kid in class that he or she isn't all alone—to show the one black kid that, too."

I wish it were possible to convey to would-be censors that writing about something isn't the same as promoting it!

Howard Reeves, who's an editor at Hyperion in New York, says "The very idea [of censorship] is revolting. The worst is this guy in Queens"—Frank Borzellieri, chair of the District 24 School Board in Queens, NY, who tried unsuccessfully last spring to ban all multicultural books from the schools. His effort was reminiscent of the one in 1992 banning the Rainbow Curriculum, which included *Heather* and *Daddy's* and led to the firing of Chancellor Joseph A. Fernandez. Sasha Alyson of Alyson Publications told me that was his worst censorship experience. "The potential was so huge," he said; "a real precedent. The biggest school system in the country saying we'll address gay issues—and then backing down."

Some campaigns against gay books for kids that fall short of actual censorship are equally alarming—as are threats against authors of gay books. "I'm going to go right on burning your books!" the minister who burned **Annie** shouted at me when I visited Kansas City last spring. Worse, I recently heard about an author who was threatened with an end to his picture book career if he published a gay anthology on which he was working. After Jacqueline Woodson's new book was mentioned in *Out* magazine, a clergyman "warned" his congregation against it. Woodson then got letters from 32 sixth graders saying in effect that they'd never buy any more of her books and Woodson's publisher ran into distribution and book club difficulties. "In the beginning," said Woodson, "I didn't know if they [Scholastic] were on my side. . . . [But] they wrote a wonderful letter of support. They're going to stand behind the book."

Woodson's editor, Dianne Hess, echoes this. "The company is 100% behind Jacquie's new book," she told me, and pointed out that the flap "wasn't real censorship."

Not "real censorship" either, but equally unsettling is the fact that, according to Diane Wachtell of the New Press, some suburban stores have refused to stock her company's YA anthology *Growing Up Gay,* and an educational materials catalog has refused to offer it. And also disturbing is an experience Cristina Salat had with her manuscript for *Living in Secret* about a girl who is kidnapped from her father by her lesbian mom and her mom's lover. "Before Bantam took it," says Salat, "a big house was interested in it for a movie, if I cut the lesbians and anything to do with race. So I didn't do it, and they didn't do it." That's a hard decision for an author to face, especially when it's her first book.

A hard-fought attempt at actual censorship was levied recently against the fairy tale collection *The Duke Who Outlawed Jelly Beans* by Johnny Valentine and other Alyson books in Dayton, Ohio. According to Mark Willis, Community Relations Manager for the Dayton and Montgomery County Public Library, last fall a parent who discovered that the stories in *Duke* involved kids with same-sex parents taped a handwritten note to the book, saying "Warning: This book contains homosexual themes." Then, says Willis, "She alerted the media, who interviewed a lot of people and ran a series on the situation at 6 and 11 two nights in a row." The leader of a small Christian sect, Spirit of Life Christian Center, who Willis said holds an annual Halloween book-burning, urged his followers to complain about the book—and that set off a brouhaha involving angry phone calls and the distribution of a flyer accusing the library of making pornography available to kids. The library sent out some complaint forms, and got about 12 back; most respondents admitted that they hadn't read the book. Library staff then reviewed all the Alyson children's books they had and voted to keep them; the would-be censors appealed, and eventually, after noisy public meetings, the library's Board of Trustees unanimously supported the staff's decision.

Most libraries have specific policies about complaints, and those that do usually have an easier time dealing with them. Ellen Fader, who's Public Library Consultant of the Library Services Division for the State of Oregon, says "Virtually every Oregon public library that's had a challenge has had a policy in place." In 1988-1989 (the library's fiscal year runs from July 1 to June 30), Fader's office documented 4 challenges to gay adult and kids' books. In '89-'90, 3; in '90-'91, 2; in '91-'92, also 2. In '92-'93, the year that Ballot Measure 9 hit Oregon, the figure jumped to 35—44% of the year's total challenges.

This year—July 1, 1993-June 30, 1994—there were only 6 documented challenges to gay books in Oregon, so it appears that things have calmed down a little there. But since conservatives in Oregon gathered enough signatures last summer for a ballot measure prohibiting the expenditure of government funds on anything that "promotes" homosexuality, that could be the calm before the storm, even if, as may have happened by now, the court has ruled against it. "The catch," says Fader, "is that anything that doesn't decry homosexuals would be considered promoting."

The Boston Public Library, says Joanne Goodman, children's librarian at the Field's Corner branch, "has no written policy on censorship." Their unwritten policy, she explains, is that "people are responsible for censoring themselves. Parents should select what their kids read," and the rationale for not having a written policy is that "we'd be stuck with it. . . . This way we can be more flexible. We listen to complaints, and they

[those who complain] can put it in writing." A parent recently complained that Isabelle Holland's *The Man Without a Face* is "horrible and disgusting and shouldn't be on the shelves," Goodman says. "We told him we don't censor, and told him he could put his complaint in writing and send it to the main library. He didn't. Most people don't pursue it. I think the thing to do is to listen to people."

Most people in the literary community agree that no one has the right to censor anyone, even though one may want to. As Judith Krug points out, if one cares deeply about one's own value system, one is, at least potentially, a censor. Lesléa Newman adds, "Once any form of censorship is okay, we [gay people] will be the first to be censored. . . . The answer is to protect the First Amendment but to fight like hell when something's expressed that you don't believe in."

As Michael Thomas Ford, formerly an editor at Macmillan and now freelancing, pointed out last February in the trade magazine *Publishers Weekly* even among gay or gay-sympathetic publishers, there seems to be a certain amount of resistance to publishing gay kids' books. This also bothers David Gale, now an editor at Simon and Schuster, who worked for a time on Marion Dane Bauer's new YA anthology *Am I Blue? Coming Out From the Silence.* "A lot of [publishers] don't buy gay books because they say there's no market for them," Gale said. "Gay books require extra work—more than just doing the book and giving it to regular channels."

"Gay books are the black books of the 90s," Mike Ford points out. "Editors say 'We'll publish this because it's gay. It's the PC thing to do.'—or they'll say 'We can't do this because it's gay.'"

Susan Korman, Cristina Salat's editor at Bantam Books for Young People, brings up an interesting peripheral point about book clubs, which represent a large part of the sales of many children's publishers, and which, especially at the middle grade level, turn away from anything to do with sex. "There will definitely be some resistance," she said, "to selling [*Living in Secret*] to a book club." I asked her if that would influence Bantam in acquiring a book. "No," she said. "If it was a good book and we believed the author had a career, it wouldn't make us reject it."

What about self-censorship on the part of the authors? Surely that's one of the most dangerous by-products of attacks on books. Everyone I talked to resists it—but many find it hard.

"The way [censorship] affects us is in our pocketbooks," says Cristina Salat, "until we're financially secure. . . . I want to do this full time, and it's very hard. . . . I can refine informational details, but I can't change a character once it's come to me."

"I'm doing an adult book now, and it's so much easier,"

Jacqueline Woodson told me. "I think a lot before I sit down to write a YA book."

The popular notion, of course, is that censorship increases sales. "Terrific!" was the first response of a number of my writer friends when I told them *Annie on My Mind* had been burned. "Wonderful! Think of the books you'll sell."

Well, okay, I did think of that, a little, and it's true that I was told all the bookstores in Kansas City were soon sold out of *Annie*. Although I haven't seen any rise in my royalties as a result, it *is* nice that people who wouldn't ordinarily be exposed to *Annie* have read it and have apparently been affected positively by it.

But even though that can be "the silver lining in the cloud," as Sasha Alyson puts it, it doesn't mean publishers or authors can afford to shy away from fighting it when it occurs.

"The author has to be willing to go out there and refute what's being said," feels Cristina Salat, and Jacqueline Woodson says, "I don't believe censorship is good for anyone. . . . It's going to impact on people who haven't got their stuff together yet, who aren't published. The publisher is going to censor new stuff. . . . I want there to be other books out there like mine."

Mike Ford called the increase in sales that censorship can bring "a two-edged sword. . . . If it gets a book out there and gets people to read it, I guess that's a good thing. But if [a book is] read just because it's banned, it isn't so good. To write or publish a book so it'll be banned or controversial is dumb, and has nothing to do with art." But, he went on, publishing a book because you believe in it even though it's going to be banned "is an act of courage."

Publishers and writers are often the last to know when a book is challenged. First to know, though, are the librarians. They're the ones who face the angry patrons, who replace and repair the books removed or damaged by people who decide to take matters into their own hands, and who sometimes even lose their jobs because of censorship issues. And yet many of them fight tirelessly to keep controversial books—our books—available, and to educate the public about the threat that censorship represents.

Cathi Dunn MacRae, YA librarian at the Boulder, Colorado, Public Library, has an advisory board of middle and high school students who were so horrified to learn about book banning that they were inspired to write a program called "Don't Read This!" which includes information on censorship, book talks on challenged books, and skits—including one featuring *Daddy's Roommate*. They've performed the program a number of times, despite the fact that four schools cancelled bookings after seeing the script, and despite threats of disruption. Having their play about censorship censored and threatened rocked many of the students. "It was a neat experience," says MacRae, "because the kids were learning [about censorship] first hand."

The Oregon Intellectual Freedom Clearing House, for which Ellen Fader is Coordinator, issues an annual report on challenges in Oregon and tries to help libraries and schools deal with them. They also provide consulting services and workshops about intellectual freedom. Organizations like the American Library Association, People For the American Way, the National Council of Teachers of English, the Coalition Against Censorship, the American Civil Liberties Union, and others, are all doing their part—but that doesn't mean the literary community can afford to leave all the work to them.

Perhaps we, as queers, are uniquely equipped to fight the efforts against our books. As victims of homophobia, we know firsthand the ignorant, narrow, illogical and controlling thinking that leads to censorship.

How can we fight it?

"By not giving in to it," says David Gale, and, adds Mark Willis, through "a lot of education" and by showing people that "if they could ban everything that offends someone there wouldn't be much left." Sasha Alyson points out, "It's important for people to show up at their library hearings and be heard." Michael Willhoite urges us to write and illustrate "books that are so good they are their own defense," and Cristina Salat suggests "Buy stuff you think is controversial to show the publishers that it sells. And keep putting it out there."

"The Christian right has come together," says Jacqueline Woodson. "We have to do the same. We can't say 'I'm going to make a lot of money.' We have to think of ourselves as a community and come together and fight this now. . . . We can't be selfish and think of personal gain."

The pre-Stonewall fight was hard on many levels, but it looks as if the post-Stonewall-25 fight is going to be even harder. Our enemies are more organized now, and sneakier. They are attacking us on many fronts—and one of them is censorship of books for children and young adults. Make no mistake: this is not a trivial scrap. It is an early battle in what must not become a full-fledged war.

TITLE COMMENTARY

📖 *BERLIN, CITY SPLIT IN TWO* (1971)

Kirkus Reviews

SOURCE: A review of *Berlin, City Split in Two,* in *Kirkus Reviews,* Vol. XXXIX, No. 1, January 1, 1971, p. 8.

Without pictures or map, not only "bleak and dreary" East Berlin but the whole city presents an uninviting prospect—but the book's major flaw remains the stress on contrasts between the two sectors, tempered only towards the close, and on dramatic aspects of the split. Moreover the summary history is studded with simplicisms that amount to evasions: to say that "Socialism, which often appeals to the poor," took hold in the 1890s is a misstatement of the strong radical strain, that "Germany and Austria-Hungary started World War I" is almost equally obscurantist. (The appended definitions of ideologies flounder on the level of 'democracy is our system, inherited from the Greeks.') Even in the more developed sections on post-World War II and the blockade there is much that is unclear (the precipitating currency reform is not related to West German economic integration) while the many tales of hardship and daring stemming from the border-closing are both old and, considering the overall detente spurred by Willy Brandt, untimely. Indeed, recognition that the status quo may be regularized—following brief mention that East Berlin has progressed—is about the only enlightenment this has to offer and its chief advantage over David Knight's 1967 *First Book,* a more general, well-illustrated examination giving equivalent prominence to the Wall.

WHAT HAPPENED IN MARSTON (1971)

Publishers Weekly

SOURCE: A review of *What Happened in Marston,* in *Publishers Weekly,* Vol. 199, No. 17, April 26, 1971, p. 60.

What Happened in Marston when a senseless killing leads to racial violence is narrated by 13-year-old Davey, whose friendship with a young boy from the ghetto precariously places him in the middle of a black-white confrontation. The major portion of the book centers upon the boys' friendship, from its tenuous beginnings at the so-called integrated school to a firmer relationship as each explores the other's way of life, with the last chapters focusing on the violent eruption of tension. *What Happened in Marston* can and does happen in cities everywhere, and Nancy Garden has done an admirable job of examining both sides of the story.

Zena Sutherland

SOURCE: A review of *What Happened in Marston,* in *Bulletin of the Center for Children's Books,* Vol. 25, No. 1, September, 1971, p. 6.

"Some of the kids in my class don't think I should tell this story to anyone, but I think I should," Dave begins. He'd never thought of himself as prejudiced, but when a black child came into the eighth grade class, Dave felt uncomfortable when Joel was assigned the next seat.

But, as Dave puts it, in time "the walls came tumbling down" and the two became good friends. Picked up by police for prowling around a deserted house, the boys are treated with noticeable difference. Then the class is given disciplinary measures because "someone" cheated, the implication being that it was Joel; he takes the test over and gets a very high grade but no apology from the teacher. When there is a violent incident (a policeman shooting a black child who is running, after a store theft) a riot ensues in which both boys become involved. In the end, Joel tells Dave he is going to change schools, because he doesn't want people to think he is ashamed of being black, and that he won't be seeing as much of Dave, although they'll still be friends. The story is realistic and candid, although it gives a rather grim view of policemen and teachers. It is capably written, but is weakened by its purposefulness, albeit in good cause, giving the impression of being a deftly fictionalized case history rather than a story.

Janet C. Polacheck

SOURCE: A review of *What Happened in Marston,* in *School Library Journal,* Vol. 18, No. 1, September, 1971, pp. 2916-17.

David Bellinger, a white ninth-grader, relates the events following the admission of black Joel Garth to his class as a token of integration. It's all here: the nice WASP starting with antagonism, then moving toward friendship with Joel and paying his first visit to a Negro home. The wonders of interracial friendship miraculously generate a ferment of understanding. Thus, when the inevitable riot breaks out, David and another WASP convert, Beany, are caught in the middle and with great courage try to defend Joel and his family. At the end of the book, Joel decides to go back to his original black school and David resolves to educate *his* race about liberty and justice for all. The book's plot has been manufactured to accord with the sermon on social problems which begins it; the result is cardboard figures set up only to be knocked down and, for the most part, a waste of book budget.

THE LONERS (1972)

Kirkus Reviews

SOURCE: A review of *The Loners,* in *Kirkus Reviews,* Vol. XL, No. 21, November 1, 1972, p. 1245.

Souped-up sentiment about Paul Windsor who comes from a straight family (they're horrified to hear him call his brother a "stuck-up . . . screwed-up bastard") and Jenny who just drifts (she's almost anonymous—parentless?) into his life—fey, wistful, sometimes tearful, Jenny. She understands many things better than he does (his grandfather has had a stroke—one has to accept that "living is dying") and she has done some other things, like smoking pot or dropping acid. Gramp dies; Jenny and Paul "hurt" each other; she gives him a "tiny bluet" before his last exam; he takes an acid trip with her but she comes down only to be sent back to that other kind of hospital, having apparently failed to "know how I am inside." *Tres triste,* or is it really?

VAMPIRES (1973)

Kirkus Reviews

SOURCE: A review of *Vampires,* in *Kirkus Reviews,* Vol. XLI, No. 5, March 1, 1973, pp. 261-62.

Garden tries hard, maybe too hard, to assimilate all possible references to the theories about our ghoulish friends. Besides summaries of "Carmilla" and *Dracula* and folklore stories and superstitions (some of which seem to be about mere ghosts rather than vampires *per se*), she includes possible historical counterparts (the Countess Bathory who bathed in blood) and real phenomena which may account for vampire legends (porphyria, premature burial, even TB). All European vampires can (or is this mere speculation?) be traced back to the first woman Lamia/Lilith who was believed to attack infants at night, but in an ecumenical gesture the author demonstrates that non-Christians can also be vampires—citing the Malayan *penanggalen,* the Ashanti *obayifo* and the West Indian *loogaroo* (which is French for werewolf, but nevertheless counts here as a vampire). Despite all the scientific and mythological evidence, there are still plenty of unexplained toothmarks, undecomposed bodies, and at least one documented case of a pernicious anemia sufferer in Brooklyn with an insatiable craving for human blood. . . . It's enough to curdle yours.

WEREWOLVES (1973)

Kirkus Reviews

SOURCE: A review of *Werewolves,* in *Kirkus Reviews,* Vol. XLI, No. 7, April 1, 1973, p. 400.

With some reluctance we approach *Werewolves,* the "Weird and Horrible" companion of *Vampires.* No doubt Lippincott and Ms. Garden are undertaking their investigations in the spirit of fun and, up to a point, they are fun. But just what are these "well-documented reports of small children being suckled and cared for by wolves" that are referred to as fact? Are we really supposed to believe that poor Giles Garnier, Peter Stumpe, and Pierre, Georges and Antoinette Bouget, executed for being witches/werewolves were really guilty? Garden never says so explicitly, but she certainly encourages us to imagine that they might have been. As for the scientific basis of lycanthropy, there's cannibalism induced by nutritional defects (reported in grisly, if not "well-documented" detail), porphyria (also, apparently, a chief cause of vampires), and rabies. Either this is non-fiction, or it's a collection of superstitions retold simply to throw a good scare into us. It's a mistake to try to have it both ways.

WITCHES (1975)

Donald A. Colberg

SOURCE: A review of *Witches,* in *School Library Journal,* Vol. 22, No. 2, October, 1975, p. 98.

Garden sketches popular attitudes—primarily negative—toward witches and witchcraft from Greco-Roman days to the present and, in particular, details the persecution and execution of witches during the German Inquisition and the Salem witch trials (the two chapters on those events are the best in the book). While the writing is generally clear and the organization sensible, the chapter on voodoo is obviously filler and the final chapter on "Witches Today" is so positive (witches appear as a normal, everyday feature of American life) that some parents and patrons may object. In the burgeoning occult market, however, Garden's book is one of the better titles.

Kirkus Reviews

SOURCE: A review of *Witches,* in *Kirkus Reviews,* Vol. XLIII, No. 20, October 15, 1975, p. 1189.

Still another recapitulation, with two paragraphs on the Loudun possession, an eighteen-page chapter on events at Salem, another on the Inquisition, a few curiosities from the *Malleus Maleficarum,* and a listing of "famous" witches from Circe and Medea on. There's no attempt to provide a viewpoint or any ideas and when Garden does try to make sense of the phenomena her shallowness shows. She reports "two theories" on witches—they are either pagans or devil worshippers—but draws no connection between the two. And as for research she is content to scan the obvious sources and let it go at that, offhandedly concluding that "it seems unlikely that there was very much human sacrifice, if any" in New Orleans voodoo ceremonies. Very little reprocessing here, if any.

Sally C. Estes

SOURCE: A review of *Witches,* in *The Booklist,* Vol. 72, No. 5, November 1, 1975, p. 358.

A lively account of the origins and development of witchcraft throughout the world, primarily in Western civilizations, from Circe and Medea to contemporary witches who practice various forms of pagan religions. Garden includes discussion of medieval beliefs in Europe and Great Britain, tribal African and native American witchcraft, Inquisition tortures, the tests used by witch finders, the Black Mass and other sabbat rites, spells and healing recipes, and voodoo practices and ceremonies. A balanced objective introduction for junior high and high school age readers.

FOURS CROSSING (1981)

Paul Heins

SOURCE: A review of *Fours Crossing,* in *The Horn Book Magazine,* Vol. LVII, No. 4, August, 1981, pp. 431-32.

In a note the author states, "This book is based on things that *could* have happened, not on things that *did* happen." Thus she gives a certain kind of historical and geographical verisimilitude to her narrative, which combines realism and fantasy with varying degrees of success. After the death of her mother, Melissa Dunn goes to live with her grandmother in Fours Crossing, a small town in New Hampshire, and becomes aware of strange happenings caused by a religious rift in the community at the time of its settlement in the seventeenth century. Although the townsfolk march around the green carrying a pine tree on the first day of spring, winter fails to give way to a milder season; and Melissa and her friend Jed discover that an old hermit, who has stolen one of her grandmother's antique silver plates decorated with esoteric lettering, is uttering incantations to keep springtime away. The consanguinity of the townsfolk, the spry cheerfulness of Melissa's grandmother, and the friendly relationship between the boy and the girl are brought to a climax in a somewhat melodramatic but genuinely exciting episode: the abduction and imprisonment of the teenagers in a root cellar by the malevolent hermit. But one wonders whether the putative transplantation of medieval beliefs to a seventeenth-century New England town provides a sufficient basis for the failure of the seasons to change.

THE KIDS' CODE AND CIPHER BOOK (1981)

Harry C. Stubbs

SOURCE: A review of *The Kids' Code and Cipher Book,* in *The Horn Book Magazine,* Vol. LVII, No. 4, August, 1981, pp. 457-58.

I am not sure that cryptology is really a science rather than an art and was tempted to classify the book with the computer ones. The only mechanisms mentioned, however, are the Scytale cylinder and the Cardano grille; and since neither of them is as complex as even an abacus, it seemed safer to separate the categories. Still, encoding and enciphering messages do bear a noticeable resemblance to the simpler levels of computer programming. The book covers only the elementary aspects of the subject but does this extremely well. An amusing narrative is threaded through the presentation, and even though it is rather less believable than a good science-fiction tale, it will probably stimu-late young readers into tackling each mysterious message as it comes; for the lazy, there are solutions at the end of each chapter. Bibliography, glossary, and index.

Phillip Morrison and Phyllis Morrison

SOURCE: A review of *The Kids' Code and Cipher Book,* in *Scientific American,* Vol. 267, No. 6, December, 1992, p. 152.

The experiences of Captain Snow, a cipher expert under sail, and his missing son, Samuel, doing their best to avoid pirates, offer a fictional frame for codes and ciphers. The strength of the book is its admirable practicality for kids. Its first, very simple ciphers—nothing more than backwards spelling—demonstrate the sensible schemes of adding nulls to text, suppressing cases and word spaces and other devices to confuse the unwanted reader. Quickly the scrambling becomes more complicated: twisted paths drawn on a graph-paper plain text, for instance. Then we see the classical transpositions, Caesar's shifted alphabets, checkerboard ciphers and more, all in service as coding and decoding practice.

The menu changes from letter hash toward writing with strange symbols: Pigpen corners and dots, Morse, Ogham, Runes, musical notes, Holmes' Dancing Men. At last the forms combine into one tough message. On to simple code and cipher machines a kid can build and use. Start with the telephone dial, proceed to stencil-like grills and to movable St. Cyr alphabet tapes. There are strong hints on organizing effective and patient work, answers for problems and a good annotated list of other books. This book for young enthusiasts is meant as a guide to ingenious action, not as a history of adult codes nor an exploration of much mathematics of substitutions. Oh, yes, very easily: TA TSAL EHT ETARIP EGRUOCS SI DEDNE.

ANNIE ON MY MIND (1982)

Roger D. Sutton

SOURCE: A review of *Annie on My Mind,* in *School Library Journal,* Vol. 28, No. 10, August, 1982, p. 125.

"Then a funny thing happened. We looked at each other, really looked, I mean, for the first time, and for a moment or two I don't think I could have told anyone my name, let alone where I was." Liza Winthrop, a high school senior, is speaking here of her new friend Annie Kenyon in the beginning of a lesbian love story closer in spirit to Maureen Daly's *Seventeenth Summer* than to Sandra Scoppettone's *Happy Endings Are All Alike.* The young women meet one afternoon in the Metropolitan Museum of Art and quickly become best friends. Although a mutual physical attraction is manifest from the start, Liza and Annie become lovers only after an extensive, wonderfully romantic courtship. By allowing readers to see Annie and Liza first as detailed, vivid characters and then as lovers, Garden gives the relationship a solid resonance that until now has been absent from this genre. Liza and Annie's affair and its repercussions are skillfully developed through Liza's narration in straightforwardly simple, unironic prose. Her struggle to admit her feelings for Annie and subsequently to admit her sexual orientation, "Liza, Liza Winthrop, you are gay," is convincing; and the happy ending, "Annie—I'm free now. I love you. I love you so much!" is a boon for young gay readers who are *not* going through a phase. A significant book, this departs from the fact-packed preachiness of the problem novel to become instead a compelling story of two real and intriguing young women. There have been many books for teenagers, fiction and nonfiction, that give lots of useful and accurate information about homosexuality; here's one that tells *what it feels like,* one that has, finally, romance.

Judith N. Mitchell

SOURCE: "Loving Girls," in *The ALAN Review,* Vol. 10, No. 1, Fall, 1982, pp. 32, 34.

Liza [in Garden's *Annie on My Mind*] is, relatively speaking, a child of privilege. She lives in a secure, well-lighted home, and is educated in a private school which she has attended all her life. The school has begun a fund-raising effort as a last-ditch attempt to stay open. Against that genteel, but increasingly desperate backdrop, the unfolding of the love between Liza and Annie seems particularly imperiled. Annie, by contrast, is poor. Her father drives a taxi, and her school reminds the reader of the first half of the movie *Brubaker,* full of guards and grim overtones.

Nevertheless, when the two girls meet, they fall utterly in love. In fact, one of the ways Garden's novel departs from its antecedents is in the chronicling of the first raptures of romantic love. Both girls are by turn eloquent and taciturn; they both tend to babble of the other when separated; in short, no standard element from the more usual boy-meets-girl scenario has been omitted.

What sets *Annie* apart is both the shared sex of the lovers and Garden's gift for combining the exquisite with the inexorable consequences. And, there are gentle, deeply-satisfying moments, as when Liza realizes that in the ideal kitchen as far as she is concerned, Annie will always be there to feed the cats. The plot dictates that the fate of the girls and of their love will be enmeshed with the struggles of the school to look its best. When discovery occurs, both girls are appalled, but Garden gives Liza a partial victory over the forces of fear and loathing. In fact, the novel opens with Liza and her attempt to impose perspective and focus on her shame. She has been unable to respond to Annie's letters until she retraces their story for herself. The novel's resolution, in which the two arrange to spend their first vacation together, is possible only after Liza has lived inside of and accepted her sexual identity.

That men may love other men, and that boys may love other boys comes as no surprise to anyone who keeps up with adolescent literature. However, the attention given to novels written for adolescents with male characters has failed to extend to the contribution of authors who portray for us the love of one girl for another. For us, teachers and librarians, the knowledge that these books exist may be a neutral or even a positive force. For some parents, perhaps, that knowledge may seem an affront to their values. But for today's young adults the knowledge that these books exist may be fraught with emotion. In *Annie on My Mind,* Nancy Garden argues for these novels when she poignantly captures the relief-cum-gratitude of Liza and Annie, who read Isabel Miller's *Patience and Sarah,* seeking from its pages an imprimatur, an affirmation of their worth, and the validity of their love for each other.

English Journal

SOURCE: A review of *Annie on My Mind,* in *English Journal,* Vol. 73, No. 7, November, 1984, p. 61.

Liza Winthrop, an intelligent and successful high school senior from a wealthy section of Brooklyn, meets Annie Kenyon, a working-class girl, who is a senior at a public school in the city. The two girls quickly become friends, then slowly and sometimes painfully acknowledge that their relationship has both a romantic and a sexual component.

Nancy Garden's characters are complex and real, and her portrayal of their emotions, joys, and struggles is sensitive and honest. Throughout the book, being gay is equated with love rather than sex, and the upbeat tempo of the ending is warm and affirming.

Much of the affirmation comes from two lesbian teachers who serve as healthy homosexual models for Liza and Annie. When these two women lose their jobs after their sexuality is revealed, they react without shame, guilt, or bitterness. In the face of bigotry and discrimination, they remain true to themselves and their relationship and provide Liza and Annie with a valuable lesson.

The overall positive treatment of female homosexuality outweighs the punishment of the teachers, thus this well-written book would make a most welcome addition to any adolescent library. Unfortunately, the close pairing and the unattractiveness of the two girls on the hardback's dust jacket may turn off many teens. The Books for Young Adults program at the University of Iowa found that the students who read this book generally will do so only after the cover is removed.

Jessica Yates

SOURCE: A review of *Annie on My Mind,* in *The School Librarian,* Vol. 37, No. 3, August, 1989, p. 114.

Middle-class New Yorker Eliza Winthrop encounters another seventeen-year-old girl in the Metropolitan Museum of Art, and they instantly become friends. As they share their favourite places in New York, like museums and parks, Liza the narrator (recalling all this a year later) drops hints that they are not only soul-mates but falling in love. 'It felt a little as if we'd found a script that had been written just for us.' You can also guess what the girls have yet to discover, that two of Liza's schoolteachers are lesbians. Annie already suspects she is gay, but for Liza this is the first time she's been in love. Their first kiss is on page 92, with more than half the book still to go. Then comes the guilt; the decision to go on meeting but keep their love secret; recognition of sexual-genital desire; joint reading of *Patience and Sarah.* Then Liza is engaged as the spring vacation cat-sitter for her two favourite schoolteachers. . . .

With their own private place for loving, they have two weeks of heaven, until they are discovered by the scandal-mongering school secretary. Liza's place at college is threatened; so are the teachers' jobs, and she has to decide whether to tell the truth about her love for Annie. This is a beautiful love story which takes the time, unlike many teenage novels, to describe the growth of the lovers' intellectual and social companionship before physical desire takes command. As with Deborah Hautzig's *Hey Dollface,* this book illustrates how difficult it is for sensitive teenage girls to find a partner, and how lesbianism can be right for them, even if it is, as Liza's mother pleads, only a phase.

Two further points. Originally published in the USA in 1982, the book includes an ear-piercing scene. Condemned by teachers as unhygienic, the practice would carry an AIDS warning today. And the story ends with Liza and Annie reaffirming their vows, though love at seventeen doesn't usually last for life, whatever your sexual orientation. Still, I hope school librarians will make this book available to readers from whatever age they judge suitable—and recommend it to teaching colleagues too.

William Sleator

SOURCE: "Annie on My Mind by Nancy Garden," in *Censored Books: Critical Viewpoints,* The Scarecrow Press, Inc., 1993, pp. 80-6.

To begin by demolishing what will almost certainly be a basic misconception about this book: *Annie on My Mind* does not idealize or encourage homosexuality. On the contrary, it is an often painful account of the very serious problems that can result from a homosexual experience. These problems are not only encountered by the teenage protagonists, but also by two adults involved in a long-term homosexual relationship. No one can argue that this book might influence readers to experiment with homosexuality. The book will instead make it very clear to readers that homosexual behavior often causes great suffering.

I also want to dispense right away with what will probably be another cause for concern: there is no explicit sex in this book. No one reading this book will learn anything about actual sexual practices. It is important to emphasize that most teenagers—whether parents realize it or not—have already learned about such things from conversations with their friends, and of course from movies and television. They will not learn about them here.

I must quickly add that although *Annie on My Mind* does not paint a rosy picture of homosexuality, it doesn't condemn it either. The gay people in this book are not pathological misfits. These characters are different from heterosexuals in only two essential ways: they love members of their own sex; and to live in a manner that is natural for them they must deal with a society that often brands them as freaks—and punishes them severely.

The three-dimensional and mostly positive portrayal of gay characters may be one of the most difficult aspects of the book to defend to some people. But I can only point out that if the book were moralistic or preachy, if it were an obviously slanted tract depicting homosexuals as either virtuous martyrs or evil sickos, then it would have no credibility or interest for teenagers, who tend to be skeptical by nature. The fact that gay characters are depicted realistically and often sympathetically only emphasizes, and makes more compelling and moving, the point that homosexual behavior means risking harsh consequences.

The story is a highly believable account of what happens to two teenage girls who begin to realize, with great difficulty and hesitation, that they have feelings of love for one another. Liza, the protagonist, meets Annie, a girl her own age who goes to a different school, at a museum. Their common interest in art and the middle ages is the initial basis for their friendship. Liza's parents are affluent, her father a professional; she attends a private school. Annie's family are Italian immigrants with menial jobs; she goes to a large inner-city school. They both learn a great deal from the differences in their backgrounds.

Much of the plot concerns the situation at Liza's private school, Foster Academy. The headmistress is a stern and forbidding woman who believes that students should be disciplined for minor infractions of often arbitrary rules, and also that students should report such infractions, even when they are innocent mistakes that cause no real harm to anyone. We learn quickly that Liza, who is student council president, is a highly-principled young woman who is willing to put herself on the line for what she believes, even at the risk of getting in trouble herself.

Foster Academy is in financial difficulties. A fund drive is in progress. Any hint of scandal at the school could result in the failure of the fund drive, and the closing of the school.

The affection between the girls progresses very, very gradually. Liza does not even realize what her feelings mean until well into the book. Nothing physical happens until it is clear to them both that they love each other emotionally. In fact, both girls have great difficulty even admitting to these feelings, aware of the great stigma attached to them which adds to the credibility. The physical contact is very tentative at first—a touch, a hug. It is also entirely mutual—neither "seduces," or puts any kind of pressure on, the other. Implicit here—though never stated directly—is the fact that nothing would happen if *both* girls did not want it to. No one can "make" someone else gay if the inclination is not there already. Eventually both girls are able to admit that they very much want to express their feelings completely. But there is, of course, no place where they can make love.

Ms. Widmer and Ms. Stephenson are two of the most popular and accomplished teachers at Foster Academy. They share a house, but no student has ever been there until the headmistress asks the teachers to "volunteer" their house for a student council meeting. At the meeting, Liza learns that the two teachers are going away over spring break, and the boy who usually takes care of their cats is not available. Liza feels comfortable in the house, it is not far from where she lives, and without thinking much about it offers to feed their cats herself. Not until the first day that Annie goes to the house with Liza to help her feed the cats do they realize that now they do have a place.

The lovemaking, as I've already said, is handled with great delicacy and no explicit details. What is emphasized is that it is an expression of love, not merely sex, and is entirely mutual. It is beautiful for both of them.

From books they find in the master bedroom, and because of the way the bedrooms are furnished, the girls realize that the two teachers are lovers and seem to have been together for quite a long time. The vacationing teachers, of course, do not know about Annie, have not influenced Liza in any way, and have no idea what is going on in their house.

Liza and Annie are discovered by the prying school secretary and another student, under conditions that make it obvious they were in bed together. An uproar ensues. The headmistress is terrified that if a scandal occurs it will kill the fund drive and the school will have to close. She tells Liza's parents, which is of course a very painful situation for Liza. For the first time in her life she lies to her parents, telling them that she and Annie were merely "experimenting," and that there was no "real" sexual contact between them. Annie, who goes to a different school and is not involved in the scandal, does not tell her parents, not wanting to hurt them. Liza is suspended from school. She and the two teachers are

required to attend, separately, a disciplinary meeting of the school board of trustees. The board will decide if the incident should go on Liza's permanent record, and whether or not MIT, which has accepted Liza as an architecture student, will be informed of it. Not only is the experience itself humiliating, it is also possible that her relationship with Annie will have a disastrous effect on her entire life.

It is decided that no disciplinary action will be taken against Liza. When she returns to school, many of the students avoid her, others make nasty remarks—though a few of them are understanding and treat her no differently than before.

The two teachers do not get off so easily. It is naturally assumed—erroneously—that they influenced the two girls. They are fired from their jobs and the incident is put on their records, meaning they will never be able to teach again. They are excellent teachers who have inspired many students. Though completely innocent, their lives are now irrevocably changed. Yet the two teachers do not blame Liza and Annie for their misfortune. They tell them that bad things often happen, they can deal with them—it would only be unbearable if they couldn't stay together.

During her first semester at MIT Liza thinks about Annie all the time. Annie, who is studying at Berkeley, has written Liza a letter, but Liza is unable to answer it. Finally, after going through the whole experience in her mind, and knowing that she still loves Annie, she telephones her. The book ends on a positive note; the two of them will be together over Christmas vacation.

It's a curious phenomenon that many parents believe the only way teenagers will find out that sex exists is by reading about it in books. They seem to feel that if they keep books that mention sex away from kids, then kids will never think about sex or want to experience it. The real truth, as anyone who understands teenagers knows, is that peer pressure, the media, and especially adolescent biology itself all combine to guarantee that teenagers will naturally be curious about, preoccupied or even obsessed with sex—even if they never read a single word about it.

So why are some parents so afraid of books? One reason is that these people are aware of the power of literature. They are correct that literature is powerful, but in my opinion they are incorrect as to the nature of its power. They're afraid that literature will influence behavior, when in fact it is peer pressure, and the attitudes of society as reflected in the popular mass media, that have the strongest influence on the way teenagers want to appear, the way they dress and talk, the way they behave with others.

The power of literature is not that it directly influences behavior (except perhaps for political tracts) but that it conveys information. And good literature, by which I mean the kinds of books we are discussing here, conveys accurate information. TV commercials and music videos aren't interested in accuracy—they're interested in selling products any way they can. Other teenagers aren't interested in accuracy—they're interested in coming across as cool and with it. They want to appear to be knowledgeable about the world—and about sex—and to create this impression they often convey information to their peers that is full of dangerous misconceptions.

This is why it is so important that young readers have access to books that will give them a true and accurate picture of the world. But that is not necessarily a line of reasoning that will change the minds of people who want to ban books. In fact, the opposite is often true: it is the information in books that many concerned parents feel is so dangerous.

Since they don't seem to be thinking about the fact that kids are *already* being bombarded with information from so many other sources—remind them. Make it very clear to people who want to protect kids from books that all kids are constantly being fed details about sex, and other controversial subjects, from the media and from their friends. And it is this irresponsible and often false information, *not* the information in good books, that can be truly dangerous to them. Even the most protective parents must realize that they can't isolate their kids from Madonna videos, or from other kids at school who will encourage them to experiment with sex. It is the accurate and unbiased information found in good books that will help to counteract these influences, and give kids a basis for making wise and responsible decisions.

But this line of reasoning may still not have much effect on people who want to ban *Annie on My Mind* because of its specifically homosexual content. Homosexual behavior is highly stigmatized in this society—*especially* among teenagers. Derogatory slang words for homosexuals are just about the worst insults teenagers can inflict on each other. Unlike drugs and heterosexual behavior, which are often regarded as glamorous by young people, teenagers see homosexuality as a brand of shame, probably the most potent reason for being cruelly ostracized. Everyone knows how obsessed adolescents are with peer approval and acceptance. To imagine that reading a book might be enough to motivate a teenager to experiment with behavior that is already so powerfully stigmatized by much more pervasive and controlling influences is so illogical that it verges on the fantastic.

How can you get this fact across to adults who want to keep this book off the shelf? You could just point it out to them, but they may still resist the logic of it. I can suggest several other strategies. However, first I must emphasize that I have far less contact with people who want to ban books than do librarians and teachers. I'm just throwing out ideas for you to think about.

But it seems to me that simply *asking* adults if reading

this book would influence *them* to change their sexual orientation might give them pause for thought. If they argue that teenagers are more susceptible to suggestion, then ask them to consider this question in the context of how they felt as teenagers. Would this book have compelled them to engage in behavior they found personally repugnant, and that would cause most people to treat them as outcasts?

Perhaps this strategy is too personal and direct. Much more important questions to ask are: Why would anybody—especially teenagers—*want* to be gay? What is the attraction of homosexuality? Anyone who seriously considers these questions will have to admit that our society views homosexuality as unattractive, for the reasons given above—which are also emphasized in *Annie on My Mind.*

The fact is that the attraction and rewards of *hetero*sexuality are so overwhelming and undeniable that there can be only one reason anyone would risk losing them—and that is if the risk is inevitable. If it were possible to choose between being straight and being gay, faced with society's sanctions, most people would not choose to be gay. Reading *Annie on My Mind* will do nothing to alter that fact.

What this book *will* do is tell readers a story involving lesbian characters who may be quite different from what they have probably heard about lesbians from their peers or other unreliable sources. The gay characters in this book are ordinary fallible people who have no choice but to express their love in a way that makes many people hate and fear them. To lead satisfying lives under these conditions requires strength and courage. But the book is not a diatribe proclaiming that all gay people are innocent victims who behave perfectly in every situation; they make mistakes, and with luck they can learn from them. Like all good novels, *Annie on My Mind* is more than anything else a believable story about particular individuals.

I have so far said nothing about what effect this book might have on the very small percentage of young readers who do have homosexual feelings. I don't know whether bringing up this issue in defense of the book will help to keep it on the shelf or have the opposite effect (it is not up to me to make that decision) but it should be mentioned here. *Annie on My Mind* will be a blessing for teenagers who are becoming aware that they may be homosexual, and terrified because of it. Once again, it will not encourage them to be actively gay; the book is very clear about the problems gay people must resolve. But it will also let them know that being gay does not necessarily mean one is depraved or mentally ill or condemned to a life of misery and humiliation—which are the messages they have probably heard from other sources. It will show them that gay people can have loving, long-term relationships, that they can have satisfying lives and be productive members of society—that they are different from other people only because of whom they love. It is not an overstatement to say that this information may well save some teenagers from much anguish and self-hatred, and perhaps even do a little to help them adjust successfully to their sexual orientation. But gay readers are not the major issue here.

I'm not sure *any* book can convey to teenagers the astonishing concept that being exactly like everybody else may not be the most important thing in life. But this book might possibly stimulate them to take another look at peer pressure, and to begin to question the validity of judging people on the basis of arbitrary opinions. Whatever readers of this book choose to believe about homosexuality, in a broader sense they will see an example of what it means to be different and experience how it feels to be treated as an outcast. And if they do gain an inkling of compassion from reading this book, then that can only improve their own lives and the lives of those around them.

WATERSMEET (1983)

Mary M. Burns

SOURCE: A review of *Watersmeet,* in *The Horn Book Magazine,* Vol. LIX, No. 5, October, 1983, pp. 580-81.

Set in a small New Hampshire town, the story—a sequel to **Fours Crossing**—builds upon events from the earlier novel in considering the influence of the past upon the present. Nearly a week has elapsed since the kidnapping of Melissa Dunn and her friend Jed Ellison by the crazed hermit who serves as the community's forest keeper, a hereditary position which originated in the seventeenth century. And with his capture and the release of the children, a seemingly endless winter suddenly melts into spring, suggesting that the hermit possibly possesses power to control weather. But the improvement in climate proves a doubtful blessing, for melting snows and heavy rains flood most of the village. To complicate matters, Rhiannon, a mysterious young woman, moves into an abandoned cottage and becomes a divisive element in the community since many of its inhabitants suspect that she is allied with the hermit. Even Jed, influenced by malicious gossip and the developing friendship between his widowed father and Rhiannon, seems willing to think ill of her. Despite his warnings Melissa continues to believe that the woman is a positive force for good—a trust severely tested as the hermit's trial approaches. A succession of events provides a battleground for conflict between the old ways and the new as the hermit manipulates ancient rituals and contemporary fears into an attack on stable community institutions. The novel's strength derives from the author's ability to develop setting and tension; its weaknesses lie in a dependence upon the first book and the less than satisfying reconciliation of fantasy and reality. For those willing to suspend disbelief, however, the flaws are counterbalanced by readability and pace.

PRISONER OF VAMPIRES (1984)

Publishers Weekly

SOURCE: A review of *Prisoner of Vampires,* in *Publishers Weekly,* Vol. 227, No. 4, January 25, 1985, p. 94.

A crypt-like chamber in an old library is the place where a nice boy, Alexander Darlington, is researching vampirism for a school project. When Alexander meets an obliging stranger, Radu, Garden's latest thriller becomes so suspenseful that even steely-nerved readers may scream in fright. Radu is a descendant of the original count of ill fame. His offer to give Alexander source material on his assignment puts the boy in a spell that forces him to help Radu victimize Peggy, the older Darlington child. Thanks to Alexander's brave friend Mike and a wise old neighbor, Mrs. Potter, the villain is done in and the prisoners are saved. The subtly humorous details in Chessare's scary pictures reflect Garden's witty account of events in the characters' lives as ordinary people. The leavening of tensions is welcome in the entirely believable drama.

Trev Jones

SOURCE: A review of *Prisoner of Vampires,* in *School Library Journal,* Vol. 31, No. 6, February, 1985, pp. 73-4.

A melodrama that has all the elements monster lovers want—fangs, bats, bites and blood. Garden tells of the deadly plight of Alexander, a boy noted for his fanatical interest in horror stories and films. A school project that requires primary sources leads him to a private library for rare material on vampires. He is fascinated by, yet fearful of, Radu, the man he meets in the basement (crypt?) where the materials are kept but attributes his uneasiness to his overactive imagination. Each exposure to Radu brings him closer to becoming a vampire, as Radu implants in Alex' mind the true sequence of events regarding Dracula and his contemporaries, as well as the errors in the accounts by Sheridan Le Fanu, Bram Stoker and others. While readers will know exactly what is going on, it is not unbelievable that Alex is oblivious to what is happening because of the power Radu wields over him. The spell is not limited to Alex alone, however, as Radu and his accomplice attack young women, causing a strange "flu" epidemic in which one girl dies. In a wildly terrifying conclusion, Alex is locked in the crypt with the vampires as they plot their escape, using Alex to return them—in their coffins—to their beloved Walachia. A coded message to his best friend, an elderly neighbor's knowledge of garlic, crosses and grains to subvert vampires plus a break-in bring it all to a breath-taking halt. It's a chilling, gory and absurdly funny story with perfectly suited black-and-white illustrations. Horror fans will love it.

Ilene Cooper

SOURCE: A review of *Prisoner of Vampires,* in *Booklist,* Vol. 81, No. 15, April 1, 1985, p. 1119.

Twelve-year-old Alexander Darlington is a vampire buff, and so the undead seem a natural choice for his research project. He finds out more than he bargained for, however, when his studying takes him to the basement of an old library where he meets Radu, a red-lipped specter of a man who has a taste for rare roast-beef sandwiches. It doesn't take long for Alex and his friend Mike to realize something unsavory is going on here. Unfortunately, Radu and his family soon have Alexander at least partially under their influence, and so his lucid moments become fewer and farther between. The "flu" epidemic sweeping the town is the result of the vampires' blood-sucking ways; when Alexander's sister, Peggy, becomes a victim, Al must finally try and cast off the spell so he can save her. Overly long and at times convoluted, this still has an otherworldly appeal that cannot be denied. Garden walks a thin line between spoof and spookiness and, for the most part, carries off the whole affair with aplomb. With its intriguing subject matter, creepy cover, and accessible opening chapters, the book should have no trouble finding an audience.

PEACE, O RIVER (1986)

Bryna Fireside

SOURCE: A review of *Peace, O River,* in *The Horn Book Magazine,* Vol. LXII, No. 1, January, 1986, pp. 91-2.

Nancy Garden's book, *Peace, O River,* to be published in 1986 by Farrar is a valiant attempt to help teenagers understand the tremendous difficulties faced by those who would seek to solve difficult problems through direct nonviolent intervention. When the two communities of River View, which is intellectual and middle class, and Hastings Bay, which is blue collar and working class, square off in the battle of which town will become the dumping ground for a nuclear waste disposal plant, Kate Kincaid has already learned that the foundation for violence had been in place for generations. At first her one-woman efforts to bridge the gap between the two communities through her friendship with Pippa Brown in Regional High are met with a combination of derision from kids on both sides of the river and an ambivalent yearning to see if she can really bring it off. But for each small step in the direction of unity that Kate achieves, there is a terrible component of violence, first to her brother, then to Pippa, and to her most cherished childhood friend. Although the story is compelling, the author fails to convince the reader that nonviolent action based upon principles of respect and love for one's enemy can ever be effective. Garden's characters fail not because their cause is just or unjust but because neither they nor the reader come to understand anything about the theory of nonviolent intervention. If *Peace, O River*

doesn't quite succeed, it certainly raises some important questions.

Kirkus Reviews

SOURCE: A review of *Peace, O River,* in *Kirkus Reviews,* Vol. LIII, No. 1, January 1, 1986, p. 52.

A powerful, beautifully written novel that explores such issues as small-town prejudice, pacifism, and nuclear waste dumping, as well as teen friendship, love, disillusionment, and despair.

Kate, 16, and her family are glad to return to rural River View, Mass., after four years in Providence, R.I. Kate reestablishes her close friendship with her best childhood pal and soon-to-be-first-love, Jon, and discovers that her former classmates have become attractive teens. Kate also finds herself in the middle of an undeclared war at school between the well-to-do River View kids and the supposedly "tough" kids from Hastings Bay, a working-class town across the river. This traditional enmity, shared by adults and teens, is augmented when it's discovered that one of the towns will be chosen as a nuclear waste site. Kate defies convention, befriending Pippa, a Hastings girl. She also appoints herself peacemaker, and with Pippa's and Jon's help throws mixed parties and conducts summit talks with the male teen ringleaders of both factions, remaining obsessed with her mission even after older brother, Dan, is beaten up by Hastings boys. Kate's successes at peacemaking are shattered when Pippa is almost raped by Rab, a River View bully. This incident also destroys an attempt by Kate's father to convince both towns to stand together to try and keep the waste site out. It's only after Jon is killed during a final, desperate teen summit called by Kate that both towns begin to understand the importance of promoting peace and unity.

Garden has presented likable characters caught in a microcosm of the tragic "them/us" situations taking place in the world. Readers will see clearly how such situations develop and will be inspired to think about possible solutions.

Hazel Rochman

SOURCE: A review of *Peace, O River,* in *Booklist,* Vol. 82, No. 13, March 1, 1986, p. 973.

The ongoing feud between two small Massachusetts towns on opposite sides of the river—poorer, blue-collar Hastings Bay and affluent River View—is focused on their common high school. But sophomore Kate, returning to River View with her academic family after four years in the city, is determined to make peace. She becomes best friends with Pippa, a Bay classmate; dates Pippa's macho but sensitive brother, Nick; organizes parties so that students can get to know each other; and, with her father, tries to get the two towns to combine in resisting a proposed nuclear-waste disposal site in the area. Her gentle childhood friend Jon warns her of the danger, the ugly elements on both sides that perpetuate the hatred. When her brother is beaten up and Pippa is attacked and nearly raped, Kate faces grave doubts about her peace-making role and quarrels with her mother and with Nick about where her responsibility lies; then the escalating violence leads to Jon's accidental drowning—which ends the fighting. There are several good scenes (Kate's desperate effort to resuscitate Jon; her appeal at his funeral that "his death be worth something"). However, the characterization is thin; though Garden talks about intense relationships, she doesn't show them. The novel's main interest lies in the conflicts about ideas—is it "heartless" to care more for the general good than for family and friends? Is it "bossy" to try to change things? Does total pacifism always make sense, locally and globally? Young adults will be moved by the candid dramatization of complex issues and values.

Merri Rosenberg

SOURCE: A review of *Peace, O River,* in *The New York Times Book Review,* March 2, 1986, p. 29.

In *Peace, O River,* a somewhat grim, unrelievedly message-driven novel, Nancy Garden uses the contemporary issue of nuclear waste to propel what is essentially a thinly veiled cautionary tale about class and social status.

When 16-year-old Kate Kincaid returns to her childhood home of River View, after a four-year sojourn in Providence, R.I., where her father was the head of a college history department, she finds that the tranquil small town of her Massachusetts childhood has been transformed into a battleground worthy of "West Side Story."

During her absence, the normal tensions of childhood have metamorphosed into a chilling, deadly feud between the middle-class, college-bound River View teenagers and their working-class counterparts from Hastings Bay. When Kate innocently befriends Pippa Brown, a girl from the proverbial wrong side of the tracks, Kate herself becomes the focus of the escalating hostilities.

Kate assumes the self-appointed role of peacemaker in an effort to bring the feud to an end. Yet, as she ruefully discovers, the fight has been going on too long to be easily discarded. As Jon, her childhood friend and now boyfriend, observes, "It's like some kind of holy war, going so far back people just concentrate on their differences and clash with each other without thinking much about why."

The teenagers' antagonism mirrors the schism between the communities' adults, with the haves contemptuously dismissing the have-nots, and the Hastings Bay residents resenting those of the affluent River View. Matters reach a crisis because of the proposed installation of a nuclear waste disposal plant upstream from River View, and the rift is cleverly exploited by those who want to build the plant. For instead of working together to defeat the project, each side clings to self-interest, with predictably dire consequences for all involved.

As for Kate's peacemaking overtures, they are thwarted and mocked. Although Jon wistfully dreams of "kids from both sides being friends. If there were more Kates and Pippas, the whole thing might go away," that dream, which could be a model for the adults, dissolves when Kate's brother, Dan, is attacked and her best friend assaulted. The two sides eventually abandon their senseless feud, but not until after the teenagers confront one another at the river and there is an accidental death.

Miss Garden is a prolific author for young adults who has previously tackled such taboo topics as lesbianism in *Annie on My Mind.* She is clearly at ease and assured in dealing with the violence of the adolescents' world she depicts here. Although she resorts to a maudlin device to resolve the crisis, *Peace, O River* is an effective, if discomfiting book.

Betsy Hearne

SOURCE: A review of *Peace, O River,* in *Bulletin of the Center for Children's Books,* Vol. 39, No. 8, April, 1986, p. 147.

Kate's family moves back to the small town of River View that they had lived in until four years earlier, when Kate was twelve. Her best friend, Jon, is still loving and reliable, and Kate begins to wonder if she is moving from loving him to being in love with him. Jon is one of the very few peers who takes no sides in the feud that rages between the towns, especially between "Viewers" and the adolescents of neighboring Hastings Bay. Kate decides she will end the feud and tries to bring the two factions together, her efforts mirroring the dispute between the towns about the location of a proposed nuclear storage site. An apparent accord is reached by the teenagers when Jon is accidentally drowned while a peace talk is going on, the participants being on boats in the river. There is one small non-event that is barely credible (Jon has been scarred by a knife with a "T" for traitor because he made a friend in the other group but didn't inform the authorities) but the plot and the characters are on the whole solid, the writing style is smooth, and the double indictment of hostility is trenchant.

Barbara Chatton

SOURCE: A review of *Peace, O River,* in *School Library Journal,* Vol. 32, No. 8, April, 1986, p. 96.

Kate, 16, moves back with her family to the small New England town in which she spent her childhood, where she discovers, much to her dismay, that the high school is divided by hostile feelings between students from communities on each side of the river. Kate decides to try to make peace when she discovers she has inadvertently befriended a girl from the other side of the river. Kate's peacemaking campaign is complicated when a nuclear-waste recycling plant is scheduled to be built in one of the towns, alienating the adults of the two towns. Both the problem at the high school and the issue of the waste plant build to a climax when a tragedy strikes in the midst of Kate's peacemaking campaign. This book's strength lies in its characterization of insiders and outsiders and of haves and have nots. Kate's perception of the problems of her community and her ability to empathize with both sides as she tries to find solutions are believable. Her attraction to two very different young men, both of whom have had their integrity tried by day-to-day life, is believable. In addition, Garden has used the metaphors of peace and war effectively to help delineate the difficulties of seeing issues as black or white. Several violent incidents and an attempted rape play roles in the novel but are not graphically described. These are essential to creating the mood of the novel and are presented with discretion. Garden provides rich background and texture in her story of conflict among high school students.

Sherry Blakely

SOURCE: A review of *Peace, O River,* in *Voice of Youth Advocates,* Vol. 9, No. 2, June, 1986, p. 78.

Sixteen-year-old Kate and her family return to the small New England town of her childhood after a near-fatal heart attack forces her father into early retirement. The "twin" towns of Hastings Bay and River View are on the opposite sides of the river with Hastings Bay considered the "wrong side of the tracks." Kids from both towns attend the regional high school and a long-standing feud exists between them, the severity of which even forbids the friendship between two kids from the different sides without strong ostracism from peers. Kate, with the objectivity of a newcomer, befriends Pippa from the wrong side of the river and sets out to end this pointless feud of long-forgotten origin. Trouble between the two towns intensifies and becomes complicated by the fact that a nuclear waste dump is planned to be located in one or the other. This, of course, brings the adults into the fray as they battle to keep the dump out of their respective towns.

The attempted rape of Pippa and another's death occur before the people involved can see the idiocy of their division. The potential for didacticism is strong in this story, but Garden avoids it to a great degree by making the actions of Kate and her supporting cast believable through well-developed characterization. Young adults will especially identify with Kate's depth of feeling and the portrayal of the power and pervasiveness of peer pressure. The book is also a beautiful study of friendship, especially that between Kate and her childhood blood-brother Jon.

THE DOOR BETWEEN (1987)

Kirkus Reviews

SOURCE: A review of *The Door Between,* in *Kirkus Reviews,* Vol. LV, No. 13, July 15, 1987, p. 1069.

Continuing the saga of the seasons begun in *Fours Crossing* (a small New Hampshire town where Celtic traditions and magic still vie with modern customs) and *Watersmeet,* Melissa, 13, discovers that as True Keeper she must make a dangerous journey to the Otherworld.

With the passing of summer, there are changes. Melissa's Dad has been appointed Keeper of the Forest. But, though he's a loving parent, his notions for developing the forest tract (beginning with the destruction of the root cellar that is actually a Celtic temple) prove him a false Keeper. Jed, now in high school, is so involved in new concerns that he is less of a support. Gran is failing. Harvest festival and Halloween provide the arena for the Hermit, escaped from jail and lurking in the background, to send forth the menacing Hunt until Melissa confronts him in the Otherworld and frees the town from his persistent threats.

If this sounds like the middle of a long tale, it is. Clearly, winter is expected to produce a fourth volume. Meanwhile, readers of the earlier volumes will want this one in spite of its problems: Celtic beliefs are less comfortable in Garden's sketchy New Hampshire than in Cooper's vividly evoked Britain; characters have ambiguous roles to no apparent purpose; and the magic is less than compelling. Still, this is at least as strong as the earlier volumes, is fairly well paced, and may serve as a bridge to Cooper's more substantial fare.

Publishers Weekly

SOURCE: A review of *The Door Between,* in *Publishers Weekly,* Vol. 232, No. 29, July 24, 1987, p. 187.

Continuing the story begun in *Fours Crossing* and *Watersmeet,* Garden's new novel puts Melissa at the crossroads of youth and womanhood—at a time when she has the chance to prove herself as the true Keeper who will join the Old Ways with the New. Even before Melissa is sure of her destiny, the hermit who clings to the Old Ways has beset Fours Crossing with problems in the form of wild, destructive dogs, through which bullets—even silver ones—pass. Melissa wins the hermit over with a newfound compassion and maturity. Despite evocative descriptions of a New England town under siege, the story has problems for readers unfamiliar with the other books. There is a laborious retelling of key elements from the past. These contribute to the suspense of the story, but the sheer bulk of references to earlier events ultimately renders the plot more dependent on the other books, rather than less.

Zena Sutherland

SOURCE: A review of *The Door Between,* in *Bulletin of the Center for Children's Books,* Vol. 41, No. 2, October, 1987, p. 27.

Third in a fantasy series (*Fours Crossing, Watersmeet*) set in a small New Hampshire town, this follows the traditional pattern of the struggle between good and evil as Melissa and her friend Jed pursue the mystery of a pack of vicious ghost dogs and try to avert the doom planned for Fours Crossing by the evil hermit of the earlier books. Garden is a writer with strong narrative sense, so that her story has good flow and pace; what her novel lacks is clean structure and the ability to stand on its own rather than depend on iterated references to past events.

Barbara Elleman

SOURCE: A review of *The Door Between,* in *Booklist,* Vol. 84, No. 1, November 1, 1987, p. 476.

The supernatural events besieging Melissa's small New Hampshire town—spun out in *Fours Crossing* and *Watersmeet*—erupt once again. Foreshadowed by the wicked hermit's howling dogs and old, dying Caleb's dire warnings, the action spirals to a climax on Halloween night. With the dog Ulfin, her pet sparrow hawk Llyr, and her friend Jed standing by, Melissa enters the door to the Otherworld, where she meets the fearful hermit and bravely defies him. Although she returns with the stolen Ancient Tools, relics of Fours Crossing's ancestors, bringing peace and normalcy to the village at least for the nonce, both she and Jed know that the fight against their adversaries is not over yet. Garden tempers her good-versus-evil story with touches of homeyness (cocoa in Gram's kitchen and children's three-legged races), a meshing that doesn't always fit comfortably. Nevertheless, Melissa is a resourceful character, and readers of the first two books won't want to miss the third saga in this projected quartet.

Virginia Golodetz

SOURCE: A review of *The Door Between,* in *School Library Journal,* Vol. 34, No. 4, December, 1987, pp. 99-100.

As in the two previous books in this series, *Fours Crossing* (1981) and *Watersmeet,* strands of Celtic mythology and pagan rituals are woven into a modern-day fantasy. Thirteen-year-old Melissa Dunn continues her struggles with the mad hermit who persists in his determination to destroy her tiny New Hampshire village. He is convinced that the people must be punished for growing lax in following the Old Ways, rituals brought by Celtic settlers in the late 1600s. The hermit's evil power becomes evident as Melissa encounters phantom-like hounds that terrorize the villagers, frightening spirits that try to lure her into dangerous situations, and the disappearance of Ancient Tools that have magical powers. Melissa, who is related to the original Keepers of the Old Ways, is set in the task of traveling through the door between the Upper World (living world) and the Otherworld (place of the dead), where she must pass trials to prove her worthiness to become the next Keeper. A mood of suspense and powerful magic pervades the story until almost the very end, when the climax is weakened by a prosaic solution for housing the Ancient Tools. Significant events from previous books are well integrated, allowing this one to stand on its own. Readers interested in fantasies involving Celtic mythology may want to read others, such as Bond's *String in the Harp,* Cooper's "The Dark Is Rising" series, and Garner's *The Owl Service.*

MYSTERY OF THE NIGHT RAIDERS ("Monster Hunters" Series, 1987)

David Gale

SOURCE: A review of *Mystery of the Night Raiders,* in *School Library Journal,* Vol. 34, No. 3, November, 1987, pp. 104-05.

Tedious and mundane rather than suspenseful and eerie, Garden's first book in her new series has no bite. The story—three preteens, using Sherlock Holmes as a role model, investigate the mysterious cause of the malady killing a herd of cows—is laboriously told. When, more than halfway through, they find that vampires are responsible, the abrupt shift is jarring. Neither section is successful, though, as the realistic possibilities are dull and the supernatural explanation is not well developed. When dealing with poisons and cow parasites, the children speak intelligently—and unrealistically—to professionals. Yet when they decide to risk their lives by confronting the vampires, they rely on half-remembered scenes from old movies. For all of the problems with the stereotyped human characters, the vampire characters are even more clichéd, wavering uneasily between serious and tongue-in-cheek descriptions. Considering that Garden has written convincingly about vampires in the past (*Prisoner of Vampires*), this lifeless book is a big disappointment.

Publishers Weekly

SOURCE: A review of *Mystery of the Night Raiders,* in *Publishers Weekly,* Vol. 232, No. 20, November 13, 1987, p. 71.

This is the first Monster Hunters Case, a book that exhibits Garden's talent for spooky tales. Brian's visit to his grandparents' farm isn't as carefree as in the past; the cows are dropping dead of unknown causes, which could bring on financial ruin. A Sherlock Holmes fan, Brian hopes to discover the killer and is joined by Numbles, a scientist, and Darcy, an impetuous athlete.

None of them is prepared for the possibility that something supernatural is behind the deaths of the cows, until it looks as if Brian has become the next dish on a vampire's menu. The story falters only once, when the sleuths outwit the vampires too neatly. After an eerie and suspenseful build-up—and a beautifully evoked Vermont setting—the ending may disappoint but will not dissuade readers from seeking out Monster Hunters Case #2.

MYSTERY OF THE MIDNIGHT MENACE
("Monster Hunters" Series, 1988)

Kirkus Reviews

SOURCE: A review of *Mystery of the Midnight Menace,* in *Kirkus Reviews,* Vol. LVI, No. 20, October 15, 1988, p. 1526.

A light mystery, sequel to *Mystery of the Night Raiders.*

Brian, an eighth-grade swimmer and Sherlock Holmes enthusiast, befriends new kid Ralph, a gangly, socially inept joker with a problem of premature hairiness. When their Central Park apartment building yields such clues as pigeon carcasses, gray hair on the elevator buttons, and eerie midnight howling, Brian summons his old friends and fellow monster-hunters Darcy and Numbles—who suggest that a werewolf is the culprit. Is it the lycanthrope Mareck, the evil teenager living on the roof—or is it, possibly, poor hirsute Ralph, who lately has taken to growling at people?

Unfortunately, there is a tendency toward cuteness here: the chapter entitled "The Second Body," for instance, refers to a pigeon, not a person; and although there are red herrings, Brian does not really engage in deductive reasoning like his hero—rather, he is in the right place at the right time. Meanwhile, Darcy and Numbles, mostly out of town, contribute little to the investigation but make it back in time to help enact a brave rescue. Swimmers will enjoy the authentic swim team details and the splashy finale.

Li Stark

SOURCE: A review of *Mystery of the Midnight Menace,* in *School Library Journal,* Vol. 35, No. 4, December, 1988, p. 103.

The dead pigeon on the sidewalk *could* have died of natural causes—or it could have been killed by wolves which escaped from the Central Park Zoo. The wolves are recaptured, but animal killings continue, and escalate in severity. Brian begins to suspect werewolves—but who? Ralph, a new boy in school, is awfully hairy and produces chilling growls as a dog in the school play. Mareck is a sinister teenager with pointed teeth. Brian

and his friends eventually solve the mystery in this second "Monster Hunters" adventure, and most readers will be several chapters ahead of them. The action drags on tediously. Only those who can accept werewolves on Central Park West or are particularly interested in the New York City setting are likely to persist to the end. Overall, this is a disappointing entry from a usually first-rate writer.

Phillis Wilson

SOURCE: A review of *Mystery of the Midnight Menace,* in *Booklist,* Vol. 85, No. 8, December 15, 1988, p. 709.

Are there werewolves in Central Park? Or, as seems more likely, are the wolves who escaped from the Central Park Zoo responsible for the unexplained demise of various small creatures? Eighth-grader Brian decides to find out. As he assembles the clues, a pattern of attacks emerges that is suspiciously akin to the moon's cycles. Ralph, a new friend in his apartment building, becomes a suspect as does a sinister, aloof older boy who lives in the penthouse. Brian calls on his friends Darcy and Numbles for advice. They research information on werewolves and finally devise, in a race against time, an elaborate scheme to catch the creature. Garden weaves enough clue fragments, false leads, and subplot activity into her tale to keep readers guessing about the final outcome.

JoEllen Broome

SOURCE: A review of *Mystery of the Midnight Menace,* in *Voice of Youth Advocates,* Vol. 11, No. 6, February, 1989, p. 284.

In this second in the "Monster Hunters" series, monster hunting has become an acquired summer skill for Brian and his two Vermont chums, Darcy and Numbles. But now, summer is at an end and Brian is back home in New York City to begin school as an eighth grader. School seems normal enough but inexplicable events keep occurring on the homefront right in his own apartment building, like the discovery of two dead pigeons, a gray dog on the roof, fur caught on the elevator button, and that new boy in the building with an overabundance of body hair. All of the weirdness falls into place if a werewolf is at large. Naturally, Brian needs his Vermont buddies to help him out on this one. When the friends are reunited in the "Big Apple," the werewolf stalking begins in of all places—Central Park—at night!

This is a creepy, moody piece for lovers of the genre and big chuckles for the more skeptical among us. These everyday kid detectives are just a little too crafty and cool or is it that their parents are unbelievably unobservant ninnies who unleash the children on the city or is it the other way around?

📖 *MYSTERY OF THE SECRET MARKS* ("Monster Hunters" Series, 1989)

Molly Kinney

SOURCE: A review of *Mystery of the Secret Marks,* in *School Library Journal,* Vol. 35, No. 14, October, 1989, pp. 117-18.

In a private girl's school in Maryland, Darcy Verona, 13, finds the ingredients for the third case of the Monster Hunters Club. Unexplainable events—flying strawberries, strange tappings, a mysterious code written on stable walls, and a runaway horse—all directed at her roommate, Ro, convince Darcy that a poltergeist is at work. Aided by fellow members, Brian and Numbles, Darcy unravels the mystery surrounding her roommate and the tragic boating accident that killed Ro's family. The code, an important part of the mystery, becomes lost in the jumble, and at climax, everything falls conveniently into place. The supernatural, the code, and the young detectives should have great appeal to children, but this is a fairly typical series mystery, moving jerkily from start to finish without much character development. A possible addition for libraries in which others in the series have been popular.

Marlene Kuhl

SOURCE: A review of *Mystery of the Secret Marks,* in *Voice of Youth Advocates,* Vol. 12, No. 5, December, 1989, pp. 275-76.

A spooked horse, flying turnips, invading frogs, and a mysterious cipher are among the strange phenomena the Monster Hunters encounter in their third adventure. Darcy is a resident at Fox Ridge School where she rooms with Rowena, whose parents and twin sister died in a recent boating accident. Rowena appears assured of winning the equestrian medal for Fox Ridge until a series of unusual events begin to occur. Twice her horse is let out of the barn and the strange x and o cipher appears on the wall of the stall. Then, during competition, the horse's tightly braided mane and tail come undone. At first Tina, a competitor, is suspected of sabotaging Rowena's bid for the award but the reappearing cipher and other strange events, all directed at Rowena, lead Darcy to conclude that something supernatural is taking place and that this is a case for the Monster Hunters. She calls in her cohorts from the two previous adventures and they successfully solve the mystery.

This series does a nice job of blending elements of mystery, humor, and parapsychology. The cipher is logical but still challenging (it is included as an appendix). Mystery and psychic phenomena fans will enjoy this title. The other titles in the series are *The Mystery of the Night Raiders* and *The Mystery of the Midnight Menace.*

Phillis Wilson

SOURCE: A review of *Mystery of the Secret Marks,* in *Booklist,* Vol. 86, No. 8, December 15, 1989, p. 830.

Fans know they can count on Garden for out-of-this-world characterizations when her monster-hunting gang stalks the supernatural. This time it's a poltergeist whose funny, then increasingly vengeful antics, appear directed at Darcy's boarding school roommate, Rowena. Ro, as she's called, was recently orphaned in a sailing accident when her parents and twin sister drowned. Messages written in cipher accompany the pranks, prompting Darcy to call in her friends, Brian and Numbles. For readers willing to go along with the premise of a ghostly apparition, the stunts are cleverly rendered within a boarding school setting, and the psychological circumstances as to which twin actually drowned brings forth a theme of self-acceptance. A letter-cipher symbol key is provided.

📖 *LARK IN THE MORNING* (1991)

Kirkus Reviews

SOURCE: A review of *Lark in the Morning,* in *Kirkus Reviews,* Vol. LIX, No. 10, May 15, 1991, p. 670.

A gay teenager hides two runaways while trying to help the more disturbed youngster find a reason to live.

Even before she takes on Lark and her brother Jackie, Gillian Harrison is having trouble managing the fact that she's gay, hasn't told her close-knit family, and will soon be leaving her beloved Suzanne to go to Oregon State. But when she finds two kids camping out in an old hut and living by stealing food and blankets from summer cottages, she can't bring herself to report them: they've already been betrayed too often, especially by their own abusive father. Still, helping them poses risks: Lark, a mercurial, intense 15-year-old, plans to commit suicide as soon as Jackie is safely housed with their aunt. When Gillian leaves a note for her already-worried family—they have no idea why she has been so secretive and unlike herself—and drives the two to New Hampshire, she's terrified that she isn't doing what's best.

Like Lisa and Annie in Garden's **Annie on My Mind** (1982), Suzanne and Gillian are likable girls trying to deal responsibly with their sexual preference. Here, their story is almost a backdrop to Lark and Jackie's tale—or would be, except that theirs isn't entirely in the foreground either. Nevertheless: an involving, smoothly written novel with believable characters and engrossing issues.

Roger Sutton

SOURCE: A review of *Lark in the Morning,* in *Bulletin of the Center for Children's Books,* Vol. 44, No. 10, June, 1991, p. 236.

It's her last summer before college, and Gillian is spending it with her family at their summer cottage. Someone has broken into the cottage, taking food and bedding—and Gillian's diary, which contains details of her growing awareness of her lesbianism and her love affair with best friend Suzanne. Garden's *Annie on my Mind* was a groundbreaker in its romantic treatment of a gay theme; the present book is notable in that it presents a gay relationship as just one (and a subordinate one, at that) story element. The central plot concerns Gillian's befriending of Lark, a younger girl who with her little brother has run away from an abusive home. Lark is a tough but ultimately vulnerable stereotype of the Gilly Hopkins mold; the dialogue between Gillian and Lark is windy and therapeutic, as Gillian convinces the bitter girl that the world is not necessarily a terrible place. Despite Suzanne's dire (and sensible) warnings not to get too involved, Gillian takes the two children to their kindly aunt in New Hampshire, leaving the younger girl feeling much better about herself: "Some of what you said began making sense, and I began feeling maybe I was okay after all, and maybe there were some good things around after all . . . I—I think I do want to be alive." The love story between Gillian and Suzanne is also talky, but authentically so, and gay and straight kids both will find them an easy pair to like.

Dona Weisman

SOURCE: A review of *Lark in the Morning,* in *School Library Journal,* Vol. 37, No. 6, June, 1991, pp. 122, 125.

Gillian Harrison, 17, is looking forward to her sixth consecutive quiet summer in Pookatasset, Rhode Island with her parents. Things take an unexpected turn when they find that their cabin has been broken into, although the thieves have taken only food and household needs. When Gillian discovers that her diary, with revelations about being in love with her best friend, is among the missing items, she worries about who the thieves might be and what they might do with the diary. She discovers that the culprit is a suicidal young girl and her five-year-old brother who have fled their abusive alcoholic father and are trying to reach their aunt's home in New Hampshire. By interweaving the issues of child abuse, suicide, runaways, and homosexuality with ethical questions regarding helping "outlaws" and lying to family and friends in order to protect others, Garden offers readers much food for thought. Even the inconsistent credibility of the story reinforces the ideas that there are often many ways to handle a situation, that mistakes are often made along the way, and that it is difficult to untangle a web once it has begun. Many readers will question the resolution of the problems, but few will escape personal reflection while reading this novel.

Publishers Weekly

SOURCE: A review of *Lark in the Morning,* in *Publishers Weekly,* Vol. 238, No. 25, June 7, 1991, p. 67.

Gillian's family arrives at their summer home to find it has been burglarized, and Gillian is horrified to discover that her diary is one of the stolen items. But when she accidentally locates the thieves—two abused, runaway youngsters—she doesn't mind sharing her food, clothing and even the contents of her diary. Garden attempts to combine two unrelated plot lines that cross paths but never quite merge. Her novel's most vividly written portions concern Gillian's romantic attachment to her best friend, Suzanne; unfortunately it is given short shrift through brief letters and action that has occurred largely in the past and has little bearing on Gillian's adventures with the runaways. Uncharacteristically slow-moving for this author, the runaways' story generates neither sympathy nor interest. However, the persistent reader will likely wade through the lugubrious plot to see Gillian and Suzanne's relationship through to its conclusion.

Stephanie Zvirin

SOURCE: A review of *Lark in the Morning,* in *Booklist,* Vol. 87, No. 21, July, 1991, p. 2040.

Even though she still hasn't told her parents that she's a lesbian, Gillie is comfortable enough with her sexuality to have confided in her longtime friend, Brad. But she does have a secret she's keeping even from him. She's discovered two abused runaways—little Jackie and his older sister, Lark—living in a hut on Gillie's parents' property, and she's afraid that if she turns them in, 14-year-old Lark will kill herself. Young adult novels with lesbian protagonists are rare; that makes this book worthy of notice. But that's not enough to counteract the slow-moving story, which is loaded with melodrama about "The Problem" (Lark found out about Gillie's being gay when she stole and read Gillie's diary) and about how "unhappy people are." Though forced, Gillie's struggle to find a safe haven for Lark and her little brother is easy enough to read, and characters are adequately sketched. But whether readers will care about what's going on is questionable.

Rebecca Sue Taylor

SOURCE: A review of *Lark in the Morning,* in *Voice of Youth Advocates,* Vol. 14, No. 3, August, 1991, p. 170.

After graduation, 17-year-old Gillian Harrison spends the summer as she has spent many others, at the family cottage in rural Rhode Island. It is a good summer, filled with the comfort of knowing that her life is working out as she had hoped. Gillian will be going to Oregon to forestry school in the fall, a goal she has worked toward for several years. Her best pal Brad, has grudgingly accepted her revelation of a committed and intimate relationship with Suzanne, her childhood best friend. He is honest that he is disappointed but is working hard to understand the type of life that Gillian and Suzanne hope to build for themselves. Gillian has a close and loving relationship with parents whom she respects. She hasn't told them yet about her new relationship with Suzanne, but she is pretty sure they will accept it when she does. All of Gillian's contentment and feelings of "all is right with the world" are shattered when she discovers that two young runaways are hiding in an old hut not far from the family cottage. Lark and Jackie have been stealing from cottages in the area in order to survive and the police are pushing hard to solve the burglaries.

Much of the tension of the story revolves around Gillian's dilemma over what is best for Lark and Jackie and whether she should involve adult authorities in helping to solve their problems. By the end of the story Gillian has lied to her parents and Brad and withheld information from Suzanne in her attempts to "do what's best" for these two children running from an abusive home.

Garden, author of the remarkable *Annie on My Mind*, again creates an honest and realistic look at love, truth, and responsibility. Gillian and Suzanne are mature young women from stable homes who have come to accept what they are and reach for what they want. In contrast, Lark's confusion and despair are all the more apparent. Particularly poignant are the scenes between Gillian and her family as they try to "fix her up with boys" and she ponders how and when you tell your parents the truth, and why and when you don't—a significant question that many young people must eventually face.

MY SISTER, THE VAMPIRE (1992)

Sally Estes

SOURCE: A review of *My Sister, the Vampire,* in *Booklist,* Vol. 88, No. 21, July, 1992, p. 1931.

Garden takes the traditional vampire story and weaves it into a shivery tale for kids. Their parents called away and their aunt suffering from a sprained knee, 12-year-old Tim and his sisters, Sarah, 13, and Jenny, 5, are on their own at the family's somewhat isolated summer cottage at Starfish Harbor, Maine. Their first crisis is a houseful of bats; the second is the mysterious wasting illness that strikes Sarah's friend Emily and then Sarah herself as well as other children in the area. Finally comes the realization of the root of the problem and the nature of the elusive new owners of deserted Spool Island. Along with the chills and thrills are well-realized, likable characters whose interactions, both sibling wrangling and support, ring true; the absence of adult supervision is believable; and the resolution of the vampire dilemma is satisfying as well as true to the genre. Sure to be popular with those who like to be scared but not terrified.

Publishers Weekly

SOURCE: A review of *My Sister, the Vampire,* in *Publishers Weekly,* Vol. 239, No. 30, July 6, 1992, p. 56.

This novel—whose subject is handled more seriously than its title suggests—concerns Tim, 12, who worries that his sister Sarah may actually become a vampire. A profusion of bats in their summer cabin brings in two peculiar exterminators. Shortly thereafter, Sarah appears under the same hypnotic spell as their friend Emily, who has become so pale, gaunt and listless. Emily's brother John, convinced of strange goings-on in the Maine resort town, joins Sarah and Tim in ferreting out the truth. Garden's main protagonists are quick-witted and courageous, yet deceptive: they fib to their temporarily absent parents about being under the guardianship of an aunt who, in fact, has postponed her visit. The dialogue often sounds strained and the essentially bizarre story is slow in starting. It grows needlessly convoluted (a drug-runner theory, for example, is thrown in as a possible reason for the strange goings-on), but there's enough tension overall to appease SF/horror fans.

Lyle Blake Smythers

SOURCE: A review of *My Sister, the Vampire,* in *School Library Journal,* Vol. 38, No. 9, September, 1992, p. 252.

Unexpected events leave Tim, Sarah, and their younger sister, Jenny, alone and unsupervised at their family's summer cabin in Maine, where their pleasure in having total freedom is dampened by frightening incidents. Hundreds of bats invade the house; the girl in the neighboring cabin is wasting away, haunted by disturbing dreams; and Sarah seems to be developing the same symptoms. Dark strangers appear in the community, using a formal and stilted form of speech suggesting that English might not be their native language. Then Tim and Sarah face the fact that the bites on their necks are not from mosquitoes and that vampires have come to Starfish Harbor. Can the kids track them down and destroy them before Sarah becomes a full-fledged bloodsucker? Prim, rigid Great-aunt Clara seems to be a deliberate stereotype intended for comic relief, and the adult vampires are straight out of an old horror movie, but this scary adventure has likable child characters, good dialogue, and a nice relationship between the two sets of siblings in the neighboring cabins. Readers will figure out what's going on long before the kids do (and they take a ridiculously long time to see the light), but this could work in the book's favor by building suspense as the characters slowly put all the clues together and move toward the exciting climax. Acceptable entertainment if you don't analyze it too closely.

MYSTERY OF THE WATCHFUL WITCHES ("Monster Hunters" Series, 1994)

Chris Sherman

SOURCE: A review of *Mystery of the Watchful Witches,* in *Booklist,* Vol. 91, No. 11, February 1, 1995, p. 1004.

In their fifth case together, monster hunters Darcy Verona and her friends Numbles and Brian must unravel two mysteries: they have to find out who's trying to create a modern-day witch-hunt with Darcy's eccentric Aunt Eleanora as the target, and they need to learn how the Salem witch trials are related to what's happening in their town. In the process, they risk their own lives by traveling back in time to witness the trials of Martha Cory and Tituba. They also encounter a ghost who aids them in their efforts and learn the truth about Aunt Eleanora. Laced with accurate information about the Salem trials, Garden's story is an entertaining, fast-paced mystery, with steadily building tension that will keep the pages turning.

DOVE AND SWORD: A NOVEL OF JOAN OF ARC (1995)

Kirkus Reviews

SOURCE: A review of *Dove and Sword: A Novel of Joan of Arc,* in *Kirkus Reviews,* Vol. LXIII, No. 19, October 1, 1995, p. 1428.

In the winter of 1429 a young peasant girl from the French village of Domremy sets off to do the unthinkable: to lead an army that will wrest the throne from the Britisher who rules France and restore it to the French dauphin, Charles, in the process ending the bloody Hundred Years War. Jeanne d'Arc's story is told by Gabrielle, a girl learning the art of healing and midwifery. Gabrielle joins the Maid, as Jeanne is called, because her skills are desperately needed on the battlefield. Disguised as a lad, she observes Jeanne's successes and the ultimate treachery that result in her death at the stake for heresy.

Not just another retelling of a familiar episode—in the hands of Garden, the entire historical period comes brilliantly alive. The pert and plucky Gabrielle delivers readers into a peaceful village life and then vividly summons the carnage of war. In the process, she grows up too soon, just as the Maid dies too young. In a season of plenty for fine historical fiction, Garden's gripping, gritty tale ranks as one of the best.

Publishers Weekly

SOURCE: A review of *Dove and Sword: A Novel of Joan of Arc,* in *Publishers Weekly,* Vol. 242, No. 42, October 16, 1995, p. 62.

Venturing far from the contemporary Brooklyn setting of her *Annie on My Mind,* Garden takes up the story of Joan of Arc—and proves that she is as compassionate and imaginative with the vagaries of 15th-century French history as with the problems of 20th-century gay teens. Wisely, she centers her novel on a fictional character, Gabrielle, who comes from the same village as "Jeannette" and who follows her into battle, serving as a medic. Accordingly Garden need not convince the read-

er that saints have spoken with Jeannette and sanctioned her mission; it suffices that Gabrielle believes this. Instead of emphasizing religion, the author brings into high relief the dramas of daily life in rural homes, in combat, in sheltered convents. Gabrielle, who serves as narrator, is essentially a modern creature—she chafes at the inferior status of women, wants a career as a healer, abhors war (Jeannette nicknames her "friend dove")—and her views act as a bridge between the reader and the unfamiliar mores of a remote past. While Garden fills her narrative with the ringing voices of soldiers proclaiming the glory of their campaigns, she employs Gabrielle's more cautious tones to send an anti-war message. Her strategically plotted novel achieves the highest goals of historical fiction—it vivifies the past, robustly and respectfully, then uses its example to steer the audience toward a more courageous future.

Ann W. Moore

SOURCE: A review of *Dove and Sword: A Novel of Joan of Arc,* in *School Library Journal,* Vol. 41, No. 11, November, 1995, p. 119.

The "sword" refers to Joan of Arc, the feisty, impatient 17-year-old who—guided by the voices of saints—leaves her small village to free France from the English. The "dove" is a fictional teenager, Gabrielle, a friend of Joan's who uses her healing skills to aid French soldiers. Gabrielle is an intelligent, clever young woman who loves, mourns, ponders, and learns a great deal in the course of the novel. She narrates the story, which begins with Joan's first visions in 1425 and ends with her death by fire six years later. This is a fascinating and well-written historical novel, filled with rich details, evocative descriptions, and interesting characters. It is a masterly addition to the recent medieval fiction by Karen Cushman, Frances Temple, and others. However, there are minor problems. The map omits more than it includes and is poorly designed. Although most unfamiliar terms are defined in context, there are a few glaring exceptions. It's hard to keep track of the many characters, and some are carefully introduced only to suddenly vanish. Finally, not all of Garden's facts agree with established research on Joan, most notably the reasons she was burned at the stake.

Roger Sutton

SOURCE: A review of *Dove and Sword: A Novel of Joan of Arc,* in *Bulletin of the Center for Children's Books,* Vol. 49, No. 5, January, 1996, p. 158.

Different in tone and scope from Barbara Dana's *Young Joan,* which recreated only Joan of Arc's early life, *Dove and Sword* is an old-fashioned historical epic, told in the voice of that most convenient of narrators, the fictional friend to the famous. Gabrielle is accompanying Jeanne d'Arc's mother Isabelle on a pilgrimage to Le Puy, where she convinces Isabelle to allow her to join her friend Jeanne, who has already left home on her mission and is raising an army in Tours. To keep safe from rapacious advances, Gabrielle disguises herself as a boy, serving as a page and healer in Jeanne's army; the disguise nevertheless does not prevent Gabrielle from conducting a passionate romance with the young nobleman Louis. Due to some awkward insertions of historical information into conversations, the book moves slowly, and the dialogue often has the ring of costume drama: "'Gabrielle,' Pierre cried urgently, 'do not linger! The brigands may still be nearby!'" Still, Gabrielle, the "dove" of the title, is an appealing foil to the fiercer Joan (the sword), and Garden introduces some feminist themes and questions into the story that are enlightening without becoming anachronistic.

Mary M. Burns

SOURCE: A review of *Dove and Sword: A Novel of Joan of Arc,* in *The Horn Book Magazine,* Vol. LXXII, No. 2, March, 1996, p. 206.

Writing with passion and concern, Garden has constructed a readable, well-paced historical novel focusing on the life, mission, triumphs, trial, and execution of Joan of Arc. Most of what is known of Joan's life comes from the records of her trial for heresy as well as from the chroniclers of the period, as noted in the introduction. Garden's novel is enriched by considerable research into the social and political history of the times and by an examination of the arms and armor of the period. By presenting Joan through the eyes of a fictional friend, Gabrielle, the novel allows for latitude of interpretation without skewing facts. Gabrielle's accessible narration of events provides a bridge between twentieth-century readers and Joan, the peasant girl of Domremy whose insistence on the authority of her visions enabled her to ensure the coronation of Charles the Dauphin as the rightful king of France. Uneducated but intelligent, untrained in the science of warfare but a superb military leader, a child who rose above the strictures of society and gender to become celebrated as a hero and a worker of miracles, Joan remains an enigma, a challenge, and an inspiration. Garden captures this ambivalence in Gabrielle's account of her journey with Joan's army as a healer, her romance with a young nobleman whose tragic death epitomizes the inevitable loss of lives attendant on military ventures, and her witnessing of Joan's death at the stake as a witch and heretic. At the conclusion of her narrative, she who once followed Joan and who had played at war as a child utters a plea for peace very much in tune with contemporary—or rather, universal—attitudes.

📖 *GOOD MOON RISING* (1996)

Kirkus Reviews

SOURCE: A review of *Good Moon Rising,* in *Kirkus Reviews,* Vol. LXIV, No. 16, August 15, 1996, p. 1234.

Following a successful stint in summer stock, Jan fully expects her drama teacher, Mrs. Nicholson, to give her the best part in the school play, *The Crucible.* After auditions, however, a new girl gets the role. Hurt though she is, Jan admits that Kerry is perfect for the part and reluctantly accepts the job of stage manager. Jan works closely with all the cast members, including the arrogant male lead, Kent. She also coaches Kerry, finding herself more and more attracted to her. The feeling is reciprocal, and it isn't long before Jan and Kerry are in love, a fact they attempt to keep secret. Kent, however, who harbors a dislike of Jan, launches a vicious campaign of rumor and innuendo, first among the cast and then throughout the school. Meanwhile, Mrs. Nicholson succumbs by degrees to cancer, leaving Jan to direct the play, which further infuriates Kent. What opened as a tender tale becomes a story of the outrages heaped on any teenager suspected of being different, although Kent's deep, almost pathological hatred, chalked up much later to homophobia, is never adequately explained in the early pages. This is not *Annie on My Mind* (1982) revisited, but it covers similar territory.

Claudia Morrow

SOURCE: A review of *Good Moon Rising,* in *School Library Journal,* Vol. 42, No. 10, October, 1996, p. 147.

Jan is a high school senior, just back from summer stock and hoping for the role of Elizabeth in the school production of *The Crucible.* When a new student named Kerry gets the part, Jan's larger-than-life mentor, Mrs. Nicholson, assigns Jan to be stage manager instead. Then, as stand-in director when Mrs. Nicholson falls ill, Jan coaches Kerry. Eventually, the two realize that they are sexually attracted to one another. Other cast members notice, too. Some harass them, threatening the success of the play; others think it's nobody's business. Told in third-person narrative, this is a straightforward story of teen romance with a '90s twist. It gets off to a slow start, but tension builds as the young women receive increasingly disturbing hate messages. They finally "come out," affirming their feelings and undercutting the clique that had targeted them. Allusion to Salem witch hunts of the 17th century is obvious but effective, and the novel is well paced. Some may call this story a rehash of Garden's *Annie on My Mind,* but it's more of an update. Although M.E. Kerr's *Deliver Us from Evie* is stronger, *Good Moon Rising* will find grateful readers among some of the same kids who appreciated that book.

Sally Estes

SOURCE: A review of *Good Moon Rising,* in *Booklist,* Vol. 93, No. 3, October 1, 1996, p. 340.

Another lesbian love story by the author of the widely praised and widely condemned *Annie on My Mind* (1982), this novel, set in a small New Hampshire town, will have more immediacy for YAs since it is not cast in a retrospective mode. High-school senior Janna Montcrief is sure she will get the part of Elizabeth Procter in this year's junior-senior play, Arthur Miller's *The Crucible;* but enter Kerry Socrides, new junior and a dead ringer for Elizabeth. Bitter at first at being appointed stage manager instead of getting the role, Jan comes to realize her directing potential and thrills to the feeling of putting a patchwork of scenes together to create a total, powerful play. She also gets to know and like Kerry by coaching her and gradually becomes aware that her feelings for Kerry go beyond friendship. The love relationship between the two girls evolves tentatively until the first quick, soft kiss on the lips. The sex scenes lack explicitness beyond the fumbling fondling typical of teen romances. As Jan and Kerry begin spending more and more time together, suspicions arise, and gay baiting begins, led by the determinedly macho Kent. Characterizations ring true, with one exception: Jan's summer stock gay friend, Raphael; although he plays a pivotal part in the girls' coming out, we just don't get to know him well enough to get beyond the stereotype; also, his letter to Jan seems contrived to get AIDS information across. Otherwise, the school scene, the play rehearsals, the interactions between characters, and the support the girls get when they finally squelch the rumors by coming out are natural and believable. Garden offers no easy answers: true, the gay bashers are suspended, but what will happen when they return to school, and how will the student body at large react to Jan and Kerry's love?

Publishers Weekly

SOURCE: A review of *Good Moon Rising,* in *Publishers Weekly,* Vol. 243, No. 44, October 28, 1996, p. 83.

A lesbian romance takes center stage as a high school mounts a production of *The Crucible* in this sensitive if not altogether convincing drama. Jan begins her senior year with her confidence primed from years of starring roles and a stint in summer stock; she is stunned when a new girl, Kerry, gets the lead in the play and she herself is made the assistant to Mrs. Nicholson, the drama teacher. Her anger and jealousy evaporate quickly as she and Kerry get to know each other and discover a powerful mutual attraction. And when Mrs. Nicholson withdraws due to grave illness, Jan realizes the teacher has been preparing her to step in as director. Trouble arises in the form of Kent, the male lead, who is unaccountably homophobic and who appropriates the anti-witch rhetoric of *Crucible* characters to start a campaign against Jan and Kerry. Garden's descriptions of teenagers confronting their gay sexuality are just as affecting and candid here as in her *Annie on My Mind,* but the book as a whole is less successful. The author takes shortcuts in characterizing the supporting cast, rendering them as fairly predictable types rather than individuals: the faithful friend, the quaint maiden aunt, the flamboyant retired actress. Kent in particular is underdeveloped; as a result, parallels between the hysterical witchhunting

of the play and Kent's anti-gay malice seem programmatic rather than provocative.

Marilyn Bousquin

SOURCE: A review of *Good Moon Rising,* in *The Horn Book Magazine,* Vol. LXXII, No. 6, November, 1996, pp. 743-44.

Before Jan Montcrief and Kerry Socrides even realize they are in love with each other, Jan's affectionate wannabe-boyfriend, Ted, jokes, "You two got some kind of secret society going or something?" But Kerry's whimsical response, "It's called the SSS—Secret Society Society," turns out to be no joke. Because when superstud Kent, who plays lead opposite Kerry in their small-town high school's production of *The Crucible,* suspects that the young women are lesbians, he leads the cast in a relentless barrage of harassment. Tormented and terrified, Jan and Kerry exercise their only apparent option: they publicly deny their relationship. The irony is that the harder they work to hide their relationship, the more strained and tense it becomes. By spotlighting Jan and Kerry's struggles—both within themselves and with each other—as the obvious, painful result of imposed silence, Garden illuminates the significance of Audre Lorde's proverbial, "Your silence will not protect you." She takes us inside the dynamics of homophobia so that we not only sympathize with Jan and Kerry for unwittingly spawning their own "secret society," but we realize our outrage at how this guise of protection endangers their integrity. Ultimately, unlike Annie and Liza who were [mercilessly] victimized by homophobia a decade and a half ago in *Annie on My Mind,* Jan and Kerry challenge it with mature, determined style. And, even though Garden occasionally interrupts their passionate story with textbook information about homophobia and sexuality, she never abandons their essential romance, which, in the end, promises us that a "good moon still rises."

Janice M. Del Negro

SOURCE: A review of *Good Moon Rising,* in *Bulletin of the Center for Children's Books,* Vol. 50, No. 4, December, 1996, p. 134.

Jan, a high-school senior, is just back from summer stock and looking forward to getting the lead role in the school production of *The Crucible.* But the arrival of a new girl, Kerry, brings more than one surprise: Kerry gets the part Jan wanted, and Jan falls in love with her. This is pretty standard stuff in the high-school romance genre, the only curve being that Jan and Kerry are momentarily stunned at discovering they're lesbians. The characters are stock—the drama coach who is dying of cancer, the homophobic male lead who's going to kiss Kerry "like a real man," the flamingly gay actor who advises Jan about homosexuality, and Jan's former boyfriend who is a paragon of acceptance and support all fall into predictable place, their lines down pat. The "outing" of Jan and Kerry and the following antagonism, while not pleasant, basically fizzles out due to lack of interest, and everybody lives happily ever after in rosy clouds of tolerance. Clichés and naïveté abound, but then that's what romance novels are all about.

Jennifer Fakolt

SOURCE: A review of *Good Moon Rising*, in *Voice of Youth Advocates,* Vol. 19, No. 5, December, 1996, pp. 269-70.

Garden, who gave us one of the first honest, sensitive portrayals of two young women in love in the brilliant *Annie on My Mind,* offers us another thought-provoking story of homosexual love. Crafted with integrity and empathy, *Good Moon Rising* brings us the romance of Jan Montcrief and Kerry Ann Socrides—and it is destined to be as controversial as its ground-breaking predecessor.

Jan, beginning her senior year in high school, has her heart set on the part of Elizabeth in the fall production of Arthur Miller's *The Crucible*. It will be Jan's last big play of her school career. When Jan loses the part to the graceful new student, Kerry, and must settle for a role as stage manager, she is bitterly disappointed. Jan's resentment vanishes, however, as she begins to realize the creative aspect inherent in managing and directing, and as she gets to know Kerry, whom she coaches in lines and blocking during their spare time. Their instant friendship metamorphoses into a deeper relationship—love. Jan experiences an awakening, an understanding of her true identity, which explains her confused dreams, and why she cannot be more than a friend to her chum Ted. Jan is confronted with the growing suspicion of the rest of the cast about her relationship with Kerry; the hostility of the play's arrogant male lead, Kent; the tragic death of her long-time mentor, drama coach Mrs. Nicholson; the mistrust of Kerry's Aunt Elena; as well as hateful notes and phone calls. The strength of Kerry's and Jan's love is put to the test. They face difficult choices: to make their love public and take both the criticism and support it elicits; to keep their love a secret, pretending to be straight; or even to stop loving.

Jan's and Kerry's relationship is elegantly played out against the backdrop of *The Crucible,* which Mrs. Nicholson calls a play "about misguided power and the cruelty of falsehood and about the sin of blindly following the common herd." *Good Moon Rising* is a case of art imitates life imitates art: Garden uses the energy of Miller's powerful drama to parallel the tensions in the high school, and in Kerry's and Jan's lives and minds. The attitudes of many of the students against homosexuality mirror the fanatical beliefs of seventeenth-century witch hunters; accusations, persecutions, fear, and prejudice boil to the surface, forcing Kerry and Jan to decide whether to submit to pressure to fit in with the majority, or to be true to themselves and their hearts.

The choice Jan and Kerry make to embrace the truth and their love is one of affirmation. It marks a beginning: the rising of the good moon, of promise. Many obstacles are left unresolved—the critical opinions of the girls' families remain, for instance—but there is anticipation of joy ahead as well.

Garden never plays us false. Jan and Kerry are unique, relatable characters, whose emotions are portrayed with sincerity. *Good Moon Rising* does not have the radiance that *Annie on My Mind* flashes with; instead, it possesses a more thoughtful shine of truth and hope. The love of Jan and Kerry, true but fragile, survives its first trial by fire and emerges the stronger for it. Here is an important, sensitive addition to the increasing body of excellent gay and lesbian fiction for young adults.

Additional coverage of Garden's life and career is contained in the following sources published by Gale Research: *Authors and Artists for Young Adults,* Vol. 18; *Junior DISCovering Authors; Something about the Author Autobiography Series,* Vol. 8; and *Something about the Author,* Vol. 77.

Mel Glenn

1943-

Swiss-born American author of fiction and poetry.

Major works include *Class Dismissed! High School Poems* (1982), *Class Dismissed II: More High School Poems* (1986), *Back to Class* (1989), *My Friend's Got This Problem, Mr. Candler: High School Poems* (1991), *Who Killed Mr. Chippendale? A Mystery in Poems* (1996).

INTRODUCTION

Teacher and writer Mel Glenn brings firsthand knowledge of his audience into his widely-acclaimed poetry and fiction for junior high and high school readers. Glenn is best known for his poetry anthologies that provide snapshots of high school life as seen from the eyes of students. His poems are written in free verse, using uncomplicated language that makes them accessible to many adolescents who would otherwise steer clear of the genre. He is praised for his realistic portrayal of high-school life and his unique ability to capture adolescent experiences from the students' perspectives. As Luvada Kuhn notes, "All characters are fictional but their struggle to bring the world into focus is real, totally honest, and realistically appealing." Glenn presents high school life in a straightforward, no-holds-barred fashion, and addresses often unpleasant topics head-on. His subject matter varies widely from history tests, prom dates, and first loves to divorce, suicide, and murder. His characters, as diverse as his themes, are "engaging, very real kids" of different races, religions, and sexual orientations. What makes Glenn's poetry so meaningful is his close connection with the age group he portrays. Chris Sherman commented that "Glenn's years as an English teacher have given him a sure ear for the dialogue of adolescents and an understanding of the problems that bedevil them." Glenn understands adolescence as a common experience that binds people together across age groups. "Though styles and fashions may change," he once remarked, "there are certain common denominators in being a teenager that connect all generations—the feelings of being alone, different, in love, in conflict with parents. No matter how old we grow there will always be a part of us that will be sixteen years old."

Biographical Information

Born in Switzerland, Glenn moved with his family to the United States in 1945—his father, a doctor, was a U.S. citizen. "If I have one picture of my father," Glenn commented, "it is one of him sitting at the dining-room table writing in English (and sometimes Yiddish) on yellow legal pads. If there is a gene on my chromosomes that shouts 'writer,' it is one that he passed on to

me." Glenn was raised in Brooklyn, New York, and grew up watching baseball, especially the Brooklyn Dodgers, and playing basketball in the local park. Glenn's love of sports ultimately fueled his writing career. While a student at New York University, he worked as a reporter for the school newspaper. He covered games at Madison Square Garden and wrote feature stories and columns. "I thought at the time I would become a journalist," Glenn recalled. However, journalism was not to be Glenn's trade. He graduated from college with a B.A. in 1964, a year that was darkly veiled in the aftermath of a national tragedy: the November, 1963 assassination of President John F. Kennedy. Following Kennedy's death, Glenn joined the Peace Corps, and it was during this period that he embarked upon the profession that would ultimately provide the subject matter for his successful poetry and fiction. "I became an English teacher in a small town in Sierra Leone, West Africa," he explained. "I found out, between bouts of dysentery and rains that lasted for days, that I really loved teaching. I loved it all—the class discussions, marking reports in fractured English. But most of all I loved the students I taught." Indeed, Glenn's love for his students manifested itself in his later poems told from their perspectives. He went on to earn a M.Sc. from Yeshiva University in 1967, and later took a teaching position with a junior high school in his native Brooklyn. In 1970, he joined the teaching staff of Lincoln High School, the same school from which he had graduated. He also married another teacher, Elyse Friedman, on September 20 of that year. Glenn still teaches at Lincoln and lives in New York City with his wife and two children, Jonathan and Andrew. In 1982, with the publication of his first poetry anthology, *Class Dismissed! High School Poems*, Glenn launched a successful writing career.

Major Works

Class Dismissed! High School Poems is a collection of seventy free-verse poems, each written in first person and bearing as its title the name of a fictitious student. The poems explore a wide range of experiences: a first kiss, a rejected invitation to the prom, a pregnancy. The collection is illustrated with black-and-white photographs of teenagers. Several years later, Glenn followed this anthology with its sequel, *Class Dismissed II: More High School Poems*, which also contains seventy poems in the same format, covering topics such as a first car, a first love, divorce, and rape. A *Kirkus Reviews* critic highly praised the collection, saying, "These monologues are so immediate and true to the real concerns of this age group that they beg to be shared with both young people and their parents." *Back to Class*, another poetry anthology, follows the same structure, but adds poems told from the point of view of teachers and faculty members, as well, with themes ranging from romance to retirement. In praise of Glenn's style, a contributor to *English Journal* said of this collection, "Glenn captures through sentence structure, word choice, and divine inspiration the three-dimensional maze through which kids wander." He followed these successes with *My Friend's Got This Problem, Mr. Candler: High School Poems*. This collection chronicles a week in the life of high school guidance counselor Mark Candler. Each poem introduces a student who comes to talk to Mr. Candler. Glenn again adds something new, with several poems about parents' meetings with Mr. Candler as well. Praising Glenn's ability to bring his fictional characters to life through poetry, Diane P. Tuccillo commented, "In your mind you can 'see' Mr. Candler responding and in between the lines you can 'hear' his reactions." Another poetry anthology with a slightly different twist is *Who Killed Mr. Chippendale? A Mystery in Poems*. In this collection, Glenn translates the classic "whodunit" motif into his famous format of poetry vignettes that chronicle the reactions of various people to the murder of English teacher Robert Chippendale. This time, Glenn stretches far beyond the limits of his previous works, including poems not just from students, faculty members, and parents, but from police officers and other members of the community as well. By the end, the killer has been discovered and apprehended. In *Mr. Chippendale*, "Glenn delivers," as Sharon Korbeck recognized, "a starkly realistic view of modern high school life."

Awards

Class Dismissed! High School Poems made the American Library Association (ALA) Best Books for Young Adults list and received the Society of Children's Book Writers' Golden Kite Honor Book plaque, both in 1982. *Class Dismissed II: More High School Poems* made *School Library Journal*'s Best Books list in 1986 and received the Christopher Award in 1987. *My Friend's Got This Problem, Mr. Candler* made ALA's Best Books for Young Adults list in 1992. *Who Killed Mr. Chippendale? A Mystery in Poems* was one of ALA's Top Ten Best Books for Young Adults in 1997.

GENERAL COMMENTARY

Karen Kutiper

SOURCE: "Poetry for Young Adults," in *The ALAN Review*, Vol. 13, No. 2, Winter, 1986, p. 19.

"I can go home again," said Mel Glenn, author of *Class Dismissed*, an award winning collection of original poems. Glenn currently teaches English in the same Brooklyn high school from which he graduated. Using the *Spoon River Anthology* as a philosophical base, Glenn's own collection is a series of sensitive mini-portraits of high school students. Noting that teen-agers today have the same questions and same problems as previous generations, even though times change and fashions change, Glenn told the ALAN audience that the main purpose of his collection was to help students find a clearer image of themselves. He also encouraged teachers to let students write about themselves in order to develop this clearer image.

TITLE COMMENTARY

📖 *CLASS DISMISSED! HIGH SCHOOL POEMS* (1982)

Stephanie Zvirin

SOURCE: A review of *Class Dismissed! High School Poems*, in *Booklist*, Vol. 78, No. 20, June 15, 1982, p. 1361.

English instructor Glenn has put together his own special class of high school students via 70 first-person poetry profiles that capture some of the best and some of the worst about being a teenager. Kevin McDonald's world brightens when a girl kisses him; Grace DeLorezo expresses loneliness and fear at the thought of her pregnancy; Lisa Goodman moans over her "averageness";

Allen Greshner aches when his invitation to the prom is refused. Glenn even includes several interrelated poems—Christine Leader regrets the theft of her necklace while, on the next page, Thomas Kearns congratulates himself on its theft. The poems are spare, plainspoken, and revealing expressions about adolescence, laced with touches of humor and poignancy. And each conjures up a vivid, individualized image that gives life to the students on Glenn's fictitious roster. Readers need not be poetry enthusiasts to appreciate this unpretentious, on-the-mark offering.

James H. Campbell

SOURCE: A review of *Class Dismissed! High School Poems,* in *Voice of Youth Advocates,* Vol. 5, No. 3, August, 1982, p. 44.

At first I thought these verses were *by* high school students. Later I discovered they were *about* high schoolers and by a balding, pipesmoking, ex-Peace Corps high school English teacher. The verses poignantly utter what high schoolers (hopefully) feel, think, write. Any parent would enjoy them, too. Snapshots of students interspersed are superior to the cover photos.

Zena Sutherland

SOURCE: A review of *Class Dismissed! High School Poems,* in *Bulletin of the Center for Children's Books,* Vol. 36, No. 1, September, 1982, p. 9.

For each poem in this collection, the title is the name of an adolescent student; photographs of teen-age boys and girls illustrate the book. Many of the poems are related to school: peers, teachers, hopes for college, or to events that took place in a school setting (ripping off a girl's gold chain in the hallway, pulling a prank in Spanish class) but most are about the worries, interests, and experiences that are common in the adolescent years. Each poem is in first person, free verse that is direct and concise, candid in tone and varied in subject and attitude. Not great poetry but good poetry written with perception and sympathy.

ONE ORDER TO GO (1984)

Stephanie Zvirin

SOURCE: A review of *One Order to Go,* in *Booklist,* Vol. 81, No. 3, October 1, 1984, p. 211.

The last place Richie Linder wants to be is in school. He would much rather be stretched out in front of his TV set or better yet working on a local newspaper. But dissatisfaction with school is only a symptom of Richie's actual difficulty. His real problem is his father, a short-tempered, obstinate man who is more able (and seemingly more willing) to converse with the customers of his luncheonette than he is to communicate with his own son. The attentions of an oddball girl classmate give Richie some welcome relief from problems at home, but matters there continue to worsen until the issue of college causes a father/son blowup that can't be ignored. The pace is rather slow here, but principal characters are distinctive and credible (Richie comes across as more mixed-up than right about everything, and his father is shown to have a less abrasive side kept hidden away), and Glenn deftly manages to bring the story to a close on a positive note without resorting to a pat resolution.

Deborah M. Locke

SOURCE: A review of *One Order to Go,* in *School Library Journal,* Vol. 31, No. 4, December, 1984, p. 89.

Richie Linder, 17, views high school as a boring trial, and he longs to drop out and pursue his vague ambition of becoming a news correspondent. The barrier to this and all of Richie's plans is his dictatorial father. Concerned and ambitious for Richie's future, Mr. Linder is nevertheless gruff and quarrelsome, failing continually to give affection or support to his son. He demands that all of Richie's free time be spent working in his luncheonette. Bolstered by the support of his new friend, Lana—herself an aggressive, eccentric misfit who is also unhappy at home—Richie determines to confront his father with his own plans for his future. Glenn's first novel unfortunately lacks the perception, sensitivity and poignancy of his award-winning book of poetry for YAs, *Class Dismissed.* Characterizations and relationships, although colorful, are not well developed, and the story's final scenes are disappointing. Teachers and parents suffer under Glenn's pen, although the novel's most sympathetic character is a sincere and helpful guidance counselor. Accessible to poorer readers, *One Order to Go* may appeal to YAs who share Richie's dissatisfaction with school and difficult relationships with parents, but they will gain few new insights here.

PLAY-BY-PLAY (1986)

Zena Sutherland

SOURCE: A review of *Play-by-Play,* in *Bulletin of the Center for Children's Books,* Vol. 39, No. 8, April, 1986, p. 148.

This is a sports story and it does have some game descriptions, but—despite the title—the book is not a series of game sequences precariously held together by thin threads of plot. It's a robust story about a boy who feels that he is average, has ups and downs in his family relationships, and an even more see-saw record of best-friendship. Jeremy is in fourth grade, he's the narrator, and he always feels eclipsed by best friend Lloyd, a superior athlete and vocal about it. When excited, Lloyd is derisive about Jeremy's performance, and Lloyd is usually excited during a game. All this comes to a head when a new gym teacher introduces the class to soccer. The boys learn that girls can be good players and good sports, Lloyd learns to restrain himself, and Jeremy learns to be tolerant in a story that has good pace and balance, and that is convincing as the product of a fourth-grader.

Kirkus Reviews

SOURCE: A review of *Play-by-Play,* in *Kirkus Reviews,* Vol. LIV, No. 7, April 1, 1986, p. 545.

Readers who like Matt Christopher's sport stories will find more of the same here, though they will have to make their way past extended episodes of breast-beating on the part of the main character before they get to the action.

Jeremy is not particularly athletic, a fact of which best friend Lloyd often reminds him. But when a new gym teacher introduces soccer, Jeremy feels this might be one sport he can play well, and though he suffers doubts, in the clutch he comes through. Characters are all much simplified and sound older than the fourth-graders they are supposed to be. Jeremy also seems too self-analytical; he spends part of the first chapter telling us how average he is, and later he says—actually says!— "I want to feel good about myself."

The author does show how individual effort and teamwork can dovetail, and readers who understand Jeremy's frustration will also enjoy his sense of accomplishment.

Carolyn Phelan

SOURCE: A review of *Play-by-Play,* in *Booklist,* Vol. 82, No. 18, May 15, 1986, p. 1395.

Glenn depicts the relationships that exist and evolve among the members of Jeremy's fourth-grade class as well as among the members of his family during the weeks when the class is learning to play soccer. Jeremy, typically the last one chosen for the basketball team, is glad to find a new sport. In hopes of excelling, he practices at home and, though he doesn't score the winning goal in the Big Game, he does contribute to his team's victory. Although Glenn tries to show some character development in his protagonist, such as in Jeremy's early flat statement, "Girls stink," which eventually gives way to the admission that the girls helped the team in the final game, it comes off sounding a bit wooden. Much better are his depictions of generally unsympathetic characters such as Jeremy's friend Lloyd, whose bursts of outrageous anger are totally convincing, or Jeremy's father, a rather stiff person who finds it easier to give his son sententious advice than the most perfunctory display of affection. A somewhat uneven novel with a sports theme and an appealing dust jacket showing a likable group of boys and girls playing soccer. Since they appear to be around twelve years old,

the book may find an audience among older readers despite the author's potentially limiting choice of fourth graders.

Publishers Weekly

SOURCE: A review of *Play-by-Play,* in *Publishers Weekly,* Vol. 229, No. 22, May 30, 1986, p. 67.

There's plenty of tenderness in this down-to-earth story about an average boy who wants to be more than average. When a new coach introduces soccer at school, Jeremy sees his chance. As in most rousing sports stories, team effort and friendship are the things that really matter, but the practices and games are clippingly handled and carry those themes. Jeremy has more talent than he knows—not just for accurate kicking but for loyalty, perception and forgiveness. He has to be strong to stand up to his best friend Lloyd, a sports nut who "gets crazy and says mean things" when he competes. Although the author never settles whether girls are welcome or not on the motley team, he is sensitive to Jeremy's need for encouragement and warmth from his father and coach.

Robert Unsworth

SOURCE: A review of *Play-by-Play,* in *School Library Journal,* Vol. 32, No. 10, August, 1986, p. 92.

Jeremy is no athlete, or so he believes. But soccer is for everyone, and when the new gym teacher introduces it to Jeremy's fourth-grade class, Jeremy finds that he can not only hold his own but also that he can help win the big game against the school's best. Jeremy's problem comes from friends like Lloyd, who plays for nothing but winning; the conflicts between the boys are the basis of the plot. Other than that Jeremy is given a nice family and an ordinary life; there is even a sister with whom he fights, in this case an older one. Competently written, yet the story is unlikely to hold the interest of any but the easiest-to-please, especially since it involves a sport that is hardly new to many schools today.

CLASS DISMISSED II: MORE HIGH SCHOOL POEMS (1986)

Kirkus Reviews

SOURCE: A review of *Class Dismissed II: More High School Poems,* in *Kirkus Reviews,* Vol. LIV, No. 19, October 1, 1986, p. 1522.

Another group of 70 poems about the high-school experience, from the author of the acclaimed *Class Dismissed!* Brief vignettes in voices of fictional characters capture youth's pathos, humor, boredom, rebellion and aspirations: Elizabeth, whose play goes unread because she's too shy to share it, and Craig, whose paper is dismissed as plagiarism because it's too good; Candie, so pretty no one sees beyond her face; dropouts and the college-bound; paired points of view: twin brothers; Vinnie, who describes his car as he would a girlfriend, and Mary, who's bored with an overextended relationship with Vinnie; Jennie Tang and David Klein sharing real love opposed by all their parents; Justin's empathy for his divorcing parents, contrasted with Mary Louise's rebellious anger at hers—Glenn ranges among the many intense experiences suffered in coming of age. Simply phrased in the vernacular of youth, these monologues are so immediate and true to the real concerns of this age group that they beg to be shared with both young people and their parents. The occasional portrait photos speak as eloquently as the poems.

Kathleen D. Whalin

SOURCE: A review of *Class Dismissed II: More High School Poems,* in *School Library Journal,* Vol. 33, No. 4, December, 1986, p. 116.

As in **Class Dismissed,** the subjects of these poems are fictional adolescents based on actual students. The 70 poems are fresh and crisp; they cut to the bone of adolescent life. The book is in perfect balance, with Glenn's honest poetry set in clear print with a clean layout and Michael J. Bernstein's striking photographic portraits of teenagers. Whether presenting "Ian Sinclair's" view of the future ("That fallout makes for nuclear winter /and winter kills") or "Hayes Iverson's" flush of sports ("The ball is up / Universe waits") or "Min Than's" relocation to America ("I write letters to my father /Telling him of my progress /I have not heard from him in over one year /I hope he is alive"), each poem makes its subject live. From homework to relationships to proms to graduation to life beyond—the class may have been dismissed at the end of the book, but the poems remain firmly in readers' minds and hearts.

Booklist

SOURCE: A review of *Class Dismissed II: More High School Poems,* in *Booklist,* Vol. 83, No. 7, December 1, 1986, p. 567.

Glenn, whose first **Class Dismissed** evoked angst-ridden adolescence through free-verse profiles of a mythical group of teens, is back with another round of students (and a few grads this time) who are grappling with the same stuff of life. Concerns of Glenn's new "class" range from religion, romance, and sports success to rape, divorce, and the bomb; the first-person perspectives are still by turns funny, poignant, joyful, and right on the mark. Yet lines such as "I'd rather bask / In the warm glow of her candle-lit face" may be too schmaltzy for even the most romantic-at-heart teenager, and the stylized e. e. cummingsish inclusions (absent from the first book) seem more interesting as exercises in writing poetry than as insights into adolescence. Despite these preten-

sions, however, Glenn's class of '86 has simplicity and candor going for it and will likely find a comfortable home right next to its predecessor.

Roger Sutton

SOURCE: A review of *Class Dismissed II: More High School Poems,* in *Bulletin of the Center for Children's Books,* Vol. 40, No. 6, February, 1987, p. 107.

In this well-intentioned collection, Glenn has written 70 first-person poems, each attributed to a fictional high school student, many accompanied by a photograph of the "poet." (This may cause confusion among some readers.) While the poems do speak to adolescent concerns—school, romance, family, the future—they do so in the shallow and banal style of lesser contributions to the school paper: "I know that people are/ Starving in Africa . . . But I got my own problems . . . If I don't get the car tonight,/ My social life is history./ The world stinks." That adolescents write like this is beyond dispute, but in reading, they are certainly capable of greater sophistication than this collection offers.

Luvada Kuhn

SOURCE: A review of *Class Dismissed II: More High School Poems,* in *Voice of Youth Advocates,* Vol. 9, No. 6, February, 1987, p. 297.

Wendy wants a "slow, easy ride to maturity," while Nolan looks in the funhouse mirror and says "I wonder if I'll ever see a clear image of myself." This sequel to the earlier **Class Dismissed** presents 70 new poems based upon the emotional lives of students. All characters are fictional but their struggle to bring the world into focus is real, totally honest, and realistically appealing.

Full-page, black-and-white photographs by Michael Bernstein capture the determination and vitality of youth. The poetry grabs the reader and doesn't let go. Young people will relate to these poems, recognizing themselves and their peers, delighting in the humor and poignancy of these poetry profiles. Teachers will find the book useful with students in creative writing or in poetry evaluation and appreciation sessions. The author's honest approach is inspiring.

📖 *BACK TO CLASS* (1988)

Kirkus Reviews

SOURCE: A review of *Back to Class,* in *Kirkus Reviews,* Vol. LVI, No. 20, October 15, 1988, p. 1527.

A new series of ingenuous, blank-verse vignettes from the author and photographer of the **Class Dismissed** collections. Glenn gives each of his 65 subjects—all fictional high-school teachers or students—an individual voice, though many have needs, problems, or strengths in common: fears of standing out from the crowd or of failure; resentment against parental control or life in general ("I have been in this school for ten years . . . too long"); or anxiety over social expectations ("The only important questions are:/How far to go,/How far to let him go,/How far to let yourself go . . . "). Some face life with brash confidence, others are obviously heading for a fall ("I don't have time to study history./I'm making it instead"), but in general the tone is upbeat and hopeful. As in the previous books, candid, lively black-and-white photos portray natural-looking teenagers and older adults in relaxed poses. The simple language and clearly stated themes make this accessible to the most unpracticed poetry reader.

Stephanie Zvirin

SOURCE: A review of *Back to Class,* in *Booklist,* Vol. 85, No. 7, December 1, 1988, p. 634.

The author of *Class Dismissed* and *Class Dismissed II* adds teachers to the high school roster he conjures up for his latest book of poetic profiles. There's a sprinkling of enthusiasm among his newest subjects: an instructor who truly loves his work, a student who knows what he wants from life, another grateful for a patient teacher. By and large, though, the composites are a struggling lot, coping with worries about their futures, grappling with personal problems—adoption, suicide, romance, retirement—and alternately tuning in and out within the boundaries of each classroom. The poems range widely from the poignant to the precious. The accompanying black-and-white photographs provide substance, and Glenn's unadorned acknowledgment of familiar concerns gives the volume charm and appeal.

Kathleen Whalin

SOURCE: A review of *Back to Class,* in *School Library Journal,* Vol. 35, No. 5, January, 1989, p. 98.

Back to Class offers the same clear, fresh insight into the adolescent world as Glenn's earlier books of poems, *Class Dismissed* and *Class Dismissed II.* This collection of 65 poems includes the thoughts, pains, and hopes of high-school students and, for the first time, of some of their teachers. Mr. Henry Axhelm, math teacher whose hobby is ham radio ("It's nice to talk to people/Who are far away") is contrasted with Mr. Joshua Cantor, who teaches physics ("I like the state I'm in/Teaching the laws of nature/ In an ordered universe"). Glenn uses the language of each subject to illuminate the person's interior world. The wonder of this is the reality of the personalities. Bernstein's black-and-white photographic portraits capture the feelings of the poems. But, beyond the photos, the people live because of the words, words that create real thoughts of real people.

Elizabeth A. Belden and Judith M. Beckman

SOURCE: A review of *Back to Class,* in *English Journal,* Vol. 78, No. 2, February, 1989, p. 84.

Mel Glenn has produced a third book of seventy free-verse poems providing authentic insights into the world of adolescents. In this volume he adds teachers and groups poems into subject fields such as English, fine arts, special education, and counseling.

Glenn captures through sentence structure, word choice, and divine inspiration the three-dimensional maze through which kids wander, searching, often futilely, for warm strokes of acceptance.

Student teachers beginning to grapple with the confusing psychology of adolescents will update their faded high-school memories with this book's balance of humor, poignancy, and hard realities. Teachers will immediately recognize themselves and peers, especially the special ed teacher Joan Gladstone. Kids reading Glenn's poems attest to the honesty of his soul-deep understanding of their celebrations and frustrations.

Tony Manna

SOURCE: A review of *Back to Class,* in *Voice of Youth Advocates,* Vol. 11, No. 6, February, 1989, pp. 300-01.

Having previously given us two popular collections of poetry—*Class Dismissed* and *Class Dismissed II*—poet-high school teacher Glenn has set out once again to capture the psychology, spirit, and machinations of the emotionally-charged everyday world of a public high school. This time around Glenn infiltrates the lives and sentiments of a varied assortment of individuals who populate the halls and classrooms of the Everyschool he has fashioned out of the stuff of real life. The collection contains over 60 brief, mostly free-verse poems which, according to Glenn's introductory note, provide "fictional composites of the many students and teachers I have worked with through the years." The collection's overall structure is both intriguing and tightly-knit: each of the 15 sections opens with a first-person narrative poem in which a teacher or one of the school's support staff talks about his or her life within and outside of school, thereby setting the stage for the first-person revelations of several students who have close contact with the adults we just encountered. Throughout, Glenn reveals the personal insights of both professionals and students who are disaffected, or cynical, or turned off as well as those who are dedicated, or hopeful, or quite content to be where they are—emotionally, physically, and psychologically. In terms of its design (it is enhanced with photographic portraits of some of the people Glenn introduces), its subject matter, and its voice, the collection is well tuned. But in terms of its literary value, it often runs headlong into serious artistic trouble. For one, some of the poems slip into melodrama ("Mr. Joshua Cantor" and "Jaime Milagros"), condescension ("Mr. Robert Winogard" and "Diana Marvin"), sentimentality ("Mr. Henry Axhelm"), or triteness ("Andrea Pulovsky"). And—largely because much of the material is so mired in the particular that it fails to embrace the kind of universals that we expect good poetry to illuminate— there is the issue of whether many of the revelations are in fact poetry rather than the rendering of personal feelings, however deeply felt they may be, in poetic form and structure. There is little here of the type of compression and compactness which allows the poet to suggest a network of meanings far beyond the surface meanings which the words and thoughts supply. Also absent from far too many of these portraits is the type of vivid imagery which helps us to forge crystal-clear pictures of thought and feeling and action. Often, the poems tell about, rather than show, the pleasure and pain Glenn so carefully observes.

SQUEEZE PLAY: A BASEBALL STORY (1989)

Kirkus Reviews

SOURCE: A review of *Squeeze Play: A Baseball Story*, in *Kirkus Reviews*, Vol. LVII, No. 4, February 15, 1989, p. 292.

More than a year after their triumph on the soccer field *(Play-by-Play)*, Jeremy and his athletic friend Lloyd have a new problem: a teacher with a mission. Mr. Shore may be new to the school, but he takes command from the first day—organizing the class into "squads" and "platoons," delivering lectures on competitive spirit, barking out orders and blame. The other sixth-graders roll their eyes and try to adapt, but Jeremy slowly comes to a boil. Shore then organizes a pair of baseball games with archrival Penwell Prep and "suggests" that everyone sign up for the team; even Jeremy, a poor player, feels pressured to join. Penwell wipes them out in the first game; but after some intense practice, Jeremy's team comes back in the second when he overcomes his fear of the inside pitch and delivers the winning run. Glenn contrasts Shore's ineffectual bullying and frequent losses of temper with the calm wisdom of Jeremy's new friend and sounding board, Mr. Janowicz, a gentle old storekeeper who faces loneliness, would-be vandals, and a heart attack with quiet courage. By the end, Jeremy has gained some self-confidence; Shore, if not completely reformed, has at least been shown that his way isn't the only way to learn; and readers will have observed all this while enjoying both brisk sports-action and spirited conversation between Jeremy and his friends. Themes and lessons stick out all over this, but don't slow the pace.

Todd Morning

SOURCE: A review of *Squeeze Play: A Baseball Story*, in *School Library Journal*, Vol. 35, No. 9, May, 1989, p. 104.

The characters from *Play-by-Play*, Glenn's earlier novel about soccer, are back in a baseball novel. Sixth-grader Jeremy and his classmates are faced with a hard-driving teacher, formerly a military man, who wants the class to learn discipline. He challenges a local prep school to two baseball games, and sets up a series of intense practice sessions to get ready. This proves difficult for Jeremy, who is not a natural athlete. Jeremy receives good advice, however, from the man who owns a local card shop. The somewhat complicated elements of the plot move along swiftly, and the descriptions of the baseball action are exciting and accurate. Characters are believable, and, as in all good sports fiction, they learn more about both themselves and the game that they play by the book's end.

Carolyn Phelan

SOURCE: A review of *Squeeze Play: A Baseball Story*, in *Booklist*, Vol. 85, No. 18, May 15, 1989, pp. 1648-49.

Entering sixth grade, Jeremy and his classmates encounter a strict teacher who announces his intention to mold their minds through hard work, discipline, and baseball. Shy of pitched balls after being hit in the eye, Jeremy rebels. But when he is ostracized by his classmates, he discovers the pain of exclusion and learns to fight his fear. As in Glenn's previous book about the same children, *Play-by-Play*, Jeremy's best friend, Lloyd, is his foil. Subplots involving family relationships and Jeremy's friendship with a fatherly older man give the story dimensions beyond the struggles seen in the classroom and on the baseball field. Although the story occasionally seems contrived, the clearly drawn characters and conflicts will keep readers involved.

Zena Sutherland

SOURCE: A review of *Squeeze Play: A Baseball Story*, in *Bulletin of the Center for Children's Books*, Vol. 42, No. 11, July-August, 1989, p. 275.

There's a new sixth-grade teacher, and Jeremy and his classmates soon learn that Mr. Shore is a martinet whose barking voice and rigid discipline extend beyond the classroom to the baseball diamond. Jeremy, who tells the story, becomes increasingly resentful as Mr. Shore persists in domineering and bullying his team. It is the protagonist's elderly friend Mr. Janowicz, a gentle but far from timid Holocaust survivor, who has the courage to confront Mr. Shore at the end of a game in which, despite Shore's hostility, Jeremy's class wins when Josie is brought in as a relief pitcher. The characters are convincing, the writing style is adequate, the situation is handled with insight; the weaknesses of the book are the structure (predictable and monotonous) and the slow pace.

MY FRIEND'S GOT THIS PROBLEM, MR. CANDLER: HIGH SCHOOL POEMS (1991)

Kirkus Reviews

SOURCE: A review of *My Friend's Got This Problem, Mr. Candler: High School Poems,* in *Kirkus Reviews,* Vol. LIX, No. 15, August 1, 1991, p. 1010.

Drawing on their experience as high-school teachers, Glenn and Michael J. Bernstein continue their series of vignettes of urban teenagers, begun with *Class Dismissed!* In his usual simple, natural language, Glenn captures the emotional concerns and conditions that dozens of students bring to "Mr. Candler," a fictional school counselor: Ivy Hayden doesn't know what to do when her mother hits her; the world will end if Miki London doesn't do well in the baton-twirling tryouts; a new transferee glibly promises to stay out of trouble; several teens separately declare their love/hate for a teacher, or their attraction for one another, in nearly identical words. The poems are well matched with Bernstein's seemingly casual black-and-white portraits, catching natural, unfeigned expressions. The poet's vision is upbeat: problems are there to be solved, anger and confusion can be worked through, the future is always promising.

Barbara Chatton

SOURCE: A review of *My Friend's Got This Problem, Mr. Candler: High School Poems,* in *School Library Journal,* Vol. 37, No. 9, September, 1991, p. 288.

This collection follows the successful format and style of Glenn and Michael J. Bernstein's earlier collaborations, *Class Dismissed,* and *Class Dismissed II,* and *Back to Class,* using black-and-white photographs of young people along with first-person monologues about their lives and concerns. This volume focuses on a series of visits with Mr. Candler, a high school guidance counselor. Glenn uses a device he has employed before with some success—pieces that give contrasting points of view on the same experience, adding the thoughts of parents this time. As in the previous works, readers meet a variety of students struggling with academic, career, social, family, and personal problems. All of the young people are sympathetically portrayed. Some of the parents appear to have created insoluble problems for their children, but most are as concerned and struggling as their offspring. Candler, who has the last word, provides a reassuring message—that there will be a caring adult to listen when these youngsters need one.

Chris Sherman

SOURCE: A review of *My Friend's Got This Problem, Mr. Candler: High School Poems,* in *Booklist,* Vol. 88, No. 2, September 15, 1991, p. 134.

Mel Glenn has done it again. His fourth book of poetry about high school students is another winner. This time, the reader follows guidance counselor Mark Candler through the course of a school week, as he meets students and parents who come for advice, come to complain, or come just to shoot the breeze. Glenn's years as an English teacher have given him a sure ear for the dialogue of adolescents and an understanding of the problems that bedevil them, and in relatively few lines, he's able to empathetically depict each of Candler's visitors.

Diane P. Tuccillo

SOURCE: A review of *My Friend's Got This Problem, Mr. Candler: High School Poems,* in *Voice of Youth Advocates,* Vol. 14, No. 6, February, 1992, p. 394.

The team of Glenn and Michael J. Bernstein have once again produced a unique collection of free-verse poems and photographs to which teens can relate. Like *Class Dismissed!, Class Dismissed II,* and *Back to Class,* the poems focus on feelings, experiences, and perspectives. This time, the poems are directed to Mr. Mark Candler, high school guidance counselor. Not only do the students express their concerns, fears, joys, and impressions to Mr. Candler, but parents, by phone, do too. Many of the poems "play" off of each other. For example, one poem is from the viewpoint of a girl who likes a particular boy, the next from the viewpoint of that boy. Another poem is the exuberant discovery of a girl's 92 on a difficult history exam contrasted with her brother's discovery—a 29 on the same test. Sometimes it's a poem giving a parent's view of a situation with a son or daughter. Individual poems have a stark intensity that will strike a chord of recognition and compassion in teenagers, i.e., the poems about the girl whose father had money for her brothers' college education but not hers; the boy who is embarrassed about his parents who, unlike his friends' parents, are still romantic after 25 years of marriage; and the girl who is being sexually harassed at the job she badly needs. Through all the poems, and clear black-and-white photos of teenagers, it is interesting how, in your mind, you can "see" Mr. Candler responding and between the lines you can "hear" his reactions. Finally, the reader meets Mr. Candler in the very last poem and photo and, not unexpectedly, finds him to be a generous man, tired at the end of a long week but willing to counsel one more student who shows up at his door as he's leaving. This is the most cohesive and best of the Glenn/Bernstein books to date.

WHO KILLED MR. CHIPPENDALE? A MYSTERY IN POEMS (1996)

Kirkus Reviews

SOURCE: A review of *Who Killed Mr. Chippendale? A Mystery in Poems,* in *Kirkus Reviews,* Vol. LXIV, No. 9, May 1, 1996, pp. 688-89.

A respected teacher's murder on school grounds sparks a series of free-verse reveries and comments from a large cast of students, colleagues, police officers, and members of the local community in this unusual, provocatively oblique whodunit, subtitled "A Mystery in Poems."

As in Glenn's most recent collection, *My Friend's Got This Problem, Mr. Candler,* voices, attitudes, and concerns are realistically varied: Youthful optimism alternates with fear or disillusionment, pre-packaged opinions with thoughtful observations, anguish with disinterest. Chippendale is remembered largely with affection, a competent teacher who, every now and then, made a difference, sometimes to the good (Celia Campbell) and sometimes bad (Delia Campbell). The contributors/suspects include Angela, a counselor who fell in love with Chippendale years ago; Leah, a teenager who claims she had a fling with him (but whose veracity is suspect); and violence-prone, emotionally numb Mike, who, despite enough circumstantial evidence by the end to arrest and convict him, never admits much. He's a chilling character—but is he guilty? And what about Leah's admission? *Does* anyone get the whole story? Let readers decide, as they appreciate the multiple ironies here, search for clues, and look for echoes of their own peers and teachers in these vignettes.

Stephanie Zvirin

SOURCE: A review of *Who Killed Mr. Chippendale? A Mystery in Poems,* in *Booklist,* Vol. 92, No. 19, June 1 & 15, 1996, p. 1688.

Teens who have enjoyed Glenn's previous free-verse peeks at contemporary high-school life, such as *My Friend's Got This Problem, Mr. Candler,* will probably want to see this one, even though it is not as successful. Violence, a top concern among today's teens, is the unifying theme, and the idea of presenting a mystery in free-form verse should have great appeal. The aftermath of the unexplained shooting death of a high-school teacher is presented through the eyes of a variety of different people—students in his classes, investigating cops, a counselor with whom he had an affair. Unfortunately, even accounting for Glenn's attempts to differentiate the characters, the poetry is painfully turgid at times ("black holes appear in the constellation of my memories"), and his story lacks punch. His previous, more intimate books, which present characters and problems more varied and more emotionally compelling, will continue to draw readers long after this one is forgotten.

Sharon Korbeck

SOURCE: A review of *Who Killed Mr. Chippendale? A Mystery in Poems,* in *School Library Journal,* Vol. 42, No. 7, July, 1996, p. 98.

High school English teacher Robert Chippendale is shot and killed one morning while running on the Tower High track before class. Moments earlier, he'd had a confrontation with a shadowy figure in a red-hooded sweatshirt. That's all readers learn early on in this mystery in poem format. But more than a whodunit, this unique offering explores a multitude of issues in its pages. Single-page conversational poems are presented, each of which bears the name of a different student, teacher, or community member touched by the murder. Not only do the poems clue readers into the characters' personalities and sensibilities, but they also provide a telling commentary on the attitudes toward violence reflected in our society at large. The cast is large, ranging from students who loved or hated "Mr. C" to guidance counselor Angela Falcone, who ties the book together. An epilogue takes readers 13 years into the future to show what the characters, including the murderer, are doing with their lives. Glenn delivers a starkly realistic view of modern high-school life. A clever idea, executed in a thoughtful, compelling, and thoroughly accessible manner.

Publishers Weekly

SOURCE: A review of *Who Killed Mr. Chippendale? A Mystery in Poems,* in *Publishers Weekly,* Vol. 243, No. 28, July 8, 1996, p. 85.

Glenn's diverse collection of free verse describes the aftermath of the murder of an English teacher at Tower High School. Focusing on the feelings and opinions of the characters more than on suspense or action, the text cleverly embraces varied narratives—a press memo, a police interview, a letter from the Board of Education—but consists mainly of the dramatic monologues of students and staff at the school. "I hope his soul goes straight to heaven./What that man did for me,/ . . . / He made feel smarter than I am" says one; "I hope his soul goes straight to hell,/ What that man did for me,/ . . . /He made me feel stupider than I am," says that student's twin. The girl who had a crush on Chippendale, the students he encouraged or flunked, the guidance counselor who loved him—all are represented in one-page poems. Clues and red herrings drop somewhat obviously, and the killer is apprehended in one of the final poems. While the format allows Glenn license to experiment with different voices, the verse seems like a plain-spoken prose text divided up arbitrarily into line lengths to resemble poetry. The language is gritty and colloquial, but the characters aren't individuals so much as types. However, YA readers who share Glenn's taste for heavy irony might enjoy the Spoon River-esque storytelling.

Deborah Stevenson

SOURCE: A review of *Who Killed Mr. Chippendale? A Mystery in Poems,* in *Bulletin of the Center for Children's Books,* Vol. 49, No. 11, July-August, 1996, pp. 372-73.

Average Mr. Chippendale, long-time high-school English teacher, is shot dead by a sniper as he runs on the school track, and the school is in an uproar. In first-person free-verse poems, each about a page long, Glenn depicts the responses of Mr. Chippendale's students, his colleagues, the neighbors, the detective on the case, and others; the result is a cumulative picture of Mr. Chippendale and high-school life that suggests things are more complicated than they appear and that eventually leads to the revelation of the murderer's identity. It's an original approach, and there's plenty of drama and emotion in everybody's secret lives (Mr. Chippendale and the guidance counselor had been in love, and Mr. Chippendale was currently having an affair with a student, to say nothing of the battles with alcohol, danger, and low self-esteem undergone by the students); the double-voice poems, where a character's thoughts are contrasted with his or her words, are effective and intriguing. Other poems, however, often hammer relentlessly on a central metaphor or image and rely on cheap irony, and the contrivances of the situation and of its mystery impede the story. This has a certain dark but undemanding appeal with its look inside everybody's secret souls.

Sally Kotarsky

SOURCE: A review of *Who Killed Mr. Chippendale? A Mystery in Poems,* in *Voice of Youth Advocates,* Vol. 19, No. 5, December, 1996, p. 287.

English teacher Mr. Chippendale is gunned down as he runs the track of Tower High School. The investigation begins, rumors fly, and secrets are revealed. What makes this murder mystery different is that it is told entirely in poems. Students who didn't like the teacher express their indifference to his murder, teachers wonder who among them will be next, a confused counselor questions her own true feelings toward him.

This unusual introduction to poetry is more than a murder mystery. It is a profile of society; a high school society in which gossip is the gospel and the school is divided along immigration lines. Representatives from many countries speak out, mainly on the value placed on education in their homelands. Rosina Robles writes, "In my home country,/When the teacher walks into the room,/We all stand up and say, 'Good morning, sir.'" Others, however, express their anger toward the number of immigrants in the community, like Bill Jones: "Too many foreigners 'round here,/They should all pack up/and go back/where they came from."

The problem with this book is that it tries to be too many things at once. The murder mystery is lost in the large number of poems dealing with immigration views. The underlying mystery as to whether Mr. Chippendale had an affair with a student or always harbored feelings for Ms. Falcone, the counselor, is lost. But what is really lost is Mike Curry's true reason for committing this crime. While we know the motivation in the end,

we have no feeling for it throughout the book. This book will appeal to the student needing to work with poetry who is not interested in the classic poets.

THE TAKING OF ROOM 114: A HOSTAGE DRAMA IN POEMS (1997)

Kirkus Reviews

SOURCE: A review of *The Taking of Room 114: A Hostage Drama in Poems,* in *Kirkus Reviews,* Vol. LXV, No. 3, February 1, 1997, pp. 222-23.

A veteran high-school teacher cracks, holding his class at gunpoint on the last day of school in this drama-in-poetry from Glenn. Writing in conversational free-verse trains of thought, Glenn probes the hopes, fears, conceits, and moods of students, officials, and bystanders, introducing each of the hostages with a series of vignettes that trace the evolution of a particular idea or relationship through four years of school and to the beginning of class that fateful day. Fond of playing with language and irony—e.g., pairing poems in which the speakers express opposite views in nearly the same words—the author keeps the focus so firmly on individuals that the plot is really only a pretext for a series of earnest character portraits. From Morton Potter's determined assault on his weight problem to Denise Slattery cooing to her unborn child, readers will find plenty of familiar peer attitudes and situations with which to identify and to ponder. The teacher's own voice is heard in a handful of despondent poems: "I speak./Who listens?/ I teach./Who cares? . . . There's little I have done to make a difference." After the teacher's capture, police find a clipping in his pocket describing his 27-year-old son's apparent suicide by drowning. An arresting, if undeveloped, premise cements a gallery of recognizable high-school seniors fretting about—or blowing off—their pasts and futures.

Elizabeth Bush

SOURCE: A review of *The Taking of Room 114: A Hostage Drama in Poems,* in *Bulletin of the Center for Children's Books,* Vol. 50, No. 7, March, 1997, pp. 247-48.

Gimmickry outguns content in this overdrawn compilation. The action begins at the opening of a June school day, as seniors with their minds on graduation shuffle through a slow-moving yearbook line and muse (in a poem apiece) on their current states of ennui and on life beyond Tower High School. But it's gonna be a bad day—veteran history teacher Mr. Wiedermeyer has finally snapped, and he holds his first-period class at gunpoint while he slips notes under the door that provide clues to the large and small personal tragedies that have brought him to this pass. Between the takeover and the all-too-easy, relatively bloodless rescue, Glenn plods through some one hundred pages of poems (five for each hostage) retracing each student's Tower career. And what a carefully balanced bunch of stereotypical students they are. Tramps, nerds, immigrants, underachievers, womanizers, jocks—they're all accounted for, elevating teen banality and egocentrism to new heights ("Let me outta here./ Man, am I gonna party tonight"). Occasionally an image will flash and grip, tantalizing the reader with the possibilities of Glenn's premise ("Private tortures/ Ending in public spectacle./ Serpentine demons/ strangling common sense"). The bulk of the verse, though, is flat prose broken into lines ("I feel restless/ And horny/ Pretty much all of the time./ . . . I think I'll take a shower, a cold one./ Then maybe I'll do a little math homework").

Debbie Carton

SOURCE: A review of *The Taking of Room 114: A Hostage Drama in Poems,* in *Booklist,* Vol. 93, No. 13, March 1, 1997, p. 1154.

Glenn uses first-person narrative poems to relate an ongoing story. This time, however, the teacher is the villain. Mr. Wiedermeyer, longtime history instructor, is holding his senior history class hostage at gunpoint. The story unfolds through one-page poems contributed by students in the class, with five poems from each student—one for each year spent in high school and one about the dramatic day. Through notes to the administration, Mr. Wiedermeyer reveals himself as a committed but exhausted teacher for whom a personal tragedy has tipped the balance. Some of the student characters are stereotypes: the gay student (who has AIDS) dreams of going to Paris; the Chinese immigrant's main concern is fitting in; and the girl who came from parochial school is boy-crazy. However, the topic and the format are fresh and unusual, and Glenn branches out in the poems themselves, employing interesting typographical devices such as shaped poems. This is somewhat longer than Glenn's previous books, but the tense plot and clever format will hold readers.

Marjorie Lewis

SOURCE: A review of *The Taking of Room 114: A Hostage Drama in Poems,* in *School Library Journal,* Vol. 43, No. 4, April, 1997, p. 137.

At 8 a.m. on June 16th, the seniors are lined up in the courtyard waiting to receive their yearbooks. Some flirt. Some daydream. Some are impatient. All of them will be in first-period history class where their teacher, Mr. Wiedermeyer, will lock the classroom door, brandish a gun, and hold them all hostage. Glenn's proven ear for the cadence of speech is exercised here with great skill while telling the story of each character's life and preoccupation. The many points of view expressed, the typographical versatility, and the creative use of white space all add interest to the unfolding story of the tragedy of a teacher's life and the vivid stories of his students. Unfortunately, melodrama supplants real drama. Stereotypical portrayals spoil any real involvement, and predictability destroys the suspense. The Jewish student is being pushed by his parents; the Asian student is hellbent toward success; the one with artistic talent thinks he is gay; one is pregnant; one is abused, etc. And the reporters are uncaring and aggressive; the parents scream and yell; and the administration bumbles along. The selections lack the conceits that heighten the enjoyment of traditional poetry—metaphor, simile, alliteration, onomatopoeia. But they're never boring and often very clever. YAs will find their interest piqued and reluctant readers particularly will be drawn to the excitement of design and content.

JUMP BALL: A BASKETBALL SEASON IN POEMS (1997)

Kirkus Reviews

SOURCE: A review of *Jump Ball: A Basketball Season in Poems,* in *Kirkus Reviews,* Vol. LXV, No. 16, August 15, 1997, p. 1305.

Basketball dreams shatter when a high-school team bus goes out of control on an icy road in this latest novel-in-poems from Glenn. The course of Tower High's championship season becomes clear through the musings of a gallery of players, groupies, teachers, parents, and bystanders; the author expertly creates dramatic tension with early hints of the tragedy to come, but the voices he creates are largely focused on their own lives and concerns of the moment. Those voices are not as strong and distinct as some messages and strokes of broadly brushed irony, e.g., two pages after Rayanne Walker declares how hard she's worked to raise her son, and how hard he works to earn college money, he is killed in an attempted robbery—and his memorial service is just another item, along with the Spring Concert and the scores, in the school's morning announcements. Though Glenn's language is largely conversational, he breaks occasionally into quick, rap-like rhythms, or even concrete poetry, evoking the feel and pace of basketball action rather than conventionally describing it. His fans will find the characters falling into familiar types, and though at its best the poetry is exciting, some superficial, indifferent adults and the imminent crushing of so many hoop dreams give the story a bitter, discouraging cast.

Randy Meyer

SOURCE: A review of *Jump Ball: A Basketball Season in Poems,* in *Booklist,* Vol. 94, No. 4, October 15, 1997, p. 394.

In his latest "story" in poems, Glenn introduces a chorus of distinct voices from an inner-city high school—basketball players, parents, teachers, and friends—each with a personal take on the sport and dreams for the future. He uses this lean format to create memorable, often troubled characters who will continue to live in readers' imaginations even after the book has been completed. A scattering of seemingly unrelated poems (from a weatherman, a bored teenager in a rural town, a 911 operator), which do not fit into the chronology of the other poems, builds a sense of foreboding. More than a book of sports poetry, this is a quick read with a lot of impact. It is also a richly emotional book that brings readers face-to-face with issues in their own lives, such as heartbreak and violence.

Sharon Korbeck

SOURCE: A review of *Jump Ball: A Basketball Season in Poems,* in *School Library Journal,* Vol. 43, No. 11, November, 1997, p. 128.

"To all my old-fogy colleagues,/Who seem to think that/Basketball has assumed some/Inordinate celestial weight/In the educational firmament,/I have a simple message: 'Get a life!'" That phrase from physics teacher Fiona Sullivan is just one of the realistic viewpoints presented in Glenn's story, told in free-verse poems. *Jump Ball* captures the pulse of the basketball season—on and off the court—in poignant, honest, and well-spoken glimpses into the many personalities who work and play at Tower High School. The Tigers have a hot point guard, Garrett James, who is destined for the NBA—but he has to make it through high school first. A lot of demands are placed on him by school, fans, media, etc. Garrett's popularity affects everyone. His coach believes, "Publicity is a poison,/Like a cup of wine/That can raise a man to drunken heights/Only to crash him down into frightening depths." Teenage crushes, pregnancy, homelessness, and the glamorization of athletes are all examined here. Tower High's championship season is chronicled in fine, easy-to-read vignettes interspersed with broadcast accounts of the games. The insights of the players and adults are cleverly penned. They're sure to interest sports fans or just those desiring a look into human nature. The startling, tragic event that grips the team at the end of the season will keep young people reading to learn the fate of the troubled and terrific Tigers.

Additional coverage of Glenn's life and career is contained in the following sources published by Gale Research: *Contemporary Authors New Revision Series,* **Vol. 49; and** *Something about the Author,* **Vol. 93.**

Susan Kuklin

1941-

American author and photo-illustrator of nonfiction and picture books.

Major works include *Thinking Big: The Story of a Young Dwarf* (1986), *Fighting Back: What Some People Are Doing about AIDS* (1988), *What Do I Do Now? Talking about Teenage Pregnancy* (1991), *Speaking Out: Teenagers Take on Race, Sex, and Identity* (1993), *After a Suicide: Young People Speak Up* (1994).

INTRODUCTION

An accomplished photojournalist, Kuklin blends her photographic talents with a penchant for dramatic storytelling to create moving, informative nonfiction works for young people, from preschoolers to young adults. She is best known for a number of hard-hitting books on difficult and controversial topics facing teens, with subjects ranging from teen pregnancy to suicide, from dwarfism to AIDS, and from prejudice to the fight for human rights. Kuklin is celebrated for her insight and the emotional intensity of award-winning titles such as *Fighting Back: What Some People are Doing about AIDS* and *Thinking Big: The Story of a Young Dwarf,* in which she reveals the human drama behind the statistics, making such subjects at once readable and informative. Beverly Robertson praised *Fighting Back,* for example, as "an emotionally wrenching story that is accessible to teens because it is about individuals, not numbers." Kuklin takes an investigative approach to many of her subjects, presenting personal testimonies of men and women who have experienced difficult challenges in their lives.

Though many of Kuklin's books are aimed at a junior high and high school audience, she has also written and photo-illustrated a series of works for younger readers, introducing them to potentially scary situations—from a first visit to the dentist to attending nursery school. Noted for their realism, detail, and attractive formats, these works combine photojournalism techniques with medium format photography to recreate actual experiences of a young child going to the doctor, the dentist, etc. All of Kuklin's works project her mission: to raise awareness and never lose sight of the human subject when dealing with difficult themes and topics. "When I get down to it," she once commented, "my books revolve around one rudimentary question: how do ordinary people deal with unusual, sometimes extraordinary, situations. . . ? I simply report my subject's choices and values, trying hard not to add editorial comments. For a person who loves sappy, happy endings, letting my subject 'go' can be trying. So far, I've been lucky. My subjects have come through wonderfully."

Biographical Information

Born in Philadelphia, Pennsylvania, Kuklin's earliest memories are of attending opera, ballet, and theater performances with her family, and of many hours spent at the library. "I fondly remember looking at long wooden shelves filled with books thinking that I must read all of them before I grow up," she recounted. She later attended New York University as a drama student and spent her summers as an apprentice at Philadelphia's Playhouse in the Park and Joseph Papp's New York Shakespeare Festival, working in minor roles or backstage and rubbing elbows with actors such as Jessica Tandy and Geraldine Page. In graduate school, also at NYU, her desire for an on-stage career began to wane and was eventually replaced by an interest in directing. "While acting taught me how to interpret a part," she recalled, "directing forced me to look at the big picture which included a visual appreciation of the art. I learned about framing, position, lighting, movement, etc. These fundamentals later became intrinsic aspects of my approach to photography and non-fiction writing." After college, Kuklin supplemented her income as an actress by working as an English teacher in New York City schools. She married in 1973 and moved to Tennessee where she taught film and took up photography, first as a hobby and then as a profession as her photos began to sell. Working with Planned Parenthood, she produced a photo essay, "Appalachian Families," on some of the mountain families of the region. She eventually landed her first children's book contract, taking photographs for *The Story of Nim, a Chimp Who Learned Language* (1979), and later for a photographic essay of a new ballet by choreographer George Balanchine. Thereafter, she found assignments for major magazines. While she enjoyed magazine work for a time, she yearned to delve deeper into subjects, something that her work on *Nim* had allowed her. She found the opportunity of getting back into children's books with *Mine for a Year* (1984), this time as an author. "Children's books enable me to spend lengthy periods of time with a specific subject," Kuklin explained. "Having the opportunity to meet and become close to people who I would not otherwise have the opportunity to meet is fascinating and fun."

Major Works

Kuklin's first work, *Mine for a Year,* launched her career of human interest books for young readers. It is the true story of Doug, a puppy candidate for a seeing-eye dog, and a foster child named George who will help train the dog for one year. This book takes an unusual twist in that George himself suffers from failing eyesight and might one day need a dog like Doug. A reviewer for *Bulletin of the Center for Children's Books* concluded that readers may be "impressed by the candor and directness of the text." The positive reception of this first title encouraged Kuklin to search for more human interest topics, and she next told the story of Jaime Osborn, an eight-year-old dwarf, in *Thinking Big*. Elizabeth S. Watson noted the "well-integrated" text and photos, and that the book should be a "real" addition to the limited resources on children with special needs. Kuklin garnered further praise for the joyful spirit that infuses these works, and for teaching her readers how disadvantaged children can lead normal lives. With *Reaching for Dreams: A Ballet from Rehearsal to Opening Night* (1987), Kuklin was able to indulge in her love of ballet with a book length study of how ballet is made—following the Alvin Ailey American Dance Theater in preparation for a new ballet. In a similar vein, she realistically portrays commonplace experiences in the lives of preschoolers in works such as *When I See My Dentist* (1988), which follows a four-year-old on her first visit to the family dentist. In *Going to My Nursery School* (1989), a little boy talks about a typical day at his day-care facility, while in *Going to My Ballet Class* (1989), a little girl describes a pre-ballet class at the Joffrey Ballet School. In these and other similar works, Kuklin attempts to remove the fears from possibly scary situations or to increase the excitement of a new experience. Reviewers have applauded the engaging first-person narratives and attractive, color photographs of these books, as well as the inclusion of several pages of advice for parents on the topic of each book.

In *Fighting Back: What Some People are Doing about AIDS,* Kuklin follows volunteers for the Gay Men's Health Crisis around New York City as they visited their clients with AIDS, run errands, clean, and cook for them. A *Kirkus Reviews* contributor found *Fighting Back* a "moving portrayal of a dedicated team of volunteers." Others noted Kuklin's skillful, nonjudgmental inclusion of information about AIDS and AIDS prevention. Similarly, in *What Do I Do Now?: Talking about Teenage Pregnancy*, Kuklin interviews teenagers from different socioeconomic backgrounds to explore the impact pregnancy had on their lives, presenting information about birth control, adoption, and abortion without overshadowing the first-person perspectives of her subjects. Teenagers also discuss sex and other sensitive topics in *Speaking Out: Teenagers Take on Race, Sex, and Identity*, a compendium of interviews with students in a culturally and racially diverse New York City high school. Critics found Kuklin's interviewees shockingly forthright about the experience of labeling—for race, sexual orientation, weight, and other factors—and how it affects their sense of identity. Likewise, *After a Suicide: Young People Speak Up* is a series of interviews with young people who not only attempted suicide themselves, but were affected by the suicide of those close to them. William R. Mollineaux concluded, "The book merits its greatest praise for being a suicide deterrent, for I believe that any reader contemplating suicide will reconsider this final act." In *Irrepressible Spirit: Conversations with Human Rights Activists,* Kuklin investigates human rights issues by presenting first-hand accounts of those who have experienced such abuses. Tracey Kroll regarded *Irrepressible Spirit* as "a quality book that will stir strong emotions and raise awareness."

Awards

The Story of Nim, a Chimp Who Learned Language was recognized as an Outstanding Science Trade Book for Children by the National Science Teachers Association in 1980. *Mine for a Year* was honored as a Notable Children's Trade Book in the Field of Social Studies by the National Council for Social Studies and the Children's Book Council in 1984. *Thinking Big: The Story of A Young Dwarf* was named a Best Book of the Year by *School Library Journal* and the International Board on Books for Young People, both in 1986, and a Children's Book of the Year by Child Study Association of America in 1987. *Reaching for Dreams: A Ballet from Rehearsal to Opening Night* was selected as a Best Book of the Year by the American Library Association and the New York Public Library, both in 1987. *After a Suicide: Young People Speak Up* was designated a Best Book by the American Library Association, a Best Book for Reluctant Young Adult Readers, and a Best Book of the Year by the New York Public Library, all in 1984. *After a Suicide* also received the Suicide Prevention Award at the 11th Annual Regional Survivors of Suicide Conference at the Robert Wood Johnson Medical School. *Irrepressible Spirit: Conversations with Human Rights Activists* was named a Choice Book for 1996 by the Cooperative Children's Book Center and received the Christopher Award in 1997.

TITLE COMMENTARY

📖 *MINE FOR A YEAR* (1984)

Zena Sutherland

SOURCE: A review of *Mine for a Year,* in *Bulletin of the Center for Children's Books,* Vol. 37, No. 11, July-August, 1984, p. 207.

Told from the viewpoint of George, who for one year is responsible for the care and training of a puppy destined to become a guide dog for the blind, this has a subtle poignancy because George fears he himself is going blind (he has poor vision, but learns in the course of the book that it won't get worse) and because he is one of the many foster-sons of a warm, motherly single woman. The photographs, which are of good quality, corroborate the love George expresses for his dog and make more graphic the details of the training the puppy gets. Readers may be interested in the training program, conducted under the auspices of the 4-H Club, as well as impressed by the candor and directness of the text.

Denise M. Wilms

SOURCE: A review of *Mine for a Year,* in *Booklist,* Vol. 81, No. 1, September 1, 1984, p. 67.

Doug is a puppy candidate to become a seeing-eye dog; George is the foster child who, as part of a 4-H program, will be Doug's master for a year until formal seeing-eye training begins. George's narrative expresses his excitement and involvement with Doug and also educates readers in the kind of training these puppies receive early on. There is an added emotional factor as well; Doug is special to George not only because he's a seeing-eye-dog candidate, but also because George has a vision problem and worries that he himself may become blind and one day need a dog like Doug. Accompanying photographs are uneven in quality. Some are inexcusably blurry or grainy, while others are quite sharp and well composed. The human-interest appeal here is great; the book will work well as an accompaniment for units on the blind—or as interesting nonfiction for independent readers.

Charlotte W. Draper

SOURCE: A review of *Mine for a Year,* in *The Horn Book Magazine,* Vol. LX, No. 5, September 10, 1984, p. 607.

George, along with the other foster children who live with Evelyn Henderson, participates in Puppy Power, a 4-H project that places puppies with families for a year before they are trained to be guide dogs for the blind. George's first puppy is Doug, a black Labrador retriever. The boy tells of Doug's care and feeding, his obedience classes, and his antics on the farm while black-and-white photographs document the year of socialization which will determine Doug's aptitude for professional training. It is a period of maturation for George as well as for Doug. In his thirteenth year George reports, "By early spring, Doug was full grown . . . I was changing too. Each morning I checked my face for whiskers." George has fun dealing with Doug. But his commitment to the dog's training has a further dimension, for the boy suffers from cataracts and fears that he himself may need a seeing-eye dog later in life. The camera records a George more authentic than the one the author sets forth in speech; occasionally, the boy's account sounds stilted. But the importance of Puppy Power to all its beneficiaries is clear. The emotions explored, including the bond between George and his foster mother and his loss of Doug at the end of the year, add depth to a well-paced account of the early training of a guide dog.

Carole B. Kirkpatrick

SOURCE: A review of *Mine for a Year,* in *School Library Journal,* Vol. 31, No. 2, October, 1984, p. 158.

As a 4-H project, 12-year-old George raises a Labrador Retriever puppy destined to become a guide dog for a blind person. Participants in this program socialize their puppies, teaching them to get along with people and to obey rules so that at the end of the year they can be trained as guide dogs. George has a special interest: he has had several cataract operations and may lose his vision some day and need a guide dog of his own. The love between George and his dog, Doug, comes through clearly in the first-person text and in the well-integrated large black-and-white photographs. In addition, the book addresses the fears and feelings of an adolescent, as George tells Doug his concerns and thoughts. A very readable book that may lead readers to explore getting involved in such a project.

📖 *THINKING BIG: THE STORY OF A YOUNG DWARF* (1986)

Zena Sutherland

SOURCE: A review of *Thinking Big: The Story of a Young Dwarf,* in *Bulletin of the Center for Children's Books,* Vol. 39, No. 9, May, 1986, p. 170.

A photodocumentary essay focuses on eight-year-old Jaime Osborn and her family, who belong to Little People of America because Jaime is a dwarf. "Think Big" is the organization's motto. The writing is straightforward, the tone matter-of-fact and candid; the book explains how dwarfs differ from midgets and how Jaime copes with clothes that are too big, chairs that are too high, stairs that are too steep. She's a lively child who faces problems with cheerful honesty, and the account shows how important the support of a loving family is. An epilogue explains the genetic cause and discusses Jaime's physical problems in the past and the future, and possible social problems she may have during the teen years, as most adolescent dwarfs do. This does a good job of providing information simply; it should help readers understand that having a disability doesn't make another child different in any but a physical sense.

Kirkus Reviews

SOURCE: A review of *Thinking Big: The Story of a Young Dwarf,* in *Publishers Weekly,* Vol. 229, No. 22, May 30, 1986, pp. 65-6.

Kuklin has produced the first photo-essay to profile the life of an achondroplastic dwarf, and she's done an inspiring job. Eight-year-old Jaime is neither ashamed nor professionally cute. She proudly exclaims, "Hi, this is your lucky day. You've just met your first dwarf." Kuklin looks at ways Jaime is the same as other youngsters (she likes to have her hair curled, and reads to her little brother), and ways she is different (she is double-jointed and less bothered by the cold than average-size people). Jaime's problems being teased and needing special medical care aren't ignored; guidance from her gentle family and from Little People of America helps. There's an epilogue for adults; readers of all ages and sizes will be intrigued and enlightened. The book is special in every sense.

Elizabeth S. Watson

SOURCE: A review of *Thinking Big: The Story of a Young Dwarf,* in *The Horn Book Magazine,* Vol. LXII, No. 4, July-August, 1986, p. 466.

One of the few titles concerning dwarfism, **Thinking Big** will be a real addition to the available resources concerning children with special problems. The text and photographs are well integrated and clearly show Jaime in some situations where, because of her short stature, she needs help and in other situations where she is able to adapt. The author writes in a straightforward, unemotional tone while effectively creating a positive and reassuring mood. She explains both the medical problems and adjustments that Jaime, her parents, and her schoolmates must make to accommodate her in everyday activities. Several references are made to the Little People of America, to which Jaime and her parents belong. An epilogue gives further information on dwarfism for teachers and parents.

Margaret C. Howell

SOURCE: A review of *Thinking Big: The Story of a Young Dwarf,* in *School Library Journal,* Vol. 32, No. 10, August, 1986, pp. 83-4.

A photo story about an eight-year-old girl who is a dwarf. Although Jaime's body is normal size, her limbs will always be short. This book reveals her relationships with her family and her friends and the difficulties she must face. It is told with compassion and humor, as Jaime takes off her shoes to climb into the refrigerator to get food on the top shelf or slides down the steps on her bottom because the steps hit her at the knees. Her little brother is five and already head and shoulders above her, but she is still his "big sister" and reads to him. She takes part in all normal activities, such as Brownies and playing in the park, but when she is selling Girl Scout cookies someone must go with her to ring the doorbells. Kuklin also notes special characteristics of dwarfs, like double-jointedness and the fact that all of the fingers of each hand do not touch. The good-quality black-and-white photographs illustrate the strong family support that Jaime receives. An afterword in smaller type ex-

From Thinking Big: The Story of a Young Dwarf, *written and photographed by Susan Kuklin.*

plains dwarfism and offers more background on Jaime's life. A positive book that should be of interest to libraries as it covers a subject about which little has been written.

Elizabeth Gillis

SOURCE: A review of *Thinking Big: The Story of a Young Dwarf*, in *Appraisal: Science Books for Young People*, Vol. 19, No. 4, Fall, 1986, pp. 60-1.

An appealing eight-year-old dwarf named Jaime is the focus of this account of the daily life of a child who is different from her peers. A dwarf has a body that is normal in size but with shorter limbs (as opposed to a midget who is a smaller replica of his/her contemporaries). How Jaime manages everyday life is shown with sensitivity. Coping with relationships with others and with medical problems (weight gain, leg bone curvature) is described. Plentiful black-and-white photographs show Jaime climbing stairs with an awkward gain, having her younger brother reach for things, and when he is not available, getting up on the bottom refrigerator shelf and down again quickly before her bare feet get cold. The text also emphasizes the things she can do well, such as her art work. Jaime can also get up easily without using her hands from sitting on the floor, as her brother cannot, because she is double-jointed. But that term is not explained. A bright resourceful child, Jaime handles life well in an oversized world. An epilogue explains more fully the medical and psychological problems such children have. The causes and types of dwarfism are described. A good way to tell young children that a dwarf is a normal child in most respects.

John R. Pancella

SOURCE: A review of *Thinking Big: The Story of a Young Dwarf*, in *Appraisal: Science Books for Young People*, Vol. 19, No. 4, Fall, 1986, p. 61.

Jaime Osborn is eight and she is a dwarf. Her genetic affliction, achondroplasia, causes short limbs on an average-sized body. This photoessay should speak for all physically handicapped as they cope with life's needs, physical barriers, siblings and parents, schoolmates, doctors, and mundane daily routines that everybody else probably takes for granted. Jaime's beautiful face and bright smile and her positive and poignant comments, such as "Hi, this is your lucky day. You've just met your first dwarf," will surely heighten the awareness of all readers, young and adult. There is an appropriate plug for a national organization called Little People of America, an information-sharing and social group, whose motto is "Think big." This is a joyful book, not a morbid biography of a disadvantaged child growing up. Highly recommended as general library reading.

REACHING FOR DREAMS: A BALLET FROM REHEARSAL TO OPENING NIGHT (1987)

Stephanie Zvirin

SOURCE: A review of *Reaching for Dreams: A Ballet from Rehearsal to Opening Night*, in *Booklist*, Vol. 83, No. 13, March 1, 1987, p. 1005.

"Morning ladies and gentlemen. Everybody here?" With those words stage manager Keith Simmons greets senior members of the Alvin Ailey dance company and begins the formal day for onlooker Kuklin, a photojournalist present to chronicle what goes on as dancers rehearse a new ballet. And what a treat her observations are. Piecing them together with unposed black-and-white photographs, Kuklin provides a vibrant record of behind-the-scenes intensity—from the rigors of learning a role to individualizing it and reworking it to fit into the scheme of the whole that is presented to an audience on opening night. While Kuklin observed, she also listened, and she incorporates what she heard—candid comments and responses to questions about work and background—to lend a sense of the individual dancers as well as of some of the other people involved in production. In fact, she gives equal time to people and process, intricately tied as they are, and the result is a wonderfully unpretentious close-up that teenage balletomanes will adore.

Kirkus Reviews

SOURCE: A review of *Reaching for Dreams: A Ballet from Rehearsal to Opening Night*, in *Kirkus Reviews*, Vol. LV, No. 5, March 1, 1987, p. 383.

This stunning book is a must for anyone who already enjoys dance, and should bring many others to appreciate the art of ballet. Kuklin has followed the construction of a ballet named *Speeds*, choreographed for the Alvin Ailey troop by Jennifer Muller, with camera, tape recorder, and soul. Muller had performed the dance for years with her own troop, but now she and her dancers instruct the Ailey troop in its movements, nuances and rhythms. Since the Ailey troop does mostly jazz-oriented pieces, they feel apprehensive, yet challenged by the modern dance involved. Through Kuklin's perception, always finely tuned to the personalities, we see the dancers work, strive and gradually become comfortable with each section of the work.

We can hear the music and see the dance by the completion of this intense, involving book. Kuklin interviews the various dancers and pinpoints their individuality so that the reader feels a strong identification. The intense effort expended, the constant striving for improvement, much often with pain, the brutal drive of rehearsals, the technical difficulties from costuming to lighting are all justified by the transcendence of the performance. The reader truly feels art has been created. The photography, also by Kuklin, is a moving and splendid testimony to the dedication, the joy, the beauty of these dancers and their art. Not to be missed.

Zena Sutherland

SOURCE: A review of *Reaching for Dreams: A Ballet from Rehearsal to Opening Night*, in *Bulletin of the Center for Children's Books*, Vol. 40, No. 8, April, 1987, pp. 149-50.

Kuklin describes, in a staccato text, the long process of learning and rehearsing a ballet. In a photographically illustrated text, she gives detailed information about the procedures, the problems, the dancers (Alvin Ailey American Dance Theater) and the support staff, and the backgrounds and personalities of the dance company. There's a modicum of dialogue, quite a bit of cited reminiscence (usually about a dancer's childhood and training) and a great deal about the ballet itself, choreographer Jennifer Muller's *Speeds*. Occasionally the text becomes intense or repetitive, but true balletomanes will probably enjoy every detail. A glossary of dance terms is provided.

Amy Kellman

SOURCE: A review of *Reaching for Dreams: A Ballet from Rehearsal to Opening Night*, in *School Library Journal*, Vol. 33, No. 80, May, 1987, p. 114.

Through sharp photographs and a lucid text, Kuklin reproduces the adventure of professional dancers learning a new piece. With choreographer Jennifer Muller, readers get to know the dancers of the Alvin Ailey American Dance Theater, who are preparing to perform *Speeds*, a 30-minute dance in 8 sections. The process of learning the steps, interpreting them, and creating a total experience in costume on stage in front of an audience takes seven weeks. The tedium of repetition and the impatience of not seeing the work as a whole and finally the excitement of knowing that "the ballet will work" are articulated by the dancers and reinforced by the clear black-and-white photographs that capture the dancers at rest and in motion. All that is missing is a videotape of their performance of *Speeds*.

Elizabeth S. Watson

SOURCE: A review of *Reaching for Dreams: A Ballet from Rehearsal to Opening Night*, in *The Horn Book Magazine*, Vol. LXIII, No. 3, May-June, 1987, p. 357.

Susan Kuklin has produced a stunning book that reads like a novel and is illustrated with striking black-and-white photographs. Her subject is the Alvin Ailey American Dance Theater, one of the foremost modern dance companies in the world. She chronicles nearly two months of their preparations for staging the new ballet, *Speeds*,

by guest choreographer Jennifer Muller. The hard work, pain, and frustrations of dancers' careers are evident but well balanced against the beauty, excitement, and grace that appear in the performance. The narrative is smoothly integrated with dancers' comments that range from observations on the work in progress to remarks about their backgrounds and aspirations for their careers. Tension builds as the time for the opening approaches and the personalities of the various dancers emerge. The business end of the company and technical aspects of performance, such as lighting and costuming, are included. The book provides an insightful look at modern dance, not usually the focus of ballet books for young people.

Margrett J. McFadden

SOURCE: A review of *Reaching for Dreams: A Ballet from Rehearsal to Opening Night*, in *Voice of Youth Advocates*, Vol. 10, No. 5, December, 1987, p. 250.

A delightful book, this gives the reader an insight into the seven weeks it took the Alvin Ailey American Dance Theater to prepare for a performance. There are many, many pictures of the various members of the group as they stretch, exercise and rehearse various parts of the ballet. An insight into the camaraderie of this particular group is fascinating as is the effort to make each ballet a "human" endeavor. Instead of submerging the individual person to the plot of the dance, the choreographer integrates the humanness of that person into each step. The result is another moving ballet by this world-acclaimed group. Although the writing is at the junior high level, students (or browsers) at any age will enjoy the pictures and commentary. There is a brief glossary of theatre terms, no index.

WHEN I SEE MY DENTIST; WHEN I SEE MY DOCTOR (1988)

Kirkus Reviews

SOURCE: A review of *When I See My Dentist; When I See My Doctor*, in *Publishers Weekly*, Vol. 233, No. 11, March 18, 1988, p. 84.

These two photo-essays cover potentially threatening situations in a painless—even fun—fashion. Thomas, an adorable four-year-old, has to have a check-up at his doctor's. Erica, also four, needs to have her teeth cleaned and X-rayed for cavities. The photographs convey, in ways no drawings could, what a doctor's and dentist's office look like, the myriad procedures that take place there, and the reasons behind those routines, with some of the hard words spelled phonetically in the margins or simply defined. Kuklin has included rather serious-looking pictures with less formal moments; this accounts for her reassuring tone, which neither white-washes the truth nor makes the visits sound too scary.

Kirkus Reviews

SOURCE: A review of *When I See My Dentist; When I See My Doctor,* in *Kirkus Reviews,* Vol. LVI, No. 8, April 15, 1988, p. 620.

Appealing full-color photo essays provide information and reassurance about routine visits. The clearly written texts are accurate without being overwhelming; the photos convey a sense of warmth and comfort, with relaxed and smiling kids, moms, and medical personnel. Specialized tools are photographed both close up and in use; a pronunciation guide near each picture helps with unfamiliar terms like stethoscope and sphygmomanometer.

Erica's visit to the dentist includes talk about proper brushing, teeth cleaning and scaling, a fluoride treatment, a gum examination, and X-rays. After each procedure, she gets a sticker; and at the end of the visit, she gets a balloon. (Parents might want to alert their dentist or provide a disclaimer if this is not the local practice.) In [*When I See My Doctor,*] the doctor examines Thomas' eyes, ears, throat, and lungs. He receives oral vaccine and a blood test, and has his blood pressure taken, and finally receives a sticker and a hug. The doctor and dentist are both male, while their assistants are female. Both titles should be popular and useful.

Carolyn Phelan

SOURCE: A review of *When I See My Dentist; When I See My Doctor,* in *Booklist,* Vol. 84, No. 17, May 1, 1988, p. 1525.

Illustrated with excellent, full-color photographs, these two picture books give a realistic view of visits to the dentist and doctor. Each takes a four-year-old child through a typical checkup. Erica's trip to the dentist includes visiting his assistant for teeth cleaning, a brushing lesson, and an explanation of how sugar harms teeth. As Dr. Steve examines and x-rays her teeth, he explains every procedure to Erica. An interesting feature of both volumes is the use of close-up photos of medical instruments, properly labeled with correct pronunciations. For example, when Thomas visits the doctor, the nurse takes his blood pressure: "She wraps a wide band around my arm and pumps it up until it feels like a big squeeze." A large photo shows Thomas stretching out his arm for the blood pressure cuff, while a smaller photo shows the entire instrument hanging on the wall. Among the many books on visiting doctors or dentists, these are notable for their realistic approaches, relatively detailed texts, and attractive formats. They are somewhat more informative than most and will appeal to a slightly older child.

Lucy Young Clem

SOURCE: A review of *When I See My Dentist; When I See My Doctor,* in *School Library Journal,* Vol. 34, No. 11, August, 1988, pp. 89-90.

Both of Kuklin's books will be useful in preschool collections, but *When I See My Dentist* is particularly well done. Four-year-old Erica is having a routine checkup and cleaning. The first-person narrative explains the procedures in terms that preschoolers can understand, without being condescending. Both words and pictures have a comfortable, reassuring tone. Only relatively painless routines are covered. The tools used for each stage of the examination are shown in clearly-labelled illustrations. The book stresses good dental hygiene and preventative measures. *When I See My Doctor* follows a similar pattern. Again, no painful procedures are included, although Thomas does have a blood test and an oral vaccination. The outstanding feature of both books is the photographs, which are clear, colorful, natural, and unposed. They show relaxed children and adults in attractive, nonthreatening surroundings.

TAKING MY CAT TO THE VET; TAKING MY DOG TO THE VET (1988)

Denise M. Wilms

SOURCE: A review of *Taking My Cat to the Vet; Taking My Dog to the Vet,* in *Booklist,* Vol. 85, No. 1, September 1, 1988, p. 80.

Kuklin's color photographs and simulated first-person narratives show what happens to a dog or a cat when it goes to the vet for a checkup. Each book features a child—a young boy in *My Cat* and a young girl in *My Dog*—who accompanies the pet to the office and into the examining room, where it is subjected to the gentle scrutiny and shots that are the stuff of animal checkups. The mood is friendly; the vets know the right thing to say to both child and animal, and the sharp color photographs are well composed and instructive. An added benefit is the dialogue between vets and owners that subtly teaches children some of the medical signs of a healthy or sickly animal. Attractive, effective photo essays, especially for youngsters who are about to become pet owners.

Zena Sutherland

SOURCE: A review of *Taking My Dog to the Vet,* in *Bulletin of the Center for Children's Books,* Vol. 42, No. 2, October, 1988, p. 45.

Large print and uncrowded pages, plus the age of the narrator as indicated in the photographs, make [*Taking My Dog to the Vet*] seem more appropriate for the independent reader than for the preschool child indicated (in the review slip) as the intended audience. Minal and her mother take their cairn terrier, Silver, to the vet's for a checkup; it is Minal who stands by and helps during the examination, as Dr. Kuhlman explains each procedure and its resultant information. Useful for pet owners, but static in tone, this is clearly written; the color photographs, while clear, tend to become repetitive.

Betsy Hearne

SOURCE: A review of *Taking My Cat to the Vet,* in *Bulletin of the Center for Children's Books,* Vol. 42, No. 5, January, 1989, p. 126.

In a companion to *Taking My Dog to the Vet,* young Ben tells readers [in *Taking My Cat to the Vet*] about taking his cat Willa, adopted as a kitten from the A.S.P.C.A., to the veterinarian for a standard checkup. The vet, a woman, explains her way through the examination, testing Willa's eyes and ears, taking her temperature, trimming her nails, and giving her shots. The dialogue rarely strains to be informative, and the large color photographs are well composed and businesslike. The author/photographer steers clear of sentimentality, gives listeners a preview of procedures that can be intimidating if not scary, and lists suggestions for a successful visit to the vet, including tips for preparation, waiting room, exam room, and return home. Too bad the cat can't read them.

Elizabeth S. Watson

SOURCE: A review of *Taking My Cat to the Vet; Taking My Dog to the Vet,* in *The Horn Book Magazine,* Vol. LXV, No. 1, January-February, 1989, p. 91.

Illustrated with photographs in color. Attractive and useful, these companion volumes for young pet lovers feature first-person narratives by the owners themselves. The same office is the site for both books, but different veterinarians—one male, one female—examine the pets. The dog and cat are healthy animals taken for regular preventative examinations, so the visits are positive experiences for both pets and owners. The photo essays combine simple, straightforward text with excellent photographs shot from a variety of perspectives and distances. Each book includes a final section, "Keys for a successful visit to the vet," which is tailored to fit the specific type of pet. A welcome duo appropriate for younger readers.

📖 *FIGHTING BACK: WHAT SOME PEOPLE ARE DOING ABOUT AIDS* (1988)

Publishers Weekly

SOURCE: A review of *Fighting Back: What Some People Are Doing about AIDS,* in *Publishers Weekly,* Vol. 234, No. 20, November 11, 1988, p. 57.

Photojournalist Kuklin spent nine months following the lives and deaths of Gay Men's Health Crisis volunteers and their clients (the word victim is not used) with AIDS. The result is exactly what the title implies— a realistic, yet moving discussion of PWAs (people with AIDS) trying to live with the disease, and the cross-section of helpers who provide household help and emotional comfort. The strength of the book lies in its real people—both volunteers and PWAs hail from across the spectrum—gay and straight, men and women, teens. Their backgrounds and feelings are clearly expressed in these pages—a PWA who had led a degrading life of addiction, now rehabilitated; AIDS dementia; a marriage of friendship between a gay and a straight person; volunteers who burn out, drop out of the program (and sometimes return); the prejudice of the AIDS issue, from family and friends. AIDS transmission and prevention are gracefully folded into narrative and dialogue; this is an excellent, compassionate addition to the growing AIDS library that may inspire more people to volunteer. Further, in view of Kuklin's own body of work, this comes across as her strongest, most skillfully wrought project yet.

Stephanie Zvirin

SOURCE: A review of *Fighting Back: What Some People Are Doing about AIDS,* in *Booklist,* Vol. 85, No. 8, December 15, 1988, p. 700.

Kuklin has put together the first teenage book on [AIDS] that revolves entirely around people. Though uneven and somewhat fragmented, it is, nonetheless, a moving, totally unaffected combination of interviews, personal profiles, and photographs, drawn together from Kuklin's nine-month interaction with a PWA (person with AIDS) support group associated with New York City's Gay Men's Health Crisis organization. Kuklin uses one man's struggle with AIDS to provide a connective context of sorts, but her real focus is on "buddies," the GMHC team members (some of whom have AIDS themselves) who lend emotional support, cook meals, and help their "clients" in myriad vital ways. Their honest testimony— filled with laughter, guilt, anger, and tears—is the heart of the book, which takes the tragedy of AIDS out of the laboratory and puts it squarely into everyday life. Thirty black-and-white photos are planned.

Kirkus Reviews

SOURCE: A review of *Fighting Back: What Some People Are Doing about AIDS,* in *Kirkus Reviews,* Vol. LVI, No. 24, December 15, 1988, p. 1813.

A moving portrayal of a dedicated team of trained volunteers in New York City, members of GMHC (Gay Men's Health Crisis), who are working to help people with AIDS or ARC (AIDS Related Complex) "regain control of their lives by, among other things, helping with their day-to-day chores." Kuklin captures the emotions both of the volunteers (who are called "buddies") and of their "clients": anger, helplessness, fear, humor, love, courage. The "buddies" not only cook and do laundry; they also help with financial problems, are willing listeners, provide companionship at a friend's funeral, and meet to give one another support. Kuklin interviews both clients and buddies; there are thumbnail sketches of a punk-rock hairdresser (female), AIDS researcher, lawyer, actor, nun, and a longtime drug addict.

A powerful, thought-provoking look at people struggling with a contemporary problem and trying to make a difference.

David Gale

SOURCE: A review of *Fighting Back: What Some People Are Doing about AIDS,* in *School Library Journal,* Vol. 35, No. 6, February, 1989, p. 106.

Kuklin adds to the growing body of AIDS-related literature with this moving documentation of a group of people who volunteer to help people with AIDS by providing support for them and doing their daily chores. The volunteers, a team of "buddies" for New York City's Gay Men's Health Crisis, are a diverse group of men and women, straight and gay, who have chosen to make a difference in the fight against AIDS. The portraits of the volunteers and their clients show the physical and emotional strain that can come of dealing with a debilitating illness daily, while they also reveal depths of courage and strength. Kuklin includes much information regarding the transmission of the HIV virus, antibody testing, orthodox and alternative treatments, and aspects of day-to-day living with the disease. Powerful black-and-white photos of the people mentioned in the book make the stories all the more personal. The book humanizes a serious disease about which many are prejudiced, and it encourages understanding. Certainly this book should be shared widely among people whose lives have been affected by AIDS. The level of commitment shown by the team of buddies and the spirit of the PWAs will speak to everyone, and *Fighting Back* may encourage more people to join the fight.

Roger Sutton

SOURCE: A review of *Fighting Back: What Some People Are Doing about AIDS,* in *Bulletin of the Center for Children's Books,* Vol. 42, No. 7, March, 1989, pp. 174-75.

While there have been many commendable books for teens about AIDS, its causes, symptoms and prevention, this is the first one to tell—with candor and detail—what it is like to live with the disease. Susan Kuklin spent nine months working with a team of volunteers from the Gay Men's Health Crisis organization in New York. These volunteers (straight, gay, young and old) are "buddies," helping people with AIDS with shopping, cooking, cleaning, talking and listening. More than anything, one sees from Kuklin's account that there is no strict division between the helpers and the helped (called "clients"); instead, there is reciprocal attention and friendship among people sharing a common concern. Some of the buddies have AIDS themselves; one straight buddy, Kachin, is thinking about having the AIDS test because she wants to have children someday. "Take someone with you when you are tested," says her client Michael. "Don't go alone." Perhaps surprisingly, there is plenty of humor in this book. Manuel wants a wild haircut before he dies, so while his mother wails in dismay, friend Stephen gives him a bright orange Mohawk. Sister Kathleen, a Franciscan nun, gives safe-sex lectures and demonstrations. "Oh, I use a banana. It's the second best model." Stories weave in and out: brave, funny, irritated and angry, sad but never mawkish, and the book closes with Kachin and Michael's inspiring visit to the AIDS quilt on display during the march on Washington for gay and lesbian rights. Kuklin's organization of material is fluid and fluent, her black-and-white photographs give faces to the voices, and, wisely, she lets her subjects speak for themselves. Says one buddy, relieved and surprised that his AIDS test was negative: "My interest in AIDS hasn't changed. I used to think, that's me. Now I look at these young kids and think, why should it be them?"

Beverly Robertson

SOURCE: A review of *Fighting Back: What Some People Are Doing about AIDS,* in *Voice of Youth Advocates,* Vol. 12, No. 1, April, 1989, p. 59.

Fighting Back reports the events of a nine-month period that the author spent with a team of volunteers for the Gay Men's Health Crisis (GMHC) in New York City. Volunteers, called "buddies," are each assigned a PWA (person with AIDS) for whom they run errands, cook meals, clean, and/or just visit with. The buddies come from all walks of life, with one, Sister Kathleen, being a Franciscan nun, and another, Kachin, a Japanese immigrant. Even with their diverse origins, the volunteers are united by their commitment to the physical and emotional welfare of their PWAs. Inevitably, emotional attachments develop that make deaths very difficult to face, often requiring that some buddies take time off between assignments.

Personalizing the AIDS crisis by focusing on individuals rather than facts and statistics provides a unique and effective mechanism for learning about AIDS. Becoming acquainted with buddies, doctors, PWAs and their families emphasizes the fact that we must face this epidemic and fight back, because it has, or will eventually touch the lives of everyone.

Fighting Back is an emotionally wrenching story that is accessible to teens because it *is* about individuals, not numbers. Their courage and dedication is an inspiring tribute to everyone now desperately fighting this, as yet, incurable disease.

GOING TO MY BALLET CLASS (1989)

Kay McPherson

SOURCE: A review of *Going to My Ballet Class,* in *School Library Journal,* Vol. 35, No. 13, September, 1989, p. 241.

Jami attends beginning ballet class (or pre-ballet, as it is called here) at the Joffrey Ballet School. The material covered is very much like that in Sorine's *Our Ballet Class*. However, Sorine's book has black-and-white photographs of a class full of all-white girls, while Kuklin's full-color photographs show girls from the major ethnic groups and a little boy. The text is adequate and gets its point across clearly, but the book does not expand on materials currently available.

Carolyn Phelan

SOURCE: A review of *Going to My Ballet Class*, in *Booklist*, Vol. 86, No. 2, September 15, 1989, p. 185.

Although actual ballet lessons do not usually begin until the age of eight, pre-ballet classes are available to younger children in many communities. Those children are the audience for this book. Kuklin, whose previous books include *When I See My Dentist, Taking My Cat to the Vet,* and *Reaching For Dreams,* now takes children to the Joffrey Ballet School. Written in the first person from the point of view of Jami, a student in pre-ballet, the text describes her experiences, from dressing for class to the ending bow honoring her teacher. Boys as well as girls participate. Kuklin's clear, full-color photographs bring the experience to life. The simplicity of the background and the leotard-clad children's dress allow her to focus effectively on the actions and expressions of the students and teachers. A final note to parents, "How to Choose a Ballet Class," provides sound advice to those considering lessons for their children. A handsome book on a subject seldom approached at the beginning level.

Nancy Vasilakis

SOURCE: A review of *Going to My Ballet Class*, in *The Horn Book Magazine*, Vol. LXV, No. 5, September-October, 1989, p. 639.

The image of grinning children obviously having a great time is the prevailing impression one derives from this appealing, sure-to-be-loved photo-essay for budding ballet stars and their parents. The first-person text follows Jami through her preballet class at the Joffrey Ballet School. Photographs in full color are reassuringly multiethnic and nonsexist, as we see Dad combing Jami's hair into its ballet bun and young Edward practicing his cartwheels. The photos set the visual tone for the narrative, which establishes that a well-run ballet class for young children contains a healthy mix of discipline—"We sit in our circle, not talking, with straight backs, straight legs, and pointed toes"—and fun, "After all this standing still . . . Paul [the pianist] plays very fast, and we run all around the room." Type and pictures contribute to create a spacious, unified look, with an occasional full-page photograph adding dramatic interest. An afterword for parents on how to choose a ballet school is a welcome addition, offering some sound and detailed practical advice.

Zena Sutherland

SOURCE: A review of *Going to My Ballet Class*, in *Bulletin of the Center for Children's Books*, Vol. 43, No. 2, October, 1989, p. 36.

Color photographs show young boys and girls in a ballet class for beginners; the pictures are technically good and visually appealing as well as informative. The text is simply written in first person, so that facts about lessons and positions and steps are always from a child's viewpoint. The book concludes with a section (in smaller print) addressed to adults, giving some use-ful advice on choosing a ballet class and on researching what's available and has a good professional reputation.

GOING TO MY NURSERY SCHOOL (1990)

Denise M. Wilms

SOURCE: A review of *Going to My Nursery School*, in *Booklist*, Vol. 86, No. 22, August, 1990, p. 2176.

Because attendance in nursery school or day-care facilities is becoming so routine, there is plenty of room for books to help children prepare for that experience. Kuklin takes her young viewers on a tour of New York's First Presbyterian Church Nursery School, where a little boy named Heath Reinhard settles in to enjoy his day. Color photographs show him participating in a variety of activities, all the while following the rules of polite behavior. Kuklin provides a lengthy, substantive afterword addressed to parents advising them on what to look for in a well-run preschool. . . . Kuklin's is a fine production, more informative than Rockwell's and as handsomely designed as Rogers'. Definitely worth having, especially if demand is strong.

Kirkus Reviews

SOURCE: A review of *Going to My Nursery School*, in *Kirkus Reviews*, Vol. LVIII, No. 15, August 1, 1990, p. 1096.

The author of several other attractive picture-book photo-essays depicts a typical day with a class that has a laudable range of activities. One unusual feature: this relatively affluent city school has a rooftop playground. Three sensible pages on choosing a school are appended for adults. A good model, well presented.

Zena Sutherland

SOURCE: A review of *Going to My Nursery School*, in *Bulletin of the Center for Children's Books*, Vol. 44, No. 2, October, 1990, p. 35.

In a fine photo-essay, the narrator, one of a class of

four-year-olds, tells a lot about policies and procedures through his simple description of his own day. Heath mentions his own separation anxiety in the first days ("I didn't want my dad to leave"), but now that stage is over, and it is clear that he is happy and busy. The teachers are firm about rules, friendly and welcoming, comforting when a child is distressed. Heath talks matter-of-factly about sharing, but he doesn't say that this is imposed. The color pictures are of an excellent quality; a thoughtful postscript is addressed to parents. Informative and cheerful, this maintains the child's voice in a way that increases the accessibility of the recorded experiences. An unusually good introduction to the great mystery of what goes on at a nursery school.

Liza Bliss

SOURCE: A review of *Going to My Nursery School,* in *School Library Journal,* Vol. 36, No. 11, November, 1990, pp. 104-05.

A realistic glimpse of a day at a New York City nursery school, focusing on the activities of a class of four year olds. Readers follow Heath as he visits his cubby; says goodbye to his father; decides on an activity; cleans up; and enjoys snack time, playground time, and circle time. His security and his freedom to make choices are emphasized. There is a sea of wellgroomed white faces—the Oshkosh set—the Peters, Katies, and Andrews with fathers looking spiffy in business suits as they drop off the kids. There's a largely suburban ambiance until the class goes outdoors to their rooftop playground with city buildings all around. The text is topped off by several pages of advice to parents about how to select appropriate nursery schools. Colorful photos give a view of the school from all angles. They're extremely inviting and full of the children's activity and creativity. Wrapped up in delightful endpapers featuring a bright display of preschoolers' marker drawings, this is a good-looking, cheerful package. It's loaded with as much information, presented both verbally and visually, as preschoolers can absorb. And it gives an upbeat impression of nursery school as an experience. Its only limitation stems from the unicultural background depicted.

WHAT DO I DO NOW? TALKING ABOUT TEENAGE PREGNANCY (1991)

Kirkus Reviews

SOURCE: A review of *What Do I Do Now? Talking about Teenage Pregnancy,* in *Kirkus Reviews,* Vol. LIX, No. 11, June 1, 1991, pp. 730-31.

The author-photographer of *Fighting Back: What Some People Are Doing about AIDS* (1989) takes a similar investigative approach in interviewing young women and men of varied socioeconomic groups, affiliated with a wide spectrum of agencies. The emerging picture is both optimistic and discouraging, but a repetitive pattern stands out: immaturity, of the pregnant teens and often of their parents as well (for instance, a woman who refers to her grandchild as her son). Time and again, the baby changes a couple's relationship; almost always, the attitude of the young mother's mother is pivotal to whether the girl will choose to abort, to keep the baby, or to put it up for adoption.

Matter-of-factly, Kuklin spells out the daily routines of these young mothers. The message isn't lost: this is no picnic. Adeptly, she folds information in—e.g., you *can* get pregnant again before your period returns. Throughout, there is emphasis on building a support system, whatever the decision. A fine job.

Libby K. White

SOURCE: A review of *What Do I Now? Talking about Teenage Pregnancy,* in *School Library Journal,* Vol. 37, No. 7, July, 1991, pp. 94-5.

Kuklin interviewed teens and their families from many racial, ethnic, and socioeconomic backgrounds, as well as medical and counseling personnel of organizations that assist those facing unplanned pregnancies. From these interviews and her observations of a Planned Parenthood unit, an adoption agency, a facility that performs abortions, and a hospital clinic, she presents in a clear and detailed style the pros and cons of options available to pregnant teens and their consequences. Some descriptions of procedures are graphic; accounts of the difficulties of those who kept their children and of those who opted for adoption also pull no punches. A particularly ugly episode relates the abuse and ostracism suffered by a teen who gave up her child. Kuklin is frank about her sympathies for the Planned Parenthood approach. Her experiences with pro-life groups are chronicled with negative connotations. She touches on a currently volatile issue about which she is uneasy—parental notification in teen abortions. Solid information, soberly presented, without moralization or strident activism.

Laura L. Lent

SOURCE: A review of *What Do I Do Now? Talking about Teenage Pregnancy,* in *Voice of Youth Advocates,* Vol. 14, No. 3, August, 1991, p. 190.

Kuklin's book on the choices teenagers make after they discover that they are pregnant is phenomenal. Part of what makes this book so terrific is that before Kuklin began writing, she spent two years interviewing pregnant teens so she would be able to accurately present their individual situations. In my opinion, her diligent research and her selection of first-person accounts pay off because she successfully portrays the anguish that each teen must feel when she discovers she is pregnant, and the further turmoil that the teen undergoes when she considers and finally decides on having an abortion, giving the baby up for adoption, or raising the child herself. As a result, most readers will feel empathy for the plights of these young women.

Besides arousing the reader's emotions, the author educates her audience about a very real problem in American society—teen pregnancy. To her credit, Kuklin does not attempt to judge any of these young women or to anger the reader. Her motivation is simple—to inform her audience, not to moralize. She also includes a glossary of anatomical and medical terms at the end of the book so that no question is left unanswered. The glossary is an invaluable source for teen readers who may not understand a term, and who are too shy to ask for a definition.

I think any reader—be that person a teen or an adult—will be interested in what these teens have to say about why they make the choices they do when faced with the prospect of motherhood. This book is easy to read; however, it is somewhat depressing so I found myself putting it down and coming back to it a lot. Nevertheless, I highly recommend it to teens; parents; teachers; and people, in general, who are concerned with the skyrocketing rate of teen pregnancy. Because I cannot convey the emotions of pregnant teens in this review, I can't do the book justice. This is a book that simply must be read to gain an understanding of the problem.

Betsy Hearne

SOURCE: A review of *What Do I Do Now? Talking about Teenage Pregnancy,* in *Bulletin of the Center for Children's Books,* Vol. 45, No. 3, November, 1991, pp. 66-7.

Pregnant adolescents (23.9 percent of U.S. teenage girls have been pregnant by the time they're eighteen) come from a wide spectrum of ethnic and socio-economic backgrounds, a fact to which Kuklin has paid careful attention in her interviews here. White, black, Hispanic, rich, poor, educated, or ignorant, these subjects have an overwhelming problem in common and are often articulate in voicing it. They also vary in their reactions and decisions, from the uncertain 13-year-old who is pregnant with her second child to the decisive 18-year-old having her second abortion or the 17-year-old who insists on personally handing over her baby to adoptive parents. The experiences these girls describe are more informative than a factual compendium and manifestly convincing of the need for birth control education. Kuklin has balanced background information with the subjects' own words in a natural flow to ease young readers through a series of stories that may help prevent them from becoming a statistic. Names have been changed for confidentiality, but clear black-and-white photographs portray several of the teens who kept their babies.

GOING TO MY GYMNASTICS CLASS (1991)

Stephanie Zvirin

SOURCE: A review of *Going to My Gymnastics Class,* in *Booklist,* Vol. 87, No. 22, August, 1991, p. 2150.

Eighty rolls of film taken on two visits to a New York City fitness center yielded the wonderful photographs for the latest in Kuklin's ongoing series. Young Gaspar Caro provides the unaffected voice of the text, which focuses on the experiences he and eight pre-school-age classmates have while practicing exercises and routines in their beginners' gym class. As usual, the photographs count as much as the text. Here, they show a gym bright with color and alive with movement, and they introduce various activities, clearly showing the hard work involved. They also capture the children's nervous anticipation as they await their turns, registering, forever, the exhilaration and pride on young faces after the kids accomplish each task—whether it be warming up like an *X* or an *I* or jumping joyously on a springboard.

Zena Sutherland

SOURCE: A review of *Going to My Gymnastics Class,* in *Bulletin of the Center for Children's Books,* Vol. 45, No. 2, October, 1991, p. 42.

One of the members of a beginning gymnastics class, Gaspar is the putative narrator of a simple, direct continuous text in which Kuklin describes basic exercises and defines a few terms. There isn't that much needing definition, partly because nothing complicated is going on, and partly because the color photographs make procedures clear. There is but one instance in which a term is used (sitting "in pike") and explained but not shown. Two teachers are shown working with nine young children (of both sexes), encouraging but not rushing them, reminding them to be careful as well as to use correct technique. Everybody seems to be having fun, and this book may well encourage children to try it themselves.

Janice C. Hayes

SOURCE: A review of *Going to My Gymnastics Class,* in *School Library Journal,* Vol. 37, No. 12, December, 1991, p. 111.

A look at the experiences and excitement of gymnastics lessons through the eyes of a young beginning gymnast. A light sense of humor is apparent as the boy tells about his lessons. The dialogue and narrative style is clear, lively, and quite engaging. Beautiful full-color photographs of children participating in the class are found on every page. Simple tumbling and equipment skills are presented along with safety procedures on appropriate clothing, spotting, and sequencing of skills. This is sure to appeal to children interested in this sport, and . . . it would be an appropriate book for spectators.

📖 *HOW MY FAMILY LIVES IN AMERICA* (1992)

Heather Vogel Frederick

SOURCE: "Salad Bowl of Storybooks," in *The Christian Science Monitor,* January 1, 1992, p. 10.

In a trio of photo essays, photographer Susan Kuklin records the lives of three children—Sanu, an African-American girl, Eric, a Hispanic-American boy, and April, an Asian-American girl. First-person text and abundant photographs give *How My Family Lives in America* a sense of immediacy and make this an especially welcome introduction to diverse cultural and ethnic traditions.

Kirkus Reviews

SOURCE: A review of *How My Family Lives in America,* in *Kirkus Reviews,* Vol. LX, No. 4, February 15, 1992, p. 257.

A multicultural consciousness-raiser in which three children, each with at least one parent who did not grow up in the U.S., describe some of their adapted family customs. Food is a common theme: Sanu's African father invites friends over for a special meal of *tiebou dienn,* eaten on the floor from a common bowl, and "while we eat, we hear stories about our parents when they were little in Senegal and in Baltimore"; Eric enjoys baseball, the merengue, and especially *arroz con pollo y habichuelas* with his Puerto Rican family; Taiwanese Chin Lan ("My name in America is April") has cold sesame noodles, *tsu ma liang mein,* in school, and take-out pizza for dinner. The young narrators, speaking in an easy, unforced way, invite readers to see them both as individuals and as proud members of ethnic groups, but not, ultimately, as so different from children anywhere. The practices they describe are a well-chosen blend of the exotic and the mundane, enhanced by many lively, natural-looking color photos. Recipes at the end.

Alexandra Marris

SOURCE: A review of *How My Family Lives in America,* in *School Library Journal,* Vol. 38, No. 3, March, 1992, p. 231.

A glimpse at how three families impart a sense of ethnic identity to their children. Five-year-old Sanu's father is from Senegal. Her mother grew up in Baltimore. Sanu and her father buy food for a traditional dish he will prepare and share with other relatives. Eric and his mother were born in New York City, while his father is from Puerto Rico. When relatives gather at their house, they like to dance the merengue. April's parents were born and raised in Taiwan. On Saturdays she and her siblings go to Chinese school to learn calligraphy. All three families live in middle-class urban settings. All three children have sensitive, caring parents; two of them have strong ties with extended families. Religion is not discussed directly, but there are hints of Christian backgrounds in two cases. Each child's first-person narration is simple and uncomplicated, with occasional humorous touches. One can almost hear them speaking. The full-color photographs are well composed and serviceable. As there is a growing demand for books depicting multicultural heritages, this one will be useful.

Hazel Rochman

SOURCE: A review of *How My Family Lives in America,* in *Booklist,* Vol. 88, No. 13, March 1, 1992, pp. 1282-83.

In loosely connected photo-essays with large, clear type and cheerful color pictures, three children—an African American, a Hispanic American, and a Chinese American—talk about their families. Each child has at least one parent who did not grow up in the U.S. There is pride in the traditions they keep alive from the old country as well as in their American culture. For example, Sanu's father was born in Senegal, and she loves his African clothes and customs. She's proud of her mixed heritage—from him and also from her American grandmother—and she likes to tease him, "You're in America now." Eric's father is from Puerto Rico and so are all his grandparents. April's parents are from Taiwan. She speaks Mandarin, and on Saturdays, she goes to Chinese school, but her family enjoys pizza as much as Chinese noodles. Food is always a rich part of cultural identity, and Kuklin focuses a lot on table manners and special dishes, and at the back in small type, she includes a special family recipe from each group. The photos are clear, informal, affectionate, upbeat. It would have been nice to have a white family, too, so as to avoid any distinction between "them" and "us." But all kids will see the richness in diversity and the connections among the human family.

Roger Sutton

SOURCE: A review of *How My Family Lives in America,* in *Bulletin of the Center for Children's Books,* Vol. 45, No. 8, April, 1992, pp. 212-13.

In a spacious format that will work well for both the preschool listener and independent reader, Kuklin's newest photoessay presents three young children growing up in bicultural circumstances. Sanu's father is Senegalese, her mother black American; Eric's father is from Puerto Rico, his mother is an Hispanic-American born in New York; April's parents were born in Taiwan. Each of the chapters is told through the voice of the child, a device Kuklin manages less self-consciously than most. Says Eric, "when my parents are at work, my mommy's mommy, Nana Carmen, takes me shopping at the *carniceria,* the Spanish meat market. I get to pay." The profiles casually blend everyday America (playing baseball, eating pizza) with specific cultural activities (Sanu's

From Reaching for Dreams: A Ballet from Rehearsal to Opening Night, *written and photographed by Susan Kuklin.*

Senegalese clothing, April's Chinese calligraphy). Definitions aren't always clear, with Sanu, for example, seeming to call herself African-American because her father is African, a more restricted usage than that currently in vogue, and Kuklin does not make the distinction between Puerto Rico and the foreign countries of Senegal and Taiwan. Still, the level, amount, and kinds of cultural detail (lots of eating, for example) are appropriate for the intended audience, and Kuklin's color photos show happy families, lively parties, and tasty foods. One recipe from each family is appended, but a don't-do-this-alone note should have been included, particularly for a recipe that involves deep-frying a whole stuffed fish.

SPEAKING OUT: TEENAGERS TAKE ON RACE, SEX, AND IDENTITY (1993)

Susan Dunn

SOURCE: A review of *Speaking Out: Teenagers Take on Race, Sex, and Identity,* in *Voice of Youth Advocates,* Vol. 16, No. 2, June, 1993, pp. 116-17.

Bayard Rustin High School for the Humanities is the most culturally diverse school in New York City; racially it is one-fourth white, one-fourth African-American, one-fourth Asian, and one-fourth Hispanic. The author spent a year at the school interviewing students and faculty members and observing a racially mixed student body. As she states, she "specifically wanted to explore issues related to prejudice, stereotyping and identity."

The book is a collection of interviews with students from all different races and backgrounds, discussing their experiences in dealing with prejudice and racial stereotypes. When asked about stereotypes they encounter every day, Asian students say that they all feel pressured to do well in school because "everyone knows Asians are smart"—good at anything that has to do with math, physics or science. Asian teens are further divided within themselves as ABC's (American-born Chinese) or FOB's (Fresh off the boat). The African-American students retaliate by saying that they are all subjected to the stereotype of being good dancers, that they all supposedly steal and sell drugs and belong to gangs. Within the black groups the darker skinned students complain that their lighter skinned peers think themselves superior. The author interviews not only students from different races; also included is the overweight girl who wonders if she'll ever get a boyfriend, and the gay teen who can't bear to tell his peers his secret. As he reveals to the class in an anonymous note that he asks the teacher to read aloud, it's hard enough to deal with his family's negative reactions, much less to tell his friends at school and risk alienating them as well. Then there's the stutterer who, after spending seventh and eighth grade not talking at all because of his handicap, constantly has to work to prove that he's not stupid just because he can't get the words out sometimes.

Many of these testimonies are heart-breaking, some are uplifting, some are terrifying; every single one is memorable. All the teenagers agree that they are tired of being stereotyped, tired of being made to feel like an "other" rather than an insider. The problem is that no one really knows what to do about it. Becoming more tolerant is a start. So, hopefully, is reading this book.

Kirkus Reviews

SOURCE: A review of *Speaking Out: Teenagers Take on Race, Sex, and Identity,* in *Kirkus Reviews,* Vol. LXI, No. 11, June 1, 1993, p. 723.

The author of *Fighting Back: What Some People Are Doing about AIDS* (1989) gets at the heart of subtle encounters with prejudice during a year at Manhattan's multiethnic Bayard Rustin High School. Her interviews, plus observations of classes and clubs, bring out the roles parents play (positive and negative) in perceptions of self and others as experienced by African-Americans, Latinos, Caucasians, Asians, multiracial kids, short kids, fat kids, stutterers, homosexuals, immigrants, and "special-ed" youngsters. As might be expected, the more talk of differences there is, the more the students realize commonalities. Guided by excellent teachers committed to keen probing about multiculturalism and recognition of diversity (and perhaps influenced by the reporter in their midst), their mixing becomes less superficial. Kuklin definitely captures the edge/excitement/hope/despair of contemporary New York. Splendid b&w portrait photos.

Donna Weisman

SOURCE: A review of *Speaking Out: Teenagers Take on Race, Sex, and Identity,* in *School Library Journal,* Vol. 39, No. 7, July, 1993, p. 108.

The teenagers of the title are multiracial students from various socioeconomic backgrounds at Bayard Rustin High School for the Humanities in New York City. Their candid comments are occasionally predictable, but more often are revealing and thought-provoking. Clearly the contents could be used as discussion starters in classes not only in conjunction with specific subjects, but also as a way of exploring the differences in attitudes in other regions of the country. High quality, full-page black-and-white photographs of some of the staff members and student body are included. Librarians and teachers will need to make YAs aware of this title through booktalks, displays, and other devices as the topic is not an especially common one.

Stephanie Zvirin

SOURCE: A review of *Speaking Out: Teenagers Take on Race, Sex, and Identity,* in *Booklist,* Vol. 89, No. 22, August, 1993, p. 2061.

Of all Kuklin's interview-style books, including *What Do I Do Now?* (1991), about teenage pregnancy, this will have the widest audience and leave the greatest impact because its setting is one of the places kids identify with the most—their school. It is the result of a year's worth of observation of students and faculty at Manhattan's Bayard Rustin High School for the Humanities, a public school with a fairly evenly distributed student population comprising Asian and African Americans, whites, and Latinos. Kuklin listened in on classroom and school-club discussions and interviewed individual students and teachers in an attempt to gauge prejudice among today's young adults.

Exposing frustration as well as anger lurking beneath the school's surface, she has captured a wide range of feeling—from the opinion of the young NAAWP (National Association for the Advancement of White People) member who declares, "So many things are unfair. All the emphasis is on the African-American person who is oppressed in America. What about the poor oppressed whites?" to that of the girl who admits, "I know that prejudice is one of those things we have to face. But I wish that the club [the school's Humane Humanity Club] wouldn't talk about it so I wouldn't have to know about it." The students and teachers speak candidly about many things related to identity—being short, having a speech impediment, being gay, being in a special education class—but race and cultural diversity are the primary topics, and what readers learn will either shock them considerably or validate what they already know. The book offers no answers—Kuklin in no way interjects her own views. It does, however, make clear the insidious nature of prejudice, and it will inspire readers to think about the stereotypes they have acquired from their parents, from television, from their friends, and from what they read. Although rather arbitrary in its mixing of reported classroom conversations and personal profiles, the book is, nonetheless, an excellent springboard for class discussion, in addition to being an extraordinarily compelling reminder of the power of words to hurt and to heal. Excellent black-and-white portraits of some of the people with whom Kuklin speaks give character to the voices.

Roger Sutton

SOURCE: A review of *Speaking Out: Teenagers Take on Race, Sex, and Identity,* in *Bulletin of the Center for Children's Books,* Vol. 47, No. 2, October, 1993, p. 49.

As Kuklin notes in her introduction, Bayard Rustin High School for the Humanities in New York is the perfect place to find kids to talk about the importance of race, class, gender and self-identity in their lives. The student body at Humanities is a fourth each white, Latino, African American and Asian American, and the school has a conscious commitment to help students bridge ethnic and other borders. Through a variety of first-person portraits and wide-shots of classes and clubs in action, Kuklin demonstrates the effects that the multiple "isms" have in kids' daily lives. "This has to be more than a conversation about sweet and sour pork," cautions one Chinese American student, and the issues debated here—having a boy/girl friend of a different race, confronting prejudice in friends and teachers, interracial violence, balancing immigrant family expectations with American customs—have real bite. As in her *Fighting Back* or *What Do I Do Now?*, Kuklin allows her subjects to speak for themselves, even when it's a white boy explaining why he joined The National Association for the Advancement of White People, or a gay kid saying that he wished he was a girl: "Girls get more attention. Girls can be sexy and flirty." Voices we don't think of as "minority"—a fat girl, a stutterer—also speak their pieces and will widen readers' understanding of what being "different" can mean. Black-and-white portraits of the interviewees have a candor and immediacy missing in yearbook pictures, and many teens will see themselves within these pages.

FIGHTING FIRES (1993)

Carolyn Phelan

SOURCE: A review of *Fighting Fires,* in *Booklist,* Vol. 89, No. 21, July, 1993, p. 1971.

Clear, full-color photographs feature the equipment and operations of today's firefighters, shown and described as they carry out individual jobs as parts of specific crews. As up-to-date as the fire truck's computerized cab is Kuklin's explanation of terms such as *roof man* and *outside vent man:* "All fire fighters are nicknamed *men* because in earlier days only men had these jobs." That sounds quaint and logical in context, but eventually leads to this sentence: "When the *nozzle man* needs a break, she moves to the back position. . . . " That's enough to make any grammarian whimper. Kids will be more absorbed with the photos than with the text, though, and that's Kuklin's strong point. A good resource for primary grade classrooms studying community helpers and for preschool fire-engine buffs.

Eldon Younce

SOURCE: A review of *Fighting Fires,* in *School Library Journal,* Vol. 39, No. 9, September, 1993, p. 225.

This is just the book for those youngsters who are fascinated by fire engines. Its bright, full-color photographs vary in size from quarter to full page. Most of the action shots look a little staged, but are not stiff. Kuklin's prose reads easily and smoothly. Unfamiliar words and important terms are printed in boldface and defined in context. Wide margins frame both text and illustrations. No female firefighters are discernable in the pictures, but the author uses "he" and "she" constructions. The volume concludes with a page entitled "What To Do," which covers some tips for fire prevention and in case of fire. An excellent title to use with a community social-studies unit and during fire prevention week.

FROM HEAD TO TOE: HOW A DOLL IS MADE (1994)

Deborah Stevenson

SOURCE: A review of *From Head to Toe: How a Doll Is Made,* in *Bulletin of the Center for Children's Books,* Vol. 47, No. 9, May, 1994, pp. 291-92.

Autumn is a rosy-checked, nattily dressed doll, presumably available in your local toy store, and this photo-essay (reminiscent of Kathryn Lasky's *Dollmaker,* although Kuklin deals with mass production and writes for younger readers) shows how she came to be, following her through her design, molding, eye-setting, hairdressing, and costuming. Kuklin focuses on the specific craftspeople along the doll-making line, allowing Wellington the eye-installer ("'All the time I'm making a doll I look at her and say, "How ya doing?" To me, this is a little baby'") and Greta the dresser ("Dolls are great because they smile back—they don't talk back") to comment on the work and the final product. Kuklin is a talented documentarian and she seems inspired by the slightly peculiar situation here: the conversational text is lively and entertaining, and the photos, filled with disembodied heads and naked doll-butts as well as tidy doll dresses, have a surreal charm. Kids who believe dolls to be small people may find some scenes (such as the eyeball being thrust into Autumn's bald but lipsticked head) a little alarming, but the let's-see-how-it-ticks school of youngster will get a kick out of all the mechanical details and the posterish double-spread filled with eyeballs staring right at the reader.

Stephanie Zvirin

SOURCE: A review of *From Head to Toe: How a Doll Is Made,* in *Booklist,* Vol. 90, No. 17, May 1, 1994, p. 1598.

Nowhere has Kuklin better demonstrated her facility with a camera. The wonderful pictures she's gathered here bring process and people together. The jacket photo, a fetching picture of a pretty doll's face, will be a spectacular draw for doll lovers. The clear, full-color photographs inside the book, which include many close-ups (a particularly arresting one is a double-page spread of dolls' eyes), are equally striking as they guide us through a factory to witness the dollmaking process—from the pen-and-paper design of the character to the tying of the costume's last perfect bow. Kuklin adds an attractively personal element to the text by naming each worker pictured and by including a few direct quotes. The book design is well thought out, with an eye-catching interplay of large and small photographs and enlarged type surrounded by plenty of pleasing white space. A book certain to enchant the doll lovers among us—adults as well as children.

AFTER A SUICIDE: YOUNG PEOPLE SPEAK UP (1994)

Stephanie Zvirin

SOURCE: A review of *After a Suicide: Young People Speak Up,* in *Booklist,* Vol. 91, No. 4, October 15, 1994, pp. 409, 417.

Turning to the emotional issues involved in suicide survival, Kuklin focuses not simply on people whose attempts to kill themselves fail, but also on friends and family left behind when a death attempt succeeds. With artless candor, "survivors" who've lost loved ones (mostly older YAs, some college age), explain the obvious as well as the many subtle ways their lives have been altered by death: the shock, the stigma, the loss of trust and self-esteem, and the guilt of not knowing or helping enough. Careful not to ignore the complex issues that prompt suicide, Kuklin also includes the words of two people who courted death (one who struggled with substance abuse, another with sexual orientation) as well as a mock-up of a conversation that took place on a suicide hotline. As usual, her editorial hand is light (she has left in the harsh language and raw sentiment) yet firmly directed. There is a sense that healing is possible, but readers will find the riveting detail and candor of the accounts more impressive than images of recovery; the surprisingly rocky road for people left behind is clearly and sympathetically revealed, as is the wrenching torment of those whose lives have spun out of control.

Libby K. White

SOURCE: A review of *After a Suicide: Young People Speak Up,* in *School Library Journal,* Vol. 40, No. 12, December, 1994, p. 135.

Kuklin attempts to support survivors in confronting the social stigma and isolation that suicide engenders; hopes to convince young people that killing themselves is not the solution to their problems; and urges teens who suspect that someone they know is at risk to talk with that person about it. The introduction traces historical attitudes toward suicide. Part one consists of interviews with surviving siblings, parents, classmates, teachers, and counselors. Part two offers powerful interviews with two young men who were deeply depressed and survived suicide attempts. Both now lead positive and constructive lives. An addendum that describes the work of a volunteer hotline is realistic but upbeat. The black-and-white photographs are of high quality and are natural complements to the well-organized, well-written text. The further reading list includes fiction as well as non-fiction. Many books on teen suicide discuss aspects of the effects on survivors, but Kuklin's is the only one that considers their predicament so thoroughly, sympathetically, and intelligently.

Elizabeth Bush

SOURCE: A review of *After a Suicide: Young People Speak Up,* in *Bulletin of the Center for Children's Books,* Vol. 48, No. 5, January, 1995, p. 170.

Interviews with families of suicide victims and with persons who attempted suicide probe survivors' struggles to cope with grief and guilt and their efforts to find some single, definitive reason why the suicide chose death. With sadness, anger, or detachment, siblings, friends, and children of victims speak of the stages of mourning, the benefits (and failures) of support groups, and their ultimate inability to discover a compelling motivation behind the death; other interviewees address the psychological turmoil that brought them to make a suicide attempt and the road back to stability and recovery. A skilled interviewer and sensitive photographer, Kuklin allows the personalities as well as the situations of the subjects to emerge, which results in a credible and eminently readable diversity of voices. Although the text is accessible to middle-grade readers, the range of interviewees' ages—late teen to adult—tends to limit the interest level of the work to a junior-high audience and above. Addenda on the operation of a crisis hot line, suggestions for further reading, and a generalized outline on "where to get help" (whether for survivors or potential suicides is unclear) are included.

William R. Mollineaux

SOURCE: A review of *After a Suicide: Young People Speak Up,* in *Voice of Youth Advocates,* Vol. 17, No. 6, February, 1995, pp. 359-60.

While spending a year in a New York City high school researching *Speaking Out: Teenagers Take on Race, Sex, and Identity,* Kuklin was surprised to discover how often teenagers brought up the topic of suicide. Thus, the idea was conceived for this pertinent and necessary book which vividly and candidly describes the efforts of suicide survivors (those who have attempted suicide and survived, and the family or friends of a person who has committed suicide) to cope.

The book is divided into two parts. Part I is concerned with survivors who are family members, friends, and schoolmates, while Part II focuses on a person who attempted suicide and another who considered it. The addendum is comprised of two composites created from hotline calls by people who threatened suicide, and shows how getting potential suicide victims to talk can help them confront their problems.

Kuklin's reasons for writing the book are threefold: "to help other survivors; to encourage people who are feeling suicidal to talk about it with a professional or a trusted adult; to help people understand that suicide is never a way to solve problems." In all three endeavors, she is exceptionally successful without being preachy! The book merits its greatest praise for being a suicide deterrent, for I believe that any reader contemplating suicide will reconsider this final act.

📖 *KODOMO: CHILDREN OF JAPAN* (1995)

Roger Sutton

SOURCE: A review of *Kodomo: Children of Japan,* in *Bulletin of the Center for Children's Books,* Vol. 48, No. 8, April, 1995, p. 279.

Kodomo means children, and here Kuklin focuses on seven of them to give a picture of contemporary Japanese child-life. Each child gives a brief first-person narrative (whether interviews were conducted through a translator is not stated) telling of school activities or participation in traditional customs such as a tea ceremony or martial arts. Kuklin's decision to divide the book by locale (three kids from Hiroshima and four from Kyoto) and, additionally, to concentrate on schooling in Hiroshima and customs in Kyoto inadvertently gives the impression that the second city is more fun than the first; "About Hiroshima" and "About Kyoto" pages give information about the cities but are only tangentially related to the interviews. There's also a page on Japanese writing at the end, and explanations of facts glanced at in the text are placed in the margins, looking like captions to the color photos but in fact functioning as footnotes. (An explanation of yen, for example, is placed next to a photo in which the only currency to be seen is a U.S. greenback.) This isn't as pulled-together a presentation as we've come to expect from this talented photojournalist, but the book is quite browsable and the excellent photos offer their own rewards—expect particularly heavy wear on the pages that show nine-year-old Keiko and eight-year-old Masaaki at their respective martial arts classes.

Lauren Peterson

SOURCE: A review of *Kodomo: Children of Japan,* in *Booklist,* Vol. 91, No. 15, April 1, 1995, p. 1391.

Seven Japanese children are the guides for this informa-tive, insightful look at daily life and traditional Japanese customs and culture. Nozomi describes his noisy math class, where the teacher calls out addition problems and students scramble to find the answer on their abacus. Beautiful Ai tells of the special importance of her kimono, once her mother's, and explains the painstaking process of putting it on. Keiko and Masaaki enjoy the physical and mental strength that comes with their study of kendo and judo, and Masako and Natsuko delight in calligraphy and Japanese dance. The many full-color photos, some with lengthy captions, capture the individuality and intelligence of these spirited youngsters and, at the same time, allow readers to see that Japanese and American cultures are actually more alike than different.

John Philbrook

SOURCE: A review of *Kodomo: Children of Japan,* in *School Library Journal,* Vol. 41, No. 8, August, 1995, p. 148.

Kodomo, meaning child or children, describes the everyday lives of 6 girls and 1 boy, ranging in age from 8 to 14, in contemporary Japan. The first section. "A Way of Life," focuses on daily activities in Hiroshima; the second, "Traditional Activities," on sports and the arts in the ancient capital of Kyoto. Each part opens with evocations of nature and closes with a brief description of the city involved. In between, the children introduce themselves. Those from Hiroshima describe shopping, school life, the complexities of donning a kimono, and setting up for the Doll Festival. The Kyoto section features youngsters working at kendo and judo, mastering calligraphy, and studying the tea ceremony and traditional dance. Though supposedly first-person narratives, the presentations are fairly uniform—only one child seems to have a distinct voice and personality of her own. The full-color photographs are excellent, lively, and sometimes humorous, capturing the variety and individuality of these young people far better than the text. The typeface chosen to introduce each subsection is not distinct enough, making for some momentary confusion. Judith Elkin's *A Family in Japan* presents more in-depth information, though Kuklin's title has better photos.

📖 *FIREWORKS: THE SCIENCE, THE ART, AND THE MAGIC* (1996)

Deborah Stevenson

SOURCE: A review of *Fireworks: The Science, the Art, and the Magic,* in *Bulletin of the Center for Children's Books,* Vol. 49, No. 7, March, 1996, pp. 232-33.

Except for a few nervous dogs, almost everybody likes fireworks, and Susan Kuklin gives eager audiences a chance to know incendiary displays a bit better. Focusing on the Grucci family, the "First Family of Fireworks," the book gives a basic explanation of the making, storing, exploding, and choreographing of fireworks, including some description of the different varieties and how they are achieved. The text is not as strong as it might be: readers who don't know what actually makes fireworks flammable won't learn it here, the technical discussions tend to be dauntingly dense, and it can be difficult to discern just what part of the text a photograph is illustrating. The real glory here lies in the photographs: Kuklin shows pyrotechnics at their most splendiferous and varied, with gold-and-blue spiders, silver tourbillions, and the Grucci trademark, split golden comets, streaking through the dark skies and lighting up Shea Stadium below or enhanced by the glittering skyline behind them—in fact, real-life fireworks may be rather disappointing by comparison. Readers may not get all the information they'd like here, but for sheer oohs and ahs per page, this is a firecracker.

Kathleen McCabe

SOURCE: A review of *Fireworks: The Science, the Art, and the Magic,* in *School Library Journal,* Vol. 42, No. 4, April, 1996, p. 146.

"Ooooh! Ahhh!" The appreciative cries of delighted onlookers are almost audible in this visually appealing book on the fireworks produced by the Gruccis of Long Island, New York. Kuklin takes readers right into the factory where the family and longtime employees load the shells that will ultimately become Roman candles, blue and golden spiders, white waves, and more. The clear text describes the mechanics of fireworks and follows the pyrotechnicians as they prepare for a show. The stars of this book are the full-color photographs. Glorious explosions almost burst from the pages, just as the Gruccis' finales fill the night sky. . . . Kuklin's title will delight young and old while filling a serious void.

Kirkus Reviews

SOURCE: A review of *Fireworks: The Science, the Art, and the Magic,* in *Kirkus Reviews,* Vol. LXIV, No. 11, June 1, 1996, p. 824.

Young and old alike will enjoy meeting the Gruccis, dubbed "The First Family of Fireworks," and learning all the details involved in staging a fireworks show. Readers learn that the Gruccis love their business, which dates back to 1850. None of them, however, is able to explain exactly what makes the work more of a calling than a job, although certainly part of the answer can be found in the trademark fireworks they detonate at every show, to honor deceased family members. Actual preparations for a show require infinite care: Made by hand, the fireworks in a twenty-minute display may require two days' work; employees wear only cotton, to avoid sparks of static electricity. Many of the full-color photographs illustrate the fireworks detonated during a show, while the text defines all the jargon of the business: aerials, breaks, and reports. The book concludes with a brief history of fireworks.

Some of the posed photos of the Gruccis have a stilted, silly quality, and Kuklin can become so gushing that the book reads like a public relations piece. The subject of fireworks, however, is so inherently exhilarating that readers will easily forgive her for getting a little carried away.

Stephanie Zvirin

SOURCE: A review of *Fireworks: The Science, the Art, and the Magic,* in *Booklist,* Vol. 92, No. 19, June 1 & 15, 1996, pp. 1710, 1712.

As she did in her 1994 book *From Head to Toe* (about doll making), which was written for a slightly younger audience, Kuklin takes readers into a small business operation that manufactures a product of interest to kids. Her focus here is on the Grucci family, whose fireworks business and pyrotechnic displays have earned them the title "First Family of Fireworks." As usual, Kuklin's photos are fascinating and crystal clear, catching not only the spectacle of a well-staged fireworks show but also the preliminary work that goes on behind the scenes. The text, however, is problematic in both its explanations and its organization. Information about the Grucci family, placed in an afterword, would have been better at the beginning, and although Kuklin tries to personalize the text, speaking often of family members (and quoting them at times), the individuals shown in the erratically captioned photos are not always easily identified through the accompanying text. Readers will be intrigued by explanations of fireworks in the making, but there are no diagrams to ease them through the intricacies. Yet, with relatively little information available about fireworks, this may answer some questions, and the photos are guaranteed to attract browsers.

📖 *IRREPRESSIBLE SPIRIT: CONVERSATIONS WITH HUMAN RIGHTS ACTIVISTS* (1996)

Tracey Kroll

SOURCE: A review of *Irrepressible Spirit: Conversations with Human Rights Activists,* in *School Library Journal,* Vol. 42, No. 4, April, 1996, p. 162.

This collection of conversations with 10 human-rights activists records atrocities committed around the globe. Kuklin touches on such tragic events as the Tianamen Square massacre, the Bosnian War, and incidents in Haiti, as well as the issues such as the death penalty and slavery. At the end of each of the personal narratives, the writers give their own messages to the world. Each narrator offers a passionate and moving story; all are compelling and intense in their descriptions. This is a quality book that will stir strong emotions and raise aware ness, but it will take a mature audience to under stand the messages of the activists and the intent of the graphic details.

Susan Dove Lempke

SOURCE: A review of *Irrepressible Spirit: Conversations with Human Rights Activists,* in *Booklist,* Vol. 92, No. 17, May 1, 1996, p. 1503.

In her introduction, Kuklin names some human rights: "The right to live, the right to free speech, the right to practice the religion of one's choice, and the right to equality before the law." For each of 11 activists, she gives the background of human rights abuses in the activist's country, and then stands back to let her interviewee speak in a conversational, first-person voice. Kuklin has chosen her subjects and the details they reveal with great finesse, giving enough detail to substantiate the horrors of rape, torture, and murder but not overwhelm young readers. The stories are heartfelt and heartrending, but all end with a message from the activist; for example, a lawyer investigating child abuse in Jamaican jails says, "Don't be afraid to speak up. Ask questions. Never doubt that you are important. Your words, your actions can make extraordinary differences." Readers will find the book depressing, but with the personal messages and the list of addresses of human rights organizations, they may find it inspiring as well.

Deborah Stevenson

SOURCE: A review of *Irrepressible Spirit: Conversations with Human Rights Activists,* in *Bulletin of the Center for Children's Books,* Vol. 50, No. 1, September, 1996, p. 19.

Eleven activists from countries all over the globe tell their stories here: some, such as China's Li Lu and Cuba's David Moya, are witnesses to their own persecution as well as that of their compatriots; others, such as Ivana Nizich (who describes her fact-finding in Bosnia) and Joe Ingle (who uses the example of a specific inmate to discuss his opposition to the death penalty in the U.S.), fight against injustices they feel fortunate to have been spared. Kuklin breaks the accounts up into seven chapters, which focus on subjects such as "The Right to Freedom of Expression," "The Right to One's Life," and "The Right to Vote." The testimony (which frequently tells of teenage experiences or addresses the status of children) makes compelling reading; the voices here are intense and individual, and they often demonstrate a vigorous sense of humor in counterpoint to their very serious subject. The interviewees' brief autobiographies and final messages don't preach but instead show how commitment can be translated into action in many different ways and by many different people. Far more energizing than series nonfiction about global strife, this will offer teens an idea of the varied forms "good works" can take and how challenging and exciting they can be. Additional material about Human Rights Watch (the organization with which most of the interviewees are affiliated), a list of other human-rights organizations, endnotes, and a bibliography are included. Kuklin's photographic portraits of the activists are interspersed with occasional photographs of the situations they hope to change.

Additional coverage of Kuklin's life and career is contained in the following sources published by Gale Research: *Contemporary Authors,* Vol. 130; and *Something about the Author,* Vol. 95.

Michael Morpurgo

1943-

English author of fiction, picture books, retellings, and short stories; editor and anthologist.

Major works include *The War Horse* (1982), *Why the Whales Came* (1985), *King of the Cloud Forests* (1988), *Waiting for Anya* (1990), *The War of Jenkins' Ear* (1993).

INTRODUCTION

The prolific author of works in a variety of genres and styles, Morpurgo is respected as an author of books for preschoolers, primary and middle graders, and young adults that reflect his insight, sensitivity, strong sense of place, and lyrical prose style. Morpurgo writes historical fiction, realistic fiction, animal stories, fantasies, picture books, and easy readers as well as retellings of classic English legends; in addition, he has edited and contributed to several anthologies. Acknowledged for the originality, inventiveness, and thought-provoking quality of his books, which range from young adult novels with serious themes to exciting adventure stories with heart-rending endings for middle graders to picture books and easy readers laced with fantasy and humor, Morpurgo is often celebrated for his vivid evocation of the English countryside and his realistic and empathic portrayals of animals. He often uses the rural landscape around his home in Devon as the setting for his works, which are noted for their authentic portrayal of farming, village, and seaside communities. Characteristically, Morpurgo places his young male and female protagonists in situations that call upon their courage, loyalty, and self-confidence. Demonstrating a strong environmental consciousness, Morpurgo explores conservation themes in a number of his works; he also addresses such issues as tolerance and brotherhood, the hardships of war, the battle between good and evil, and the positive results of determination and hard work. As a prose stylist, Morpurgo is admired for the beauty of his writing, which is described as lean yet elegant; as a reteller, he is praised for staying faithful to his sources while placing them in a contemporary frame. Some observers call Morpurgo an old-fashioned, sentimental writer, a designation for which he has been both celebrated and criticized. While a few of his works have been viewed as contrived—especially those that end by having children reunited with parents presumed dead or missing and others that use a human or animal character as a deus ex machina—most of Morpurgo's books are considered unusual, distinctive stories that are both satisfying and affecting. Called "a master storyteller" by Ann Jenkins and "an excellent teller of tales" by a reviewer in *Junior Bookshelf*, Morpurgo, according to Anne Wood "perfects his own special brand of storytelling with each new novel." A critic in the *Children's Fiction Sourcebook* noted of

him, "Undoubtedly a leading figure in the field of children's books, Michael Morpurgo has quite a following. He writes for a large age range, and there is a real sincerity in his writing which gives added weight to what he has to say."

Biographical Information

Born in St. Albans, England, Morpurgo was educated at King's School, Canterbury, a grammar school in Sussex that he later used as the model for Redlands Prep School in his novel *The War of Jenkins' Ear;* he credits his time at school for introducing him to the struggle between social classes as well as to the experience of being part of a small, insular community. Morpurgo attended King's College in London, becoming a teacher after graduation. He married Carol Allen, the daughter of English publisher Allen Lane; the couple have three children and own three farms. With Carol Allen, Morpurgo founded Farms for City Children, a program in which inner-city youngsters are exposed to country life and given the opportunity to learn about agriculture. Several of Morpurgo's books have been written in conjunction with the

National Trust, an organization responsible for the preservation of English landmarks, historic sites, and natural habitats.

One of Morpurgo's most controversial works, *The War of Jenkins' Ear,* is based on an incident from his grade school years. The story of how a modern English schoolboy becomes involved with a fellow student who claims that he is Jesus Christ, *The War of Jenkins' Ear* has been compared to such books as *Lord of the Flies* and *The Chocolate War* for its realistic depiction of the inner dynamics of a group of boys. "At my school," Morpurgo explained, "one of the boys gathered a group around him, including me, and we all believed this boy had healing powers. We had a little camp in the park and set ourselves apart from other people. Eventually, we were discovered and then beaten for our blasphemy. I always remembered this boy, so I incorporated a Christ-like figure into the story." Morpurgo also noted that he "wanted to explore belief and disbelief, as well as faith and superstition" in the novel. In an interview with Morpurgo, Ilene Cooper commented that he takes "as much care with the small details of [his] writing as with the large ones," an attribute for which he is consistently praised. Morpurgo responded, "In order for me to believe the story absolutely, I have to imagine it as closely as I possibly can. I'm a very visual writer. I have to have very clear pictures in my head, and it's the little things. . . that draw me into an intimacy with the story. I find I write better if I am close to it."

Major Works

Morpurgo's first award-winning title was *War Horse,* a historical novel for young adults featuring a half-thoroughbred English farm horse that becomes a hero of World War I. Based on a true story and told in the first person by the horse, the narrative describes how Joey, sold to the British army in 1914, endures battles and bombs and proves his courage in his work as a cavalry mount, artillery mover, and ambulance puller. Captured by the Germans, Joey works for them until he is returned to his beloved master Albert, the son of his original owner. Often compared to *Black Beauty, War Horse* was called "a most accomplished piece of storytelling" by Margery Fisher. A critic in *Booklist* called the book a "compelling and universal piece of historical fiction," adding that it is "genuinely affecting in its testament to the hardships of war and the fidelity of enduring friendships." Sue May praised *War Horse* as "a testament to the stupidity of war." *Why the Whales Came,* a historical novel for middle graders that is again based on a real incident, is one of Morpurgo's most popular works. Set in 1914 on the Isles of Scilly off the southwest coast of England, the story outlines how two children break the tradition of prejudice that has existed on their island for a generation. When a whale is beached on the island of Sampson, the siblings Grace and Daniel, joined by an elderly deaf recluse called the Birdman whom the children's parents have forbidden them to see, save the whale and break the island's curse. Called a

"highly original story, both in subject and presentation" by Marcus Crouch and "a wonderful story" by Eileen Cowie, *Why the Whales Came* was made into a film called *When the Whales Came* in 1989.

Morpurgo switches his setting from England to Nepal for *King of the Cloud Forests,* a young adult novel that is considered among his best. In this book, fourteen-year-old Ashley Anderson, the son of an American missionary, escapes from the Japanese invasion of China by traveling through Tibet and Nepal to safety in India. While on his journey, Ashley is separated from his guide, the Tibetan doctor Uncle Sung, and left alone in a Himalayan mountain hut. Rescued by yetis—intelligent, apelike creatures who live in a utopian society high in the mountains—Ashley is taken to be their king, especially since he resembles a former visitor on whom they had bestowed this title. After reluctantly leaving the yetis, Ashley travels to England, is reunited with Uncle Sung, and meets Sir Edward Lely, the man who lived with the yetis years before and who has recently won the Nobel Prize for medicine. At the end of the novel, Ashley plans to return to the cloud forests to search for the yetis. Compared to such works as *The Man Who Would Be King, Lost Horizon,* and *The Time Machine, King of the Cloud Forests* was praised for its lively narrative as well as for Morpurgo's believable characterization of the yetis. A critic in *Kirkus Reviews* called the novel an "unusual, well-told yarn" while a reviewer in *Booklist* noted that the plotting, pace, and characterizations "are all superb" and concluded that *King of the Cloud Forests* is "a top-notch offering—especially to boys who think books are boring."

In *Waiting for Anya,* a historical novel for young adults set in the French Pyrenees during World War II, Morpurgo represents the bravery and humanity of wartime as well as its tragedy. After the young shepherd Jo meets Benjamin, a Jewish man hiding in the mountain home of his mother-in-law, the boy is drawn into a plan to help smuggle Jewish children across the border to safety in Spain. Benjamin waits hopefully for the arrival of his daughter, Anya, from Paris. After the Germans occupy the village, Jo and the other members of his community assist Benjamin in one more daring mission into Spain before the man is captured and sent to Auschwitz. At the conclusion of the novel, Benjamin's daughter Anya finally appears in the village and is taken to safety. Marcus Crouch called *Waiting for Anya* "an intensely exciting story guaranteed to keep a sensitive reader on the edge of his chair"; the reviewer concluded, "There have been many Second World War stories for the young, none of which deals more convincingly with its perils and dilemmas." A critic in *Kirkus Reviews* commented that the story "achieves special resonance in its depiction of the innocent and guilty living side by side, setting into uneasy alliance while learning the unwelcome lessons of war."

The War of Jenkins' Ear is perhaps Morpurgo's most well known work. Set in England in the early 1950s, the novel describes how Toby Jenkins, a student at Redlands

Prep School, becomes the disciple of Simon Christopher, a new boy at the school who claims to be the reincarnation of Jesus Christ. Christopher, who makes predictions and proclaims that he possesses healing powers, thwarts a potentially violent battle between the prep school boys and the local village lads, among other good works. Despite his devotion to Christopher, Toby denies his friend's capabilities when called to testify in a trial by the Redlands administration. Christopher is expelled for blasphemy, but his influence lingers: his followers convince their classmates that further bloodshed with the villagers is unnecessary, and the terminally ill daughter of a Redlands teacher is miraculously cured. D. A. Young claimed, "I found this book impossible to put down" and concluded that Morpurgo "may have set himself an almost impossible task but he has succeeded most wonderfully." A critic in *Kirkus Reviews* called *The War of Jenkins' Ear* "a rare novel that has the capacity to teach its potent lessons of altruism to many readers." Kenneth L. Donelson, praising the story as "a wise and wonderful book," noted that if it "serves no other purpose than to make students wonder about the spiritual side of humanity, it will be worthwhile."

Morpurgo received the prestigious Smarties Medal for *The Butterfly Lion* (1996), a novel for middle graders that interweaves supernatural fantasy and historical fiction and is both a reminiscence and a story-within-a-story. The narrator recalls the time when, as an unhappy ten-year-old who had run away from school, he learns from an old lady about another schoolboy from sixty years before. This boy, Bertie, spent his earliest years in Africa, where he bonded with an orphaned white lion cub he calls White Prince. Forced to leave Africa to attend school in England, Bertie is devastated when White Prince is sold to a circus. As an adult, Bertie becomes a decorated hero in World War I; after returning to England, he is reunited with White Prince and brings the animal to his home. When the lion dies, Bertie and his wife spend forty years creating a giant chalk likeness of White Prince on a hillside. At the end of the story, the young schoolboy learns that the old lady who told him the story was Bertie's wife, a woman who had died many years ago. "It is not often," wrote D. A. Young "that one turns the final page of a story with a reluctance similar to waking up with the total absorption of a vivid dream"; the critic concluded that the story is "language put to its finest use."

Awards

War Horse was named a runner-up for the Whitbread Award in 1982 while *King of the Cloud Forests* was a runner-up for the Carnegie Medal in 1988. Three years later, *Waiting for Anya* was named a runner-up for the Guardian Award. In 1995, *The War of Jenkins' Ear* was named the Top of the List selection for Youth Fiction by *Booklist* as well as a Best Book selection by *School Library Journal*. *The Butterfly Lion* was awarded the Smarties Gold Medal in 1997.

TITLE COMMENTARY

📖 *FRIEND OR FOE* (1977; reprinted, 1984)

Margery Fisher

SOURCE: A review of *Friend or Foe,* in *Growing Point,* Vol. 23, No. 5, January, 1985, p. 4369.

There is inevitably some didactic purpose behind historical stories, even those which purport to be open narratives of adventure. The intention behind *Friend or Foe* is to serve the cause of peace by suggesting that all men are brothers. To this end the story works well. It tells how two London boys are evacuated during the blitz and settle happily with a moorland farmer in Devon. Happily, that is, until they are woken by gunfire, see a German plane vanish behind the hills and join the Home Guard and other local forces in an exciting but unavailing search. Days later the boys themselves find two Germans hiding—find them in circumstances that call for a difficult decision, for one has rescued David from drowning in a swollen river. Who is the enemy? becomes a desperate question, finally solved for the boys when one of the airmen, wounded and ill, decides to go with [David] to the farm as his captive, and the other [airman] fails in his effort to reach the coast undetected. The boys emerge as heroes and the farmer and his wife, who guess their share in the event, accept their motive for stealing food for the fugitives. It is an easy way out, perhaps, but the story is framed for young readers and the simple conclusion does make a very necessary point.

📖 *THE NINE LIVES OF MONTEZUMA* (1980)

Margery Fisher

SOURCE: A review of *The Nine Lives of Montezuma,* in *Growing Point,* Vol. 19, No. 4, November, 1980, p. 3776.

To claim that the family pet is a member of the family is as valid a half-truth as the claim that it 'understands every word I say'. Michael Morpurgo writes about an individual animal in *The Nine Lives of Montezuma,* combining sentiment and close observation in measured tones which seem addressed as much to adult cat-lovers as to the young. The onward movement of the farming year lies behind the story of a kitten, reprieved when it is found starving, survivor of an unwanted litter. Montezuma demonstrates the tenacity of his breed by surviving also the righteous retribution of Sam the yard-dog after he has stolen his bone, several days buried in snow with sheep, a territorial battle with an invading cat and a hit-and-run accident on the road, dying quietly in advanced age but leaving one particular descendant with a characteristic white patch on its ginger throat. Continuity, in fact, is the theme of a book whose quiet description of a cat's life is also the story of two generations in a farming family. There is no anthropomorphism here, unless one is pedantic enough to count one or two incursions into Montezuma's 'thoughts', and the neat, precise background of country weather and country ways is supported by the firm outlines and unassuming elegance of Margery Gill's drawings.

D. A. Young

SOURCE: A review of *The Nine Lives of Montezuma,* in *Junior Bookshelf,* Vol. 44, No. 6, December, 1980, p. 294.

Montezuma is a farm cat and his story is told without sentimentality, though not without sentiment and with the style and confidence that has been so evident in the many excellent examples of this genre which seems to belong in a unique way to English writing.

Cats are so independent and have none of the jolly romping characteristics of dogs. They keep themselves to themselves; take life seriously; know what they are about; and tolerate humans for the use they can be to them. Each of the nine chapters deals with a narrow escape in Montezuma's life. They spring from experience and close observation. His thought processes, although put in words, are always feline. The people on the farm who grow up alongside Montezuma are presented as characters too and allowed to engage the interest of the reader in a way which adds to the richness of the story.

The story can be recommended with confidence to cat-lovers of all ages.

Adrian Jackson

SOURCE: A review of *The Nine Lives of Montezuma,* in *Books for Keeps,* No. 80, May, 1993, p. 14.

In nine sections we have the lives of Monty (for short) the cat. He's a survivor and a great fighter, a natural hero, growing in age and craft. There's insight and skill enough to make much more of this than just a sentimental pet lover's tale. It's a simple idea, but very well done with the sections neatly carrying the reader through a series of dramatic adventures with every assurance, for the first eight lives, that things will come out right at the end of the chapter.

MISS WIRTLES' REVENGE (1981)

Josephine Karavasil

SOURCE: "Matters of Rhythm and Register," in *The Times Literary Supplement,* No. 4121, March 26, 1982, p. 347.

Successfully outside the mainstream, with its well-conceived layout and narrative verse form, is *Miss Wirtles' Revenge.* Its large format was probably dictated by Gra-ham Clarke's original etching, figured on the last two pages of the book and used as a context for the granny to tell her story of a courageous little heroine. The dark brown script, while adding to the book's beauty, is very readable, the letters well formed and clear, and the story itself swings along at a remarkable pace. Changes of rhythm in the verse are often used for dramatic impact though occasionally the meaning of a word is stretched just to get the rhythm right. This is indeed a granny's tale with something to offer. A girl is ranged against a whole class full of boys and wins throughout, but the final position is that of the peopleists: "Battles are fun, and have to be won, / But nobody wins the war".

WAR HORSE (1982; U.S. edition, 1983)

Margery Fisher

SOURCE: A review of *War Horse,* in *Growing Point,* Vol. 21, No. 4, November, 1982, p. 3989.

Inspired by records showing the role of cavalry in World War I and by a particular painting in a village hall, the author has followed up the history of Joey, a farmhorse commandeered for the army in 1914 and enduring bombardment, capture, exposure and fear as he is drafted for work with ambulance or gun, learning to work for different masters but keeping the memory of the first human to become a true friend. Told in the first person in a grave, rhythmic style reminiscent of *Black Beauty,* this is a most accomplished piece of story-telling, full of sympathy for an animal manipulated by man but preserving its dignity.

Sue May

SOURCE: A review of *War Horse,* in *The School Librarian,* Vol. 31, No. 1, March, 1983, p. 54.

Earnestness is most excusable in **War Horse,** in which Joey, the war horse, tells his own story of the First World War, and no one could expect such a sorely-tried animal to laugh at his own misfortune. I believe the author's explanation that the book was inspired by a real painting of a real horse. It *is* second-hand writing, but there is a genuine affection for brave animals, and for people devoted to them, which will be capable of jerking more than a tear or two from readers of ten and over who share the fancy. It is also a testament to the stupidity of war, and any methods of getting that message over to the age group must be welcomed. Joey is the friend of the good guys on both sides, whose first thoughts at the end of each blood-spattered day are of a bucket of cool water for their faithful mounts. The reader who follows Joey's fortunes thus far will nod agreement. Straight from the horse's mouth is as good a medium as any for this message—at least for younger readers. The ghost of Black Beauty watches over it all, particularly the implausibly happy ending; but in fairness any other ending for Joey would be hard to take.

David A. Lindsey

SOURCE: A review of *War Horse,* in *School Library Journal,* Vol. 30, No. 2, October, 1983, pp. 160-61.

Set in the English countryside and the frontlines of World War I France, Morpurgo's effort strains for pathos, descends into bathos and overworks its cliché-ridden plot that is filled with cardboard characters. Joey, an anthropomorphic, tri-lingual, half-thoroughbred farm horse, tells his own story of how he went from being Albert's beloved draught animal to a horse that served as a cavalry mount, ambulance puller and artillery mover; this tale also includes his stints as a Frenchman's plow horse and a prisoner of war before being reunited with Albert and returning to Devon to live happily ever after. Morpurgo's use of this "first-horse" technique makes the foregoing ludicrous.

Kate M. Flanagan

SOURCE: A review of *War Horse,* in *The Horn Book Magazine,* Vol. LIX, No. 6, December, 1983, pp. 711-12.

The story of Joey, a farm horse turned war hero, is told in the first person—ostensibly, by the horse. Bought by a Devon farmer who treated him roughly, Joey realized at once that in the farmer's son Albert he "had found a friend for life." Boy and horse were inseparable until World War I broke out and Albert's father sold Joey to the British cavalry. Joey had fine bloodlines that stood him in good stead during months of arduous training. He found comfort in the kindness of the soldiers and in the companionship of Topthorn, a splendid black stallion. But the cavalry was no match for machine guns and barbed wire, and the squadron was decimated in an attack. Captured by the Germans, Joey witnessed the war from their side, pulling ambulances and artillery. Toward the end of the conflict, Joey ended up in a British veterinary hospital, half-dead from wounds and starvation; but by happy coincidence he was reunited with Albert and survived to return to Devon. Written with an eloquent, old-fashioned grace, the book does not gloss over the horrors of war but focuses on the goodness found in people on both sides. Permeating the story is the courage of the horse and his undying devotion to the boy who loved him.

Karen Stang Hanley

SOURCE: A review of *War Horse,* in *Booklist,* Vol. 80, No. 11, February 1, 1984, pp. 814-15.

In a style akin to that of Anna Sewell's classic *Black Beauty,* the horse Joey relates the story of his life in a compelling and unusual piece of historical fiction. Speaking in the first person, Joey begins by describing the auction that took him away from his mother at the age of six months. Joey's new owner is short-tempered and sometimes cruel, but the man's son, Albert, becomes Joey's protector and dearest friend. When Joey is sold to the British army at the start of World War I, Albert mourns but promises Joey that he will find him again. Upon being shipped to France, Joey witnesses the rout of a hopelessly outmoded British cavalry squadron, is captured, and draws German ambulance carts and artillery. Joey's wartime experiences are described with such authenticity that even his eventual reunion with Albert does not seem improbable. Although some readers will be put off by the manner of narration, the story is genuinely affecting in its testament to the hardships of war and the fidelity of enduring friendship.

Diane G. Yates

SOURCE: A review of *War Horse,* in *Voice of Youth Advocates,* Vol. 7, No. 1, April, 1984, p. 32.

The first years of the young colt Joey's life were happy ones, brought up on an English farm, cared for and loved by the farmer's son Albert. When the First World War comes, Joey finds himself trained as a cavalry horse. His first rider is shot out from under him almost immediately; he survives many more battles carrying a kind but poor rider; he is captured and used as a cart horse carrying wounded German soldiers to the hospital. This life is much better than his later experiences pulling a gun cart. Only after a narrow escape from death is Joey re-united with his first master, Albert.

Young animal lovers will respond to this anthropomorphic tale of a brave horse that was originally published in Great Britain in 1982 and is based on a true story. The message about the futility and carnage of war comes across loud and clear. The characters, both human and animal, that die in the war are all the best and brightest of their generation. It is quibbling to complain that the horse understands both English and German and thus makes it confusing at times to know which side has him in tow. But writers of books for children need to be just as careful about that sort of thing as other writers do.

📖 *THE WHITE HORSE OF ZENNOR: AND OTHER STORIES FROM BELOW THE EAGLE'S NEST* (1982; U.S. edition, 1985)

Hazel Rochman

SOURCE: A review of *The White Horse of Zennor: and Other Stories from Below the Eagle's Nest,* in *Booklist,* Vol. 82, No. 2, September 15, 1985, p. 137.

A magical giant horse from the ocean, a benevolent storytelling witch, and powerful little "Knocker" folk change the lives of farmers and children in five stories about a remote coastal town in Cornwall, England. In one story a physically deformed boy, taunted and alone, learns to swim and finds a home with the seals. In another, a greedy farmer is taught to respect the land by the little folk who upset his animals and bring him near to ruin. The language is somewhat sophisticated for a young audience, but the Cornwall setting is vividly evoked, and some romantic fantasy readers will love the magic that happens in the caves, on the moors, and along the wild rocky shore.

Gale Eaton

SOURCE: A review of *The White Horse of Zennor: and Other Stories from Below the Eagle's Nest,* in *School Library Journal,* Vol. 32, No. 6, February, 1986, p. 88.

Set in contemporary Cornwall, these short stories have an old-fashioned flavor of sentimental pathos. All are more or less tinged with the occult. Two involve Knockers, the little folk who bring luck to farmers; one is about a determined child who makes her way home through a storm only to find that her grieving family cannot see her ghost. In another, an ostracized boy with a twisted foot swims off to live with the seals. These tales portray a world in which kindness is a rare virtue, and good ends are sometimes achieved by dubious means: the Knockers use something very like blackmail to persuade farmer Barbery to respect his land, and the child Kate relies on a rather deceitful capitalist venture to help Miss Marney, a witchy recluse. The characters seem remote, and the dialogue is unconvincing. Children will be better served by real Cornish folk tales or by Eleanor Farjeon's longer and more sophisticated *Martin Pippin in the Apple Orchard.*

Margery Fisher

SOURCE: A review of *The White Horse of Zennor: and Other Stories from Below the Eagle's Nest,* in *Growing Point,* Vol. 30, No. 4, November, 1991, p. 5609.

The five tales in this collection, first published in 1982, evoke the Cornish landscape with legends about huge rocks, the mysteries of the sea and the shape-changing of seals. The author advises readers to take the stories in order and the last one, 'Mad Miss Marney' explains why, as it describes a lonely woman who talks to herself and dresses in corn-sacks and tells how young Kate, animal-mad and unafraid of 'the witch' establishes friendship with her over their care for a wounded raven. A repository for local legends, Miss Marney wins the trust of the village through her gift of healing in a final tale which draws together the threads of the rest and ties them firmly to the present. Lively in style and wise in conclusions, the tales certainly deserve a continued life for the pleasing of readers in the middle years.

📖 *TWIST OF GOLD* (1983; U.S. edition, 1993)

Margery Fisher

SOURCE: A review of *Twist of Gold,* in *Growing Point,* Vol. 22, No. 5, January, 1984, pp. 4183-84.

The potato famine of the 1840s . . . provides a starting point for *Twist of Gold,* another tale of the testing of childhood, but it is only a starting point as far as the plot goes, for Sean and Annie O'Brien (with the help of a dragoon, an enemy in occupation but a friend out of compassion for their desperately ill mother) set sail for America to find their father, who has gone to make a home for them away from Ireland's misery. Helpless in their youth, the children reach their goal finally through their own courage and determination and also with the help offered to them, first by two benevolent elderly sisters in Boston and their disreputable gambler brother, and then by an old prospector who sets them on their final, desperate miles. The journey on the ship and from East to West by riverboat and wagon train gives the book a panoramic view of America a century ago in varied scenes where the family heirloom, an ancient torque lost and found again in dramatic circumstances, provides a narrative link and also stands as a symbol of the family unity which is the theme of a touching and inventive adventure story.

Geoffrey Trease

SOURCE: "In Quest of Adventure," in *The Times Educational Supplement,* No. 3524, January 13, 1984, p. 42.

Twist of Gold might have been subtitled "The Luck of the Irish". Sean and Annie are near death in the 1847 famine. Saved by one of the hated English dragoons, they sail in a hellhole of an emigrant ship to seek their father in America. Episodic adventures are strung together as in a parent's extempore bedtime serial. Perils press, but there is always a new *deus ex machina,* as though Olympus had a dozen on stand-by. Sole survivors of shipwreck, the children beg in the streets of Boston until rescued by a benevolent black and adopted by the kind ladies who employ him. Next, a quixotic colonel sells his beloved Missouri paddle-steamer to take them on the long wagon-trail to California. When they are dying (of thirst, this time) in the desert, an equally altruistic trapper sacrifices a season's pelts to help them on their way—though fortunately they immediately discover a huge gold nugget with which to recompense him. Need I say that they find their father and that even mother, whom they left on her death-bed, is already in California to welcome them? The publishers should issue coat-hangers with each chapter for the suspension of our disbelief, but less critical children will lap up the rich sentiment.

Publishers Weekly

SOURCE: A review of *Twist of Gold,* in *Publishers Weekly,* Vol. 240, No. 3, January 18, 1993, pp. 469-70.

When, in the Ireland of 1847, "a sudden blight . . . reduced the countryside to a pungent mass of black rot and left the people starving," an English dragoon helps

Sean O'Brien, 13, and his 10-year-old sister, Annie, to leave their ravaged homeland. Following an eventful sea voyage from Cork to Boston, the youngsters struggle across a rough, new America to find their father in California. With only the family "torc"—an ancestral golden medallion given to them by their dying mother—for protection, the children are dealt life lessons along the way in both the goodness and the inhumanity of man. Sentimental in the best sense of the word, this epic journey gathers momentum as the children draw ever nearer their destination. As the pace pours on, the story loses some of the beauty and lyricism of Morpurgo's musical dialogue, and conflicts are resolved a little too conveniently; but the novel remains a colorful, engaging, Dickensian read to its happy and affecting conclusion.

Renee Steinberg

SOURCE: A review of *Twist of Gold,* in *School Library Journal,* Vol. 39, No. 2, February, 1993, p. 94.

History and wonder combine in this novel that uses the Irish potato famine of 1847 as its core. Readers will come away from it with an understanding of the dreadful conditions in Ireland that prompted so many to find a new life in America. What detracts from the story are the plot contrivances. The novel begins in County Cork where the O'Briens are suffering through the effects of the famine. Three siblings have already died and Sean and Annie's mother's death seems imminent. Their father has gone to America and has promised to send for the family when he reaches California. Rather than starve while waiting for him, the youngsters head to America with only their lucky family heirloom, a golden torc, to protect them. Their adventure begins on the ship crossing the Atlantic. Morpurgo's descriptions of the conditions on board and those they find in Boston and on their cross-country journey are realistic. The precious torc becomes the catalyst for the relationships that develop in their travels. Characters are either good or evil, and each time it seems that Sean and Annie have lost everything, a twist of fate and just the right person come along to move them toward their ultimate goal. The most outrageous turnabout comes at the end when the youngsters finally reach California, find their father, and discover their mother there as well. This book has much to offer as historical fiction, but the plot development is too artificial. Conlon-McKenna's *Wildflower Girl* is a more successful choice for fiction dealing with the same theme.

Betsy Hearne

SOURCE: A review of *Twist of Gold,* in *Bulletin of the Center for Children's Books,* Vol. 46, No. 7, March, 1993, p. 221.

Like Marita Conlon-McKenna's *Wildflower Girl,* this is a story of survivors from the Irish famine immigrating to America, but unlike McKenna's more realistic work, this is filled with fortunate coincidences that repeat themselves in a contrived pattern. In defiance of army regulations, a British dragoon keeps Sean and his sister Annie from starvation; a ship's officer and a fiddler conspire to retrieve the O'Briens' golden torc from an evil captain and help the two children become the only survivors of a wreck; two rich sisters and their black servant ("I's can see I's gonna have to keep my eye on you two") rescue the children from the Boston streets; a riverboat colonel restores the torc, stolen again, and gives up his life for the children's safety; a mountain man rescues them from the desert and offers to give them half the gold he's found; Indians return the torc (stolen once more); and finally, after crossing the continent to California, the children find not only their father, but also their mother, whom they thought had died back in Ireland. Despite occasional information loading, the writing is competent, the characterizations are consistent, and the action is fast paced, but to impose such tidy plotting on historical fiction distorts the difficult immigrant experience into an unlikely adventure.

LITTLE FOXES (1984)

Margery Fisher

SOURCE: A review of *Little Foxes,* in *Growing Point,* Vol. 23, No. 2, July, 1984, p. 4283.

For Billy Bunch nature is a compensation for a bleak life as a foundling unhappy at school and hardly encouraged by a succession of cold-hearted foster-mothers. A deserted churchyard by a ruinous abbey and an adjacent canal provide the boy with a refuge from an unfriendly world and by chance he finds a role in life when some of the animals he loves to watch—a family of kingfishers, a swan battered by teasing boys and the survivor of a gassed litter of foxes—seem to need his help. *Little Foxes* is perhaps a little too much of a good-luck story but Billy's flight from civilization, when the fox he is secretly tending is threatened, is described in such vivid detail and the sounds and smells of the country are so strongly evoked that the tale does achieve a kind of authenticity even when the good fairy (in the shape of a nature-loving couple ready to take Billy on in place of their dead son) turns up rather predictably in the end. Apart from the interweaving of crisp, vital description the black and white illustrations [by Gareth Floyd] add a special veracity to the book; the artist has realized the boy and his animal friends in direct, unsentimental terms which establish their existence and their needs successfully for the reader.

G. Bott

SOURCE: A review of *Little Foxes,* in *Junior Bookshelf,* Vol. 48, No. 5, October, 1984, p. 220.

Billy Bunch never had a chance. Deposited on the police

station steps as a baby, he is shunted from one cold foster home to another; friendless, uninterested in school work or games, he finds solace and satisfaction in the wild wasteland by the ruined chapel. He rescues a cygnet and adopts several fox cubs; he steals food for his beloved animals but when the den is destroyed he runs away with the only fox cub left alive. He avoids capture, accepting hardship and loneliness uncomplainingly, and finally finds a haven. If the ending is rather sentimental, it is no more than Billy's due: we leave him knowing that his future is secure and happy with his new-found friends. Billy will rouse a sympathetic response in young readers, not only because he is an orphan, badly treated and battered by circumstance, but also because his fellow-feeling for outcast animals releases a determination and sense of purpose that more than compensate for his unfortunate origins and early misfortunes.

Patricia Manning

SOURCE: A review of *Little Foxes,* in *School Library Journal,* Vol. 34, No. 1, September, 1987, p. 181.

Abandoned at birth, Billy Bunch, now ten, has lived in a string of foster homes. He stutters, does poorly in school, and has no friends, finding consolation in an abandoned churchyard and its environs where he watches birds and other wildlife. It is here that he rescues a deux ex machina in swan shape from some vicious boys, and is miraculously cured of his stutter. He also finds a family of foxes, and when the vixen is run over, Billy rescues one of the cubs and runs away with it (aided and abetted here and there by the d.e.m.). Ultimately, Billy finds a home and a family, the fox returns to the wild, and the d.e.m., "her mission accomplished at last," heads for the swannery. This is overwritten in spots and has other weaknesses to boot (Billy, portrayed as a keen nature observer, fails to notice the swan's bright red leg band for months). As it stands, this plot is too contrived to be convincing.

📖 *WHY THE WHALES CAME* (1985)

Margery Fisher

SOURCE: A review of *Why the Whales Came,* in *Growing Point,* Vol. 24, No. 4, November, 1985, p. 4524.

A conservation theme puts *Why the Whales Came* firmly in the present as far as readership goes but the events described take place in 1914 and in the unusual setting of the Scilly Isles. Gracie and her boon companion Daniel live on Bryher and go to school on Tresco but in that particular year their attention is mainly directed towards the small adjacent island of Samson, by reputation suffering from a curse which had brought poverty and hardship to its inhabitants and finally left it desolate. The history of Samson is eked out bit by bit to the

children by the Birdman, a recluse whose friendship they had won against the wishes of their parents. Isolated by deafness and happier with nature than with people, he sees old wrongs seemingly repeated when he and the children find a stranded whale on Bryher; before they can get it back into the water the villagers, already suspicious of his way of life and ready to label him Hunlover in the hysteria of coming war, arrive ready to exercise an ancient right to slaughter the whale as well as its companions cruising anxiously offshore. The crisis is resolved through the common sense and courage of Gracie's mother and her friends; the surprises of that uneasy year have forced the community to look at things in a new light. Well told as far as events go, the book is notable also for a broad, natural balance of old and young characters and a rich vein of descriptive writing that brings the place vividly before the mind's eye.

Marcus Crouch

SOURCE: A review of *Why the Whales Came,* in *Junior Bookshelf,* Vol. 49, No. 6, December, 1985, p. 279.

The scene is Bryher in the Isles of Scilly, the time 1914, the theme two children breaking the tradition of prejudice that has stunted their parents.

Gracie and Daniel have been forbidden to have any contact with the Birdman, a sinister recluse on whom most of the ills of the island can be laid. Chance allows them to discover that he is not a malign influence but a sad, wise, lonely man haunted by the tragedy of the past. The Birdman came from the now deserted island of Samson which was abandoned by its inhabitants partly because of its inhospitable nature, partly because of the ill-luck associated with it. When, during the World War, a whale beaches itself on Bryher and the islanders come in force to harvest this unexpected crop, the Birdman breaks his rule of silence and tells them that all the troubles of Samson sprang from a similar destruction of wild life. The men of Bryher take the warning, the whales are saved, and the Birdman goes to sea for the last time.

The success of Michael Morpurgo's novel comes not so much from the story, adequate though this is, but from its portrait of the two children and from its exploration of the blend of superstition and communal spirit existing in an isolated settlement. Mindless hostility to anything out of the ordinary, represented in the figure of Big Tim, Daniel's brutal elder brother, and unity in the face of an alien authority, represented by the 'Preventative', the custom's men who claim the jetsam which the islanders regard as theirs by right, these are powerfully and convincingly presented. And although there is little formal scene-painting, the reader is left in no doubt that the hero of the story is Bryher itself, sharing that role, perhaps with the sea which, in the last passages of the book, gives up Gracie's father, who had been reported lost in action in the War.

A highly original story, both in subject and presentation, which somehow just fails to involve the reader in the joys and griefs of its protagonists.

Anne Wood

SOURCE: A review of *Why the Whales Came*, in *Books for Your Children*, Vol. 20, No. 3, Autumn-Winter, 1985, p. 21.

Michael Morpurgo perfects his own special brand of storytelling with each new novel. Essentially he is a romantic. Beauty of landscape, feeling for animals and for times just past, the turn of the century, colour all his work but nowhere better than in this new novel. Set in the Scillies, principally Bryher, it is built around the true story of why the island of Samson was abandoned. There will be extra spice for children in knowing that all these locations exist and can be visited today, including the island of Samson with its deserted cottages each with its pile of limpet shells beside the door. Only the old mysterious and frightening "Birdman" knows what disasters overtook Samson. He now lives a solitary existence on the island of Bryher where children are forbidden to speak to him. Daniel and Gracie disobey. The growing relationship between young and old, innocence and experience, at a time when even the life of this very small island community is overshadowed by the outsize tragedy of World War I lifts this book above the level of adventure story, though it is a breathtaking read. It is an ideal book to take children from the sheer enjoyment of reading stories to the pleasure of discovering what literature can be about.

Nicole Irving

SOURCE: "Sea-Fearing Folk," in *The Times Literary Supplement,* No. 4318, January 3, 1986, p. 22.

Why the Whales Came is both an adventure story with a tantalizing mystery at its centre, and an unpretentious account of the everyday life of a young girl on Bryher, one of the Isles of Scilly, in 1914.

Gracie Jenkins, the lively, impetuous narrator, is ten; her parents, simple, hard-working people, live, as do all their neighbours, off what the sea and the land provide. Gracie and her friend, Daniel, are inseparable. All too often, they have to take the boat to school on nearby Tresco; they also often help their parents, gathering driftwood or fishing for bait for the lobster-pots; but as soon as they are free, they are off playing with the miniature boats which Daniel has built with Gracie's help.

Parts of Bryher are out of bounds to them: even more forbidding than the steep cliffs and treacherous sea is the Birdman, an old man who lives in a lonely cottage with his animals. He is from the neighbouring island of Samson, and the mysterious and unexplained curse of Sam-

son is attached to him. Thus when Gracie and Daniel's usual place of play is invaded by swans and the children stray towards the Birdman's cottage, it takes Daniel's sensible and logical attitude to persuade Gracie to discount the less likely tales told about the recluse and the curse.

The friendship grows between the Birdman, Daniel and Gracie, with Daniel learning to communicate with the kind, sensitive old man, who is neither mean nor terrifying but deaf. The two children contrive to spend much of their time with their new, secret friend. The curse of Samson, however, remains unexplained, and Gracie has still not overcome all her fears. The war brings matters to a head: Gracie's father joins up, and life becomes hard. Daniel and Gracie help out by getting a catch of fish and this turns into a dangerous adventure as fog descends on their boat leaving them marooned on the dreaded Samson. When, immediately after their return, news arrives that Gracie's father is lost, presumed dead, the children feel they have brought the curse on their families and they are spurred on by these events to uncover the Birdman's secret. He reveals that the curse began with a massacre of whales by the people of Samson; a beached whale now offers an opportunity to redeem this misdeed. The villagers must save the whale and chase the entire shoal into the open, sacrificing the meat and ivory they could provide.

Michael Morpurgo's story is well paced and well rounded; at the end, there are dramatic moments as the villagers are swayed, with the help of Gracie's mother, towards doing the right thing; there is sadness as the Birdman disappears and, we assume, dies, although the qualities which set him apart make this a fitting—and moving—conclusion; there is joy as Gracie's father returns after all, confirming, in the children's minds, the lifting of the curse. But the story is good in more subtle ways too: Morpurgo is a delicate writer who trusts his readers to weigh up the evidence and draw their own conclusions. A variety of conflicting views of the war are hinted at; women's strengths and courage play a crucial part; the islanders are not presented as simple-minded and greedy, but as a hard-working comunity to which the sea occasionally brings good fortune. Michael Morpurgo's world is not black-and-white: it is, without contrivance, rich, complex and thought-provoking.

Eileen Cowie

SOURCE: A review of *Why the Whales Came*, in *The School Librarian,* Vol. 34, No. 1, March, 1986, p. 52.

This is a wonderful story about two children living on one of the Scilly Isles in 1914. It tells how they befriend a social outcast who, having initially terrified them and the rest of the islanders, turns out to be a remarkable old man, full of wisdom and kindness. Eventually they have to defend him against the other boys on the island in a very exciting episode. The whales do not appear until late in the story, but when they do they provide the answer to a lot of the mysterious legends which have been accumulating over the years.

Cindy Darling Codell

SOURCE: A review of *Why the Whales Came,* in *School Library Journal,* Vol. 33, No. 6, February, 1987, p. 82.

Set in the Scilly Islands off the coast of England in 1914, this is a retelling of a local story that contains legendary elements. Ten-year-old Gracie and her friend Daniel unintentionally make contact with the island pariah, the Birdman, when he kindly returns their lost toy boats and leaves shell messages in the sand. Gradually the children realize that this strange man has been victimized because of his deafness and the personal tragedy that has befallen him. He shares with them his mission to lift the old curse from neighboring Samson Island and his desire to protect all its people. External events and internal pressures pit the islanders against the Birdman in a climactic struggle, and the children must find a way to save their own island, as well as the people whom they love. Masterful use of parallelism heightens the sense of drama. While the rest of the world wars against martial enemies, the islanders wage daily war against the sea and the sky, economic hardship, and governmental idiocies. Morpurgo's language is lean, yet lyrical. His descriptive paragraphs let readers taste the salt of the sea and feel the grit of the islanders' lives. More importantly, he allows the Birdman to grapple with an almost cosmic desolation and miraculously turn it to hope.

📖 *TOM'S SAUSAGE LION* (1986)

J. Nicholls

SOURCE: A review of *Tom's Sausage Lion,* in *Junior Bookshelf,* Vol. 50, No. 2, April, 1986, p. 70.

"It was Christmas Eve when Tom first saw the lion. His mother had sent him out to fetch the logs, and there was a lion padding through the orchard with a string of sausages hanging from its mouth . . . " From this unlikely but highly intriguing opening Michael Morpurgo's tale unfolds skillfully, becoming more and more involved as it proceeds. His style is engaging and accessible—deceptively simple, in fact, concealing skills in dialogue, characterization and plot structure which are only appreciated fully in retrospect. Nine year old Tom's continuing difficulties in persuading family, school or police to believe his story threaten to lead to much more serious consequences until an unexpected meeting with the local butcher's daughter leads to a more systematic plan. Michael Morpurgo is an excellent "teller of tales". This one deserves a wide audience and should make compulsive reading for many young readers.

Margery Fisher

SOURCE: A review of *Tom's Sausage Lion,* in *Growing Point,* Vol. 25, No. 3, September, 1986, pp. 4667-68.

At first nobody believes young Tom when he claims to have seen a lion carrying a string of sausages in its mouth and, which is worse, Tom's own dog is suspected of being responsible for local sheep-worrying. The boy has no way of stopping his father from shooting the dog when it is found beside dead sheep but he can at least hide the wounded animal in a disused cottage and, with the help of his school friend Clare, keep it fed. While Tom is asleep near the cottage the 'lion' appears, a pet and friendly puma which he triumphantly leads to school to discomfit the bad-tempered teacher who had teased the boy with his skepticism. It is flattering to children, this kind of victory for the young over adults, but it is in no way improbable, for the glimpse of life on the moors is enough to give this short tale for newly fledged readers a satisfactory solidity.

Nigel Spencer

SOURCE: A review of *Tom's Sausage Lion,* in *Books for Keeps,* No. 46, September, 1987, p. 20.

The adults in this story behave all too realistically and the reader cannot but help feel sympathetic towards the unfortunate hero who has to face their spleen. This is a thoughtful, didactic book about a boy who sees a lion, but who is disbelieved by everyone—except a young girl. Michael Morpurgo skillfully blends the harsh attitudes of adults with the dogged determination of the hero, and the bleak weather and moorland landscape add their atmospheric value.

The victory experienced at the story's climax is doubly appreciated; the reader who has become so involved can now relax as justice visibly triumphs. This is a good book for 9+ children. Definitely worth having in school.

M. Carter

SOURCE: A review of *Tom's Sausage Lion,* in *Books for Your Children,* Vol. 31, No. 2, Summer, 1996, p. 10.

This is a lovely book—just right for the rising eight year olds. One evening Tom sees a lion in the back garden: a lion with a string of sausages hanging from its mouth. No one believes Tom: no one takes him seriously even though it's Christmas Eve and a spirit of charity prevails what with Aunty Rose and Uncle Bertie coming to tea. School friends tease him, his teacher gives him lines—you know the picture. But enter Clare who wears glasses fixed together with Elastoplast. Clare, being a butcher's daughter, is a very useful ally: she brings meat to trap the lion. Each night Tom watches for the lion . . .

not knowing that the lion is watching for Tom . . . What happens: Aha! Just beg, borrow or steal the book and you won't be disappointed. It's concise, masterly and the prose lopes along—just like a lion.

📖 JO-JO THE MELON DONKEY (1987)

Kirkus Reviews

SOURCE: A review of *Jo-Jo the Melon Donkey,* in *Kirkus Reviews,* Vol. LV, No. 23, December 1, 1987, p. 1677.

A sentimental story, set in Renaissance Venice, about an ugly, ragbag of a donkey and a little girl who loved him more than she loved all of the horses in the kingdom.

When Jo-Jo jauntily sets out with his master to sell melons in front of the Cathedral, everyone laughs at him and refuses to buy his melons. But the Doge's daughter notices Jo-Jo's sad, kind eyes, and wants him for her friend. When her father announces that he will buy her any horse she wants, she chooses Jo-Jo the donkey. Angered by her choice, her father sends her to her room in disgrace. But when Jo-Jo sneaks into town late that night and the two of them save the town from an unexpected flood, the humble donkey becomes a hero—and the Doge allows his daughter her wish.

With a nice blend of humor and sadness, Morpurgo brings to life the vibrancy of 16th-century Venice, while [Chris] Molan's vivid mixed-medium illustrations add to the poignancy—and triumph—of Jo-Jo's tale.

Amy Spaulding

SOURCE: A review of *Jo-Jo the Melon Donkey,* in *School Library Journal,* Vol. 34, No. 8, April, 1988, p. 87.

Jo-Jo, a donkey in 16th-Century Venice, is bullied by a cruel master and belittled by the elegant people who laugh at him as he stands beneath handsome golden horses. It is only when the Doge's daughter takes one of his melons and pats his head that the snobbish people will buy. The story combines aspects of *The Ugly Duckling, Cinderella,* and *The Little Hero of Haarlem.* First the little donkey, who so wishes for more than his humble station in life, is championed by the daughter of the Doge, and then he saves the people of Venice by braying loudly enough to warn them that the sea is coming in. The writing style follows that of the literary fairy tale, being at once simple and elegant. The illustrations fit the story perfectly. Vivid colors (mostly watercolors) follow the rich palette of Venetian painters of the era, with bright golds, reds, and greens that seem to reflect the strong light of the Mediterranean. The impressionistic style suggests an opera or ballet set. A pleasant addition to picture book collections for older children.

Chris Brown

SOURCE: A review of *Jo-Jo the Melon Donkey,* in *The School Librarian,* Vol. 36, No. 2, May, 1988, pp. 54-5.

Michael Morpurgo resisted the description of Jo-Jo as a melancholy melon donkey, but harsh treatment and heavy work do create a woebegone being whose Venetian master moves up-market by setting up his wares in St. Mark's Square. There Jo-Jo comes to the attention of the Doge's daughter, though the awesome figures of the four golden horses of Venice seem to overshadow his donkey dreams. Just as his yearnings may apparently be realized a twist in the narrative occurs, which makes this picture book somewhat long and complex for younger readers. However, my younger listeners were entirely engrossed, even in the midst of one of those school afternoons of constant upheaval. Indeed, the book would find a place through the entire primary age range, particularly as the well-shaped text is accompanied by lush illustrations of such magnificence that the pages shimmer with the heat and glory of the city

Marcus Crouch

SOURCE: A review of *Jo-Jo the Melon Donkey,* in *Junior Bookshelf,* Vol. 52, No. 4, August, 1988, p. 180.

Jo-Jo the Melon Donkey is a story of the Doges' Venice. A downtrodden donkey earns a hard living selling melons in the market at the bidding of a hard master. Looking for bigger profits they take their wares to St. Mark's Square, where it becomes apparent that they have gone too far up-market. When the Doge's little daughter takes a fancy to Jo-Jo and buys a melon, fortunes change. The future of Jo-Jo and the royal child become involved with that of the city itself and, with the help of the golden horses of St. Mark, Jo-Jo finds fame as well as happiness. Michael Morpurgo's story is rather long for picture-book format, but it is exceedingly well told, and Chris Molan's pictures are so full of fine and absorbing detail that they sustain interest. They are full of brilliant Adriatic light, set against gorgeously glowing colours of the Renaissance.

📖 CONKER (1987)

Margery Fisher

SOURCE: A review of *Conker,* in *Growing Point,* Vol. 26, No. 5, January, 1988, p. 4927.

Nick's grandmother had a way of solving problems and taking the sting out of troubles. When their old Alsatian had to be put down she helped the boy to get over the shock and when the local bully attacked him now that he no longer had a guard dog, she instructed him so well in the art of conker-fights that Stevie Rooster's arrogance was shattered; but the best thing she ever did was to guess what lay behind Nick's question about a maltreated dog and to do something about it. Pleasingly direct prose is allied to small painted scenes [by Linda Birch]: from both comes an authentic picture of people and places in a 'Banana' book for first solo reading notably persuasive and accessible.

Donald Fry

SOURCE: A review of *Conker,* in *The School Librarian,* Vol. 36, No. 1, February, 1988, pp. 20-1.

In *Conker,* Nick lives with his granny, and the story begins with the death of their much-loved dog. When Stevie, the Conker King, says something cruel about the old dog, there is a short fight which Nick loses; but with Gran's expert help he later humiliates the King in a conker contest. At the same time, Nick has come to the rescue of another Alsatian dog, cruelly treated, and finally is able to have him for himself. The story is simply and movingly told, and will engage young readers in thinking about important feelings. The narrative is expertly handled. The conker victory is not the ending Nick wants, though it is for a time of most interest to his gran and the reader. It is the dog that matters, and in a satisfying last moment we finally understand the full meaning of the story's title.

Frances Ball

SOURCE: A review of *Conker,* in *Junior Bookshelf,* Vol. 59, No. 1, February, 1995, p. 23.

Nick lives with his grandmother and Pooch, an old Alsatian. Their usually settled life is disrupted when Pooch dies and the school bully teases Nick about it. The conker season has started, and Grandma decides to use her old 'conker magic' to defeat the bully. A chance visit then provides an opportunity for them to rescue a neglected dog. He looks quite like Pooch, and their life returns to its old routine.

[*Conker* is] suitable for newly independent readers. The story is told simply and clearly, with events and reactions to them, charted with care. The sadness of the opening gradually passes as Nick and Grandma find ways to overcome their difficulties. By the end, they are ready to enjoy the company of a new pet.

KING OF THE CLOUD FORESTS (1988)

A. R. Williams

SOURCE: A review of *King of the Cloud Forests,* in *Junior Bookshelf,* Vol. 52, No. 1, February, 1988, p. 51.

Whether the reader truly believes in the existence of the Yeti or not he/she may well find Michael Morpurgo's Yetis credible. They are drawn with a consistency which makes their common ethos and code of conduct very real. Before Ashley Anderson becomes a temporary resident in their society he has an adventurous flight from his father's Chinese mission in the face of advancing Japanese armies. The overland journey to India is hard and hazardous with many moments of high suspense. When Ashley finds himself high in the Himalayan ranges and like to be frozen to death he is not only rescued by the Yeti but finds himself a god, albeit a homely kind of god, among them. When he regains contact with 'real' human beings his escape is tinged with regret. Above all, their innate gentleness is a salutary contrast to the world in which he has to grow up. Life at the Mission as well as life on the march carries a convincing flavour. In Ashley's adopted Tibetan 'Uncle' Sung the author has created with restraint a character who too easily could have slid into the passé image of a fairy godfather; he is too practical for that.

Jacqueline Simms

SOURCE: "Magic Man," in *The Times Literary Supplement,* No. 4429, February 19, 1988, p. 200.

"I am called Ashley Anderson," begins the boy-narrator, swiftly pitching us into this marvellous adventure story, which will surely become a perennial favourite with the nine-to-thirteen age-group for whom it is intended, and with older readers too. When the invading Japanese Army bombs Ping Ting Chow, where Ashley's father is a strict but pragmatic missionary, Ashley is entrusted to Uncle Sung, a wise Tibetan Buddhist, who was a medical assistant on the Mission. Together Ashley and Uncle Sung set out on their long journey through China, intending to cross the Himalayas into India. Ashley travels as Sung's son, his face darkened with "a mixture of crushed charcoal and cocoa", and pretending to be dumb lest he betray himself as a "foreign devil" or (to use the Tibetan expression) a "philling". After several risky incidents, his disguise is seen through by a lama, who—remarking on his blue eyes, untypical height and "giant feet of a yeti"—prophesies that Ashley will become "a king of the cloud forests".

And so it turns out. When Uncle Sung fails to return from a search for food, Ashley is rescued from his snow-bound yak-herders' hut by a huge, red-furred creature, who is one of the legendary yetis, known only by their footprints but said to live higher up in the Himalayas than any other creature. "Red" carries Ashley to the yetis' colony, where to the boy's confusion he is treated as if he were a long-lost hero. The intelligent and affectionate yetis insist, in their simple imitative speech, that a photograph they have in their possession of a young man, apparently dressed in a cassock, is— that Ashley is—"Leelee", and they seem to expect him to be able to serve as a doctor and magic man among them. Happy as he is in this paradisal existence, Ashley feels increasingly fraudulent, and eventually he knows he must somehow leave the yetis if he is not to disillusion them.

Michael Morpurgo writes with a well-judged mixture of compression and relaxation. Long stretches of time and space are covered in no more than twenty pages, in sentences alive with particularities. If the later stages of the story flag a little, after Ashley manoeuvres his departure from the yetis, meets up with Uncle Sung again (the only part of the story that doesn't quite ring true), and eventually travels by sea to his maternal grandmother's home in England, then that can only be because they are bound to be less exotic than what preceded them. Children perhaps will accept this more realistically than adults who may be enchanted by the account of the "good place" left behind.

But who was Leelee, the young man in the photograph? This mystery is unexpectedly solved when he is identified as a pupil in his "Housey" uniform of Christ's Hospital (which a few alert readers will already have detected, as the photograph is teasingly reproduced on the back of the book's jacket), the now elderly Nobel Prize winner for medicine, Sir Edward Lely. He and Ashley meet and at first cautiously, then with great relief, share their experiences. The story ends with Lely's letter to Ashley saying that if ever he should go back to the yetis, "then try to tell them that we were not gods and that there is no magic, only the truth they already know".

Tony O'Sullivan

SOURCE: A review of *King of the Cloud Forests,* in *The School Librarian,* Vol. 36, No. 2, May, 1988, p. 66.

As the Chinese government leaves Peking and moves west in the face of the advancing Japanese army, Mr Anderson, an American missionary, evacuates Ashley his son from the danger. He trusts his close friend Uncle Sung to protect Ashley on the journey from China to India through the mountains of Tibet, but they are separated in a snowstorm. Ashley is found by a group of Yetis who welcome him as 'Leelee', their long-lost king. Gradually he comes to understand the Yeti way of life and to appreciate the virtues of this race set apart, so that when he finally escapes from the Cloud Forests to England he finds that he is no longer at ease in the old dispensation and yearns for the land of content.

This is a very satisfying book. The Tibetan scenes are vivid and the story is full of memorable incidents. I was reminded a little of *Lost Horizon* and rather more of *The Time Machine*—for the Yetis grow on Ashley in the way that the Eloi fascinate the Time Traveller. Yet this novel is not derivative. The moment when Ashley has to choose whether to stay with the Yetis or to leave them is movingly described. Many incidents linger in the memory long afterwards. I recommend *King of the Cloud Forests* very highly. It is a novel that will be enjoyed by a

wide age group and I, for one, will go in search of other works by this author.

Kirkus Reviews

SOURCE: A review of *King of the Cloud Forests,* in *Kirkus Reviews,* Vol. LVI, No. 10, May 15, 1988, p. 764.

Accompanied by Uncle Sung, an old Tibetan doctor, Ashley (14) leaves his missionary father and escapes the Japanese invasion of China by traveling through Tibet and Nepal to India. While Sung scouts for food, Ashley is left alone in a hut high in the mountains. Ill, hungry, and snowed in, he is in despair for his life when he is rescued by yetis—giant, hairy, big-footed humanoids who prove to have a simple but idyllic culture. Mistaking Ashley for an earlier visitor whose photograph they still treasure, the yetis treat him as their king; but in time he realizes that even his limited knowledge may contaminate their purity, so he escapes and continues his journey to Britain.

Ashley's brisk narrative, though it is brief and easily read, has the charm of ruminative, old-fashioned adventure novels told in the first person. The yetis' appeal has more to do with their Shangri-La-like life than with being "Abominable Snowmen," but they hold fascination both ways. Morpurgo makes a thoughtful, anti-imperialist statement in Ashley's fear of becoming the yetis' "false god," later reinforced by Uncle Sung's comment to Ashley's condescending aunts: "There is often much truth in simplicity." The discovery of the yetis' earlier visitor, now an aged doctor, rests on too improbable a coincidence, but it does neatly round the story. An unusual, well-told yarn.

Ilene Cooper

SOURCE: A review of *King of the Cloud Forests,* in *Booklist,* Vol. 84, No. 21, July, 1988, p. 1840.

Readers will be immediately intrigued as the narrator, Ashley Anderson, recounts how, at age 14, he was caught in the middle of the Japanese invasion of China. On the insistence of his physician-missionary father, Ashley leaves with Uncle Sung, a trusted aide who will chart their arduous journey across the Himalayas to India. The trip is even more difficult than imagined, with hunger, illness, and ravenous wolves adding to the danger. When Uncle Sung goes off to find food, Ashley is sure he is going to die alone; to his amazement, he is rescued by a band of yeti—abominable snowmen—who seem to recognize him as someone they have known, perhaps worshipped, before. While this excels as a gripping adventure story, it is also a keen psychological drama, reminiscent of Kipling's "Man Who Would Be King." As in that tale, a powerful predecessor has become part of the natives' lore, making the unmasking of the newcomer a distinct possibility. Ashley reluctantly leaves before that can happen. Reunited with Uncle Sung, Ashley travels to England where he meets the man who lived with the yeti, and though their reunion is hopelessly contrived, the story is so action packed that readers will hardly care. Plotting, pace, characterizations (of both humans and yeti) are all superb. A spellbinding read-aloud and a top-notch offering—especially to boys who think books are boring.

Mary Mueller

SOURCE: A review of *King of the Cloud Forests,* in *School Library Journal,* Vol. 35, No. 1, September, 1988, pp. 200-01.

When the Japanese invade China in the 1930s, 14-year-old Ashley Anderson, son of western missionaries, is forced to flee with longtime family friend Uncle Sung. With Ashley disguised as Sung's son, the two begin the dangerous trip across the Himalayas to India. Ashley is injured and becomes separated from Sung. He is rescued by the yeti (abominable snowmen), who nurse him back to health and show him some old human artifacts, including a photo of a boy who looks like him. They view his arrival as the return of their god-like "Leelee," and their faith in him is complete. Ashley eventually finds the pressure of leadership to be too much and escapes. He is reunited with Sung, and they make their way to Ashley's grandmother in England, where Ashley solves the mystery of "Leelee" when he meets Sir Edward Lely, who had lived with the yeti many years before. Years after his escape, Ashley is still obsessed with the yeti and plans to return to the cloud forests and search for them. This is a gentle fantasy in which the yeti seem very real and are portrayed as intelligent, kindly creatures. Most of the humans are somewhat one dimensional, but the action moves swiftly. Even though some events happen too neatly, Morpurgo ties up all the loose ends. Both fantasy and adventure fans will enjoy Ashley's story.

📖 *MY FRIEND WALTER* (1988)

Margery Fisher

SOURCE: A review of *My Friend Walter,* in *Growing Point,* Vol. 27, No. 5, January, 1989, p. 5117.

To bring history into friendly relation with young readers Michael Morpurgo has used Sir Walter Raleigh as an historical figure round whom to arrange fictional characters, some past and some of our time. Bess Throckmorton, who is ten, is escorted to London from her home in Devon by her aunt to join in a reunion of their extensive family. On a visit to the Tower Bess goes to look at the room where Raleigh was imprisoned and there on a roof walk he appears to her, explains that he is an ancestor and that he was wrongfully executed, and enlists her help in getting his confiscated property back for the family. Back in Devon, the 'ghost' causes the

child some embarrassment as he tries to drive the farm tractor, smokes the family out with his pipe and ruins fishing lines at the riverside. Besides, he has claimed and stolen a golden orb from the Crown Jewels and this the terrified Bess has to hide, in the farm dung-heap. Apart from the humour of such incidents and the ingenious way the problems of the resident ghost are solved to the benefit of the family, *My Friend Walter* moves easily through certain historical events, introducing details of Tudor life in a pleasantly instructive way.

R. Baines

SOURCE: A review of *My Friend Walter,* in *Junior Bookshelf,* Vol. 53, No. 1, February, 1989, pp. 33-4.

Ten-year-old Elizabeth Throckmorton goes to London with her aunt to attend a mysterious family reunion, and whilst there meets the ghost of Sir Walter Raleigh. This spirit longs to return to Devon where he was once a boy, and does so by travelling in the back seat of Aunty Ellie's car, apparent only as a faint smell of tobacco.

Michael Morpurgo's spectre troubles the instincts of the family dog and is not above scaring rogues by materializing and then removing his head, but he is basically a practical spirit, catching fish with a borrowed rod and riding about the countryside on horseback. The means by which Sir Walter enables the Throckmortons to raise the money to buy the farm which was his birthplace strain credulity to its limits, but the book tells a sufficiently agreeable tale for the reader to be willing to suspend disbelief.

📖 *MOSSOP'S LAST CHANCE* (1988)

G. H.

SOURCE: A review of *Mossop's Last Chance,* in *Junior Bookshelf,* Vol. 53, No. 4, August, 1989, pp. 176-77.

One of the Jets series which have become very popular with the young emergent reader. The books use a variety of techniques to get the child interested in the printed word from speech bubbles to lists and word patterns. In my experience children seem to love reading the books and really enjoy the different forms of presentation. Reluctant readers are drawn to them. I have worked in classrooms where they have been passed around the class from child to child. *Mossop's Last Chance* is a great favourite. Mossop, the farm cat, just wants to sleep rather than go out and catch mice. He is, however, given one last chance by the farmer. All day long Mossop hunts for the mice but he is too old and his heart is not in it. Eventually Albertine the Goose provides him with a plan which seems to do the trick. An excellent book for children who have just started to read.

▭ *MR. NOBODY'S EYES* (1989; U.S. edition, 1990)

Margery Fisher

SOURCE: A review of *Mr. Nobody's Eyes,* in *Growing Point,* Vol. 28, No. 4, November, 1989, pp. 5241-45.

Harry Hawkins and the chimpanzee Ocky both have good reason to run away. Harry, at odds with an insensitive stepfather and a mother preoccupied with a new baby, always in trouble at school with the dreaded Miss Hardcastle, has provided an escape for himself by furnishing a half-ruined basement room next to his home with broken furniture from a bomb site. When one night, after an unusually distressing row at home, he finds the chimpanzee lurking in his room, separated from the Italian circus performer who has become Ben's friend, it seems natural that the two of them should take up residence together, the boy putting in token appearances at home and at school. The whole enterprise is spoiled when Ocky's random digging reveals the fin of an unexploded bomb; an allotment hut offers another safe home for her for a time but at last the only hope for the fugitives is to make their way to Bournemouth to that queen of landladies Aunty Ivy. A stolen ride in a goods train brings the boy into the country where his wrenched ankle is tended by a gypsy family who seem friendly enough until Zak, with his eye on possible cash, reveals their identity; nor is Aunty Ivy as willing to shelter the pair as Ben had hoped. In the end the boy realizes that Ocky must be restored to her owner and that mysterious being, none other than the mysterious Mr. Nobody of the circus ring, helps him to find the courage to go home and make a better effort to fit into his family. The boy's character comes through a simple narrative spiced with details of England not long after the second world war and the author draws a warm humour from the unlikely alliance of a wayward animal and a perplexed boy.

Marcus Crouch

SOURCE: A review of *Mr. Nobody's Eyes,* in *Junior Bookshelf,* Vol. 53, No. 6, December, 1989, pp. 298-99.

Characters in fiction, like actors, appear with animals at their peril. Whenever Ocky the chimpanzee is in sight, the plight of Harry Hawkins takes its rightful place in the scheme of things. Harry meets Ocky and his old minder when, putting off a scene with stepfather, he takes the long way home from school. Harry has a hard time. Mother has saddled him with a second father distantly related to Mr. Murdstone and a horrible second grandmother. School work has gone down the drain, and he is at the mercy of a sadistic schoolma'm. Ocky and the circus life in which she is involved are attractive. When Ocky enters his life again, without the old circus clown, he adopts her and keeps her in his hideout—perilously set up among the next-door ruins (the time is

shortly after the War in which Harry's Dad was a hero and a casualty). Father Murphy, Harry's confessor and confidant, has to betray his secret, and Harry and Ocky go on the run.

The ingredients of the story, stated so baldly, are commonplace. Michael Morpurgo, however, is an old hand at story-telling, and he knows how to breathe life into old themes. His study of Harry, a malcontent at war with his world and clinging to memories in preference to realities, is sympathetic and convincing. Perhaps the transformation of Bill from Murdstone monster to good companion is acceptable if we assume that the earlier image is in Harry's mind rather than in fact. But we must not be too serious in approaching what is mainly a good yarn, full of vivid incidents, plenty of drama and suspense. It will be read with much enjoyment, especially by those who don't take kindly to much of current fiction for young teenagers.

Publishers Weekly

SOURCE: A review of *Mr. Nobody's Eyes,* in *Publishers Weekly,* Vol. 237, No. 3, January 19, 1990, p. 110.

In trouble at school and at home, Harry can do little to please his demanding stepfather; Harry's mother, preoccupied with her new baby, has no time to spare for her eldest son. Harry's world is lonely until he meets two circus performers: Signor Blondini and Ocky, a chimpanzee. When Ocky escapes from the circus, Harry hides her in his secret den, but a complicated chain of events forces the pair to run away from home. Together they hop freight trains, live with gypsies and take part in a terrifying adventure. In a happy ending that may strike some readers as abrupt, Harry gains his stepfather's respect and returns home determined to turn over a new leaf. Perceptive writing, strong characters and scenes of breathless suspense combine to produce an overall compelling novel.

Ilene Cooper

SOURCE: A review of *Mr. Nobody's Eyes,* in *Booklist,* Vol. 86, No. 17, May 1, 1990, pp. 1708-09.

Set in post-World War II England, this melancholy story grapples with the adjustment a child must make when he loses a parent. Harry's father died a hero's death in the war, and no one can take his place, certainly not Bill, his mother's new husband. Needing a haven from his troubled life—a new baby brother, an unsympathetic teacher, and, of course, the ubiquitous Bill—Harry fashions a hideout for himself in a bomb shelter. It becomes the perfect place to keep Ocky, a trained monkey who has escaped from the circus. Harry knows Ocky means a lot to her owner, Signor Blondini, but Harry feels he needs Ocky more; and when his life begins unbearably closing in, he and Ocky run away. For a story of such intense emotion, Morpurgo's pace is surprisingly leisurely. He slowly fashions settings and characters—and there are many—as Harry tries to flee from a situation that can only be dealt with head-on. Well written and thoughtful, the story demands a discerning reader who will take the time to understand Harry and empathize with his problems.

Carol A. Edwards

SOURCE: A review of *Mr. Nobody's Eyes,* in *School Library Journal,* Vol. 36, No. 11, November, 1990, p. 117.

It's the '50s and Britain is recovering from the war. Harry's life is a mess. Miss Hardcastle has singled him out as a troublemaker in school, and at home his mother's husband and mother-in-law are preparing for the new baby. No one seems to notice him unless he is in trouble. One day Harry meets Signor Blondini and his chimpanzee companion, Ocky. When he runs into Ocky alone, he takes him back to his secret hideaway in a bombed-out, condemned house. In no time, Ocky and Harry are on the run as a number of events conspire to make Harry distrust everyone around him. In the end, after much excitement and travail, the stepfather proves to be kind and Harry heads happily home. This could have been a gripping novel with logical character development as Harry slowly learns about trust, love, and his own obligations to others. Unfortunately, the whining tone in the early chapters leaves readers with little sympathy for Harry. The ending is abrupt, as readers are not adequately prepared for Harry's sudden discovery that his stepfather and family do care about him. Adventure and suspense abound in this historical (well, to kids the '50s are history) novel, yet little of that time period or the realities of stepfamilies are conveyed. Best for readers who demand fast-paced action and are less concerned about appealing and convincing character growth.

📖 *JIGGER'S DAY OFF* (1990)

Margery Fisher

SOURCE: A review of *Jigger's Day Off,* in *Growing Point,* Vol. 29, No. 4, November, 1990, pp. 5414-15.

The naturalistic rural backing of *Jigger's Day Off* is contradicted partly by the toyland atmosphere of Mudpuddle Farm, suggested in outrageously grotesque black and white illustrations [by Shoo Rayner], but still more unnatural are the extraordinary events of the one day in the year when Farmer Rafferty's dog is allowed a holiday. Accustomed to spend this day off quartering the harvest field, hoping to catch the animals left in the last areas of standing corn, Jigger determines to end the series of failures by allotting sentry posts round the corn to horse, cows, pigs and the rest of his farmyard friends; the idea might have succeeded if old one-eyed Mossop, the farm cat, had not dozed off and left a clear path for resourceful mice, hedgehogs and rabbits to steal away

from danger. The format of this extravaganza, in the small blocks of text surrounded by illustrations or set under strip-pictures with speech-balloons, makes this book especially suitable for hesitant beginner-readers.

Frances Ball

SOURCE: A review of *Jigger's Day Off,* in *Junior Bookshelf,* Vol. 54, No. 6, December, 1990, p. 281.

Jigger is a farm dog enjoying a day off at harvest-time. While the farmer cuts the corn, Jigger waits for all the small animals trapped in the last patch. His plan is foiled when some sheep escape and he is called to work. He leaves a few friendly farm animals on guard but they let his supper escape. Eventually, he gets over his disappointment and enjoys a rest as the day ends.

The story is suitable for reading aloud or for children with some experience of reading stories. The cover has a colour illustration, other illustrations are black and white and they are combined with the text in some very imaginative ways. Trails of letters follow the combine harvester round the field, sounds come from machinery amid smoke and sparks, animals call to each other from a range of speech bubbles, and cockerels, clocks and calendars chart the passing of time. This form of presentation enhances a pleasant story and would be particularly suitable for children aged about seven to nine who are becoming aware of the many ways in which words can be organized.

📖 *WAITING FOR ANYA* (1990; U.S. edition, 1991)

[In the following essay, Morpurgo discusses the origins of Waiting for Anya, *a story set on the Franco Spanish border in the Pyrenees during World War II.]*

Michael Morpurgo

SOURCE: "The Making of Anya, or A Tale of Two Villages," in *Children's literature in education,* Vol. 24, No. 4, December, 1993, pp. 235-39.

Magicians are not supposed to give away their secrets. It is hardly in their own interest, nor in the interest of their fellow wizards. Magicians who blab are likely to be zapped. Writers, who are after all magicians of a kind, are generally of a less vengeful, less vindictive nature—mostly. Some like myself are so utterly perplexed by the magic of making stories, by its precocious unreliability, that we constantly seek to rationalize it, to explain it somehow. This way, we hope, we might discover the secret of ourselves for ourselves and become "proper" writers, not mere storytellers or wordsmiths. There are dangers. The secret, once revealed, may spoil forever the trick, may lobotomize the spell. We may, by robbing the story of its essential mystery, invalidate it quite and its creator with it. It's a risk I shall take.

The trouble is that I am just as intrigued by how a story is made as by the story itself; and because I have as yet failed to unlock the mystery, I feel quite content and secure enough to tell you the story of the making of *Anya*. A writer is a prospector. A prospector may find gold by accident or on purpose, by a mere glance at a glinting river bed or by years of laborious back-aching panning. He may never find gold at all. Of course, what a prospector does with his gold is another matter. He could drink it, invest it, pawn it, or bury it.

I found gold in the making of *Anya* by accident, a lucky *coup d'oeil,* followed by some industrious panning. It is up to others to say whether I used my gold wisely or not.

The making of *Anya* is the tale of two villages in southwest France in the foothills of the Pyrenees. I was not looking for a story. My son had just been married to a wonderful French girl—he's fairly wonderful, too. We had had a glorious wedding in the garden of an ancient manor house in the Béarn, tricolours and union jacks flying above us, English beer and French wine flowing in abundance. The entente was never more cordial.

After it was all over, we decided—my wife, Clare, and I—to spend a few days in the Pyrenees. Our new French family suggested an area very close to the Spanish border, a small village called Lescun. From here we could walk into Spain easily. I had this childish fantasy that I might one day stand with one foot in one country, one in another. Here was my chance.

We got lost, of course, and found ourselves instead approaching a place called Bourse. Beside the road, Clare noticed a sign, a picture of a bear with an arrow pointing off the road. By this stage, we were going to follow any arrow we came across—anything that pointed somewhere. Besides, the bear was intriguing. Bourse, we decided, was an unremarkable little village except for a fine old church. But just beyond the church was a cage, a large cage with yet another picture of a bear and another arrow. We left the car and discovered in a hut at the back of this cage a rather ragged looking European bear. He greeted us warmly, so warmly we were happy to have the bars between us. A bear's breath, I discovered, is not a bear's most endearing asset. The notice on the cage read, "JoJo European Bear," and below a brief account of how JoJo came to be there.

A small boy had been playing by a stream some fourteen years before and had felt something touch the back of his neck. Turning round he discovered a baby bear. Being a well-read sort of boy, Paddington and Pooh foremost in his mind, he was not in the least frightened. He clasped JoJo to him and took him into the village. There they fed and cared for the orphan bear, and he very soon became one of them; his mother had been shot it seemed. He played with the children, and he grew. He grew and he grew, until he was so big that, friendly as he was, people began to be worried he might do someone some damage. They built a cage for him,

and that was why there was so much honey for sale in the village, with a picture of JoJo on every label. They had made the best of him, poor raggedy old thing.

We tried to stay in the village, but they shook their heads and pointed us to a village higher up the mountainside: Lescun. Ah, that's where it was. We left JoJo pacing up and down and headed for Lescun. As we entered the hotel lobby, the first thing we noticed was a bearskin hanging on the wall, and large black-and-white photographs of a bear hunt, circa 1940. I was beginning to tingle. Wild horses would not have driven me away. We found a room and stayed.

The next day we put on our walking boots, bought some cheese, and made for the mountains. I noticed as we left the village that a dog was following us, shadowing us, a great white mountain dog. I noticed, too, that every house in the village was divided, half for stock—great arched barn doors—and half for the farming family. Every house had a walled yard around it for a sheepfold.

The dog was still with us. Once outside the village, we saw women sitting in the fields, knitting, with sheep all around, their bells jingling in the cool morning air. At any moment I was expecting Julie Andrews to come cavorting down the mountainside in full song. What were those women doing? I keep sheep on my farm in Devon in the southwest of England. I know about sheep. You don't sit in fields with them, knitting; Clare dared to ask, because I didn't. She was a shepherdess, said the lady in the flowery headscarf. A shepherdess! That's picture book stuff. The milking sheep were higher up the mountain, she went on. These were the young sheep. If we went all the way to Spain, we'd come across her son in his hut with one hundred milking sheep, and pigs to lap up the whey. We couldn't miss him.

To cut a long walk short, we found him and his sheep and his pigs. We stayed and watched him milk his sheep and make his cheese. Every summer since he was sixteen, he'd spent up in these mountains in this hut, milking the sheep twice a day. Once a week, he'd lead a donkey down to Lescun loaded with the cheeses he'd made. I listened and looked, enthralled. Afterwards, I went up the last peak and stood with one foot in Spain and one in France, and Clare took a photograph of me all kinglike and astride the world. The great white dog stayed with us all the time.

That evening, after dinner, we went into the little church, read the names on the war memorial, wonderful names; Horcada was one (a name I subsequently borrowed for the story). I lay in bed and began my dream time. I had a shepherd, I had bears, I had cheese, I had a great white dog. Maybe we should stay for a few more days, Clare said. She liked it. I did not argue.

The following day I began to ask questions: Do you still shoot bears? No. Was the village occupied in the last war? Yes, by frontier guards. They took over the house by the church, the priest's house. There were people trying to escape into Spain to avoid being sent to Germany to the camps. If you were caught helping them you were shot. Was anyone in Lescun caught? No. And if I wanted to know more I should see the former mayor of Lescun; he was a boy during the war. So we went knocking on doors and found him. As he was a farmer, like me, we could talk farming together, my French improving all the while as we drank his wine and ate his pâté. The Germans were in Lescun for two years, he said. No problems. They kept to themselves, as did the Lescunois—as much as possible. There were jovial anecdotes of boys caught out after curfew. There was a cross by the side of the road below the village. What was that for? Either he didn't understand me or he wouldn't say. I wasn't sure which. I left Lescun, my head full of dreams, dreams I did not yet know would hatch into a story.

Further investigation with my French family gave me more cause, more pause, for thought. They had lived through the Occupation. One confessed to a sneaking admiration for these all-black German knights with their wonderful uniforms, their fair hair, their blue eyes. I heard tell of a young husband taken prisoner by the Germans when France fell, of his return home sick after three years. I heard of a Jewish doctor who waited two years in a "safe" house in the Pyrenees for his wife to join him. Then, believing she was dead, he left for Spain, and the United States. He went to live in Chicago, and after the war, his wife turned up: She'd been in a camp. Yes, there were camps in France, too. At Gurs, not thirty kilometres from Lescun, they rounded up local Jews, escaping Jews, and sent them back to Germany for "processing." I visited the camp. I saw the gravestones. I wept inside.

For a year—and my dream time is never less, I find— I thought of little else. For an Englishman to write a story of the occupation of France seemed absurd, impudent, presumptuous. Yet I had to do it. I sat down and wrote it as I had dreamed it. *Waiting for Anya* was born. They call it *Anya* in France, where I am grateful that they seem to like it. Recently I went back and presented the shepherd and the former mayor with their copies. The great white dog was no longer there.

Marcus Crouch

SOURCE: A review of *Waiting for Anya,* in *Junior Bookshelf,* Vol. 55, No. 1, February, 1991, pp. 35-6.

Here is an intensely exciting story guaranteed to keep a sensitive reader on the edge of his chair which is also rich in the qualities which make for critical approval.

The scene is the French Pyrenees, the time following the surrender of French forces in the Second World War. Lescun seems far away from the war zone, important only to those who have relatives dead or in prison. Jo's father is among the prisoners, and Jo carries on

with a man's work with the sheep while attending the village school. Chance brings home to him the meaning of war when he meets a young Jew hiding in a mountain farm and waiting for Anya, his daughter who will one day reach this rendezvous and so escape into Spain. It should not be too difficult. Papa's hut is so close 'you could spit into Spain'. Then the Germans come, garrison the village and patrol the frontier. What makes it more difficult is that the Germans are not to be hated. The Lieutenant is gentle and cultured, the men third-class soldiers and good-humoured. Before long villagers and their enemies are living in harmony. Meanwhile at the Widow Horcada's farm the refugee children are growing in numbers, but Anya is still to come. Credulity is not strained as the story moves to its predictably tragic climax.

Mr. Morpurgo writes with much economy, both of word and of emotion. No need to pile on horrors. The terror is in the circumstances, the remedy in the characters of the opposing communities. It is in the end the spirit of Lescun and its people that brings about the limited success of their plans. Here is a writer who has no need of heroes or villains. His characters carry out their roles because of, and in spite of, their limitations. He draws the magnificent scenery, and assesses its influence on these mountain folk, with equal restraint. No purple passages here, just honest, sensitive writing at the service of a great story. There have been many Second World War stories for the young, none which deals more convincingly with its perils and dilemmas.

Betsy Hearne

SOURCE: A review of *Waiting for Anya,* in *Bulletin of the Center for Children's Books,* Vol. 44, No. 7, March, 1991, p. 172.

A World War II adventure story set in Vichy, France, this centers on a young shepherd, Jo, who becomes involved in smuggling Jewish children across the border from his mountain village to Spain. Morpurgo has injected the basic conventions of heroism and villainy with some complexities of character—especially in one of the German soldiers who befriends Jo, and in Jo's father, who returns from prison camp to become, briefly, a depressed and abusive alcoholic. The ending is a mixture of tragedy and triumph, reflecting the capricious fate of wartime victims. Independent readers will appreciate the simple, clear style and fast-paced plot of the book, which will also hold up well in group read-alouds, commanding attention to ethics as well as action.

Margery Fisher

SOURCE: A review of *Waiting for Anya,* in *Growing Point,* Vol. 29, No. 6, March, 1991, p. 5485.

The day Jo saw the dead bear brought triumphantly into the village, the bear which he had been the first to locate on the Pyrenean slopes near the sheep-herds, was the day when he made two discoveries in the hills—the discovery of the deserted bear-cub and of the man who had taken over its feeding. Red-headed Benjamin, secretly domiciled with his mother-in-law, a widow feared and distrusted by the villagers, is engaged in smuggling Jewish orphans over the border into Spain while he waits to be joined by his daughter Anya, separated from him as they fled together from the advancing Nazis. Jo's unobtrusive visits to the widow's farm become increasingly dangerous when the Germans occupy the village in order to locate and block the escape route. The escapes go on and the boy has to realise the risks to himself and the village; at the same time he finds that the enemies round him are not all the same in their way of dealing with the subversive activities in the village. There is action enough, in chases, escapes, hidings and meetings, to satisfy the most avid reader of adventure for its own sake but the patterns of human confrontations and of the bitter constraints of war is one which intelligent young readers will find as absorbing as the courage and resource of young and old in a community whose geographical position made it especially vulnerable in World War II. Superb mountain views and a sure sense of everyday life come through the growing perceptions of a boy whose responsibility for the sheep in his charge is drastically broadened by the perilous events he endures.

Kirkus Reviews

SOURCE: A review of *Waiting for Anya*, in *Kirkus Reviews*, Vol. LIX, No. 5, March 1, 1991, p. 320.

Lescun, France, during WW II is the setting for this latest work by the author of *Mr. Nobody's Eyes.*

Jo is a shepherd with a tendency to doze on the job—until a close encounter with a bear cures him while simultaneously leading to his acquaintance with Benjamin, son-in-law of the Widow Horcada, who lives up on the mountain. Meanwhile, Benjamin, waiting to be reunited with daughter Anya, leads other Jewish children over the mountains into Spain. The last-minute occupation of Lescun by the Germans threatens all; still, a final group of children are helped before Benjamin is captured and sent to Auschwitz with a child who refuses to be parted from him.

Never depending on stereotype, Morpurgo builds a sort of magic-amidst-the-war oasis in his descriptions of region, seasons, village, and people. While harrowing journeys like these have become familiar, this particular story achieves special resonance in its depiction of the innocent and guilty living side by side, settling into uneasy alliances while learning the unwelcome lessons of war.

Susan M. Harding

SOURCE: A review of *Waiting for Anya*, in *School Library Journal*, Vol. 37, No. 4, April, 1991, p. 122.

In a village in southern France, only a few miles from Spain, Jo discovers that the Widow Horcada is sheltering Benjamin, her Jewish son-in-law, who is helping to smuggle Jewish children over the border. He is also waiting for his own child, Anya, from whom he was separated. When a garrison of German soldiers is sent to occupy the village in order to stop the flow of refugees into Spain, Benjamin needs the cooperation of the entire village to save the children. What Jo and the others learn, though, is that the Germans are human and that there are more similarities than differences among them. Readers do not see battles, but will witness their effects when Jo's father returns a sick and bitter man; they do not see the horrors of the death camps—it is enough to know that those who are taken away will not be seen again. Everything is seen through the eyes of one young, compassionate boy. There are no villains and no larger-than-life heroes, just human beings following what conscience or duty tells them is right. In its understated style and gentle telling of a harsh lesson, the story is reminiscent of Lois Lowry's *Number the Stars.*

Kathryn L. Havris

SOURCE: A review of *Waiting for Anya*, in *Voice of Youth Advocates*, Vol. 14, No. 2, June, 1991, pp. 98-9.

An encounter with a bear leads 12 year old Jo into a world he did not know existed right in his own backyard. In the countryside of Vichy France in World War II, war has not invaded the village except the men have gone to war and Jo's dad has been captured and is a prisoner of war. Jo has to become the man of the family since Grandpère is too old. When he discovers the bear, he also discovers that the Widow Horcada's farm has become a station on the underground movement of Jewish children into Spain. Her son-in-law is a Jew and he is facilitating the escape of the children while looking for his own daughter Anya from whom he was separated on their flight out of Paris. When the Germans come to occupy the village, Jo's help to the Widow Horcada, carrying food supplies to the very hungry escapees, endangers both him and her. But Grandpère gets involved, and then the whole village, when the Germans virtually shut down the border escape route. Only a ruse by everyone allows the escapees to depart.

Well paced and evenly written, this WWII/Holocaust story has adventure, drama, and pathos. Jo is a likable young man caught up in events he doesn't understand but realizing that one person can make a difference. His growth from a daydreaming shepherd boy to a willing participant in the daring escape ruse pulls the book together. Boyish pranks and adult realizations illustrate the difficult cycles the young go through to mature. The adult characters, although mostly incidental to the story, are well drawn and the German corporal who knows something is fishy but turns a blind eye is a special touch. Following the lines of his other novels, Morpurgo again creates a competently written story that places children into a situation that they did not create but have to deal with anyway, and demonstrates effectively its influence on their lives and those around them.

Ellen Fader

SOURCE: A review of *Waiting for Anya,* in *The Horn Book Magazine,* Vol. LXVII, No. 4, July-August, 1991, p. 458.

Readers will find plenty to satisfy them in an action-packed historical novel that takes place during World War II in Vichy, France. Young shepherd Jo discovers that Widow Horcada's son-in-law, Benjamin, is hiding Jewish children at her farm near Jo's town, Lescun, and smuggling them over the border into Spain. Benjamin waits for his daughter, Anya, to arrive, assisted by the underground network that guides children to his door-step; before they were separated two years ago while fleeing Nazi fire in Paris, the father and daughter vowed to meet at the farm. While Benjamin's mission is obviously risky, it is made more so when the Nazis suddenly move in to occupy the little town. Jo has secretly and single-handedly been delivering supplies to the farm despite the law that anyone caught helping fugitives will be shot; when the need arises, the entire town of Lescun becomes involved in helping one final group of children escape to safety in a daring plan literally carried out under the noses of the enemy army. While Benjamin and Léah, a young girl who refuses to be parted from him, ultimately die at Auschwitz, the sadness is tempered with joy when Anya finally does appear at the conclusion of this gripping, clearly written story. Morpurgo's characters rise above the two-dimensional, giving young people much to ponder in the areas of good versus evil and hero versus villain. A first-rate choice for reading aloud or for curriculum enrichment.

COLLY'S BARN (1991)

Marcus Crouch

SOURCE: A review of *Colly's Barn,* in *Junior Bookshelf,* Vol. 55, No. 6, December, 1991, p. 253.

Banana Books, of which this is one, are for competent readers who are not yet ready for a full-length book but who deserve to be treated with respect. Michael Morpurgo has a story about the inhabitants of an old and decaying barn, who include a barn owl, sundry swallows and Annie, a little girl whose Grandad had once been the farmer here. Father has different ideas. There is much sound observation in the story, but the conclusion I feel is pure sentimentality. Would any working farmer be deflected from the course he regards as prudent by a dream owl and a dead bird? The book is beautifully written with many colourful new words to add to a growing vocabulary, and Claire Colvin's coloured drawings are delightful.

Margery Fisher

SOURCE: A review of *Colly's Barn,* in *Growing Point,* Vol. 30, No. 5, January, 1992, pp. 5631-32.

In *Colly's Barn* a barn owl and a swallow communicate in words and co-operate in a human rather than an avian manner but in a logical relation to the human behaviour which underpins the tale. Young Annie is set to clear out an old barn which her father wants to knock down though Grandad believes it could serve usefully for years ahead, as it has provided nest sites for Screecher and Colly in the past. The two birds make common cause against the human threat, which becomes all the more critical after a storm has made a hole in the barn wall. With the help of local swifts and house-martins, a mud and plastering exercise is carried out; this timely repair, and Annie's plea after she has picked up a dead swallow, brings a reprieve for the old building. Improbable, certainly, in some ways but the tale touches the conscience and with the help of pleasing coloured scenes [by Claire Colvin] it seems on the wavelength of young readers in country or town who have regard for the welfare of animals.

THE SANDMAN AND THE TURTLES (1991; U.S. edition, 1994)

J. Jarman

SOURCE: A review of *The Sandman and the Turtles,* in *Books for Your Children,* Vol. 27, No. 1, Spring, 1992, p. 19.

Dadci—he's Cornish—tells Polly, Michael and Barry about the Sandman, who has been stranded on a nearby beach for hundreds of years. Brought over from Ireland in a coracle pulled by three giant turtles, the coracle now forms the base of the local lighthouse and the turtles have become the three turtle rocks out in the bay. When Polly and Michael find the Sandman, Polly remembers something else Dadci said—that the Sandman will only wake up when someone loves him enough to feed and look after him. She persuades Michael to help her help the Sandman and the legend comes to life. It's a magical story convincingly told by Michael visiting his cousins on their farm in Cornwall, and it's generously illustrated in black and white by Shoo Rayner who brings out the humour.

Marcus Crouch

SOURCE: A review of *The Sandman and the Turtles,* in *Junior Bookshelf,* Vol. 56, No. 3, June, 1992, pp. 113-14.

Michael Morpurgo follows his blockbusting *Waiting for Anya* with a trifle light as air. Mike, who tells the story, goes on holiday to Uncle Rob's farm by the sea in Wales, confident that it will be fun. It is, and more. As his cousin Barry is laid up with a broken leg, Mike is saddled with little Poppy who is seven and 'bouncy like a puppy'. An immutable tradition here is the bedtime story by grandpa (Dadci) who has such loved and familiar material that the children always join in. Two stories dominate: the Sandman, an Irish giant who sailed across the sea in a coracle towed by three giant turtles, and Sergei Ivanovitch Prokovief, a Russian merchant captain who shipwrecked here and ended his days as lighthouse-keeper, living on tea and Welsh cakes. Sure enough, the coracle is still there, upside down and looking like a rock with a lighthouse on it, and other rocks represent the Sandman and his turtles. At Polly's insistence Mike builds a Sandman, not a sandcastle, and when the tide comes in their desperate efforts to save him from destruction put life into him. The Sandman gets up and eats their picnic, and this holiday will be like no other.

Mr. Morpurgo wastes no time persuading us to believe in his inventions. He is satisfied to get the maximum of fun and excitement out of them. The Sandman is a bit like the Snowman without Raymond Briggs' pictures and almost as endearing. Perhaps the whole thing would have done better as a picture-book, but it does well enough to give much gentle pleasure. All the characters appear sharply etched, especially the dreadful Poppy, and the author keeps up the pace of his cheerful narrative.

Susan DeRonne

SOURCE: A review of *The Sandman and the Turtles,* in *Booklist,* Vol. 91, No. 1, September 1, 1994, p. 44.

This delightful fantasy, set on a seaside farm in Wales, tells of one special summer when fairy tales come true. Michael visits his cousins every year and looks forward to the tradition of Grampa's nightly bedtime stories. All the children learn them by heart, so Michael knows "the script" when some of the best characters come to life. Spurred by Grampa's tale of the Sandman, Michael and young Polly craft an enormous form on the beach and are frightened as well as delighted when the sand creation wakes up. Michael must then decide how much about his and Polly's incredible adventures with the Sandman he should tell his cousins and the adults. A warmly written tale that will be a great read-aloud for families.

Publishers Weekly

SOURCE: A review of *The Sandman and the Turtles,* in *Publishers Weekly,* Vol. 241, No. 45, November 7, 1994, p. 79.

A pitch-perfect delivery brightens this familiar-seeming tale about stories that come true. Visiting his relatives at their farm in Wales every summer, Michael looks forward to Gramps's storytelling, "like a long, happy sigh at the end of each day." The stories are so much a part

of the fabric of the summer that when Michael takes his seven-year-old cousin, Polly, to the beach and creates a Sandman like the one Gramps has described, it does not entirely surprise them that the Sandman wakes up and eats their picnic. Determined to help the Sandman return to his native Ireland, they enlist the help of another character from Gramps's repertoire. Predictably, the family reacts to Polly's progress reports with good-natured disbelief (Michael carefully evades the issue). Consequently there is some satisfaction when the various characters reveal themselves to Gramps and Aunt Eleri, especially when Aunt Eleri proves herself a worthy hostess by producing miraculous quantities of tea. Inextricably linking summer holidays with magic, Morpurgo casts a spell with his ambient dialogue—the Sandman's brogue and the British inflections rise from the page like music.

Kirkus Reviews

SOURCE: A review of *The Sandman and the Turtles,* in *Kirkus Reviews,* Vol. LXII, No. 22, November 15, 1994, pp. 1539-40.

Michael spends the summer in Wales with his Uncle Rob, Aunt Eleri, Gramps, cousin Barry, and Barry's little sister, Polly. Usually when he goes to Wales, Michael spends his time playing with fun, athletic Barry. But Barry has a broken leg, Polly wants Michael's company on the beach, and Michael's vacation turns out differently from the way he expects. One thing hasn't changed, though—Gramps's stories. Before bed the family gathers around and listens to Gramps talk about the Sandman and his Turtles who sleep rocklike on the beach, and of Sergei Ivanovich Prokofiev, the Russian sailor who lost his ship and crew and became the lighthouse keeper on nearby Coracle Rock until he turned himself into a seagull and flew home. Polly is young enough to believe her grandfather's stories. So when she and Michael go to the beach, she fully expects the Sandman to wake up before the tide comes in—and he does. The family doubts Polly, but when Sergei Ivanovich Prokofiev Jr. shows up with his Russian submarine and joins them for tea, the rest of them are convinced.

A diverting fantasy from Morpurgo.

THE WAR OF JENKINS' EAR (1993; U.S. edition, 1995)

Ilene Cooper with Michael Morpurgo

SOURCE: "The Booklist Interview," in *Booklist,* Vol. 92, No. 9-10, January 1 & 15, 1996, p. 816.

BKL: *Can we assume you spent your school days in a place like Redlands, where* **Jenkins' Ear** *is set?*

MORPURGO: Yes, there's an awful lot of autobiography here. At the age of seven, I went away to a school in Sussex very similar to Redlands. Lots of the atmosphere I tried to convey in the book came from there. Certainly, I wanted to get across the intensity of a small community shut away from the world. Rather extraordinary feelings can build up in that situation between students and students, and teachers and students.

There was another thing I gleaned from that particular episode in my life. It was my introduction to class war. The schoolboys and the village boys had fights and difficulties; walking along cow paths, we'd hurl insults at each other. It was an indication that there were people out there who didn't like you because of the way you spoke, and we didn't like them, either. And while things have changed since the 1950s, class still seems to me to be a cancer that riddles our society.

BKL: *So did this story begin as a tale about the British class system?*

MORPURGO: Partly. I always wanted to address this problem in a novel. But there had to be something else to it because the class system has been dealt with very well in other books. However, there was another memory that was hovering around in my head. At my school, one of the boys gathered a group around him, including me, and we all believed this boy had healing powers. We had a little camp in the park and set ourselves apart from other people. Eventually, we were discovered and then beaten for our blasphemy. I always remembered this boy, so I incorporated a Christ-like figure into the story.

BKL: *One of the remarkable things about this book is that it deals seriously with the question of faith.*

MORPURGO: I wanted to explore belief and disbelief, as well as faith and superstition. While my background is not particularly religious, I did go to church when I was young. I am a believer, but I'm not quite sure what I believe in—I'm still working that out. However, I've never really understood why a believer would demand the proof of miracles. If Jesus really is the Son of God, why must he wave a handkerchief and perform magic?

BKL: *How much did you believe in Christopher?*

MORPURGO: I believed more and more as the main character, Toby, came to believe. As I wrote the story, I was swept along on the same wave. Just like Toby, I wanted to believe. That's why writing the end of the book was so tricky. I didn't want to do anything that would tie the story up with a nice little ribbon. At the end of the book, I desperately wanted Christopher to be who he said he was, but I also wanted to leave possibilities open.

BKL: *At the book's conclusion, there is a scene where Christopher is dismissed from school. Have you thought about what happened to him after he was sent home?*

MORPURGO: When I started writing the book, I had it in my head that he was being sent to this school where he didn't want to be, and he would try his best to get out. I assumed he would run away, which he did, and be sent back. My theory was that if he was a con man, he was doing things that would get him kicked out of school. So, one original possibility was that he went home and said, "Yeah, I've done it." But as I wrote the book, it began to take on a life of its own. The characters took the story where it was going. I have found that is what happens with the books that really work. I suppose now I think Christopher is out there doing some extraordinary work, living for his principles.

BKL: *You seemed to take as much care with the small details of your writing as with the large ones. For instance, readers first get an inkling about what kind of boy Christopher is when he takes a stand about not eating the skin on rice pudding, and we really get a visual image of that pudding.*

MORPURGO: In order for me to believe the story absolutely, I have to imagine it as closely as I possibly can. I'm a very visual writer. I have to have very clear pictures in my head, and it's the little things, like the daddy longlegs crawling about in that scene, that draw me into an intimacy with a story. I find I write better if I am that close to it. For instance, I've just done a book about an Irish pirate woman. It takes place on an island off the west coast of Ireland. In order to do it properly, I had to go live on this very bleak island.

BKL: *Some people have compared this book to* The Chocolate War *or even* Lord of the Flies. *What do you think of those comparisons?*

MORPURGO: I hadn't read *The Chocolate War* until after I finished *Jenkins' Ear.* Someone who read my book suggested it to me. I can see the similarities. A British reviewer said that *The War of Jenkins' Ear* had echoes of *Lord of the Flies.* I was very pleased by that because it's a book I've long admired. When you read *Lord of the Flies,* it sends permanent shivers down your spine.

BKL: *This book is very British in voice and, of course, in setting. Do you find it a problem when a story so grounded in its place is published in another country?*

MORPURGO: I think it's a mistake when publishers try to Americanize. The great thing about books that come over here is that kids learn about America. Any child who reads Judy Blume knows instantly that she doesn't live in Surrey. Nor do I think it's a problem when unfamiliar words or phrases come up. When American children begin reading this book, they probably won't know what *toffs* or *oiks* are. But they're about to find out.

Joanne Schott

SOURCE: A review of *The War of Jenkins' Ear,* in *Quill and Quire,* Vol. 59, No. 7, July, 1993, p. 59.

Toby Jenkins hates Redlands Prep School, but the new boy at school turns everything upside down. After what Toby thinks is an epileptic seizure, Christopher reveals that he has visions of Jesus telling him he is His reincarnation. Christopher has been told to start his work, and he makes Toby his first disciple. An unlikely second disciple is Hunter, the school's Captain.

Christopher responds to nothing in the expected way, fears no punishment. He even deescalates the hostility between the school and the village boys, which is due partly to Toby's violation of school boundaries. Christopher makes predictions and claims he can heal. He is finally expelled for blasphemy, having been betrayed by one of the boys he trusted, while Toby and Hunter are made to deny publicly their belief in him.

A strict school of 40 years ago makes a credible setting and gives scope for the complex relationships Morpurgo uses to examine questions of belief and credulity, deception and self-deception, loyalty and the pressure of doubt, and much more. Nothing is truly resolved or disproved; the reader might well wonder what things would be like if there were a Second Coming.

D. A. Young

SOURCE: A review of *The War of Jenkins' Ear,* in *Junior Bookshelf,* Vol. 57, No. 4, August, 1993, pp. 155-56.

Once started I found this book impossible to put down. Set in a Sussex Preparatory School the incredible story unfolds itself with such accurate detail that even the reader finds no difficulty in sharing Jenkins' belief that the new boy Simon Christopher could be, must be and is in fact a second manifestation of Jesus Christ. Amid the humdrum everyday affairs of Prep School life, so convincingly portrayed that one can almost smell the stale cabbage as its aroma is wafted from kitchen to corridor, hints of Simon's mission intrude themselves into the lives of this closed society with the insistence of a dripping tap.

The prep-school boys and the village lads are at loggerheads. The 'toffs' and 'oiks' become involved in an escalating confrontation which builds up into open warfare threatening to turn to bloodletting violence. Stones are thrown; staves are sharpened into spears; prisoners are taken and the air pulsates with hatred and revenge. Simon, alone, stands for sanity and strangely has the power to frustrate the slide into violence. Jenkins is his first confidant and their friendship becomes a blood-brotherhood.

Not only does Jenkins have to cope with all the traumas of prep-school life; the iron will of the Headmaster; the need to hold his own with his peers; his homesickness and his loyalty to Simon but he is also fascinated by Wanda, the daughter of the school cook, who is, of course, an 'oik' as is her brother, the leader of the 'oik' contingent.

When Simon's claims become known to the Headmaster the school assembly becomes a re-run of the trial before Pontius Pilate as the Headmaster demands a public recantation as the price of avoiding expulsion. Simon stands firm but his two disciples fail him. He is expelled but they are allowed to remain after being suitably beaten in the Headmaster's study for their blasphemy.

Was Simon really a healer? His 'miracles' could easily be passed off as 'coincidences'. Yet, as he promised, the child of one of the teachers did recover from an illness diagnosed as terminal.

Like *The Lord of the Flies* this is a story about children but its true brilliance is perhaps only within the grasp of an adult reader. The prep-school milieu is really only so meaningful and evocative for those who have successfully escaped from it. So too, an essential ingredient is an awareness of the similarities between what happened to Simon and what happened to Christ.

The author may have set himself an almost impossible task but he has succeeded most wonderfully.

Michael Lockwood

SOURCE: A review of *The War of Jenkins' Ear,* in *The School Librarian,* Vol. 41, No. 4, November, 1993, pp. 156-57.

The setting is a prep school in Sussex and the year is 1952. Simon Christopher, a new boy from a 'council school', makes friends with Toby Jenkins who is returning unwillingly at the start of a new term. Through Toby's eyes we witness this friendship turn into discipleship as Christopher declares himself to be Jesus Christ in his second coming and wins Toby's belief through apparent miracles, healing and visions. Christopher has come to try to bring peace in the war of the book's title between the village boys and the public schoolboys. The narrative concludes with an absorbing scene where the biblical parallels become more pronounced as Christopher is betrayed, tried and sent 'home'. Toby then has to decide whether to deny his master like Peter in the Gospels.

The novel succeeds in recreating the intense, stifling atmosphere of the English boarding school, but some parts of the story don't work. Even given the historical setting, the class war between Oiks and Toffs is not convincing, and the romantic attachment between Toby and kitchen girl Wanda even less so. Older readers, however, will find it a thought-provoking and slightly disturbing read.

Tim Rausch

SOURCE: A review of *The War of Jenkins' Ear,* in *School Library Journal,* Vol. 41, No. 9, September, 1995, p. 219.

The new term at Redlands begins routinely for Toby Jenkins, except for the presence of a new boy, Christopher, who confidently stands up to the headmaster. After his initial clash with authority, Christopher becomes a model student and befriends Toby. He tells Toby of his many visions, reveals that he is the reincarnated Jesus Christ, and vows to try to save the world. Aware of Toby's doubt, he promises that a miracle will occur. Several days later, Toby becomes his first disciple. When the students become embroiled in a war with the local village boys, it is Christopher who becomes the voice of peace, tolerance, and love to both sides. School officials eventually find out about the young man's claims, expel him for blasphemy, and force Toby to renounce him publicly or be expelled himself. Worried about his parents' reaction, he forsakes Christopher as a fraud, though in his heart he still believes in him. Through vivid and memorable characters, rich details of the rural setting, and ample dialect to spice the interesting dialogue, Morpurgo captures the flavor of an English boarding school in the 1950s. He tackles provocative themes, dealing with the issues of hate, revenge, prejudice, and especially faith in an intelligent and fresh manner. While this novel is likely to be controversial, it will interest YAs and will assuredly provide them with numerous discussion possibilities.

Kirkus Reviews

SOURCE: A review of *The War of Jenkins' Ear,* in *Kirkus Reviews,* Vol. LXIII, No. 17, September 1, 1995, p. 1285.

Morpurgo chooses a British preparatory school in the 1950s as the unlikely setting for the second coming of Christ in an engrossing, imaginative tale. Although Toby dreads another year at the strict and austere Redlands, his anxieties fade in the face of his friendship with Christopher, a new boy who is brave enough to stand up to the overbearing headmaster and compassionate enough to reassure a homesick younger boy. When Christopher admits his belief that he is Jesus Christ, Toby is stunned, but in the face of various miracles and foretold events, his skepticism shatters into the faith of a true believer. Toby becomes ensnared in a series of skirmishes between the Redlands students and the locals that threatens to flare into all-out war. Christopher's attempts at peace-keeping work, but he is expelled for claiming to be God. His example prevails, and the cadre of Redland boys who followed Christopher convince their fellows that further bloodshed will settle nothing.

Morpurgo is unhindered by the undeniably British locale and characters: He has written a rare novel that has the capacity to teach its potent lessons of altruism to many readers.

Kitty Krahnke

SOURCE: A review of *The War of Jenkins' Ear,* in *Voice of Youth Advocates,* Vol. 18, No. 5, December, 1995, pp. 307-08.

Intriguing! That's the word that comes to mind when reading this book. Imagine that you were told that Jesus had returned to earth and was enrolled in a boys' school in England. Would you believe it? Unruly, untamed, and undisciplined boys to test Christ. What a great sample of society to represent humanity.

The year is 1952 but it may as well be 1995. Toby Jenkins has attended Redlands (prep school) for a number of years and each fall he feels the same dread. He misses home, the hugs, his bed, and the silence and space needed to do his own thinking. At Redlands he is thrown in with bullies, sleeps in a large dorm room and eats with everyone. The teachers are of little help and can barely cope. They have their own problems and resort to corporal punishment. The dread of the first day is almost too much for Jenkins. But this year a new boy, Simon Christopher, is in the dining room. Right from the start he is different. He refuses to eat what is in front of him; he questions the rules, and stands up to the authorities. Somehow he escapes punishment. As the weeks go by he continues to question the rules and judgments, feeling they are too severe, and unjust. He also questions the actions of the boys feeling they are too brutal and lacking compassion. And finally he tells Toby that he is Jesus and can perform miracles. When Christopher calmly tries to stop a war between the town boys and those of the school by walking between them as they are flinging stones at one another, Toby thinks that maybe this boy is Jesus. Christopher "creates" some miracles to help Toby see the "truth." But soon the teachers find out about Christopher's beliefs and expel him so that he will not corrupt the minds of the students. Toby of course becomes confused, especially when as Christopher is being taken home, the biggest miracle of all is revealed.

The premise of this book may be hard to accept but it is handled extremely well and will cause readers to stop and wonder how they would react to someone like Christopher. Would the media overexpose him, would we prejudge him, or would we give him space and allow this gentle and nonviolent man to change our lives? Good questions—great book—maybe we will all stop and do some thinking. There is a lot of action, a super beginning and memorable characters. This is a winner.

Kenneth L. Donelson

SOURCE: A review of *The War of Jenkins' Ear,* in *English Journal,* Vol. 85, No. 7, November, 1996, pp. 133-34.

In 1951 at Redlands Preparatory School in Sussex, England, Toby Jenkins returns to school. He meets Simon Christopher, who gains fame or notoriety by standing up to the headmaster at the first meal of the fall term. Toby's shock is nothing compared to what he feels when Christopher tells him privately that he is Jesus Christ returned to earth. Not only that, but he promises Toby a miracle to prove his identity. Toby is sure that Christopher is either mad or sick, and Christopher responds:

> He tells me that I am him reincarnated, come back. I am Jesus, and like he did before me, I have to try to save the world. And today he told me that the time has come, that I have to start my work right away, and with you at my side. You will be my Peter, my Rock, my first disciple.

Toby may still think Christopher is crazy, but after they become blood brothers, he begins to wonder who is crazy—Christopher or Toby or the rest of the world. A river runs between the school grounds and the local town, and a war of sticks and stones has gone on between students and town kids as long as anyone can remember. Christopher sets out to make peace between the two sides, and despite being stoned by a local boy, he gains peace of sorts and picks up several admirers, school boys on the verge of accepting his statements of divinity.

Someone finks to the headmaster about Christopher, who in a public setting accuses Christopher of blasphemy. The penalty is expulsion from Redlands Preparatory, and Christopher leaves. Toby and a fellow student betray Christopher at the public meeting, and neither can forgive himself or the other for the betrayal though they know that Christopher has forgiven them. Then a miracle that Christopher has promised comes true and leaves the schoolboys and readers unsure what to think.

Morpurgo makes the local setting believable and almost attractive. Characterization is excellent—we may not quite know what to do with Christopher, but Toby is a real boy, unsure of himself and falling in love and despising authority and fearing it.

David Ruenzel in "Old-Time Religion" in the March 27, 1996, *Education Week* argues that religion ought to be brought back into the public school, not to indoctrinate anyone but to help young people understand how people believe in many religions. An April 17, 1996, follow-up letter to the editor agreed with Ruenzel's point but argued that in today's political climate, studies of religion are unlikely in public schools. Books like *The War of Jenkins' Ear* may be the closest we can get to talking about religions. In many ways, it's a wonderful and wise book, and if it serves no other purpose than to make students wonder about the spiritual side of humanity, it will be worthwhile.

📖 *THE DANCING BEAR* **(1994; U.S. edition, 1996)**

Gill Roberts

SOURCE: A review of *The Dancing Bear,* in *Books for Keeps,* No. 88, September, 1994, p. 8.

7-year-old Roxanne, who lives alone with her 'dour and unloving' grandfather, where life is ruled by the mountains, sheep, snow and drought, finds and adopts Bruno the bear cub. Initial opposition is calmed by the unique relationship bear and child develop. Then media interest and the outside world intervenes: Bruno is to become a performing, dancing bear and Roxanne a singing star. It's a very moving tale told in the first person, which gives it still more credibility and pathos. The complexity of issues surrounding 'animals in captivity' is underlined by the simple reporting narrative. A memorable read.

Ann Jenkin

SOURCE: A review of *The Dancing Bear,* in *The School Librarian,* Vol. 42, No. 4, November, 1994, p. 153.

This is a delightful story by a master storyteller. A little girl, an orphan, lives high in the mountains. She is lonely, with only her rather bad-tempered, surly grandfather to look after her. One day, she finds a bear cub and her life changes. Bruno becomes her constant companion, and although the villagers are sheep farmers, the bear is safe until a film crew arrives. They need a dancing bear.

A gentle, moving story, in which all our sympathies are engaged. It would be excellent for juniors to read for themselves, or for a teacher or parent to read to them. It raises questions which children will feel strongly about: loneliness, the place of animals in the human world, the effect of outside influences on a small village community. This book deserves to be read many times.

Kirkus Reviews

SOURCE: A review of *The Dancing Bear,* in *Kirkus Reviews,* Vol. LXIV, No. 6, March 15, 1996, p. 450.

Readers of Morpurgo's *Waiting for Anya* . . . which also featured an orphaned bear cub, may feel this novella is set in the same tiny, sheepherding village in the French Pyrenees. Roxanne, a sweet girl who sings like an angel, adopts a gentle abandoned cub that adores her. Years later, when a famous pop singer and his entourage arrive to make a music video based on "The Pied Piper of Hamelin," Roxanne is given a starring role; she is soon charmed away to a life of fame and fortune, leaving her beloved bear behind. The morning after her departure, the bear is found dead, upright in his cage as if staring after Roxanne.

This is an affecting story, certainly, but the bear's sudden death is melodramatic, and Roxanne is such a sympathetic character that her sudden neglect of home ties is scarcely credible. However, the Pied Piper theme is thoroughly developed, and the misty black-and-white drawings [by Christian Birmingham] echo the pervasive melancholy of the text.

Kathy East

SOURCE: A review of *The Dancing Bear,* in *School Library Journal,* Vol. 42, No. 5, May, 1996, p. 114.

A teacher narrator lovingly recalls the fate of Roxanne, a talented young girl from a mountain village who is best known for raising a bear cub and bringing notoriety and wealth to her gruff grandfather. When a film crew comes to town to put together its own music video version of the *Pied Piper* using Roxanne and the bear, the appeal of fame and seeing the world lures the girl away. The next day the bear dies. The storyteller says, "There's a lesson to be learned, if one just listens to my tale." This tightly constructed short story has a gentle tone, but is likely to appeal more to adults, who will relate to the elderly narrator and his style, than to children. Charcoal illustrations are soft and blurred, spare and yet suggestive enough to assist readers in visualizing additional details in order to keep the story in mind.

SNAKES AND LADDERS (1994)

Steve Rosson

SOURCE: A review of *Snakes and Ladders,* in *Books for Keeps,* No. 88, September, 1994, p. 11.

Deft characterisation by Michael Morpurgo enables him to take a fairly conventional 'escaped animal in school' story and introduce the themes of single-parent families, frail elderly relatives and mental bullying in *Snakes and Ladders* with illustrations by Lesley Smith. Wendy is small, thin and quiet and is known as 'weedy Wendy' and 'weepy Wendy', especially by the awful Simon McTavish. Her decision to take Grandad's pet snake Slinky to feature in the class Interesting Things Exhibition inevitably leads to problems but all is resolved happily—including the trouble with Simon.

S. M. Ashburner

SOURCE: A review of *Snakes and Ladders,* in *Junior Bookshelf,* Vol. 58, No. 5, October, 1994, p. 175.

Here is one of the 'Banana Books' series which the publisher describes as 'bright, funny, brilliantly imaginative stories . . . for newly fluent readers'.

This story tells of how a timid and rather insecure young girl, Wendy, becomes much more popular and confident when the pet snake which she takes into school becomes 'top exhibit' in an 'Interesting Things' show.

The plot is fairly exciting, and the characterisation is good, especially of Wendy and of Simon, her chief antagonist. The language is straightforward, with reasonably varied vocabulary.

The colourful illustrations break up the blocks of text, so that it seems less daunting to young readers. They add little otherwise to the story.

The book could be used in conjunction with class discussions on bullying, on the problem of shyness, and on feeling different: Wendy seems to be the only one in her class with no father at home.

ARTHUR, HIGH KING OF BRITAIN (1994; U.S. edition, 1995)

Neil Philip

SOURCE: "The Matter of Britain," in *The Times Educational Supplement,* No. 4088, November 4, 1994, p. 16.

T.H. White wrote that, "A man who copied out the Morte d'Arthur in morse code would still be an important literary figure". The Arthurian stories are deep in the grain of our culture, and every new retelling or reworking adds to the heritage.

Oddly enough, King Arthur himself is, in the medieval sources, often a rather bland figure. The exciting adventures and moral dilemmas are reserved for knights such as Gawain, Lancelot, and Percival. It was White himself who first put Arthur effectively at the forefront of his own story, in that flawed masterpiece *The Once and Future King.*

Now Michael Morpurgo has gone a stage further. In *Arthur, High King of Britain,* Arthur gives his own firsthand account of the rise and fall of the Knights of the Round Table. Arthur is represented as an old man, living a hermit's existence outside time, waiting for the call to lead his nation once more, and brooding on his ancient wrongs. He saves a modern boy from drowning, and tells him the whole story.

This is a noble and daring concept, and for the most part it serves Morpurgo and his story well. The Arthurian stories are notoriously hard to weave into a single coherent narrative. Even Malory, attempting to create a "hoole book", actually produced a series of distinct tales. For the modern reteller, the multitudinous contradictions and alternatives in the source material are difficult to reconcile, while some key elements—Arthur's incest with his half-sister Morgause, begetting his nemesis, Mordred; Guinevere's adulterous affair with Lancelot—create problems of presentation in a children's book.

Michael Morpurgo solves these structural and thematic problems with grace and aplomb. He makes Arthur's bastard son, the bitter-and-twisted Mordred, and Lancelot's, the pure-at-heart Galahad, into a perfectly balanced pair. He portrays an unexpectedly tender relationship between the young Mordred and the childless Guinevere. He writes movingly of the cross-currents of love and friendship in the Arthur-Lancelot-Guinevere triangle. And he manages to interweave the spiritual Grail quest with the emotional disintegration of Arthur's earthly kingdom. This is the best-organized Arthur I know.

It is also at many points, especially as it moves to its climax, strikingly well-written. Where the relentless unfolding of the story provides its own momentum, Morpurgo's prose dances vividly across the page. Moments of high drama, such as Sir Lancelot's account of a dragon-slaying, are conveyed with a quick thrilling exactness. When action isn't carrying the narrative urgently along, the narrative tone can break down. Morpurgo doesn't always maintain the sense of a speaking voice, and Arthur's normally direct speech can suddenly stiffen into a sentence such as, "It is true that hyperbole was not unknown at Camelot." The occasional failed joke, cliched phrase, or clumsy sentence may be inevitable in a book as ambitious as this. There are, however, whole scenes that don't catch fire. For instance, there is an oddly flat account of Lancelot's miraculous healing of the wounded knight Sir Urré, proving him to be the best knight in the world. In Morpurgo's version, this is a triumphal occasion. After Lancelot pulls the rusty sword from Urré's leg, "Lancelot held the blade up in front of him and offered it to him with a smile. 'Yours, I think', he said, as the hall erupted with joyful cheering."

In Malory's version of the same incident, Lancelot feels unworthy to be the vehicle of God's mercy to Sir Urré. After the healing, "Than kynge Arthur and all the kynges and knyghtes kneled downe and gave thankynges and lovynge unto God and unto his Blessed Modir. And ever sir Launcelote wepte, as he had bene a chylde that had bene beatyn!" An emotional and psychological resonance has been lost, here, for no gain.

No writer tackling the "Matter of Britain" can now hope to make the kind of definitive statement Malory made, but it is possible to add a personal charge and a personal slant to the old stories. This, Michael Morpurgo has done. He treats the source material with respect but he makes his own story out of it, and in doing so he turns a series of adventures into the tale of one great Adventure—the attempt to create a heaven on earth, and its inevitable doom. He does not, like so many retellers, simply paraphrase Malory; nor does he, like Roger Lancelyn Green, attempt to represent the whole range of Arthurian literature.

The use of Arthur as narrator allows Morpurgo to concentrate on the central figures and their emotional tangle, and bring them alive for the modern reader. Michael Foreman's full page illustrations, by turns mistily romantic and unexpectedly vigorous, complement a book that is at once full-blooded and action-packed and suffused with sadness and regret.

S. Bates

SOURCE: A review of *Arthur, High King of Britain,* in *Books for Your Children,* Vol. 30, No. 1, Spring, 1995, p. 17.

Every once in a while a special book is produced; the partnership of Morpurgo and Foreman has produced something very special indeed. This setting and introduction to the Arthurian Tales has a simplicity and clarity that takes the reader straight to the Isles of Scilly and the magic of those islands.

A boy wants to walk the causeways between the islands; the task is quite plausible and the reader sets out with the boy. In the fog the adventure takes on a fantastic quality and we are drawn into a world of legend and spellbinding stories. The technique of telling a tale within a tale works wonderfully and the stories read easily aloud to groups, or privately. The language is well chosen and flowing, written with a confidence that denotes a writer who knows how to practise his craft. The illustrations capture the spirit and mood of the text superbly. Michael Foreman has used wet on wet, wistful watercolours, and it is this technique that has made them so mysterious and enticing. He also mixes pictures that suggest times long past with vibrant, dramatic scenes of the knights' deeds. My readers and I have studied the pages over and over. A true winner!

Heather McCammond-Watts

SOURCE: A review of *Arthur, High King of Britain,* in *Bulletin of the Center for Children's Books,* Vol. 48, No. 9, May, 1995, p. 317.

It's hard to resist an Arthurian legend in full-fledged regalia (complete with an extra-large trim size), and this majestic vision of the glory days of Camelot is enticing indeed. The sweep of this version encompasses a rich array of beloved stories (Excalibur, Guinevere, Launcelot) as well as some of their noteworthy yet lesser-known kin (Tristram and Iseult, Gawain and the Green Knight, Percivale). Although he offers no source notes, Morpurgo has clearly done wide research, and he weaves a tapestry of different tales from different time periods. He follows in a time-honored tradition of adaptation and abridgement, but he never neglects the integrity and authenticity of the stories he tells. The framing device is simple: a modern boy stumbles onto a remote island where he is cared for by an ancient man claiming to be Arthur Pendragon. Arthur tells the boy his life story in an almost painfully honest retrospective. He is a complex character: an impetuous youth, an august yet sometimes rash ruler, a jealous lover, and a tortured man trying to live up to his epic persona. It is a heady mix, but [Michael] Foreman illustrates the weighty legend with a lighter touch. His soft watercolor scenes are pricked with a cool freshness; blues, greens, golds, and purples shimmer together into variances of seasonal changes, windswept hilltops, and shadowed castles.

Morpurgo's storytelling is graced with smooth transitions and sharp-witted asides that serve the mythic tales well. This is a far cry from *The Sword in the Stone*'s lightheartedness; it's the real thing—darkness and all—and budding Arthurian devotees may want to read this as a tantalizing precursor to *Le Morte d'Arthur*.

Helen Gregory

SOURCE: A review of *Arthur, High King of Britain,* in *School Library Journal,* Vol. 41, No. 7, July, 1995, p. 89.

This clear and riveting narrative of one of our greatest legends begins with a 20th-century boy rescued from drowning by an old man who introduces himself as Arthur Pendragon. After 1400 years of isolation, the old man tells his story from childhood in Wales to his death at Camlann with final transport to the half-world of Lyonesse. Afterwards, the boy, returned to ordinary existence by a mysterious boat, finds that in real time he's been gone only a few hours but still has the remnant of Camelot that Arthur gave to him—an acorn. The modern boy helps focus the story, giving it relevance, while Arthur's first-person narrative humanizes him more than other versions of the legend. This telling never falters; takes only three side trips to scenes Arthur had not witnessed (Gawain, Tristram, and Percivale's stories); and moves smoothly through this epic of honor, violence, and human frailty without flinching. Foreman's vivid full-page watercolors, predominantly in his trademark blues and greens, maintain the magic, capturing the beauty and mystery of Camelot and the chaos of its sad demise. Storytellers and artists cannot resist bringing Arthur back from exile; it's an adult saga that fascinates children. Morpurgo and Foreman have brought the High King of Britain back alive. This retelling stands with the best.

Chris Sherman

SOURCE: A review of *Arthur, High King of Britain,* in *Booklist,* Vol. 91, No. 22, August, 1995, p. 1947.

Morpurgo's retelling of nine familiar stories about Arthur Pendragon and the Knights of the Round Table is beautifully presented and certain to attract browsers. It is Morpurgo's faithfulness to the original stories, however, and the fine writing that captures all the adventure, drama, and tragedy that will engage readers. Arthur himself tells the tales to a 12-year-old boy, who awakes in Arthur's cave after attempting to walk the seabed to the Eastern Isles. As the boy recovers, he learns how Arthur became king, hears the legend of Excalibur and the adventures of the knights, and finds out about the end of Camelot. Although the Green Knight appears in armor when he is described wearing different attire, Foreman's hazy watercolors are usually a perfect complement to the dreamy, bygone-times quality of the stories.

Marcus Crouch

SOURCE: A review of *Arthur, High King of Britain,* in *Junior Bookshelf,* Vol. 59, No. 4, August, 1995, pp. 147-48.

There have been several ventures into the Arthurian world in recent years, and Michael Morpurgo faces competition. In his favour is a very lavish production, a large page and coloured plates by Michael Foreman, and the support of the National Trust. Morpurgo's contribution is a deliberate modesty. No attempt here to match Rosemary Sutcliff's eloquence. He meets the violence, the tragedy, incest and adultery, in the same quiet tones. His voice is that of Arthur himself, a novelty among treatments. The story is framed with invented prologue and epilogue which set the scene and the mood and fill in the events which followed the ultimate tragedy. A very clever treatment is played down stylistically in Arthur's voice which is quiet and which avoids excess of emotion. The selection of episodes is careful too. With so much to be contained within eleven chapters what goes in is most important, and the writer is successful in blending sequences of events. Most of what matters most is in, including the Grail and Gawain and the Green Knight, Tristram and Iseult, and each is tied into the mainstream story.

GHOSTLY HAUNTS (editor, 1994; U.S. edition, 1997)

Susan Dove Lempke

SOURCE: A review of *Ghostly Haunts,* in *Booklist,* Vol. 93, No. 14, March 15, 1997, p. 1236.

To celebrate the 100th anniversary of Britain's National Trust (which conserves historic buildings and natural beauties), children's book author Morpurgo solicited a collection of supernatural stories from some of Britain's leading children's writers, each of whom uses a National Trust site as the setting. From Dick King-Smith, we have a spooky tale narrated by a chicken; Joan Aiken writes of a lily protected from moneygrubbing publicity hounds by a ghostly guardian; and Terence Blacker offers a tale that humorously connects vampires and the National Trust. As delightful as some of the stories are, particularly for Anglophiles, many will fall flat for American children, who will not recognize such ironies as the infant Thomas Hardy being saved by a ghost from the future, who has a copy of *Tess of the d'Urbervilles*.

BLODIN THE BEAST (1995)

James Riordan

SOURCE: A review of *Blodin the Beast,* in *The Times Educational Supplement,* No. 4109, March 31, 1995, p. 15.

Blodin the Beast is rare among children's picture books in its skillful blend of word and picture, evidently based on an integral conception which the author and artist share. Michael Morpurgo, storyteller and moral philosopher, is known for his poetic imagery and terse style. Here he presents an old theme of a young boy's quest to save his people from a dragon-like beast who "drinks only oil and breathes only fire". With the aid of a magic carpet woven by the wise Shanga, the boy journeys alone and finally conquers evil: so triumphs the wisdom of age and the courage of youth.

This apparently simple story is delightfully illustrated by Christina Balit, an accomplished artist and teacher whose dramatic pictures betray her versatility as both actor and playwright. Here she combines wide undulating vistas with intricate collage-type miniatures—like a gaudy red carpet against an expansive sun-scorched plain—thereby drawing attention to the magical amidst the mundane. One curious aspect of the book is the relegation of women to the role of bystanders or porters for the men.

Ted Percy

SOURCE: A review of *Blodin the Beast,* in *Books for Keeps,* No. 92, May, 1995, p. 30.

In Michael Morpurgo's **Blodin the Beast,** hideous Blodin stalks the land condemning its inhabitants to slavery or death by the fire he breathes, which is fuelled by their labours, for his thirst for oil is unquenchable. There's one wise man in a so far untouched village who knows how to destroy Blodin. In a classic combination of wisdom and faith, Old Shanga and young Hosea succeed—at the cost of Shanga's life—in ridding the land of its tyrant and forging a fairer future. I've never seen a style like Christina Balit's but her contribution to this book is immense. Her tenebrous images of Blodin are made all the more menacing because she never shows us all of him—he's woven into the landscape and remains always a partial mystery. This is one terrific book which deserves a lap of honour, and anyone who wants to regard it as an allegory for our times will find in it plenty to justify such a claim.

Marcus Crouch

SOURCE: A review of *Blodin the Beast,* in *Junior Bookshelf,* Vol. 59, No. 3, June, 1995, pp. 95-6.

Here is a disturbing story, told with lots of pictures but with a long and challenging text too, of a remote time and place but with allegorical implications for today. Blodin the Beast has ravaged the land until only one village has escaped his attentions. The inhabitants have a choice, to die or to be his slaves. Only old Shanga and his son are prepared to face death in freedom. Shanga must finish the carpet which is his life's work. 'There is more than wool in this carpet.' In the one day and night that remain Shanga finishes his work. He sends his

son to escape over the mountains with the carpet, while he holds the beast in sleep. When he awakes he kills the carpet-maker and pursues his son, but Shanga's spirit is still awake and Blodin is killed. There is a new life ahead. Powerfully written, interpreted with detailed pictures of monster and rich land, here is a book to read often and to ponder. No joke this.

Julie Blaisdale

SOURCE: A review of *Blodin the Beast,* in *The School Librarian,* Vol. 43, No. 3, August, 1995, p. 109.

Blodin, the all-consuming monster, is stalking the earth, laying waste all before him in pursuit of oil and wealth. All but one village has been destroyed and its fate lies in the hands of Shanga, the oldest and wisest inhabitant, and Hosea, a young orphan. Using their combined skills of wisdom and courage, they defeat Blodin and return the land to its people. Told in the language of the storyteller, this fable for modern times speaks directly to children about the beauty of our planet and its impending destruction at the hands of the weak and greedy. Christina Balit's individual, stylised illustrations employ evocative water-colour to contrast Blodin's blue and grey landscapes with the fresh, glowing hues of the natural world.

📖 ***THE WRECK OF THE ZANZIBAR* (illustrated by Christian Birmingham, 1995; U.S. edition illustrated by Francois Place, 1995)**

V. Bierman

SOURCE: A review of *The Wreck of the Zanzibar,* in *Books for Your Children,* Vol. 30, No. 2, Summer, 1995, p. 23.

Told in the form of a diary given to the author after the death of his great Aunt Laura, its contents make a fascinating and moving story set in 1907. Laura Perryman chronicles the hard life of the fisher folk of Bryher, in the Scilly Isles. On her fourteenth birthday she spotted a three masted schooner fast on the rocks—the islanders set sail to salvage her, bringing work to the island for several weeks. But its captain spun tales of faraway shores and after a family argument, her brother Billy sailed away with Captain Hannibal and the 'General Lee'.

It's a wonderful story of people struggling in the face of poverty and a harsh environment and their relationship with the sea, which can bring life as well as destruction. It is illustrated with memorable black and white pictures [by Christian Birmingham]; a truly special book.

Marcus Crouch

SOURCE: A review of *The Wreck of the Zanzibar,* in *Junior Bookshelf,* Vol. 59, No. 4, August, 1995, p. 148.

This is a short book by Morpurgo standards but by no means a slight one. The secret lies in the pattern of the book. A man attends his great-aunt's funeral and is rewarded with a bequest—her manuscript diary for 1907, written in pencil and adorned with the writer's own pencil drawings. She claims to be a better artist than writer, but on this evidence she is both. She, like the rest of her family, comes from Bryher on Scilly, and from childhood she was familiar with the sea and all its ways. Here, for a few months, she records the events of a harsh life. Laura is a girl of great spirit and resolution. She wants to play a full part in island life, but tradition and her father are against her. She cannot become a member of the crew of the gig, however much an extra pair of hands is needed, as they are when her brother Billy leaves in search of adventure. Terrible weather continues until nothing faces the islanders except abandonment of home and tradition. Then help comes in the Scilly way, with a wreck. Laura has her brief moment of glory.

The book is bigger than its 120-odd pages. Beautiful timing throughout. Symbolically the longest chapter is not about the wreck but an account of how Laura, with help from her eccentric Granny May, saves a stranded turtle from hungry gulls and no less hungry humans. The scene and the time are remote beyond imagining, but in its way Bryher is a microcosm of the wider world, and here is an account, no less truthful for being fictional, of people living together and finding some kind of modus vivendi.

Kirkus Reviews

SOURCE: A review of *The Wreck of the Zanzibar*, in *Kirkus Reviews*, Vol. LXIII, No. 20, October 15, 1995, p. 1498.

A great-aunt's childhood diary opens a window to the past in this introspective, deeply felt story by Morpurgo. The year 1907 is a hard one for the Perrymans: 14-year-old Laura's beloved twin brother Billy runs away to sea; the only milk cows die; and great storms devastate the islands. Starvation is a real threat, but when Laura finds a stranded leatherback, she hides it until she can help it back to the sea. Salvation comes in the form of a shipwreck: From a cargo vessel, the islanders salvage live cattle, lumber, goods, and Billy, home to stay. [Francois] Place's small, frequent watercolors feature windswept littoral scenes and lonely figures, echoing the text's focus on the Perrymans' grief and the isolation of the island. Laura takes an active role in the rescue; her courage lights up a small, tidy drama.

Publishers Weekly

SOURCE: A review of *The Wreck of the Zanzibar*, in *Publishers Weekly*, Vol. 242, No. 44, October 30, 1995, p. 62.

Morpurgo spins a tale as compelling as it is unusual in its setting and plot. The story unfolds in journal entries and watercolor illustrations made by 14-year-old Laura Perryman in 1907 and 1908. She tells of her life on storm-battered Bryher Island, among Britain's Scilly Isles, where her family's survival depends on the mercy of the elements and, especially, the sea. This winter is particularly harsh, with the family's cows sickening and dying, the weather destroying houses and boats, the food stores dwindling and Laura's twin brother, Billy, running away to join a ship's crew. All anyone can hope for is a shipwreck, that the people of Bryher might salvage its cargo. As bleak as Laura's days are, she is gentle enough to protect a sea turtle that might otherwise serve as food, and hopeful enough to dream of rowing in the island gig despite repeated declarations that a girl will never be allowed to handle one of the oars. Laura gets her chance in a dramatic storm and shipwreck, and she helps save the island. A hearty, old-fashioned survival tale that should appeal equally to both sexes.

Joanne Kelleher

SOURCE: A review of *The Wreck of the Zanzibar*, in *School Library Journal*, Vol. 41, No. 11, November, 1995, p. 105.

The diary of Laura Perryman, 14, describes the fateful year of 1907 on the Scilly Isles off the southwest coast of England. Laura yearns to row in a gig alongside her father and the other men when they salvage ships that run aground, but he refuses to let her do so. Conflict within the family increases when her twin brother runs away to sea; she blames her father for his flight. A violent storm in the autumn destroys most of the islanders' homes and the residents consider leaving forever. As a feeling of hopelessness engulfs Laura, she finds a large turtle beached on the sand. Symbolically, her feelings of helplessness will be mitigated if she can save it, and her grandmother aids her in this quest. As December approaches, another storm hits and a wreck is sighted. Laura finally gets her chance to row, and her brother is among the rescued seamen. The goods aboard the *Zanzibar* restore prosperity to the island, and Billy's return signals new harmony within the family. The action in this short novel builds slowly toward the final chapter. Billy declares at the end, like Dorothy, " . . . there's nowhere else in the world quite like Scilly, nowhere like home." To believe the happy ending is to subscribe to the explanation offered by Laura's granny—the rescued turtle is repaying a debt. Bright watercolor illustrations scattered throughout do much to enliven the text. In all, a story that's well written but that has limited appeal.

Roger Sutton

SOURCE: A review of *The Wreck of the Zanzibar*, in *Bulletin of the Center for Children's Books*, Vol. 49, No. 4, December, 1995, p. 135.

When his great-aunt Laura dies and leaves Michael her diary, he learns the secret of her most coveted legacy: "Zanzibar." While Morpurgo cagily keeps Zanzibar's identity a secret until the last pages of the brief novel, he intrigues us with Laura's story of growing up on Bryher Island, one of the remote Scilly Isles, which in Laura's girlhood was struck with a series of natural and personal disasters that seemed destined to drive all the island families back to the Cornish mainland. There's a taste of fantasy here and a touch of Grace Darling but mostly a story of a girl determined to get herself and her family through hard times, creating a local legend as she does it. Watercolor vignettes are inconsistent in style but open up the page design.

Elizabeth S. Watson

SOURCE: A review of *The Wreck of the Zanzibar,* in *The Horn Book Magazine,* Vol. LXXII, No. 2, March-April, 1996, p. 198.

The story begins as a family gathers in Great-Aunt Laura's island cottage after her funeral to receive the elderly lady's few bequests. She has left her diary to her grandnephew, Michael; as he reads it, we begin a backward glance at an earlier time. Michael has grown up unable to solve the mystery of his great-aunt's wooden tortoise, Zanzibar. Where did it come from? And how did it get to Laura's front yard? In a beautifully executed tale enhanced by delicate watercolor sketches [by Francois Place], we learn of a terrifying shipwreck, of Laura's brother, and of her greatest dream and how it was realized. The slight volume makes a solid impact on the reader, who will finish the book with a satisfied smile.

📖 *MUM'S THE WORD* (1995)

Eileen Ireland

SOURCE: A review of *Mum's the Word,* in *The School Librarian,* Vol. 44, No. 1, February, 1996, p. 21.

In this further story of the inhabitants of Mudpuddle Farm (including Mossop, the cat with the one and single eye), all is not as it should be. Egbert, the grumbly goat, is missing. The only animal unconcerned about the elusive Egbert is Albertine, the goose. When Egbert returns at supper time, saying he'd been 'Just visiting', Albertine is suspicious. In the days which follow, Egbert appears to have undergone a personality change: instead of grumbling, he is joking, singing and dancing, eats the entire contents of the carrot field, and then starts on the apples. While the other animals try to cope with the transformed Egbert and find out what has been happening, all Albertine will say, knowingly, is 'Mum's the word'.

The play on words, which gives the book its title, will probably need to be explained to children, as will the

expression 'an inscrutable smile'. The illustrations [by Shoo Rayner] are delightful—apart from Egbert, who seems more donkey than goat.

Marcus Crouch

SOURCE: A review of *Mum's the Word,* in *Junior Bookshelf,* Vol. 60, No. 3, June, 1996, p. 112.

This revelation of queer doings down on the farm comes in the 'Jets' series, and is very much the result of close collaboration between Morpurgo and his illustrator Shoo Rayner. In fact Rayner has a share in telling the story as well as finding the right images for Albertine the goose, Mossop the one-eyed cat, Jigger the almost-always-sensible sheepdog, and the many other residents of Mudpuddle Farm. The names give away the secret that this is a comic story, not too closely related to real life, and with no serious objective. There is room for a book which delivers its frivolous message with animation and a touch of style, and that is what we have here, modestly priced for hardback and sure of a welcome from children halfway through their primary-school life.

📖 *MUCK AND MAGIC: STORIES FROM THE COUNTRYSIDE* (editor and contributor, 1995)

Catherine Byron

SOURCE: "Animal Magic in a Strange Universe," in *The Times Educational Supplement,* No. 4157, March 1, 1996, p. 12.

Muck and Magic is a collection of newly-commissioned short stories by some of our best children's writers—an inspired idea by Beefeater Children's Novel author and farmer Michael Morpurgo to raise both the profile and funds of his charity Farms for City Children. The book itself will entertain young readers from city or country, with distinctive stories from storytellers such as Berlie Doherty, Ted Hughes and Dick King-Smith. My own favourite was "Derek Dungbeetle and the Lost Lover" by Alick Rowe.

B. Clark

SOURCE: A review of *Muck and Magic,* in *Junior Bookshelf,* Vol. 60, No. 2, April, 1996, p. 82.

Written in support of "Farms for City Children," the charity established by Clare and Michael Morpurgo, there are eleven stories and their subjects and styles vary considerably. "Black and White" by Rachel Andersen is about a town boy who is afraid of the dark in the country which is difficult for him as he has to make notes on the lunar eclipse at 4.40 a.m. Berlie Doherty takes us to a fox's lair in "Bella's Den". There is the totally irresponsible school bully who disregards the country law, but gets his comeuppance when he becomes a scarecrow in Anthony Horowitz's "Scared".

There are fantasies like Ted Hughes' look into the future called "Key to the Universe" and Joanna Lumley's charming "Secret Stones", and a very different fantasy based on a rat rebellion called "The Rats of Meadowsweet Farm" from Dick King-Smith. Elizabeth Laird's "Mr. Hesbini's Garden" stresses the comfort of growing plants to a young boy who has been present during a bomb attack, and a contemporary fantasy in contemporary expressions by Alick Rowe called "Derek Dungbeetle, the Lost Lover".

One of the most appealing is Bel Mooney's "Hector's Great Escape" in which a little town boy Sam makes a pet of the local ram who runs into the road, and is saved by Sam's quick action. Ian Strachan has a sad but topical story of a grandfather forced to move from his farm, but the tale is brightened by the brewing romance of his grandson to the prospective purchaser's daughter; the title of this one is "Everything Must Go".

The editor's own story is of a remarkable young boy very attached to horses who becomes known to Lisa who teaches him how to model figures by using strips of cloth dunked in plaster. Together they work on a figure for the parish church called the Rising Christ. The boy goes away for a short spell and returns on the day when their figure is to be unveiled only to find that Lisa has been very ill, and that his arrival is just in time for the funeral.

📖 THE GHOST OF GRANIA O'MALLEY (1996)

Deborah Stevenson

SOURCE: A review of *The Ghost of Grania O'Malley*, in *Bulletin of the Center for Children's Books*, Vol. 49, No. 9, May, 1996, pp. 309-10.

Jessie loves her life on the small Irish island of Clare, but she resents the way other people treat her as different because of her "lousy palsy," which makes it difficult for her to keep up physically. She finds allies in her American cousin Jack, over in Ireland for the summer, and in the ghost of pirate Grania O'Malley (biographized in Emily Arnold McCully's *The Pirate Queen*), who headquartered for a time on the island. Soon the trio faces not only Jessie's private problems but the threat of ecological devastation as the Big Hill, the island's spiritual heart and the home of Grania's castle, is slated for destruction in order to hunt for gold within. There are some appealing ideas here and a romantic setting, and Jessie's growing camaraderie with Jack is warmly depicted. Unfortunately, between Jack, his family problems, Jessie, her physical and social difficulties, Jessie's parents fighting over the fate of the Big Hill, and Grania O'Malley, the book's many plot elements cause it to sprawl; more unfortunately, the great pirate queen is disappointingly mundane, stripped of most of her glamorous danger despite her flashy appearance. Still, . . . readers who enjoy a good island drama will appreciate Jessie's fight for her home.

Kirkus Reviews

SOURCE: A review of *The Ghost of Grania O'Malley*, in *Kirkus Reviews*, Vol. LXIV, No. 10, May 15, 1996, p. 749.

Even an unusually vivacious ghost can't brighten this lackluster tale of young people fighting to preserve the scenic beauty of their Irish island. Though hampered by cerebral palsy, Jessie, 10, stubbornly keeps trying to scale Clare Island's Big Hill—and succeeds at last, thanks to some sudden and startling help from the cheery ghost of a 16th-century pirate, Grania O'Malley. Jessie then faces a fresh challenge when a developer brings in earth movers to mine Big Hill for gold. When Jessie, with a visiting American cousin, leads a march to the summit for a faceoff, Grania and her ghostly crew drive the bulldozers over a cliff. The developer goes quietly, placated perhaps by the suggestion that he "mine" Big Hill's springs for designer water (to be named, of course, for Grania). The island's formerly depressed economy gets a boost from ghost-hunting tourists.

These are neat twists but still shrink-wrapped. While Jessie is a spunky main character, paired with a colorful figure in Irish history (O'Malley's checkered career is covered more thoroughly, and just as admiringly, in Emily Arnold McCully's *Pirate Queen*, 1995) who is literally and figuratively a kindred spirit, readers looking for the strong atmosphere of Morpurgo's ***The Wreck of the Zanzibar*** (1995) or the captivating magic of ***The Sandman and the Turtles*** (1993) will be disappointed.

Carolyn Phelan

SOURCE: A review of *The Ghost of Grania O'Malley*, in *Booklist*, Vol. 92, No. 19, June 1 & 15, 1996, p. 1720.

From the Big Hill on Clare Island, which Jessie struggles to climb despite her cerebral palsy, she can see the ocean, the bay, and the mainland of Ireland. Soon a struggle over the hill itself divides the islanders, and even Jessie's family, into two camps: those who support destroying the Big Hill in hopes of economic development, and those who struggle to preserve the hill and all it represents. Into this realistic story strides the larger-than-life ghost of Grania O'Malley, the Irish pirate queen, who's ready to give up her legendary treasure for the hill she loves, and willing to do more when that's not enough. History and fantasy weave in and out of the story, inextricable and convincing within the realistic, contemporary setting. The book's conclusion brings a sense that an enormously important, unwieldy, and difficult problem has finally come right. An interesting change of pace for Morpurgo, whose *The War of Jen-*

kins' Ear was *Booklist*'s 1995 Top of the List winner for youth fiction.

Jane Gardner Connor

SOURCE: A review of *The Ghost of Grania O'Malley,* in *School Library Journal,* Vol. 42, No. 7, July, 1996, p. 85.

Realism and fantasy are artfully blended in this novel set on an island off the Irish coast. Jessie struggles with cerebral palsy, but her hardest battle is against those who continually remind her of her limitations. Unbeknownst to anyone, she climbs the Big Hill that dominates Clare Island. There she appreciates the splendid view and feels the magic of a special place. There, too, she hears for the first time the voice of the long-dead female pirate, Grania O'Malley. Jessie's world is soon disrupted both by the arrival of Jack, an American cousin, and by the news that a mining company has acquired rights to cut off the top of Big Hill to search for gold. However, Grania O'Malley is determined to save it, involving Jessie and Jack in her plans. In a climactic confrontation, Jack makes a heartfelt plea that results in the community ascending the hill en masse to defend it. O'Malley and her pirate band join in to create a triumphant victory. There is a lot going on in the story; however, Morpurgo combines the many elements successfully. Jessie is an appealing character who grows in self-confidence and in the eyes of others. Jack's sojourn to Ireland helps him see what is important so that he can return home able to face his own problems. The appearances and actions of the pirates are convincing, and several minor characters are distinctly portrayed. An appealing, well-told story.

A. R. Williams

SOURCE: A review of *The Ghost of Grania O'Malley,* in *Junior Bookshelf,* Vol. 60, No. 4, August, 1996, p. 159.

The ghost of a seventeenth century female Irish pirate is the guiding and eventually the controlling element in this story of ten-year-old Jessie's success in preventing the industrial exploitation of her unspoilt island home. As a cerebral palsy victim Jessie has to battle with her handicap at every turn of events in school, at home and on the island at large. Her American cousin Jack, on a protracted visit, gradually becomes her ally and close friend. The reader has to accept the practical interventions of Grania O'Malley and her pirate crew although they do not provide an easy solution to the island's problem and in the end it is Jessie's defiance in support of her mother's opposition to the sacrifice of the island's uniqueness which changes everyone's mind.

Apart from Jessie and her 'lousy palsy' the tale has an interesting environmental challenge and a sterling character in Jack who fits happily into the lives of Jessie's family and the school. His cheerfulness offsets Jessie's constant dismay at being 'left out'.

THE BUTTERFLY LION (1996; U.S. edition, 1997)

Irene Babsky

SOURCE: A review of *The Butterfly Lion,* in *The School Librarian,* Vol. 44, No. 3, August, 1996, p. 108.

Written in a warm, clear style and evoking the wonderful relationship between a boy and a lion cub, this book is as masterly as we have come to expect from such a distinguished children's writer. The story spans two continents and two lifetimes and is brought to life through the narrative of a lonely young boy, who makes friends with an old lady when he attempts to run away from school. The thread of the narrative is linked forwards and backwards through time by the relationship between another boy long ago and a lion cub that he befriends. They are parted; the boy goes to boarding school in England, and the young lion is sold to a circus. Then they meet many years and a world war later and their story is carried forward by the old lady and the runaway boy into the present. A delightful story beautifully supported by Christian Birmingham's sensitive pencil drawings; and a wonderful read for anyone between 8 and 12 years old. The text is worthy of close attention for its insights into friendship and loyalty.

D. A. Young

SOURCE: A review of *The Butterfly Lion,* in *Junior Bookshelf,* Vol. 60, No. 5, October, 1996, p. 204.

It is not often that one turns the final page of a story with a reluctance similar to that of waking from the total absorption of a vivid dream. The mechanics of the printed page and even the illustrations have become transparent and we have lived through the passage of some sixty years in goodly company.

Michael Morpurgo has blended the theme of that strange bonding which can take place between man and beast with wartime heroism and the deeply felt romance of committed love. The narrator recalls the time when he was the unhappy ten year old who ran away from school into the arms of a stern old lady. She takes him home for hot scones and tea and tells him of another runaway schoolboy whom she met some sixty years before. Bertie had spent the first eight years of his life in Africa. It was there that he looked after the orphaned white lion that was to play such a large part in his life. Bertie grows up in time to fight in the 1914-1918 war, winning a VC and surviving into peace-time marriage with his war wounds and White Prince his tame lion. When White Prince died, Bertie and his wife created a giant chalk figure on the hillside which is sometimes covered with blue butterflies for a brief moment.

Such a brief summary does an injustice to the exquisite telling of a simple story. Michael Morpurgo has a talent for the quiet understatement which he has exploited to the full in this charming piece. Not a word is wasted. It is language put to its finest use. The delicate pencil illustrations will come into their own on the second and subsequent readings when familiarity with the text allows a more relaxed approach.

Publishers Weekly

SOURCE: A review of *The Butterfly Lion,* in *Publishers Weekly,* Vol. 244, No. 19, May 12, 1997, p. 76.

Winner of a Smarties Gold Medal, Morpurgo's cozy, well-executed British novel may not survive the jump across the ocean—the climax depends on a casual reference likely to be lost on American readers. The story, about a boy who gives his white lion immortality, moves gracefully through frequent switches from past to present, from first to third person, from the English countryside to pre-WWI South Africa. A boy runs away from his strict boarding school ("It was a diet of Latin and stew and rugby and detentions . . . and chilblains . . . and semolina pudding"), only to meet an old woman who invites him in for tea. There, fed delicious scones, he looks out the window upon the hillside to see a huge shape of a lion, switching from white to blue. How did it come to be there? The old woman tells him the remarkable story of Bertie, who as a boy found a white lion in Africa and was later obliged to give him to a European circus. Magic enters the novel at an appropriate moment, and the conclusion is sweet. But unless readers can picture "the famous White Horse on the hillside at Uffington" (an enormous, ancient image carved into chalky ground), they will have difficulty imagining an adult Bertie and his wife carving out a similar picture of the white lion or of blue butterflies alighting on it en masse to "drink on the chalk face"—concepts critical to the book's conclusion.

Kathleen Squires

SOURCE: A review of *The Butterfly Lion,* in *Booklist,* Vol. 93, Nos. 19 & 20, June 1 & 15, 1997, p. 1704.

In this story within a story, readers listen along with a 10-year-old boy as a friendly old widow, Millie, tells about her dead husband, Bertie, who grew up in South Africa with a white lion as his pet and only friend. Devastated when his father sells the lion, Bertie vows to find the beast again one day. The story sounds hokey, but Morpurgo evocatively captures the South African landscape and presents young, lonely Bertie's heartbreak and his blossoming friendship and love for Millie with genuine emotion and tender poignancy. Eventually, a reunion does come after Bertie goes off to fight the war in France. When the lion finally dies, Bertie and Millie honor it by carving a monument that attracts beautiful blue butterflies. With just the right mix of tension and romance, this short, sophisticated novel will appeal especially to animal lovers.

Gebregeorgis Yohannes

SOURCE: A review of *The Butterfly Lion,* in *School Library Journal,* Vol. 43, No. 8, August, 1997, p. 158.

Elements of fantasy and fiction are woven into this fast-paced adventure. A student runs away from boarding school and meets an elderly lady, whom he later discovers is a ghost. She tells the story of another boy, Bertie, who grew up long ago in Africa and eventually became her husband. Lonely and neglected by his parents, he rescues an abandoned white lion cub and cares for it, gradually forming a close bond. After some years the boy's parents abruptly decide to send him to school in England and sell the lion. Bertie attempts to save the animal by returning it to the jungle, but it has lost its ability to survive in the wild and returns to the only home it has known. A French circus owner buys the lion, and the boy vows never to forget him. Twelve years later, Bertie fights in World War I and is decorated for rescuing wounded comrades. In a small French town he finally finds his lion, starving and near death, and the two friends are reunited. Heartened by the woman's tale, the student returns to school. This touching story is well written and emotionally satisfying. Readers will be drawn to this fascinating tale of a unique friendship between boy and beast. In addition to being a successful adventure story, the book demonstrates the value of character—of keeping promises, standing up for one's beliefs, and courage under fire.

ROBIN OF SHERWOOD (1996)

Kirkus Reviews

SOURCE: A review of *Robin of Sherwood,* in *Kirkus Reviews,* Vol. LXIV, No. 15, August 1, 1996, p. 1155.

The story of the hero of Sherwood Forest is retold in this compelling, heartwarming, illustrated adventure book for older children. This team deftly removes Robin from his pedestal and sets him in a realistic and exciting recreation of King John's despotic realm. Readers will learn that Robin's father inspired the lad's heroism by risking his own life to feed starving villagers; they'll see how Robin and Marion first met, and discover that the young beauty was also heroic and a talented swordswoman; and they'll witness the cruelty and suffering inflicted on the kingdom by King John's greed. Unfortunately, the opening and closing chapters, which tie the story to the present, seem unnecessary, bookends nailed on without the punch of the epic itself. [Michael] Foreman's drawings convey a jaunty, adventurous feel, well-suited to the tale: They evoke the lush green of an earlier British countryside, and also capture the ferocity of battle, minus the gore. Resonant and satisfying.

Publishers Weekly

SOURCE: A review of *Robin of Sherwood*, in *Publishers Weekly*, Vol. 243, No. 33, August 12, 1996, p. 84.

Another Robin Hood retelling? Why not, if it's created by the distinguished team that crafted *Arthur, High King of Britain*? Why not, if Morpurgo succeeds, as he does, in bringing together the isolated episodes of the legend into a coherent story following Robin Hood from childhood to his death? This Robin is driven into the Forest to join the "Outcasts" when his father is blinded by the Sheriff's men. Familiar stories, like the Nottingham archery contest, develop naturally out of the conflict between Robin's growing band and the evil Sheriff. Eventually, after decisively defeating the Sheriff's soldiers, Robin goes on an exciting journey to Austria to ransom King Richard. Robin appears as a heroic but decidedly human figure, with his family always important. There are a few moral twists: the Outcasts are disabled, disfigured or sick people "cleansed" from their villages by the Sheriff, and Marion herself is an albino, one of the "mutations," as she terms them. But these innovations are unlikely to slow the book's intended readers as they are swept along by a well-paced narrative and lively characterizations, aided by Foreman's loosely modeled, dynamic watercolors of key scenes.

Carolyn Phelan

SOURCE: A review of *Robin of Sherwood*, in *Booklist*, Vol. 93, No. 3, October 1, 1996, p. 350.

Morpurgo recounts the story of Robin Hood as a tale within a tale. In the modern-day framework story, a boy tells of a storm that uprooted a massive, beloved oak tree. Among the roots he finds a silver arrowhead, a long curved stick, a horn, and a human skeleton. He faints and dreams of Robin, who flees to Sherwood when the Sheriff's men catch him poaching. Robin goes on to rescue his father from the Sheriff's prison, joins the Outcasts who live in Sherwood, marries Marion, who bears him a son, and has many other adventures. Most of the characters and events are familiar, though many are somewhat changed from their traditional versions. The dream device allows Morpurgo some latitude in his storytelling, and readers will gladly grant him more, since this involving narrative works so well. In the last, moving scene, the boy (clearly a descendant of Robin and Marion) reburies the skeleton, the bow, the arrowhead, and the hunting horn. In the earth above the grave, he plants an acorn from the fallen tree. Called a companion volume to Morpurgo's *Arthur, High King of Britain*, this large-format book also features Foreman's sensitive, dynamic line-and-watercolor artwork. A fine, original piece of storytelling, faithful in spirit to the legend of Robin Hood.

Deborah Stevenson

SOURCE: A review of *Robin of Sherwood*, in *Bulletin of the Center for Children's Books*, Vol. 50, No. 5, January, 1997, p. 181.

A contemporary young boy finds Robin Hood's great tree uprooted after a storm, then drifts into dreams of Robin's adventures. Robin Hood here is a poor man's young son, driven to the Outcasts of Sherwood when he rescues his father from a death sentence. Marion, Much, Friar Tuck, Little John, and the others all get their stories, and Robin and his band engage in the usual duping of the sheriff and restoration of King Richard, until eventually vengeful treachery ends his life. The book includes no source notes, so it seems that it is Morpurgo himself who has added eugenics to the Sheriff's evil practices: like many of the Outcasts, Marion is an albino, and others are similarly physically differentiated or disabled; Robin and Marion's young son is also not a typical part of the legend. Between the contemporary framework, the Sheriff's xenophobia, and the stately style (which often has Robin displaying various shades of twentieth-century angst), this has a somberness that saps the energy from the legend; the earnest members of this collective are hardly Merry Men. There's really not enough magic or character development to make up for the absence of panache, but this greater sense of oppression does have its historical merits. A plethora of Foreman's watercolors adds movement to the text, as swiftly drawn Outcasts lurk amid the trees or gallop through the night. This isn't a particularly noteworthy take on the classic, but kids eager for Robiniana might enjoy the trek through the familiar forest.

Nancy Zachary

SOURCE: A review of *Robin of Sherwood*, in *Voice of Youth Advocates*, Vol. 19, No. 6, February, 1997, p. 330.

An outstanding new version of the Robin Hood legend is paved with exquisite watercolor drawings, making its oversized form and detailed narrative an excellent choice for read-aloud purposes.

This story is unearthed when a boy steps outside his home to check on the condition of his favorite tree following a storm. He finds a silver arrowhead, a long stick, a horn, and skeletal remains. A faint-and-dream sequence grabs the readers, and charismatic, benevolent Robin Hood springs to life. Saving his father from the evil Sheriff of Nottingham and Sir Guy of Gisbourne, Robin joins forces with the Outcasts, collects his band of merry men, and falls head over heels in love with Marion, in between fighting for the poor and the good of England. Original plot twists and character alterations (like Marion as an albino cagot) allow this tale to unfold magically. Robin's ultimate demise at the hand of the wicked Abbess of Kirkleigh is sadly portrayed in text and illustration, but the triumph of good over evil is the overwhelming sentiment. Shelve this treasure alongside

Howard Pyle's and Ian Serrailler's classic folktales about Robin Hood.

Maurice Saxby

SOURCE: "Making Sense of Life: New Interpretations of Old Tales," in *Magpies,* Vol. 12, No. 1, March, 1997, pp. 18-19.

Michael Morpurgo has chosen to use the chronicled exploits of the folk hero, Robin Hood, as the basis for a one hundred and twenty three paged time-slip novel that has been given visual brilliance by the watercolour paintings of Michael Foreman and which is produced in picture book format. Of the legendary outlaw, hero of a multitude of ballads and stories, there has been much conjecture. A proverb dated about 1405 declares *Many talk of Robin Hood that never bent his bow.* But those same exploits have long fired the imaginations of schoolboys, scholars and sages. So it is legitimate enough for Morpurgo to take the bones of the story and to flesh them out into a costume drama which is also framed in a surreal time-slip dream of a twelve-year-old Robin on a storm-ridden, violent and seemingly interminable night. *And this time Robin promised to himself he would dream his dream right to the bitter end* even if that dream *foretold his own death.* But it is the way of dreams to have strange twists and turns, bizarre details and surreal events. So when the framing dream turns into the story of Robin Hood it is a somewhat technicoloured version, with added sentiment (Marion who has healing hands tends Robin's father blinded by the Sheriff of Nottingham) and a love story (Marion is an albino who believes that God has brought her and Robin together).—*'I was just thinking that I love you.' 'I know you were,' Marion laughed. 'I just wanted to hear you say it.'* Personally, I prefer the less cluttered versions in which the earthiness of the outlaws (here they are 'outcasts') predominates. But if those of us who were brought up on the terse but robust tales of Robin Hood can put aside our prejudices and accept this as a romantic romp there is much to be enjoyed: such as when a spy infiltrates the camp and acts as a cover for *a poor abbess and a dozen or more ragged nuns* who are really agents of the scheming Sir Guy of Gisborne—a wretched lot, wonderfully pictured in Michael Foreman's forest-green illustration. Indeed Foreman brings magic to an elaborated plot which has all the trappings of the Robin Hood movie that once helped lessen for me the tedium of a long international flight.

BEYOND THE RAINBOW WARRIOR: A COLLECTION OF STORIES TO CELEBRATE 25 YEARS OF GREENPEACE (editor, 1996; U.S. edition, 1997)

Mary Jo Drungil

SOURCE: A review of *Beyond the Rainbow Warrior: A Collection of Stories to Celebrate 25 Years of Greenpeace,* in *School Library Journal,* Vol. 43, No. 6, June, 1997, p. 122.

To commemorate the 25th anniversary of the founding of Greenpeace, 18 popular children's authors and illustrators have contributed their work to this anthology of ecologically sensitive stories. Times and settings range from medieval Europe to modern-day New Zealand to a post-apocalyptic desert region. While each selection carries a clear message regarding the importance of preserving Earth's natural resources, writing style and plots vary widely. Morpurgo's **"The Beastman of Ballyloch"** seems like an old-fashioned Scottish folktale, while Anthony Horowitz's "Dragon Soup" is a comedic send-up of Arthurian legends with lively illustrations by Quentin Blake. The "Rainbow Warrior" stars in James Riordan's tale of a hero who keeps his people from becoming consumed by greed. The powerful "A Singer from the Desert Came" reveals a young girl's growing awareness that her people, descended from nuclear-holocaust survivors, are wrong to keep outsiders from sharing the secrets of their green oasis. Other contributors include Joan Aiken, Paul Jennings, and Margaret Mahy. Brief biographical information and a description of the Greenpeace organization conclude the book. This collection could be used effectively for assignments on ecology or conservation. The stories are also compelling enough to stand on their own.

Additional coverage of Morpurgo's life and career is contained in the following sources published by Gale Research: *Contemporary Authors,* Vol. 158; and *Something about the Author,* Vol. 93.

Donna Jo Napoli

1948-

American author of fiction and nonfiction.

Major works include *The Prince of the Pond: Otherwise Known as De Fawg Pin* (1992), *The Magic Circle* (1993), *The Bravest Thing* (1995), *Zel* (1996), *Stones in Water* (1997).

INTRODUCTION

A renowned professor of linguistics whose credentials include Georgetown University, the University of Michigan, and Swarthmore College, Napoli is an expert on language and its origins. She brings her knowledge and ardent love of language to her fiction for middle-grade and young-adult readers. Writing in such genres as fantasy, mystery, realistic and historical fiction, Napoli employs a blend of lyrical and precise language to craft stories of hope and inspiration. Eccentric humor and whimsical charm also have a prominent place in her works; in *Soccer Shock* (1991) and its sequel, *Shark Shock* (1994), the young protagonist has magic freckles that can both see and talk, and in *The Prince of the Pond: Otherwise Known as De Fawg Pin,* a prince suffers the odd misfortune of being transformed into a frog with a speech impediment. Several of Napoli's other books for middle-graders are realistic in setting and plot, featuring school-age protagonists who overcome various anxieties and disappointments. *When the Water Closes over My Head* (1994) addresses a boy's fear of drowning, while in its sequel, *On Guard* (1997), he worries that he will be overshadowed by his siblings, but gains self-confidence and the respect of others after he discovers he is good at fencing. However, Napoli is perhaps best known for her works for older readers, having produced several titles, including *The Magic Circle* and *Zel,* that retell fairy tales with an original twist. According to Betsy Hearne, Napoli "flexes her proven talent for unexpected viewpoints, builds strong pace with compressed vigor, and evokes powerful sensory images," while Lisa Dennis noted that Napoli's "writing and the clarity of her vision" make stories like *The Magic Circle* "fresh and absorbing." She has also written historical fiction, such as *Song of the Magdalene* (1996), an account of the life of biblical figure Mary Magdalene, and the critically acclaimed *Stones in Water,* about an Italian boy's survival and escape from a German labor camp during World War II. While Napoli refuses to preach to children, her books offer them what she hopes is a clear message: "I do not hesitate to present [children] with the sadness of mortality and the horrors of wickedness—but I always try to leave them with a sense that whether or not they can change the problems in life, they can find a way to live decently and joyfully," she explained. "Hope is an internal matter. I strive to cultivate it in my readers. Children offer fertile ground."

Biographical Information

Napoli was born in Miami, Florida, in 1948, the youngest of four children. By the time she was thirteen, she and her family had lived in thirteen different houses that her father, as a contractor, built on speculation and subsequently sold. Though she remained in the same school, her neighborhood changed often, and she grew up feeling like an "outsider," having constantly to make new friends. The school library, with its likable and helpful staff and vast selection of reading material provided a haven for Napoli in her elementary school years, and by high school she excelled in French, Latin, and math. She later attended Radcliffe, then the name of the women's college at Harvard University, where she earned a bachelor's degree in mathematics in 1970, and a Ph.D. in Romance linguistics—combining her love of languages and math—in 1973. Although she had been encouraged by an instructor at Harvard to pursue a writing career, Napoli decided that doing so, at this point, would not be practical; having started a family with husband Barry Furrow, she wanted a job with a more certain paycheck so that her children would have a more comfortable existence than she had as a child. While working toward full professorship in linguistics, she held positions as lecturer and assistant professor at Smith College, the University of North Carolina, and Georgetown University. Nevertheless, during the late seventies and early eighties Napoli wrote and edited several books pertaining to her field, including such titles as *Elements of Tone, Stress, and Intonation* (1978) and *Syntactic Argumentation* (1979). But it was not until 1988 that her first book for children was published. Inspired by her family's frequent visits to Italy, *The Hero of Barletta* is a retelling of an Italian folktale in which a clever giant saves his town from an advancing army. Since then she has written over fifteen books for children and adults, has contributed to poetry books such as *The Linguistic Muse, Meliglossa, Lingua Franca,* and *Speaking in Tongues,* and has produced numerous professional articles on linguistics.

Major Works

Napoli's *The Prince of the Pond: Otherwise Known as De Fawg Pin* offers a new twist on the frog-prince motif often used in fairy tale. In this story, a prince is transformed into a frog by a witch and is soon befriended by a female frog called Jade, who shows him how to survive pond life. The two fall in love and have tadpoles together, but are not destined to live happily ever after; instead Napoli explores themes of grief and loss as the heartbroken Jade witnesses a kiss between a human princess and her beloved frog, who then becomes a prince again. Observing that the tale was both accurate and enchanting, a *Kirkus Reviews* critic commented that *The Prince of the Pond* has "an astonishing amount of in-depth natural history cleverly enmeshed in its endearing, screwball charm." Napoli's first young-adult novel was inspired by her own daughter's question of why so many evil female characters can be found in fairy tales. She wrote *The Magic Circle* as a prequel to the Hansel and Gretel fairy tale, with the intention of giving the witch a history to explain her wickedness. As in several of Napoli's other works, an old story is told from a fresh angle: in recounting her former life as a devoted mother, a pious servant of God, and a healer, the witch is portrayed as a compelling and sympathetic heroine, who has been tricked by the devil's minions and forced to embrace evil herself. *The Magic Circle* contains vivid imagery informed by nature and folklore, and Napoli's talent for creating suspense is showcased when, in the book's final pages, Hansel and Gretel meet this witch, who has purposely removed herself from civilization to avoid the temptation of devouring children.

Napoli shifts from the fairy-tale genre to realistic fiction in *The Bravest Thing*, in which themes of death and loss are again explored. Ten-year-old Laurel must deal with the death of her pet rabbit's litter of bunnies, her aunt's bout with cancer, and her own diagnosis of scoliosis. The novel conveys the message that life's obstacles can seem less daunting if faced head on and ends on a note of hope: Laurel successfully nurses the only surviving bunny to maturity and is offered a job by the local

veterinarian. Reminiscent of *The Magic Circle* but narratively more complex, Napoli's novel *Zel*—based on the Rapunzel story—is another complete refashioning of a dark fairy tale. The novel has three different narrators: Zel, who is imprisoned in a tower; the prince who wants to rescue her and Zel's foster mother, the witch who holds her hostage. By changing the point of view with each new chapter, Napoli is able to delve into the psyches of her characters, each of whom is verging on madness. According to *Publishers Weekly*, "the genius of the novel lies not just in the details but in its breadth of vision. Its shiveringly romantic conclusion will leave readers spellbound." *Stones in Water* marks a brave departure from Napoli's previous fiction. Set in Europe during World War II and narrated by a young Venetian boy who is forced into the war against his will, this historical novel is based on the life of an actual veteran. Napoli proves once again that she is an excellent researcher and masterful storyteller, as Roberto recalls the atrocities he both witnessed and experienced firsthand while working in a German labor camp alongside his Jewish friend Samuele. What emerges, however, is Napoli's belief in the prevailing goodness of people; against the backdrop of the unspeakable acts by Nazi soldiers, Roberto and Samuele make great sacrifices for each other and for the strangers they encounter. Praised by reviewers as an intense and gripping story, *Stones in Water* is certain to leave an indelible impression on readers of all ages.

Awards

The Prince of the Pond: Otherwise Known as De Fawg Pin was selected as a Children's Book of the Year by Bank Street Child Study Children's Book Committee in 1993, and received the New Jersey Reading Association's Jerry Award in 1996. *The Magic Circle* was regarded as a Best Book Selection by *Publishers Weekly* and received a Blue Ribbon Book designation from *Bulletin of the Center for Children's Books*, both in 1993. *When the Water Closes over My Head* was selected as a Children's Book of the Year by Bank Street Child Study Children's Book Committee in 1995. *Jimmy, the Pickpocket of the Palace* received the same designation in 1996. *Zel* was voted the Best Book Selection by *Publishers Weekly* and *School Library Journal*, and received a Blue Ribbon Book designation from *Bulletin of the Center for Children's Books*, all in 1996.

TITLE COMMENTARY

📖 *THE HERO OF BARLETTA* (1988)

Nancy A. Gifford

SOURCE: A review of *The Hero of Barletta*, in *School Library Journal*, Vol. 34, No. 11, August, 1988, p. 84.

Nico is teased for being too big, too strong, too fast for all the boyhood games, but when the town of Barletta is attacked by a strange army, Nico uses his size to good advantage. Crying on the bridge as the army approaches, Nico explains that everyone teases him for being so small. The enemy decides it would be wiser to retreat. Simple vocabulary, strong story line, and a direct telling make this a good choice for beginning readers. Illustrations are only adequate, alternating pale black-and-white line drawings with full-color pictures. Tomie dePaola's *The Mysterious Giant of Barletta* is a more attractively illustrated version of the same folktale, but it serves a different readership. Beginning readers who may have heard dePaola's tale now can have their own version to read independently.

SOCCER SHOCK (1991)

Kirkus Reviews

SOURCE: A review of *Soccer Shock*, in *Kirkus Reviews*, Vol. LIX, No. 18, September 15, 1991, pp. 1225-26.

Brainy Adam wants desperately to make the fifth-grade soccer team but doesn't have much chance until star player Grayson offers lessons in exchange for math tutoring—and, more importantly, Adam discovers that a lightning bolt's near miss has left him with the ability to hear the freckles on his knees talking, so that he has an efficient early-warning system on the playing field. The freckles really steal the show here, whether they're telling Adam that the ball's coming his way or the swing's about to break, or just commenting aimlessly on the gum under desks. Despite having to cope with classmate Kim's aggressive pursuit, Adam is feeling fine—until he temporarily skins off Gilbert, his best freckle, and has to face the soccer tryouts without his secret weapon.

A well-written story with an affectionate, tolerant cast, a little elementary math and soccer instruction, and a funny premise.

Denise Krell

SOURCE: A review of *Soccer Shock*, in *School Library Journal*, Vol. 38, No. 4, April, 1992, p. 118.

Do talking freckles sound far-fetched? It is an unusually fantastic twist, yet this lighthearted novel succeeds with genuine characters in a believable setting, wound into an otherwise realistic plot with lots of childlike experiences. Even the freckles become credible. Adam is an average, likable kid who wants to make the soccer team, but he is better at math. Garrison is assured of making the team but his poor math skills embarrass him. In the weakest segment of the book, lightning strikes close to Adam and he hears voices. Two chapters later, in a humorous sequence in the bathtub, he discovers that his freckles talk only when there's a proper conductor—in this case, water from his ears to his spots—and that he is the only one who can hear them. Although he bribes them into helping him play his chosen sport better, Adam never becomes the best player, nor does Garrison truly excel in math. Instead, they are heroic in smaller, more personal ways—sticking to their goals and accomplishing them. Johnson's black-and-white drawings capture many of the comic moments.

THE PRINCE OF THE POND: OTHERWISE KNOWN AS DE FAWG PIN (1992)

John Peters

SOURCE: A review of *The Prince of the Pond: Otherwise Known as De Fawg Pin*, in *School Library Journal*, Vol. 38, No. 10, October, 1992, pp. 118, 120.

When a female frog comes upon an attractive but very confused male sitting near a pile of human clothing, she's appalled to see that his feet tangle when he tries to leap, that his tongue keeps falling out of his mouth, and that he doesn't seem to know the first thing about frog behavior or predators. Though she does persuade him to eat bugs, he never learns to speak clearly, with "I'm De Fawg Pin" being a typical utterance, and he stubbornly clings to odd ideas (e.g., that the young must be cared for). He also demonstrates reckless, very unfroglike courage, and while rescuing one of his 50 offspring, he suddenly disappears. "Pin's" companion never does figure out what's going on, but readers will; his situation and reeducation is defined in broad, comic strokes against an accurate, almost technical, picture of pond ecology. The froggy characters are clearly delineated, and their feelings for one another are genuine, to the point that many readers may greet the prince's reversion to human form with mixed emotions. Ornamental borders and [Judith Byron] Schachner's pictures of goggle-eyed, expressive frogs in detailed, natural settings give the book a formal, dignified look that plants the tongue even more firmly in cheek.

Kirkus Reviews

SOURCE: A review of *The Prince of the Pond: Otherwise Known as De Fawg Pin*, in *Kirkus Reviews*, Vol. LX, No. 19, October 1, 1992, p. 1259.

Poor Jade (or Jade-to-be, since "de fawg pin" has yet to name her): she's faced with a big, beautiful frog—such legs!—and he doesn't seem to have the foggiest notion about what to do with his tongue, or how to leap or avoid danger. She even has to teach him to mate, and then he insists on personally raising at least 50 of his hundreds of children. Still, though he never masters r's, l's, and s's (hence "Pin" for "Prince"), he leaves his aristocratic mark on the pond world, as a hag-bewitched prince should. He also leaves Jade with the 50 tads when a passing princess accidentally plants a kiss on his proboscis.

Just when you thought it was safe to go back to the pond, another change is rung on the frog prince; this time, readers' sympathies will be with the frog's first wife, left with 50 upwardly mobile children. Nicely complemented by Schachner's charmingly whimsical (and anatomically informed) drawings, a book with an astonishing amount of in-depth natural history cleverly enmeshed in its endearing, screwball charm.

Publishers Weekly

SOURCE: A review of *The Prince of the Pond: Otherwise Known as De Fawg Pin*, in *Publishers Weekly*, Vol. 239, No. 50, November 16, 1992, p. 64.

This variation on "The Frog Prince" is told by Jade, a watchful female frog who teaches the bewitched royal how to survive in the pond. Jade eventually becomes a frog wife and mother to a school of tadpoles. The romance between these two characters, somewhat convoluted and tinged with adult sensibilities, changes Jade's outlook and alters the traditional habits of the frog world. Incorporated into the story are absorbing observations about pond life from a factual perspective. However, Pin's attempts to humanize the frog world are questionable, as his eventual return to human form in front of his amphibian family leaves them saddened and bereft. The story is further weakened by an ongoing, supposedly comic device: the Prince, due to a problem with his tongue, indulges in a kind of baby talk, so that his words emerge as "fawg" for *frog* and "obteh" for *lobster*. Aided little by Schachner's rough-hewn black-and-white drawings (a few witty, some repetitious), the story, sadly, does not measure up to its premise.

Betsy Hearne

SOURCE: A review of *The Prince of the Pond: Otherwise Known as De Fawg Pin*, in *Bulletin of the Center for Children's Books*, Vol. 46, No. 5, January, 1993, pp. 153-54.

Point of view is all here, and Napoli uses it to involve the reader in a touching story narrated by a female green frog who befriends the large, bewildered male appearing suddenly under a human hat. He is bewildered, readers realize, because he's just been turned from prince to frog by a witch. He cannot talk properly (*r*s, *s*s, *th*s, and *l*s are beyond the power of his newly long tongue); he doesn't realize who his enemies are; and he eventually teaches the narrator, whom he names Jade, how to love both himself and their tadpoles—only to be transformed back into a human by a princess' kiss before Jade's very eyes. Froglike, she has no idea what happened ("Where was my beautiful Pin?") which makes readers feel for her all the more. The consistency and mini-drama of a frog's-eye view (one at a time), coupled with a poignant ending that doesn't shy away from loss, makes this an animal fantasy that fairy tale readers will relish. The prince's lisp occasionally becomes wearing, but it will

be fun to read aloud, and the humor of Jade and Pin's developing relationship keeps sentimentality at bay. Schachner's numerous ink-and-wash drawings go far in supporting the characterization; they're skillfully drafted, combining anatomical fluidity, witty expression, and subtle modeling of light and dark values, all to handsome effect.

Carolyn Phelan

SOURCE: A review of *The Prince of the Pond: Otherwise Known as De Fawg Pin*, in *Booklist*, Vol. 89, No. 10, January 15, 1993, p. 909.

The frog prince motif has inspired many books, but few as original as this novel, told from the point of view of Jade, a female frog. Jade meets the prince when he first becomes a frog, but she never quite catches on that he's more than just a frog. Pin (as the Prince calls himself, hampered in his speech by a long, fat tongue attached at the front of his mouth) is handsome, but strangely ignorant of everything from the joys of eating insects to the importance of avoiding reptiles, so Jade must teach him the ropes. Pin's bewilderment with pond life is matched by Jade's confusion with Pin's ways. Eventually, when the opportunity of kissing a princess presents itself, Pin leaps at it and disappears from Jade's life forever. Sometimes amusing and always convincing, this light fantasy raises questions about animals' thoughts and behavior and also explains a good deal about the lives of frogs. Lively drawings appear throughout the book, adding to its appeal for younger readers. An unusual choice for reading aloud in the classroom.

Jo Goodman

SOURCE: A review of *The Prince of the Pond: Otherwise Known as De Fawg Pin*, in *Magpies*, Vol. 10, No. 1, March, 1995, p. 26.

The traditional *The Frog Prince* is a favourite target for post-modern reconstruction. In this deliciously ironic version the author takes seriously the dilemmas imposed upon a SNAG (Sensitive New Age Guy) prince who suddenly finds himself to be a frog. Fortunately he proves attractive to a determined female frog; she takes him in hand, overcomes his squeamishness about flies, and they both learn a great deal from the relationship. One wonderful episode involves the prince's determination to be a good father to their tadpoles—an attitude new to the frog world!

Here is a story to be enjoyed on a number of levels. It is amusing for young listeners and readers, but also contains a gently satiric look at SNAGS, and the implications of changes in social attitudes; there is plenty here too for a serious study by older readers interested in post-modernism. This American edition is most attractively presented with generous layouts, decorative borders, and an appropriate illustration at almost every opening. Great for sharing with a class or family, this is a book which offers lasting enjoyment for both children and adults.

THE MAGIC CIRCLE (1993)

Betsy Hearne

SOURCE: A review of *The Magic Circle,* in *Bulletin of the Center for Children's Books,* Vol. 46, No. 8, April, 1993, p. 260.

Napoli turns from the hilarity of her last book, **The Prince of the Pond,** to a dark tone and highly charged plot developed as a kind of prequel to "Hansel and Gretel." The heroine of this first-person, present-tense narrative is called "Ugly One." Twisted in body but kind in heart, the devoted mother of an illegitimate daughter, she's a woman whose interest in healing lures her from midwifery into sorcery. Finally, the demons whom she has commanded trick her into becoming a witch, and she flees their initiation rite of eating a child, only to be confronted, after years of lonely resistance, by two succulent children in the isolated woods where she has sought shelter from her appetites. Napoli flexes her proven talent for unexpected viewpoints, builds strong pace with compressed vigor, and evokes powerful sensory images—at one point, the witch uses her iron teeth to bite off her tongue, which flies across the hut and writhes in a corner on the floor. As brief as the novel is, each aspect is vividly realized with details such as the narrator's compulsive sweeping to clean away the spiders that spy on her movements. Intense overall, this has an ending that will guarantee it a place in the hearts of young adult gothic fans. It is in many ways a groundbreaking book, treating demonic evil seriously and flying in the face of politically correct revisionist history about women falsely accused of witchcraft. Although the community does react with conventional ignorance and hatred toward this social outcast, it is the narrator's own pride that proves her downfall. The scene where she breaks the magic circle to retrieve a coveted ring is gripping enough to make a reader want to stop reading so she won't do it. When she and her daughter are tied to the stake—where she makes a demonic pact to save her daughter from the flames—we perceive the sinister underside of a magic lightly played out in books such as McKinley's *Beauty.* Gwen Strauss' *Trail of Stones,* the poetic retelling of fairy tales from the antihero's viewpoint, or Patricia Wrightson's *A Little Fear* make more apt companions to **The Magic Circle.**

Publishers Weekly

SOURCE: A review of *The Magic Circle,* in *Publishers Weekly,* Vol. 240, No. 24, June 14, 1993, p. 73.

A midwife-cum-sorceress known simply as the Ugly One narrates this riveting tale of how, tricked by the devil's minions, she lost her gifts for healing and was forced to become a witch. Escaping from the stake, where she is about to be burned, she ekes out a solitary existence in an enchanted forest—until she takes in two wandering children named Hansel and Gretel. As she did in **The Prince of the Pond,** Napoli gives a classic fairy tale an entirely new twist, at the same time incorporating absorbing details about medieval religious beliefs. The witch's "true" history as a devoted mother and pious servant of God renders her a compelling and entirely sympathetic figure, a heroine courageously fighting the evil spirits that have invaded her once-pure life. The Hansel and Gretel motif, carefully woven into the story, emerges as a surprise for the reader, albeit a surprise that has been fully prepared. The author's extraordinary craftsmanship and originality never flag, and even the archetypically fiery ending for the witch acquires a new dimension. A YA novel of genuine magic and suspense, this will captivate adults as well.

Kirkus Reviews

SOURCE: A review of *The Magic Circle,* in *Kirkus Reviews,* Vol. LXI, No. 12, June 15, 1993, p. 789.

The author of **The Prince in the Pond** (1992) leaps from that comic take on "The Frog Prince" to a dark, deeply thoughtful novel whose gifted, driven, and wholly sympathetic protagonist is Hansel and Gretel's witch. The hunchback known as "Ugly One" is a midwife who becomes a healer when she learns to draw, with a blessed object, a magic circle that cannot be invaded by the devil's minions; from safely within it, she can command them to leave their victims. But the demons eventually trick her with a ring she hopes to give her beloved daughter, now of an age to marry. Now the sorceress who has commanded devils becomes a witch subject to their demands; still, with great care, she avoids the potent temptation to devour a child, which would complete her damnation. Hansel and Gretel's arrival, in the novel's last pages, is a cruel test; with extraordinary artistry, Napoli shapes a conclusion in which the witch finds redemption by collaborating with a clever Gretel, who senses the meaning of her fiery death. Writing in a beautifully honed first-person present and summoning splendid imagery well grounded in folklore, psychology, and the natural world, Napoli delves into the mind and heart of a fascinating figure embodying Faust and Marguerite in one—a nurturer and lover of true beauty whose inner being is never truly corrupted by the dangerous knowledge she dares to exert on others' behalf. Richly poetic yet accessible and immediate; pungent and wise; mesmerizing.

Sally Estes

SOURCE: A review of *The Magic Circle,* in *Booklist,* Vol. 89, No. 21, July, 1993, p. 1957.

Napoli offers an unusual treatment of the Hansel and Gretel story, which she tells from the viewpoint of the witch, known here as the Ugly One. The first full half of the story takes place before she becomes a witch— when she is only an ugly, hunchbacked midwife/sorceress who dotes on her beautiful young daughter, Asa. Eventually ensnared by the demons she summons to work her healings, the Ugly One flees deep within a distant forest "where no human being will dare to tread," feeling that if she is not in the presence of humans, she can do them no harm. She bedecks her cottage with candies, as Asa had decorated their house with mints, silently raging against the demons for all she has lost and using the energy she once focused on healing to keep the devils at bay and their incessant voices out of her head. Inevitably, Hansel and Gretel arrive at her doorstep. At this late point, the story pretty well follows the original Grimm tale, with an emphasis on the uncompromising grimness (pun intended). In this telling, it's Gretel who's the stronger of the siblings, and her relationship with the Ugly One stands as counterpart to that between the Ugly One and Asa. After an almost idyllic four weeks in which the witch comes to love Gretel as a daughter, the two children discover the witch's cache of jewels and plan to leave her to return home. Once more the demon voices resound in the Ugly One's head, "Eat them, eat them, eat them." She cannot stop herself from trapping the children and caging Hansel, but she can scheme to save them. And out of despair, both hers and the children's, comes redemption and forgiveness, with the witch willing Gretel to push her into the fire that supposedly awaits Hansel. With its focus on the mother/witch and its dark echoes of childhood fears of abandonment, it's difficult to predict the audience for Napoli's novel, but it is decidedly for an older group than is her *Prince of the Pond.*

Lisa Dennis

SOURCE: A review of *The Magic Circle,* in *School Library Journal,* Vol. 39, No. 8, August, 1993, p. 186.

A new perspective on a traditional tale, Napoli's richly imagined, somber story illuminates a possible "history" for the witch in "Hansel and Gretel," and is sure to change readers' view of this much maligned figure forever. A strongly medieval flavor permeates setting, characterization, and tone. The "Ugly One" is a hunchbacked woman who lives with her daughter in a small village. Her healing power, she believes, is a God-given gift that enables her to cast out demons from the sick. Her downfall comes when she falls prey to one of the devils' cleverly plotted temptations. Transformed in an instant from healer to witch, she resists her fate and flees to a faraway land "where wolves eat grandmothers and young beggar girls are princesses for a night." There she immerses herself in work and solitude to escape the demons' terrible urgings to eat children, an act that will tie her to them forever. She decorates her house with candies in memory of her daughter, unintentionally luring Hansel and Gretel to her. From this point, the story is both familiar and different. The woman genuinely cherishes the children, who learn to love and trust her,

to their peril. When the inevitable ending comes, it is not a victory for them, but rather the Ugly One's ultimate triumph and redemption, as well as another bitter parting. The strength of Napoli's writing and the clarity of her vision make this story fresh and absorbing. A brilliantly conceived and beautifully executed novel that is sure to be appreciated by thoughtful readers.

Rosie Peasley

SOURCE: A review of *The Magic Circle,* in *Voice of Youth Advocates,* Vol. 16, No. 3, August, 1993, p. 169.

This is an imaginative variation on the classic *Hansel and Gretel* tale. Napoli's witch begins as a loving mother and a healer, doing only good and serving God as best she can. In one lightning moment, because of one covetous action, she becomes the pawn of devils and must serve them as a witch. The major elements of the classic tale are all included and explained in light of Napoli's twist—the cottage bedecked with sweets, the bone Hansel uses to fool the witch, and the climax in which the witch is shoved into the hot oven. Told from the point of view of the witch, who is indeed a bedeviled but sympathetic character, this brief novel is beautifully and sensitively written. The reader empathizes with the "Ugly Sorceress" as she loses her battle with evil but triumphs at her death in the closing pages. Napoli presents a powerful, effective alternative to the traditional tale and may tantalize young writers to try their hand at alternative renderings of well-known stories.

Pam Nealon-LaBreck

SOURCE: A review of *The Magic Circle,* in *Kliatt,* Vol. 29, No. 6, November, 1995, p. 18.

This ALA Best Book for YAs is the story of the witch from *Hansel and Gretel* before she retreats to her candy-covered house in the forest. The hunch-backed Ugly One is a midwife living with her daughter, Asa, on the edge of a village. Convinced by an older acquaintance, the Ugly One decides to try her hand at healing. She uses her own spirituality to create a magic circle from which she chases the demons out of the sick. And then she is tricked. The demons tempt her out of the security of her circle with a beautiful ring. No longer does she have control over them. Instead, she is transformed into the Ugly Witch—now at the mercy of the demons. Sentenced to death by her fellow villagers, the demons agree to save her daughter, also slated to die, if the Ugly Witch will serve them. Understanding her first act of submission is to eat a child, the Ugly Witch agrees and then removes herself from society and retreats to a cottage in an enchanted forest to escape her temptation. She spends her days in isolation boiling sweets to decorate her cottage until one day she hears the voices of children as they eat the candy off her house. Napoli has created a compelling and complex historical background for one of the archetypal characters in literature. This creative new focus redefines a classic fairy tale as it sympathetically portrays one who has always represented evil. YA readers will enjoy revisiting this well-known tale from a new perspective.

WHEN THE WATER CLOSES OVER MY HEAD (1994)

Hazel Rochman

SOURCE: A review of *When the Water Closes over My Head,* in *Booklist,* Vol. 90, No. 9, January 1, 1994, p. 827.

Mikey is about to start fourth grade, and he can't swim. He's good at sports, but he doesn't like water. He's scared he'll drown. His older sister's teasing doesn't help. His parents try to give him support, but his fear has become such a big thing—especially now that summer has come and swimming lessons loom—that at times it seems as if sadness and disappointment are everywhere. Of course, he does finally learn to swim, and it's a great triumph; but this is far from a predictable problem novel. Mikey is part of a warm, messy family, with parents who are loving (and sometimes grumpy) and siblings who can be a pain in the neck. Gender roles also subvert formula: Mikey's older sister is jealous that he cooks better than she does. His little brother Calvin likes to dress up in necklaces and lipstick; at first Grandma is appalled, but Mikey defends Calvin, and Grandma accepts the fact that "attitudes have changed." The story is told in a series of tightly structured, cinematic episodes, with dialogue that captures the daily tangle of close relationships as people bicker about breakfast cereal and also confront elemental issues of grief and rivalry and love. Kids will want more stories about this family.

Kirkus Reviews

SOURCE: A review of *When the Water Closes over My Head,* in *Kirkus Reviews,* Vol. LXII, No. 1, January 1, 1994, p. 72.

By a gifted author (whose first three children's books range from *Soccer Shock,* 1991, to a hilarious frog-prince takeoff—*Prince of the Pond,* 1992—to the splendidly dark, intricately structured *The Magic Circle,* 1993), a genial family story that, in its forthright good humor and succinct handling of real issues, recalls Betsy Byars. Mikey, nine, hasn't learned to swim; his natural reluctance to go under water is exacerbated by a history of failure, embarrassment, and an insensitive teacher who literally throws children in. Meanwhile, Napoli portrays the kind of family every child should have: parents who know how to lay down the law cheerfully; four energetic, curious kids whose bickering is just one facet of their mutual affection. In addition to his phobia, the otherwise plucky Mikey is fascinated with weapons, to his mother's consternation (there's a delightful sequence involving rubber bands he gleans around the house and fash-

ions into a slingshot, only to have a younger sib dismember it to sort the bands by color). In the end, with the help of some non-interfering advice from Mamma and Grandma, Mikey faces down his fear. The connection Napoli makes between this and with his preoccupation with guns and knives is almost too direct, but—since Mikey's family is one where such things are explicitly discussed—it's in a believable context. A funny, easily read story that boys and girls alike should take to like ducks to water.

Publishers Weekly

SOURCE: A review of *When the Water Closes over My Head,* in *Publishers Weekly,* Vol. 241, No. 8, February 21, 1994, p. 255.

Its rather frightening, downbeat title aside, this is a decidedly uplifting story. The day before his family leaves to visit Grandma and Grandpa in Iowa, nine-year-old Mikey packs his clothes, taking special care to leave his bathing suit behind. Terrified of swimming, he is determined to avoid the water. But he has no such luck. His parents have signed him up for lessons, and it seems that swimming is on the agenda at every turn ("Does everyone in the world have to have a pool or a watering hole or some other stupid place to drown?"). Punctuating her book with much lighthearted banter and realistic sibling bickering, Napoli (*The Magic Circle*) deftly delivers a worthwhile message to youngsters having trouble overcoming a fear and making a leap—into the water or elsewhere. Heeding the advice of his mother and grandmother, Mikey learns to think positively and act confidently (and to swim). Napoli's snappy dialogue and compact sentences—and [Nancy] Poydar's animated drawings—make this a good selection for reluctant readers.

Carol Schene

SOURCE: A review of *When the Water Closes over My Head,* in *School Library Journal,* Vol. 40, No. 3, March, 1994, p. 223.

Mikey Nelson, nine, is afraid of the water. He and his family are spending their vacation in Iowa at his grandparents', and he knows that they are all expecting him to overcome this fear and learn to swim. He finally does so when he saves a little girl from drowning. Although young readers might relate to the boy's apprehension, it seems to take forever for him to resolve his problem. The plot is constantly diverted by incidents that may or may not give Mikey new insights into his dilemma. He is surrounded by didactic adults and bickering siblings. Even the family dog's main function seems to be to annoy everyone. Mikey worries about death and unknown dangers and expresses his anxiety and frustration with name calling and occasional swearing. He keeps trying to arm himself—first with a superdeluxe slingshot, then with a knife, and finally with a toy gun about which he says, "'With a gun in my hands I feel ready.'"

Although there are lighter moments in the story and the child's self-esteem eventually takes a turn for the better, this contemporary story is too convoluted and wordy to appeal to most youngsters.

Deborah Stevenson

SOURCE: A review of *When the Water Closes over My Head,* in *Bulletin of the Center for Children's Books,* Vol. 48, No. 1, September, 1994, pp. 21-22.

Mikey, a soon-to-be fourth-grader, is looking forward to his family's summer trip to his grandparents' Iowa home, but he's dreading another fact of summer: swimming. Mikey's older sister, Victoria, swims "like a frog," and his younger brother and sister don't seem bothered by water, but Mikey is petrified of pools, lakes, ponds—anyplace where he might go underwater and never come up. His failure as a swimmer seems to make him a failure generally, since "it seemed every time he turned around, someone or something was ruined or lost or dead." Eventually Mikey finds himself mastering tasks in swimming lessons, and he gains confidence from his family and from saving a classmate in trouble. Napoli writes a lively and funny family story but treats Mikey's terror and self-doubt with the respect they deserve. Her characterization and emotional dynamics, as with her portrayal of the cheerful, thoughtless swimming teacher who hurls Mikey into the water and Mikey's bitter rage afterward, will strike a chord with all sufferers of unreasoning terror. The book's an easy and entertaining read, and since everybody could use some confidence-building, the story's point will reassure the wet and dry alike. Black-and-white illustrations, with lively lines and subtle shading, appear throughout the book.

SHARK SHOCK (1994)

Frances Bradburn

SOURCE: A review of *Shark Shock,* in *Booklist,* Vol. 91, No. 4, October 15, 1994, p. 427.

Shark Shock offers a lighthearted but realistic look at the fears contemporary children encounter as they grow up. In this companion to *Soccer Shock,* Adam and his family head to New Jersey for a well-deserved summer vacation. Only Adam is reluctant. His friend Grayson presented a horrifying report on sharks before school was out, and now Adam fears for his life. Over the course of the summer, Adam learns that, although he can't deny his fears, he can put them in perspective just as his new-found friend Seth does. Seth, two years Adam's senior and blind since a waterskiing accident when he was 10, continues to explore and experience life in spite of his natural fears. The effective multidimensional characterization of Seth, actually a secondary character, moves this book from an optional purchase of lighthearted humor to an important one of diversity, empathy, and understanding.

Kirkus Reviews

SOURCE: A review of *Shark Shock,* in *Kirkus Reviews,* Vol. LXII, No. 22, November 15, 1994, p. 1540.

Adam is back with a new fear and a different band of talking freckles. In *Soccer Shock* (1991), Adam used his unique ability to hear his freckles conversing to help him play soccer. Now he wants them to warn him if there are sharks in the water at the Jersey beach where he is spending the summer with his parents and sisters. The only problem is that his freckle pals, Gilbert and Frankie, have stopped talking—at least, Adam can't hear them anymore. Adam figures that if he can sensitize his ears he can talk with them, but he isn't about to get nearly hit by lightning, like he did the first time. Adam tries everything he can think of, from static shocks to putting hair conditioner in his ears, but he only succeeds when he nearly electrocutes himself while playing a video game under a sprinkler. Then his freckles start talking with a vengeance, only they aren't Gilbert and Frankie but the hostile female beauty marks on his shoulder. They are no help at all when it comes to sharks. They trick Adam whenever they can. When a blind boy, Seth, hears Adam conversing with the recalcitrant beauty marks, he and Adam strike up a conversation and become friends. Seth helps Adam tame his spots and overcome his fear of the water, and Adam gives Seth the understanding he needs to accept his blindness. A weird, meandering tale.

Maggie McEwen

SOURCE: A review of *Shark Shock,* in *School Library Journal,* Vol. 41, No. 1, January, 1995, p. 109.

Adam can hear his freckles and beauty marks conversing. Using an electrical conductor to make contact with them, he finds these "friends" to be very helpful. So, naturally, when his family takes a seaside vacation, he turns to them to warn him about the presence of sharks. For days he hears nothing, but eventually learns that the beauty marks (female) have overthrown the freckles (male) and refuse to allow them to speak. Without the support of his freckles, Adam is too fearful to go in the water. Moping on the beach, he finds a new friend in a lonely boy who was blinded in an accident, and together they both grow in self-acceptance and confidence. The strong portrayal of their relationship contrasts with the utterly preposterous plot. The gender war between the adult-sounding beauty marks and freckles stretches credibility to the breaking point—their stilted talk of revolution seems out of place and dated. Nonetheless, Napoli does a creditable job of developing her characters. Adam's family life and the characters' feelings, relationships, and growth are well handled and believable. This light read will appeal to children who have an appreciation for the absurd, particularly when it occurs in a warm, supportive environment.

JIMMY, THE PICKPOCKET OF THE PALACE (1995)

Ilene Cooper

SOURCE: A review of *Jimmy, the Pickpocket of the Palace,* in *Booklist,* Vol. 91, No. 14, March 15, 1995, p. 1331.

In *The Prince of the Pond* (1993), a prince becomes a frog named Pin. Now, the tables are turned, as Jimmy the frog, Pin's son, becomes a boy. The best audience for this will be readers of the first book, who can hop into the action without trying to wade through back story. They will enjoy Jimmy's awkward transition from amphibian to boy (he keeps wanting to ingest insects), but they may wonder why it takes both Jimmy and the prince so long to figure out what readers are well aware of—their shared froginess. The story gets a little tedious before the bittersweet conclusion, in which Jimmy realizes that his dad is really a human at heart. Illustrated [by Judith Byron Schachner] with many pen-and-ink drawings, the book, with its good-size print, has an easy, accessible look.

Betsy Hearne

SOURCE: A review of *Jimmy, the Pickpocket of the Palace,* in *Bulletin of the Center for Children's Books,* Vol. 48, No. 10, June, 1995, p. 355.

The author of *The Prince of the Pond* follows with a sequel as Jimmy, the smartest of the "fawglets," is transformed into a boy through the magic of a wicked hag and the kiss of a spoiled princess. The tone here is not as fresh and witty as in the first book. There's heavy emphasis on the mechanics of the transformation, and readers already know what it takes Jimmy so long to figure out: first, that he has been transformed; and second, that the empathetic prince is really his father, changed from frog back into his original princely shape. The real suspense is not in what will happen to the threatened pond or the evil hag, which is predictable, but in what form Jimmy and his father will choose to remain. That question is answered in a climactic deliverance: "I had wished that the ring would turn each of us who touched it into what we really were at heart. . . . The ring had turned me into a frog. The ring had turned the hag into an iron rock. . . . Would the ring turn him into Pin again? Was my daddy a frog at heart?" In a brave ending, we read in the last sentence the poignant fact that parents and children must sometimes separate according to differences of the heart.

Sally Margolis

SOURCE: A review of *Jimmy, the Pickpocket of the Palace,* in *School Library Journal,* Vol. 41, No. 6, June, 1995, p. 112.

Pin, the *Prince of the Pond* left his frog family unintentionally in Napoli's first amphibious plunge when he was kissed by Marissa, a princess. Now his venturesome son Jimmy leaves home to find the magic ring that will save the family pond from the curse of their old nemesis, the hag. As he hops into the palace, he is captured by the hapless princess Sally, Marissa's preteen sister. When Sally kisses his wounded leg, Jimmy finds himself in unsteady human form. The kindest of the palace inhabitants is Marissa's husband-to-be, a prince whose unusual empathy with frogs includes a taste for bugs. Jimmy must betray this friend to steal the magic ring from his pocket. Of course, the prince is Pin, who faces a bittersweet choice between his human and frog lives and loves. Napoli balances the comic possibilities of Jimmy's struggles with his human form with his deeper feelings of loyalty, courage, and honor. In an echo of his father's plight, he has two female admirers—Gracie, a frog, and Sally, whose rough handling spells doom for all pets. The ultimate strength of the book lies in Napoli's rich descriptive powers that include a respect for biological accuracy. Schachner's black-and-white illustrations enhance especially the transformation from frightened frog to goggle-eyed boy. This sequel is as engaging and unpredictable as its predecessor.

Publishers Weekly

SOURCE: A review of *Jimmy, the Pickpocket of the Palace,* in *Publishers Weekly,* Vol. 242, No. 24, June 12, 1995, p. 61.

Napoli picks up where she left off in *The Prince of the Pond,* in which a prince turned frog regains his royal corpus only after starting a large and loving frog family. The star of this new adventure is Jimmy, the prince's frog son, who attempts to save the pond from a witch's wicked machinations. His mission leads him to a nearby palace, where an encounter with an ill-tempered princess transforms him into a human boy (being told to stand up, Jimmy confides, "Slowly I straightened my legs. Standing was so strange. Even with my human body, I didn't see why people did it"). Misunderstandings pile up in this lighthearted romp, only to be swept away with comic legerdemain. The bittersweet undertones of the first novel (and of Napoli's even more memorable *The Magic Circle*) are replaced by broad humor and almost slapstick sequences. Sure to amuse the target audience.

THE BRAVEST THING (1995)

Deborah Stevenson

SOURCE: A review of *The Bravest Thing,* in *Bulletin of the Center for Children's Books,* Vol. 49, No. 2, October, 1995, p. 64.

In her ten years, Laurel has had an array of pets ranging from newts to parakeets, and while her care of them has been excellent, she has had more than her fair share of pet tragedies. She's thrilled to acquire a rabbit at long last, and she adores Bun Bun, but even Bun Bun proves to be a source of pain: Laurel carefully arranges to have her bred, but then Bun Bun refuses to mother her babies and they all die. Laurel rises to the occasion when the rabbit abandons her second litter, feeding (with her family's help) the six babies with an eyedropper, and while most of the babies eventually die, Laurel does triumphantly raise Blossom to adulthood. This is one of the more straightforward books about fragile pets and the joys and sorrows of pet ownership; Napoli permits a certain amount of humor in the situation (such as Laurel's boa constrictor who was killed by the mouse he was supposed to eat) but is honest and understanding about the unpredictable fates of such animals. Laurel's interaction with her family and her best friend, Charlotte, gives detail to the picture; subplots about Laurel's aunt's cancer and her own diagnosis of scoliosis emphasize the *carpe diem* theme but don't overwhelm the main story. Laurel is realistic and appealing in her devotion to her animal husbandry, and readers will appreciate her success.

Susan Oliver

SOURCE: A review of *The Bravest Thing*, in *School Library Journal*, Vol. 41, No. 10, October, 1995, p. 138.

A number of serious subjects are touched upon in this novel, but none of them is fully explored. Ten-year-old narrator Laurel is an animal lover, but in spite of the support of her parents and a working knowledge of the library, pet after pet dies, sometimes due to her ignorance. Napoli makes light of the situation as Laurel tries again, this time with a baby rabbit. Over the course of the time that Bun Bun matures and mates, Laurel has a scare following a scoliosis test at school and her aunt undergoes cancer treatment. Neither disease is clearly explained, and although Laurel's mother is troubled by these events, neither she nor her husband ever emerges as a solid character. Bun Bun neglects both of her litters and all of the baby rabbits but one die in spite of Laurel's desperate attempts to save them. Though she does manage to nurse that one to maturity and learns enough about rabbits for the local vet to offer her a job, this is neither a particularly believable story nor one that will teach readers about responsible pet care or the real impact of life-and-death issues.

Julie Yates Walton

SOURCE: A review of *The Bravest Thing*, in *Booklist*, Vol. 92, No. 3, October 1, 1995, p. 317.

For 10-year-old Laurel, pet ownership ushers in some profound lessons in mortality. When Laurel's new rabbit, Bun Bun, refuses to nurse her first litter, the babies die. Devastated, Laurel mates Bun Bun again, but once

more the rabbit ignores her babies. Laurel feeds and cares for them herself, and one of the six, Blossom, survives against all odds. Echoing this theme of survival are two subplots: Laurel is diagnosed with scoliosis and her Aunt Lizzy with cancer. Through these trials, Laurel learns to accept what is inevitable and to challenge what is not. Laurel is a sensible, believable protagonist, and her repeated confrontations with illness and death may help readers face similar situations. Be warned, though: the book starts slowly, and its body count feels depressingly high until near the end when things turn more upbeat and the lessons of Laurel's experience clarify.

ZEL (1996)

Kirkus Reviews

SOURCE: A review of *Zel*, in *Kirkus Reviews*, Vol. LXIV, No. 9, May 1, 1996, p. 691.

A passionate, painful elaboration of the story of Rapunzel, from the author who did the same for Hansel and Gretel in *The Magic Circle* (1993).

Here again, the "witch" is the tragic figure: A woman unable to bear children but unable to exist without a child sells her soul for an eldritch power over all plants, bullies her terrified neighbors into giving up their newborn daughter, and spirits her away to a remote Swiss farm. Lovingly nurtured, Zel grows into a joyful, creative child, wholeheartedly devoted to the only mother she knows until she meets Konrad on a rare visit to town. Brutally torn between love and need, the witch imprisons Zel, and watches in anguish as the child's sanity begins to slip away with the seasons. Writing in present tense, using three alternating points of view, Napoli (*Jimmy, The Pickpocket of the Palace*, 1995, etc.) makes each incident immediate, each character's needs and longings sharply felt. She adheres closely to the traditional plot and, to a story already abrim with symbol and metaphor, she adds even more. This rich, complex reading may require an adult's sensibility and level of experience to absorb fully, but it powerfully renders the tale's inherent terror and tragedy.

Publishers Weekly

SOURCE: A review of *Zel*, in *Publishers Weekly*, Vol. 243, No. 25, June 17, 1996, p. 66.

As she has done for *The Frog Prince* and *Hansel and Gretel*, Napoli here visits her magic upon the tale of Rapunzel, creating a work of depth and beauty. In mid-16th-century Switzerland, Zel, on the threshold of adolescence, accompanies her mother on a rare trip from their remote cottage to the village. By chance she meets a youth named Konrad; unknown to her, he is the son of the count, and he is charmed by her apparent simplicity and forthright manner. Napoli gently guides the reader through the inevitable consequences of this meeting, mining every movement in the fairy tale for its psychological treasures. Zel's mother, no longer a routine villainess, has sacrificed everything, even her soul, for the witchcraft that enables her to have a daughter; a desperate fear of Konrad's attentions drives her to imprison Zel in the famous tower. Isolated, Zel wavers between recognition of her mother's sacrifices and her own fury, and wanders into madness. Konrad, meanwhile, must discover the difference between love and obsession. Napoli imagines the precise quality of the mother's supernatural powers, the colors of the stones in Zel's tower, the rustle of the trees in the forest. But the genius of the novel lies not just in the details but in its breadth of vision. Its shiveringly romantic conclusion will leave readers spellbound.

Betsy Hearne

SOURCE: A review of *Zel,* in *Bulletin of the Center for Children's Books,* Vol. 49, No. 11, July-August, 1996, pp. 381-82.

Reminiscent of Napoli's *Magic Circle* but narratively more complex, this fictionalization of Rapunzel switches points of view—by chapter—between the heroine, her witch/foster-mother (whom she knows only as Mother), and Konrad, the prince who loves her. Although the dynamics of the relationship are explored with modern sensibility, the setting itself is a remote, folkloric Swiss Alpine mountainside well suited to the magic that Mother wields over trees and plant life, including the irresistible lettuce that once brought her a longed-for baby girl. Soon the intensely happy mother-child relationship becomes a prison, first figuratively and then literally, as Zel enters adolescence and discovers attractions—especially Konrad, whom she meets during a rare visit to the closest village—that threaten to lure her away. Napoli has done an admirable job of getting into the heads of the main characters, all of whom at one time or another verge on madness: Mother because of her possessive jealousy, Zel because of her isolation in the tower, and Konrad because of his obsessive search. The original Rapunzel can in fact be seen as a story of child abuse, and Napoli renders that aspect with vivid realism. The witch's redemption is ingeniously subtle (whereas her recollection of acquiring Rapunzel seems too explanatory), and the conclusion of Konrad finding his true love, complete with twins, and regaining his sight because of her healing tears is triumphant.

Bruce Anne Shook

SOURCE: A review of *Zel,* in *School Library Journal,* Vol. 42, No. 9, September, 1996, pp. 227-28.

This retelling of the story of Rapunzel is no simple fairy tale retold for the entertainment of children. Instead, it is a searing commentary on the evil that can result from human longings gone awry. Napoli sets the novel in 16th-century Switzerland and alternates the various char-

acters' points of view. Zel and Count Konrad's narratives are presented in the third person, while Mother tells her own story. All are told in the present tense. Readers learn that the barren mother's obsession for a child drove her to give herself up to eternal damnation in order to have a daughter. Now, she seeks to keep the child away from the world so that the innocent girl will choose her mother above all others. That this will mean Zel's damnation also does not deter Mother in the least. When the inevitable happens and Zel meets the young man, Mother locks her away in a tower. Unlike most versions, this story realistically portrays the dismal effects of isolation on the girl's mind and spirit. She goes quite mad but is still able to accept Konrad's love when he finds her at last. Konrad's transformation from arrogant noble to a man with an obsessive love for a girl he barely knows is less realistic but follows the traditional story line. In his final confrontation with Mother, evil appears to have triumphed. Even the eventual "happily ever after" ending cannot clear the air of the darkness that pervades this tale. Mother's fatal possessiveness and the horror of Zel's life in the tower are the dominant themes that readers will remember. This version, with its Faustian overtones, will challenge readers to think about this old story on a deeper level. It begs for discussion in literature classes.

Hazel Rochman

SOURCE: A review of *Zel,* in *Booklist,* Vol. 93, No. 1, September 1, 1996, p. 118.

As she did in *The Magic Circle* (1993), a retelling of the Hansel and Gretel story, Napoli humanizes the witch in the fairy tale. This time the novel is based on *Rapunzel,* the setting is fifteenth-century Switzerland, and the story is told in the present tense from three alternating points of view: the happy peasant girl, Zel, about to turn 13, eager, creative, daring; the young nobleman who falls in love with her and wants to marry her; and her mother, who loves Zel so much that she is driven to lock her beloved daughter in a tall tower because she cannot bear to let her go. Only the mother's narrative is in the first person; she's at the center of the story. Her intense tenderness for Zel is never in question; in the wild, beautiful mountains she has raised a wonderful child. But gradually we learn that the loving mother is also a witch—and why. Barren, in anguish, 13 years earlier she had made a pact with the devil and had stolen another woman's baby. Now she sees that child, Zel, fall in love, and the desperate witch uses lies and black magic to try to keep her daughter. The storytelling is poetic and languorous, especially in the Zel chapters, which show Zel cavorting in the natural world and then held in stasis for two years in the imprisoning tower. Teens may not fully understand the childless woman's yearning. What will move them profoundly is the pull of possessive love, the coming-of-age drama from the parent's point of view. Above all, there's the shocking realization that even the best of us, given the need, will sell her soul.

Roger Sutton

SOURCE: A review of *Zel,* in *The Horn Book Magazine,* Vol. LXXII, No. 5, September-October, 1996, p. 603.

Inevitably looking over its shoulder at **The Magic Circle,** the author's meditation on "Hansel and Gretel," *Zel* is a re-visioning of "Rapunzel," told in turns by the girl in the tower, the witch who keeps her there, and the prince who would take her away. The writing, although always sensuous in description and perceptive in shading character, is less concentrated than in **The Magic Circle,** and it's a bit of a wander as we move from Zel's early idyllic life with the witch to the old bargain (and its recumbent tragic destiny) that leads Zel to her tower. What powerful chapters come then, though, culminating in a stunning sequence of three encounters: between Zel and her prince, Zel and "Mother," and Mother and the prince in a struggle for the heart of Zel and life and death. While sometimes unduly hazy and with a telescoped last chapter, this is a book that transforms myth without flippancy, honoring the power of its roots.

Sarah Flowers

SOURCE: A review of *Zel,* in *Voice of Youth Advocates,* Vol. 20, No. 1, April, 1997, p. 44.

This retelling of Rapunzel explores the story from three points of view: that of Zel (Rapunzel), Mother, and Count Konrad, the young man who loves Zel. The most gripping story—and the only one told in the first person—is Mother's. Far from being the stereotypical wicked witch, Mother is a barren woman who trades her soul for the "way with plants" which enables her, ultimately, to acquire the thing she wants most in all the world—a daughter. She adores Zel, and raises a happy and loving child. When Zel is thirteen, however, and has just met Konrad, Mother moves Zel to a tower to keep her safe and pure until she can convince Zel to freely offer her own soul in exchange for magical powers and thus remain with Mother forever. Napoli describes Zel's descent into madness in the tower and her journey to recovery and forgiveness afterward in simple but effective language. Konrad's years-long search for Zel is also the story of his growth from boy to man. This is an exceptional book that fans of McKinley's *Beauty* will love. It is also a moving exploration of the age-old question: "What will I do—and what will I give up—to achieve my heart's desire?"

SONG OF THE MAGDALENE (1996)

Kirkus Reviews

SOURCE: A review of *Song of the Magdalene,* in *Kirkus Reviews,* Vol. LXIV, No. 17, September 1, 1996, p. 1326.

Napoli (*Zel*) turns from folklore to the Bible for inspi-ration, and crafts a brutal, challenging tale.

Living with her widower father, Miriam roams the countryside, sings from the treetops, and acts in other ways inappropriate for the women of Magdala. She suffers seizures (probably epileptic ones) and, believing she is possessed, keeps them a secret, so that she will not become an outcast. She is drawn to Abraham, son of a servant, who is almost completely paralyzed and therefore mistakenly thought to be an idiot; in exchange for her friendship, he teaches her to read, using songs from the Torah. Their feelings deepen into love; Abraham dies knowing that Miriam carries their son. Later, in a shocking scene, Miriam is raped, suffers another seizure, and miscarries. In her subsequent travels away from and then back to Magdala for a certain famous meeting, Miriam prays, sings, and meditates, trying to make sense of her life and future. As is true of the protagonists in Napoli's **The Magic Circle** (1993) and **Zel,** Miriam's trials make her a tragic figure but also strengthen her, freeing her from the physical and intellectual restraints imposed on those of her sex. The novel may not easily find an audience: Its length, stiff prose ("The yellow jasmine winds through the trees behind us in such profusion you think they are [sic] the sun itself"), and deliberate pace will prevent many readers from appreciating the intelligence with which Napoli develops her themes and characters.

Ilene Cooper

SOURCE: A review of *Song of the Magdalene,* in *Booklist,* Vol. 93, No. 3, October 1, 1996, p. 333.

Napoli has made a career of telling familiar stories from a fresh perspective. In this work, she fashions a history for a familiar name, whose story has been untold. With richness of detail and depth of feeling, Napoli introduces the biblical figure Mary Magdalene, who is hardly mentioned in the New Testament, and there are questions over which biblical episodes refer to her. Here, Miriam is the daughter of a well-to-do Magdala widower whose household includes a servant and her crippled son. Because of his physical affliction, the village assumes Abraham is an idiot as well, but Miriam knows him as the bright, sweet young man who teaches her to read and to sing the Song of Songs. When she begins to suffer fits, he tells her that she is pure, not demon ridden as she fears. Eventually, they become lovers, but Abraham dies, and the child Miriam is carrying, dies when she is raped. Miriam, who has always been considered odd, moves away to live with relatives, until they observe her suffering a fit; then she goes alone into the Judean wilderness, where she tries to make sense of her life. That happens when she meets the healer Joshua, and that's where the book ends. Lyrical writing and layered characterizations more than make up for some small inconsistencies in the plot, but the very elegance of the story may restrict the audience. Napoli's inclusion of issues of the ancient world—the treatment of women and the infirm religious practices, societal pressures— also means the book demands a reader who can both comprehend philosophical ideas and appreciate nuance to truly recognize all the story has to offer.

Shirley Wilton

SOURCE: A review of *Song of the Magdalene,* in *School Library Journal,* Vol. 42, No. 11, November, 1996, p. 124.

Napoli has created two stories in this intriguing novel. One is the creation of a plausible explanation for the brief mentions of Mary Magdalene in the New Testament. The second is that same tale seen as a story of a young woman who finds herself an outsider. The narrative is rich with modern issues of gender, disability, violence against women, and spirituality. Miriam describes her life from age 10 to 16 when she is deeply troubled by the occurrence of "fits," which over the years come upon her 7 times. She is driven in her loneliness to explore nature and to learn the songs and poetry of her faith. Her closest relationship is with severely disabled Abraham. As teenagers, the two become lovers, briefly, before he dies. Pregnant, Miriam withdraws into herself until, after being raped, she loses the child and is forced to seek shelter elsewhere. In her travels, she hears of the great healer Joshua, or Jesus. At the end of the tale she finds him; she is cured of the seven devils and becomes a follower of the Master. Knowledge of ancient Hebrew culture, an ability to express the feelings and anguish of an intense young woman, and skillful weaving of plot and character create a gripping novel that is hard to put down. The necessity of finding an ending compatible with the Biblical scene in which Mary Magdalene first appears does in the end constrain a plot that is otherwise highly inventive and complex. Napoli has taken up a challenging and possibly controversial topic and created an interesting book that should lead readers to look further into both Old and New Testament histories.

Publishers Weekly

SOURCE: A review of *Song of the Magdalene,* in *Publishers Weekly,* Vol. 243, No. 45, November 4, 1996, p. 77.

Imagining the youth of Mary Magdalene, this novel is easily Napoli's (*Zel*) riskiest; unfortunately, it is not one of her most successful. Miriam, daughter of a wealthy Jewish widower in Magdala, is 10 when the novel opens and is about to have her first seizure. Miriam's experiences over the next eight or nine years build up in her a rage at social injustice as well as solidarity with the sick and suffering, therefore preparing her for the fellowship of Joshua, "the healer that the Romans called Jesus"; whom she meets in the final passages. Miriam suffers more seizures; loves a "cripple" despite popular belief that the diseased are "inhabited by demons"; buries

her lover; discovers herself pregnant; is raped so violently that she miscarries; and is sent out of Magdala for her own safety. The effort as a whole is lumpy. The pacing seems clotted around climactic moments, while the tone rarely goes beyond an uncomfortable mix of quasi-archaisms ("The fierce purity of our passions knotted us together on the Creator's earth" describes sexual intercourse). The plotting, too, suffers from conflicting impulses toward periodicity (e.g., the belief in demons) and contemporary sensibilities (Miriam's surprise and outrage at the men's prayer of thanks for not being born women). Readers may come away with new thoughts about a different era, but insights into a powerful Biblical figure are few and far between.

Deborah Stevenson

SOURCE: A review of *Song of the Magdalene,* in *Bulletin of the Center for Children's Books,* Vol. 50, No. 5, January, 1997, p. 182.

Young Miriam sometimes finds her life very confusing, but no one seems interested in answering her queries. What is the meaning of love? What is the meaning of the fits she sometimes falls into? Why are there limits placed on her merely because she is a woman? Her growing friendship with Abraham, the son of the family servant, brings her comfort but more questions: Abraham is loving and wise, but an outcast because of his palsy. Eventually her questioning leads her to Galilee, to meet the healer and prophet Joshua, and to carve her place in biblical history as Mary Magdalene. This isn't as successful as Napoli's fleshing out of legendary characters in *Zel* and *The Magic Circle;* the story here moves with painstaking slowness and lacks the atmospheric and mystical appeal of those works. The depiction of Miriam/Mary as possessing a fairly modern mindset and being misunderstood rather than sinning is interesting, but it does mean that her redemption by Jesus is essentially superfluous and therefore undramatic. It's still a provocative imagining about one of the most famous women in the New Testament, however, and readers may enjoy sharing Napoli's "what ifs." A brief note explains the author's sources.

Libby Bergstrom

SOURCE: A review of *Song of the Magdalene,* in *Voice of Youth Advocates,* Vol. 19, No. 6, February, 1997, p. 331.

Biblical references to Mary of Magdalene are few. In her lyrical, intense style, Napoli fills in these brief mentions by imagining the life of Mary before she was healed by Jesus. Miriam, as she would have been called in first century Palestine, suffers from fits which others, and even she herself, believe are signs of demon possession. However, Abraham, a twisted, crippled "idiot," convinces her that she suffers a disease of the body. While Miriam finds this knowledge liberating, it doesn't change the society around her. When she becomes pregnant with Abraham's child before his death, she is labeled a prostitute and is brutally raped, causing a miscarriage. She leaves Magdala, only to return later to try to find the healer, Joshua (Jesus). Still unable to accept her, the villagers begin to stone her. She is saved and healed by Joshua, and the novel ends where the Biblical accounts start, with Mary as one of the followers of Jesus.

The sheer beauty of Napoli's descriptions of Miriam's thoughts and feelings are sometimes a shortcoming. She appears too insightful for her age. She is ten when the first fit occurs, yet her thoughts are those of an adult. Often, too, modern sensibilities creep in; Miriam easily leaves behind the beliefs and customs with which she would have been surrounded since she was born. These points detract from the book's sense of realism. However, the power of Napoli's investigation into the human psyche will draw YA readers into this book; Miriam is a character they will not soon forget.

ON GUARD (1997)

Kirkus Reviews

SOURCE: A review of *On Guard*, in *Kirkus Reviews*, Vol. LXIV, No. 23, December 1, 1996, p. 1740.

Having overcome his fear of drowning in *When the Water Closes over My Head* (1994), Mikey advances further down the road of self-discovery when he witnesses a fencing demonstration and catches the fever. It's perfect: He can indulge his interest in weapons while truthfully assuring his parents that it's a sport, and not fighting. Meanwhile, he shores up his battered, middle-child's self-esteem and creates a class report on the history of swords that he hope will win the Olympic medal his fourth-grade teacher hands out every week. To his delight, Mikey has an aptitude to match his enthusiasm, and what he learns in his first few classes about balance, strategy, sensitivity, and sportsmanship pays immediate dividends—not just on the practice floor, but in a series of more conventional situations into which Napoli places him: dealing with a bully, nurturing a new friendship, and holding his own in his busy, good-natured family. The author writes authoritatively of this unusual martial art, and lays on lessons with a light hand.

Hazel Rochman

SOURCE: A review of *On Guard*, in *Booklist*, Vol. 93, No. 8, December 15, 1996, pp. 726-27.

In *When the Water Closes over My Head* (1994), fourth-grader Mikey struggled to overcome his fear of deep water and learn to swim. Now he takes up fencing, and several chapters tell about his training in balance, footwork, and strategy. Mikey discovers that it's sweet to

win and horrible to fail and that lots of things aren't fair. As in the first book, it's his family interaction that is the heart of the story: the sibling rivalry and protectiveness, the combination of irritation and love. Much of the story is told in dialogue, and it rings true, but it may be hard at times for young readers to work out what's going on and what everyone really means. Many scenes seem to have been written for a play and would work beautifully performed as readers' theater in the classroom. Then kids would recognize how any family's dinner table conversation can sound like absurdist comedy, each speaker locked in a private code. "Can't we have a normal conversation?" Mikey's sister shouts. The answer is "What?"

Deborah Stevenson

SOURCE: A review of *On Guard*, in *Bulletin of the Center for Children's Books*, Vol. 50, No. 6, February, 1997, p. 217.

Fourth-grader Mikey (from *When the Water Closes over My Head*) is back, and he's out for a medal. To be more specific, an Olympic medal—which his teacher gives at the end of every week to a student for a particular skill, achievement, or quality. Feeling middled-out as the second in his four-kid family, Mikey despairs of ever being special enough to merit a medal until he discovers the sport of fencing. He's hooked (though his mother's afraid he'll be stabbed) and begins lessons immediately, finding that the confidence and skill in his new métier is starting to pay off in noncombatant life as well. Napoli is excellent at depicting Mikey's general tendency towards uncertainty, his frustration at his lack of family stardom, and his passionate attachment to his new field (his dedicated obsession matches that of any young balletomane); the portrayal of Mikey's growing friendship with a new boy, Bill, is deftly drawn, evincing wisdom about the perplexities and pitfalls involved in youthful alliances. Especially with its lure of an offbeat and glamorous sport, this will please many young readers who understand the difficulty of parrying the world's thrusts.

John Sigwald

SOURCE: A review of *On Guard*, in *School Library Journal*, Vol. 43, No. 5, May, 1997, p. 138.

When Victoria, a sixth-grader, laments, "Can't we have a normal conversation?" during yet another trying dinner full of apparent non sequiturs from her "demented" younger siblings, readers get a sympathetic view of the charming chaos in her family. Actually, it's Victoria's brother Mikey who is the focus of Napoli's subtle lesson in strategy. Mikey has great balance but little self-confidence, and he has yet to win one of the Olympic medals that his fourth-grade teacher awards weekly to a student for achievements ranging from "readiness" to "best research project." On a class visit to the science museum, Mikey is mesmerized by the silent speed and gracefulness of a couple of fencers putting on an exhibition. He badgers his mother to let him take lessons, but he's insecure enough not to advertise his new interest. Youngsters will be drawn to the details of this exotic sport and will chuckle at Mikey's interfamily banter. A bully, an overweight friend, a persistent little brother, and a henpecking older sister all have their place in Napoli's suburban world. So do pretty mouths, runny noses, a raft, a pair of sunglasses, and chocolate chips in oatmeal. What a pleasant potpourri.

TROUBLE ON THE TRACKS (1997)

Kirkus Reviews

SOURCE: A review of *Trouble on the Tracks,* in *Kirkus Reviews,* Vol. LXV, No. 2, January 15, 1997, p. 144.

Zach is constantly embarrassed by the antics of his younger sister, Eve, a child whom most adults find charming. But when Eve shows off once too often, the siblings—traveling alone in Australia—end up in a confrontation with a pair of bird-smugglers. The thieves throw them off a train in the middle of the outback; Zach and Eve need to survive their ordeal and stop the smugglers, too. Napoli works hard in the first half of the book to present Eve as a trial to Zach, and succeeds a little too well: Eve's behavior is so improvident that it's hard to believe she's been released from adult supervision, and Zach remains a commentator, without a personality of his own. By the time the children are battling giant lizards and scorpions in the desert, readers may have lost interest, and exciting action scenes can't quite bolster the ending, in which Zach and Eve learn to get along, the crooks are foiled, the bird is freed, and the children are heroes.

Hazel Rochman

SOURCE: A review of *Trouble on the Tracks,* in *Booklist,* Vol. 93, No. 11, February 1, 1997, p. 941.

Napoli moves here from the domestic comedy of *On Guard* (1996) and the languorous dramatic fantasy of *Zel* (1996) to a high-spirited contemporary adventure. Two Americans, Zach, 13, and his younger sister, Eve, are tourists on a 22-hour train ride speeding across the Australian desert. On board the luxurious train they discover two bumbling, dangerous smugglers, whose loot is not diamonds and gold but a priceless, endangered species of cockatoo. In a fight with the thieves, the kids are thrown off the speeding train and have to find their way back through the desert night; but with ingenuity and guts, they do return to fight again, get the smugglers, and free the endangered bird. Zach and Eve also battle with each other, and their sibling rivalry, irritable and affectionate, is a rueful counterpoint to the exotic survival action.

Deborah Stevenson

SOURCE: A review of *Trouble on the Tracks,* in *Bulletin of the Center for Children's Books,* Vol. 50, No. 7, March, 1997, p. 253.

Thirteen-year-old Zach finds his chatterbox younger sister, Eve, incredibly annoying, and she's been even more so on the family's trip to Australia, what with her newfound obsession with ornithology that leads her to strike up conversations with strangers and perform birdcalls at the most awkward of moments. Now the siblings are traveling sans Mom on The Legendary Ghan, the famous old train from Alice Springs to Adelaide, and they get into deep trouble when they happen onto the illegal smuggling of a rare bird—and some violently protective smugglers. This is a traditionally unlikely middle-grades adventure, with unsupervised kids trouncing villains in an appealing setting. The contrivances start to mount up, and the ornithology and ecology intrude beyond their necessary places in the plot. Napoli strikes a fresher chord, however, in Zach and Eve's relationship: the sibling dialogue is authentic and the characterization (Eve really *is* annoying) credible. There's also more genuine threat here than usual for this level of mystery, so readers who want some real danger but not a really thick book may be on the right track with this one.

Connie Tyrrell Burns

SOURCE: A review of *Trouble on the Tracks,* in *School Library Journal,* Vol. 43, No. 3, March, 1997, p. 190.

Like most older brothers, 13-year-old Zach is embarrassed by his feisty 10-year-old sister, Eve. While their anthropologist mother does field-work at an Aboriginal settlement in Australia, the siblings take a trip on "The Legendary Ghan," a famous train that travels across the desert from Alice Springs to Adelaide in 22 hours. Aboard the train, they discover, through Eve's extensive knowledge of Australian birds and her friendliness, two bumbling yet frightening men trying to smuggle an endangered cockatoo to Adelaide. What begins as an effort to save the bird becomes, for Zach and Eve, a dangerous and exciting struggle to save their own lives. They are thrown from the train by the criminals, wander hours in the desert in search of assistance, and help to uncover a bird-smuggling ring that threatens Australia's natural treasures. Told from Zach's perspective, the novel is exciting, yet funny. The book's real strength, however, and the heart of the story, is the interaction between the two youngsters. Rivalry mixes realistically with protectiveness, irritation with love.

STONES IN WATER (1997)

Publishers Weekly

SOURCE: A review of *Stones in Water,* in *Publishers Weekly,* Vol. 244, No. 36, September 1, 1997, p. 106.

This gripping, meticulously researched story (loosely based on the life of an actual survivor), set in Europe during WWII, is told from the point of view of a Venetian boy forced into war against his will. Roberto's quiet life as a gondolier's son ends abruptly the day he sneaks off to see a movie with his older brother and two friends, Memo and Samuele. German soldiers raid the theater and take the boys captive, and Roberto is immediately separated from his brother. Roberto and his two friends are carted by train across the border and quickly learn that although the Germans are allies, they consider the Italians dispensable (Nazi soldiers shoot three Italian boys on a train platform). Roberto is concerned for his own safety, but he is even more fearful for his Jewish friend Samuele (Roberto and Memo flank him when Samuele urinates, to hide his circumcision). When the train finally halts, Roberto and Samuele manage to stay together, while Memo is sent to a different camp.

In the first half of the novel, Roberto describes the abominations he and Samuele both endure and witness as they are sent from one work camp to the next. At one, the boys build a large pen that the Germans later fill with Jews; horrified, Roberto puts himself at great risk to smuggle food daily through the barbed wire to a starving girl and her sister. The second half recounts Roberto's lone escape across Ukraine's barren landscape after Samuele dies fighting for a pair of German boots. Napoli's (*Song of the Magdalene*) graphic depiction of the boys' inhumane treatment counterpoints their quiet nurturing of each other's spirits. Roberto gives half his food rations to Samuele (because a boy who knows Samuele's secret is confiscating his food), and Samuele helps Roberto fall asleep by telling him comforting stories from the Old Testament.

Napoli portrays a war in which resisters and deserters are the real heroes. In her choice of an innocent boy as first-person narrator, she gently leads readers through a gradual unfolding of events until they come face-to-face with the scope of the war's atrocities. Children will be riveted by Roberto's struggle to stay alive—and to aid others along the way—against enormous odds. And adults may never view WWII the same way again.

Hazel Rochman

SOURCE: A review of *Stones in Water,* in *Booklist,* Vol. 94, No. 3, October 1, 1997, p. 333.

From her rich, dark fairy tale fantasies and light contemporary novels, Napoli turns here to historical fiction about the young Italian boys forced to work as indentured laborers for the Nazis during World War II. Roberto, 13, and his Jewish friend, Samuele, are rounded up with other boys and transported to harsh work camps. The two keep each other alive (no one must see that Samuele is circumcised), and they try to help starving Polish Jews in a barbed-wire holding pen. When Samuele dies, Roberto runs away, and the book's second half becomes a survival adventure as he narrowly escapes Germans, wolves, freezing cold, and starvation to make his way back to join the Italian partisans. The history is well-researched, but much of the long escape adventure reads like an episodic docunovel: we know there will always be some lucky chance to save him (a boat, a fellow deserter, etc.). It is the friendship story and the little-known history of the Italian child laborers that will hold readers, who may imagine what it was like to be a civilian caught up in a war you wanted no part of, fighting an enemy much like you.

Marilyn Payne Phillips

SOURCE: A review of *Stones in Water,* in *School Library Journal,* Vol. 43, No. 11, November, 1997, p. 122.

Napoli, who has written in a variety of genres—fantasy, mystery, realistic fiction, legends—demonstrates that she has mastered historical fiction as well. Sneaking into the cinema to see an American Western during World War II has grave consequences for Roberto, a Venetian middle-school student, his brother, and two friends. The young male audience is trapped by German soldiers and transported by train out of Italy as cheap forced labor. The first project, constructing a tarmac, goes smoothly, despite wretched living conditions. Separated from his older brother, timid Roberto relies on his quick-thinking friend, Samuele. Both realize the necessity of hiding Samuele's Jewish identity from their captors and fellow prisoners. When a "shipment" of Polish Jews arrive and are penned near the labor group, Roberto uses his ingenuity to help feed two Jewish girls with his meager rations. After Samuele is beaten to death trying to save Roberto's scavenged boots, Roberto escapes. He is a displaced gondolier trying to navigate his boat on a modern Styx, a hellish river journey with slim chances for survival. Few books view the Holocaust from this vantage point; few readers are familiar with the Venetian/Italian connection to the work camps. Others will be interested in this story as survivalism from the worst kind of nightmare. Many children will be ensnared by the author's paean to the art and value of storytelling. Samuele's legacy is the nourishing stories that keep Roberto alive. An intense, gripping tale.

Betsy Hearne

SOURCE: A review of *Stones in Water,* in *Bulletin of the Center for Children's Books,* Vol. 51, No. 6, February, 1998, p. 214.

Since very little World War II literature for children has dealt with the experience of the Italians, this account of two Venetian boys abducted by their ostensible allies, the Germans, for slave labor provides an unusual look at the war. Roberto and his Jewish friend Samuele are rounded up in a theater, forced onto a train, and transported to German territory where they are overworked, starved, frozen, and beaten. Although the friends do their best to protect each other, Samuele is ultimately killed by his fellow captives for his boots. More unlikely but also more intriguing is Roberto's subsequent escape by foot and boat through Soviet territory to the Caspian Sea, where he falls in with a Roman deserter on his way to the Mediterranean to join the partisans. Despite the realistic depiction of victims shot and imprisoned, the reader is kept at an emotional distance by quickly developed scenes and flat characterization (plus an overly swift, unsatisfying conclusion). Still, this has the tone of an adventure story and it depicts some dramatic events, so it may capture some readers. In an introductory section of acknowledgments, the author describes the story as "based loosely (very, very loosely) on experiences of Guido Fullin" and discusses her research.

📖 FOR THE LOVE OF VENICE (1998)

Kirkus Reviews

SOURCE: A review of *For the Love of Venice,* in *Kirkus Reviews,* Vol. LXVI, No. 8, April 15, 1998, p. 584.

Percy, 17, is spending the summer in Venice with his engineer father, his artist mother, and his endearing brother, Christopher, 6. Percy misses the sailing and soccer he left behind in Massachusetts until he meets Graziella, who sells him gelato and offers him other things to think about. Napoli expertly weaves a number of strands: the Venetians' love and loathing for the tourists who keep the city alive; the delicate and ever-threatened ecological balance of the lagoon; the darkness of violence planned with the purest of motives. The city's radiance is captured in small, stunning moments: fireworks over the water on a festival night; a dark alley doorway that opens into a palace with cherubs on the ceiling; the taste of new olive oil. A wild summer storm and two small boys lost in it, the suggestion of a first sexual encounter, and the odd exhilaration of new places and experiences drive the story, even as Percy tries to find his place as an American in Graziella's deeply Venetian life. All the while, Napoli never lets the message about the city's fragile existence overwhelm the story or the delicacy of the romance.

Jane Van Wiemokly

SOURCE: A review of *For the Love of Venice,* in *Voice of Youth Advocates,* Vol. 21., No. 4, October, 1998, p. 276.

When teenage Percy finds out he is to spend the summer in Venice, Italy, with his engineer father, artist mother, and six-year-old brother Christopher, he is not too happy—he'd had visions of sailing around Cape Cod. Percy's father has been assigned to help design a seawall floodgate project to prevent flooding in Venice. On his first day in Italy, Percy changes his mind when he meets ardent Venetian Graziella working in an ice cream store and immediately wishes to become better acquainted. Fortunately, she also works as a counselor at Christo-

pher's Italian camp. As their romance progresses, Percy discovers that Graziella is part of a radical group trying to drive tourists out of the city to make jobs and real estate available for Venetians. The group plans to blow up the floodgates, but nature intervenes with a storm and a flood, making for an exciting ending.

Having recently visited Venice, I can verify that the city is indeed full of tourists. Graziella's perspective might make readers stop and consider the consequences of tourism, and how one deals with unfavorable political and social realities. Napoli wonderfully evokes the sights, sounds, and feel of Venice—as Percy wandered through the narrow, sometimes dank streets, I felt I was there too. Fascinating cultural tidbits that are scattered throughout the story are painlessly absorbed without being didactic. There is much to like in this novel: Percy's parents, who obviously love their children and want to do well by them; [Percy's] relationship with Christopher, which has just the right amount of big brother exasperation, and love; and Percy's championing of a "slow" child at Christopher's camp. All these add up to an appealing and thought-provoking read.

📖 CHANGING TUNES (1998)

Carol A. Edwards

SOURCE: A review of *Changing Tunes,* in *School Library Journal,* Vol. 44, No. 8, August, 1998, p. 164.

Eileen's world is drastically altered by her parents' separation and impending divorce. Arriving home after school one day, the gifted 10-year-old musician discovers all of her father's belongings are gone—including the beloved piano that she thought belonged to the whole family. Her mother then arranges for her to practice on the old piano in the school auditorium. Adjustment is hard, and even more difficult because Eileen is unwilling to tell her best friend, Stephanie, about her family situation. When Mr. Poole, the school janitor and fellow music lover, listens to her play, somehow her problems seem more bearable. Music, Mr. Poole, and when given a chance, Stephanie, gradually ease Eileen into the changes required. Eileen strongly resembles many children in her reluctance to see the world from any viewpoint but her own. Her struggles are quietly portrayed and the situation is uncomplicated by other issues, although there is a nice counterpoint made by an elderly neighbor caring for a new grandchild. Perhaps this simplicity increases the desire for a stronger sense of the music that Eileen obviously feels is so important. Readers who are true music lovers will find the descriptions of its restorative power inadequate and there may not be enough plot to hold those who are not.

Additional coverage of Napoli's life and career is contained in the following sources published by Gale Research: *Something about the Author Autobiography Series,* Vol. 23; and *Something about the Author,* Vol. 92.

(Rosina) Ruth (Lucia) Park

1922(?)-

(Full name is Rosina Ruth Lucia Park) New Zealand-born Australian author of fiction, picture books, poetry, and plays.

Major works include *The Harp in the South* (1948), *The Muddle-Headed Wombat* (1962), *Callie's Castle* (1974), *Playing Beatie Bow* (1980), *When the Wind Changed* (1981), *My Sister Sif* (1986).

INTRODUCTION

Although her first major published works were for adults, Park has enjoyed both critical and commercial success in Australia and throughout the world for her picture books for primary graders and her novels for young adults. She is best known for her compelling narrative style that infuses history, fantasy, romance, and adventure into eloquent stories of Australia, New Zealand, and the South Pacific region. Park is praised for her humorous style in creating endearing and lovable characters in her picture books for younger children—particularly *The Muddle-Headed Wombat*. She is further recognized for her direct prose and skill in creating believable characters and settings in her young adult fiction—frequently exploring themes of change, growth, and transformation through adolescent characters who, often confused and angry, must learn to cope with the emotional demands of their lives. "Confronting change in oneself and those around you is the emotional core" of Park's writing, Kerry White explained. Park integrates contemporary characters and themes within extraordinary settings to create an atmosphere of place and feeling that appeals to adolescents' interest in the exotic and adventurous and mirrors their own coming-of-age experiences. Her works also display her keen sensitivity to human weakness and folly: no matter how base her characters are, they are, according to C.H. Gratton, "never lacking in humanity."

Biographical Information

Born in Auckland, New Zealand, Park came from a storytelling family of Irish, Scottish, and Nordic ancestry. As a small child, she traveled with the Maori road crews led by her father, a road builder. She spent much of her time living in tent camps in the surrounding rainforest where she dramatized and enacted the tales of Scottish history her father told her. When a depression in New Zealand brought her father to bankruptcy, Park moved to distant and exotic Glen Afra to stay with an aunt and uncle. She revealed in her autobiography *A Fence around the Cuckoo,* "I cannot emphasise sufficiently the importance of my early life as a forest crea-

ture. The mindset it gave me has dominated my physical and spiritual being. The unitive eye with which all children are born with was never taken away from me by the frauds of civilisation; I always did know that one is all and all is one."

Park went on to attend St. Benedict's College, Auckland University, and New Zealand University. She began her professional career editing the children's page for the newspaper *Zealandia,* and later served as the children's editor of the *Auckland Star.* Of her experience as an editor, she learned that "what adults would like children to read, they simply don't." She further explained, "My one criterion is whether children like to read my books; if they didn't, I'd stop writing them. . . . I always try out a children's story on a group . . . usually kindergarten." Beginning in 1941, Park worked in Australia as a reporter for the *Sydney Mirror.* In 1942, she married writer D'Arcy Niland and began a family of her own that eventually included five children. She also wrote for *Children's Session,* broadcast by the Australian Broadcasting Corporation (ABC), for twenty-five years. During this time, she created her muddle-headed wombat for several episodes, which yielded at least a dozen books about the adventures of the bungling marsupial and his equally inept friends.

Major Works

Before gaining notoriety as a children's author, Park earned a reputation as an adult novelist. Her first book, *The Harp in the South,* chronicled an Irish family's life in the slums of Sydney. Published in 1948, the novel was a critically acclaimed best-seller and was reissued later for a young adult audience. Park followed *The Harp in the South* with other novels and plays for adults, including *Poor Man's Orange* and *The Witch's Thorn.* Her works for children and youth, however, differ in their focus and eclectic style. She typically combines devices from several genres to develop suspenseful, exciting stories about very human characters. "I like children enormously," she once commented, "and have spent much of my life with them, as teacher, children's editor, and finally mother. I like interesting and amusing children, and this is why I wrote children's books. . . . Writing for children is different from writing for adults and much more difficult. Most adult writing is designed to expand the inner world of the reader. Children's writing is the reverse. For a child, all the doors of his imaginative vision open outwards; the content of the story is the marvelous world beyond these doors, the style is what opens them for boys and girls too small to reach the knobs." Beginning with *The Muddle-Headed Wombat,* Park created a series of picture books for younger children about a fanciful marsupial and his friends, setting their adventures in the treetops, the snow, at school, on holiday, in the springtime, and on a rainy day. A young boy's talent for making scary faces is put to good use in *When the Wind Changed,* another picture book. Young Josh, whose awful face can chase away a growling dog and get a yelp of fright out of his grandmother, rushes to his father's workplace, a local bank, to scare a bank robber.

Among her works for young adults, *Callie's Castle* concerns a ten-year-old Australian girl who is having difficulty coping with the stress of living in a new home with her step brothers and sisters who seem to get all of the attention. With the help of her grandfather, Callie finds a place of her own—the turret room—in the big Victorian home. Park later published *Callie's Family* (1988), a sequel in which thirteen-year-old Callie is on the verge of losing her beloved tower room to her younger brother Dan. On reviewing *Callie's Family,* Margery Fisher acknowledged, "Nobody is better qualified to bring humor and sharpness to such a tale than Ruth Park."

Considered by many reviewers to be Park's best book, *Playing Beatie Bow* takes its title from a Scottish schoolyard game. The novel tells of fourteen-year-old Abigail who experiences mixed emotions over her mother's decision to reunite with her father, a man who had previously abandoned his family. Abigail travels through time with a young girl named Beatie Bow, back to Sydney, Australia, in 1873. Taken in by the close-knit Bow family, Abigail learns about the importance of family, love, and responsibility that brings her to an acceptance of herself and her place in her own contemporary world. "This book is many things," reported a *Junior Bookshelf* reviewer, "time-shift adventure story, study of Victorian colonial life, penetrating examination of adolescence, social document. More than the sum of these, it is a heart-warming and joyous tale, absorbingly interesting and true to the core." Critics applauded Park's writing in *Playing Beatie Bow* for its intensity, which made the time travel acceptable and the adventure believable. Park's accurate rendering of period clothes and furniture also portrayed the Victorian era vividly. According to the *Catholic Library World, Playing Beatie Bow* "is, without question, one of the most carefully crafted novels . . . for young readers. Every aspect is carefully tied together and at the very end every item completely comes together to form a unique whole."

Park dabbles in elements of fantasy in *My Sister Sif,* developing an undersea city with merpeople, dolphins, and dwarves and where humans have special aquatic adaptations to communicate with sea creatures. Set in Sydney in the year 2000, the story is narrated by fourteen-year-old Erika who lives with her two older sisters. Erika and her sister Sif contrive to escape to the home of their childhood on the remote island of Rongo where Sif falls in love with a young marine biologist. Park explores ecological issues as Erika and Sif discover that their island home is threatened by human intervention.

Awards

In 1948, *The Harp in the South* received the *Sydney Morning Herald* Prize. *Callie's Castle* earned recognition in 1975 as a runner-up for the Australian Book of the Year. *Playing Beatie Bow* won numerous literary awards, including Australian Children's Book Council Book of the Year in 1981, and the *Boston Globe-Horn Book* Award, Parents' Choice Award in 1982. In the same year, *Playing Beatie Bow* was recognized as an IBBY Honour List book and runner-up for the Guardian Award. *When the Wind Changed* received the Young Australians Best Book Award for a picture story book in 1986.

TITLE COMMENTARY

📖 *THE HOLE IN THE HILL* (1961; U.S. edition published as *Secret of the Maori Cave,* 1964)

Margery Fisher

SOURCE: A review of *The Hole in the Hill,* in *Growing Point,* Vol. 1, No. 4, October, 1962, p. 59.

Ruth Park in [*The Hole in the Hill*] tells how two

children, newly come to a farm in the North Island of New Zealand, explore a cave and find a really spectacular treasure, a Maori war-canoe of great antiquity. The Maori feeling for the ancestral past, the swamp and tussock setting, are finely described, and the book is well produced, with charmingly decorative pictures; as an admirer of Ruth Park's novels, I am sorry to have to say that I found the story a little dull, depending too much on brother and sister talk and oddly lacking in point.

The Junior Bookshelf

SOURCE: A review of *The Hole in the Hill,* in *The Junior Bookshelf,* Vol. 26, No. 5, November, 1962, p. 267.

Brownie Mackenzie and her brother Dunk go with their father from New South Wales to investigate a lonely farm in New Zealand, which their father has inherited. Left alone at the farm, the children hear some strange noises, find the attitude of the local Maoris mysterious and not wholly friendly, and then fall into a cave which leads them into eerie circumstances before the solution to the mystery is found. Miss Park savours and loves her words and this story is rich in a vocabulary that conveys vividly and suddenly an atmosphere of place and feeling. Sometimes this wealth of words overflows and satiates the reader, obscuring the story itself. For the most part, however, the enthusiasm is controlled and gives depth and stringency to a story that has originality, some knowledge of character, and obvious sincerity.

Virginia Kirkus' Service

SOURCE: A review of *Secret of the Maori Cave,* in *Virginia Kirkus' Service,* Vol. XXXII, No. 17, September 1, 1964, p. 897.

Brownie, 14, and her younger brother Dunk are sent on ahead and alone to the New Zealand farm left by a great-uncle along with the directive that there is "something . . . more valuable than gold" to be discovered there. In spite of frightening noises in the night, wild pigs, bats and a fall in a pothole, the children explore the cave to which the latter leads. They are joined by a Maori boy who is just as interested in and anxious to protect their eventual find, a statue, an old vessel and inscribed tablets of infinite archaeological significance and tribal, sacramental value. The likable youngsters keep the story animated and Miss Park, an experienced novelist, handles it with ease.

📖 THE ROAD UNDER THE SEA (1962; U.S. edition, 1966)

The Junior Bookshelf

SOURCE: A review of *The Road under the Sea,* in *The Junior Bookshelf,* Vol. 27, No. 4, October, 1963, pp. 217-18.

This story of Manuhune, a Pacific island, opens with a vivid picture of a hurricane. Immediately the reader gets the full flavour of such a typical tropical event, and throughout the story the atmosphere is well maintained— the superstitions of the islanders, and the visits to the old "taunga" or wise man.

Added to the tension of the life there, the father of young Nancy Kemp, the heroine of the story, is believed to have been lost at sea recently with one of the old island fishermen, and the brother of two young English visitors to the island. The arrival of the scuttled schooner—washed up in the bay after the storm— awakens suspicion as to the truth, especially as the sole known survivor—supposed to be suffering from loss of memory at the island hospital—does not act in a genuine way. After a skillful build-up of mounting tension, the missing sailors are discovered, and all ends happily.

Virginia Kirkus' Service

SOURCE: A review of *Road under the Sea,* in *Virginia Kirkus' Service,* Vol. XXXIV, No. 1, January 1, 1966, p. 10.

An adolescent mystery entertainment for girls featuring underwater detection and aerated dialogue. The setting is an island in Polynesia. It has to be. Anywhere else there wouldn't be the taboos that keep the proper island from being investigated right at the start instead of right at the end. There, Nancy's sea captain father, his native crewman and a passenger have been surviving like Robinson Crusoes after the schooner was sabotaged, while at home, a few sea miles away, his daughter and his passenger's sister are wildly surmising. Childlike natives submit happily to the directives of the two teenaged girls, who get to the bottom of *The Road under the Sea,* which leads to archaeological discoveries of even greater significance than the artifacts that were central to the author's last—*The Secret of the Maori Cave.* A South Sea burble.

Jane Manthorne

SOURCE: A review of *Road under the Sea,* in *School Library Journal,* Vol. 12, No. 9, May, 1966, p. 172.

The disappearance of their relatives in the waters off Manuhune in the Cook Islands sends four young people on a search which leads to an underwater city. Their adventure revives unanswered questions about the pre-Polynesians—the Manuhunes, Long-Ears, and workers in stone. The authentic island customs, the personalities of Polynesian characters, and the atmosphere drawn from the author's familiarity with the South Pacific are of far more interest than the suspense or villainous activity. Not impressive, but diverting reading. Recommended.

Margery Fisher

SOURCE: A review of *The Road under the Sea,* in *Growing Point,* Vol. 2, No. 5, October, 1967, p. 236.

Yet another story of Lost Atlantis, but the discovery of the hidden city under the Pacific waters is less important than the conflict between the good archaeologists and the men out to make money from ancient history. The action involves one character after another, as Nancy, the Captain's daughter, Tiare, their Polynesian servant, and English Phoebe, all try to find out where the schooner has gone and who the unknown survivor may be. There are some decorative drawings but the story itself disappointed me because with all the twists of personal relationship, there seemed too little room for the atmosphere of place which Ruth Park is so well qualified to establish.

AIRLIFT FOR GRANDEE (1964)

The Times Literary Supplement

SOURCE: "Packed Lunches: Food for Young Readers," in *The Times Literary Supplement,* No. 3303, June 17, 1965, p. 500.

Children who have just learnt to read to themselves are probably better catered for than they have ever been. Books for sevens and eights pour from the publishing houses, most of them well-produced, and, by today's standards, fairly cheap. They are, to put them at their lowest estimate, reading fodder for the voracious young reader, and they provide a reviewer with food for thought.

The particular examples under review have been selected for their family backgrounds. Most of them are enlivened with adventures, credible or otherwise, but with some claim to the title, "real-life stories." No witches. No fairies. No talking animals. No history. Although children are the central characters, it cannot be said that many of them remain in one's mind. Certainly, books of this length offer little scope for presenting characters in depth. Writers fall back, rather readily, upon stereotyped figures: little boys who are always shouting, and little girls who adore ponies. Grandee, the prize ram of Ruth Park's story, seems a more rounded figure (in every sense) than any human. . . .

Ruth Park's **Airlift for Grandee** brings farming really down to earth. Its setting is a large Australian sheep station. Through the children's fault, Grandee, the prize ram, gets out of his paddock and makes off into the bush, and Antonia and her brother Buff have to accept responsibility for getting Grandee back. This proves a tough job, for the ram is a cunning and wilful animal. The chase through the bush and the return of Grandee in a helicopter, subsequently to undergo the indignity of being "shore", make excellent reading, and this is one of the best-told stories in the collection.

If the only living creature that emerges from these books with a clearly defined character is a prize sheep, what else should one look for? Obviously, the quality of the story-telling, and in putting this second to the characters, it is not implied that it is secondary in importance.

THE MUDDLE-HEADED WOMBAT ON HOLIDAY (1964)

Margery Fisher

SOURCE: A review of *The Muddle-Headed Wombat on Holiday,* in *Growing Point,* Vol. 14, No. 2, July, 1975, p. 2674.

Tabby makes a small caravan for Wombat's birthday. Towing it behind his bike, the Wombat takes his friends for a "pickwick" to the seaside, with a night stop that brings out the worst in the exacting Tabby and the best out of the bush mouse who, if the smallest of the trio, is certainly its dominant member. Small adventures by water and land fill one more pleasing instalment of the adventures of three amusing Australian friends, as individual in their talk as in Noela Young's drawings of them.

THE MUDDLE-HEADED WOMBAT IN THE TREETOPS (1965)

Margery Fisher

SOURCE: A review of *The Muddle-Headed Wombat in the Treetops,* in *Growing Point,* Vol. 4, No. 7, January, 1966, p. 639.

There is a rackety humour, too, in **The Muddle-Headed Wombat in the Treetops,** the third adventure of Wombat and his friend Tabbycat, and their associate Mouse. They are "he" while Mouse is only "it," but it is the Mouse who has the most definite personality. Tabby Cat, a boastful creature, has tired of his friends and builds a tree-house to escape from them; as the story proceeds, the cat gets into one sort of trouble after another and ends by admitting that he couldn't do without blundering Wombat or the piratical, bossy Mouse. The humour, partly verbal, partly implied in the action, is most endearing and has a touch of *The Magic Pudding* about it. Pictures in one colour and black effectively underline the temperaments of the three creatures as indicated by the author.

The Junior Bookshelf

SOURCE: A review of *The Muddle-Headed Wombat in the Treetops,* in *The Junior Bookshelf,* Vol. 30, No. 2, April, 1966, pp. 116-17.

Tabby Cat, in an attempt to find some privacy, builds

himself a house in a tree, believing that his two friends, Mouse and the Muddle-headed Wombat, won't be able to disturb him there. He is mistaken, however, and finds no privacy at all. After sundry adventures, the three of them are marooned in the tree-house during a storm, and eventually Tabby Cat decides that he needs his friends.

There are some funny episodes in the book, and the Wombat is quite a lovable character, but the hypochondriac cat soon becomes a bore.

THE MUDDLE-HEADED WOMBAT IN THE SNOW (1966)

Margery Fisher

SOURCE: A review of *The Muddle-Headed Wombat in the Snow,* in *Growing Point,* Vol. 6, No. 5, November, 1967, p. 1012.

Tabby, enriched by a birthday, takes Mouse and Wombat for a holiday to the Snowy Mountains; the possibilities of animals on skis are exploited in a whimsical manner. The idiosyncratic chat of the animals and a comic entanglement with a lorry-load of cats alone remind me that Ruth Park is an experienced and skilful writer; the humour of the Wombat stories, otherwise, seems to me very laboured, and the plots, as such, almost non-existent.

THE SIXPENNY ISLAND (1968; U.S. edition published as *Ten-Cent Island,* 1968)

Kirkus Service

SOURCE: A review of *Ten-Cent Island,* in *Kirkus Service,* Vol. XXXVI, No. 1, January 1, 1968, p. 6.

Dad's new job takes the Gales from Portland, Maine, to Sydney, Australia; winning an island in a ten-cent lottery takes them to the Great Barrier Reef off the Queensland coast. Situation and setting are promising but the characters are not: Donald, about fifteen, is a selfish boob who asks "What about my milk" when the family proposes to camp out on the island; fourteen-year-old Paula is afraid to speak to strangers; twelve-year-old Sam, dubbed *robot* by his family because he's methodical, steady and quiet, at least doesn't act like a baby. Once they're on John Drunkard Island, however, things begin to improve; after various complications that could have happened back home (an eccentric recluse scientist, three poor, touchy almost-orphans), the lot of them organize to locate a valuable shell ("just about the rarest shell in the world") that was pitched into the lagoon unknowingly; selling it will enable them to turn John Drunkard and near-by Chinkapook into a tourist resort, where the Gales can remain and the orphans can thrive. Donald has toned down, Paula has toned up, and the flat story has acquired some local features, but it takes time.

Nancy Young Orr

SOURCE: A review of *Ten-Cent Island,* in *School Library Journal,* Vol. 14, No. 8, April, 1968, p. 130.

An American family newly arrived in Australia wins a coral island in a lottery and so decides to spend a few months there for a modern Swiss Family Robinson adventure. The loveliness of the island and the fascination of its marine life are vividly portrayed, as the three young people explore, go swimming under water, and 12-year-old Sam, the youngest, pursues his mania for shell collecting. The challenge of adapting to primitive living conditions and encounters with a dolphin and a shark, a killer wave, and with three children struggling on their own to exist on a neighboring island provide exciting adventures. In a short time the island transforms sullen, unhappy Donald, shy Paula, and their tense father, and all welcome the prospect of a permanent life there. The Australian author obviously has an intimate knowledge of and love for coral reefs, and the clarity of her descriptions and the romance of the unusual background make this a better-than-average nature and family story.

The Times Literary Supplement

SOURCE: "Tests of Initiative," in *The Times Literary Supplement,* No. 3475, October 3, 1968, p. 1115.

More distant but still warm and sunny, **The Sixpenny Island** of Ruth Park's Australian story is set in the Great Barrier Reef, and if the doings on it are less hilarious, it, too, is an enjoyable place to lose oneself for a while. The Swifts, an English family living in Australia and not enjoying it much, unexpectedly win the tiny, uninhabited John Drunkard Island and set off for the summer to explore it. Dad, with his neck in plaster from falling on the steps of the aircraft before he even set foot in Sydney, and Mick who is still regretting England, friends and university, seem determined at first not to enjoy it. To Mum and Paula it is all their dreams come true. For twelve-year-old Sam, John Drunkard is a living laboratory, complete with a not-so-tame boffin whom the family find already installed.

Much of the charm of this simple story lies in the members of the Swift family as individuals. They come alive as a family in a way all too rare in children's books, especially shy, imaginative Paula and scientific Sam, often known to his family as N.29. It is Sam who by precipitating their friendship with the crusty Professor Brisley and by finding the Domina Maris shell, makes it possible for them all to keep their Sixpenny Island and by doing so to help the fatherless Gartreys from the twin island of Chinkapook to keep theirs.

Ruth Park writes very well and this book can be recommended for all those feeling the early prickings of the wanderlust.

N. Danischewsky

SOURCE: A review of *The Sixpenny Island,* in *Children's Book News,* Vol. 3, No. 6, November-December, 1968, p. 329.

The story begins with "the second important thing" that happened to the Swift family when they arrived in Australia. Sam and Paula become joint owners of John Drunkard, a small island off the Great Barrier Reef; they win it in a sixpenny lottery. Father and Donald, in rare agreement, want to sell it; Sam wants to study its marine life; Paula just wants to see it. Mother says, "I suppose everyone dreams of having a private island of his own," and begins to marshall her arguments. A fortnight later the family is living on "The Sixpenny Island." The vitality and directness of the writing makes an immediate impact—yet one is never conscious of the author: all one's vivid impressions of the island come naturally through the characters and events. Any child with a really absorbing interest of his/her own will understand Sam's passionate committal to the study of marine biology; he is a memorable character drawn with great insight and affection. One could wish all such children to find a Mr. Brisley as he did. There is a very skilled economy in the storytelling; Ruth Park has written an entertaining book that will satisfy the insatiable appetite for things-to-happen of the nine- to eleven-year-old, without sacrificing characters for events. She has an unerring eye for what is important to the story and a ruthless disregard for irrelevant background padding.

The Junior Bookshelf

SOURCE: A review of *The Sixpenny Island,* in *The Junior Bookshelf,* Vol. 32, No. 6, December, 1968, p. 382.

Mr. Smith having fractured his neck on arrival to take up an appointment in Australia is the freak factor which enables and incites his family to take up temporary residence on a tiny island off the coast of Queensland. Not that they emulate the Swiss Family Robinson to any great extent though improvisation and a certain amount of roughing it ensue. One easily accepts that in Australia it is possible to win an island with a sixpenny lottery ticket and after that anything goes. For someone who likes to combine fiction with information this is just the book from which to learn about the flora and fauna of remoter lands, especially as one member of the family is mad about biology and encounters (and disturbs) a noted professor of the same, squatting on the island. Each member of the family finds the opportunity to indulge a dream before the demands of school and work reimpose their restrictions on the adventure—until the next holidays, of course. Their sojourn is not without danger of the sort to be expected in a tropical demiparadise but all hazards serve to cement new friendships and to develop the characters of the visitors, as all good stories of living under difficulties should. Good fun and good value.

NUKI AND THE SEA SERPENT: A MAORI STORY (1969)

The Junior Bookshelf

SOURCE: A review of *Nuki and the Sea Serpent: A Maori Story,* in *The Junior Bookshelf,* Vol. 33, No. 3, June, 1969, p. 164.

There is sound stuff in this story of a little Maori boy who told lies—or stories—and suffered some tribulation before being appointed Village Storyteller. The manner of the narrative is rather pedestrian. It provides, however, a starting point for Zelma Blakely's most excellent pictures. Perhaps she sentimentalizes Nuki and his friends, but the New Zealand motifs are rendered beautifully and the whole thing carried out with panache. Through an entertaining and attractive tale children, and not only the youngest, will be led to the realization of an exotic and most fascinating culture.

The Times Literary Supplement

SOURCE: "Maori Lines," in *The Times Literary Supplement,* No. 3513, June 26, 1969, p. 698.

In *Nuki and the Sea Serpent* the story is perhaps more important than the pictures, attractive though these are. Nuki is a Maori boy whose inventive imagination conjures up blood-curdling tales, such as the one about "wild men with long pink hair who jump out on travellers and eat them up, crunch-crunch." Sent away for disturbing the people with these fantasies, he encounters a monstrous but good-natured Sea-Serpent (an appreciative listener, too) and Nuki proudly returns to the village with his improbable friend. A handsome book; the strong ornamental pictures with their folk-print look enrich the tale.

THE MUDDLE-HEADED WOMBAT IN THE SPRINGTIME (1970)

Margery Fisher

SOURCE: A review of *The Muddle-Headed Wombat in the Springtime,* in *Growing Point,* Vol. 9, No. 9, April, 1971, p. 1717.

Spring affects Wombat and his friends with discontent. How can they be different? The solution is simple. They put on a performance of *Cinderella* for a bush audience, with Tabby as the Prince and the mouse as a surprisingly waspish Cinderella. The Wombat is a hit as the Fairy Godmother but perhaps not as he intended, for his conjurations never come out quite as they should. However, the performance is greatly enjoyed and the friends agree they have 'changed' enough to satisfy their restlessness. There are other adventures in the book too—an amusing encounter with three Wolf Cubs and a meeting with Rich Jim Crumble, a cantakerous bandicoot—one of the best animal characters in the saga. The zest and slapstick of these stories are right in the *Magic Pudding* tradition and the Wombat's exploits always have a topsy-turvy logic that is most satisfying.

The Times Literary Supplement

SOURCE: "Animal Magic," in *The Times Literary Supplement,* No. 3605, April 2, 1971, p. 388.

It is one of the characteristics of the best fantasy that what happens is both unexpected and inevitable—mad, perhaps, but consistently so. When Ruth Park, in her most recent story about her muddle-headed wombat, says that the audience at the play sit on the grass, "because, of course, animals don't need chairs," she strikes one of the many wrong notes in these pale Australian versions of Winnie-the-Pooh. If they don't need chairs, does the wombat need his hat (without which he is never seen) or the sick bandicoot his bed? Oh, reason not the need. Consistency is the thing. When Mouse is shocked at the idea of having smoke in the play, one sees the public-spirited beware-of-bush-fires Ruth Park appearing over the fantasist's shoulder. But 22 pages earlier Mouse is nonchalantly lighting a match to scare away a magpie.

There is some amusing invention in the book but the whimsy is often painful. "I wish I wasn't wicked, treely ruly I do," says the wombat. The cat is inclined to sniff, as we are, but it is equally given to coyness: "Oh, Mouse, won't you give your own dear pussy a little treat?" A. A. Milne may also have been accused of whimsy but his nursery toys had a great deal more character than these Antipodean animals.

CALLIE'S CASTLE (1974)

Margery Fisher

SOURCE: A review of *Callie's Castle,* in *Growing Point,* Vol. 13, No. 8, March, 1975, pp. 2579-80.

One of the most frequent criticisms of stories for children in the early reading years—which these days can be anything from six to eight or even higher—is that they offer them a trivial or insipid view of life. These are years of discovery, when children become aware of all kinds of new relationships and pressures, and perhaps stories can help them a little, not by giving them examples or drawing heavy conclusions but simply by showing all manner of alignments, encounters and surprises within the framework of stories to be read for enjoyment. . . .

The problem in *Callie's Castle* will be familiar to any large family. Callie Cameron at ten is expected to be kind to her younger brother, Dan, a cantankerous convalescent, and to her little half-brother and sister, who are mischievous and destructive. She wants, and needs, privacy, and when the family moves to a big old Victorian house in a suburb of Sydney her dreams seem to be coming true, for her grandfather, a retired builder, plans with her sympathetic stepfather to turn the turret into a room for her. But can she really exclude Dan, who is jealous, or Gret and Rolf who are noisily inquisitive? And if she does, will she really enjoy her retreat? Again, behind vivid, persuasive domestic detail there is a firm, unostentatious point about human relations.

R. Baines

SOURCE: A review of *Callie's Castle,* in *The Junior Bookshelf,* Vol. 39, No. 2, April, 1975, p. 126.

In an Australian family of four, only Callie is the child of her mother's first husband, who died young. She is ten years old, and the stress of moving to another house, even though it is an attractive one, brings to the surface emotions Callie cannot handle. She quarrels with her best friend, her relationship with her half-brother deteriorates, and she is on the verge of rejecting her loving step-father for the photograph of a man she cannot remember. In her distress she turns to her paternal grandfather, a practical, understanding man. He manages to find and renovate a neglected room in a turret of the family's new home which can become Callie's refuge through the tumults of adolescence.

Margaret Carter

SOURCE: A review of *Callie's Castle,* in *Books for Your Children,* Vol. 21, No. 3, Autumn-Winter, 1986, p. 13.

Fiction with a difference for fluent readers of 8 years upwards. Set in Australia—with enough skillful background to be interesting but not intrusive. When Callie's family move into a different home, Callie finds all sorts of things going wrong, schoolwork, quarrels with friends and family. It's the *no-one understands me* stage. Fortunately, Grandpa's help is enlisted—Grandpa is the father of Callie's *real* dead father—on to which a second family has been happily grafted, and Grandpa finds the ultimate treasure—spare space in the empty cupola of the house which he turns into a retreat for Callie.

How Callie learns to share her castle with both its previous owners and her own demanding smaller brother and sister mirrors her own growth and change. How refreshing to read a book where family pleasures and squabbles are so truthfully detailed without technicolor frenzy.

THE MUDDLE-HEADED WOMBAT AND THE INVENTION (1975)

Margery Fisher

SOURCE: A review of *The Muddle-Headed Wombat and the Invention,* in *Growing Point,* Vol. 14, No. 9, April, 1976, pp. 2849-50.

Two kinds of humour coalesce in the tales of the Muddle-headed Wombat. First, the animals are endowed with one human characteristic apiece—Mouse is conceited, Tabby is insecure and touchy and the Wombat lives up to his adjectival prefix. The simple assumption of human speech and behaviour brings about a series of banana-skin situations which are never too much at variance with the true nature of the animals. In *The Muddle-headed Wombat and the Invention* it is easy enough to believe that Tabby, on holiday with an uncle, should have collected a wardrobe of trendy clothes and learned to drive a car, and just as easy to accept that the Wombat, eager to use the book of "Things to Make" given him by the cat, should build a cart which is used successively, and dangerously, as a land and sea vehicle and finally as a shelter, after a local magic-maker has brought the desired rain. In this new book the usual black-and-white pictures, which have always offered the same kind of daft, casually amusing details as the text, have been given an overlay of colour which somehow forces one to consider the characters as animals rather more than is desirable for the particular kind of jokes that keep the sequence of stories going.

THE GIGANTIC BALLOON (1975; U.S. edition, 1976)

R. Baines

SOURCE: A review of *The Gigantic Balloon,* in *The Junior Bookshelf,* Vol. 40, No. 3, June, 1976, p. 148.

Shopkeeper Mr. Hoy sells more than his competitor Mr. Jones because his advertising is better—until Mr. Jones hits upon the idea of obtaining a balloon to trail an advertising banner. The balloon arrives safely, but without a balloonist, which gives Mr. Jones' persecuted assistant, the hero of this book, a chance to volunteer for the position. With the help of his dog he overcomes Mr. Hoy's attempts at sabotage and sails away to adventure, loyally towing an exhortation to shop only at Jones' behind him.

It is a lively, original tale, recorded in a well produced book. The large illustrations are coloured in a wide variety of pastel water colours, so that Victorian interiors are enlivened by many hues, and crowd scenes look superficially like appealing patchwork quilts. It is a pity that all the characters have such ugly faces.

Publishers Weekly

SOURCE: A review of *The Gigantic Balloon,* in *Publishers Weekly,* Vol. 210, No. 5, August 2, 1976, p. 114.

Mother Ruth Park is lucky to have her daughters, Kilmeny and Deborah, collaborating with her by producing the fetching color pictures in her book. The scene is 19th-century Sydney, Australia, where rival shopkeepers

try to invent ads which will put each other out of business. Peter Thin (an abused employee), comforts himself and his dog, Belle, with visions of a rosy future. His tyrannic boss, Jones, hires a balloon and balloonist from France to fly a streamer with the legend, "Shop Only at Jones's" and Peter—who rechristens himself Pierre Maigre—volunteers to fly the craft when the balloonist is a no-show. Chicanery on the part of the other merchant almost defeats the daring act but Belle comes to the rescue and she and her friend are off to a new life in the wild blue yonder. It's a funny book with funny pictures.

Allene Stuart Phy

SOURCE: A review of *The Gigantic Balloon,* in *School Library Journal,* Vol. 23, No. 2, October, 1976, p. 100.

Another tale of a schlemiel who finally makes good. Peter Thin, harassed assistant of business shyster J. J. Jones, overcomes an assortment of rascals to become Pierre Maigre, fearless balloonist, who sails away to fortune with his faithful dog, Belle. Published first in Sydney, Australia, this is a pleasant period piece recalling the days of overstuffed parlor furniture, maids in uniform serving tea, handlebar mustaches, etc. The caricatures of the villainous Victorians and Our Hero (who bears a strong resemblance to Stan Laurel) are crisp and, at times, hilarious, making . . . *Balloon* a breezy, open-ended adventure.

Ethel L. Heins

SOURCE: A review of *The Gigantic Balloon,* in *The Horn Book Magazine,* Vol. LIII, No. 2, April, 1977, p. 152.

From Australia comes a madcap Victorian farce about two rival shopkeepers—Mr. J. J. Jones, of J. J. Jones's Gigantic Emporium, and Mr. Alexander Hoy, of Hoy's Palace of Fashion and Universal Providers. Each proprietor tried to outsmart the other in persuasive advertising until Mr. Jones ordered from France an enormous balloon which would trail a hundred-foot-long banner, saying "SHOP ONLY AT JONES'S, CHEAPEST AND CHOICEST." But because of Mr. Hoy's treachery, the French balloonist never appeared; and Peter Thin, Mr. Jones's fearless young assistant, jumped in to take his place. Once again, Mr. Hoy plotted to ruin the ascent, and again he was foiled as Peter's dog came to the rescue and the magnificent balloon rose and floated over the city. Broadly humorous, full-color illustrations by the award-winning artists of *Mulga Bill's Bicycle* [Kilmeny and Deborah Niland] stretch the hyperbole of the text. The wildly caricatured figures and the wickedly impudent children are worthy of Tomi Ungerer while, in ludicrous contrast, the endpapers show pink and blue birds and the disappearing balloon sweetly silhouetted against an evening sky.

WHEN THE WIND CHANGED (1980; U.S. edition, 1981)

Publishers Weekly

SOURCE: A review of *When the Wind Changed,* in *Publishers Weekly,* Vol. 219, No. 5, January 30, 1981, p. 76.

Josh discovers that making a scary face reduces the fierce dog next door to quivering jelly, and his success encourages the lad. He practices until he has turned his face into a truly hideous sight, disregarding his father's warning that a strong wind will make the condition permanent. It does. Josh covers his face and rushes to the bank, where he finds his father at the mercy of an armed robber. The thief is so terrified of the boy that he is easily overcome, and that is the quirky story Park tells, giving it a final mirthful twist when the wind changes just as Josh's father demonstrates his skill at creating fearful expressions. Niland's pictures are a riot of strong colors, particularly notable when they show the faces inhumanly contorted.

Kirkus Reviews

SOURCE: A review of *When the Wind Changed,* in *Kirkus Reviews,* Vol. XLIX, No. 5, March 1, 1981, p. 281.

A joke. A pretty dumb joke. There's this boy, Josh, who makes horrible faces. He scares the dog next door, and his grandmother. His mother asks him "not to try his faces on the people in the street because it would not be good for Dad's business." His father is a bank teller. He warns Josh that "if you're making a face and the wind changes it will stay that way." When he does, and it does, he heads for the bank—face covered—to see if his Dad knows "some more." A bank robber, seeing his face, drops his gun; and just then the wind changes again (yes, inside the bank), and Josh's face returns to normal. But that night on TV, Dad makes a face too, and "Just then the wind changed." The faces are gruesome, all right, but making faces is a lot funnier in the flesh.

Zena Sutherland

SOURCE: A review of *When the Wind Changed,* in *Bulletin of the Center for Children's Books,* Vol. 34, No. 9, May, 1981, p. 178.

First published in Australia, a story about a boy who discovered that the faces he made were awful enough to frighten a ferocious dog. His grandmother screeched when he showed her; his mother who "was not a screecher," asked him not to make faces on the street because it would be bad for Dad's business. Unfortunately, just as Josh was making his newest, improved Awful Face, the wind changed and he was stuck with it. Fortunately, he

came into his Dad's bank and frightened away some robbers. Unfortunately, just as a pleased Dad was showing Josh the Awful Face he had made as a boy, the wind changed. The pictures are in bright, cartoon-like pastels, the faces more grotesque when contorted than funny; the story is slight, a bit contrived, but adequately told and mildly funny.

PLAYING BEATIE BOW (1980; U.S. edition, 1982)

Margery Fisher

SOURCE: A review of *Playing Beatie Bow,* in *Growing Point,* Vol. 20, No. 4, November, 1981, pp. 3966-67.

On the (unfortunately) rare occasions when Ruth Park writes for young readers, she abates none of her exuberance and gives fully of her skill in creating believable characters and settings. Her prose has always been very direct and concrete, with a particular edge of idiom in dialogue, and this is very evident in *Playing Beatie Bow,* which casts the same spell of authenticity that I remember holding me fast in my discovery of *One-a-pecker, Two-a-pecker.* As that superb novel took me to the Otago goldfields in the last century, so now Ruth Park moves from the Sydney of the present to the same streets in 1873, writing so pictorially and with such intensity that we seem to be walking with fourteen-year-old Abigail up a steep alley which she has never noticed before and into a world 'full of strange smells, horse manure and tidal flats, wood smoke, human sweat, and an all-pervading odour of sewage.' She is following 'the little furry girl' she has seen standing wistfully on the fringes of the group game of 'Beatie Bow' currently fashionable in the park. But who is, or was, Beatie Bow? And why has Abigail been brought into the past to speak to her? There is a tangible link between the generations, a piece of yellowed crochet found in a bag of jumble which Abigail's mother had bought for the trendy junk-shop she started after her husband left her. With its design of flower and leaf, the piece is exactly right for the long dress Abigail has contrived from an Edwardian curtain from the same bag of jumble. When Abigail is drawn by skinny Beatie into her family, with its troubles of poverty and disease, the old grandmother is planning the crochet piece as part of the meagre trousseau for kindly, plain Dovey, who is to marry the handsome sailor Judah. Abigail's irruption into the Tallisker family comes near to wrecking Dovey's happiness but Grannie, Hebridean by birth, has the Sight, and she enlightens Abigail about her translation in time and the responsibilities it entails. Grannie does not know, however, that Abigail as well as being bound by ties of heredity to the poor family in the Rocks, is open to the call of the past because of the turmoil in her mind after she learns that her father wants to come back to them. Past and present flow into one another, as the Harbour bridge seems to appear and disappear, not like a conjuring trick but as a symbol of time interacting and as the focus of Abigail's surprised observation. The spirit of old Sydney—the wooden buildings, the clothes, the hardship—comes unerringly through the taut, forceful words of this fine book.

Ann Evans

SOURCE: "Extensions of Reality," in *The Times Literary Supplement,* No. 4103, November 20, 1981, p. 1354.

To build a story for ten to twelve-year-olds around the supernatural is to court disaster; the successful ghost story for this age group is such a rarity. . . .

The ghost in *Playing Beatie Bow* is its heroine, Abigail Park. Against the disturbing background of her parents' broken marriage there moves an ingenious plot in which the fourteen-year-old schoolgirl is spirited back to the Sydney of a hundred years ago; there she is required to live in the home of young Beatie Bow, who subsequently gave her name to the playground game in Abigail's school. Beatie's grandmother recognizes in Abigail the Stranger who alone can perpetuate their family gift of clairvoyance.

How she achieves this is turned into a story of suspense and excitement, rich in humanity, shrewd observation and wit. Abigail herself is a character in the Dido Twite tradition: tender-hearted despite an astringent tongue, vulnerable behind a tough exterior, she has the courage of ten and a breezy optimism to go with it. As the pivot of the plot, she is the book's chief delight, followed closely by the marvelously Dickensian portrait of the Victorian family with whom she has to live. An exuberant book, written with confident expertise and richly deserving the popularity it will surely have with ten to twelve-year-old girls.

Marcus Crouch

SOURCE: A review of *Playing Beatie Bow,* in *The Junior Bookshelf,* Vol. 46, No. 1, February, 1982, p. 36.

Here is one for the Opies. Children are playing in a Sydney street. They chant:

> 'Oh, Mudda, what's that, what can it be?'
> 'The wind in the chimney, that's all, that's all.'
> 'Oh, Mudda, what's that, what's that can you
>   see?'
> 'It's the cow in the byre, the horse in the stall.'

And then:

> 'It's Beatie Bow, risen from the dead!'

Among those watching is Abigail, a teenager, confused and distressed by the break-up, and then by the promised revival, of her parents' marriage. There is also a 'little furry girl' who is—wait for it!—the real Beatie Bow, a child alive in 1873. Somehow, out of the air of the Sydney tower-blocks, modern children have snatched the hundred-year-old story of a slum child and her aspirations.

Abigail chases the 'furry girl' and finds herself back among the turmoil and filth of Victorian New South Wales, sharing the life of Beatie Bow and her family until she has fulfilled her role as the Stranger who will guarantee the survival of the 'Gift' which the family has brought from their original home in Orkney. She shares their lives, falls in love, and, in a magnificent climax, completes her task and is allowed to return to her own times.

Here a lesser writer would have left it. But Abigail has been involved in this strange adventure for her own sake as well as that of the Bow family. Experience and suffering have taught her how to meet the problems of her own life. She is, although in modern terms she has been away only seconds, older, wiser and more tolerant. Then in a masterly last chapter, all the loose ends are drawn together and Abigail is allowed her reward.

This book is many things: time-shift adventure story, study of Victorian colonial life, penetrating examination of adolescence, social document. More than the sum of these, it is a heart-warming and joyous tale, absorbingly interesting and true to the core. Miss Park's best book, I think, and she has written many, all good. I commend it to all readers, irrespective of age, and especially to mixed-up adolescent girls who are trying to find a chart through the murky waters of their private lives.

Dorothy Atkinson

SOURCE: A review of *Playing Beatie Bow,* in *The School Librarian,* Vol. 30, No. 1, March, 1982, p. 56.

This book won the Australian Children's Book of the Year Award for 1981. It is a time-slip with a difference, beginning with a fourteen-year-old girl in Sydney. Troubled by her parents' problems, she watches a Sydney street game, a kind of 'Poor Mary,' but the sheeted 'rise up' figure is that of Beatie Bow. With Beatie, Abigail goes back into the life of Victorian Sydney, a time-slip which is brought about by a knock on the head from the edge of a doorstep (the same device as in *A Traveller in Time*). Sydney in 1873 is an interesting place, nowhere better described than in the paragraph on Sydney Harbour, but our heroine is soon recognised by the Bow family (immigrants from Orkney) as having 'the Gift': she is fey. They will not let her return to her own time until a prophecy is fulfilled. She does get back, but not before she has fallen in love with one of the family. She loses him, but finds him again 'in her own time,' so this is a story with a happy ending. It has a most agreeably unusual setting and atmosphere, it is full of detail about the clothes and furniture of the time, and it does not present Sydney in 1873 as a gentle place.

Zena Sutherland

SOURCE: A review of *Playing Beatie Bow,* in *Bulletin of the Center for Children's Books,* Vol. 35, No. 8, April, 1982, p. 156.

'Beatie Bow' is the name of a game that Abigail sees younger children playing, and she notices one waif-like girl who watches but never joins the play. Abigail's fourteen, resenting the fact that her mother is more than willing to take back the husband who'd deserted her for another woman, resenting even more her parents' decision to move from Sydney to Norway. That's the realistic setting out of which emerges a fantasy named the best Australian children's book of 1981. In this beautifully crafted time-slip story, the waif proves to be the Beatie Bow for whom the game was named—but she doesn't know why her name is known. Only when Abigail goes back to Beatie's time, a century ago, does a pattern emerge that answers both their questions. This lively story has action, suspense, strong characters, and an ingenuous knitting of past and present, so that each affects the other.

Anita C. Wilson

SOURCE: A review of *Playing Beatie Bow,* in *School Library Journal,* Vol. 28, No. 9, May, 1982, p. 65.

An Australian prize winner, *Playing Beatie Bow* is a time fantasy set in present-day Sydney. Fourteen-year-old Abigail Kirk is embittered and confused upon learning that she and her mother are to be reunited with her father, who had abandoned the family several years earlier. Abigail finds herself in the Sydney of the 1870s after seeing a children's game, "Beatie Bow," named after a famous Victorian schoolteacher who is still a child when Abigail enters her world. Abigail discovers that she has been sent into the past to preserve "the gift," or ability to foretell the future, which runs in the Bow family. During her stay with the Bows, Abigail falls in love for the first time and begins to understand the pain and complexity of romantic love. As she comes to perceive and carry out her task in the Victorian world, Abigail acquires sufficient maturity to handle the risks and challenges posed by her parents' attempted reconciliation. She also experiences both the vitality and the horror of Victorian working-class life, which is vividly and authentically portrayed. Too many loose ends are resolved too quickly, but the story is notable for its skillful integration of a contemporary problem novel with an element of fantasy.

Ilene Cooper

SOURCE: A review of *Playing Beatie Bow,* in *Booklist,* Vol. 78, No. 19, June 1, 1982, p. 1315.

Abigail Kirk, a 14-year-old Australian girl, was distraught when her father left her mother for another woman. Now that her parents want to reconcile, she is furious and more than a little wary of letting his love back into her life. In the midst of this confusion Abby begins watching the playground children playing a game, Beatie Bow, and at the same time she notices a small, oddly dressed girl hovering at the fringes of the sport. It is this child, the original Beatie Bow, who brings Abby back in time to Victorian Sydney. Once there, Abby finds her life inexplicably intertwined with the Bows—the deranged father, a candy maker; handsome Judah; defiant Beatie, eager for learning and ready to fight for it; saintly Dovey; and most memorable, Granny Tallisker, whose gift of ESP and prophecy identifies Abby as the Stranger come to influence the family's destiny. In a league with the best time fantasies, Park's setting is embellished with such rich detail it becomes real. When Abby is shanghaied by a legless cripple and brought to a rotting warehouse inhabited by lowlifes and grotesques, the episode is so finely crafted the reader's terror feels as great as Abby's. Once Abby fulfills her destiny, she returns to her own time infinitely wiser about the meaning of life and love; the ending, totally unexpected and sweet as the treacle sold in Mr. Bow's shop, perfectly rounds out the fantasy. A dazzling tour de force.

Barbara Jo McKee

SOURCE: A review of *Playing Beatie Bow,* in *Voice of Youth Advocates,* Vol. 5, No. 3, August, 1982, p. 35.

Named the best children's book of the year in Australia in 1981, this is a compelling mystery story of 14-year-old Abigail and her trip into the Australia of a hundred years ago. Abigail, going through conflicting emotions because of her parents' separation, follows a small strange girl who appears in her neighborhood and ends up in another time dimension with her. Her Victorian family feels that she has been sent to them to revive their gift of prophecy and refuses to try to get her home again until this is done. During her stay with this family she falls in love with the brother and rescues two of the family members from a raging fire. She finally gets back to her own world, and her love story has a happy ending. Page-turning story with lively characters—a sure hit with . . . students.

Nancy C. Hammond

SOURCE: A review of *Playing Beatie Bow,* in *The Horn Book Magazine,* Vol. LVIII, No. 4, August 2, 1982, pp. 407-08.

Adopting an expressionless face and a loner's lifestyle when her adored father walks out with another woman, Abigail builds barricades so that "not even her mother should know what she was like inside", she becomes a captive in her own egocentric prison. Furious when her mother announces with unbridled happiness that her father wants them to live with him again and move to

Norway, disgusted by this response, and worried that they may be abandoned a second time, she cuttingly remarks, "'And now for the violins'"—and threatens to go to boarding school. In the Australian award-winning time fantasy, an old crocheted piece and a playground game, "Beatie Bow," spur her to follow a Victorian child, Beatie Bow herself, down a Sydney alley and into her 1873 world—a century away in time yet only five minutes from Abigail's home. Accepted as an amnesic immigrant by Beatie's loving family, who feel responsible when their father accidentally injures her, Abigail is nurtured by Granny, a fairy godmother figure; plays a crucial role in the Bows' family story; and discovers herself in love, unlocking her self-centeredness. Life in Sydney in two very different periods is vividly described. Neither time is idealized; paralleling the stench, lack of sanitation, and diseases of the Victorian world are the loneliness and alienation of her modern life. Although the contemporary episodes seem a bit manipulated, the reader's dominant response is delight, as a skillful storyteller unfolds a rich, tightly meshed fantasy. While conscious of women's liberation and choices, she chooses to tell a romantic story of the power of love.

James A. Norsworthy

SOURCE: A review of *Playing Beatie Bow,* in *Catholic Library World,* Vol. 54, No. 5, December, 1982, p. 225.

Abigail Kirk, a fourteen-year-old, is watching a group of children playing a strange game called Beatie Bow. She notices an odd child watching and when Abigail tries to follow her, she ends up back in time one hundred years. There in the past Abigail learns that the child she followed was in fact Beatie Bow who was trying to figure out why children of the future would be playing a game using her name. While searching for a way to return to her own time, Abigail becomes quite involved with the Bows and their belief in "the gift"—the supernatural explanation for why Abigail had come from her time to the past. Set in Australia, this is, without question, one of the most carefully crafted novels of recent years for young readers. Every aspect is carefully tied together and at the end every item completely comes together to form a unique whole. Those who love adventure, a hint of romance or just a good story will be captivated by this book. Highly recommended for grades six through nine.

Thelma Davey

SOURCE: A review of *Playing Beatie Bow,* in *Books for Keeps,* No. 40, September, 1986, p. 25.

This 1981 Australian Children's Books Award winner is both historical and contemporary. Abigail at 14, still numbed by a sense of betrayal (her father left when she was 10), is appalled by her mother's decision to live with him again. She time-slips to 1873, is cared for by

Orkney immigrants, now New South Welshmen,—trapped too, since she's the stranger who will ensure that the family gift survives. Victorian Sydney is made wonderfully vivid. Its squalor and its humanity astound Abigail. She, the other characters and their stories are compelling and convincing. I enjoyed the book enormously and had a good sniffle at the end when past and present connect.

⌂ *MY SISTER SIF* (1986; U.S. edition, 1991)

M. Hobbs

SOURCE: A review of *My Sister Sif,* in *The Junior Bookshelf,* Vol. 51, No. 4, August, 1987, pp. 184-85.

Ruth Park's story begins normally enough: two orphaned sisters being looked after in Australia by an elder one and her husband. Sif is homesick for the Polynesian island where she was brought up, so that Riko, the narrator, helps her run away back to Rongo by selling a rare shell. This brings an American marine biologist after them, and he and Sif fall in love. At this point it becomes clear that this is science fiction: the girls' mother is still alive, but living under the sea with their Nordic-looking brother Stig. The fantastic element is partially explained away, however, and the book's real purpose emerges, to bring home the terrible destruction and distortion of marine life caused by atomic experiment in the Pacific Ocean and by dumping chemical waste at sea. Teenage Riko can understand the speech of dolphins and whales though, unlike Sif, she cannot breathe well under water, and she sees and hears of deformed births, and of cracks in the seabed oozing poison. Sif's death is part of the penalty also, and Riko is writing in the future, when dedicated biologists and teachers are at last hoping to educate children to use modern technology to restore and recreate instead of destroy. This imaginary account is much more immediate even than horror photographs of the effects of sea pollution; it creates understanding of the dangers from the creatures' viewpoint. But the book is much more than a vehicle for propaganda. The people are real, from the drunken old doctor and his Polynesian Mammy Ti, who brought up the girls after their father's death, to Sif's tender love affair and Riko and her problems with a pygmy Menehune admirer. It is also about possessiveness, on many levels, from their selfish mother to Riko herself, who cannot bear to lose Sif to Henry. One hopes the optimism of the conclusion about human nature is justified.

Chris Stephenson

SOURCE: A review of *My Sister Sif,* in *The School Librarian,* Vol. 35, No. 4, November, 1987, pp. 356, 358.

This is a strange mixture of lyrical fantasy and Greenpeace campaigning. The story begins with two sisters running away from school in Sydney to return to Rongo, their remote island home in the Pacific. Sif, the elder sister, falls in love with an American shell-collector called Henry. Little by little the elements of fantasy are introduced. With Henry, the reader learns that the mother of the girls is a mermaid, that menehune (fairy folk) inhabit the island, and that the sisters are able to exchange thoughts with dolphins and whales. Then the narrative takes an ominous twist. Environmental pollution is endangering all marine life. The sea-people are forced to leave Rongo for a safer habitat, and Sif must choose between following her mother and staying with Henry. Tragedy follows. Sif dies, and the pollution theme is pushed to its logical conclusion as the earth itself reacts massively to the misuse of modern technology (no, nothing as drastic as the bomb—just the usual industrial waste and damage to the ecosystem). But the book ends on a note of optimism, with Henry and Sif's sister Riko picking up the pieces: Riko as a marine biologist and Henry as a writer on the theme of planetary support.

Margery Fisher

SOURCE: A review of *My Sister Sif,* in *Growing Point,* Vol. 28, No. 4, November, 1989, pp. 4885, 4889.

Since we all rebel instinctively against didacticism in fiction, the introduction of alternative worlds or species can be useful in allowing moral statements to be made obliquely. Recently, one social problem in particular, the exploiting of animals by Man, has been in the forefront of speculative fiction. . . .

Ruth Park has . . . used the theme of racial isolation in *My Sister Sif,* imagining that in prehistoric times a kind of purposive evolution has enabled certain people to live in and under the sea. Not mer-people but humans with a special metabolism. Erika and her siblings are living in Australia in the twenty-first century. Their father is dead and their mother prefers to stay on the small Pacific island of Ronga; Erika and Sif lodge in Sydney under the guardianship of their older sister, in whom the sea-element is so slight that she distrusts their special gifts. Visiting Ronga in the holidays, both Erika and her beloved sister Sif have to redefine their relationship. A marine biologist setting up a research programme is gradually let into their secret but his love for Sif is doomed, for she is dying on land and must return to the element with the strongest influence on her. Besides, the sea is becoming increasingly polluted; called on to help dying whales and dolphins, with whom Erika and Sif communicate freely, finally threatened by a volcanic eruption and tidal wave, the sisters are parted; Sif and her sea-living mother and brother move to a safer but bleaker island in northern seas, while Erika returns to the city world to which her body is better suited. The broad picture of an endangered Pacific, topical and timely, is subordinated to the interplay of human feelings and attitudes. Among the piles of best-selling trash offered to teenage readers, this look into the future should be a rare experience, enclosed as it is in a properly constructed and deeply considered novel.

Zena Sutherland

SOURCE: A review of *My Sister Sif,* in *Bulletin of the Center for Children's Books,* Vol. 44, No. 8, April, 1991, pp. 201-02.

Erika begins her story with "These things happened when I was fourteen years old," and goes on to describe the reasons she and Sif, who is seventeen, were unhappy living with a married sister in Sydney since their father, a Scandinavian seaman, died. Their mother was still on the home island, Rongo. Separately, each of the sisters makes her way back to their beloved Rongo; then Erika is fearful that the American scientist who has come to Rongo and fallen in love with Sif will learn their secret. Are they really descendants of a sea people? Does their mother really live in a submarine city and talk to sea creatures? Themes of pollution and conservation are smoothly incorporated into a story that very deftly blends realism and fantasy so that each reflects the other and neither dominates. As she did in **Playing Beatie Bow,** which was voted the Australian Children's Book of the Year, Park has put together a strong plot, solid characterization, and a colorful setting to create a narrative with depth and lucid style.

Ruth M. McConnell

SOURCE: A review of *My Sister Sif,* in *School Library Journal,* Vol. 37, No. 5, May, 1991, p. 94.

As she did in **Playing Beatie Bow,** Park creates a believable world within a world—this time an undersea one of merpeople in telepathic contact with sea creatures; and an underearth one of menehune, a race of dwarfs who live in burrows and fear fire. Set in the near future, this ecological fantasy begins when the narrator, Riko, was 14, and her older sister, Sif, was unable to cope with city life in the home of their married sister in Australia. Riko engineers their return to their remote islet home and, with adolescent fear of change, tries to scotch the growing attraction between Sif and a persistent marine scientist who has come for rare shells. There are some wonderful and funny scenes as he gradually grasps their half-sea connection, and even visits the undersea city where Riko's brother and mother live. But greater change threatens as pollution wrought by humans encroaches, deforming sea life and threatening the Earth itself. Well plotted, the last chapter is a bit anticlimactic but satisfying as summary. There are enchanting scenes of beauty and danger; perceptive, expressive writing; and vividly drawn characters.

Kirkus Reviews

SOURCE: A review of *My Sister Sif,* in *Kirkus Reviews,* Vol. LIX, No. 10, May 15, 1991, p. 675.

In another beautifully written story by the author of **Playing Beatie Bow,** an adult Erika ("Riko") narrates events in 2000 A.D. when she was 14, imaginatively linking environmental concerns with a plausible explanation of mermaids as humans with special adaptations (e.g., webbed fingers), but with lungs and sophisticated technology to maintain their undersea cities; the "tail" is a sort of wet suit.

Daughters of a mermaid (Marika) and a Scandinavian seaman, Riko and Sif, 17, are unhappily living with a bossy older sister in Australia; until their father's death, they had lived on an island near Tahiti, where they were friends with dolphins and could visit their mother. Riko plans to become a marine biologist, but Sif pines for the sea; deeply concerned, Riko contrives to take her back to their beloved paradise. They find it threatened by man's depredations: whales and porpoises are tragically born dead; the sea people plan to migrate to a cold, desolate, but safer place, and Marika wants Sif to join them. Sif is torn: she realizes how precious she is to Riko and has also fallen in love with Henry, a young scientist they have both learned to trust.

Like many of the poignantly evoked sea creatures, Sif doesn't survive, losing her life in a dramatic undersea climax. In a final chapter/epilogue, people are finally stirred by the earth's impending death (and by Henry and Riko's well-informed pleas) to give up their greed and begin to reclaim their environment. A compelling novel with unique, memorable characters and a thoughtful message.

Mary Hedge

SOURCE: A review of *My Sister Sif,* in *Voice of Youth Advocates,* Vol. 14, No. 2, June, 1991, p. 100.

Narrator Erika tells about her paradisiacal life on Rongo, a small Pacific Ocean island, in the year 2000 when she was 14. She has a special concern for her sister Sif, age 17, who is more frail than she and who is at the age when marriage is possible. The girls' parents, their Scandinavian father and Polynesian mother, separated when Erika was four. At the beginning of the book the girls are living with their mean older sister Joanne in Sydney, Australia. Erika successfully figures out how she and Sif can escape back to their homeland, and they then remain on Rongo where they hunt sea shells and swim with friendly dolphins and whales. Other people who inhabit the island include a small menehune tribe, who are sometimes called Stone Age people, and sea people, who are sometimes born with webbed fingers and wear mermaid-like tails while swimming. At the end of the story, Sif drowns. Finally, in the last chapter, Erika, now an adult, comes back to visit Rongo.

The book appeals to one's senses and longing for a slower-paced, back-to-nature, and almost magical life. The cover, with the girls grasping dolphins' fins as they swim near their island, sets the mood and place of the story. The story is not entirely plotless, yet it is more about Erika's feelings and perceptions of life as she grows.

The book is for teens who are contemplating the meaning of their lives, who like the exotic, or who can be convinced that a fast-moving plot is not always important.

CALLIE'S FAMILY (1988)

Valerie Alderson

SOURCE: "Room for Growth," in *The Times Educational Supplement,* No. 3805, June 2, 1989, p. B8.

It would seem that the foam of Aussie soaps is now surging out of the television screen to invade the children's book shelves. *Callie's Castle* (the first in the series) was a gentle, highly-commended story of everyday Australian folk for readers in that difficult 9-12 age-range, which explained Callie's need to find a place in the noisy, crowded family that was only half her own. For Callie's real father died when she was a baby and Callie's mother married again. Callie's three half-siblings, two boys and a girl, exhibit all the intrusive beastliness that can be inflicted by young family members on their "elders," spoiling treasured possessions, invading "territory." Callie's "castle" was the small room that Callie's real grandfather found for her and which was declared out of bounds to the other children until Callie was too big to climb the narrow stairs any more.

Now, in *Callie's Family,* three years have passed. Callie's grandfather has died, leaving a big gap in all their lives, but especially in that of her apparently irrepressibly exuberant sister Gret, who is hiding a mess of fears about loneliness and death. Rolf, the baby, has grown into a bouncing schoolboy with an equally bouncing dog, and Dan—the brilliant, but "delicate" next in line for the castle—is as unpleasant and snide a character as ever as he waits for "hips and pimples" to herald Callie's move into adolescence.

Callie's Family traces, with great sensibility, this thorny passage, in which all the family gradually reach a greater maturity and understanding of each other. The biggest leap forward is made by Callie herself, who not only discovers her true place in the family set up, but also finds the maturity to put away childish things and pass on her castle to Dan with a good grace. Dan, too, learns to overcome his rather unpleasant characteristics and to cooperate in a true spirit of friendship, while Gret, having admitted her weaknesses, learns she can depend on her family to understand and support her in conquering them. Only Rolf is as yet unchanged except by years—maybe he is being saved for the next episode.

Margery Fisher

SOURCE: A review of *Callie's Family,* in *Growing Point,* Vol. 28, No. 3, September, 1989, p. 5208.

The eldest child of a family has a special need for privacy and in *Callie's Castle* Ruth Park told the story of a girl's claim on an octagonal tower room in an old house in Sydney which her family took over with relief at having enough space to dispose of four children all with a strong sense of their rights. Now in *Callie's Family,* we renew acquaintance with her at thirteen, almost too well grown to be able to negotiate the narrow spiral staircase to the refuge which, by agreement, she will have to cede to her impatient step-brother Dan. Almost reconciled to losing the room, however valuable it still is to her, she does not find it so easy to endure the disappointment over a journey to Denmark; her step-father's sister has offered to finance a visit for him and one of the children and though Callie is not a blood-relation she feels confident that she is the one to make best use of the experience. She and Dan are often at odds and the rivalry now becomes noisy and ill-natured until circumstances make it clear that in fact the youngest child, placid Rolf, is to accompany his father. This is one of those domestic tales which depend for their interest not on surprising events or eccentric characters but on a perceptive, good-hearted view of a family coping with the emotional demands of a second marriage and a mixed family while carrying on the everyday life of an Australian city. Nobody is better qualified to bring humour and sharpness to such a tale than Ruth Park and children who found the first book a congenial read will certainly want to catch up with the family in the sequel.

JAMES (1988)

Marcus Crouch

SOURCE: A review of *James,* in *The Junior Bookshelf,* Vol. 55, No. 6, December, 1991, pp. 240-41.

Ruth Park, a veteran on the Australian literary scene, is equally at home with picture-stories and adult novels. *James* has taken some time to get here—it was published in Australia in 1988. Despite some local scenery its appeal is universal in its quiet humour. James is a lucky boy; he goes to school by ferry-boat. One day he misses the boat and decides to walk. Never having been told that you can't walk on water he does quite well—'He liked the way the sea dented under his shoes in a rubbery way'—until a helpful dog decides to rescue him. Pip has taught him a lesson about human limitations, and James resists the temptation to fly or somersault over telephone wires. Ms Park tells the story with deadpan seriousness, and in exquisitely balanced style. Deborah Niland's illustrations, very flat and in bright primary colours, may leave little to the imagination, but they are done with skill and humour. Altogether a charming minor work of an important writer.

THINGS IN CORNERS (1989)

Elisabeth Brewer

SOURCE: "Shadows of the Mind," in *The Times Educational Supplement,* No. 3842, February 16, 1990, p. 59.

In *Things in Corners,* Ruth Park chooses urban or suburban settings but adds an extra dimension, a concern with family relationships which gives these tales an underlying seriousness. Most of the young protagonists suffer from problems associated with their sense of identity and their inability to communicate. Ruth Park understands the resentments and bolshiness of adolescents, especially of boys. She effectively suggests fear, panic and mystery, but is best of all on feelings of loneliness, uneasiness, irritation and exasperation. While telling an exciting tale, she manages to show how families get on each other's nerves, and how one awkward member can ruin everyone's enjoyment. In these stories, love, tolerance and understanding struggle against hostility and obtuseness. Ruth Park subtly represents psychological problems in terms of the supernatural, in ways which could help young readers to come to terms with their own difficulties. This book . . . makes excellent reading.

Margery Fisher

SOURCE: A review of *Things in Corners,* in *Growing Point,* Vol. 29, No. 1, May, 1990, pp. 5335-36.

Among the images used in fiction to designate states of mind and to deepen emotion, ghosts and appearances depend especially on atmosphere conjured out of details of place and weather, of domestic appurtenances homely but capable of astonishing power. Illusion is all. . . .

The *Things in Corners* described—hinted at, rather—by Ruth Park are appearances or emanations created by human anxieties and sometimes by human malice. When a boy recovering from glandular fever sees a shapeless creature huddled in the lift, we guess it has appeared because of his own blocked memories of being put into care as a small child, memories wakened in the solitude of convalescence. Another boy at odds with his step-father sees the freedom so strongly desired in a new light after he has watched an old woman actually flying from the roof which has become a refuge for him; the extraordinary happening is believable because the boy's state of mind becomes so real to the reader. The elaborate mystification of 'What kind of Lady was Auntie Bet?' reveals all kinds of greed and selfishness in a family when the house left to them by a rich aunt seems suddenly endowed with dangerous influences. The ordinary becomes strange and alarming in finely wrought tales which show how an experienced writer can create atmosphere without any crude exaggeration of style or content.

Kirkus Reviews

SOURCE: A review of *Things in Corners,* in *Kirkus Reviews,* Vol. LIX, No. 2, January 15, 1991, p. 109.

From the talented author of *Playing Beatie Bow,* five satisfyingly long stories in which the supernatural plays a small, sometimes menacing, part.

An old fur viciously defends the home its vanished mistress willed to her nice nephew and his family; the face of the mad long-ago owner of an old car is glimpsed in a rearview mirror while a reenactment of his tragic crime threatens; an adopted boy is terrorized by a creature, in the corner of his elevator, which turns out to be a hallucination caused by the trauma of losing his birth mother; another apartment-dweller observes a lonely old woman who, buoyed by faith in her own potential, has learned to fly. The eerie elements are intrinsic to the stories and intensify their suspense, but Park's greatest achievement is her unique families, each made up of thoroughly individual characters who are all likable despite some resounding quirks and faults.

An outstanding collection, to savor, ponder, and read again.

Betsy Hearne

SOURCE: A review of *Things in Corners,* in *Bulletin of the Center for Children's Books,* Vol. 44, No. 7, March, 1991, p. 174.

Five long short stories project the supernatural with a fictional force that will make readers feel right at home—or rather on edge—in the Australian settings. In the first tale, a boy's anger at being abandoned takes the form of a mournful, brown-eyed blob that appears whenever he gets on an elevator. In another, the spirit of a disturbed man haunts all the subsequent drivers of an old touring car in which he drowned himself and his family. The most powerful tale centers on a fur collar that comes alive at night and bites what it doesn't like. The young human protagonists are mainly discontented by some family situation, and their characterizations are sharp and true. The author of *Playing Beatie Bow,* one of children's literature's finest time-travel novels, continues to give fantasized fiction the hard edges of believable realism.

Molly Kinney

SOURCE: A review of *Things in Corners,* in *School Library Journal,* Vol. 37, No. 5, May, 1991, p. 112.

Australian author Park has penned five stories of psychological horror. One tells of a boy who becomes terrified of elevators after encountering a blob with brown eyes. Another relates the tale of a haunted car that affects people's personalities. Inheriting a house from a relative is the theme of one of the stories. Hideous sibling rivalry and divorce are portrayed. The hazards of flying and the freedom it brings are the components of another. This is not the book for traditional horror fans. The plots are there but are bogged down in detail, and the endings are either convoluted or abrupt. The mood and tone are often uneven, leaving readers unsatisfied with the outcome. This works to an advantage, however, when interpreting the psychological aspects of each story. Characterization is often developed through dialogue that includes many Briticisms, making comprehension difficult. *Things in Corners* might be enticing to Stephen King readers as its selections bear a slight resemblance to the fright master's short stories, but the connection will have to be introduced.

Rosemary Moran

SOURCE: A review of *Things in Corners,* in *Voice of Youth Advocates,* Vol. 14, No. 2, June, 1991, p. 112.

These five short stories by a prolific Australian author make an interesting book. Although each story has a slight element of the fantastic, overall the stories are about young people maturing and dealing with their lot in life. In the title story, a young boy overcoming a serious illness begins to see a scary blob in the corner of his apartment building's elevator. Eventually he sees his need to overcome his feelings of rejection by his natural mother who gave him up for adoption when he was a baby. In **"Where Freedom Is"**, a young man, whose mother has left him to live with his sister while the mother goes on an overseas assignment, learns the secret of true freedom from a crotchety old neighbor. All the other stories have young people facing difficult family situations and learning from something out of the ordinary.

The stories are set in Australia, and some of the terms will be unfamiliar to American readers; however, this doesn't detract from the effect of the stories. Readers anticipating an evening of scary horror stories will be disappointed, but those who like stories with a little bit of a twist at the end, and slightly scary plots will find this collection just their cup of tea.

Adrian Jackson

SOURCE: A review of *Things in Corners,* in *Books for Keeps,* No. 69, July, 1991, p. 12.

Children who go straight for 'spine-chilling' titles are often disappointed. The real interest in these five long stories is the way that strange happenings transform children's lives. There's a range of settings and unusual incidents (my favourite is the flying old lady), but the focus is on the children who are caught up in the loss or separation of parents and cope with the frustrations of relationships and try to cement new ones. An impressive lightness of touch here.

Carol Hill

SOURCE: A review of *Things in Corners,* in *The School Librarian,* Vol. 39, No. 3, August, 1991, p. 116.

Australian writer Ruth Park delves into the dark corners of the mind to pull out these five stories of ghostly and extraordinary experiences. In each one, the main character is a young person with the sort of problem that can produce psychological and frightening upsets. For Theo Dove, the thirteen-year-old in the first story, it is the discovery of a bundle of pulsing, jelly-like substance in the corner of a lift that is the start of a period of terror and claustrophobia. When old Mrs Oliver plunges into space and flies away into the night, it is Gideon who sees her and has to come to terms with this strange phenomenon. In all these stories, the young people concerned are challenged with fears and confrontations that must be overcome. Their emotions are detailed with skill and their characters invested with reality.

Additional coverage of Park's life and career is contained in the following source published by Gale Research: *Something about the Author,* **Vol. 93.**

David Wisniewski

1953-

American author and illustrator of picture books.

Major works include *The Warrior and the Wise Man* (1989), *Elfwyn's Saga* (1990), *Rain Player* (1991), *Sundiata: Lion King of Mali* (1992), *The Wave of the Sea-Wolf* (1994), *Golem* (1996).

INTRODUCTION

Wisniewski's lavishly-detailed cut-paper illustrations have carved him a unique niche among picture-book authors and illustrators. Written for preschoolers and elementary graders, his original stories are based on folklore from a variety of ancient settings and cultures, from Jewish to African to South American Indian. He has thoroughly researched each tale, so that his books are vibrant not only with the color and drama of the stories and their illustrations, but with fascinating details of the traditions and beliefs of these cultures. In *Rain Player*, the Mayan chief wears traditional ceremonial garb that is explained as part of the story, and the illustrations reflect the flavor of Mayan art. Of *Sundiata: Lion King of Mali*, a reviewer for *Publishers Weekly* stated, "Historically accurate images are sharp without starkness, expressive of raw power and delicate fragility by turns, and full of strong dynamism and motion. Bright rainbow colors capture the fabrics of Africa, and the text's patterned boarders are suggestive of kilim rugs." Wisniewski's stories all speak of heroic feats accomplished against great odds because of the protagonist's virtue. Often there is a contest between the protagonist and outside forces of destruction—from nature, magic, or evil acts of human beings—that only can be overcome by the powers of spiritual wisdom and the forces aligned with it. "I try to create richly detailed, obsessively accurate, original folk tales set in ancient cultures, but with modern messages," Wisniewski commented. "I consider the work my ministry, my service to others." Ellen Fader praised *Elfwyn's Saga* as "A truly original offering that will give back to today's children some of the mythic element that Joseph Campbell said we are missing."

Wisniewski's experience with shadow puppets is the root of the dynamic and evocative illustrations for which he is celebrated. Using colored cut paper, he painstakingly details, cuts, layers, positions, assembles, and then carefully lights his pieces, creating the depth and drama that make them so unique and highly praised. Reviewers speak of his pictures as magical and perfectly aligned with the essence of the story, giving each page "depth and dimension." A reviewer for *Publishers Weekly*, in discussing *The Warrior and the Wise Man*, described Wisniewski's "[b]lack silhouettes . . . set against boldly colored figures and background," as "achieving a fine

sense of movement and tension and suggesting at once the particular and the epic." Kay E. Vandergrift, writing about the same book in the *School Library Journal*, said enthusiastically of the illustrations that they created the sense of looking into a panoramic box. T. Griffiths further commented, "Everyone who picked up this book, whether child or adult, immediately put out their hand to touch the pages, so effective is the art work." Jane Resh Thomas's review of *Golem* commends his work as artistry at its finest: "Cut-paper illustrations are usually novelties rather than art, but this is art of a high order, if not magic."

Biographical Information

The son of a U.S. Air Force career officer, Wisniewski was born at South Ruislip Air Force Base in Middlesex, England. After attending the University of Maryland as a theater and art student, he studied to become a clown at the Ringling Brothers and Barnum and Bailey Clown College. For four years he worked professionally as a clown, both with Ringling Brothers and Barnum and Bailey Circus and with Circus Vargas before being drawn into the world of puppetry. He became a puppeteer for the Maryland National Capital Park Planning Commission, after which, with his wife, Donna, he created and became co-director of the Clarion Shadow Theatre in Laurel, MD, a position he still maintains. His interest in creating original folktales finally surfaced in 1989 with his first book-length creation, *The Warrior and the Wise Man*. Wisniewski and his wife currently direct, design, and illustrate for Clarion Graphics, their own publishing house.

Major Works

Wisniewski's books are all original stories based on motifs and legends from a variety of traditional cultures. Set in ancient Japan, *The Warrior and the Wise Man* examines the respective merits of wisdom versus physical strength as two brothers, sons of the emperor, vie for the throne. Given the task of gathering the five elements, Tozaemon, the warrior, fulfills his mission with destructive force, thereby angering the elemental demons. Toemon, the contemplative, repairs the damage done by his brother and in the end saves Tozaemon, the emperor, and the entire kingdom from the fury of the avenging demons, his wisdom winning him the throne. *Elfwyn's Saga* is another original folktale, based this time on Icelandic legend and history. Anlaf, the clan leader, incurs the jealous wrath of Gorm the Grim who curses him. Because of this curse, Anlaf's daughter, Elfwyn, is born blind, but the Hidden Folk protect her and bless her with the deeper vision of wisdom. When Gorm brings a giant magic crystal as a peace offering, only Elfwyn, unaffected by the visions it creates, can see its hidden evil. She destroys the crystal, saves her people, and lifts the curse, thus receiving her sight.

The third of Wisniewski's books takes place in the ancient land of the Mayans. In *Rain Player,* Pik, the chief's young son, challenges the rain god Chac to a game of pok-a-tok—a cross between soccer and basketball—to determine the fate of his drought-stricken people. When Pik seeks help from his father, the chief reminds him of the gifts bestowed on him as an infant: the strength of the Jaguar, the speed of the Quetazl bird, and the wisdom of the underground river Cenote. Pik seeks the counsel of these protectors, and they help him to win the game and bring rain to the people. The story of *Sundiata: Lion King of Mali* takes place in the ancient African trading empire of Mali. More authentic than Wisniewski's other tales, Sundiata is based on oral tradition rather than being wholly original. It follows the story of Sundiata, a thirteenth-century Malike prince who neither talks nor walks for the first seven years of his life. When Sundiata's strength suddenly appears, his mother fears for his safety in the kingdom and flees with him into exile. After ten years, Sundiata returns with an army from the nations that helped him and defeats the invading sorcerer king to regain his rightful place on the throne of Mali.

The Wave of the Sea-Wolf was inspired by a myth of the northwest native American Tlingits. Kchokeen, a Tlingit princess, is blessed with a vision of a powerful Sea-Wolf who creates giant waves in the bay. This vision confers upon her the ability to predict—by the trembling of the earth, the roar of the sea, and the howl of a bear—the violent ocean waves caused by the Sea-Wolf's movements. Her warnings allow the fishermen of her village to safely navigate the waters that have been so destructive in the past. All is well when the first European explorers arrive and begin trading for furs, but when the strangers' greed threatens the homes and lives of her people, Kchokeen must summon the power of the Sea-Wolf to save them.

Golem, for which Wisniewski received the Caldecott Medal, is set in the Jewish ghetto of sixteenth-century Prague and is a retelling of the golem legend of Jewish folklore. According to the legend, the *tzaddik*—the most righteous man—possesses the power during times of trouble to create and control the golem, a clay creature brought to life to protect the Jewish people. As the persecutions in Prague become severe, the Rabbi (the *tzaddik*) is instructed in a vision to raise the golem to protect the people from the Blood Lie, the rumor that Jews mixed the blood of Christian children with flour to make *matzoh*. With the word *emet* (truth) engraved on his forehead, the golem, or Joseph as he is called, captures those planting false evidence of the Blood Lie and brings them unharmed to the authorities. Joseph turns back the rioters massed to destroy the Jewish neighborhood and protects the Jewish people until the emperor agrees to protect them himself. Since the golem has fulfilled his purpose, the Rabbi must return him to clay; however, Joseph has seen the beauty of the sunset and felt the joy of life, and begs that it not be taken away. In the end, the Rabbi sadly preserves the clay that shaped the golem.

Awards

The Wave of the Sea Wolf and *Golem* were each cited by *The New York Times* as one of the Ten Best Illustrated Books of the Year in 1994 and 1996, respectively. Both *Elfwyn's Saga* and *Sundiata: Lion King of Mali* were awarded Notable Children's Trade Book in the Field of Social Studies by the National Council for the Social Studies and Children's Book Council. In 1997, Wisniewski won the Caldecott Medal from the American Library Association for *Golem*.

AUTHOR'S COMMENTARY

[The following is Wisniewski's acceptance speech for the 1997 Caldecott medal for Golem, *which he delivered in San Francisco, CA, on June 29, 1997, at the annual conference of the American Library Association.]*

David Wisniewski

SOURCE: "1997 Caldecott Acceptance Speech," in *Journal of Youth Services in Libraries,* Vol. 10, No. 4, Summer, 1997, pp. 373-77.

Back when I was a circus clown with a tent show, there was a guy called the Arrow Man. His job was to tack up paper signs with red arrows printed on them all along the route to the next town, so the performers and crew could find their way. This fellow did his job very well. He never made a mistake. And he really secured those signs; even in the worst weather, the red arrows could be seen flapping from lightposts and exit ramps, bedraggled and torn but always there, a tattered assurance to all concerned that they were on the right track.

Despite his excellent record, there were times I doubted the Arrow Man. Not on the well-posted hops between neighboring towns or within big cities, but on the long hauls—over flat, featureless plains and twisting mountain roads, whenever there were scores of miles between pointers.

And sometimes that doubt got the better of me. I'd turn off the highway, looking for local assurance. Eventually, a rusty gas pump tended by a wizened elder named Slim, Buzz, or Junior would come into view. After absorbing my request for guidance, Slim-Buzz-Junior would squint, spit, wipe his hands on an oily rag, and always say the same thing: "Son, it's the next exit."

And, sure enough, the next exit would be festooned with red arrows.

In a career that's careened from circus-clowning to shadow puppetry to picture books, early off-ramps have been a great temptation. Sometimes, there weren't any red arrows. Other times, the road disappeared.

But here's a terrific indication that, despite numerous detours and stop signs, I'm on the right track. Being awarded the Caldecott Medal for *Golem* is a wonderful honor and I'm very grateful for it. It's much prettier than a beat-up red arrow. And the people who give it are so classy. At dinner tonight, not one of them used an oily rag, squinted, or even spat.

After the announcement, many people asked me if I was excited. I was, but the initial burst soon dimmed. As more folks inquired, I began to wonder if I was excited enough. Then, I realized, "Yes, of course, you are." It had simply transformed—to a steadier, more quiet glow, just as satisfying but easier to sustain.

My wife, Donna, and I have been self-employed in the arts for almost twenty years. We've managed to maintain a steady upward course despite changes, challenges, disappointments, and victories. It helps to keep good things in perspective as much as bad.

Donna is excellent at this.

One time at home, she took a breathless call from a teacher totally undone by the fact that we answer our telephone like all other mortals.

"Is this where David Wisniewski lives?" she queried.

"Yes," Donna replied.

"Oh, my!" said the teacher. "Are you his secretary?"

"No," said Donna. "I'm his wife."

"Gracious!" said the teacher. "That must be so exciting!"

Donna said, "Occasionally."

Another reason for perspective is that I'm still new at this in a lot of ways. Yes, *Golem* is my sixth book, but it and all the others have been achieved without standard training. As a self-taught artist and writer, I rely on instincts developed through years of circus and puppet performance to guide a story's structure and look. It's worked well so far, but there's still plenty to learn. At least I don't doubt the outcome as much as I used to. When my first effort, *The Warrior and the Wise Man,* got great reviews, I said to Donna, "Gee, I hope they don't find out that I'm not a real writer."

But the greatest rationale for perspective concerns the nature of awards. The Caldecott Medal, like all other honors, isn't a glorious destination. It's a glorious indication, brightly marking a turning point on a continuing course. Gold rather than red, metal instead of paper, it serves the same purpose (albeit in much grander terms) as those weathered signs that guided me across the country earlier.

Cheering as it was to spot those red arrows, I didn't pull over, set out a deck chair, and wave to the show from the median strip. The boss wouldn't have liked it. It's still not a good idea, because now the editors wouldn't like it. Treating the Caldecott as an end in itself would mean the journey's over and complete, and—my goodness—there's still an awful lot to do.

Backstage at Ringling Brothers, I overheard a reporter question Gunther Gebel-Williams, the animal trainer who headlined the show for decades, about his energetic performances and nonstop training schedule.

"Don't you ever relax?" she asked.

Gunther looked at her as though she had three heads.

"You can relax when they throw dirt in your face," he replied.

I take a similar attitude toward book illustration. Actually, with my obsessive-compulsive art style, I have no choice. It's the only way to meet a deadline within the decade specified by the publisher.

Though demanding, making words and pictures fit and flow in narrative harmony is enormously satisfying. Few other professions are as metaphysical: the thoughts and images of one mind are transformed into a solid object, which, when opened, conveys them to thousands of other minds. What a privilege! What an opportunity! What a responsibility . . .

That's why I enjoy epic tales. There's so much to them; huge canvasses teeming with character, adventure, and romance which, when flung back, reveal an equally luxuriant superstructure of history and culture. When properly balanced, epics operate like enormous machines, with the thoughts and actions of individual characters meshing with the giant gears of society and civilization in perfect synchronization.

And they take you places.

When I was a kid, I remember so well being transported by big stories. The first was in first grade: Dr. Seuss's *McElligot's Pool,* an undersea tale of bizarre creatures that had me gazing suspiciously at puddles and bathtubs for months. Comic books came next; sometimes short on character, but with enough interplanetary upset to make up for it. These were followed by Classic Comics, simplified graphic versions of novels by Charles Dickens, Jules Verne, and H. G. Wells, inspiring me to tackle the densely printed pages of the real things later on. By fourth grade, I was a regular commuter to other worlds: *20,000 Leagues under the Sea, A Journey to the Center of the Earth, The War of the Worlds, The Time Machine,* and everything ever written by Ray Bradbury, Robert Heinlein, and J. R. R. Tolkien.

So, I figure that if I'm going to lavish all this time and energy designing a ticket, it should take the buyer someplace worthwhile.

The first ingredient in constructing that someplace is language. The words must serve the world of the story. And because that world is other than our own, the words seldom have the comfortable cadence and vocabulary of contemporary English.

Sometimes that causes complaint. "Why do you use such big words?" some students and teachers ask.

Actually, the words aren't so much big as underused. On that basis, they can be unfamiliar. I'm not a fan of using big words when little ones will do. However, as a culture, we're rather lazy with language. Lack of variety and imprecision abound. Books are the last repository of specific language. So, when a more exotic word refines a phrase or adds subtlety and grace to a sentence, I'll give it the nod over its more common cousin.

The second ingredient is mission. The characters must engage in something that matters greatly—to them and to the family, village, clan, or nation they love and are part of. The execution of this mission forces the characters into a conflict, which, to resolve, demands they stand, if not on their own resources, on principles beyond themselves. Then, if I've adequately humanized the characters in the few broad strokes allowed within the text limits of a picture book, the readers will not only willingly suspend disbelief, but give the story their heart. They will invest themselves emotionally. An author cannot be granted a greater gift than this.

When creating this emotional fulcrum, I often think of an excerpt from Percy Bysshe Shelley's *Prometheus Unbound,* a piece committed to memory for its simple and majestic reasoning:

> To suffer woes which Hope thinks infinite,
> To forgive wrongs darker than Death or Night,
> To defy Power which seems omnipotent,
> Neither to change, nor falter, nor repent,
> This is to be good, great and joyous, beautiful and free.
> This is, alone, Life, Joy, Empire, and Victory.

This thought has powered all my books. At one point, I got concerned about it. I asked my excellent editor, Dinah Stevenson, if I was writing the same story all the time and just changing the characters' clothes.

She replied, "No. The individual against great odds is one of the great themes of literature, and you can spin endless variations off a theme. And, besides that, I would be the first to tell you if you were repeating yourself."

The final ingredient is the happy ending. Not for its own sake and the pleasant conclusion of a comfortable tale, but because a principle has been called into action, and that principle must prove itself. Life has laws, and these laws of life must stand by the one who requested their assistance as truly and faithfully as the one willing to sacrifice everything for their aid.

Of course, one might reasonably say, "Well then, you really blew it with *Golem.* There's no happy ending there."

On the contrary, there is: the persecution of the Jews of Prague ended, at least for a time, and the community survived. But this triumph is deeply shaded by sacrifice: the melancholy demise of the clay giant who was the flawed instrument of their salvation.

In his wonderful essay *On Fairy-Stories,* J. R. R. Tolkien writes,

> . . . the joy of the happy ending . . . does not deny the existence of . . . sorrow and failure: the possibility of these is necessary to the joy of deliverance; it denies (in the face of much evidence, if you will) universal final defeat . . . giving a fleeting glimpse of Joy, Joy beyond the walls of the world, poignant as grief.

I regard striving for and transmitting these glimpses of Joy to be the highest calling of this profession. It's for this reason that a Japanese sage is awarded the kingdom when wisdom overrules force; that a blind Viking girl's bravery regains her stolen vision; that a Maya ballplayer's skill saves his people from disaster; that a prince of Mali overcomes overwhelming odds to lead an empire; that a desperate rabbi successfully calls upon divine salvation.

And it's also the reason for the Caldecott—to point beyond the walls of the world, to wrest attention away from the extraordinary hustle and bustle of everyday life in order to acquaint an eager audience with the quiet beauty of a book—a book that, for the duration of its spell, may provide a fleeting glimpse of an existence more pure and powerful than the one we presently know.

I've had a lot of help achieving these stories. The greatest has been and continues to be from my wife, Donna, whose loving support has been constant, even when I didn't deserve it. This honor is hers.

I want to thank Dilys Evans, the resolute artist's representative who was gracious enough to look at a fledgling artist's meager portfolio ten years ago and say, "Why not? Give it a go!" And who has been a source of great encouragement and advice ever since.

Dorothy Briley of Clarion Books has my great gratitude for agreeing with Dilys Evans and giving an untried artist a chance.

Dinah Stevenson, editor extraordinaire, has been instrumental in refining six books of my words and pictures with the fiery red of her flashing pencil. My deep appreciation for your grand sense of story and unwavering eye for composition.

Thanks are also due art director Anne Diebel, production supervisor Andi Stern, photographer Lee Salsbery, and the indefatigable staff at Berryville Graphics.

And, of course, thank you to the members of the 1997 Caldecott Committee for choosing *Golem.*

GENERAL COMMENTARY

Dilys Evans

SOURCE: "David Wisniewski," in *The Horn Book Magazine,* Vol. LXXIII, No. 4, July-August, 1997, pp. 424-26.

I met David Wisniewski at a children's book conference in Washington, D.C., in 1987. I had just finished a speech about the fine art of children's book illustration and had moved on to the portfolio review section of the program. David's portfolio was the high point of the entire day. I went carefully through his samples of cutpaper illustrations with an occasional remark from him—but words were really immaterial. He had said everything in his pictures. I asked him what he most wanted to do with this remarkable art form, and he said, "Tell good stories." We talked about the technical aspects of his work and about his graphic art experience, and that was all I needed to know about this earnest young man with a ready smile.

Even then he knew the importance of story and the power of the picture. He had a great sense of fun and a definite goal in mind, and his artwork was quite simply magnificent. My advice to David Wisniewski that afternoon was: "Go home now and call Dorothy Briley at Lothrop, Lee & Shepard and tell her I told you to make an appointment to see her." Meanwhile, I called Dorothy to tell her to expect his call, and to let me know what she thought about his work. *The Warrior and the Wise Man* was published by Lothrop in 1989, and now, eight years and six books later, *The Golem* has captured the 1996 Caldecott Medal.

When David was in high school, he concentrated on both the performing and visual arts, and then went on to the University of Maryland to study drama. While there, he attended a talk about Ringling Brothers and Barnum & Bailey Circus Clown College, and he was so intrigued that he knew he had to find out more. He spent the next two years with the circus and found it to be fascinating, hard work, and tremendous fun! He traveled around the country the next year with the Circus Vargas, the largest tent show in the nation, but by the end of the season he realized that the solitary traveling life was not for him.

Returning home to the Washington area, he found a puppet theater troupe and was interviewed for a position by Donna Harris; six months later, they would be married. It was in this environment, under the guidance of his future wife, that he learned all about puppetry, costume making, set design, and finally shadow puppetry, an ancient performance art where flat jointed characters perform against a screen lit from behind to create the shadow forms. David was now able to explore his sense of drama and storytelling to the fullest, and he learned new and exotic folktales that would later fuel his picture books.

In 1980, David and Donna left the troupe to form their own company, The Clarion Shadow Theatre, for which they created thrilling adaptations of "Rikki-Tikki-Tavi" and "Kaa's Hunting" from Kipling's *Jungle Book.* They even ventured into puppet pantomimes set to classical music, and by the end of their first year they were performing at The Smithsonian Institution's Discovery Theater and the Kennedy Center's youth and family program.

In 1984 the troupe was awarded its first Henson Foundation grant, an award established by the late Jim Henson "to foster excellence in the field of American puppetry." This grant enabled them to stage a grand adaptation of Mussorgsky's *Pictures at an Exhibition,* which was highly acclaimed at theater festivals in California and Florida and won a citation of excellence from UNIMA (Union International de Marionette).

By 1985 they were awarded a second Henson Foundation grant and were commissioned by the Smithsonian to create a production of "Peter and the Wolf." It had been a thrilling five years, but the hectic schedule brought both David and Donna to yet another turning point in their lives. It was now time to concentrate on raising their family. They established Clarion Graphics, a graphic design company, which enabled them to work at home.

With Donna's previous training as a graphic designer and David's growing skills in illustration, they pursued clients in the performing arts and education areas. Their daughter Ariana was now four years old, and son Alexander was born that year. At this point David felt he needed another creative challenge to fill his life, and he began to work on some ideas for a children's book. He had a wealth of information and story to draw upon from his life experiences, and the portfolio I saw that day in Washington reflected a remarkable diversity coupled with natural intelligence. I knew he was bound to succeed, not only by the contents of his portfolio but by the intensity of purpose that was evident in our conversation. So I am particularly happy that my friend David proved me right! And also because this year's Caldecott committee recognized a book created with cut paper and collage, the most demanding of disciplines. To be able to take such an exacting medium and translate a tale with great scale and drama, color and passion, is a formidable achievement, and it proves that this art form truly embraces the standards of the fine art of illustration.

In the creative process, David Wisniewski is first and foremost a storyteller. When the manuscript for the text is deemed perfect, he proceeds to do the first pencil sketches on layout paper, followed by more detailed black ink. Once the drawings are approved by the editor, he uses a color marker to establish color consistency, adding to the growing mood of the book. Then detailed tracings are made, one for each spread, and these are the final compositions. Each spread is then transferred, with carbon, to colored papers, and the cutting, positioning, and assembling with double-stick photo-mounting and foam tape takes place. For each book David uses between eight hundred and one thousand blades for his X-Acto knife.

The final and most important step in the procedure is the lighting. Working closely with Lee Salsbery, who has photographed all of his books, David carefully lights each spread for the full dramatic effect. The lighting must be perfect to insure that depth, illusion, and color are at their best in the final transparencies that will be sent to the printer. In the tradition of all great artists,

David Wisniewski makes it look so easy, and he tells me there are still more surprises ahead.

TITLE COMMENTARY

📖 *THE WARRIOR AND THE WISE MAN* (1989)

Publishers Weekly

SOURCE: A review of *The Warrior and the Wise Man,* in *Publishers Weekly,* Vol. 235, No. 12, March 24, 1989, p. 70.

This original folktale, set in ancient Japan, explores the merits of strength and wisdom through a contest for the throne. The emperor instructs his twin sons to gather the elements. Warlike Tozaemon seizes his objects by force, cutting a swath of destruction and enraging the guardian of the elements, Demons. The contemplative Toemon chooses to repair his brother's damage rather than accumulate booty. In the end, it appears Tozaemon has won the kingdom, but a final twist demonstrates to both the emperor and his bellicose son the superiority of diplomacy and wisdom over mere strength. Wisniewski has woven traditional motifs into an entertaining and instructive parable, which he brings to life skillfully with dramatic cut-paper illustrations. Black silhouettes are set against boldly colored figures and background, achieving a fine sense of movement and tension and suggesting at once the particular and the epic.

Kay E. Vandergrift

SOURCE: A review of *The Warrior and the Wise Man,* in *School Library Journal,* Vol. 35, No. 8, April, 1989, p. 93.

An original tale based on the warrior/wise man theme. Wisniewski's research into Japanese art, culture, and religious history is revealed in the details of the illustrations. And what illustrations they are! The exquisite fine lines and perception of depth truly add new dimension to the art of paper cutting. Bold black silhouettes and multiple tones of basic earth hues accentuate these qualities and create the sense of looking into a panoramic box. The tactile quality of the work is such that one can almost feel the sharpness of the paper's edge. At the same time, these pages reflect power and a luminous quality reminiscent of a film cell. There is both continuity and dramatic contrast from page to page as seen in the color shifts from one scene to the next. On first glance it appears that very different palettes were used for different pages, but a closer look reveals that the dominant colors in some spreads had highlighted previous pages. The first double-page spread captures the essence of dramatic contrast as the warrior brother is pictured in an actively charged pose on one side and the wise brother in a quietly serene one on the other. A large tree between ties these scenes together and symbolizes the strength of the twins' relationship, which is also one of the strengths of this story. Although wrongheaded, the warrior brother is not portrayed as thoroughly evil; thus the bond between the brothers can be maintained, and finally they can live together in wisdom and harmony. A brilliant first book.

Kirkus Reviews

SOURCE: A review of *The Warrior and the Wise Man,* in *Kirkus Reviews,* Vol. LVII, No. 8, April 15, 1989, p. 632.

An original fairy tale that draws extensively on Japanese culture. An emperor sends his twin sons on a quest for five eternal elements—earth, air, fire, water, cloud—each guarded by a mighty demon; the one who best fulfills the quest will be the next emperor. The warrior, Tozaemon, quickly seizes each of the five, leaving disruption and anger in his wake; his thoughtful and gentle brother, Toemon, follows after, helping the guardian demons to repair the damage and receiving their gifts in return. Tozaemon claims the inheritance, since he retains all five elements, while Toemon has used all but

one of his in his work of reconciliation. But the demons have sent armies to pursue Tozaemon; and after Toemon has dispelled them by using his one remaining element plus all of Tozaemon's, the emperor recognizes his superior wisdom.

In a meticulous note, Wisniewski explains how he has incorporated themes and images from medieval Japan here; the result is an exciting, well-told story that convincingly delivers its 20th-century message. The cut-paper illustrations are outstanding: bold, dramatic, in striking origami-paper colors, incorporating intricate detail and photographed so that the paper's edge provides a delicate white outline. A beautiful first book from a highly accomplished artist.

Carolyn Phelan

SOURCE: A review of *The Warrior and the Wise Man,* in *Booklist,* Vol. 85, No. 17, May 1, 1989, p. 1556.

In this impressive first book, Wisniewski creates striking, full-color artwork with intricately cut papers. His mastery of silhouette reflects his background in shadow puppetry, and his creation of patterns through overlaid cuts and in juxtaposing bold, flat areas of color demonstrates a broad artistic sensibility. Reminiscent of a folk-

From The Wave of the Sea-Wolf, *written and illustrated by David Wisniewski.*

tale, this original story describes the quests of the twin sons of the emperor of Japan for five magical elements of the world: earth, water, fire, wind, and cloud. The brother who returns first will inherit the throne. The warrior brother recklessly steals each of the five elements from the demons who guard them. His wise twin rides behind him, repairing the damage and earning the demons' gratitude. After both brothers have returned to their father, the castle is besieged by the armies of the demons. The wise brother defeats them through cunning and becomes his father's heir. Illustrating this satisfying story with considerable dramatic flair, Wisniewski has created a riveting picture book.

Ethel L. Heins

SOURCE: A review of *The Warrior and the Wise Man,* in *The Horn Book Magazine,* Vol. LXV, No. 4, July, 1989, pp. 479-80.

An original story with echoes of familiar folkloric motifs has been energetically told and dramatically illustrated. Presenting the age-old antithesis between brute force and rational behavior, the story, set "long ago in Japan," tells of an emperor's twin sons—one, a brave and fierce warrior, and the other, a humble wise man. Because the aging father cannot decide which of his sons should be his successor, he sends them forth in quest of the "five eternal elements"—magical manifestations of earth, water, fire, wind, and cloud—each one guarded by an army under the leadership of a monstrous demon. Five times the war-like brother seizes his prize, leaving behind wanton destruction; five times the thoughtful brother makes amends and is justly rewarded, until at last he returns home and saves not only his twin but the emperor and the whole kingdom from the fury of the demons' avenging soldiers. The striking cut-paper illustrations, executed and reproduced with virtuosity, make use of black silhouettes against emotionally charged colors that modulate and change from page to page and create a dynamic, almost cinematographic effect. In a detailed end note Wisniewski explicates the visual references to be seen in the costumes, decorations, and artifacts and thus establishes the historical, religious, and artistic authenticity of his work.

Zena Sutherland

SOURCE: A review of *The Warrior and the Wise Man,* in *Bulletin of the Center for Children's Books,* Vol. 42, No. 11, July-August, 1989, p. 286.

Tozaemon was the greatest warrior in Japan; his twin brother Toemon was the greatest sage. In this folk-like story, Wisniewski uses the traditional folklore patterns of the setting of tasks: whichever brother first returns with the five elements should succeed their father as emperor. The writing style is fluent and well-paced; the nicely-integrated illustrations are bold and dramatic, done in beautifully detailed cut-paper technique that combines color and—in effective contrast—black silhouettes. On a few pages, a dark background makes the print less easy to read.

Jane Resh Thomas

SOURCE: A review of *The Warrior and the Wise Man,* in *The Five Owls,* Vol. III, No. 6, July-August, 1989, pp. 89-90.

As so many kings before him have done in traditional stories, an emperor sends his twin sons out into the world to determine who shall inherit the throne. They are like one another in everything, except nature and temperament. Tozaemon is the greatest warrior in the land, and Toemon the greatest wise man. The emperor commands his sons to bring him the elements from the realms of earth, air, fire, water, and cloud, which are guarded by demons and their armies.

In each realm, Tozaemon forcefully seizes the prize, unmindful of the chaotic consequences. Toemon puts things right, each time using one of the elements that his reason and generosity has won. The warrior returns to claim the throne. Although the wise man comes home empty-handed, only he can repel the armies that have pursued the warrior. Toemon wins the empire when his father realizes that "strength, though vital, must always be in the service of wisdom."

As he explains in a note, David Wisniewski has drawn on the zen and the samurai traditions for his first book. His marvelous cut-paper illustrations make it a commanding debut. One of his pictures employs some sixteen papers of different colors. The human figures are black silhouettes, with some edges cut at an angle that results in a narrow white outline and the illusion of light. Other figures cast a slight shadow. Paper has been made to look like water and fire and mist. The pictures are fascinating and beautiful.

Cut-paper illustrations are usually novelties rather than art, but this is art of a high order, if not magic. Were the prizes for illustration mine to give, Wisniewski would certainly win one.

T. Griffiths

SOURCE: A review of *The Warrior and the Wise Man,* in *Books for Your Children,* Vol. 25, No. 3, Autumn, 1990, p. 13.

Everyone who picked up this book, whether child or adult, immediately put out their hand to touch the pages, so effective is the artwork. In an explanatory note, David Wisnieswaski explains how the pictures were built up from layers of cut paper, and that eight hundred blades were used in the production of this book. The story, set in ancient Japan, tells of how an Emperor has two sons, one the greatest warrior in the land and the other the greatest wise man. He sets them both a challenge to bring him the five eternal elements from which the world is made, Earth, Water, Fire, Wind and Cloud, and the son who achieves this first will rule the kingdom after him. Both brothers set about the task in completely different ways and, as might be expected, wisdom ultimately triumphs over force.

📖 *ELFWYN'S SAGA* (1990)

Kirkus Reviews

SOURCE: A review of *Elfwyn's Saga,* in *Kirkus Reviews,* Vol. LVIII, No. 15, August 1, 1990, p. 1093.

Wisniewski's *The Warrior and the Wise Man* was an extraordinarily accomplished debut; here, he creates another original story based on legend—an Icelandic tale about a girl, Elfwyn, blind since birth because her father, Antar, was cursed by Gorm, a warlike Viking who coveted Antar's fertile settlement. When Gorm brings an apparently conciliatory gift—a pillar of crystal that destroys prosperity when "each member of the household received a vision of a wish unearned or a dream unattainable"—Elfwyn is protected from the false visions by her blindness; always self-reliant, she contrives to haul the crystal to its destruction, restoring her family's good fortune.

An excellent note explains the author's historical sources, which he has blended skillfully into his lively story. His unique cut-paper illustrations, in brilliant yet subtle colors, are both decorative and powerful, vibrant with action yet delicately expressive. A beautifully wrought book.

Publishers Weekly

SOURCE: A review of *Elfwyn's Saga,* in *Publishers Weekly,* Vol. 237, No. 35, August 31, 1990, p. 67.

In his latest story, Wisniewski dives into the history and myths of Iceland and emerges with an original saga, inspired by Viking lore, that explains the origins of the northern lights. Elfwyn, daughter of a Viking settler, is born blind due to a curse placed on her family by Gorm, a rival. Later, because she cannot see, Elfwyn is not drawn under the terrible thrall of Gorm's crystal, a spiteful gift whose visions fill Elfwyn's kinsmen with discontent. She alone is able to shatter it—sending its dust into the heavens, where it becomes the aurora borealis. Wisniewski's prose resonates with the majesty of legend, and his handsome, dramatic cut-paper illustrations add dimension to a splendid tale.

Connie C. Rockman

SOURCE: A review of *Elfwyn's Saga,* in *School Library Journal,* Vol. 36, No. 10, October, 1990, pp. 120, 122.

A mesmerizing picture book for older readers, this story

unfolds in a perfect blend of text and illustration. The Hidden Folk of frost and fire guide a Viking ship of settlers to a safe harbor, but deter a warrior ship from landing there. In anger, the warrior leader, Gorm the Grim, pronounces a curse on the peaceful Anlaf and his kin, causing Anlaf's daughter to be born blind. The child Elfwyn grows happily under the protection of the Hidden Folk, learning to use her other senses to make up for her blindness. In Trojan Horse fashion, Gorm presents Anlaf with a gift, a huge crystal in which all see a reflection of themselves in some unattainable position—younger, prettier, wealthier. The crystal causes discontent in all except Elfwyn, whose blindness makes her immune to its evil. When the others neglect their duties to continue gazing into the crystal, Elfwyn uses her pony to topple it. The splinters pursue her until she is rescued by the Hidden Folk, regaining her sight when the splinters crash into a boulder, thus ending the curse. This powerful story is based on elements of legend and history of the settlement of Iceland that are discussed in an extensive author's note at the end. Wisniewski's distinctive cut-paper illustrations are exquisitely rendered in rich and glowing colors. His portrayal of the people is especially compelling, with details of facial expression reflecting character and plot development. A truly original offering that will give back to today's children some of the mythic element that Joseph Campbell said we are missing.

Ellen Fader

SOURCE: A review of *Elfwyn's Saga,* in *The Horn Book Magazine,* Vol. LXVI, No. 6, November, 1990, p. 737.

Loosely based on Icelandic legend and history, this original story is full of elements and motifs—magic, the battle between good and evil—that entrance young people. Elfwyn, the daughter of Anlaf Haraldsson and his wife, Gudrun, is born blind because of a curse placed on "Anlaf and all his line" by the evil Gorm the Grim. Blessed and protected by the Hidden Folk, Elfwyn grows up to be wise and, according to her mother, "'sighted in other ways.'" When Gorm presents the clan of Anlaf Haraldsson with a huge crystal—"I bring you this to make amends for the harsh feelings of the past"—only Elfwyn perceives its truth: the stone, in all its captivating glory, causes the people to become discontent with their present lot and to neglect the duties necessary to sustain life. Elfwyn demolishes the crystal—whose dust now lights up the sky as the northern lights—and destroys the original curse, regaining her sight. In a lengthy end note, Wisniewski clarifies elements of his tale, providing background information that supports his creation. In comparison to his first effort, *The Warrior and the Wise Man,* the author-illustrator has not only simplified his writing—*Elfwyn's Saga* reads much more gracefully—but also his art, which, with its liberal use of solid color backgrounds, creates a perfect stage for the unfolding of the theatrical plot. Again, cut-paper illustrations dazzle the eye and bring power and drama to an exciting folkloric tale.

From Golem, *retold and illustrated by David Wisniewski.*

Carolyn Phelan

SOURCE: A review of *Elfwyn's Saga,* in *Booklist,* Vol. 87, No. 5, November 1, 1990, p. 520.

By the author-illustrator of **The Warrior and the Wise Man,** this picture book provides the showcase for another virtuoso display of artwork. Superimposing intricately cut paper for three dimensional effects, Wisniewski creates a series of boldly colored and dramatically composed double-page spreads. Icelandic sagas of the Vikings inspired the original story. After Gorm the Grim curses her father's line, Elfwyn is born blind. Beloved of the spirits, she grows into a happy, capable child, who eventually brings about Gorm's downfall, the end of the curse, and the restoration of her sight. Finally able to see, she gains the name Elfwyn the Second-Sighted. While the text's formal language will be a disadvantage when reading the story aloud to younger children, older kids who are willing to try a picture book might find this an intriguing tale.

RAIN PLAYER (1991)

Publishers Weekly

SOURCE: A review of *Rain Player,* in *Publishers Weekly,* Vol. 238, No. 31, July 19, 1991, p. 56.

Wisniewski's latest, inspired by ancient Mayan culture, takes full advantage of his penchant for original folktales rooted firmly in well-researched fact. This interest, together with his instantly recognizable cut-paper artwork (vibrantly colored, its dramatic lighting and photography result in sharply three-dimensional images), have helped

him carve a niche in the picture book realm. Here, a boy named Pik challenges Chac, the god of rain, to a game of "pok-a-tok"—a cross between soccer and basketball—in order to avert a foretold drought that would devastate his people. Pik's father gives him three talismans to help in the play-off against the fierce sky god, and with their aid the boy is victorious. It's a satisfying tale, and Pik—a sort of Magic Johnson of the Yucatan—is the kind of impetuous hero with whom young readers will enjoy identifying.

Kirkus Reviews

SOURCE: A review of *Rain Player,* in *Kirkus Reviews,* Vol. LIX, No. 17, September 1, 1991, p. 1170.

A unique artist again creates a substantial original tale based on folkloric traditions, meticulously explained in an extensive note. This time the setting is Mayan; the protagonist is Pik, a boy who challenges his culture's fatalism in a ballplaying competition with Chac, the rain god, thus bringing relief to his drought-stricken village. Like the memorable contest in Wisniewski's **The Warrior and the Wise Man,** Pik's is monumentally heroic and made even more dramatic in the artist's spectacular three-dimensional collages. A strong adventure that will appeal to a broad age range.

Susan Scheps

SOURCE: A review of *Rain Player,* in *School Library Journal,* Vol. 37, No. 10, October, 1991, p. 106.

An unusual story of a young Mayan ballplayer who, defying the priest's prophecy of a drought to come in the year ahead, challenges the rain god (Chac) to a game of *pok-a-tok* (a Mayan basketball/soccer game played on an outdoor court). Equipping himself with the speed of a jaguar (sacred animal to his people), the strength of a beautiful long-plumed Quetzal, and the hidden power of a sacred underground spring, the boy outperforms Chac. The god rewards him by sending gentle showers after his victories on the court. Wisniewski's exquisitely rendered cut-paper illustrations—more intricately crafted than those he created for *The Warrior and The Wise Man*—contain depth and shadows, giving the appearance of an action-filled play. Their harmonious hues are those of the natural world that is the basis of Mayan existence: the browns, grays, and terra cottas of the earth; the blues of the sky and water; the ochres of the sun; and the greens of the foliage. In several places, though, the story skips from one scene to the next, as if the text were written to support the illustrations. Nevertheless, the great beauty of the volume and its lessons on Mayan culture make it a unique and worthwhile purchase.

Leone McDermott

SOURCE: A review of *Rain Player,* in *Booklist,* Vol. 88, No. 4, October 15, 1991, p. 437.

Magnificent illustrations in paper cut dominate this tale based on Mayan folklore. When the chief priest foretells a year of terrible drought, young Pik makes a boastful joke: if he were the priest, he would make Chac, the rain god, get to work. No sooner has he spoken than the thundering figure of Chac appears. Pik challenges the rain god to a match of pok-a-tok (a game resembling soccer and basketball), and Chac sets the stakes: if Pik wins, there will be rain for his people, but if he loses, he will be turned into a frog. With the help of the jaguar, the quetzal, and the cenote (an underground reservoir), Pik wins the match and secures abundant rain. Wisniewski dramatizes his story with multilayered paper constructions like no others. Swirling thunderclouds, the rain forest, and the richly costumed characters appear in bold colors and amazingly intricate detail. The visual excitement of these pictures gives the book immediate and lasting appeal. An author's note at the book's end provides extensive information on Mayan history and culture.

Zena Sutherland

SOURCE: A review of *Rain Player,* in *Bulletin of the Center for Children's Books,* Vol. 45, No. 3, November, 1991, p. 79.

Elements of Mayan legend have been combined to tell the story of a boy hero; while the tale is original, the author has used mythic elements to describe the way in which Pik, a young pok-a-tok player, challenges and bests the powerful rain god, Chac. With the help of Quetzal, Jaguar, and Cenote (all representing birthgifts),

Pik saves his land from drought. Intricate and colorful cut-paper pictures are, if at times crowded, remarkable for their design, their vitality, and their incorporation of details of Mayan art. The author's note describes briefly the complex technique used for the illustrations; it also gives information on cultural details used in the story.

Lolly Robinson

SOURCE: A review of *Rain Player,* in *The Horn Book Magazine,* Vol. LXVIII, No. 1, January, 1992, p. 64.

This original tale combines research on Mayan history and legend with a suspenseful sports story. When the Ah Kin Mai—the old village priest—predicts a year of terrible drought, a young man named Pik challenges the god of rain to a game of *pok-a-tok,* a fast-moving cross between soccer and basketball. When none of his friends want to risk playing with the powerful god, Pik enlists the help of Jaguar, Quetzal, and the *cenote,* an underground river, all of whom promise to help him win. Intricate and dramatic cut-paper illustrations powerfully re-create the foliage, landscape, architecture, and clothing of the Mayan classical period, though the complex patterns that Wisniewski uses for dust and mist are a bit confusing. An author's note provides fascinating background information on Mayan civilization and gives in-depth explanations of some of the words and phrases used in the text.

SUNDIATA: LION KING OF MALI (1992)

Linda Greengrass

SOURCE: A review of *Sundiata: Lion King of Mali,* in *School Library Journal,* Vol. 38, No. 10, October, 1992, p. 111.

An appealing biography of Sundiata, credited as the founder of the Mali empire. A lengthy author's note informs readers as to how little firsthand information on the topic is available, and that what is known has been handed down orally by *griots,* or African storytellers. Therefore, the narrative has the distinctive, if somewhat mystical, flow of an oral history. Sundiata neither walks nor speaks for the first seven years of his life, but is still named heir over his older brother. Regardless of the pronouncement, following the king's death, Sundiata and his mother are forced into exile. How the Lion King of Mali defeats his enemies and becomes the rightful ruler makes for an exciting tale. Wisniewski's characteristic artwork (vivid colored paper designs that have been intricately cut, arranged, mounted, and then photographed) add to the drama of the tale and are consistent with the folkloric tone. The characters have personality and vitality, and the setting has a texture and richness that heightens climatic moments of the story. Neither straightforward biography nor folktale, this is an interesting combination of the two. While some younger listeners may have difficulty following the somewhat choppy nature of the narrative as years fly by between the major events, older children will appreciate both the flavor and intrigue. All in all, another fine effort from a talented author/illustrator.

Kirkus Reviews

SOURCE: A review of *Sundiata: Lion King of Mali,* in *Kirkus Reviews,* Vol. LX, No. 20, October 15, 1992, p. 1318.

The dramatic story of a Malinke prince who overcame infirmity (as a child, he was lame and unable to speak), ridicule, palace intrigue, and a seven-year exile to become the savior of his people when Mali was attacked by a neighboring kingdom. Sundiata's victories ushered in a golden age of power and prosperity in 13th-century Mali. Retaining its elements of prophecy and magic, this version is "distilled" from an English translation of the epic as told by a *griot* descended from Sundiata's clan. Wisniewski's intricate cut-paper illustrations have evolved since **The Warrior and the Wise Man,** acquiring ever greater depth, detail of facial expression and figure modeling, and complexity in their vibrant color schemes. (Less successfully, the text here is set in blocks headed by decorative friezes, superimposing a jarring white rectangle on the blazing color.) A note fills in historical details, explains the *griot* tradition, and describes the research informing the art. A splendid resource; a fascinating meld of biography and legend.

Publishers Weekly

SOURCE: A review of *Sundiata: Lion King of Mali,* in *Publishers Weekly,* Vol. 239, No. 46, October 19, 1992, p. 78.

In the oral tradition of the griots (minister-like functionaries "with the wisdom of history"), Wisniewski brings to life a story of courage from the African country of Mali. Sundiata, born to the King and his second wife, "proved unable to speak or walk," and despite glowing predictions for his future he is hounded from his country. After years of exile, he is invited back to oust a tyrant and return his land to prosperity and peace. This retelling, though imbued with dignity and intelligence, proves somewhat confusing. Children may not be able to follow the convoluted series of events, while the multiplicity of characters—most with strange, hard-to-pronounce names—could well befuddle even the most assiduous reader. Wisniewski's stunning cut-paper illustrations, however, introduce to the text a striking vitality and beauty. Historically accurate images are sharp without starkness, expressive of raw power and delicate fragility by turns, and full of strong dynamism and motion. Bright rainbow colors capture the fabrics of Africa, and the text's patterned borders are suggestive of kilim rugs. An unremarkable narrative redeemed by inspired artwork.

Carolyn Phelan

SOURCE: A review of *Sundiata: Lion King of Mali,* in *Booklist,* Vol. 89, No. 7, December 1, 1992, p. 667.

In thirteenth-century Mali, a dying king passes over his healthy son to name as his heir Sundiata, a sickly young prince who is unable to walk or speak. But the king's wishes are ignored. Banished after his father's death, Sundiata grows into a courageous leader who returns to deliver Mali from an invading sorcerer king. Passed down through oral tradition, this historical account has the drama and depth of a folktale. The illustrations—elaborate collages inspired by the artifacts and culture of the Malinke—create a series of dramatic images. The intricacy of the paper-cuts and the richness of the colors and patterns give the artwork visual as well as narrative strength. In an appended note, Wisniewski discusses the history and art of West Africa as well as his research and technique for creating the illustrations. A striking interpretation.

Joanne Schott

SOURCE: "The Stuff of Legends," in *Quill and Quire,* Vol. 59, No. 2, February, 1993, p. 37.

Wisniewski has chosen to use the bare bones of Sundiata's legend from the many versions that exist in the oral tradition. The result is not so rich as some retellings but is probably closer to the historical events from which the legend grew. He acknowledges the living tradition by opening his narrative in the voice of the village storyteller.

Son of the king of Mali, Sundiata can neither walk nor speak until he is seven. His sudden strength alarms the king's first wife, who sees him as a threat to her own son's future. Sundiata's mother takes her son and flees, beginning a ten-year exile. When the sorcerer king Sumanguru invades Mali, Sundiata returns with a mighty army from the kingdoms that helped him in his exile. He defeats Sumanguru, reclaims his kingdom, and rules long and wisely.

The illustrations are made from intricately-cut paper assembled in different planes and photographed so the shadows become part of the design. The composition, variety, and total effect are striking. He has been painstaking in his research, accurately recreating images of this little-known 13th-century African kingdom.

Mary M. Burns

SOURCE: A review of *Sundiata: Lion King of Mali,* in *The Horn Book Magazine,* Vol. LXIX, No. 2, March, 1993, pp. 224-25.

The story of Sundiata has its roots in the legends of Mali, one of the great trading empires of Africa during the period corresponding to the Medieval era in Europe—from the thirteenth century to approximately the end of the fifteenth. Its principal city was the fabled Timbuktu, a center of learning and wealth. The story of Mali's emergence, dominance, and decline is skillfully summarized in an author's note appended to a dramatic account of its most famous ruler, Sundiata, who overcame physical and political obstacles to defeat a sorcerer king and transform a defeated land into a formidable power. The descriptions of Sundiata's childhood as the severely crippled youngest son of the ruler, the catalytic moment at which he endeavors to walk, his subsequent exile, and, finally, the climactic battle during which he confronts the enemy are the foundations of epic storytelling. Brilliantly colored cut-paper illustrations, combined with a carefully honed dramatic text, create a remarkable piece of theater in picture-book format. In contrast with the 1970 retelling by Roland Bertol, there is less emphasis on sorcery and on the alliance between Sundiata's would-be nemesis, Sumangaru, and the forces of evil. What seems clear from a comparison of the two versions is that the story of Sundiata and the great kingdom of Mali has been transformed over the centuries by storytellers from historical fact to epic status, much as, in Western Europe, the historical Arthur was transformed into the ruler of Camelot. Certainly, with the current interest in global understanding, Wisniewski's powerful images, unfolding like a pageant, cannot fail to stimulate a responsive chord in young audiences. Unfortunately, the placement of the text seems a disruptive element in page design, causing conflict in the eye of the beholder. One wishes that it had served as an accompaniment rather than as a series of announcements.

THE WAVE OF THE SEA-WOLF (1994)

Publishers Weekly

SOURCE: A review of *The Wave of the Sea-Wolf,* in *Publishers Weekly,* Vol. 241, No. 38, September 19, 1994, p. 71.

Drawing on myths of the Tlingit people of the Pacific Northwest, Wisniewski's dramatic tale combines folklore with history, describing the Tlingit respect for the earth and the people's first encounters with European explorers. After Kchokeen, a princess, is blessed with a vision of the mighty SeaWolf, she has the ability to predict the terrible ocean storms that have claimed so many lives in the past. For a time, her village lives safely, trading with newly arrived foreigners, but war breaks out when the outsiders turn greedy. Kchokeen must turn the power of Sea-Wolf against them in order to save her own people. Vivid storytelling is complemented by textured cutpaper illustrations that paint the forest landscape in lacy layers. Their intricacy captures the strength and dangerous beauty of the ocean, while slender silhouettes of trees against the moon are calmly awe-inspiring. Wisniewski's ability to convey both high drama and simple emotion lends a sense of authenticity to this original tale. A wise and appealing picture book.

Elizabeth Bush

SOURCE: A review of *The Wave of the Sea-Wolf,* in *Bulletin of the Center for Children's Books,* Vol. 48, No. 3, November, 1994, p. 109.

In this tale, loosely based on Tlingit lore, Princess Kchokeen has been gifted with a rare vision of Gonakadet, the powerful sea-wolf that creates great waves in the bay. Her newfound ability to predict Gonakadet's movements by clues of earth tremors, sea sounds, and bear-howling quickly bring her wealth and honor among the village fisherman, who can now safely navigate the local waters. The arrival of a vessel of white fur-traders is welcomed at first by the villagers, but when the strangers' greed threatens the homes and livelihood of her people, Kchokeen calls on Sea-Wolf for help. Double-page cut-paper collage spreads, which frequently cross the line between intricate and fussy, are bound to elicit oohs and aahs, particularly where the medium has been mounted five or more layers thick or raised to cast realistic shadows upon the background. Text insets bordered with more cutwork Tlingit designs, while appealing in themselves, tend to visually overload the already dense compositions. A lengthy but undocumented essay (intimidating with its close printed, double columned text) offers a crash course in Tlingit history and lore related to the tale, and discusses recorded geologic phenomena that shed light on possible origins of Tlingit belief in the monster thought to be responsible for turbulence in the bay. Exciting elements of killer waves and threatening aliens make this an enticing choice for independent readers, as well as a natural tie-in for school geography and earth science units.

April Gill

SOURCE: A review of *The Wave of the Sea-Wolf,* in *The Five Owls,* Vol. IX, No. 3, January-February, 1995, pp. 59-60.

The Wave of the Sea-Wolf is a visually stunning adaptation of a Tlingit myth combined with chronicles of the first European traders to visit this Pacific Northwest Coast tribe. The story is told in two parts that are woven together by the enigma of an ancient war canoe resting high above the ground, wedged in the trunk of a towering cedar tree.

Ignoring her mother's warning not to wander close to the treacherous waters at the mouth of the bay on which their village is located, the young Tlingit princess Kchokeen plunges deep into the hollow of a fallen tree wherein she finds a frightened bear cub. An enormous, rumbling wave engulfs the tree and carries the girl and bear cub far into the forest. Night falls, and, shivering with cold and hunger, Kchokeen and the cub marvel at a shimmering vision of Gonakadet, the great Sea-Wolf. Kchokeen has been given a precious gift, the ability to predict by the trembling of the earth, the roar of the sea, and the howl of a bear, the huge destructive waves that are a sign of Gonakadet's passing. The village prospers because now the fishermen can safely travel the bay and surrounding waters.

All is well until one morning, when Kchokeen is astonished to see a "huge black creature emerge from the mists of the bay." It is a sailing ship that belongs to the men from across the sea who want to trade their metal tools for the Tlingits' bountiful furs. Eventually, demanding even more furs, the traders destroy the village when the villagers refuse to hunt animals needlessly. Kchokeen consults the Sea-Wolf and then uses a canoe loaded with costly furs to entice the black ship to the mouth of the bay. The giant wave of the Sea-Wolf engulfs the traders' ship, sending it to the bottom of the sea and at the same time propelling the canoe straight into the path of a huge cedar tree. Kchokeen and the warriors ride out the wave in safety, and to this very day the war canoe is lodged in the tree trunk, lifted higher with every passing year.

David Wisniewski's intricate paper-cut illustrations evoke the grandeur of the verdant rain forests, vast misty mountains, and furious seas of the Pacific Northwest. Each detail is painstakingly cut from paper with an X-Acto knife and layered with double-stick photo mountings to give depth and dimension to this original folktale. Wisniewski has incorporated traditional Tlingit designs into his artwork and used them to decorate and define the text blocks. An extensive author's note at the end of the story provides the reader with historic, geographic, and creative information that greatly enhances the merit of this sensational picture book.

Mary M. Burns

SOURCE: A review of *The Wave of the Sea-Wolf,* in *The Horn Book Guide to Children's and Young Adult Books,* Vol. VI, No. 1, Spring, 1995, p. 61.

A lengthy author-note provides insight into the geology, history, culture, mythology, and environment of the Pacific Northwest, the setting for this original tale. A princess of the Tlingit nation is the central character. Her affinity for the traditions of her people and her sensitivity to natural phenomena are reflected in the intricate cut-paper illustrations. As always, Wisniewski's art dazzles.

GOLEM (retold by Wisniewski, 1996)

Betsy Hearne

SOURCE: A review of *Golem,* in *Bulletin of the Center for Children's Books,* Vol. 50, No. 1, September, 1996, pp. 27-8.

Heir of mythical monsters and predecessor of literary monsters, the Golem (a Hebrew word for something not fully formed, such as an embryo—or Adam, before God gave him a soul) is a legendary creature born of Jewish mysticism and Jewish persecution. Although a number of golems were mentioned in medieval Jewish lore, the Golem in . . . [this book] is created by Rabbi Judah Loew ben Bezalel in the late sixteenth century to protect the Jews of Prague from violence resulting from false reports of ritual blood sacrifice. . . . Wisniewski's version, although it is a picture book, has a text in many ways . . . complex and heavily descriptive—definitely for a readaloud audience on the sophisticated side. His dramatic paper cuttings, similar in effect to *The Warrior and the Wise Man* with its demonic forces and fiery battles, seem to involve fewer traditional graphic motifs than the Tlingit or Mayan tales he has illustrated. Nevertheless, this art has a theatrical formality that does capture the massive stiffness of the Golem and conveys the force of monumental conflict.

Kirkus Reviews

SOURCE: A review of *Golem,* in *Kirkus Reviews,* Vol. LXIV, No. 18, September 15, 1996, p. 1410.

The much honored cut-paper master turns his attention to a retelling of the story of the Golem, created by a chief rabbi, Judah Loew, to defend the Jews against the "Blood Lie" (that Jews were mixing the blood of Christian children with the flour and water of matzoh) of 16th-century Prague.

Like [Barbara] Rogasky's book, Wisniewski's exposes the slander that was embraced and widely promulgated during the Holocaust years. Loew's Golem—a sort of simple yet powerful giant made of clay with the Hebrew word *emet* (truth) on his forehead—is named Joseph and charged to "guard the ghetto at night and catch those planting false evidence of the Blood Lie . . . and bring them unharmed to the authorities." In Wisniewski's story, the Golem turns back the rampaging masses who want to destroy the Jews of Prague and is eventually returned to the clay from which he sprang. The cut-paper collages are exquisitely produced and exceedingly dramatic. There is menace and majesty in Wisniewski's use of color, and he finds atmosphere and terror in a scissor's stroke. A fact-filled final note concludes this mesmerizing book.

Susan Scheps

SOURCE: A review of *Golem,* in *School Library Journal,* Vol. 42, No. 10, October, 1996, p. 142.

Wisniewski's retelling of the golem legend varies only slightly from the traditional version recounted by Beverly McDermott in *The Golem.* It is the tale of a clay giant formed in the image of man to protect the Jewish people of medieval Prague from destruction by their enemies. His master, the chief rabbi of Prague in the late 16th century, was a highly regarded Cabbalist (a mystic). In this telling, the golem speaks with the simplicity of a child (in many versions he is mute), and he is destroyed when the emperor guarantees the safety of the Jewish people. (Traditionally, the golem goes berserk and must be returned to the earth.) A lengthy note explains the idea of the Golem and details Jewish persecution throughout history. Wisniewski has used layers of cut paper to give depth to his illustrations, many of which have a three-dimensional appearance. A wispy layer, which begins as the vapor of creation, becomes smoke from torches carried by an angry mob of armed silhouette people and horses. The colors are browns and grays of the earth, sunrise mauve, and the pumpkin and burnt orange of fire and sunset. Skillful use of perspective enhances the Golem's immense size. While the plot is stronger than in Mark Podwal's retelling, Wisniewski's text lacks the power and child appeal of McDermott's spare, well-crafted tale. Still, collections wanting another edition of the story might consider this one.

Hazel Rochman

SOURCE: "The Mythic Golem," in *Booklist,* Vol. 93, No. 3, October 1, 1996, p. 335.

Wisniewski's large picture-book version is stark and terrifying. His extraordinary cut-paper collages show and tell the shape-shifting and changing perspectives that are the essence of the story. Chanting spells from the holy books of the Cabala, the rabbi creates the giant, whose task is to protect the Jews and catch those planting false evidence of the Blood Lie. When the mob storms the gates of the ghetto, the golem is a huge Frankenstein monster who smashes the people and their weapons. But Wisniewski adds an element of melancholy to the creature (just as Mary Shelley did). This golem can talk, and when his work is done, he begs to be allowed to go on living. The pictures of the desperate giant trying to prevent his hands and face from dissolving are scenes of horror and sorrow. Wisniewski ends with a long, detailed background note about the religious roots and folklore and about the history of Jewish persecution through the ages.

Publishers Weekly

SOURCE: A review of *Golem,* in *Publishers Weekly,* Vol. 243, No. 43, October 21, 1996, p. 83.

Elaborately composed cut-paper spreads give a 3D, puppet-show-like quality to a retelling of a Jewish legend. Rabbi Loew has a prophetic vision in 1580 when the Jews of Prague are accused of mixing the blood of Christian children into matzoh: he must create a Golem, "a giant of living clay, animated by Cabala, mystical teachings of unknown power." Brought to life with apocalyptic explosions of steam and rain, the Golem seeks out the perpetrators of the Blood Lie and turns them over to the authorities. Thwarted, the enraged enemies of the Jews storm the gates of the ghetto, but the Golem grows

From The Secret Knowledge of Grown-Ups, *written and illustrated by David Wisniewski.*

to enormous height and violently defeats them with their own battering ram. Once his work is done, he pitifully (and futilely) begs the Rabbi: "Please let me live! I did all that you asked of me! Life is so . . . precious . . . to me!" Wisniewski emphasizes the Golem's humanity and the problems with his existence; instead of reducing the legend to a tale of a magical rescuer, the author allows for its historical and emotional complexity. The fiery, crisply layered paper illustrations, portraying with equal drama and precision the ornamental architecture of Prague and the unearthly career of the Golem, match the specificity and splendor of the storytelling. An endnote about the history and influence of the legend is particularly comprehensive.

Lisa Handelman

SOURCE: A review of *Golem,* in *Catholic Library World,* Vol. 67, No. 3, March, 1997, p. 60.

It is no wonder that writers of children's literature have seen fit to offer us a multitude of books on the Golem, the medieval Jewish answer to anti-Semitic blood libels and pogroms. The Golem is a powerful symbol to Jews around the world that they can have a protector even when the local community is repressive. But it can serve as a wonderful children's story as well, since it contains the various themes of giants, magic, good against evil, and other eye-widening scary stuff.

David Wisniewski's newest version certainly contains the most magnificently beautiful illustrations one could hope to see. They are paper cuts of the most intricate variety that exude old Prague in the year 1580. The incredible bird's eye view of the Golem holding back the riotous crowd is reason enough to open this book. However, this is no read-aloud for the younger set. The vocabulary and writing style are best saved for upper grades who like a good story and appreciate fine illustration. The notes at the back of the book are useful to older children who may wish to find out more information about this most turbulent time in the history of the Jewish people.

Lolly Robinson

SOURCE: A review of *Golem,* in *The Horn Book Magazine,* Vol. LXIII, No. 2, March, 1997, p. 208.

A monumental story of good and evil—and the gray areas in between—receives a dramatic presentation through Wisniewski's intricately cut colored-paper collage. The story takes place in sixteenth-century Prague, where Jews are being attacked mercilessly following the general acceptance of the "Blood Lie," a rumor that Jews are making their Passover bread from flour, water, and the blood of Christian children. To protect his people, Rabbi Loew decides to invoke the Golem, a giant made of clay. After creating the giant, the rabbi places the word *emet* (truth) on Golem's forehead. Every night Golem

leaves the walled Ghetto, catching the men planting false evidence of the Blood Lie, and delivering them to the authorities. When Golem grows larger and more violent, killing many of his enemies, the emperor guarantees the Jews' safety if the rabbi will destroy Golem. Golem tries to hold on to his animated state, but the rabbi erases the first letter from the word on his forehead, changing *emet* (truth) to *met* (death), and Golem collapses into a mound of clay. Despite his violence, Golem is a sympathetic character; like King Kong or the monster in Mary Shelley's *Frankenstein* (which this legend may have influenced), Golem is young and innocent, with a childlike ability to love and trust. The crisply cut colored-paper illustrations have been painstakingly created to show both small details and large landscapes. At times, some fussy detailing can distract the eye away from the main action, but not enough to dilute the power of the central character or the story. An extensive note provides origins and variations of the legend.

DUCKY (written by Eve Bunting, 1998)

Susan Dove Lempke

SOURCE: A review of *Ducky,* in *Booklist,* Vol. 93, No. 22, August, 1997, p. 1905.

A yellow plastic duck narrates the story of his adventures on the ocean after a ship's crate loaded with bathtub toys is washed overboard. Along with some of the other toys, the duck is swallowed by a shark, then spit out even though he and his companions are "guaranteed nontoxic." Gradually, the toys are separated by wind and wave, and the duck journeys alone for months. Eventually, he is picked up by a schoolboy and logged in by scientists. An author's note explains the real-life incident that gave rise to the story as well as the science connection. Wisniewski, last year's Caldecott Medal winner, uses cut paper to capture all the crash and motion of the ocean, and his effects are so vivid that children will need to touch the pages to make sure they are actually smooth. The bold illustrations and exciting action make the book a great story hour pick.

Roger Sutton

SOURCE: A review of *Ducky,* in *The Horn Book Magazine,* Vol. LXXIII, No. 6, November-December, 1997, p. 668.

David Wisniewski's Caldecott-winning paper-cutting talents get a comedic workout here, illustrating Bunting's slightly sly text about a plastic duck who, along with thousands of fellow bathtub toys, is washed overboard when a storm hits the freighter ferrying them across the ocean (Bunting supplies a note about the factual event that inspired the story). The duck tells the story ("Our ship has disappeared. The sea is big, big, big. Oh, I am scared!"), including an unfortunate encounter with a shark ("It shakes its head and spits us out. I expect we are not too tasty, though we are guaranteed non-toxic") and the basic existential dilemma of a bathtub toy out of its element: "I wish we could swim and get away. But all we can do is float." The ocean's currents eventually bring the duck to shore alongside many of his compatriots, and he finally achieves his destiny, floating in the security of a bubblebath. This is an out-of-the way excursion for both author and illustrator, and if Wisniewski's pictures are sometimes too weighty for Bunting's buoyant text, they are certainly splashy enough.

📖 THE SECRET KNOWLEDGE OF GROWN-UPS (1998)

Publishers Weekly

SOURCE: A review of *The Secret Knowledge of Grown-Ups,* in *Publishers Weekly,* Vol. 245, No. 6, February 9, 1998, p. 95.

Caldecott winner Wisniewski spoofs conspiracy theories in this "confidential" volume, with a jacket designed to resemble a sealed manila envelope and illustrated with intricate cut-paper collages. "As a parent, I went along with it all at first: going to secret meetings . . . preparing for the day when my kids would want to know why this and why that. But not anymore!" confesses the narrator, whose typewritten words fill a crumpled sheet of brown paper. On the pages that follow, bulletins labeled "TOP SECRET" offer classified information. For example, "Grown-up Rule #31: Eat your vegetables" is followed by "Official Reason: They're good for you." This leads to "The Truth: You don't eat vegetables because they're good for you. You eat vegetables to k. . . . " Here the document is torn as if by an enemy, and a turn of the page reveals, in oversize type: "to keep them under control!" A tyrannosaurus-style broccoli stalk marauds across the accompanying illustration, joined in its depredations by equally sinister carrots, radishes, etc. The engagingly silly formula repeats throughout, the text and the art consistent in their over-the-top humor and sure execution. The mock-official presentation gleefully contrasts with the utter ridiculousness of the "facts," just as the painstaking cut-paper technique contrasts with the loony wit of the compositions themselves. Yet, strangely, the findings seem to prove that young readers should comb their hair and stop blowing bubbles in their milk—could this expose be the work of a double agent?

Additional coverage of Wisniewski's life and career is contained in the following sources published by Gale Research: *Contemporary Authors,* Vol. 160; and *Something about the Author,* Vol. 95.

CUMULATIVE INDEXES

How to Use This Index

The main reference

> Baum, L(yman) Frank 1856–
> 1919 .... **15**

list all author entries in this and previous volumes of *Children's Literature Review:*

The cross-references

> See also CA 103; 108; DLB 22; JRDA
> MAICYA; MTCW; SATA 18; TCLC 7

list all author entries in the following Gale biographical and literary sources:

AAYA = Authors & Artists for Young Adults
AITN = Authors in the News
BLC = Black Literature Criticism
BW = Black Writers
CA = Contemporary Authors
CAAS = Contemporary Authors Autobiography Series
CABS = Contemporary Authors Bibliographical Series
CANR = Contemporary Authors New Revision Series
CAP = Contemporary Authors Permanent Series
CDALB = Concise Dictionary of American Literary Biography
CDBLB = Concise Dictionary of British Literary Biography
CLC = Contemporary Literary Criticism
CMLC = Classical and Medieval Literature Criticism
DAB = DISCovering Authors: British
DAC = DISCovering Authors: Canadian
DAM = DISCovering Authors: Modules
     DRAM: *Dramatists Module;* **MST**: *Most-Studied Authors Module;*
     MULT: *Multicultural Authors Module;* **NOV**: *Novelists Module;*
     POET: *Poets Module;* **POP**: *Popular Fiction and Genre Authors Module*
DC = Drama Criticism
DLB = Dictionary of Literary Biography
DLBD = Dictionary of Literary Biography Documentary Series
DLBY = Dictionary of Literary Biography Yearbook
HLC = Hispanic Literature Criticism
HW = Hispanic Writers
JRDA = Junior DISCovering Authors
LC = Literature Criticism from 1400 to 1800
MAICYA = Major Authors and Illustrators for Children and Young Adults
MTCW = Major 20th-Century Writers
NCLC = Nineteenth-Century Literature Criticism
NNAL = Native North American Literature
PC = Poetry Criticism
SAAS = Something about the Author Autobiography Series
SATA = Something about the Author
SSC = Short Story Criticism
TCLC = Twentieth-Century Literary Criticism
WLC = World Literature Criticism, 1500 to the Present
YABC = Yesterday's Authors of Books for Children

CUMULATIVE INDEX TO AUTHORS

Author Index

CUMULATIVE INDEX TO NATIONALITIES

Nationality Index

CUMULATIVE INDEX TO TITLES

1, 2, 3 (Hoban) **13**:109
1, 2, 3 to the Zoo (Carle) **10**:71
1 Is One (Tudor) **13**:195
1Hunter (Hutchins) **20**:151
3 and 30 Watchbirds (Leaf) **25**:127
3 X 3: A Picture Book for All Children Who Can Count to Three (Kruss) **9**:85
3rd September 1939 (Gordon) **27**:94
4-Way Stop and Other Poems (Livingston) **7**:172
10-Nin No Yukai Na Hikkoshi (Anno) **14**:40
26 Letters and 99 Cents (Hoban) **13**:112
The 35th of May; or, Conrad's Ride to the South Seas (Kaestner) **4**:123
The 60s Reader (Haskins) **39**:57
The 100-Year-Old Cactus (Lerner) **34**:130
101 Questions and Answers about the Universe (Gallant) **30**:99
121 Pudding Street (Fritz) **14**:110
The 379th White Elephant (Guillot) **22**:56
The 500 Hats of Bartholomew Cubbins (Seuss) **9**:172
729 Animal Allsorts (Oxenbury) **22**:141
729 Curious Creatures (Oxenbury) **22**:141
729 Merry Mix-Ups (Oxenbury) **22**:141
729 Puzzle People (Oxenbury) **22**:141
123456789 Benn (McKee) **38**:160
A and THE; or, William T. C. Baumgarten Comes to Town (Raskin) **1**:155
A Apple Pie (Greenaway) **6**:134
A, B, See! (Hoban) **13**:106
A Is for Always (Anglund) **1**:19
A Is for Annabelle (Tudor) **13**:194
A, My Name Is Ami (Mazer) **23**:231
A Was an Angler (Domanska) **40**:54
AB to Zogg: A Lexicon for Science-Fiction and Fantasy Readers (Merriam) **14**:199
Abby (Caines) **24**:62
Abby, My Love (Irwin) **40**:111
ABC (Burningham) **9**:39

ABC (Cleaver) **13**:72
ABC (Lear) **1**:126
ABC (Munari) **9**:125
ABC (Pienkowski) **6**:233
The ABC Bunny (Gag) **4**:90
ABC of Things (Oxenbury) **22**:138
ABC Word Book (Scarry) **41**:164
ABCDEFGHIJKLMNOPQRSTUVWXYZ (Kuskin) **4**:138
The ABC's of Astronomy: An Illustrated Dictionary (Gallant) **30**:87
The ABC's of Chemistry: An Illustrated Dictionary (Gallant) **30**:88
ABC's of Ecology (Asimov) **12**:47
ABC's of Space (Asimov) **12**:45
ABC's of the Earth (Asimov) **12**:46
ABC's of the Ocean (Asimov) **12**:45
Abdul (Wells) **16**:207
Abel's Island (Steig) **15**:193
The Abominable Swamp Man (Haley) **21**:144
About David (Pfeffer) **11**:201
About Michael Jackson (Haskins) **39**:50
About the B'nai Bagels (Konigsburg) **1**:119
About the Foods You Eat (Simon) **9**:215
About the Sleeping Beauty (Travers) **2**:176
Above and Below Stairs (Goodall) **25**:53
Abraham Lincoln (d'Aulaire and d'Aulaire) **21**:43
Abraham Lincoln (Foster) **7**:94
Abraham Lincoln's World (Foster) **7**:92
Absolute Zero: Being the Second Part of the Bagthorpe Saga (Cresswell) **18**:109
Absolutely Normal Chaos (Creech) **42**:40
Abuela (Dorros) **42**:69
Ace: The Very Important Pig (King-Smith) **40**:158
The Acorn Quest (Yolen) **4**:268
Across Five Aprils (Hunt) **1**:109
Across the Sea (Goffstein) **3**:57
Across the Sea from Galway (Fisher) **18**:126
Across the Stream (Ginsburg) **45**:16

Action Replay (Rosen) **45**:146
Adam and Eve and Pinch-Me (Johnston) **41**:87
Adam and Paradise Island (Keeping) **34**:110
Adam Clayton Powell: Portrait of a Marching Black (Haskins) **3**:63
Add-a-Line Alphabet (Freeman) **30**:76
Addictions: Gambling, Smoking, Cocaine Use, and Others (Hyde) **23**:164
Adiós, Josefina! (Sanchez-Silva) **12**:232
The Adler Book of Puzzles and Riddles: Or, Sam Loyd Up to Date (Adler) **27**:17
Adler und Taube (Kruss) **9**:86
Admission to the Feast (Beckman) **25**:12
Adrift (Baillie) **49**:6
Adventure at Black Rock Cave (Lauber) **16**:113
Adventure in Granada (Myers) **16**:142
Adventures in Making: The Romance of Crafts around the World (Manley) **3**:145
The Adventures of a Puppet (Collodi)
  See *Le Avventure di Pinocchio*
The Adventures of Aku: Or, How It Came About That We Shall Always See Okra the Cat Lying on a Velvet Cusion, While Okraman the Dog Sleeps among the Ashes (Bryan) **18**:34
The Adventures of Andy (Bianco) **19**:52
The Adventures of Charlotte and Henry (Graham) **31**:96
The Adventures of Fathead, Smallhead, and Squarehead (Sanchez) **18**:200
The Adventures of Hershel of Ostropol (Hyman) **50**:84
The Adventures of Huckleberry Finn (Moser) **49**:170
The Adventures of King Midas (Reid Banks) **24**:191
The Adventures of Lester (Blake) **31**:22
The Adventures of Lowly Worm (Scarry) **41**:171
The Adventures of Odysseus and the Tale of Troy (Colum) **36**:24
The Adventures of Paddy Pork (Goodall) **25**:43
The Adventures of Peter and Lotta (Beskow) **17**:18
The Adventures of Pinocchio (Collodi)
  See *Le Avventure di Pinocchio*

Title Index

Title Index

Title Index

Title Index

Title Index

Title Index

Title Index

Title Index

Title Index

Title Index

Title Index

Title Index

Title Index

ISBN 0-7876-2079-3

90000